HM
47   Goldsmid
.U6   Passing on sociology
G64

DATE DUE

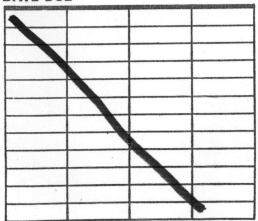

PASSING ON SOCIOLOGY THE TEACHING OF A DISCIPLINE

Charles A. Goldsmid

Oberlin College and Projects on
Teaching Undergraduate Sociology of
the American Sociological Association

Everett K. Wilson

University of North Carolina
at Chapel Hill

*I hold every man a debtor to his profession;
from the which, as men of course do seek to
receive countenance and profit, so ought they
of duty to endeavor themselves by way of
amends to be a help and ornament thereunto.*

Francis Bacon,
"Preface," Maxims of the Law

Wadsworth Publishing Company
Belmont, California
A Division of Wadsworth, Inc.

" 'Teaching is the refuge of unsaleable men and un-marriageable women. . . .' "
(Waller, 1932:61)

"A great teacher is a tough guy who cares deeply about something that is hard to understand."
(MacLean, 1974:11)

"The great teacher should care as much as any man for his subject and be able to convey his pleasure in it far better than most. . . ."
(MacLean, 1974:12)

"Teaching is the art of enticing the ego to seduce the id into its services."
(MacLean, 1974:12)

"The most basic premise of college or university education is the itch of ignorance, not the satiety of knowledge."
(Bruffee, 1978:40)

"You can no more say that something has been taught when nothing has been learned, than that something has been sold when nothing has been bought."
(Cross, 1976:52)

". . . the most dreary, the most thankless, and the worst paid profession in the world."
(Leacock, 1912:xiv)

"Pedagogy depends on sociology more closely than on any other science."
(Durkheim, 1903–11:114)

"The average curriculum, on all levels of education, consists almost entirely of some teacher's answers to problems seldom raised by the pupils."
(Cantor, 1953:200)

We Salute

Peter Filene, Paula Goldsmid, Bob Stauffer, and the other denizens of Pettigrew Hall who, set apart, were all the more together and so created a supportive, joyful place filled with ideas, both on matters of substance across fields and on teaching—not practiced as a secret rite.
C.A.G.

and

Heinz Eulau, Dick Yalman, George Geiger et al. who, in a program that joined theory and practice, themselves joined teaching and scholarship, student with instructor, in a single venture that made the old Antioch a peerless experience in higher education.
E.K.W.

❧

Sociology Editor: Curt Peoples

Production Editor: Pamela Evans

Copy Editor: Susan Rumsey

Technical Illustrator: Lori Heckelman

Set in Palatino by Bi-Comp, Inc.

Printing and binding by Donnelley

Cover photo by Paula Goldsmid

Printed in the United States of America
1 2 3 4 5 6 7 8 9 10—84 83 82 81 80
Acknowledgments for material requiring permissions precede Indexes.
Library of Congress Cataloging in Publication Data
Goldsmid, Charles A
  Passing on sociology.
  Bibliography: p.
  Includes indexes.
  1. Sociology—Study and teaching (Higher)—United States. I. Wilson, Everett Keith, joint author. II. Title.
HM47.U6G64   301'.071173   80-16574
ISBN 0-534-00914-X

CONTENTS

PART I PROBLEMS AND POSITIONS 1

CHAPTER 1 The Current Context of Sociology Instruction: Where Do We Stand? 2
- *The Past Three Decades* 2
- *The Current Situation* 5
- *What Do We Know About the Teaching of Sociology?* 18

CHAPTER 2 Dual Roles and Double Standards: How Can We Reconcile Them? 25
- *Likely Reasons for the Double Standard* 25
- *What Are the Outcomes of Standardlessness?* 29
- *Is the Opposition Real?* 31
- *What Would a Single Standard Entail?* 34
- *Applying Research Standards to Teaching: Changes in Departmental Procedures* 42

CHAPTER 3 Our Persuasions 46
- *Teaching, Learning, and the Connection Between Them* 46
- *The Effective Teacher and the Responsible Teacher* 47
- *Ten Persuasions About Effective Sociology Instruction* 48

PART II WHAT ARE THE ENDS WE SEEK? 61

CHAPTER 4 Field-related Goals 63
- *Some Field-related Goals of Sociology Instruction* 64
- *The Clear and Useful Statement of Field-related Goals* 72

CHAPTER 5 Goals Transcending Sociological Content: Critical Thinking 78
- *Developing Critical Thinking by Confronting Problems: The Rarer Pattern* 80
- *Resistance to Teaching Skills of Critical Thinking* 81
- *The Limits of Routinized Training* 83
- *Benign Disruption and Learning* 84
- *Benign Disruption and the Teacher-Student Relationship* 87
- *The Benign Disrupter at Work* 89

CHAPTER 6 More Goals Transcending Sociological Content 101
- *Gaining Knowledge: Enhanced Skills in Inquiry* 102
- *Extending Knowledge* 110
- *Reprise and Rationale* 119

PART III WHAT ARE THE MEANS WE USE? 122

CHAPTER 7 Constraints on the Means 125
- *The Bounding Walls: Influences on Sociology Instruction* 125
- *Some Options Suggested by the Constraints* 135

CHAPTER 8 Common Problems of Sociology Instruction 142
- *Sociology as a Threat to Students* 143
- *Sociology as a Failure of Nerve: Analysis over Action* 145
- *Talking in Tongues: The Academic Tower of Babel* 148
- *Sociology and Common Sense* 153
- *The Course Cycle: Periodic Difficulties* 159
- *A Final Miscellany of Problems* 167

CHAPTER 9 The Uses of Two Common
Tools   171
  The Course Syllabus   171
  Textbooks and Other Written
  Materials   185

CHAPTER 10 Three Course Patterns   200
  Lecture   201
  Discussion   218
  Personalized System of Instruction   226

CHAPTER 11 Vivifying the Class
Session   238
  Examples   238
  Audiovisual Aids (AVAs)   251

CHAPTER 12 Research Findings on the
Means We Use   271
  Paradox and Perplexity?   271
  Evidence Bearing on Teaching
  Methods   276
  Evidence Bearing on Components of
  Effective Teaching and Learning   291
  Theories of Learning—and Teaching   298
  Sociology and Effective Instruction   304
  Effective Instruction in Sociology   306

PART IV ARE THE MEANS EFFECTIVE
IN GAINING OUR ENDS?   310

CHAPTER 13 Evaluating Student
Achievement   311
  The Purposes of Testing: Why Is It Part of
  the Teacher's Role?   311

  The Teacher as Certifying Agent: What Is
  Implied?   312
  The Grade: What Does It Measure?   314
  The Grade: How Do We Contrive It?   315
  What Sorts of Instruments Can Be
  Used?   319
  What Do Testing and Grading Mean for the
  Teacher–Student Relationship?   326
  Resources: Statements and Studies on
  Assessing Student Achievement   328
  Chapter 13 Appendix: TIPS: A Response
  System   330

CHAPTER 14 Evaluating Instructor
Achievement   334
  Why Evaluate Instructors?   334
  How Do—or Might—We Evaluate
  Instructors?   338
  Student Evaluation of Teaching   347
  Peer Observation and Evaluation   358
  Resources: Literature on Evaluating
  Instructor Achievement   365
  Chapter 14 Appendix:Selected Student
  Evaluation of Teaching Forms   371

AFTERWORD   379
APPENDIX Resources for Teachers of
Sociology   382
WORKS REFERRED TO   400
INDEXES   433

PREFACE

This work was long in gestation and slow in birth. It began about thirty years ago at a school that cherished teaching (nourished by supporting scholarship) as its central task. It was stimulated by our experiences at another school where we saw rare educational practices: the separation of grading and teaching, and team-taught courses in which instructors and graduate assistants met weekly to discuss the substance of the course and how to teach it effectively. It was anticipated in a course, first offered in 1968 at Chapel Hill, to prepare our graduate teaching assistants for their first stint of independent instruction. The pace picked up as we wrote position papers for use in that course. This train of events gained momentum as we learned of others with like interests. (This was a slow discovery before 1972, the year in which the ASA Section on Undergraduate Education was established. As sociologists know more keenly than most, ideas require a social mechanism if they are to be shared and refined. And our work has been advanced, too, by assignments with the Teacher Development Group, part of an extensive ASA Project on Teaching Undergraduate Sociology. We have also been encouraged and instructed by papers appearing in a journal first published in 1973, *Teaching Sociology*. Late in appearing (several other disciplines began similar ventures four and five decades ago), this journal is the first to be wholly devoted to problems of sociology instruction.

Robert Hutchins once said of the University of Chicago that it was not a very good school, just the best there was. We think that is roughly true of this book. Past years have seen scattered and fugitive essays on the teaching of sociology, some of them quite good. The first we know of is an essay on "The Teaching of Sociology," written in 1920 by Arthur J. Todd. But until fairly recently, sociologists have studied the social conditions that affect education (usually secondary) rather than the process of teaching sociology. Durkheim's lectures in *Education and Sociology* and *Moral Education* are cases in point. So, likewise, is Willard Waller's fine book, *The Sociology of Teaching*. Our work, in contrast, fixes on problems of college and university instruction in sociology. It spans a range of issues. We know of no other work so current in its review of instructional problems and possible solutions. Nor does any other work marry ideas, data, evaluation, and examples as we have in this book.

But to say that it's the best there is, is not to say that it is very good. We hope readers will find it useful. But we are keenly aware of what it might be. As is the case with all sociologists, we are amateurs in education, despite our daily practice. When we speak about content, the goals and substance of instruction (and the operational statement of such aims), we do so confidently. But when we speak about means to reach those goals, we enter a land where we are recent immigrants, sometimes speaking an alien tongue. When we speak of evaluation, there are elements of our own field we can bring to bear. But there is an enormous range of scholarship that we have left unplumbed. Yet in exploiting our own field and progressively probing others, we've gained some assurance about teaching sociology, about typical troubles and their solutions. Although our persuasions about effective teaching are too broadly put (see chapter 3) and need, like most propositions, a statement of the conditions-under-which, we have found much in the research literature to support them (see chapter 12). As this work has developed over the years, we've become confident that we can, indeed, make fair good and good better in the teaching of sociology.

So, like the little girl in the nursery rhyme (the girl with a curl in the middle of her forehead), when we are good, we're really quite good. And when we are bad, if not horrid, we could do with a good deal of improvement.

But perfection must wait. Meantime, by

taking thought (though falling short of omni-science), sociologists can better the instructing of their students. This book works toward that end. We think it imperative to do so, both because of our respect for students and because of our commitment to sociology—a commitment expressed in Bacon's statement on the title page. Failure to sharpen its professing must condemn sociology to a poorer future than it merits and the world needs.

That last statement may seem more preposterously inflated than the cost of living. Yet that is not the case; sociology's subject matter and methods make the field supremely important. For of all our marvels—from lasers, quasars, and cloning to interplanetary travel—the greatest of our creations are the structures of human relationships that we build. They are awesome in their intricacy and in their yield for woe and joy. Sociology's subject matter thus defines a field of great import. But it also dictates methods of inquiry that invoke a great range of talent, from the parsimoniously expressed perceptions of the poet to formal mathematical estimates of linked variables. Our methods aim at increasingly accurate (if time- and place-bound) statements of humanly created structures of relationship. Hence the importance of the field, in substance and method, from which its instruction derives significance.

Not only do we speak from commitment; we speak with conviction. We know that we will sometimes seem cocky in judgment and prescription. This is not because we confuse ourselves with God, but because we approve Jerome Bruner's dictum: better to be flat-footed and wrong than guardedly indeterminate. We have the temerity to talk this way with our colleagues; for we know them as tough-minded, unwilling to accept assertion without demonstration, and as sharing our concern for improving performance in a critically important job. And so we ask readers—especially in part I—to take our assertions as first statements in a continuing conversation among peers on matters of mutual concern. (They are first statements, too, in the sense that initial positions are picked up subsequently and treated throughout the book.)

We have another plea to the reader: do not construe what we say as revealing a childlike belief that Rome can be built instanter. A reviewer of an early draft warned that some readers would react to this book by "throwing up their hands and yelling: 'What do these people want? I'm only human. I have only twenty-four hours in my day.'" This work, he suggested, is a counsel of perfection. No doubt; but why should it be less than that? Our day, too, has only twenty-four hours. Improving instruction is an ongoing task that captures a whole teaching career. Would that we ourselves, in each of our courses, consistently applied all that is in this book. It isn't so; but we try to use some of what we know about teaching and learning sociology each time we rewrite a lecture, plan the assignment on which a discussion is to be based, or design—or redesign—a course. We like to think that most days, in some small way, some element of our teaching profits from what is known about the conditions of effective instruction and learning.

Who Is the Reader?

We write to sociologists, obviously, since sociology is what we profess and need better to profess. Thus, the book may seem a private, backstage conversation among fellow sinners and sufferers. And to some extent, it is: we speak to our colleagues who seek, as we do, to teach more effectively. (And at many points—especially in chapter 2, and portions of chapters 12 through 14—we have tapped the lore of sociology to provide clues to better instruction.)

But we hope to have readers, and reactors, beyond our clan; for although the examples—especially in parts II and III—exploit sociologists' problems, opportunities, and data, none of the ideas about ends and means of instruction is peculiar to sociology. The issues broached are equally pertinent to instruction in all of the social sciences and bear, as well, on problems of teaching in the humanities and biophysical sciences. Chapters 4, 8, and 11 do treat certain issues peculiar to the teaching of sociology. However, the set of problems shared with other fields reveals an area of overlap far greater than those peculiar to sociology.

The Problem of Pronouns

We had not worked long on this book before we faced a difficult issue: what pronouns should we use in referring to students and teachers? The use of the masculine form in the generic sense, as conventionally employed, no doubt reflects and may reinforce masculine biases. Sociologists need to take care on this score: they know that inequities sometimes accompany social differentiation, and that language can be a cause as well as a product of social behavior. Two sociologists, Schneider and Hacker (1973) performed a small experiment suggesting that students tend to perceive the generic "he" and "man" as masculine. Other research indicates that gender labelling affects aspirations and evaluations (see studies cited by Kramer, Thorne, and Henley, 1978). To deal with this problem, we employ a number of strategies (which are themselves becoming conventional), such as the use of the plural and parallel construction or paired pronouns (see Rodman, 1977; and Birk and APA Task Force, 1975). But such solutions seemed inadequate when we presented an example of interchange between student and teacher and needed to use pronoun references. We decided to label such fictional teachers as female and students as male. We did this because it reverses the usual gender-role ratios in sociology (where teachers are disproportionately male and undergraduate students female), and thus reminds readers that we are not gender-stereotyping. However, we use this ploy with a major reservation. Teaching at the primary and secondary levels is traditionally a female domain, and there may still be some academics who see teaching as second-class and female, research as first-class and male.

We hope what we have written reads well and yet does not inadvertently contribute to gender-based stereotypes.

The Organization of the Book

After the introductory statements (in chapters 1, 2, and 3), the book is divided into three parts treating *ends, means,* and the extent to which means do, in fact, achieve desired ends (*evaluation*).

The first three chapters sketch the context of sociology instruction and the roles and standards through which we teach. Perhaps more than elsewhere—and especially in the statement on our persuasions—we speak our convictions. They are not baseless; they distill a good deal of experience, although necessarily restricted to two careers. And as they become more prudently refined conditional statements in later chapters, they gain the support of research evidence (see chapter 12).

In Part II, we tackle the first major problem: What are the goals of sociology instruction? These are of two sorts: those goals peculiar to sociology courses and those goals that, serving a liberal arts education, would be proper goals for any course taught under sociologists' auspices. Sociology instruction will invariably treat social structures and changes in them—demographic structure, ecological structure, class structure, power structure, institutional structures, and the like. As to nonsubstantive goals, there are countless possibilities, such as favorable attitude toward disciplined inquiry or a disposition to look for unanticipated outcomes of a social pattern. As elements of a liberal arts education, we have chosen to emphasize three goals that crosscut particular contents: (1) critical (or reflective) thinking; (2) extension of ideas (or propositions or insights) to new populations or situations; and (3) skills in inquiry. Such goals would probably be among those most sociologists would subscribe to.

Moving from ends to means, we devote six chapters to a discussion of common problems, common tools, and modes of instruction, and to the constraints that condition teaching. In chapter 12, we review research bearing on the effectiveness of different methods of teaching.

The final two chapters raise the question, How can we know how well we have done what we set out to do? Or, did the means we used achieve the ends we sought? Ultimately, the answer to chapter 13—How well did the student do?—is the answer to chapter 14: How well did the instructor do?

Throughout the book and in the appendices we provide guides to further resources on topics we discuss, as well as some to which we only allude.

Acknowledgments

This is the scheme of the book. It is a scheme that was actualized, inevitably, with the aid of others. British sociologist T. H. Marshall said that teaching is "practiced as a secret rite behind closed doors and not mentioned in polite academic society" (see Layton, 1968:vii). Alas, this is often true, and to everyone's loss. But there are exceptions to Marshall's statement; and they helped shape and sharpen our ideas.

We are especially grateful to faculty and graduate students at the University of North Carolina at Chapel Hill, 1968–1979. Many of our colleagues read and reacted to our ideas. We thank them: Professors Craig Calhoun, M. Richard Cramer, Gerhard Lenski, Krishnan Namboodiri, Robert Stauffer, Richard Simpson, and James Wiggins often provided detailed commentary on our work. Graduate students who took our Seminar-Practicum on the Teaching of Sociology not only reacted critically to what we wrote; they also brought new insights. Professor William Corsaro (now at Indiana University), Professor James Gruber (Eastern Michigan University), Professor Howard Sacks (Kenyon College), and Mr. Michael Young were particularly generous with their help.

Since 1974, we have worked with the American Sociological Association's Project on Teaching Undergraduate Sociology. A principal accomplishment of the project, one planned from the outset by its founder and director, Hans O. Mauksch, was the creation of a network of sociologists deeply concerned about effective instruction in sociology. We have benefitted from being a part of this network. Most of these sociologists did not speak directly to our work; but they helped us think about teaching.

In reworking our manuscript, we had much help. We thank four colleagues who read the first draft and provided detailed, often penetrating suggestions. They are Professors Reece McGee (Purdue University), Robert E. Stauffer (Kalamazoo College), Theodore C. Wagenaar (Miami University), and Ronald R. Watcke (Wayne County Community College).

Others who commented on one or more chapters include Professors Paul J. Baker (Illinois State University), Hubert M. Blalock, Jr. (University of Washington), Michael S. Bassis (University of Rhode Island), M. Richard Cramer (University of North Carolina), Peter G. Filene (University of North Carolina), Reed Geertsen (Utah State University), Paula L. Goldsmid (Oberlin College), Wilbert J. McKeachie (University of Michigan), Sharon McPherron (St. Louis Community College), Michael A. Malec (Boston College), Thomas J. Rice (Denison University), Lawrence J. Rhoades (American Sociological Association), Howard L. Sacks (Kenyon College), Nancy C. Saunders (San Antonio College), Charlotte A. Vaughan (Cornell College), and Sr. Kristin Wenzel (College of New Rochelle).

We appreciate the help of our editors at Wadsworth, Stephen D. Rutter and Curt Peoples, both for their useful advice on our manuscript and for their willingness to undertake this unusual, not to say risky, venture. We also thank them for placing our manuscript in the hands of Pamela Evans (Production Editor) and Susan Rumsey (Copy Editor). Beyond literacy and perceptiveness, they added a fine sense of what we were trying to do.

For the technical assistance needed to produce a usable manuscript, we thank Priscilla McFarland of the University of North Carolina and Wendy J. Looman of the ASA Projects on Teaching at Oberlin College.

About all these good friends and colleagues we will not say: to them, the plaudits for all that's good; to us, the catcalls for all the rest. That ritual division of praise and blame is both oversimple and saccharine. We are pleased, indeed, to share both with all.

C.A.G.

E.K.W.

Lake Wolsey
Manitoulin Island
July 1980

PART I
PROBLEMS AND POSITIONS

We do not carry out our roles in a vacuum. So it is with sociology instructors; our work is shaped by the situation we find ourselves in. The three chapters of part I sketch this situation from various angles.

What is the current situation? How many teachers, courses, students are there? and in what sorts of schools? What are we teaching? And who is doing that teaching? Chapter 1 offers some answers to these questions and explores some effects of time and circumstance on sociology instruction.

Most sociologists have two roles and often sense a strain between the requirements of teaching and research. In chapter 2, we explore these dual roles and the standards that govern them. We find that teaching often seems to lack standards—poorly defined goals, poorly devised means for achieving them, weakly measured outcomes, uncertainly rewarded effort. And we raise the question, Would sociology instruction be improved were we to apply to our teaching the standards that govern research?

The description of context and discussion of standards brings us to a statement, in chapter 3, of ten convictions about effective teaching. Some of our persuasions derive from applying research standards to teaching. Some stem from our experience in the classroom. All rest on reading, reflection, and eleven years of conversations.

The themes sounded in these first three chapters anticipate more concrete discussions in the rest of the book. In succeeding chapters, we specify some goals of sociology instruction and discuss the tools and techniques teachers can use in pursuing these goals. At the end of part III we review empirical evidence that relates gains in learning to various means of instruction.

Now we commence with an overview of our common enterprise, its scope and range. Every year some two million students sit in more than seventy-five thousand classes under the tutelage of twelve to fifteen thousand sociology instructors in nearly three thousand schools. Heterogeneity, as Durkheim tells us, is a corollary of increased numbers. Schools, curricula, settings, auspices, selectivity in admissions, student population characteristics (including wealth, parental education, occupational aspirations, and the like)—all these vary widely. In this first chapter, we scan the general situation embracing sociology instruction. We have not been able to treat the great diversity of settings and circumstances. So we rely on our readers, who know their local situations, to adapt those ideas that hold some promise for meeting their particular needs.

We turn, then, to our first question: How have time and circumstance shaped the current conditions of sociology instruction?

CHAPTER 1
THE CURRENT CONTEXT OF SOCIOLOGY INSTRUCTION: WHERE DO WE STAND?

Changes in time, differences in setting prompt different answers to the common quandaries we confront as teachers of sociology. What changes in the past three decades have affected sociology instruction? What, then, is the current situation? What are we teaching? What should we be teaching, as sociologists? Where are we teaching—and the related question, whom are we teaching? Who is doing the teaching? These are the questions we pose as a backdrop to succeeding chapters.

The Past Three Decades

Instruction in sociology has reflected currents of change in the larger society. Certain developments following World War II conferred unprecedented rewards on research, publication, and consulting. A likely corollary may have been diminished concern with undergraduate instruction. (One indicator is the decline in publication of articles on the teaching of sociology, especially after the mid-fifties. See Goldsmid, 1976a:233–36.) The shift in emphasis may be partly attributable to the proliferation of graduate programs as hundreds of state colleges were transformed into universities.[1] Even the smaller, private liberal arts colleges may have moved closer to the research orientations of the large universities, as some of Reece McGee's work (1971) suggests. Probably such influences were least felt in

small, four-year schools and in community colleges whose number doubled between 1945 and the mid-seventies.[2]

Three changes in the larger society affected sociology teaching. The first was demographic: a flood of postwar youth, progeny of marriages deferred until the late forties and early fifties. The consumers were so numerous, the demand so great, that the sellers could afford an indifference less possible by the mid-seventies.

A second change was political: Vietnam made campuses a refuge for those whose families could afford it. Aside from swelling the number of buyers, Vietnam heightened preoccupation with matters political, with application rather than with mastery of traditional lore. Thus an understandable concern for current issues—the civil rights movement had a similar effect—stressed action over conventional inquiries. Almost like litmus paper, textbooks reflected this change.

A third change brought rewards that minimized interest in undergraduate instruction. The bounty of the foundations, together with the establishment of NSF, NIH, HEW, HUD, and similar agencies, made available vast sums that lured scholars away from teaching, in whole or in part.[3] Research centers multiplied and battened on this unaccustomed lode. Particularly in universities, undergraduate education was jeopardized as persons well trained in research capitalized on their talents. They were able to confine themselves to the easier task of teaching graduate students,[4] linking such instruction to the research that led to publications and professional kudos. Graduate departments delighted in such an emphasis; for their visibility increased with each publication of their faculty. A school's renown, too, was enhanced by published research; administrators were slow to concern themselves with departments that treated undergraduate instruction as an irritating necessity, to be carried out by graduate students and first-term faculty. Some schools and departments justified the elevation of one task over the other, research over teaching, by identifying themselves as research places. They might contend, additionally, that the contest between the two is a zero-sum matter. What is given to creation must be withheld from transmission (an assertion that the evidence belies).[5]

This fortune-fed cultivation of a laissez-faire attitude toward teaching could not persist. Influences as remote as the balance of trade, inflation, and the shrinking dollar came into play. Circumstances differ today. After thirty years of remarkable growth, the demand for sociologists in academic roles is levelling off. Some graduate departments have reduced the size of their annual cohorts. Public funds for research and training programs are dwindling. As traineeships disappear, some feel an increasing need to finance graduate students through teaching assignments. The annual large increases in sociology course enrollments are not now so large. This seems to be so chiefly at the larger schools. Stable enrollments have been reported for schools of intermediate size; and moderate increases in smaller schools ("Undergraduate Sociology," 1975:4).

While funds in support of research and consulting diminish, the population supporting our teaching increases. In the fall of 1975, 11.5 million persons were in college, a 3-percent increase over the preceding year.

Quantity—increased numbers—poses problems of instruction, especially in large service courses. But the change is not merely quantitative. There is a high unemployment rate for teenagers, particularly blacks. Thus for some, college must be but a second choice when paying jobs are impossible to find.

Blacks are now a larger part of the college population, as figure 1.1 shows. About a million were enrolled in 1975, up 16 percent in a year's time. They remain about 2 percent under their proportion of the eighteen to twenty-four age group largely because fewer blacks than whites are eligible for college: a smaller proportion have graduated from high school.

Figure 1.1 also shows that the rate of increase in college enrollment has been greater for women than for men. In the ten years following 1965, the enrollment of women increased 100 percent; in the five years since 1970, by 45 percent. Women were 38 percent of the college enrollment (among fourteen- to thirty-four-year-olds) in 1965 and, ten years later, 45 percent.

Changes in the student population—more blacks, more women, and an indeterminate number who would be employed if they could find work—impel us to recast the form of sociology instruction. Problems of pertinence and communication emerge as we try to link the map of abstractions to the terrain of social reality—a different reality, depending on the student population. But the setting of instruction has changed, too. In recent years the burgeoning two-year colleges have come to offer sociology instruction to hundreds of thousands of students. Increased enrollment has been disproportionate in the junior and community

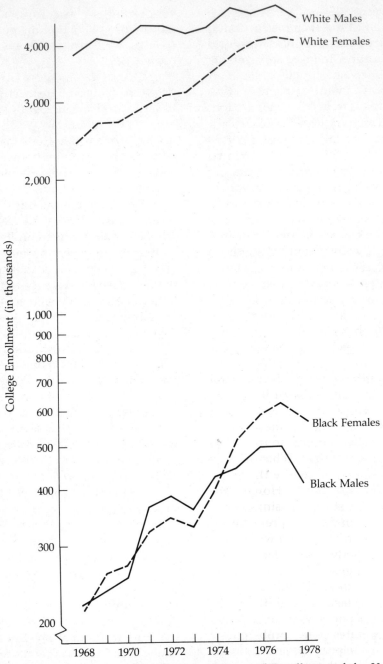

Figure 1.1 Changes in College Enrollment and Rates of Enrollment of the U.S. Population, 14 to 34 Years of Age, by Sex and Race, October 1968 through October 1978. *Source:* U.S. Bureau of the Census (1979: table 3).

colleges: between 1970 and 1975 they registered about half of the increase in undergraduates. They have more older students than do the four-year colleges. Not only do their students tend to be older: they are more likely to live in cities, and they get a less costly education.

Different student populations, different school settings change conditions of successful teaching. Financial stress, too, has had its impact on the classroom. Increasingly chary of their resources, legislators and others have pressed for accountability. This has meant, sometimes, a mechanistic specification and measurement of petty objectives. But sometimes it seems to have led to a serious reexamination and development of teaching and curriculum. And sometimes the pressure, filtering down from trustees, presidents, and deans has enabled department chairpersons to institute programs to better sociology instruction.

None of these changes affects sociology uniquely. But all have their impact on what we do. Dwindling funds for research training shift graduate students into teaching roles. Dwindling resources lead to cries for accountability: What are our aims? How well do we achieve them? Do we work a forty-hour week? How *do* we spend our time? A still increasing undergraduate population places a premium on their instruction, an obligation we are less able to treat cavalierly. More blacks, more women, some refugees from an inhospitable labor market—these changing populations change our task. The shift from a familiar student population of middle-class WASPs creates new problems of communication, relevance, and efficacy. So do new settings—the two-year colleges that register the largest share of undergraduate population increase.

Reflecting on the last three decades and considering the larger sphere of influ-

ence, we discover broad societal changes whose impact is seldom (and probably poorly) taken into account in undergraduate instruction. As instructors, we react belatedly (no traineeships for graduate students?—then let them teach) rather than using change as the appropriate reason for exploiting our intellectual legacy. Clearly we are in a favored position to tap that legacy in support of critical inquiry into the condition of the older, the urban student, women, and blacks. We have both the opportunity and the resources to make the most of change, hard though the fall from an affluent Eden may be!

The Current Situation

A Statistical Overview

Take an overview of our task. How big is the job? What resources can we tap to bring it off? Although habituated to the dimensions of Texas and the national debt, the size of the task is formidable. We have an estimated 1.8 million students each year in ten of our sociology courses, about half of these students in the introductory course (see exhibit 1.1). Most of them will have only that one exposure to sociology. One pales at the responsibility, not only to these students, but also to colleagues and the discipline. How do we represent sociology to these soon-to-be doctors, lawyers, beggarmen, thieves?

Formidable, too, is the flood of professional writing pertinent to our work, some of which must be digested: hundreds of articles and books bearing on our field—and annually produced. Fields differ in the speed at which their practitioners must run to stay abreast or stave off obsolescence. Sociology's exponential growth sets the pace well beyond jogging.

Finally, we call attention to one datum, the ratio of federal dollars spent for applied research in sociology to those invested in R & D for sociology instruction (from all sources): 89/3.3, a twenty-sevenfold difference.

What Are We Teaching? What Should We Be?

Probably none of us knows the answer to the first question, What are we teaching? If we have a hunch represented, say, in responses on a final examination, it's likely to be discouraging, relatively meaningless, or both. Even in those happy circumstances where such performances disclose mastery and perception—especially in such instances—we are driven to ask ourselves: Does this demonstrated competence largely reflect what students brought to the course? Is it my doing? Or that of their families? their peers? their books? other instructors?

A *satisfying* answer to these questions would enumerate things that a student could do after, but not before, taking a course in sociology. An *accurate* answer to these questions would acknowledge that we do not know what we are teaching. Except in a superficial and unsatisfactory way, we have no notion of the impact of our teaching on undergraduate students—enduring changes in skills, attitudes, appreciations, knowledge. This is true for individual instructors. Nor can a department estimate its aggregate impact, to say nothing of the profession as a whole. We cultivate a pluralistic ignorance stemming from our disregard of standards (quality control is for inferior enterprises such as manufacturing); our reliance on the degree as the sign of content mastery, and content mastery as surety for a talent for teaching; and our celebration of individual self-determination in the classroom, buttressed by the myth of academic freedom.[6]

One might guess what a course con-

Exhibit 1.1 The Task and the Tools: Clues to the Current Situation

How many students are there?	892,000	students are enrolled annually in a course in Introductory Sociology; 1974 ("Undergraduate Sociology," 1975:4).[7]
	1.8 Million	is the aggregate annual enrollment in the ten most frequently offered sociology courses; 1974 ("Undergraduate Sociology," 1975:4).
How many teachers are there?	5,000	instructors offer Introductory Sociology; 1974 ("Undergraduate Sociology," 1975:4).
	12,000	instructors (approximately) of sociology; 1977.[8]
How many textbooks are there?	113	textbooks in Introductory Sociology are available; 1974–1975 (Van Valey, 1975).
How many and what sorts of schools offer sociology?	92%	of all 2,652 institutions of higher education in the U.S. offer Introductory Sociology. For universities, and four-year and two-year colleges, the figures are 95%, 90%, and 94%, respectively; 1974 ("Undergraduate Sociology," 1975:4).[9]
	831	accredited four-year colleges or universities offer a major in sociology; 1971 (Shin, 1975).

	250 graduate programs are available to students of sociology, and half of these programs offer the Ph.D.; 1977 (American Sociological Association, 1977).
	6,000 graduate students (approximately) are enrolled in sociology; 1977 (American Sociological Association, 1977).
What might sociologists read to keep in touch with their discipline?	**700** articles appear annually in twenty English-language sociology journals; 1976 (Goldsmid, 1977b:345).
	170 articles appear annually in four sociology journals (*AJS, ASR, SF, SSR*); 1976 (Goldsmid, 1977b: 345).
	600 books are reviewed annually in *Contemporary Sociology*; 1976 (American Sociological Association, 1976).
What is the range of material sociology instructors need to be aware of?	**36–47** subfields or areas of concentration in sociology are identified in ASA documents; 1975 (American Sociological Association, 1977, 1976b).
How does the profession support the sociology instructor?	**42** articles on the teaching of sociology appear annually in twenty sociology journals; 1976. About half of these appear in one journal, *Teaching Sociology* (Goldsmid, 1977b:345).
	500–600 articles on the teaching of sociology have been published since 1895 (Goldsmid, 1976a:233).
	2 major sources of assistance exist: ASA Section on Undergraduate Education and the ASA Projects on Teaching Undergraduate Sociology (created in 1972 and 1974, respectively).
	36 documents on teaching are available for purchase from the ASA Teaching Resources Center.
	625 members belong to the ASA Section on Undergraduate Education (compared to 995 members in the ASA Section on Medical Sociology—the largest section); May 1979.
Do departments and institutions support sociologists in their teaching role?	**13%** of all departments offer some form of in-service teacher development activity for current faculty; 1975 (Ewens and Emling, 1975; Riechmann and Malec, 1975:299).[10]
	40% of all departments have access to in-service teacher development resources in their institutions; 1975 (Ewens and Emling, 1975; Riechmann and Malec; 1976).
	22% of all departments (24% of graduate departments) have written criteria for evaluating teaching, and substantially less than half of all departments

		have no written criteria used by either the department or the institution; 1975 (Ewens and Emling, 1975).
What percent of graduate students teach?	50%	of all graduate students are employed in some form of teaching assistantship (equal portions teach their own courses, lead discussion groups, and grade and otherwise assist faculty); 1975 (Ewens and Emling, 1975).
	60%	of all undergraduates in some major universities are taught sociology by graduate students; 1974 (Anonymous, 1974).
	32%	of all graduate departments require their graduate students to teach; 1975 (Ewens and Emling, 1975).
What percent of graduate students get some preparation for teaching sociology?	50%	of graduate departments offer some form of purposive teaching preparation for graduate students (short orientation meetings or workshops are the most common form); 1975 (Ewens and Emling, 1975).
	19%	of graduate departments offer some semester-long program or course to assist graduate students; 1975 (Ewens and Emling, 1975).
How many degrees in sociology result from these efforts?	27,670	B.A. degrees are granted with majors in sociology; 1975–1976 (National Center, 1978).
	2,010	M.A. degrees are earned in sociology; 1975–1976 (National Center, 1978).
	729	Ph.D. degrees are earned in sociology; 1975–1976 (National Center, 1978).
What funding is available in support of research and development in sociology?	$89 Million	federal dollars are spent in one year for applied research in sociology (substantially less is spent on basic research); 1971 (Baker, 1975).
	$3.3 Million (estimated)	dollars are available from all sources for research and development on teaching of sociology; 1976.[11]

veys to a student by analyzing commonly used textbooks. These are still the principal tool of instruction. Their impact may be sufficiently strong to override the idiosyncratic influence of the instructor who is sometimes simply the mediator of text-truth. (This may be one reason that Dubin and Taveggia, 1968, can report two common modes of supposed instruction, lecture and discussion, as having so little effect on learning outcomes.)

We do know something about the content of sociology texts, especially those for the introductory course. If these are taken as measures of what students learn, we know that there are gaps—matters that they do not learn and we do not teach. For example, over half of the introductory texts available in 1974 paid no more than lip service to sociological methods (Van Valey, 1975). The role of half the population, that of women, got systematic treatment in few, if any, texts available in 1971 (Kirschner, 1973). Rothman's (1971) examination of the treatment of stratification in forty-eight introductory textbooks reveals a gap between text and current work in the discipline. In examining sixteen texts published between 1951 and 1970, Baali and Moore (1972) found agreement that sociology was a science, but disagreement as to its subject matter. While such differences may be healthy for the discipline, the Baali and Moore study raises serious questions as to what it is that we are teaching.

For a general, if ambiguous, notion as to what we teach—course labels are imprecise and can be misleading—we might look at the courses commonly offered to undergraduates in sociology in the United States. Gates (1969) and others have found that, in small liberal arts colleges, the three courses most often offered are the general (Introductory) sociology course, a parallel course in anthropology (departments are often joint sociology–anthropology), and Marriage and the Family. More recently, Social Problems, Race and Ethnic Relations, and courses on crime and delinquency have been among the more frequently offered. A course in research methods is common, too, especially as a requirement for the major.[12]

Larger schools do not depart markedly from this pattern. To a common core—Introductory, Methods, Theory, and some such courses as Social Problems and Marriage and the Family—they simply add a longer roster drawn from the forty-some subfields in sociology. Many community colleges offer the common three, the Introductory, Social Problems, and Marriage and the Family. Fewer list Criminology, Race and Ethnic Relations, and other substantive courses. We think it likely that course offerings in sociology in the United States form a clear Guttman scale with high reproducibility. Table 1.1 summarizes data from major curriculum studies. (The original reports break down these summary data by school type, size, affiliation, location of school, and other variables.)

When we ask, What are we teaching? an accurate answer is likely to be disheartening. The most certain conclusion is that for any criterion of adequacy, for the achievement of the once-only student or the major, for a single course, across all courses, or across the cohort of all undergraduates exposed to sociology, we do not know the effect of our intervention. That is to say, we cannot surely attribute to the instructor's influence changes that are long enduring (say, ten years) in sensitivity to sloppy causal imputations or spurious correlations, a disposition to look for unanticipated outcomes of social action and the like. When we say that we don't know what we are doing—that we don't know about lasting effects of teacher intervention—we mean it as a simple, descriptive statement about the situation of sociology instruction (and doubtless other instruction). Of course we wish it were otherwise—and for ourselves as well as our colleagues! To learn what in fact we are (and are not) doing would entail a long period of patient inquiry, preferably among collaborating sociologists. Yet with our interest in evaluation research, it would seem possible to assess the effects of our efforts to achieve a few instructional goals we deem critical.

A second conclusion is that, in building a course or a curriculum, we seem automatically to recapitulate the past, relying on labels whose interpretations have the precision of a Rorschach ink blot. In the transmission of sociology there is an appalling ignorance of what others do, or have tried to do, with what success, among different student populations. Although we find a repeated curricular pattern among schools where sociology is taught, it seems to have developed more by imitation than cogitation. The concrete content of courses is often obscure. There is no articulation of concurrent learning experiences with sociology instruction. The separation of theory and methods from content makes for ludicrous disconnections. Nor is one assured by the declaration of prerequisites, muddily defined, that the sequence of experiences is cumulatively fruitful.

It is sobering to think that we cannot describe, certainly, what it is that we are teaching. But if we cannot describe, we can prescribe. The question, What should be taught? can be answered for core elements of the undergraduate curriculum and for different populations. It can be answered without straitjacketing the instructor or threatening academic freedom.

Why should we prescribe minimum essential learnings for certain courses, such as the introductory? There are many reasons, among them, these:

1. It helps assure a substantial introductory course—an aim all the more important when it is a large course taught by many who are often transients.

Table 1.1 Course Offerings in Undergraduate Sociology, Selected Dates, 1942–1974

	Rank Ordering of Courses					% of Departments Offering Specified Course, 1974[f]		
	1942[a]	1957[b]	1966[c]	1966[d]	1974[e]	Univ.	4-Yr.	2-Yr.
Introductory	1	2	1	1	1	95%	90%	94%
Social Problems	2	5	4	3	3	66	65	69
Marriage & Family	3	3	2	2	2	80	74	63
Social Work	4	6	9[g]	—	—	—	—	—
Criminology	5	4	6	6	5	65	58	21
Research Methods	6	—	10	7	6	78	62	2
Social Psychology	7	8	—	10	9	59	42	7
Rural	8	—	7	—	—	—	—	—
Anthropology	9.5	1[h]	3	8	—	—	—	—
Theory	9.5	9	5	4	8	68	63	0
Race & Ethnic	—	10	8	5	4	69	64	19
Urban	—	—	—	11	7	71	58	11
Juvenile Delinquency	—	—	—	19	10	44	37	6
Social Welfare	—	—	—	9	—	—	—	—
Demography/Population	—	—	—	12	—	—	—	—

Notes: Since these surveys collected data by different sampling methods and since the studies had varying response rates, the data are not strictly comparable.

[a] Kennedy and Kennedy (1942).

[b] Podell, Vogelfanger, and Rogers (1959).

[c] Gates (1969).

[d] Reid and Bates (1971).

[e] "Undergraduate Sociology" (1975), with rankings based on the percentages in the columns to the right.

[f] "Undergraduate Sociology" (1975).

[g] Introduction to Social Work only.

[h] All anthropology courses.

2. It clarifies certain objectives for the student—certain ones, but not all (some will be peculiar to the instructor teaching the course).

3. It clarifies certain objectives for the instructor and so helps that instructor in the task of developing adequate measures of achievement.

4. It helps transfer students understand what are seen as necessary underpinnings for courses beyond the introduction to the field (and especially for courses for which the introductory is said to be prerequisite).

5. It provides a basis for building a waiving examination and so enables a few exceptional students to get on with advanced work and avoid redundancy.

6. It enables the instructor to build useful learning experiences—laboratory work, field work, and the like—around the precisely stipulated objectives.

7. It enables instructors in succeeding courses to build, consciously, on what has been learned before so that the curriculum for the major becomes a sort of ogive of knowledge, a Guttman scale of learnings.

8. It gives students a gratifying (and motivating) sense of cumulative growth, of stages and progression.

9. It informs colleagues in other schools, especially those whose students may come as transfers, what is needed as a basis for succeeding courses.

The attempt to stipulate basic learnings for undergraduate work in theory, or methods, or the introductory course is sometimes resisted. It is argued, for example, that to achieve agreement on basic learnings for the introductory course, the list must be so limited and general as to be uselessly vague. As to the alternative, an extensive roster of specific learnings would list trivialities—and would never be agreed to in a discipline so varied as ours. These timorous objections are wrong. Consider one illustration. Most soci-

ologists would agree that one general aim of an introductory course would be to help students learn where to find out. This is scarcely a trivial aim for the prospective major or for others. Spelled out, it might mean knowing the existence of and the kind of data available in, say, *Statistical Abstract* or *Historical Statistics of the United States*, records in the local courthouse, indexes of major journals, and the like. Likewise, whether or not one agrees with the Davis-Moore theory of stratification, the issue is so central that most sociologists would feel that a discussion of stratification must treat this theory.

On the second point, our experience belies the contention that we can't get agreement on a fairly extensive list. Thinking about minimum essential learnings for the introductory course, members of the undergraduate studies committee at University of North Carolina, Chapel Hill put together 327 objectives under six headings: some humanistic goals, theorists to be identified, theoretical positions to be distinguished, concepts, basic facts, methodological skills, and methodological concepts. Twenty faculty members and twelve graduate students assessed these suggested minimum essentials. Three-fourths or more of faculty respondents coded seventy-six items as "an essential outcome: all students (in the introductory course) should know/learn this". Thus a quite diverse group of faculty registered marked agreement on a sizeable core of basic learnings for an introductory course. [13]

Some resistance to a public statement of core objectives for required courses may take this form. When sociologists are hired, departments implicitly express confidence in them as instructors. Hence it is gratuitous to offer, as guideline or standard, a minimal set of core objectives. Our response to this is a paraphrase of Mr.

Bumble's statement about the law: "If the department supposes that, the department is an ass." The assumption that because a person is hired as a competent sociologist that person is, ipso facto, a competent teacher is too ingenuous to take seriously. Any department can be confident only that a newcomer has probably been incapacitated for competent teaching by twenty years' exposure to poor to indifferent instruction. Any department can be sure that the newcomer is much less effective than might be. And not only the newcomer—all of us who know so little about the effects of our efforts.

In short, we find such reactions to an effort to establish minimum standards less than persuasive. It is past time for us to devise guidelines for minimal learnings for courses commonly required in our departments.

In suggesting that the core of what we teach can be stipulated, and with wide agreement among our colleagues, we want to draw a distinction between required courses and electives. We are speaking only of the former. Such courses (those required for the major or as prerequisites) have a special standing. They represent department requirements. A department must accept, to a degree not true of elective courses, responsibility for their content and their instruction.

Failure to specify minimum essential learnings has one particularly unfortunate effect: it precludes a cumulative educational experience. Instructors in courses following the introductory cannot assume a minimal base on which to build. Professor X's introductory course stresses an evolutionary, macro-societal approach; Professors Y and Z stress analysis of contemporary American society—but the former uses a functional approach, the latter a humanistic approach. Or consider a department in which one instructor's in-troductory course virtually disregards methodological issues, a second stresses temporal and cross-national comparisons, and a third instructor emphasizes skill in stating and testing hypotheses and the logic and technique of three-variable contingency tables. Our objection is *not* to the evolutionary or functional or humanistic stress, but to the fact that no instructor in later courses can assume anything about students' prior exposure, let alone mastery.

To suggest standards or minima may seem a dangerous step. Objections other than those we've raised and discarded remain. Certainly, to impose *the* correct sociology would be sad and serious, undesirable and unnecessary. Unnecessary since many concrete objectives, operationally stated (know how to use, calculate, and interpret $\overline{X}$ and SD), are compatible with all approaches.[14] In any case, the seriousness and complexity of the problem is no reason for avoiding it.

The lack of some common core in required courses precludes any sensible use of them as prerequisites, makes for redundancies, and militates against cumulativeness. Our scanning of college and university catalogs suggests that sociology has far fewer prerequisites for advanced courses than do psychology or economics. The same holds when we compare undergraduate and graduate courses in sociology. Sociology offers students far less than it should, owing to the low level of cumulativeness in our curricula. Should not an instructor in an advanced undergraduate course be able to assume that students understand the terms *class* and *socialization*, and what is meant (and not meant) when we say that two variables are positively correlated?

Aside from publicly and operationally stated course prerequisites, there are other means of promoting cumulativeness. For example, a course might have entrance, as well as exit, examinations. The content of such exams would form a statement of learnings from preceding work on which student and instructor could build. That such alternatives are administratively complex and time consuming may be true. But we are unlikely to improve our lot without such commitments and investments. In any event, the issue is cumulative intellectual growth and not prerequisites, which are only one mechanism—and as now used, a faulty one—for promoting cumulative learning.

To the first question, What are we teaching? we answered that we're not very certain. But to the second question. Can we determine what should be taught? The answer is: yes, of course. We do this, anyway, individually and privately. The imperative task is to pool a department's collective wisdom, to do the job collectively and publicly—for courses required by the department. It can be done and, as we have indicated, there are good reasons for doing so.

Where Are We Teaching? And Whom?

We teach in many sorts of settings, each with a distinctive population and each, therefore, with distinctive instructional problems and opportunities. We teach in schools of medicine, nursing, and public health, in schools of law and education. We teach in prisons and reformatories. At least 12,000 of us teach in universities, four- and two-year colleges. Such variations in the places where we teach point to variations in the attributes of those whom we teach—to differences in cultural background, antecedent education, and expectations; and to differences

in curriculum, resources, administrative procedures, and other factors that shape the process of teaching and learning. Size and type of school—university, four- and two-year colleges, private and public—differ in the proportion of students who are part-time and who are enrolled for a degree (Chronicle, 1977). They differ in the means and criteria used to evaluate faculty for promotion, raises, and tenure (Astin and Lee, 1967). They differ in graduation rates (Report, 1971:2). They differ in providing teacher development programs for their faculty—in the department or on the campus—and in their methods of training new faculty members (Riechmann and Malec, 1976:229, 301; Goldsmid, 1976a:232; Astin and Lee, 1967). They differ in the range of sociology courses offered, in requirements for the major, and in enrollment trends (ASA, 1975:4; Reid and Bates, 1971; Gates, 1969).

Contrast community college students with those at four-year schools and consider the implications for sociology instruction. The age range for community college students is much greater, and their part-time students, an increasing segment of this population, are much older. Community college students have lower test scores and lower standings in their high school classes. They are less likely to complete a two-year degree than their counterparts are to finish their baccalaureate work. Attrition in community colleges is not wholly due to poor performance: matters of motivation and money are very serious. Community college students, more of them, come from lower middle income backgrounds and are more often the first generation in their families to have the experience of higher education. In concluding a description of community college students, Monroe suggests (1972:200) that community college students tend to be *nonacademically oriented . . . more conventional, less independent, less attracted to reflective thought and less tolerant than their peers in the four year institutions (Cross, 1968:32) [and, quoting Cross, 1968:33] "were the most cautious, prudent, and controlled, most apprehensive and rigid in their concern over grades and academic standing."*

Beyond the contrast between these two groups of students, there are differences within each group. Either a two- or four-year school may be public or private, inner city or suburban or rural, may be very selective or have an open admissions policy—these in addition to a wide range of variation in student attributes within a single school.

The great range of places in which sociology is taught describes one aspect of our current situation. It alerts us to the peculiarities of our own, special teaching situation. And it impels each of us to ask: what adaptations to place and population would improve my instruction? If, for example, the situation of the community college student is as has been portrayed, then attention to their point in the life cycle, to examples drawn from the locality, and to more tightly structured courses is indicated. In any event, we cannot assume that a given mode of instruction is equally suitable for all student populations. Davis (1976:57) speaks to the need for a sensitive adaptation to population and circumstance in lecturing:

For most college teachers, lecturing is like throwing the shot: they spend all their time getting together a very heavy message and then they just fling it. Lecturing, in fact, is more like throwing a frisbee: the message has to be thrown in such a way that it can be caught and with some reasonable expectation that it can be returned.

Who Is Doing the Teaching?

The current situation in sociology is, of course, seriously shaped by those who are transmitting it. Yet, not only are we unsure about what we teach: we are haphazard as to who shall teach—despite the fact that undergraduate instruction in sociology has a critical impact on the profession. It affects the level of confidence and respect accorded sociology by the educated layman. It conveys—or should—some sense of the necessary link between knowledge and action, so affecting the willingness to invest in the sociological research needed for effective administration and legislation. And it is a means of recruiting prospective sociologists.

These outcomes are affected by the quality and allocation of teachers. As to quality, we have virtually no data on the competence or performance of sociology instructors. We have data on the highest degree earned by sociologists teaching in different types of schools, but holding the doctorate is no guarantee of superlative teaching. (One might hope that it is no obstacle.) Our view is further obscured by poor data: the methods most often used to evaluate teaching are those most removed from student learning and from the work teachers perform. Among the methods employed by schools around the country, course syllabi, examinations, test scores, and long-range follow-up of students are used far less in the evaluation of teachers than are the opinions of chairperson, dean, and colleague, and the person's research productivity (Astin and Lee, 1967). Systematic student evaluation has increased in recent years; but the quality of many instruments used is far less than one might wish—less, indeed, than that of many instruments *available*. With that caveat in mind, it is worth noting that Linsky and Straus (1973), analyzing student ratings at sixteen universities, found that sociologists were rated below average when compared with teachers in other disciplines (except psychology). The authors suggest a couple of explanations: large class size (which they, but not all researchers, find associated with low ratings) and the indefiniteness of sociological content. We are dubious. In any case, if our subject matter presents special difficulties (it may), it would still be true that sociologists have not developed teaching approaches to circumvent them.

Together with other evidence and impressions, the Linsky and Straus study convinces us that there is some room for improvement in the quality of sociology instruction. We know that few sociology departments have written standards or guidelines for teaching (Ewens and Emling, 1975). And if quality is not defined, how can we know what to aim for or the degree of our success? We know, too, that few of us have training in teaching and that few departments offer assistance. If one assumes that experience has some bearing on the quality of instruction, then we must ponder the fact that in universities, where at least a third of the teaching of sociology occurs, very large parts of undergraduate instruction are in the hands of those who have least experience—graduate students. In sum, as to the qualifications of those who teach sociology we have little evidence; but we have reason to be less than sanguine about the current situation.

What of the allocation of teachers to courses? Perhaps the most serious allocation problem is found in graduate departments. Most students whose instruction is most difficult are taught by the most transient and least qualified instructors. Let us

back away from this damning assertion to offer the argument and evidence that logically precede it.

Who shall be assigned positions of responsibility in a business, factory, agency, or classroom? The answer hinges on the nature of the product, the materials going into it, the requirements imposed by their processing, and the costs of quality control. Now we take the following propositions as true. Thinking of the distribution of knowledge at the end of, and attributable to, a given course as a product, difficulty of production *is positively related to:*

1. diversity of elements to be processed

2. scope or range of desired outcomes

3. transiency of key personnel

4. investment in material and human resources

and *is inversely related to:*

5. salience of goal to be pursued

6. understanding of the nature of the product

7. motivation to pursue that goal

8. presence of extrinsic reward and support for the producer

9. potential for intrinsic reward for the producer

Bringing these propositions to bear on our enterprise, we translate them as follows. It is harder to teach sociology effectively to the extent that:

1. students are heterogeneous in past experience and plans for the future

2. the scope of the course embraces more of sociology's forty-odd subfields

3. instructors have short-term appoint-

ments, precluding improvement based on cumulated experience

    4. classroom space and arrangements, library, audiovisual, and personnel resources represent a lower unit investment

    5. materials of sociology are less salient and pertinent to students

    6. students are ignorant of the nature of sociology

    7. a drive to master the substance of sociology is lacking

    8. there is relatively little extrinsic reward for the teacher

    9. the potential for intrinsic reward for the teacher is lower than that found in alternate ways of spending time and energy

We have just described the distinctive problems of instruction in sociology for most of our students: those to whom we offer sociology as a service course. Such courses are, above all, two: Introductory Sociology and Social Problems. In 1973/74, these two courses enrolled 1.1 million students, or 64 percent of all students enrolled in the ten most frequently offered sociology courses ("Undergraduate Sociology," 1975).

Introductory	891,980	51%
Social Problems	224,345	13
Marriage & Family	193,737	11
Seven Other Courses	431,925	25
	1,741,987	100%

Who teaches these courses? Typically, those least qualified to confront the toughest problems of instruction in sociology: the junior faculty and teaching assistants (TAs). An example: at a university where we consulted with the sociology staff, 61 percent of the 3,765 students registered in sociology courses in the fall of 1972 were in the Introductory and the Social Problems

courses. And most of these students were in classes assigned to TAs.

But is it not true that some of the young, enthusiastic, and committed who are *au courant* in their knowledge of the field may be better teachers than their elders? Why this unkindly allegation that most students are taught sociology by those least qualified to do so? For this reason: other things equal, we suspect that competence increases with experience.[15] Yet those teaching most of our students have the least experience. And members of this category—TAs, instructors, pretenure faculty—have the greatest turnover. This transiency means that there is no assurance that next year, or two years hence, the course will be improved by capitalizing on the past. *Transiency institutionalizes inexperience.*

Younger faculty and TAs tend to transmit what they've been taught, pretty much in the manner they were taught it. But the instructional mode that gets by with a homogeneous group of highly motivated preprofessionals is not likely to be effective among the heterogeneous and less motivated group in the undergraduate classroom.

The novice is more vulnerable to errors of both commission and omission. The first sort of error includes emphases eccentric to sociology, such as improving the quality of human relationships through sensitivity training. The second is seen when the instructor cannot seize opportunities presented in class sessions and extra-class work to enhance methodological acuity, or to tap pertinent research materials, or to touch related subfields in sociology, or to bridge into related content in the humanities or the biophysical sciences.

The professional training of many younger faculty and TAs pins them to sharply defined points of expertise. This they need, of course. But for teaching these large, general education courses, they also need what they lack: that breadth of experience, in sociology and in their lives, that enables them to touch students from diverse backgrounds at many points.

Finally, their assignment to these introductory courses is inappropriate since they have less time than their elders to invest in the most difficult teaching assignments. This is part of the life cycle squeeze. They are likely to be carrying a heavier teaching load—e.g., 2 and 3, even 3 and 3 courses, instead of the lighter 2 and 2 carried by senior faculty. (In *many* schools the load is heavier still!) They are under pressure to publish, to lengthen the vita as they anticipate promotion and tenure decisions. They are more recently married, more likely to have young children, less able to hire others to do household repairs for them, less able to afford summers free to reflect and plan and write.

We do not minimize the influences that have led to this situation: burgeoning enrollments in sociology, the availability of bright graduate students, the retreat of the elders after years of undergraduate servitude, the demands of graduate students for the services of senior faculty renowned in the profession. Nor do we minimize the constraints that militate against an easy solution. For example, sociology faculty at one university note that theirs is the only Ph.D.—granting school in the state. Necessarily then, that university must invest much of its resources in research and graduate instruction. What is left over is for undergraduates.

Our answer to the question, Who is teaching sociology to most students? is discouraging. Yet there are ways in which we might act to ensure a more satisfactory answer. For example, TAs and young faculty might more often be appointed to teach in their special fields. As a corollary, senior faculty should periodically accept the responsibility of undergraduate instruction, especially in the two most difficult courses, the Introductory and Social Problems. This is an obligation that need not be wholly onerous. One distinguished sociologist and member of the National Academy of Science welcomes the chance to teach the introductory course every few years. For it gives him, as he says, a chance to reshape his vision of the field and to put his specialty, demography, in context.

Another step: teaching assistants should have a chance to observe and read and ruminate about problems of instruction in sociology before they are thrown on their own. A course treating such problems should be a part of the professional training of most graduate students. It would help, too, were we to let competence in teaching enter seriously into judgments on promotion and tenure. We suggest the weight given competence in teaching be roughly proportional to that part of the total work load constituted by teaching. We should be as prompt to fire a faculty person for incompetence in teaching as for failure to produce publishable research.*

Doubtless, there are many ways of improving our situation, some of them so obvious, such as an annual faculty meeting to report and discuss innovations in sociology instruction, that their mention is embarrassing. But obvious and desirable as such steps might be, we know of departments where the obviously needed never occurs. We have yet a way to go before we can answer, more cheerily, the question, Who is teaching sociology? by saying: the trained and the competent.

* We return to this heretical proposal in chapter 14.

What Do We Know About the Teaching of Sociology?

Not enough. The lacunae are many and serious. But especially since the mid-1960s, we have learned much about sociology instruction, although it is apparent that the new knowledge is not widely exploited.[16] These conditions concern the profession since so many sociologists spend so much of their careers (and daily rounds) on teaching. To examine the literature on the teaching of sociology reveals a wide range of resources already available to sociologists. It also sheds some light on our profession's attention to the teaching role and environment.

Many of our colleagues have an answer to the question, What is reliably known about the teaching of sociology?[17] They believe (as do some academics in other fields) that little is known about what makes for effective teaching; and that research on teaching is so inconclusive or of such poor quality that there is little point in consulting it, much less acting on it. Some of our colleagues seem to take an unusual position for sociologists: that teaching and learning are not amenable to disciplined analysis, explanation and prediction. Teaching is seen as an unfathomable art for which there are few, if any, rules. Not seen as a science, no more is it seen as a craft (since crafts rest on codified and transmitted experience). If so, teaching and learning are activities and processes unique in the social world. A more sophisticated version of this position holds that teaching and learning are far too complex and uncontrollable for us to have reliable knowledge about. As rationale or rationalization such beliefs diminish the need to pay serious attention to teaching and create a convenient self-fulfilling prophecy, which can serve the self-interest of its preachers.

These beliefs are largely unsupported and unsupportable. It is true that the literature on teaching and learning contains hundreds of poor-quality studies reporting findings where no control sample has been used or where contextual effects have not been taken into account. And there are hundreds of studies that rely on bivariate tables or a dependent variable weakly measured with a pencil-and-paper test of undemonstrated relationship to the behavior under study. There are studies with strong conclusions and weak underpinnings. But while the quality of many studies on collegiate instruction (generally and in sociology) *is* poor, more recent research is far better than that done before the 1960s. It is true that the work is quite uneven; yet despite immense gaps, much is known, and reliably so. As examples, aspects of college teaching about which we have reliable knowledge include: (1) personalized systems of instruction; (2) student evaluation of teaching instruments; (3) the relationships between class size and format and learning; (4) conditions fostering higher cognitive forms of learning (e.g., problem solving, analysis); and (5) the relationship between cognitive styles and learning.[18] In later chapters where we discuss instructional goals and strategies of teaching, we will make use of this literature on college teaching as appropriate. We now turn to examine briefly that portion of the literature of most direct interest to sociologists.

The Scope of the Literature on Teaching Sociology.[19]

We estimate that, since the late nineteenth century, between 500 and 600 articles and books have been published on the teaching of sociology. It is safe to say that between 45 percent and 60 percent of this work has appeared since the mid-1960s. Since 1895 (when the *American Journal of Sociology* was first published), 191 articles on teaching have appeared in *The American Journal of Sociology*, *Sociology and Social Research*, *Social Forces*, and the *American Sociological Review;* only three of them appeared after 1965. But well over one hundred articles on teaching have appeared in *The American Sociologist* (first published in 1965) and *Teaching Sociology* (first published in 1973). In the mid-1970s, forty to fifty articles on the teaching of sociology appeared annually. This represents less than 1 percent of all articles in sociology for a one-year period. What does this literature contain?

First, many educational innovations in sociology we think of as contemporary were considered in publications more than thirty-five years ago—e.g., fieldwork, discussion-group-based courses, use of graphics in instruction, sociology correspondence courses, and high school sociology. Other early articles appeared on the use in sociology of student evaluations of teaching (1947), literature as an instructional tool (1957), film (1950), and television (1955). Curricular plans and textbooks prepared for undergraduate audiences appeared in the late 1890s.

Second, discussions of the teaching of sociology published since the 1960s concentrated on a few issues. There are:

Many Articles On

Introductory sociology
Statistics, methods and uses of the computer
Simulation and gaming
Curriculum
Preparation for teaching
Social problems courses

Few Articles On

Assessment of student learning
Grading

Teaching sociology in settings other than colleges and universities
Individualized instruction
Learning and student–teacher interaction
Sociology and general educational goals
Textbooks
Student evaluation of teaching
Specific courses, devices, or course formats

These articles vary widely in their usefulness. Many are accounts of teaching strategies or methods employed by an individual teacher. They describe what a teacher did and offer impressions as to why it worked (or didn't). Analysis and assessment often are weak and fail to take into account student or contextual variables. Comparative designs are often employed, but too often we have no measure of what really took place—for example, in the lecture class as opposed to the discussion class. Nonetheless, a number of studies appeared providing careful literature reviews, having sound quasi-experimental designs, and offering useful descriptive data. Despite the usual range of problems, there are few problem areas of teaching and curriculum where sociologists must start *de novo*. And there are several realms where we have reliable knowledge.

Curricular trends in sociology.[20]   Major studies of curriculum patterns, using national samples published in 1942, 1957, 1969, 1974, and 1975, are available. We know what courses are taught where, what courses constitute a major, and so on.

Introductory Sociology: teaching and curriculum.   Since 1965, more than sixty articles have been published describing either specific introductory courses, patterns of instruction, texts available, or outcomes of using particular instructional formats (see Davis, Goldsmid, and Perry,

1977:1–11). Among the studies are a national survey of mass instruction (Baker, 1976), a content analysis of treatment of methodology in introductory texts (Van Valey, 1975), a controlled study on teaching critical thinking skills (Logan, 1976), and a multiple regression analysis of determinants of student performance in introductory courses (Oksanen and Spencer, 1975).

Methods instruction and the use of computers in teaching. More than two dozen papers in this field include a number that report learning outcomes and an excellent descriptive literature (see Davis, Goldsmid, and Perry, 1977:12–19).

Personalized Systems of Instruction (PSI).[21] Varieties of individualized instruction (self-paced, based on explicitly stated learning objectives, unit mastery) have been shown to be more effective than conventional teaching techniques in achieving a range of learning, as well as in improving retention of content and stimulating interest in the field of study. Dozens of carefully designed studies, including a few in sociology, support these conclusions.

There are other aspects of college teaching on which we have reliable knowledge, including: the effects of class size and format on student learning of information; student evaluations of teaching, student learning, and teacher development; and the contextual effects—organizational effects—on individual student self-concept and career choice.[22] There are other matters on which our knowledge has less than firm, yet more than trivial, support, including: the influence of affective factors on learning; effects of active student involvement in the learning process; and the contribution of communication skills to teaching effectiveness.

While we know more, and more surely, we still know too little about interaction patterns in the classroom and are only beginning to see studies that go beyond teaching method—beyond, for example, comparison of lecture and discussion outcomes.[23] The yield of sociological inquiry itself has hardly been tapped for leads toward improved instruction (and not only in sociology).[24] We know little about sociology teaching with particular types of students. The interactions between student cognitive style and the learning and teaching of sociology are virtually unaddressed. Nonetheless, the pertinent research is accumulating, resources are growing, interest among colleagues is quickening. We can be sure that a larger lode of reliable knowledge will be available in the near future.

≈

When we look at sociology today there is no question about its signal achievements in a brief period. In little more than two generations' time, we have established a host of useful propositions about the conditions of status attainment; the correlates of poverty and discrimination; the impact of class on aspiration and achievement; the remarkably constant conceptions of occupational standing (with important modifications in socialist societies); the relative importance of psychic and social variables in accounting for economic development; authority and power arrangments across familial roles; concomitants of religious affiliation, participation, and devotion; the conditions of deviance, societal reaction, and its consequences; and increasingly sophisticated methods of inquiry. These are but a few examples.

And our training programs to produce the research to produce the knowledge have been increasingly effective.

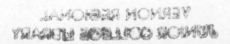

From many graduate programs, students are emerging as competent scientists. But advances in undergraduate instruction—and training for it—have been less spectacular.

To be sure, there have always been sociologists who raised questions about the outcomes of their teaching and who labored to teach responsibly and effectively. Indeed, steps toward improved teaching were taken early in the history of our discipline. Sporadically, teaching appeared on the programs of the American Sociological Society and regional associations. A course for graduate students on instruction in sociology was offered as early as 1921. But it was only after the mid-1960s that teaching concerns became institutionalized within the profession and that continuing forums for exchange of information were created. These developments include: the creation of an ad-hoc ASA committee on undergraduate education in the mid-1960s, the ASA Section on Undergraduate Education (1972), the ASA journal, *The American Sociologist* (1965) (the only large-circulation journal in sociology to carry articles on teaching after the late 1950s), *Teaching Sociology* (1973), several new state sociology associations (many of which take teaching as their central concern), and the ASA Projects on Teaching Undergraduate Sociology (1974), which have generated unprecedented efforts to improve instruction. But these new developments in the teaching of sociology are not yet widely exploited.

They will be, certainly. And the sooner the better. For we have seen that ours is a vast enterprise annually affecting millions of students. And we still cannot say with assurance what it is that we are teaching, or how such teaching might be adapted to particular aims and circumstances. We continue to assign the most difficult jobs of instruction to the least ex-perienced. Our treatment of teaching remains strangely cavalier for scholars who stress rigor and measurement in disciplined analysis. Indeed, one must be struck by the ambivalence of the sociologist's professional life, the gulf between the standards applied to creation and the standardlessness of his work as transmitter. We believe this ambivalence points to a central dilemma—and to its resolution. The matter is so critical that we devote the following chapter to the problem of our double standards.

Notes

1. It seems likely that renowned departments with their emphasis on research (Satariano, 1976) may set the style for others. Doubtless the connection between department prestige and faculty publication is a complex one, subject to change. Two articles that review much of the relevant literature are Solomon (1972) and Solomon and Walters (1975).

2. The major post–World War II expansion in community colleges occurred after 1961 (Monroe, 1972:3–4, 12–13). We think one could rank order the types of schools affected (from most to least affected) by influences that reduce concern for teaching as follows: private, renowned universities; major public universities; highly selective, private, four-year liberal arts colleges; other state universities; other private four-year colleges; and community colleges.

3. Between 1956 and 1971 there was an almost tenfold increase in federal dollars spent for contracted research with the largest proportionate increase after the early 1960s (see Baker, 1975).

4. The task of teaching graduate students is easier because, compared to undergraduates, they are rigorously selected; they bring high levels of self-motivation to their work and share goals with their graduate faculty (Wilson, 1976a:250–251; Goldsmid, 1976a:241–242).

5. Available evidence has uncovered few, if any, significant correlations (positive or

negative) between research productivity and teaching effectiveness, chiefly as defined by students. This general conclusion was reached by Eble (1972:28). Major studies are Harry and Goldner (1972), Linsky and Straus (1975), and Stallings and Singhal (1970). See also Goldsmid, Gruber, and Wilson (1977). Faculty may *feel* that the one task hinders the other. For research results clearly indicate high levels of faculty dissatisfaction with their balance of teaching and research, and the time invested and rewards received for the two tasks (Wilson et al., 1975).

6. We call academic freedom a myth to challenge the easy, stereotypical assumption of complete individual freedom in instruction. The freedom of academic choice is always constrained. Students have very little freedom; for curricula are set, and without their concurrence, the content of courses is set. They could not have genuine academic freedom, in any case, because they are ignorant of the content of the options among which choices must be made. For the faculty, academic freedom is constrained by extent of knowledge, by size of department faculty (determining range of curricular offerings and extent of specialization), by general faculty values (touching on the nature of a liberal arts education and the uses to which it should be put), by state and federal action subsidizing some sorts of scholarly activity (and not others), by the pressure of minority groups (consider CUNY's open admission policies), by the state of the budget, and by our collective representations in the United States about Communism (recall the impact of Senator Joe McCarthy—and of Sputnik on education in the United States). Academic freedom is also limited by war, by depression and inflation, by technology (consider the influence of the computer), and by the mass media.

7. Data represent extrapolation to the universe of schools from a stratified random sample of 500 of them; response rate was 53 percent; data on the pattern of nonresponse were not presented. The survey was conducted by CRM Books.

8. This estimate of number of teachers of sociology was derived as follows. There are approximately 8,000 regular members of the American Sociological Association; many teachers of sociology are not members. We doubled the ASA figure and started with a base of 16,000. A number of surveys have indicated that between three-fourths and four-fifths of sociologists work in academe. But not all sociologists working in academic organizations teach. We estimated that 90 percent of academic sociologists do some teaching. Hence: $16,000 \times .8 = 12,800 \times .9 = 11,520$. We know of some higher estimates. One direct mail company specializing in higher education has address labels for more than 17,000 sociologists (College Marketing Group, 1977). However, their definition of sociologist is not known and their list may include some persons who teach sporadically, and some who do not have training in sociology but teach it. In any event, such lists, and our estimate, do not include the very large number of graduate students who teach a substantial proportion of undergraduate enrollments in university departments of sociology.

9. These data are very close to those in three independent surveys: Reid and Bates (1971), Gates (1969), and Gates (1975).

10. The survey reported by Ewens and Emling was fielded during the spring of 1975 as part of the work of the ASA Projects on Teaching Undergraduate Sociology. Questionnaires were sent to the chairpersons of all graduate departments and to a 25-percent sample of departments in community and four-year colleges. The overall response rate (after a followup) was 55 percent, with graduate departments responding most often (75 percent) and community colleges least often (31 percent). Analysis of response patterns for two- and four-year institutions shows no statistically significant variations in the regional distribution of response or in public versus private institutions. University departments in the North Central region were far more likely to respond (91 percent); departments in the Northeast were least likely to respond (58 percent).

11. This estimate of available funding is derived as follows: We begin with the estimate that there are 12,000 teachers of sociology (see

note 8 above), and we assume that 10 percent of these teachers received a $1,000 course development grant, 1 percent received grants averaging $10,000, and .3 percent received grants averaging $20,000. To these figures is added the approximately $200,000 in grants received by the ASA Projects on Teaching. Total = $3.3 million.

12. Assessing changes in the interval between her 1969 and 1975 studies, Gates wrote (1975): "Findings indicate that there has been a substantial expansion of sociology offerings in the last five years and, more important to professional sociology, a great increase in the number of tool courses provided." By tool courses, she means Research Methods, Field Work, and other courses embracing methods of analysis including statistics, together with courses in theory and history of social thought.

13. The number of agreed-on learnings for a course is not an issue. They might be few or many, depending on the nature of the course and of the department specifying them. Above all, they would depend on those learnings on which succeeding course instructors wish to build. One might think of them as constituting 10 percent or 60 percent of the target learnings. Most of them would represent learning goals that any competent sociologist would wish to achieve in a course of a given label.

14. Such objectives are not limited to methods of inquiry, although these serve as the simplest illustrations of the point. For one set of operationally stated goals for "the sociological perspective," "thinking in sociology," and some content goals in introductory sociology, see Vaughan and Peterson (1975:13–14).

15. For some evidence, see Frey (1973).

16. It is only lately that there has been a concerted effort to improve sociology instruction in colleges and universities. (Under ASA auspices and NSF funding, a project to improve teaching materials in sociology for secondary schools ran from about 1965 to 1971.) The ASA Section on Undergraduate Education came into being only in 1972 and as late as 1976/77 had a mere 500 members, about 4 percent of the ASA membership and but 10 percent of the number teaching introductory sociology. Volume 1, number 1 of *Teaching Sociology* appeared in October 1973. The mid-seventies have brought heartening developments for those working for improved sociology instruction. Among these we have seen the flourishing ASA Projects on Teaching, an extended network of consulting and interchange among sociology departments on problems of instruction and the commitment of several state societies to such problems as their primary purpose for being. Yet there is clearly a long way to go, both in the number of those actively concerned and in the quality of their exchange.

17. The next two paragraphs are drawn from Goldsmid (1976a:237–238).

18. A brief review of studies touching on the first four areas (with citation to literature) is found in Goldsmid (1976a:238–240). For an extended discussion of research on cognitive styles and learning, and various forms of personalized instruction, see Cross (1976:111–134, 49–74). A good review on higher cognitive learnings can be found in Ericksen (1974:131–149).

19. Data cited in this section are drawn from Goldsmid (1977b; 1976a; 1976b), Goldsmid and Goldsmid (1979), and Davis, Goldsmid, and Perry (1977).

20. Major curricular studies are Reid and Bates (1971), Bates and Reid (1971), Gates (1969), Bradshaw and McPherron (1977), "Undergraduate Sociology," (1975), and Shin (1975).

21. For an excellent, detailed review of research and theory on PSI and behaviorally based modes of instruction, see Johnson and Ruskin (1977). For research and debate on PSI among sociologists, see *Teaching Sociology* (1974) and Malec (1975).

22. A brief discussion of these points is contained in Goldsmid (1976a:238–239). On contextual effects of institutions, the classic study is Davis (1966). For a recent article suggesting minor modification of that thesis and containing citations to research on these effects, see Bassis (1977).

23. Dubin and Taveggia have shown (1968) that preoccupation with teaching method only is a dead-end approach for those seeking to understand the conditions of learning. Papers in sociology that *do* focus on interaction process include Karp and Yoels (1976), and Solomon, Bezdeck, and Rosenberg (1963).

24. For some leads to such applications, see Wilson (1976a:254–260) and Goldsmid (1976a:241–242). See also Boocock (1972) and Waller (1932). In addition, some work in social psychology of teaching and learning will provide useful leads—e.g., Mann et al. (1970) and Schmuck and Schmuck (1975).

CHAPTER 2
DUAL ROLES AND DOUBLE STANDARDS: HOW CAN WE RECONCILE THEM?

We began by reflecting on general conditions that shape the teaching of sociology today. We turn now to a more immediate and pervasive influence: the ideas and values that inform the two principal aspects of our vocation, teaching and research. These ideas and values are more prominent among sociologists at major universities with large graduate departments. But the dilemma they express spills over to affect sociologists at other universities and colleges. It is instructive to reflect on our roles, which are often thought to be counter-demanding. In doing so, we will describe their antitheses, their likely sources, and their consequences, finally proposing that their opposition is superficial—that our training as sociologists can point to ways of improving our teaching and resolving a needless contradiction.

Between the two roles that dominate our lives—discoverer and transmitter—there is a curious gulf. The task that preempts most of our working hours[1] goes unevaluated, while our research and writing are likely to be assessed with the greatest care. In our research, we celebrate reason. But in teaching, we act persistently on faith. (For we assume that we are altering others' behavior and their ways of thinking. Yet the evidence on which we base this assumption is flimsy and pride-enhancing—for example, results on final examinations that demand the regurgitation of material whose relevance, reten-

tion, and ultimate use are matters of murky obscurity.) We praise the vocation of teaching while we pay on the basis of publication. Departments' reputations rest on their visibility gained through members' publications, while their bread and butter come from the hordes of anonymous students whom we think we teach. Research is held to high standards through public evaluation by competent colleagues. Teaching is virtually without standards, in part because it is a very private enterprise, seldom appraised by competent peers. In sum, the standards guiding performance in one role are reasonably clear; for the other role, the standards are scarcely articulated.

Why so?

Likely Reasons for the Double Standard

Some of our indifference to the teaching role may derive from the circumstances of past years. In the early days of higher education, there was a dearth of printed material. Professional lore resided in the minds of an elite who trained a self-selected, highly motivated minority for law, medicine, the clergy, and the military. Elements of this elitist tradition persist. We still rely heavily on the purveyor of truth. This tradition is abetted by a grading system that prompts students to record, recall, and return the truth on demand. And so it seems gratuitous to question performance in a role whose incumbents are seen as all-knowing.

Differing standards may reflect different schemes of professional socialization that separate creator from transmitter. We *are* trained as sociologists. This means that we fix on discovery. We stress problems of gaining reliable knowledge. In preparing for the research role, we deal daily with peers who are likewise engaged. Mutual aid through discussion and criticism and exchange of notes is the norm. Graduate students collaborate in preparing for certifying examinations. They do research as apprentices to faculty members. The faculty, in general, are available as consultants on research. (These include experts in affiliated research institutes.) Among all these professionals, someone is likely to serve as a useful model. Material resources are provided—office space, calculators, supplies, computers, typewriters. Thus the Ph.D. in sociology becomes reasonably sophisticated in research. And we have standards by which to judge its adequacy. Parallel support and training for the prospective sociology instructor are almost unheard of.

The sharp contrast in socialization for the two roles is paralleled by a marked difference in organizational support. At major universities, it is the research, not the teaching role, that is nurtured.[2] Research is a superior enterprise; teaching, inferior. Research merits cash and perquisites; teaching has the solace of psychic income. Research brings us our merit badges—renown, promotion, raises, tenure, and travel. Federal funds and foundation bounty affirm our conviction: it's the extension, not the transmission of knowledge, that counts. Leaves and sabbaticals are approved—for research, not for improvements in instruction. Affiliated research institutes provide research appointments, consultants, entree to funding, hardware. There are few comparable on-campus organizations in support of teaching.[3] Results of research gain publicity. New subject matter or new departures in instructional techniques seldom do. Four-year colleges often follow suit with research support funds built into the budget; and with leaves and sabbaticals on the understanding that these are for scholarly activities, to fend off the threat of obsolescence in a rapidly moving discipline. (On this score, there may be more justification for the four-year college than for the university to spend its widow's mite to stimulate scholarly inquiries.)

Another reason for our double standard stems from this proposition: standards are easier to achieve and sustain when those affected (and their circumstances) are alike, rather than dissimilar. For it is plausible that clarity and precision in standards are positively related to the homogeneity of the group. In the research situation, standards are set and kept by a group of our colleagues, typically in a subfield in which all have been trained and in which work follows accepted guidelines. But teachers are much more diverse; so, likewise, are practitioners' standards. They vary widely between colleges and universities, public and private institutions, schools predominantly white or black, urban or rural. This situation is reflected in our rating of schools and departments, remote and uncertain as such an appraisal must be. (Such ratings may be better indicators of the background and ability of students admitted than of instructional quality.)

To say that standards guiding sociology instruction vary widely is to say that we lack universal yardsticks of adequacy. But the contrast between research and teaching roles goes beyond this: standards of adequate performance are sometimes *opposed.* Consider the curious contradictions evident in table 2.1. Such contrasting occupational ideologies serve to justify exacting standards in the one role and no standards (or most ambiguous ones) in the other.[5]

There is another, critically important cause for shying away from stringent standards for teaching. The quality of instruction is endlessly improvable. Were we to invest in it what is required by the highest standards, we would be always at work, even with a course load of one! This is so for several reasons. Student popula-

---

Table 2.1 Contradictions between the Research and Teaching Roles in Sociology

In the Research Role	In the Teaching Role
1. All steps in the research process should be reported.	1. No steps in the teaching process are reported. We do little systematic sharing and comparing of instructional problems and solutions with our colleagues.
2. The welfare of one's subjects must not be compromised.	2. The welfare of one's subjects is not a salient issue.
3. The relationship between investigator and subject is a privileged one, entailing confidentiality.	3. The relationship between investigator and subject is not usually seen by instructors as problematic, although students may see it so.
4. Findings belong to the scientific community—i.e., to one's peers. They must be shared. One's work is public.	4. Findings are not shared, because they are usually impressionistic and undemonstrable. We have not been inclined to put calipers on the process of instruction and its outcomes.
5. Findings are shared, through professional journals, in order to invite criticism and correction.	5. Activities are private, not public. Teaching is carried out *in camera.*
6. More effective performance in the research role stems from peer evaluation.	6. Very seldom has there been systematic peer review. More effective performance in the teaching role cannot be based on peer evaluation.
7. Criticism, favorable or adverse, is the basis on which one's reputation rests.	7. One's reputation as a teacher must rest on unsystematic and inadequate measures: scuttlebutt, the odd complaint or praise, number of students registering, etc.
8. Criticism, favorable or adverse, is based on standards enabling peers to assess the adequacy of logic and techniques of inquiry; the adequacy of the backdrop in theory against which the research proceeds; the extent to which the inquiry advances knowledge about a given class of social phenomena; and the probability that findings may enable us to shape future events.	8. Comparable standards for evaluation are inapplicable since it is often held that: (a) good teachers are born, not made; (b) good teaching is caught (by observation), not taught; (c) it is impossible to define a good teacher since there are so many different teaching styles; (d) good teaching doesn't really matter because good students can always learn anyway; (e) practice makes, if not perfect, at least tolerable levels of teaching; (f) if one knows nothing about teaching, neither do education professors or fellow sociologists; and (g) teaching is such a complex activity, affected by so many conditions and traits that we cannot grasp the cryptic combination that makes it effective.[4]

tions differ dramatically from time to time and place to place. Teaching strategies need to change, accordingly. The discipline changes; and in sociology, maybe beyond most disciplines, the threat of obsolescence is very real. Finally, in a liberal arts program, the instructor must incessantly seek to weave sociology into the larger fabric of student experience, perhaps especially the concurrent experiences in the humanities and the biophysical sciences.

In some schools, a further reason for the lack of clearly articulated standards is that competent performance in the teacher's role doesn't carry the kudos that competent research does. And while in recent years, sometimes under duress, the teacher's role has been celebrated, the written record of research is much the more obvious basis for reward and punishment.[6]

We have already mentioned another impediment to developing standards of sociology instruction: one can't develop standards for the unseen. Each teacher, first among equals, performs his own pedagogical alchemy within the inviolable sanctuary of the classroom. Much of this is owing to the unexceptionable principle of academic freedom. And much, doubtless, results from the ever finer division of labor among colleagues and the need for administrators to manage Matters of Great Import. But the result is that each teacher is on his own. Standards, if there be any, are individual standards—almost a contradiction in terms.

Standards are lacking, too, owing to a circumstance noted in chapter 1: the inexperience and rapid turnover of those who teach most students (in introductory and other service courses). Transience works against the jelling of basic standards for what shall be taught and how.

Finally, the development of standards is resisted by those who fear the imposition of what they would call a sterile orthodoxy. This position is sometimes defended by asserting that sociologists simply don't agree on any common core of elements for, say, the introductory course in sociology. Actually, as we earlier attested, one can get ready assent to a fairly lengthy roster of learnings for such courses. Thus we interpret the assertion that nobody agrees as a defensive response—in effect, a plea to be left alone. But this assertion disregards several facts: that a statement of minimum standards will constrain but a fraction of instruction in a course; that without the public statement of instructional goals, their achievement can't be evaluated; that without a statement of desired learning goals, a student is denied the possibility of a cumulative learning experience in a series of courses, some of which are presumed to build on preceding experience; that requiring heterodox exposures may well be the orthodox standard. Such a defensive position, finally, misses the distinction between form and content. For example, to require an introductory course to treat stratification does not dictate that class distinctions be treated within work organizations, or in their ecological manifestations, or in the neocolonial relationships of international corporations.

Doubtless there are other plausible reasons for our double standard. These, in sum, are the ones we have noted:

1. We express unintended arrogance in making ourselves the central, if not the sole, source of Truth. With such an absolute posture, the relativity implied in the use of a yardstick, a standard, becomes gratuitous.

2. We are trained for the research role, but not for the teaching role.

3. Organizational resources are available for support of the one role, but not for the other.

4. Heterogeneity of audience and setting makes it hard for us to fix on appropriate standards of performance and product.

5. The standardlessness of the teaching role is supported by a know-nothing occupational ideology.

6. The lack of standards governing teaching helps us avoid the formidable task of adapting pedagogical techniques to changing circumstance and student population, and masks the threat of early obsolescence.

7. The one role is celebrated and rewarded; the other is not.

8. The privileged sanctuary of the classroom is a secret realm whose unseen activities preclude evaluation and, therefore, the development of standards.

9. Standards for teaching are hard to establish when most students are taught by the most transient and least experienced.

10. The fear of an imposed orthodoxy discourages attempts to develop exacting standards of instruction.

What Are the Outcomes of Standardlessness?

Suppose a double standard does obtain, and for likely reasons. What then? What are the consequences? The likeliest answer, we think, is this: teaching will continue to be an ill-defined process with poorly measured outcomes, enormous variation in adequacy of instruction, a mediocre mean level of performance, and students learning far less than they could and should.[7]

But students are not likely to know of their loss; for they cannot answer the question, What was missing? or the question, What might have been? And, on the other hand, the double standard brings benefits for the sociologist, the department, and the discipline. Making weaker demands of ourselves in the one role releases energy for investment in the other role. With its underpinnings of protective self-deceptions, our double standard spares us anxiety and discontent. (There is no basis for discontent when what students learn goes largely unmeasured; when what *is* measured is likely to be trivial and badly measured; and when, above all, failure to learn is exclusively attributable to student sloth, poor preparation, or institutional constraints.) Neglect of teaching benefits the department when teaching and research are seen as competing, zero-sum activities. For research, not teaching, is the scale by which many departments are judged.[8] Publications lend visibility to a department, attract highly qualified graduate students and more prominent faculty. Such departments also garner the lion's share of grant money for research and graduate training. Likewise, the discipline itself may benefit from the double standard. More research, revision and extension of past findings, improved tools of inquiry—these are indirect, though no less real, outcomes of the double standard.

Recognition of such positive effects has led several colleagues to ask how we can reasonably attack the double standard whose existence they acknowledged. They cautioned that to apply research standards to the teaching role would reduce research and publication by individual sociologists. They warned that such a situation would, in turn, entail an erosion of departmental funding, a decline in department size, and ultimately, a moribund discipline. After presenting such dire forecasts, they wanted to know how we could argue for an end to the double standard.

We can and do so argue, not because their analysis is false, but because it is markedly incomplete. It disregards not only the adverse effects of a double standard on teaching, but also the unhappy outcomes of mediocre teaching for research itself. Above all, such an analysis is insensitive to the advantage to be gained if teaching and research were to become complementary and overlapping activities, guided by a single set of standards.

Adverse Effects on Research

Poor instruction may lead to criticism of our research as trivial, or so abstract as to have no visible bearing on the needs of those who sponsor it. Research needs the criticism of the informed, not the ignorant. One might suppose that, if reporters, congressmen, and citizen lobbyists had better training in sociology (and other disciplines), they would have a better understanding of how pure research is often useful in policy analysis and decision making. They might understand, better than Senator Proxmire, how the apparently trivial can be a surrogate for a larger inquiry into isomorphic patterns of deviance. And they might be less inclined to vote for cutbacks in the level of funding for federal and state support of research.[9]

The neglect of teaching may result in less demand for sociological research by those in the professions and in government. To the extent that our students fail to understand sociology, they may, on becoming lawyers, social workers, physicians, personnel officers, and administrators, fail to exploit the findings, methods, and perspective of sociology. Particularly among government officials, defective instruction in sociology means that pertinent research findings will be disregarded and the work of these former students will be less fruitful and more costly than it need be.

Mediocre instruction can contribute

to sociology's bad press. It can lead to a disregard, by practitioners, of pertinent findings. It can also undercut support of sociology in state universities. Since the late 1960s there has been increased demand for accountability in state-supported education. Taxpayers ask if their tax-supported schools are indeed teaching their children. We know that some students discuss with parents the teaching they receive. And students tend to become taxpaying parents. They know enough of academic lore to have heard the "publish or perish" dictum. And they have some sense that research and teaching compete for faculty time. Recent legislative debate indicates that taxpayers feel their children are being shortchanged at the expense of research branded as trivial. If these taxpayers see their children suffering through courses that they think are a waste of time and money, they are likely to endorse cutbacks in appropriations for education—especially, for research.

The double standard may also hurt research by diminishing teaching's contribution to the instructor's inquiries. Adequate instruction discriminates and integrates these four elements: *theory* (big ideas), *methods* of inquiry (testing those ideas), *content*, and *practical implications*. Every course impels us to the creative task of welding these elements into a coherent whole. Such an effort has its bearing on research. It helps us identify critical lacunae in an intellectual structure. It helps us identify pertinent variables. It sensitizes us to shortcomings of past research, and so points to problems worth pursuing in our current and future research. In short—and not despite, but because of students' innocence of the field— the articulation and clarification of ideas in a public forum, the classroom, is an effort that must advance research.[10]

Adverse Effects on Teaching

Our description of dual roles leads us to conclude that, in some sociology departments, teaching is considered a necessary nuisance. Although it must be done, it steals time from the original inquiry that defines sociology and leads to professional rewards. And so it gets as little time as routine requirements permit. If one assumes that teaching is an art form, that thinking about teaching adds not a cubit to an instructor's stature, then this does not matter. And in any case, whether it matters will be forever unknown since the results of our handiwork remain unrevealed in a classic case of pluralistic ignorance.

Our view (and our experience with a few TAs) is otherwise: sociology instruction is the worse for neglect. It is a reasonable presumption that we improve our performance as sociology teachers when we: (1) think about goals of instruction—those peculiar to a course and those transcending it; (2) identify the limitations imposed by an instructional setting, and the means of circumventing them; (3) think about the course cycle—the special problems of the beginning, middle, and end of a course; (4) think about the assertion that sociology is common sense muddily expressed; (5) ponder criteria of adequacy for the course syllabus and reading materials; (6) consider the merits and liabilities of lecture and discussion procedures; (7) consider the use of PSI (personalized methods of instruction), or computer-assisted instruction, or the Keller system, or the Teaching Information Processing System (TIPS), or audiovisual aids; and (8) think about various uses of testing—to evaluate instructor performance, to guide students' work, to employ nongraded instructional devices, and to certify level of student achievement.

We waver between dismay and unbelief when a TA or faculty member asserts that taking thought on these matters has no effect on the behaviors thought about. Such a view would be summarily condemned, were the same persons treating a research problem. Would we not profit, in this instance and others, by applying to teaching the standards that guide our research? But this is to assume that teaching and research have enough in common to justify the application of similar standards. Is this the case?

Is the Opposition Real?

The double standard does in fact obtain. Although we have drawn the contrast larger than life, beliefs and behaviors informing the two roles do indeed differ, sometimes approaching a zero-sum commitment. But this is not to say that this situation need be so. Nor is it to deny that a single standard would be preferable.

Yet we think the opposition is unreal; for it does not stem from the nature of the two activities. There is, in fact, much overlap between research and teaching in the goals of discovery and transmission, the criteria of importance that guide our activities, and the procedures of seeking and teaching.[11]

The Goals of Discovery and Transmission

The purpose of research, we say, is discovery, while that of teaching is transmission. Can we really mean that there is no discovery entailed in teaching and no transmission involved in research? No one, we think, would take that view. The question, then, is this: how much overlap is there in the goals of these two processes?

The answer is: a very great deal. Every sociology paper published in a professional journal is a piece of instruction from an author to other sociologists. Were it not, the paper would not have been accepted for publication. As with classroom instruction, the lesson to be learned may be trifling or powerful. As with good teaching, the paper will commence with a problem for which available answers are unsatisfactory. (In the most interesting cases, these answers will be contradictory.) It will then enlist reason and experience to contrive a surer answer. This surer answer will be tested against available data and others' experience. The structure of a good classroom session might well resemble a well-wrought report of a good research job. For research is done for an audience whose members are to be taught and who will, in turn, raise critical questions. So, also, in the classroom. Indeed, one might make the case that the format of a research report *is* the structure of a class session, adequately taught.

One might suppose that scientists *do* research, whereas teachers *talk* about it. But surely this is an overdrawn contrast. For a very large part—in some ways, the most important part—of the research process is ruminating about, talking about, the legacy of ideas pertinent to the problem being pursued. What we call the review of the literature is not simply a record of what our predecessors have passed on to us. It is an appraisal of that legacy, a debate stimulated by negative evidence; it is clearly talking about that legacy—just as we would do in the classroom.

On the other hand, *doing*—in field work, laboratory work, classroom demonstrations—can be crucial aspects of a well-crafted course. The study of migratory workers by Professor Friedland (1969)

is a case in point. In some of our best performances as instructors, we do actual research in and through a course—research on new populations and, sometimes, testing of new hypotheses. Such was the case in the Berkeley study of parental views of local schooling carried out by Professors Hochschild and Nasatir (1973) when they combined their courses in Sociology of Education and Methods of Research. Such, also, was the case with the work of Laurence Wylie (1966) and his students in a community study in Brittany.

Transmission, then, is certainly, inevitably, at the heart of research. And discovery can be the product of a class's inquiry—in collaboration with the senior investigator, who is the teacher (see also Toby, 1972). As to goals, then, of transmission versus discovery, a thoughtful scrutiny reveals much overlap between research and teaching. *Collaborative inquiry is at the heart of both activities.*

Criteria of Importance in Research and Teaching

Do these two activities differ on what's worth doing? Some might suggest that research begins with a question of some significance, whereas teaching starts, and ends, with the delivery of an important truth. Of course, neither teacher nor investigator would accept importance as a criterion unless we could answer the question: What makes matters sought or taught important? In research, the inquiry is more important when it promises to adjudicate the claims of contending theories, when it promises to extend general propositions to new populations or circumstances; or when, following observations at odds with current generalizations, it leads us to refute or revise inherited wisdom. Is the situation different with the teaching of sociology?

If so, it is only unnecessarily—and unfortunately—so. The importance of a matter treated in the classroom might well be measured in the same way it is measured in research. Does the classroom operation promise to revise, refine, or refute lay wisdom? Does it help students adjudicate contending explanations? Does it raise propositions to higher levels of abstraction to embrace additional populations or events? Research and teaching need not—should not—differ on this score; for the extension of reliable knowledge is a criterion of importance in *both* teaching and research.

Importance may be measured a second way. We may deem our work important insofar as it speaks to practical affairs. Teaching, if not research, should bear on mundane problems of the learners' lives. It should link, somehow, with issues of the day, with problems of preference and value. Good children of Durkheim, we know that our collective troubles have their roots in social arrangements, and so we employ our discipline for systematic analysis of social problems.

So matters of the better and the worse are often proper issues that inform our work as teachers. But as sociologists? As research people? Surely the discipline itself does not respond litmuslike to the current ephemeral issues that fleetingly exercise the layman? Surely, in contrast to the professor, the researcher takes the timeless perspective, devoting himself to those problems whose solutions will most advance our efforts to distill social reality in high-level abstractions.

Ah, but it is not so. We know very well that the ready market for research in urban sociology and human ecology has something to do with the woes of New York and other cities. We can see some

sensible connection between the burgeoning research in gerontology and NIH (and the advancing years of powerful, senior congressmen). We know that extensive research in race relations has something to do with Martin Luther King and George Wallace and the civil rights movement. We know that the research of the well-travelled demographer has something to do with apprehensions about the changing size and composition of our population as these affect our peace and prosperity. And we know that research in medical sociology has flourished because of its connection with the virtuous war against sickness.

What is worth inquiring into? and teaching about? Are the criteria of importance radically different? Indeed, not. Much, if not most, research reflects societal issues. So, likewise, in teaching.

Are Seeking and Teaching Two Different Processes?

Perhaps criteria of importance, the extension of reliable knowledge and its pertinence to social issues, need not separate research and teaching. But how about the processes themselves? Does not the one inquire, the other report? Is it not true that seeking knowledge and retailing it are quite different processes?

Perhaps this is sometimes so. But to the extent that it is so, in practice, it is too bad. And perhaps it often is simply bad. Tillich (see Brown, 1971:15) was surely right: our tendency as professors is "to throw answers like stones at the heads of those who have not yet asked the questions." But tendency and practice are not justifications. Surely the aim of education, like that of research, is to get answers, however tentative, to significant questions. No doubt our teaching is too often in the declaratory, rather than the interrogative, mood. Our syllabi and the readings we require hang a set of assertions on a framework of topics. Our lectures, too, may be curiously short of question marks. But it need not—should not—be so.

Indeed, there's every reason for teaching to be otherwise and, in being otherwise, more closely matach the process of inquiry we call research. Research and teaching are alike in their dependence on the irritating power of a cerebral itch. (We will return to this old theme of Dewey's [1922] in chapter 5.)* "The most basic premise of college or university education," Bruffee (1978) writes "is the itch of ignorance, not the satiety of knowledge." Good teaching, like good research, depends on some sort of cognitive dissonance, on discrepancies, contradictions, possibilities at odds with actualities.

The process of teaching, like the process of research, requires us to pose questions that cause trouble (dissonance). Whether as investigators or teachers, we will go answer-hunting when we've posed questions. Otherwise not. Good questions, in the classroom as in research, require us to assemble cases—from the field, from the lab, from personal experience—for analysis. Good questions will lead the inquirer to look for multiple conditions, and for latent as well as manifest concomitants. Good questions will compare answers derived from controlled observation with those based on casual observation. Good questions will stimulate a pro-

cess of inquiry that is open and can be replicated by anyone who would check the adequacy of the answer. In these and other ways, the careful pursuit of significant questions reduces the spurious contrast of research and teaching. Teaching *is* seeking.

We conclude that it is a serious error, if not a mortal sin, to see teaching and research as contending, incompatible roles. If they are in fact so defined, they need not be—must not be, if we are to teach competently.

But if there is to be but a single standard, what shall it be? We answer that we professors would do well to look to the research role in which we are trained. We can estimate what changing to a single standard would mean, both generally and in details of our operation.

What Would a Single Standard Entail?

The General Transformation of Our Courses

Changing to a single standard would substitute a lot of doing for a lot of talking about. It would minimize the transmission of Truth from the omniscient and omnipotent to the ignorant and weak. It would renounce the instructional pattern practiced when we implicitly assume that listening is learning, telling is teaching. The stress would be on collaborative inquiry, with instructor as principal investigator. Changing to a single standard would mean that simple transmission of pertinent data would be chiefly through reading and other experiences arranged by the instructor, but undertaken mostly outside the brain-storming sessions and laboratory work comprising class operations. Seldom would the instructor repeat what is available in the printed word. The aim of the

* This citation is to a work of Dewey's that was first published in 1922. In our work, we used the more widely available 1930 edition. Our *Works Referred To* section lists both the edition we used and, in brackets, the first edition date. We have cited, in the text references, the original dates of publication for such "classic" works, since it is often useful to recall the year in which a concept, finding, or theory was first shared through the printed word. However, page references in these cases refer to the later edition.

course, like that of research, would be to pursue a big question with its complement of subsidiary questions.

As in the case of research, teaching would involve both theory and methods. Theory would provide a tentative answer to the central questions; and methods would be invoked as appropriate to check the adequacy of that theory through empirical probing. As in the case of research, teaching would be more adequate to the extent that it led inquirers to discover similarities in apparently different events and populations. As with research, instruction would have added significance to the extent that general findings, applied to mundane affairs, might suggest changes in policy and practice. As in research, instruction would take on a triadic form: instructor and student collaborating in the attack on a problem (rather than the too-frequently diadic, adversary relationship). As in research, the class operation would be open, public, exploiting every resource, including fellow students, that might contribute to a solution.

We stress that a good class resembles research in being a course of inquiry. And we believe that there is no sociological issue that does not have its counterpart in the experience of those whom we teach. But questions are not interchangeable in interest or value. We choose our research problems. Students might well choose theirs—i.e., choose the courses devoted to questions they wish to pursue. Thus students would be self-selected for our courses, knowing what issue will dominate the semester's work. At this point, sociology and pedagogy meet; for we would be teaching in the light of the disciplinary wisdom that asserts that the success of organizational outcomes depends on careful, selective recruiting. Hence the success of a course, the reputation of the department—and in a small way, of the discipline—is largely determined by self-selection before the course ever starts.

For most problems there are ready answers, sometimes too ready. They come from pertinent prior research, from idiosyncratic personal experience, from holy writ and other traditional sources. These explanations (theories) need to be sorted and weighed. The teacher should be pleased to have two plausible but incompatible explanations, one of which our classroom inquiry might sustain over the other.

Then, in classroom inquiry as in research, we must deal with the following questions: What indicators can we use for the variables embodied in the theory? How can we assess their validity? And how can we take their measures? On occasion we will advance the cause of our own research with students' imaginative contributions.

When, toward the end of the semester, findings are assembled, two other critical questions emerge. We ask about the extension and the application of our findings. As to the extension of our findings: If we can now describe and explain better than we could before, are there other classes of behavior that might be better understood by the same propositions? Extension is a prime criterion of importance in research. So it might and ought to be in our teaching. Keniston's theory (1965) that alienation stems from absence of a same-sex role model, and from lack of a stake in the system, is much more telling when it embraces both poor blacks and rich whites, such as those who were his subjects at Harvard. The Whiting, Kluckhohn, and Anthony study (1958) linking violent puberty rites with a protracted dependence of the male child on his mother becomes much more powerful (and pertinent) when it is extended to include gang rumbles in Chicago and Manhattan.

The second question about the application of our findings is not clearly linked to traditional research. Yet increasingly, on grounds both moral and practical, sociologists are impelled to think about the implications of their findings for practical affairs. What does it mean for public policy and legislation that we confront, again, a Malthusian disparity between available resources and the bodies to consume them? What does it mean, in practical terms, that recorded law breakers are heavily concentrated in younger age groups? How do we explain why, with the power failure in Manhattan, some people looted, while others didn't? What are the practical implications of the finding that welfare expenditures are inversely related to level of employment and other measures of prosperity?

Finally, a single standard for both research and teaching might lead us to do as teachers what we must do as researchers. We might make our findings public. A department's record for a semester would then be clearly revealed in its publication of course findings for that semester. This publication of course findings would candidly disclose the blind alleys, the roadblocks, the unanticipated outcomes, the reversals of convictions, the skills developed and lacking, as well as the confirmations, serendipitous outcomes, refinements, and extensions of propositions. As in research, the publication of work already done in past semesters and courses would set the stage for future work. What the instructor (the principal investigator) had attempted would be known, enabling succeeding instructors to build on it and increasing the probability of genuinely cumulative learning for their students.

The preceding recommendations identified some of the general features that might distinguish a course—or a unit within it—were we to apply our standards for disciplined inquiry to the courses we teach. Now let us add a few more details bearing on common teaching problems.

Specifying a Problem, Specifying Goals

As instructors following a research standard, we will make our statements of course goals as lean and precise as the statement of an hypothesis. Investigators understand the need to translate general ideas—class, integration, mobility—into operational terms if they are to know what they are saying and test what they think they know. We will not be content, under a single standard, to do otherwise in teaching as well. To state in our syllabi that we seek to impart an appreciation of the sociological perspective, or a capacity for critical thinking, or a sense of the diversity of cultures, or an understanding of the complexity of social phenomena—these statements are, at best, some first ambiguous efforts awaiting clarification. At worst, such murky statements of our goals mislead us into thinking that we know what we are talking about when, in fact, their meaning remains hidden and we are prevented from measuring our achievements. Hypotheses for research are assertions of a determinate relationship between operationally defined variables under specified conditions. In order to apply this standard to our specification of course goals:

1. We must state clearly what a student will be able to do after a learning experience.

2. We must be specific, confining each such statement to a single objective.

3. We must state the goal with a verb in the active voice, so denoting the student's action. For example, we will *not* say: "It is hoped that the heuristic value of constructing hypotheses will be brought home to the student";

rather, we will say: "The student will write an hypothesis in which independent and dependent variables are defined by their measures, the test population is specified, and control variables are indicated."

Using Theory to Explain Social Patterns and Guide Patterns of Instruction

The research problem constituting a course would require that we invoke theory in developing hypotheses as targets for testing. But also, to behave as scholars when we are engaged in teaching, we would exploit theory to guide instruction. For example, both from theory and empirical findings, we know that active participation is concomitant to commitment to a task. "If there is one thing human learning experts have agreed upon," McKeachie writes (1976:822), "it is that 'active' learning, in the sense of mental activity at least, is generally better than passive learning." Hence we will stress collaborative problem solving—laboratory work, field work, simulations, classroom demonstrations. And we will seek problems that have broad sociological significance, suggest discernible social implications, and in some transformation, touch the lives of our students.

Recalling Simmel's argument (1950) about the volatile character of the dyad and the characteristics of the triad, we will take care not to create a dangerous, dyadic relationship virtually devised in adversary terms. So far as possible, we will put the problems of the course, the assignments, and the grades outside the instructor-student relationship. Thus in alliance with the student we will work to best the third party—the problem or test administered by an outsider (ETS or perhaps the department, in the case of a departmentally required course).

Profiting from organization theory's stress on selective recruitment, we will take measures to ensure that students know clearly what awaits them, thereby assuring a degree of compatibility between their ends and means and the instructor's ends and means. And more generally, knowing about the importance of accurate perceptions and expectations in sustaining a relationship, we will take great care to clarify matters of likely concern: attendance and participation, examinations and grading, required reading, assignments, projects (and what the word *requirement* entails), the calendar of course experiences, and the like. Again, following a research standard, we might treat the syllabus (containing these statements) as we would a research instrument. We would give it a trial run to pick up reactions and ambiguities pointing to needed revision.

Identifying Variables Pertinent to Outcomes

Following a single standard we would recognize that learning outcomes, like other effects, have multiple sources. These causal influences we would try to identify, eliminating the impact of those that get in the way and exploiting those that advance the student's growth. Among these influences are variables describing the course, variables associated with the instructor, the students, the department, the school, the community, the region, and the nation. They might be represented as in figure 2.1.

Like the researcher, the teacher needs some sense of the way these variables are linked. One is wise to maximize the direct connection between the intervening variable (the course) and the dependent variable (the outcomes). On the other hand, if

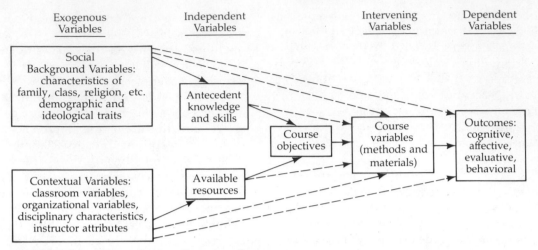

Figure 2.1 Variables Affecting Learning Outcomes.

the outcomes are chiefly the result of exogenous variables (see figure 2.1), then the course experience will seem to have been fruitless. In some instances, one might wish to eliminate the impact of contextual or social background factors. For a dispassionate study of poverty, race, or religion, one would not want analysis or conclusions compromised by level of family wealth, parental race, or fundamentalist convictions. On the other hand, as figure 2.1 suggests, background variables may be exploited to enhance the methods and materials of the course. Students from southeastern Kentucky, Tennessee, and West Virginia may, through their familiarity with coal mining communities, better understand feudal social structure if their background traits are tapped.

A standard applied to research requires that we carefully identify the relevant variables and their connections in some sort of explanatory scheme. This has a clear application to teaching. A course may be only as good as the thought invested in its design. And the design is only as good as the precise specification of pertinent variables and their likely linkages.

Sampling in Research and Teaching

Seldom do we collect data from the universe of possible subjects and situations. We must sample parts of the whole. But we so design our sample as to ensure the generality of our results.

Instructors face a comparable problem: no course can treat all problems implied by the course title within the allotted time. Instructors, one might hope, would apply like standards of sampling in selecting course materials. If they have to be partial, they can at least seek accurate representation. They might sample substance by cluster sampling, grouping sociological issues into, for example, three types: (1) those bearing on group-building (demography, socialization, family, education); (2) those treating the structures of groups so built (stratification, demographic and institutional structures); and (3) those analyzing the processes of changing structures (collective behavior, social movements, migration, race relations, science, and technology). Within each cluster, problems and data would be so sampled as to give an accurate representation of problems implied by the course title.

Although first-exposed students should probably not be caught up in professional debates about different theoretical orientations, neither should the field be misrepresented by a single viewpoint. Again, sampling is indicated—not in technical terms, but in ways that represent functionalism, conflict theory, exchange theory, and the like.

Validity in Research and Teaching

We often face the question: does a measure or an index actually represent what we think it does? And of course we constantly try to enhance the validity of our indicators.

The use of materials in teaching should be guided by similar criteria. Do the chosen materials consistently and accurately represent the ideas they are intended to reflect? For example, the talks of outside speakers often miss their mark. Unless speaker and class are carefully prepared, the burden of the outsider's statements may appear quite unrelated to the ideas students thought they were exploring. Field experiences, too, can create similar disjunctions as students aimlessly look without seeing. Different organizations of text and course sometimes increase the problem of fit between ideas and data.

The Centrality of Questions in Research and Teaching

A single standard would require us to attend to questions for teaching as we do to those developed in research. The logic of inquiry, the construction of questionnaires, and interview schedules all imply the need to pose questions significant for their theoretical implications and tractable for their empirical pursuit. Research can be no better than the quality of the questions posed. A like attention to questions (which are, after all, the justification for seeking answers—which are, after all, the reason for being in a course) would improve our instruction.

While visiting a class, we heard a teacher ask this question: "In the article you read, the author noted that rioting escalated at a certain time. When?" The answer was: at night. While that exchange could have been a starter, it ended there, with a trivial fact barren of meaning. But suppose the question had been: "Why do you suppose that rioting and general mayhem escalated at night?" We forgo testing for the trivial fact (time of occurrence) as only incidental to any significant learning. The teacher might have been able to elicit a response to the effect that cover of darkness enables one to elude authorities and escape punishment. Very well: "Are there other cases of this sort?" Students will help us lengthen the list. KKK members disguise their identities under hoods and sheets. Some organizations are secret organizations. Politicians may do much of their work in private caucuses. Thus we move toward the general proposition that social control requires identification of the actors. To escape such control, one masks his or her identity—under cover of night, by sheet and hood, by secret symbols or signs, by putting as much physical distance as possible between one's self and the control agent (as in the case of a student who seeks invisibility by retreating to the remote corners of the classroom). And we note that times of abandon, when one goes beyond the restraints of conventional conduct (as with the Mardi Gras), are times when one dons disguises (see Simmel, 1908:330–56).

Now we have moved inductively from a number of instances to the general proposition; and we have moved deductively from the general proposition to more instances. We might extend the applications (and implications) of this example further by asking how the proposition helps us explain the rank order of social distance expressed in responses to a Bogardus scale—the more distant the stranger (the more disguised), the less control, the more dislike. The same proposition might also be applied to the immigrant. With the disguise of strangeness, he weakens his host's power of control.

Were we now to state standards for adequate teaching questions (as we do for good research questions), what might they be? Here are some standards that occur to us:

1. A good question is one that requires us to assemble cases from our experience that have something in common.

2. A good question is one that, from the cases we have assembled, leads us to a general proposition that is stronger and better insofar as it:

    a. brackets cases that might seem to have little or nothing in common (the immigrant, and the night rioters in Watts); and

    b. brackets one or more cases within the student's immediate experience (the relationship between physical distance, social distance, and learning in the classroom).

3. A good question is one that helps students look for multiple outcomes and unanticipated consequences. Thus the anonymity that might be judged bad insofar as it promotes irresponsible or illegal conduct may be judged good when it offers a sanctioned regression to less demanding roles that help one recuperate and return zestfully to the demands of daily life. For example: we may deprecate anonymity when it enables one to act brutally and with impunity; but we may appreciate anonymity in the grading of student examinations so that competence becomes the only criterion at work.

4. A good question is one that is tractable: we can whittle away at it with reason and evidence.

5. A good question is one that touches, in some way, issues of the better and the worse—i.e., moral issues. We say this because we suspect that the drive to find out becomes compelling only when finding out is felt to be worthwhile.

6. A good question is better to the extent that it belongs in a set. Among a set of related questions, each individual query has enhanced pertinence, and the learning experience has an integrity not afforded by individual shotgun inquisition.

Altering the Course of Research (or Teaching) in the Light of Emerging Problems

The research person need not be inflexibly wedded to a given theory or method. It is counted a virtue to be sensitive to emerging problems and to change in favor of more adequate ideas. The teacher, too, should be aware of indicators that something is wrong and that changes are called for. The empty expressions in class, the empty responses to exam questions, the empty chairs in a classroom are crude measures of the response rate. Just as one cannot judge research findings as very useful if the response is abysmally low, the teacher's performance may be suspect if few people are engaged by the class. Attempts to find out how nonrespondents differ are indicated. One talks to them. Suggestions may be elicited on redesigning course experiences, even in midstream. Either teacher or researcher would be wrong to ignore yellow lights, for they are often followed by red ones. By then it may be too late.

Ethics in Research and Teaching

In research we recognize the possibility of harming subjects, either by acting erroneously or failing to act helpfully. In medical research, protection of subjects is thought to be guaranteed by the individual physician's adherence to the Hippocratic oath. Such a point of view, Lally and Barber point out (1974:290), expresses "an individualistic . . . bias which places excessive or exclusive emphasis on . . . the individual research physician in the protection of human subjects' welfare and rights." For sociologists that should not be enough: values are grounded in conditions of the social system, and no credo persists without the social mechanisms to applaud fulfillment and punish infraction.

But when we turn from the research role to the teaching role, we find no such concern. Adopting the a-sociological view of the doctor, respect for individual student welfare is thought to be certified by the Ph.D. This is hardly credible, and the risks are greater than those affecting research subjects. For many more subjects are involved, and the harm done is less likely to be visible or reparable.

We take the position that here, again, the process of discovery yields useful guidelines for the process of transmission. We generally accept the need of peer review of projects involving human subjects—including those in the courses we teach. We would protect our subjects by instituting some social mechanisms for review of instructor performance. And the reviewers would need some standards by which they could estimate the extent to which students are being helped or harmed. On this score, Galliher has suggested (1975:113–17) a code of ethics for teaching parallel to the ASA's ethical standards for research.

Assessing Results in Research and Teaching

The final act in a piece of research is to evaluate the extent to which the presumed causal influences produced a predicted outcome. Were we to apply this model of scholarly inquiry to our other role what would we do? Or not do? To take the second question first, we would not be so blithely certain that we are good teachers, that we had a good course last semester, or even that today's class session was great. We would routinely use pretests and posttests as crude measures of instructional adequacy. And the question would no longer be whether we are good or poor teachers, but how good or poor.*

Thus we see the antithesis of counter-demanding roles as spurious. If research and teaching have been at odds, it is because we have failed to exploit our training as sociologists in the service of instruction. But suppose we were to consider each course a research project and each syllabus a set of questions framing a course of inquiry. Suppose we treated transmission of data and ideas as handmaiden to the quest—as means, not ends. (Needed data would be transmitted through readings or through self-teaching techniques, such as Keller schemes, devised by the instructor.) Suppose teaching procedures came to resemble the disciplined search for reliable knowledge. And suppose the outcomes of inquiry were reported, as in a research operation. Then the two roles would be com-

* These are matters we return to in chapter 14.

plementary, mutually reinforcing, not conflicting.

Applying Research Standards to Teaching: Changes in Departmental Procedures

But however reasonable the rapprochement, one does not resolve the opposition of traditionally incompatible roles by waving a wand. Graduate students would need to be trained in the teaching role. And faculty recruitment and promotion would have to take into account skill in teaching, as well as scholarship.

Training for Instruction

While the exact scheme would vary among schools, adhering to a single standard would mean that graduate students would work in credit courses, or workshops, on teaching. Just as graduate departments impose requirements needed to develop and test research skills, so would students be expected to learn about teaching formats, tools, assessment procedures, types of learning objectives, student populations, and teaching techniques appropriate to them.

Supervised experience in teaching would be required. This is a parallel to the internship of the research assistant and the supervised experience of thesis and dissertation research. What we envision is a far cry from the teaching assistantship role as practiced in some graduate departments where the supervision, if there is any, is loose, carried out by a sociologist who lacks credentials appropriate to the task, and rarely subject to departmental evaluation. (In some departments, first semester graduate students with no prior teaching experience—let alone training—are thrust into the classroom to teach their own courses.)

Preparation for doing sociology typically includes a sequence of cumulative experiences: courses, prelims, admission to doctoral candidacy, dissertation, defense. Similarly, an adequate program of training for teaching would move from stage to stage upon demonstration of competence: graduate intern, teaching assistant, teaching fellow, graduate instructor.[12]

Good training requires material resources. In developing research skills, graduate students often have access to statistical laboratories, computer facilities, departmental libraries with census holdings, major research journals and books, small-group laboratories, major data sets, calculators, typewriters. Some departments have provided travel funds for students presenting papers at professional meetings. Some advanced graduate students have research assistants, and some enjoy typing services.

Parallel resources for teaching are slim—typically, 16mm projectors, slide projectors, overhead transparency projectors, and tape recorders. Resources additionally needed include: videotape equipment for the analysis of teaching performances; books and journals treating instruction in sociology and related social sciences; a few classrooms equipped with one-way observation glass; prerecorded tapes—video and audio—of situations representing typical teaching problems; and special collections of texts, transparencies, course syllabi, examination items, and the like.

The Ph.D. is granted only after the student has passed a number of certification hurdles. Available evidence indicates that no more than 5 percent of graduate departments require any certification for teaching as a part of the Ph.D. program. To apply the research standard in this instance would require certification procedures to be attached to the sequence of training experiences.

Finally, as in support of research training, graduate students would have available a qualified person as a role model and a center on campus for support of teaching. All graduate departments have faculty members who are highly skilled in research methods. Although not specifically hired for such purposes, they consult and advise and exemplify the department's commitment to research. But few departments have any specialists in teaching, and we know of only a few that have ever recruited such specialists.

Research-oriented centers offer enormous support to scholars on many campuses—for example, the Institute for Social Research at Michigan or the Institute for Research in Social Science at North Carolina. Applying the single standard to teaching would require that departments fight for and support parallel units in support of teaching. (We do find such parallel units on some campuses. An example is the Center for Research on Learning and Teaching at Michigan.)

Competence in Teaching as a Criterion for Recruitment and Promotion

How would recruitment and decisions on promotion be changed were we to invoke a single standard? In concluding our discussion with this question, we speak to the situation at four- and two-year colleges as well as universities. (In the preceding section, we were, of course, speaking only of universities with graduate departments.)

There are many means of appraising a sociologist's research: book reviews,

peer reviews within the department and from professionals elsewhere, *Social Science Citation Index,* and the like. But there is nothing comparable for teaching. Yet the evaluation of teaching has several significant uses: as a way to gather data serviceable to the instructor in becoming a more effective teacher; as a means of accounting to the department, the school, and in some cases, state legislatures; and as a way to obtain part of the information needed for departmental evaluations.

Thus decisions on hiring, retention, promotion, and salary increases would take into account, systematically, teaching performance. Measures of that performance, subjective and objective, would be regularly reviewed, revised, improved. At the point of hiring, departments would look into the evidence on the candidate's teaching abilities just as they investigate skill in research and command of field. In our experience, and by comparison with the assessment of research ability, these procedures are typically weak. To strengthen them, departments would seek letters of reference that report evidence on level of teaching experience and ability. The candidate would be encouraged to submit videotapes or audiotapes of classroom performances. During a candidate's visit, host faculty would prepare for discerning interviews that probe for sophistication in teaching techniques and theories of successful intervention— knowledge of personalized systems of instruction, computer-assisted instruction, teaching information processing systems, modular schemes, field work, laboratory methods, and the like. (See Ewens, 1976a and 1976b, for further suggestions.)

Research standards require a close fit between the problem to be tackled and the tools to be used. We are a little looser in matching instructional problems and the skills needed to solve them. Typically, the least experienced instructors teach those courses most difficult to teach—introductory courses and broad survey courses with extremely heterogeneous student populations. To apply the tougher research standard would be to realign teaching assignments.

✑

In sum, dual standards depreciate the discipline, demean our departments, and rob the instructor of the professional growth that would ensue if teaching and research were exploited as reciprocally fructifying pursuits.

To be guided by a single standard would entail a reorientation of our courses: each would become a genuine course of inquiry. It would also mean basic changes in teaching procedures and in departmental personnel practices—in training, hiring, promotion, and firing, and in faculty development programs.

The double standard for research and teaching, then, is both needless and intellectually compromising. This strong statement we will follow, in chapter 3, with some others. These persuasions will then be reconsidered and refined in succeeding chapters, but we think it well to present them forthrightly at the outset.

Notes

1. The National Register of Scientific and Technical Personnel reports about three-fourths of sociologists are employed in colleges and universities. Most, but not all of these people, teach.

2. At some smaller liberal arts colleges the emphasis may be reversed, a situation equally unfortunate for effective instruction. For research fosters a command of current studies in a field and a sense of needed tests and extension. It is hard to imagine competent in-

struction in the absence of such knowledge. (See note 10 below.)

3. On a few campuses there are such organizations—for example, the Center for Research on Learning and Teaching at the University of Michigan. There is some slight evidence suggesting that such centers have a salutary effect on teaching. See Erickson and Erickson (1979) on a teaching consultation program at the University of Rhode Island, and Davis, Abedor, and Witt (1976) on the work of Michigan State University's Educational Development Program.

4. The first six statements are taken from Mary C. Thornberry's paper, "Training Graduate Students as Teachers: The University of Michigan Experience" (1974, mimeographed). These statements will have a familiar ring for most instructors. When we put them in such a list we note that some are contradictory (compare statements 1 and 5). Some are false (for example, statement 6 is a self-serving delusion). And none is supported, which is often the case with such assertions. The double standard shows here: assertion without demonstration would be thought insupportable in research. Not so when applied to teaching.

5. We often relax standards of proof in the analysis of teaching, as in the case with these contentions. On the other hand, and ironically, we sometimes impose tougher standards when treating teaching than we do with our research. Slight findings (small r's and big p's) may be taken as suggestive in other research; but they may be minimized, if not deprecated, when, for example, they point to the slightly greater efficacy of small classes as a condition for training in critical thinking.

6. Recall, also, the esteem accorded research by department chairmen and university administrators. For its publication makes the organization visible and renowned.

7. We do not here imply that the teacher attributes or teaching pattern are the only factors affecting how much students learn, but we suspect they are important.

8. During the 1960s, the Danforth Foundation funded the annual Harbison Teaching

Awards, carrying a $10,000 honorarium. Several sociologists won that award; we doubt that many of their colleagues could identify them. Among the sociologist winners were Professors Renee Fox, Joseph Elder, and Paule Verdet.

9. We do not suggest that poor teaching is the only or the major source of attack on the social sciences. And even were college instruction as good as could be, one would still expect competition for scarce resources.

10. The reverse is true, of course. Teaching will be adequate only when informed by current research. Naive is the softest adjective one might employ to describe a colleague's view of teaching. When asked to review a manuscript for possible publication, he re-sponded: "Please send this MS. to someone else. I only teach in this field."

11. The following discussion of the complementarity of teaching and research is largely taken from Wilson (1977).

12. There are ample resources to assist departments in carrying out a program to prepare graduate students for the teaching role. See, for example, the special issue devoted to the topic in *Teaching Sociology* (April, 1976). Also, the American Sociological Association's Teaching Resources Center in Washington, D. C. has extensive materials, including a set of syllabi from teacher development courses in sociology.

CHAPTER 3
OUR PERSUASIONS

To guide and assess our teaching by the standards governing our research would resolve a frustrating dualism in our professional lives. As kin to this conviction, some other persuasions have slowly emerged through our several decades of teaching. They are not idiosyncratic; for although our own experience was their source, we have been reassured by the tardy discovery of research that generally supports our conclusions. We present our persuasions early on, both to be candid with the reader and to allow these persuasions to serve as thematic guidelines for the discussions that follow.* Since these persuasions bear on *teaching* and *learning,* we had better define these two terms.

Teaching, Learning, and the Connection Between Them[1]

Learning is what has occurred when one can now do something that he could not do earlier.[2] *Teaching* is purposeful behavior designed to bring about learning.

To teach is to create situations in which learning takes place. Learning is an outcome, the achievement of skills, information, or understanding once lacking.

It follows from our definitions that a person can be both teacher and learner, that one can teach oneself. All one need do is to specify learning goals and act purposively to achieve them. That is, we have a question and we seek an appropriate book or person for the answer. We play both

roles then, and in doing so, as Meadian theory (1934) would suggest, teacher becomes learner and learner becomes teacher. We stress the point: the teacher learns from the student. Only by internalizing student responses can instructors know what they have been saying (to their students).

Although teaching without a learner is by definition impossible,[3] the converse is not only possible, but common. We can learn without being taught by an (immediate) other. Observing a number of exchanges between blacks and whites, or men and women, in various situations can teach us that there are social hierarchies. Because we are able to state this after our observations and could not have done so before them, we say we have learned. Often the learning is casual and incorrect, even in the classroom where what is learned may be far from what the teacher intended. It may result from exposure to peers who have no intention of teaching what is learned. We have some evidence that much of the learning that takes place during college years does not involve teachers or teaching—i.e., purposeful behaviors designed to induce learning (Wilson:1971b).

We say that one has learned, not when one knows more, but when one can *do* more. For we cannot measure an increase in knowledge without somehow measuring changes in performance. Hence our definition of learning rests on the notion of measurable change. Learning, as Gagné puts it (1970:3), is an inference "made by comparing what behavior was possible before the individual was placed

* See especially chapters 8 through 12.

in a 'learning situation' and what behavior can be exhibited after such treatment. The change may be, and often is, an increased capability for some type of *performance*" (emphasis added).[4] Some teachers object to this stress on assessment of behavioral change as mechanistic and compatible only with trivial learning goals. But teaching and learning can be trivial or mechanistic with the most impressionistic assessment; and triviality is not intrinsic to measures of performance. What use is it to claim student creativity as a teaching goal if one cannot help the student recognize and rejoice in the demonstrable extent to which creative skill has been enhanced?

Learning can be demonstrated in scores of ways: student-prepared films or tapes, multimedia presentations, and various forms of oral and written performances, including examinations, oral presentations, papers, reports of field sorties, interpretations of tables or figures, insightful statements that explain apparently different social patterns, and the invention of unobtrusive measures useful as indexes. In each case the teacher, perhaps with the student, defines the learning goal and constructs measurable indicators useful in evaluating progress. Here, in passing, is an example of learning defined as knowing and learning defined as doing.

Learning Defined as Knowing

The student will appreciate the sociological perspective and will understand the social influences that bear on individual and group behavior.

Learning Defined as Doing

The student will demonstrate an understanding of the sociological perspective by analyzing a social situation not treated in class or text (such as getting a driver's license, entering high school, or observing a riot), listing and defining pertinent social variables, and creating a diagram to portray their interactions.

The Effective Teacher and the Responsible Teacher

Teaching is effective to the degree that intended learnings occur. This definition of effective teaching places much (though not all) responsibility on the teacher. Those who have taught may object that how much their students learn depends on matters over which they have little control. Student motivation and aspiration, prior preparation, size and heterogeneity of the class—these only begin the list. But this is simply to say that effectiveness will vary depending on the number and kinds of obstacles we encounter, and our ingenuity in overcoming them. Even when we disavow responsibility for our students' antecedents, we need to think about our responsibility to create accurate, detailed course descriptions, to stipulate meaningful prerequisites, to offer pretests and diagnostic tests that will help students decide whether they should register—or continue in—a course whose aims and methods they clearly understand.

Certainly the instructor is not wholly responsible for learning outcomes. Student characteristics and organizational constraints are not always predictable or controllable. But a responsible sociology instructor will look for the tools needed to do the best possible job under the circumstances. Our teaching is responsible to the degree that we exploit available research and theory on teaching to achieve our goals within existing constraints. We may not be omniscient, but we can tap all available wisdom and evidence. Research indicates that teaching is more effective when communication is clear and when students see reasons to pursue the questions being posed. Consequently, we must write our syllabi and other teaching instruments with care, then field test and revise them to improve communicability. If we hope to foster analytic skills and reflective thinking, we must attend to the evidence that such goals are best achieved through active discussion and participation.[5] This will mean small classes or sections, a case or laboratory system, situations that encourage collaborative problem solving. If instructors act on the belief that there are no alternatives to lecturing in a large introductory course with, say, 350 students, no way to practice data analysis, no means of frequent evaluative response to individual students, no chance of using active modes of learning—then they forgo the means of more effective instruction. For there *are* such options, as a number of sociologists have indicated (Baker, 1976; Baker and Behrens, 1971; Bassis and Allen, 1977; Davis, Goldsmid, and Perry, 1977:1–11).

Our notion of the effective and conscientious instructor bears on the assessment of instruction. For an informed teacher will be aware of conditions that help or hinder desired learning. These conditions become pertinent data at the time of promotion decisions. The instructor can point out that unsatisfactory student achievement—if there is any real evidence of achievement—results partly from teaching conditions (large numbers, too few TAs) that prevent the attainment of such goals as skill in building theory. Then the questions to be faced by both the faculty member and the department chair are these: Shall we change the goals? Can we alter the means? Can we devise some different relationship between ends and means?

We know that faculty cannot always shape the conditions of instruction. Some learn only a few weeks before the start of a new semester what courses they will teach. All face competing demands. In addition to their teaching, academic sociologists are expected to contribute to the discipline, to the school in which they teach (especially the department), and to the community in which they live. Teaching loads are sometimes unconscionably heavy. The amount of help available to instructors varies widely. Such constraints and competing demands on faculty are real and ubiquitous. Yet there are resources available, probably more than we commonly recognize. For teachers at the 200 schools that have faculty development programs or centers,[6] the job may be easier. And for those teachers in departments that celebrate and reward effective teaching, the task is much lightened. As we learn more about the teaching of sociology and as such knowledge becomes more readily available, instructors and their administrators have both the chance and the obligation to become more responsible and effective teachers.

These views about teaching and learning set the stage. What follows is a set of persuasions that undergirds this work and that we think should inform our teaching.

Ten Persuasions About Effective Sociology Instruction

There are many effective ways of teaching to achieve a given end. But whatever the end of instruction and whatever the means, some things promote learning, while their absence or opposites do not. Throughout the remainder of this chapter we celebrate these ten features of effective sociology instruction: (1) a command of the ideas and methods of sociology, and an ability to convey enthusiastically the importance of the field; (2) statements of objectives in operational terms; (3) a moral component in teaching and learning; (4) giving priority to questions over answers, to inquiry over expository forms of instruction; (5) emphasis on the importance of doing—i.e., the active participation of students in seeking tentative answers; (6) a genuine concern for students' intellectual growth—a concern that stems in large measure from the importance attached to sociology; (7) using the playwright or composer as model for the teacher's role, rather than God; (8) knowing how the population and the situation affect communication—and therefore, effective teaching; (9) quality control—including both subjective student evaluations and objective measures of teacher performance as revealed in student performance; and (10) using multiple modes and resources in sociology instruction.

Command of Sociological Material and Conveying Its Importance

Command of field we might take for granted. But, for two reasons, we should not: we often teach outside our fields of special competence, and we sometimes fail to keep abreast.

As instructors in the introductory course or in a course on social problems, we must go beyond our spheres of competence. Long experience, good texts, team teaching, or modular designs help us circumvent this problem. But in some circumstances it is unsolvable: we have known sociologists to carry four courses per quarter, with nine separate preparations. This situation almost insures inadequate command of subject matter in some courses.

Then there is the matter of obsolescence. A command of our field is not easily sustained. New knowledge of all sorts comes in incessant waves. (Recall the annual flood of papers pertinent to teaching sociology reported in chapter 1.) A field marked by exponential growth demands unremitting work. Unable to do this, we lose command of our field, therefore teach inadequately, and invite premature obsolescence—which comes soon enough in any case.

Beyond these facts, command of the field must be seen as worth the candle and, for students, an investment well justified because of its yield for them. Competent instructors will not impose requirements without showing, persuasively, how these requirements contribute to students' growth. How shall we convey to students how important sociology is for them as individuals?

We will show our students how the self is a social creation and how, this being so, discovery of the social influences that shape its creation brings us a surer sense of our identities.[7] To ask about any influence is to estimate what would happen in its absence. We will show our students that, in the absence of sociology, they could not see so much, so clearly. If we are sensitive to the peculiarities of a three-party relationship, we will see the divide-and-conquer process at work as a child pits parents against one another, as a student does likewise with two faculty members, and as the United States encourages contention between two Communist countries. Sociology also teaches us to see what we would otherwise overlook when it enjoins us to ferret out the unanticipated outcomes of behavior. Thus an M.A. program instituted to improve instruction in social studies had the opposite effect as able teachers with their additional training and an advanced degree moved out of teaching and into administrative posts.

In sharpening our vision, sociology helps us discover the many-layered intricacies of everyday life. And about this commonplace range of relationships we cultivate a questioning mind. For example (Wilson, 1971a:600):

> *Does a class or a course enlarge us in knowledge or wisdom? Or does it discourage a tendency toward inquiry, teaching us to substitute grades for learning? Does our system of criminal justice reduce the crime rate? Or raise it? Does regularity in religious rites promote humanity in our dealings with others? Or does it certify a conviction of superiority? Does fear of demotion, of unemployment or loss of pay drive men to work? Or to evade work more artfully? Do feelings of awe, fear and reverence give rise to religion? Or is it religion that defines and elicits these emotions? Is the American family an evolved institution best suited to breed and rear children? Or is it a chief source of blighting inequalities? And to the questioner sociology adds a warning: do not be caught by such simplistic contraries. Ask, rather, under what conditions these and other outcomes might be found.*

In demonstrating the importance of their field, effective instructors will help students see sociology's favored position between the humanities and the biophysical sciences. Applying the wiles of science to the mysteries of social arrangements, sociology constrains us to seek a deeper and surer understanding of human relationships. Not only is the field favored in the meaning of its quest and the method of its pursuit. It encourages a range of competence that stretches a person to achieve what he might not otherwise.

Effective instruction helps students see sociology as a personal benefaction since it increases their power to shape the world closer to the heart's desire. It is not enough to want to do good. "One must," as Morley put it (1901), "do it the right way." Competent instructors will, then, help students see the link between social

issues and sociological problems. The present push to develop social indicators surfaces at a time of rapid social change when our ability to control our destinies depends on our understanding social structure and social change. The stubbornly persistent problems of deprivation and unequal opportunity imposed at birth, of race, sex, age, and ethnic-linked discrimination, of urban growth and decay, of impersonal bureaucratic structures that seem to acquire a life of their own—these are socially created problems that, having social properties, require sociological solutions.

Instructors will show their students that sociology frees us from parochial restrictions. With the exception of anthropology, sociology has no peer among the sciences in opening the mind's door to the deceptively familiar world of our social arrangements. It enables a responsible questioning of the customary. It encourages us to entertain alternatives. And in the process, we achieve a better understanding of why things are as they are. "This sort of liberation," Bierstedt notes (1964:43), "in a world beset by provincialisms, by the ethnocentrisms of place and the temporocentrisms of time . . . is no mean accomplishment."

Sociology liberates us, too, from the restrictions of small academic cells, mending the intellectual fissures induced by an artificial opposition of science and the humanities. Sociology is dead center in the tradition of the liberal and liberating arts, joining the so-called two cultures, putting together in our minds matters not meant to be disjoined.

Our first persuasion, then, is this: the skilled instructor conveys, enthusiastically, a keen appreciation of the personal and social contributions of sociology. To view sociology as the queen of the sciences is not to deprecate other realms of inquiry.

Nor would we minimize interdisciplinary work; especially with undergraduates, there is no warrant for disciplinary chauvinism. But effective instruction does justify this assertion: that without a fair command of the field as a humane enterprise and as a disciplined inquiry, without an appreciation of the field where poetry and mathematics intersect and where history and biography continually join in new creations, without an understanding of the yield of this field so precisely oriented to the central issues of postindustrial society, without a grasp of the yield and promise of sociological inquiry—we can scarcely be effective teachers.

Clearcut Aims for Learning

Command of a field enables one to specify, clearly, goals for students' learning and, as a corollary, the means for reaching them. Sociologists know that the test of a big idea lies in its empirical trial; to be tested, the idea must be walked down the abstraction ladder until it can be put in operational terms—i.e., until we can operate with it, get indexes of it, measure it, vary it, manipulate it. Yet ironically, when teaching, sociologists seem about as likely as ordinary mortals to state their goals in useless abstractions that sound virtuous, but lack clear referents. With such foggy goals in mind, instructors cannot know where they are going (nor can their students), and therefore they cannot know what means to employ to get themselves there. Indeed, they can never tell whether they have in fact arrived. And arrival is the real test: does the student get there? The better instructor is the person who can help more students get farther along the road to an identifiable destination. (We note, additionally, that without

specified learning objectives, the department or administration doesn't know whom to fire and whom to retain!)

Now, we do not conceive of behavioral objectives as being restricted to matters of information such as Durkheim's birth and death dates. A common reaction by defenders of the ineffable is that a call for clarity and precision invites the trivial. In actuality, it invites hard work and long thought—impediments enough to explain adverse reactions. For behavioral objectives can be markedly subtle and sophisticated. One such objective might be the statement and evaluation of two incompatible theories explaining the strong relationship between a family's class position and measures of its children's academic achievement—provided criteria of incompatibility were sharply and publicly specified.

A final examination should approximate a statement of course objectives. But too often, even at this point, we find that the murkiness of the test reflects the spongy ambiguities of the course itself. An adequate set of behavioral objectives—perhaps a sample—should be available to students at the beginning of the course so that they know with utter clarity what is expected of them.

The Moral Component

Students need to know what is expected of them, but for instructors to say "This is what's expected," without justifying those expectations is to act capriciously, if not tyrannically. Yet this is what we often do—and what students, in their well-cultivated compliance, often accept. In fact, some things are more worth students' time than others. There is here an issue of the better and the worse. And it is not self-evident that students are better off investing their time in a given course than busying themselves some other ways.

Whether a course is justifiable hinges, in part, on how it ties into the students' past and future. It is not justifiable if it is so remote from their experience that it must be endlessly frustrating. It is not justifiable if it is so remote from anything in their future that it promises no yield in skills, perception, and understanding. Nor is it justifiable if the questions treated are either trivial in the academic field embracing the course, or in the society that embraces the discipline.

The competent instructor, then, asks about the course and every major part of the course: Is it sufficiently important to warrant imposition on my students? Is it a better way than alternate ways? The answer, if yes, must be persuasive to students as well as to instructors.

Moral considerations distinguish the competent instructor in a different way. Content chosen for a course must be better than some alternative not only because it touches students' past and future, nor simply because it escapes triviality. Moral issues are significant in social science instruction because they invest a cognitive issue with emotion and will, so heightening the drive to learn. We insist, and rightly, that desired ends can be sensibly and surely achieved only through *informed* action. But we can also insist that learning is most likely to be sought when it bears on some desired end. A perennially fulfilling and socially productive task is better than . . . hence, let us inquire into the features of bureaucratic organization. Amity is better than enmity: hence, let us consider the conditions generating prejudice and discrimination. Dependence is an invariable problem in human societies: hence, let us do studies in gerontology. Equality of opportunity is taken as good: hence, let us analyze the stratification sys-

tem and other social features that militate against it.

In sum, the competent instructor capitalizes on that ubiquitous and disruptive human trait: people's ability to discriminate and evaluate. To harness the desire for the better and the flight from the worse is to improve, to vivify instruction in sociology. To apply the principle would mean that all content areas would be crosscut not only by theory and method, but, additionally, by issues of the better and the worse—i.e., by problems of personal choice and public policy.

Questions Before Answers

Good instruction requires that questions precede answers. The aim in higher education is to get answers, however tentative, to important questions. Importance is determined by the extent to which an answer reshapes our view of the world— physical, social, and cultural. In the social sciences an important question is, above all, one whose answer throws the weight of evidence on the side of one of two competing explanations.

Nonetheless, conventional (and inadequate) instruction tends to teach by topic, not by issue. Answers are given and the question is taken for granted. We fall too easily into an expository style, using declaratory statements ("There are three principal reasons for the development we call the industrial revolution: 1, 2, and 3"). We move through a course by topic, not by problem. And in doing so we reinforce an unfortunate conception of learning as a process of ingestion, rather than a process of inquiry. We forgo the motivation that is engendered when a question leaves us in a state of imbalance. And we cloud the value of matters dealt with when one topic follows another, conveying the impression that each has equal significance.

Many practices converge to reinforce the pattern. Students are so badly trained that they do not come to a course with a few questions for which they hope to get tentative answers. Sociology texts are not organized as a set of problems for instructor and student to tackle. Nor do syllabi reflect an interrogative mood. Instead, they are organized around topics that must be, at the least, cryptic in the student's mind and about which the instructor is expected to assert the truth. We speak in declaratory rather than interrogatory statements. We confound the church with the school and, in so doing, traduce the central mission of higher education.

Of course, good questions are not easily come by. This we have already implied in our discussion in chapter 2, which compared standards for research and teaching. Indeed, most questions we put are trivial. Good questions require some preparation. Often it is only after the event that a later experience suggests the questions we should have posed earlier. Yet questions are what education is about, and good instruction hinges on their salience as points of organization.

The Importance of Doing: Active Participation in the Learning Process

Conventional expository teaching makes a cerebral blotter of the student. Such passivity is a poor condition for learning—perhaps especially for learning to learn. When, on the other hand, students are actively engaged in the pursuit of a problem, when they are gathering and analyzing the data needed to answer their questions, then learning is promoted (see McKeachie, 1976:822).

Reason and experience support this view. Over sixty years ago, Dewey argued (1916) that the customary classroom discipline impeded learning; for it restricted that bodily activity, movement, and manipulation without which the perception of meaning must be incomplete. Two years earlier, A. I. Gates (reported in Allport, 1945) had found that "learning scores jumped 100 percent when four-fifths of the subject's time was devoted to recitation rather than to passive reading." After reviewing a large number of learning studies, Haggard and Rose (1944) concluded with this law of active participation: ". . . when an individual assumes an active role in a learning situation (a) he tends to acquire the response-to-be-learned more rapidly, and (b) these response patterns tend to be more stably formed than when he remains passive."

Active participation in the process of inquiry probably has other useful outcomes that affect learning. Participation entails working with others toward a goal. In the process one is "coerced into an other-than-self orientation. There is a job to be done, a solution to be found. Undue digression or self-centered detours delay accomplishment of the job. Participation makes for action directed toward a collective problem under pressure from others to play a responsible part in solving it" (Wilson, 1954).

By active participation in the learning process we do not mean what is called, in educators' lingo, experiential learning. Obviously experience is always entailed in learning. And the experience we call empirical is always an aspect of the fruitful interplay between big ideas and their testing. That testing may take place in the laboratory. Or it may take place on a piece of paper on which the data are systematically arranged and analyzed. Or it may take place in a field experience when that experience is framed in a set of significant questions to be answered, hypotheses to be tested through the systematic gathering and analysis of data. And indeed we may invoke personal experience to check the general assertions embodied in the wisdom literature.

Relevance is at issue here, of course: the bearing of map on terrain and vice versa. But sometimes in the search for relevance, all the weight is put on experience, short-suiting reflection on that experience. Action is in; thinking is out. This is disastrous for learning.[8] Our stress on participation puts the student in an active role as collaborator, with the instructor, in the pursuit of answers to precisely put questions bearing on significant issues of theory and policy.

Demonstrable Concern for Students' Intellectual Growth

In describing conditions of effective instruction, we hardly need to point out that instructors must be concerned with the intellectual growth of their students. But perhaps it does need to be said that the concern must somehow be visible to the students through, for example, appreciation of students' contributions; real delight in example or insight from student experience; thoughtful, critical, and encouraging remarks on student papers (rather than perfunctory and uninstructive notes); suggestions for summer reading that extend the impact of the course; and relating course material to students' career plans. In these and scores of other ways, instructors' concern for students can be demonstrated. (Obviously, we are not asking instructors to assume a pious front; rather, we are pressing for the cultivation of a product, the enhancement of student learning by which the degree of our success and failure must be measured.)

The importance of a demonstrable concern for students' intellectual growth is registered in students' perceptions of the attributes of superior teachers. Some time ago we examined the conferring of distinguished teaching awards (see Goldsmid, Gruber, and Wilson, 1977). In a content analysis of 2,900 statements made by 978 students and faculty at the University of North Carolina (in support of their nominees for teaching awards) this quality of concern was among the most frequently mentioned. Concern for student mastery of course materials, enthusiastic treatment of their subject matter, and a genuine interest in students as persons were the three most often mentioned attributes of superior teachers. They were noted by a third, a fourth, and a fifth of the 978 nominators, respectively.

The Appropriate Model for the Teacher's Role

We are persuaded that our single, most grievous error as instructors is this: we teach as though convinced that we are the immediate, central, and indispensable source of knowledge. We feel—and so do our benighted students—that we alone must deliver the message, must cover the material, must perform center stage.

This may once have been acceptable when oral transmission from the wise and experienced was almost the sole source of learning. But this is surely not now the case. Now there is a curious mix of unintended arrogance and masochism in this unarticulated assumption: it places us center stage and it imposes an impossible burden. For most of us lack the omniscience—not to say the varied histrionic skills—to bring it off. Yet we often deceive and injure ourselves by acting as though, in our absence, truth would languish.

What is the alternative? Instead of using the deity as our model, we might consider the role of playwright, or composer, or conductor. With the wealth of resources now available—including students themselves—the effective teacher is one who writes the script but often stands in the wings while the performance is going on. The task of instructor becomes one of orchestrating a set of current experiences that build on students' past experience by extending—and often disturbing—the cognitions and convictions with which they start the course.

Solos in pedagogical virtuosity are hard to sustain over a semester's time. And the implicit pretension to omniscience is sure to be punctured along the way.[9] We should not deceive ourselves that effective instruction in sociology requires us to be center stage from opening curtain through all the acts. Our proper task is the artful design of a set of learning experiences, exploiting and combining the rich range of resources that our imaginations can reveal.

Knowing Our Students and Their Circumstances: A Condition of Communication

Without something in common we cannot, as the etymology of the word suggests, communicate. If we cannot communicate, we cannot teach—or learn. If students' and instructors' worlds are galaxies apart, prospects are poor for effective instruction.[10]

To know something of the social matrix in which their students' thoughts were formed would seem a natural undertaking for sociologists. Impoverished rural setting and urban ghetto, public schools and private, extension divisions, commuting campuses and ivy-walled residential colleges, schools predominantly black or white, schools disproportionately male or female, community and junior colleges and major universities—each of these implies a special population with widely differing experiences on which to build. To teach effectively we need to discover those experiences so that we can build bridges from the smaller island to the larger shore.

On matters bearing immediately on course content, a pretest sampling the final examination can provide needed data on students. Less immediately, data from students on their socially relevant characteristics will provide a comparison point for national data. We can get these data in the first week or so, holding them for use at appropriate points throughout a course. Similarly, information from past student cohorts can be used as comparison points for the current class, yielding clues to change.

The mass media commonly used by our students—newspapers, magazines, and television—provide useful points of contact. One can imagine such a goal of instruction as this: students will be able to exploit a source used by sociologists to check an alleged fact or popular (editorial) explanation found in any issue of the newspaper they usually read. Or, for any show seen on television, students will be able to identify behavior representing different patterns characterizing age, sex, class, race, or other categories; and will be able to invoke a sociologically plausible theory to explain such differences.

For American students, sports may help us communicate, while revealing the insights sociology can generate in viewing the familiar world from a new perspective. One of our graduate TAs reported:[11]

One thing I've learned this year is that a sur-prisingly high percentage of students respond to illustrations from the world of sports. (I am re-minded of Mead's classic baseball game illustra-tion.)

This semester the class period I feel best about is one in which I used Schwartz and Bar-sky's (1977) article about the home advantage for a discussion of sociological methods. . . . I asked the class whether they thought there is a home advantage. They generally agreed that there is. Then I asked them to develop explana-tions to account for it. They came up with a list that included all those discussed by Schwartz and Barsky as well as a couple of others. Then I asked: How would you go about testing these theories? After hearing their suggestions, I told them how Schwartz and Barsky did it, putting some of their data on the blackboard. I was pleased about the way students participated, and that they referred to the discussion several times later in the semester.

In sum, teaching entails communica-tion, and communication depends on some experience common to student and instructor. We should invoke the social behaviorists to enlarge our sense of the meaning of communication in sociology instruction: *we do not know what we are saying to students unless we can respond to our utterances as they will.* But we cannot know how others will respond except as we know something of the experiences that have shaped their lives and will shape their responses. To know others' experi-ences entails effort, since the instructor is separated usually by age or generation, by sex, perhaps by race or ethnic background, often by class, by region, and most often by commitment to the field of inquiry. We must, then, face the daunting question: do we really know what we are talking about to our students?

The stress on communication is not simply because we must do things *for* our students. It is not a matter of condescen-sion, of noblesse oblige. Nor is it merely a matter of enhancing our performances as instructors, although that is reason enough for improving communication. Beyond this, striving to communicate effectively with others is a condition of our own growth. For every statement bridging two experiences is a test of its strength, its abil-ity to support the weight of two lives, rather than one. It is a seeking of isomorphisms across overlapping but necessarily unique experiences. It can be the creative construction of a larger social reality. In part this is certainly what Cooley meant (1902:48, 54, 58) when he wrote:

> *. . . alone [without students' responses] one is like fireworks without a match: he cannot set himself off, but is a victim of ennui, the prisoner of some tiresome train of thought that holds his mind simply by the absence of a competitor . . . the mind lives in perpetual conversation. . . . [The sociology instructor] in proportion to his natural vigor, necessarily strives to com-municate to others that part of his life which he is trying to unfold in himself. It is a matter of self-preservation, because without expression thought cannot live.*

Measures of Teacher Performance

No less than ordinary mortals, sociologists want to know what they are doing and how they are doing. Indeed, perhaps they want to know these things *more* than others, since sociologists have a professional concern in evaluation re-search. Moreover, they are keenly con-scious of the probability of outcomes other than intended ones.

It is not until we move toward more adequate, objective measures of our influ-ence that we can claim to know what we are doing, or how well we are bringing it off.*

* This is a theme we return to in chapter 14.

More Resources for Improving
Instruction Than We Suspect

We estimate that there are some 700 articles on the teaching of sociology, some of which report empirical tests of the effectiveness of teaching techniques and strategies. From 1965 to 1979, more than four dozen articles were published on the introductory course, and an equal number on the teaching of sociological methods and statistics. Pertinent statements published in 1978 include sixteen articles, each of which describes a device to teach a sociological concept, ten articles reporting student evaluations of a sociology course (or aspects of a course), and the fifth empirical study in sociology that assesses learning gains in self-paced instruction, compared to conventional patterns.[12] Not only are there many resources, but they are increasingly accessible. The ASA Teaching Resources Center, the journal *Teaching Sociology*, the *ASA Teaching Newsletter*, and several annotated bibliographies and review articles bring these resources to our attention and provide continuing forums for discussions of teaching.

Not all our resources are in the form of printed materials. Our colleagues, students, administrators, and we ourselves are rich resources, too infrequently tapped. And there are other resources as well: the communities from which our students come and those in which we teach; the daily newspaper and television broadcasts; novels, plays, and poetry; and the whole range of experiences our students have in other courses and in their personal lives. In the appendix and elsewhere in this book, we list a broad range of resources, suggesting some of the ways they can be used.

Perhaps our most useful resource is the discipline itself—its theories, methods,

and findings. In chapter 5 we discuss an important goal of instruction in sociology—that of helping students think critically and creatively about the sources and consequences of social patterns. The social psychology of John Dewey's *Human Nature and Conduct* (1922), as well as research reviewed in chapter 12, suggests that we can best reach this goal of instruction if we disrupt the normal thought patterns of our students by revealing competing explanations for a single observation or discrepant data about the social world. Simmel's (1950) work on dyads and triads points to the use of a third party as examiner and certifying agent—in general, recasting our teaching goals so that teacher and student can work as allies in resolving problems not imposed by one of them, the teacher. Hedley (1978) suggests that we will improve our assessment of student performance if we apply to the task what we know about the sources of measurement error in research. In many articles our colleagues apply symbolic interaction theory to enhance our understanding of what goes on in the classroom (see Karp and Yoels, 1976) or to develop teaching techniques and strategies (Petras and Hayes, 1973; Spector, 1976).

Much is available to us to improve our work as teachers. Carl Taylor, in his presidential address to the American Sociological Association, plumped for fruitful collaboration between the man of knowledge and the man of action, between sociologist and practitioner. He wrote (1947:2):

> *There is no reason to believe that the average sociologist, had he spent his life in any one of the specific areas of behavior about which he generalizes [in education, for example] could not and would not make practical application of his sociological generalizations to that area of behavior and action.*

Taylor was wrong: we have every reason to believe that the sociologist-as-teacher has not made practical application to a specific area of behavior in which he spends most of his life.[13] Yet he might. Not to do so, not to exploit these resources is to waste our time: we reinvent the wheel, make avoidable errors, lose opportunities. Our instruction is less effective. Our students learn less than they might.

The task is long and hard. We are disqualified for it by our training—*unless* we put that training in research to work in the study of our intervention as teachers, the role to which most sociologists devote large parts of their careers. Along with their research training, graduate students should learn of the useful resources available to them in the career so many of them anticipate. And so should their elders.

❧

These, then, are our persuasions. We return to them throughout the book. They emerge in the teaching examples we use, especially in chapters 4 through 6, while in chapters 9 through 11 we discuss common instructional tools as means of achieving the ends embodied in some of these persuasions. In chapter 12 we consider research evidence bearing on these persuasions. And measuring teacher performance is the subject of chapter 14.

Now we turn to more immediate problems: the ends of instruction, the means for achieving them, and the assessment of the adequacy of those means. To begin at the beginning, we start at the end and ask: what are the goals of sociology instruction? These goals are of two sorts, those that are peculiar to sociology and those, such as enhanced ability to think analytically, that are shared by other disciplines. In chapter 4 we think about instructional goals peculiar to sociology.

Notes

1. This discussion draws on Boocock (1972:4–5), Gagné (1970:1–4), and Schlechty (1976:chapter 2). Our definitions differ in some ways from each of these authors.

2. We do not mean to imply a nominal scale of measurement; something is learned or it is not. Whether a nominal, ordinal, or higher scale type of measurement is appropriate depends on the learning goal in question. If the goal is simple, such as memorizing a definition or giving an example of a process, nominal scale measurement might be appropriate. But we expect that most teachers have complex, interlocking goals that can be accomplished in degree or in separate parts; hence measures of degrees of achievement, ordinal or higher scales, would be appropriate.

3. That there is no teaching without learning and that "telling is not teaching" are hardly new ideas (cf. Trumbull, 1887:chapter 2). The implications of the "telling is not teaching" position are important. It places responsibility on the teacher to do more than profess a subject matter.

4. Gagné (1970:4) adds to this definition that the change from which we infer learning "must have more than momentary permanence; it must be capable of being retained over some period of time. Finally, it must be distinguished from the kind of change that is attributable to growth, such as a change in height or the development of muscles through exercise." While omitting these factors from the text discussion, we agree with their inclusion. The matter of retention is of course important, but it simply calls for refinement of our definition of learning. Thus, the changes from which one infers learning last to a greater or lesser degree. Learning is not always permanent, and since the world and our analysis of it change, that is all to the good.

5. Research evidence on these and other factors mentioned below are cited later in this and other chapters.

6. A listing, by state, of these programs

and centers can be found in Gaff (1976) and Bergquist and Phillips (1975).

7. The following paragraphs, speaking to the first point, are drawn from a statement by Wilson (1976a).

8. We can offer an example of how the "action is in, thinking is out" principle can be disastrous for learning. In the course of consulting with administration, faculty, and students in a good liberal arts college, one student informant praised the experiential learning incorporated in the Social Welfare track. His responses illustrate the failure of experience untouched by proper preparation or post hoc reflection.

This student spoke warmly of the chance to get "meaningful learning" in a project entailing the interviewing of blacks in a nearby city. This was experience. This was relevance. In contrast with the dry and fruitless rituals of the classroom.

We asked him if he had worked long on interviewing techniques prior to his field trip. His answer was no. We asked him whether he'd had dry runs on other respondents in preparation for the field trip. Again, his answer was no. We asked him what the question was, whose answer he sought through this field experience. After some hesitation, he said that he wanted to discover whether the explanation of the blacks corresponded with that of the police (whose statements had been reported in the papers). We asked him, then, how he went about seeking an answer. He talked to the blacks, he said. Where? On street corners and wherever he could find them in one of the Negro districts of the nearby city. We asked him if he felt such locations would give him a representative sample of blacks. He didn't know. We asked what his response rate was, and he said that about one in two people he approached turned him down. We asked him if he felt reasonably confident that nonrespondents did not differ systematically from those individuals who were willing to answer his queries, but he did not know. How then, we wondered, did he know what he thought he knew?

The moral of the story is this: experience,

divorced from reflection and knowledge, leads to self-deceit. This student needed some information on developing interview items, on the meaning of reliability and validity, on probability sampling. Lacking such knowledge, he deluded himself into thinking he knew what in fact he did not know. Beyond this, he falsely celebrated one mode of instruction over another.

9. It's useful to ask what accounts for the product of a course—the knowledge and beliefs students have at the end, over and above what they had at the beginning. It's at least possible that most of the variance in knowledge among students at the end of a course can be accounted for by variance in what those students brought from prior experience. This was the view expressed by some social scientists (see Newcomb and Wilson, 1966:2,3) who examined the impact of peers (ranked as second most influential in accounting for learning). Third place in this rank-ordering of influences fell to the conventional academic apparatus. These are hunches, not data. But if there is a shred of truth in the presumed impact of peers and past experience on people's learning, then we suggest that sociology instructors should share the stage with other educationally fruitful influences.

10. Sometimes we are excessively cocky, taking as self-evident that which any competent sociologist should see as problematic: our effectiveness in altering others' (students') behavior. A young colleague arrived with his doctorate from one of our top departments. He simply transferred material from his graduate experience, a potpourri of readings from Weber, Durkheim, Marx, Pareto et al., to his introductory course. He did so with a serene sense of superiority as he contrasted the demands of his introductory section with those of other instructors. And yet, at the end of the course and despite his disenchantment with this scheme (owing to students' adverse reactions and low achievement), his chutzpah persisted. For, again, he saw his now-revised course as the ultimate answer to the introductory.

11. We are indebted to Professor Paul Lindsay for this statement on the usefulness of sports in opening channels of communication with students. He also discovered this statement by Novak (1976:33), which is to the point:

One of the most sensitive of the European professors driven to America by Hitler, Eugen Rosenstock-Huessy, observed at Harvard that his references to European stories, historical or legendary, did not illuminate for Americans the points he was making, as they did for his students in Germany. He tried for several years to find a field of examples of which his American students would have vivid personal experience. Later he wrote: "The world in which the American student who comes to me at about twenty years of age really has confidence in is the world of sport. This world encompasses all of his virtues and experiences, affection and interests; therefore, I have built my entire sociology around the experiences an American has in athletics and games."

12. See chapters 10 and 11 for further discussion of this technique—PSI, the Personalized System of Instruction.

13. We can understand why this is so. Secrecy and, therefore, pluralistic ignorance surround instruction in sociology. Consequently, there is a standardlessness of the operation, buttressed by the virtuous invoking of academic freedom. There is, also, a self-protecting disposition not to measure outcomes or to put objectives in the operational terms that would enable measurement (as would be the case in research). There is the schizziness of a profession whose practitioners are torn between creation and transmission; a profession in which the lesser rated and lesser rewarded activity of transmission supports the activity of creation. In one way or another, all of these conditions militate against the thoughtful "practical application of . . . sociological generalizations to that area of behavior and action" (Taylor, 1947:2).

PART II
WHAT ARE THE ENDS WE SEEK?

To specify instructional goals is to do at least four things. Obviously, such specification defines the instructor's aims. Three other outcomes and their implications are not so obvious. From the student's perspective, the specification of goals points to *changes to be effected* in skills and knowledge. (So signalling change is to underscore the need for initial measures of student knowledge.) It is also a first step in selecting the means best suited to achieving a given aim. Finally, such specification sets a benchmark for evaluating the extent of the *instructor's* achievement.

What are the ends we seek? Sociology instructors proclaim a wide range of goals. From reviews of course syllabi, introductory statements in textbooks, faculty responses to surveys,[1] and general suggestions about the yield of studying sociology,[2] we glean these examples. The aim is to:

1. Learn about a scholarly enterprise
   a. introduce sociology as a field of study
   b. prepare students to become sociologists
   c. convey various sociological perspectives

2. Use sociology for personal development
   a. help students understand their own lives as social beings
   b. develop skill in critical thinking
   c. promote personal growth
   d. develop skills useful in future careers
   e. develop student creativity

3. Use sociology to understand society
   a. learn about American society
   b. help students understand everyday life
   c. develop cultural awareness
   d. help students achieve practical insights into social problems

4. Achieve a variety of other goals
   a. contribute to liberal education goals
   b. transmit a body of knowledge—concepts, theories, research findings

So stated, these goals have this in common: it is hard to tell exactly what they mean. They are seriously meant and suggestive. But even within the typically terse context from which we took them, it is doubtful that students will gain a clear view of their destinations or that, so vaguely put, such statements can serve the four purposes just mentioned. Hence we will spend some time in part II (and later) on ways of specifying and clarifying goals of sociology instruction.

The goals we have listed are a mixed lot. Some embrace others. Some may apply to all students in a class, others to a subset. One way of classifying them separates sociology as means (to learn about self and society) from sociology as an end in itself. Another classification depends on whether the goals refer to the subject matter of sociology (see category 1) or to intellectual skills that transcend particular content (see categories 2 and 3). This is the classificatory scheme we use in organizing part II. Chapter 4 discusses goals peculiar to courses in sociology—not aims specific to particular courses such as Stratification, Family, or Urban, but goals that are peculiar to the discipline and crosscut all sociology courses. In chapters 5 and 6 we turn to the second category: goals appropriate, but not peculiar, to sociology. These are skills in analytical thinking (or critical or reflective thought) and, in chapter 6, skills in inquiry and in extending the fruits of inquiry. Thus chapter 4 treats some substantive (field-related) goals, chapters 5 and 6 goals of instruction that transcend the field.

To choose these goals is to omit others. But we are sure that most sociologists would agree on the importance of those we treat. We hope that our mode of treatment may provide a useful model equally applicable to other goals.

Our illustrations of teaching to meet these goals exploit but a narrow range of content—the application of a single concept, the estimation of a single social fact, and the testing of a single, elementary hypothesis. But the basic ideas are applicable when the teacher tackles larger issues, treating full-blown theories or working with students on a full-term research project, from formulation of the problem to the final report.

Although we have treated means separately (part III), our discussion of goals in part II offers some examples of the means of their achievement. But we would not wish a reader to infer that, lacking such means as we use, illustratively, the achievement of certain goals is therefore precluded. Familiarity with the literature and some ingenuity will disclose different means to achieve such ends. (These are matters we take up later.)

Our interest in part II is chiefly with the ends of sociology instruction, rather than the means of achieving them. And so we broach two questions: What are the goals peculiar to sociology instruction? And what instructional goals do we share with other disciplines?

Notes

1. Bradshaw and McPherron (1977) report on a national sample survey of departments' aims for the first course in sociology. Departments said the following statements

well describe their first course: (1) it emphasizes teaching fundamental concepts needed in subsequent sociology courses (74 percent); (2) it introduces students to the subjects that sociologists study (62 percent); (3) it introduces students to a variety of sociological perspectives (61 percent); (4) it teaches the most important scientifically established facts from sociological research (26 percent); and (5) it helps students understand everyday life (50 percent). The only marked variation by school type occurred in the last statement. This goal was more important in community colleges than in universities, with four-year colleges falling in between. Two articles that report surveys of sociology students and contain data bearing on instructional goals are Bates (1965) and Zelan (1974).

As for course syllabi, they seldom go beyond very general statements of course goals. This is confirmed by Ballantine's (1977) content analysis of 100 Introductory Sociology syllabi and our own review of hundreds of course syllabi. That introductory textbooks generally provide only vague statements of goals was found in nonsystematic reviews of texts by Professors Charlotte Vaughan and Richard Peterson and by Professor Michael Bassis.

2. The reader will find useful, general statements on goals of sociology instruction in Bierstedt (1964), Bressler (1967), Mills (1961: chapter 1), Nisbet (1976), and Page (1963). More specific discussions of goals are found in Mariampolski (1978) on humanistic goals; Kohout (1978) on goals taken from courses in the biophysical sciences; Cuzzort (1969:chapter 16) on substantive and nonsubstantive goals; Vaughan and Peterson (1975) on putting goal statements into measurable terms; Logan (1976) for a test of the degree to which sociology courses teach students to think critically (defined as logical, consistent thinking backed by evidence); Liebert and Bayer (1975) on preprofessional versus client-centered goals; and Platt, Parsons, and Kirchstein (1976) for an examination of teaching goals in 1968 and 1973 (general goals, not goals in sociology particularly). A useful overview of goals of sociology instruction is found in Stauffer's essay in Baker and Wilson, 1979.

CHAPTER 4
FIELD-RELATED GOALS

What are our aims in teaching sociology to undergraduates? We said earlier that we were less than sure about what, precisely, we are teaching our students. Sometimes we are equally uncertain about our goals and their justification. It's a difficult question. How shall we answer it?

Since our knowledge is only as reliable as the methods we use to achieve it, shall we devote much of our time to the gathering, reduction, and analysis of data? Or shall we leave that to courses so labelled? Since few students will be majors and fewer still will become professional social scientists, shall we stress the application of sociology to various vocations—business, law, social work, medicine—and to the mundane problems of daily life? Shall we stress an introduction to the field as one might in introductory chemistry? Or shall the emphasis be on problems of our society with sociology becoming, simply, the instrument of analysis? Shall we stress facts, and the empirically demonstrated connections between them—i.e., propositions? Or shall we stress the explanations of those connections—i.e., theory? To which of the various subfields of sociology[1] shall we assign greatest weight—to race, ethnicity, class, gender, age? to the various institutions (family, education, religion, polity, science)? to small group or societal analyses? to social processes such as socialization, urbanization, professionalization? Shall we emphasize goals shared by sociology and other subject areas? Or goals peculiar to the field?

These questions will have their answers (perhaps best registered in the final examination), whether by default or thoughtful planning. Sometimes they are witlessly answered as we simply recapitulate a course as it was taught us. Sometimes they are answered as an instructor-turned-missionary pushes a particular viewpoint. Sometimes they are answered by the textbook chosen by the teacher. And sometimes, we hope, they are answered through long reflection on the meaning of a liberal arts education and the contribution that sociology—even one exposure to sociology—can make to that education.

What is that special contribution? Sociological inquiries share certain things in common. Typically they start with a question that presses us to explain differences: why this way rather than that? (For example, why is there high rather than low fertility, prejudice rather than tolerance, corporal punishment of children among whites but not among plains Indians?) We look to previous explanations in experience and theory for a tentative answer. But often the answer is inadequate; so we must try to build a better one and do it in such a way that we can derive from it hypotheses to be set up as targets for testing. With skill and wisdom, the current inquiry will build on the past, refining and correcting previous knowledge and extending it to new populations or situations. Thus we are able to broaden our generalizations. The best explanation is parsimonious and embraces a wide range of behaviors, some of which might seem to have nothing in common (entering a religious order and entering the army). Sociological work is always marked by a keen concern with the logic of inquiry and the need to devise and apply the best tools possible for gathering and analyzing needed data.

Now if we are to specify goals peculiar to sociology instruction, we must ask what is distinctive about these features of sociological inquiry. And the answer must be: nothing. All disciplined inquiry can be so characterized.[2] What, then, distinguishes sociology? *That which is inquired into.* We investigate patterns of human relationships. These are the subject matter of sociology. Differences in these patterns pose our problems. Explaining the differences, their sources and consequences, is our task. To describe and explain these richly varied social arrangements, we must identify and measure dimensions that differ markedly from those pertinent to other fields—socioeconomic status (SES), type and extent of division of labor, integration (or cohesion, or solidarity), deviance, structures of power and authority, size of groups and categories—all necessarily social dimensions and not properties of individuals.[3] These dimensions are useful in the study of every social institution. A given study may examine only one dimension (say, cohesion) in a single institution (such as the family). But what brings such work within the purview of sociology is the wish to understand variations in a social dimension. And dimensions such as cohesion vary across the spectrum of social units: cohesion within a dyad (two college friends), a group (a college seminar or swim team), an organization (college), an institution (education), and a society (the United States).

Patterns (or arrangements or structures) of human relationships define the realm of sociological inquiry. Even though the source of empirical data is often the individual, the dimensions of analysis are aspects of the relationships in which the person is enmeshed. If we get measures on individual preferences, or race, age, sex, or beliefs, it is only because these are clues to the stereotypes and rules that define social relationships. (For example, young children should be in school; a woman's place is in the home—or if she is in the labor force, she should be paid less than a man.) We may study varying social patterns to help us understand variations in personal traits. (This is what the social psychologist does.) Sociological inquiry helps us understand the social sources of the self, the individual's fate as a social creation.[4] And we may study social patterns in one sector to help us understand variations in another social sector. (Thus structure of the labor force—say, proportion in extractive industry—is connected with family size.)

Some Field-related Goals of Sociology Instruction

We are distinguishing two sorts of teaching goals: those goals that bear on the substance of a particular subject (for example, explaining variation in social structures), and those goals that might be shared with any other field of study (for example, recapturing the lost ability to question the common and obvious; or developing skill in extending ideas to new situations—matters we take up in the next two chapters).

The former category, the substantive goals of teaching, derives from our conception of the field being taught. Since the task of sociology is to explain differing social patterns, their sources and consequences, our teaching goals will reflect dimensions of these social structures. What dimensions? That must depend on the problem posed, the subfield being explored, the theory adduced to offer a tentative answer, and the hypotheses derived from the theory, which become, then, the targets for testing. There are very general dimensions that characterize social structures. We have mentioned some: integration, cohesion, deviance, and social change.

But most field-related goals of sociology instruction will reflect dimensions peculiar to the specific subfield or division of sociology being taught. Thus in a course on stratification, the teacher might include learning goals touching: *basic social facts and data* such as income distribution and mobility rates; *basic concepts* useful in organizing the data, such as class, caste, status, power, intra- and intergenerational mobility; *major theories* about the sources of stratification such as the Davis–Moore (functional) explanation or the inheritance of statuses invested with privilege or poverty; and knowledge of *critical hypotheses and results of their empirical testing*—for example, the effects of education on intergenerational occupational mobility, or the effects of race and sex on income and occupation. Elsewhere we suggest approaches useful in teaching particular content, and other discussions have appeared in *The American Sociologist* and *Teaching Sociology* in recent years.

But here we are concentrating on certain instructional goals peculiar to sociology, yet transcending the content of particular subfields. Consider two basic aspects of our social arrangements, structure and change. Depending on the problem, structure may be analyzed along several dimensions: size, permeability of group boundaries, extent of internal differentiation, degree of internal integration, relationship to other social structures in the environment, arrangements for adaptation to the physical environment, and the like.

Analysis of changes in structure might prompt us to inquire into the rapidity or rate of change, the shape of the change (whether linear, cyclic, logistic, or exponential), the sources of change (both external and internal), and the kind and rapidity of response in one social sector to changes occurring elsewhere.

These two aspects of social arrangements, the cross-sectional view of structure and the longitudinal study of changes in structure, are very general. Even the dimensions through which they are analyzed are quite abstract and applicable to a wide range of issues. And that is all to the good since the higher the level of abstraction of an idea or dimension, the greater the range of reality it embraces. But of course these dimensions must be specified and applied to particular social settings and the network of relationships located in them. And that is the business of the classroom. Let us illustrate, using the notion of social structure, differing patterns of human relationships.

A Field-related Goal: Appreciating the Concept of Structure

The task at hand requires us to: (1) tap students' experience of structures: spatial and temporal arrangements of community life, bureaucratic organizations (such as that revealed by the table of organization of the college or university), class, arrangements built on discrimination between races or sexes, structures of authority both legitimate and illegitimate, etc.; (2) distill these experiences in the abstract concept of structure; (3) apply the concept, then, to some new realm, particularly to some aspect of social life under study in the particular course; and thus (4) show the usefulness of the concept as an heuristic device. For now, we fix on the third and fourth learning goals.

A teacher might convey the broad applicability and usefulness of structural dimensions by working through, with students, a comparison of three sets of social arrangements (structures) along several dimensions. The outcome might be seen in a scheme such as that in table 4.1.

Table 4.1 compares a college class, an industrial firm, and a city—three markedly different social phenomena. Yet when we apply the concept of structure (and its constituent dimensions) to them, many important facts emerge about each social pattern. Thus, increasing size alters communications (teacher–student, student–student interchange) within a classroom, necessitates more complex administrative hierarchies in an industrial organization, and leads to increased labor force specialization and centralization of administrative control mechanisms in a city. And we note that in several cases, increased size entails an outcome (e.g., communication problems) affecting all three organizations. Size, as one element of structure, is a category that transcends particular content. What distinguishes sociology is its use of such concepts to build bridges between different social patterns. Its propositions are based on similarities of form in such structures as college classroom, industrial firm, and city.

One task of the teacher of sociology is to help students discover and understand these generic features of social life. This is one significant goal in teaching the substance of sociology—in all courses, in every course.

But is this concern for transcendent dimensions and isomorphisms appropriate for the undergraduate sociology classroom? One answer is: of course it is appropriate. If this is a sociology class and if generic dimensions and isomorphisms are at the core of sociology, they surely have a place and a central one. But some teachers may object: "My students are not interested in structure and size, in transcendent anything. My students want to

talk about things that touch their lives. I think that's legitimate and would add that I want them to study social issues and large social changes that affect us all."

And so do we. In the preceding chapter, we argued for a moral component in teaching: "All content areas would be crosscut not only by theory and method, but, additionally, by issues of the better and the worse—i.e., by problems of personal choice and public policy." We also suggested that teaching is most effective when the subject matter can be related to students' past and future. Even such an abstract goal as unravelling the concept of structure (because it reflects the locus of inquiry peculiar to sociology) can be related both to the personal experience of students and to policy issues. To illustrate how this might be done in the classroom, we continue our discussion of size as a structural dimension.

A Field-related Goal: Learning the Significance of Size as a Dimension of Social Structure

Consider a class in urban sociology. The teacher asks students where they would like to live—or whether it makes any difference: "Do you care where you live? Why?" and "After college—or whenever you are about to look for your first job—will you restrict your search to certain sorts of cities or towns or communities? to a big city? to a small country place? to something in between? Or would it make no difference where your job took you?" The teacher asks students to write their answers on a slip of paper and list the reasons for their preferences.

Answers are then summarized in tables placed on the chalkboard and discussed. Some variation in preferences will emerge, and students will have reasons for

Table 4.1 Selected Dimensions of Social Structure Applied to Social Phenomena

Structural Dimensions	Social Phenomena[5]		
	College Class	Industrial Firm	City
Size	Observed Variation: 2 to 2,000 Consequences of Size: extent and types of communication will vary with size	Observed Variation: 5 to 100,000 + Consequences of Size: increased size will result in increased need for administrative coordination, increased hierarchical complexity, bureaucratic personality, communication problems	Observed Variation: 2,500 to 12 million Consequences of Size: increased size will result in increased specialization, increased number of stress points in a system requiring more specialization (roles and mechanisms) for alleviation, greater consolidation of administrative functions, variation in diversity of social groups and roles
Boundaries	Teacher-autonomy defines boundaries: variations are introduced by type of course and institutional constraints	Degree of autonomy varies with each particular firm or factory in market and related systems	Boundaries overlap only partially; fuzziness of functional boundaries
Internal Differentiation	Roles of teacher and student; subgroups within class	Roles of foreman, manager, line worker; staff and line; variation in span of control	Neighborhoods; segregation by residence, occupation, class, race, commercial activities, etc.; cellular, concentric zones, sector, multicentricity and mixes of such patterns
Internal Integration	Normative prescriptions regarding roles, participation, involvement; authority and power of teacher; leadership within class; legitimacy, degree of interdependency (e.g., between sections of large class) of TAs, student, faculty	Official and unofficial (formal and informal) normative patterns; degree of role consensus; communications; control of production work by machine flow; degree of interdependency among procurement, production, purchasing units, etc.	Functional interdependence within city; authority of political institutions; power of organized groups (such as businesses) and degree of interdependency
Relationship to Other Social Structures in Environment	College or university, state legislature, federal agencies, private foundations, other academic institutions; also, labor market and military	Other firms (some competitive) and changing markets; regulatory agencies (laws and rules)	Other, integrated territorial units (role relative to metropolitan systems and patterns of dominance)
Relationship to Physical Environment	Seating arrangements (movable or fixed), shape and dimensions of room, acoustics, temperature (as these affect distances among those present, communication, etc.)	Proximity of units within or among buildings; geographic setting of firm location (as might affect distribution, communication, etc.)	Natural: location, topography, and climate (as might affect locational patterns and interaction—subject to technical and organizational factors); Artifical: sunken highways (creating social borders)

their preferred locations. Size of place matters for them. Let us assume that the following data were obtained from the class and put on the board.

Rural or Small Town	Small Urban Place	Large Urban Place	Total
25%	55%	20%	100%

Having asked students to commit themselves to a choice and a rationale, and having encouraged discussion, the teacher points to the summary data for the class and asks students whether most Americans share their location preferences. Shortly, the teacher might provide data on actual American preferences (Elgin et al., 1974:29), so that the table now reads:

	Rural or Small Town	Small Urban Place	Large Urban Place	No Opinion	Total
Class	25%	55%	20%	0%	100%
U.S.	53	33	13	1	100%

What accounts for the differences? The class will probably conclude that its members are not an adequate sample of the population of the United States. Other data will confirm that the class is not representative: surely younger than the general population, students may be unrepresentative on other variables (education, sex, income, color, and place of residence). Do these variables matter? Do they affect locational choice? What types of data should one have to answer such questions? The teacher can provide answers or can develop them with the class. This will depend partly on how much time can be devoted to the matter at hand and partly on the teacher's goals at this point in the course.* Data are available to test

the hypothesis that people's social characteristics are related to locational preference. Exploiting such data, the expanded table would look like table 4.2.[6]

Now students have disclosed and discussed their preferences and the reasons for them, and they have compared their views with those of the larger population (and categories within the larger society). The teacher has had a chance to help students discover some important aspects of sampling and generalizing, and some social sources of preferences. Depending on the teacher's course goals, various other questions about locational preference could be introduced, such as the sources of urban imagery and changes in locational preference over time. And it would be only a few short steps to larger issues such as the meaning of community, or the effect of metropolitanization and urbanization on small towns and rural life, suburbanization, and migration patterns.

But are places of varying size actually different? If so, does city size cause these differences or is it simply correlated with them? One way to approach these questions is to ask: "Is there any optimum city size?" (Here again we invoke the moral component of learning.) The question has both personal meaning and social utility—as well as bearing on a central sociological variable, a structural dimension. If we can identify a given size range as optimal, people can use the knowledge— as citizens, in weighing a zoning decision, or as private individuals, in choosing a place to live. And there are policy questions: Should there be legislative limitations on city size? Should new towns be built to a certain size? Should tax incentives encourage labor-intensive firms to locate in communities of certain sizes? Thus the question of optimum city size provides a fine point of entry for exploring basic questions in sociology (urban) and

* In chapters 5 and 6, we will discuss such matters at length.

Table 4.2 Locational Preferences of Americans, by Background Attributes, 1971

	Rural or Small Town	Small Urban Place	Large Urban Place	No Opinion	Total
Class	25%	55%	20%	0%	100%
United States	53	33	13	1	100
Actual Residence					
Rural or small town	88	10	2	0	100
Small urban place	39	55	6	0	100
Large urban place	34	26	39	2	101
Education					
Less than high school	57	30	12	1	100
High school completed	54	32	13	1	100
Some college	47	38	14	1	100
College completed	40	38	22	0	100
Annual Income					
Under $5,000	57	32	10	1	100
$5,000 to $9,999	53	34	12	0	99
$10,000 to $14,999	45	29	11	0	85*
$15,000 or more	45	34	21	0	100
Color					
White	54	33	11	0	98
Black	33	34	33	0	100

Source: Data from Elgin et al. (1974:29).

* The error in this row total appears in the source document and cannot be due to rounding.

policy issues. A number of sociologists (and geographers and city planners) have pursued the question of optimum size and there is a substantial literature to draw on.[7] Both theory and available evidence suggest that there is no optimum size or range for all criteria of desirability.[8] Instead, the data support such intriguing conclusions as these: If you want to live in a community where you would have a low probability of illness, pick a medium-sized city; but if you might have serious illnesses, pick a very big city.

We have come quite a distance in this discussion. We started by saying that sociology is identified by its target of inquiry, patterns, or structures of human relationships. If our teaching goals are to reflect the substance of sociology, they will bear on such social features as structure. This is a very broad, field-related goal—since the concept of structure and the several dimensions that describe structure are generic, transcending particular subfields (institutions, stratification, socialization, and the like). One dimension of structure is size, and we reflected on the effects of size across three sorts of social organization: college classes, industrial firms, and cities. This concern with social structure, exemplified in the question about optimum city size, is related to personal concerns, historical developments, and public policy. Thus we can stimulate and engage the personal concerns of students and demonstrate the policy relevance of sociological inquiry. We conclude, then, where we started: one goal of the instructor is to help students discover and exploit those dimensions of social phenomena, such as structure, that define the distinctive realm of sociology.

A Field-related Goal: Learning about Boundaries as an Aspect of Social Structure

SOCIOLOGY 181:
    CRIMINOLOGY .... 3 Cr.
Second semester. Major emphasis is given to an examination of the causes of delinquency and crime. Analysis is made in terms of behavior systems, rather than legal classification. Also considered are: maturation in crime, criminal associates, policy roles and practices, the functioning of the courts and penology. Prerequisite: Sociology 100 or permission of the instructor.

We teach specialized courses such as this. And properly so. The aim of such specialized and advanced courses is to study a slice of the social world (bringing the tools of sociology to bear) or a slice of sociology (applying it to selected aspects of social life). Yet, in a liberal arts education, the instructor's goal may be to broaden students' vision by using sociology to discover similarities in social settings that seem, to the unaware, utterly different. This goal is appropriate; for like all intellectual activities, sociology seeks to deepen our understanding by broadening our assertions—i.e., by generalizing. (The generalizing is, of course, tentative and subject to testing by reason and experience.) With our students, we want to teach

In a course on:	Students will study:
Criminology, deviance, or delinquency	prisons, reformatories
Health or medicine	mental hospitals, TB sanitariums
Gerontology	old age homes
The military	military academies, bootcamp, life on naval vessels
Religion	convents, monasteries
Race relations	Bantustans (subject to South African laws enforcing apartheid)

the use of a sociological idea—for example, the notion of boundaries as an aspect of social structure—to gain insight otherwise impossible into a wider range of social arrangements. Consider the course just described, along with several others and their objects of inquiry.

It is unlikely that students in one of the six courses listed would be studying the settings listed in other courses. But each of the social arrangements listed in the right-hand column shares basic characteristics. Each is:

a place of residence and work where a large number of like situated individuals, cut off from the wider society for an appreciable period of time, together lead an enclosed, formally administered round of life. (Goffman, 1961a:xiii)

These social arrangements are what Goffman called total institutions. Each setting is all-encompassing and isolated from the larger world; in most of them, significant resocialization takes place. (It would be sad for students in a criminology course not to see the similarity between prisons, West Point Military Academy, and hospitals.)

All social systems have boundaries. Boundedness is a basic feature, and boundary permeability a basic dimension, of social structure. As with the concept of size, boundary transcends particular social contents. But although boundaries are everywhere, their permeability varies.

How might students in a course on criminology come to see some similarities of form between a federal prison, a hospital, and a military academy? How might they use the concept of boundary as a means of bridging ostensibly different social structures? The teacher might simply identify parallel characteristics and make the general point. But unless time presses compellingly, this is not the best strategy.

Better that students should discover the similarities for themselves—not simply because the process of discovery may be more fun and rewarding for them (although these are valued outcomes), but because they will learn more surely if they have a more active role. And such an approach need not be inordinately time-consuming. The teacher can proceed inductively, listing several total institutions (although not characterizing them as such) and asking students what features these organizations share. Or the instructor could move deductively, asking students to suggest central features of a prison, as one type of place where people live and work—then asking them to identify other social settings with the same characteristics. In either case, the idea of boundary and its relative permeability will emerge.

Students might be asked whether they have ever lived in a total institution, so drawing on first-hand experience. Some may have been in the military or employed by, say, a mental hospital. Some might suggest that life in a residential college or university fits the definition, at least in part. Such a suggestion would doubtless lead to reflection on differences among organizations that fit the definition of the total institution. Participation in some total institutions is voluntary (monasteries), while other total institutions have both voluntary and involuntary participants (sanitariums, old age homes).[9]

The underlying, field-related goal here is to deepen students' understanding of structure through the concept of boundary and one of its dimensions, permeability. Colleges have boundaries more permeable than those of prisons but less permeable than those of an aggregate of people waiting at a bus stop. (And what of families' boundaries? To raise this question is to introduce a social group in which membership is involuntary, ascribed, and sometimes demanding.)

The comparative impermeability of prison boundaries—and those of convents and other total institutions—imposes limits on movement and communication. Clearly these limits are imposed, in part, by rules. Now the instructor may inquire whether aspects of organizations, aside from rules, set boundaries. Do different sorts of social settings and structures have different sorts of boundaries? One might approach this question inductively or deductively.

Following the former approach, we might take a number of organizations—a football team, a church group, a retail business—and ask what sets each apart from people and groups on the outside. Thus skill, language, and interests would be seen as setting boundaries.

On the other hand, the latter approach might prompt us to ask the function of a boundary, to search, then, for cases that fulfill the function, and perhaps, after that, to specify new types of boundaries uncovered. For example, a function of boundaries is separation. What separates people other than walls or physical space? What types of things impede communication and movement? (Students might be asked to think of cases in their own lives.) Gaps between teacher and student, between parent and child suggest that age differences can separate. Thus *time* can be viewed as a boundary, separating young and old, or persons of different generational experience (Cain, 1964).

Other common social variables such as race, income, and power suggest boundaries between castes and classes. Nor is it just categories or groups of people that can be separated. Territorial units—towns, cities, metropolitan areas—can be separated by various functions, such as economic or occupational (see Hawley,

1971:329–332, passim; Schwirian, 1974). Functionally based boundaries are also used in the analysis of complex organizations (Haas and Drabek, 1973:15–17, 89–90, 233).

In sum, if our goal is to teach something of sociology's distinctive contribution, students will learn about patterns or structures of human relationships. One aspect of social structures is their boundedness. One dimension of boundedness is permeability. As with numbers or size, these aspects of social structure cut across all of sociology's subfields. Therefore learning about them and their use becomes a likely, field-related goal of sociology instruction.

The Clear and Useful Statement of Field-related Goals

We want our students not only to recognize many dimensions of social structure, but more importantly to be able to use such dimensions to bracket various settings and circumstances—to see the similarities between convent and prison, between a kindergarten class and the first year of law school, between childrearing and brainwashing. For it is only with such conceptual bridging of empirical reality that the mind gets an effective purchase on the world.

All very well, these noble aspirations, but what exactly do we mean when we say that we want our students to discover similarities of form (isomorphisms) in different social settings? How do we know that a student understands such terms? that he can use such dimensions of social structure to arrange myriad social data intelligibly and to better understand the social world? Splendid goals, muddily put, may betray our hopes for students' learning. Our goal statements, valuable and necessary as they

are, must be transformed into operational statements whose terms allow measurement. Only so can the goals for student and teacher become clear. Only so will they allow assessment of student learning and teacher effectiveness. And this would be the case even if grading were not an issue.

Understanding Marginality: Clarifying Goal Statements

Consider Professor Jones who teaches a course on race and ethnic relations. One crucial idea employed in the course is marginality. Jones has certain goals for her students; she wants them not only to understand what sociologists mean by marginality, but also to have an analytic grasp of the concept and to see that it has wide application in all sorts of social settings— and not just for members of racial minorities.

But what does it mean to understand marginality? How do we know when a student understands the term? What constitutes "an analytic grasp"? How is the instructor to know when students can see "wide application"? Jones's statement of goals suggests worthy intentions, which, we suspect, would be shared by many sociologists. But we doubt that such goal statements mean much to students. We know their uncertainty when a teacher states similar goals for a term paper or essay examination. ("Remember, I want your papers to be analytic, not just descriptive.") Nor can such vague goal statements be very helpful to teachers as they design their courses, devise ways to assess students' learning, react to students' work, and try to measure the success of their own efforts (see chapter 2).

We do not suggest that, in stating course goals, instructors can specify pre-

cisely what is to be achieved by what proportion of a class. The accuracy of a statement of anticipated achievement is a matter of post hoc determination. There is a parallel here with Mead's theory about the construction of social reality: the meaning of an act is given only in the react—i.e., in the responses of others. We may (indeed, should) work out instructional goals in accord with our knowledge of the field and our hopes for the students. But the reality that finally tests and defines those goals is the extent of their achievement. Otherwise instructors are in the position of travellers in a foreign country: they may act hopefully toward others but have no sense of the response they will get. Means and ends become disconnected; a statement of virtuous ends becomes an irrelevant piety. Only by some attempt to measure the outcomes that index our instructional goals can we improve our means (or modify our goals) and close the gap between aspirations and achievement.

Let us return now to marginality, another dimension (marginality–centrality) of social structure, the domain peculiar to sociology. What do students have to do to show an instructor that they understand the concept of marginality? With an answer to that question, the teacher has clues as to what must be done to enable each student to master the idea and demonstrate understanding. Two conventional answers to that question require that the student be able:

1. to write from memory the definition of marginality provided by the instructor

2. to recognize the definition when presented along with several erroneous or less acceptable definitions

Now we have transformed the general goal statement into an operational one. We know what the student is to learn to do. But some readers will dislike our operationalization. We hear such objections as this: "Since when is memorization or passive recall of a term regarded as understanding? That may be useful, but it's not what I mean when I say understand. I mean more than that."

Very well; so do we. But note that our hypothetical readers can evaluate our goal statement. They can tell what we mean and can call it inadequate. Because our operationalization has clear meaning and refers to specific behaviors, they can agree or disagree. In contrast, we doubt that many sociologists could have disagreed with the initial goal statement, "to understand marginality." But more important, we doubt that productive discussion about the goal could take place until that goal was expressed with the clarity of an operational statement.

If understanding marginality is more than memorizing a definition, what in fact is it? What might a student do to show understanding? Consider these two possibilities. The student will be able:

3. to write a definition of marginality using words other than those used by the instructor or text (i.e., to rephrase)

4. to provide correct examples of marginality other than those used in class (i.e., to illustrate)

Now we have four possibilities for demonstrating understanding—repeating, recognizing, rephrasing, and illustrating. If readers still find these behaviors unsatisfactory as indicators of understanding, they will wish to add or substitute others. For example, the student will be able:

5. to indicate, on a map of a metropolitan area, which group's members (among, say, Italians, Germans, and English) would be most

marginal, living in least desirable areas; and which would live farthest from city center in a desirable suburb

6. to report two critical ways in which marginality affects the children of a specific marginal group

However readers may define "understanding," we hope they will use terms as clear and measurable as those we have used in our examples.

Beyond understanding marginality, Jones's goal was for students "to have an analytic grasp of the concept and to see that it has wide application." Analysis requires that we shake out the parts or elements of some whole. When we do so, we often find that the same elements are found in other settings. And marginality-centrality is one dimension of social structure that we would expect to find in various settings. Jones wants her students to understand this generic quality and its use in analyzing structure. Her class is reading a text on race and ethnic relations that discusses only the marginality of black Americans. But the concept is useful in understanding other minority groups, including the Japanese in the United States and Jews in Europe and the United States; and it is used in the sociology of occupations.[10] Like other sociologists, Jones sees connections between marginality and status inconsistency, role incompatibility or conflict, partial institutionalization, and reference group theory.[11] This instructor also knows that various sociologists use marginality to characterize personality, status, or social and cultural groups. In sum, when Jones says she wants her students to have an analytic grasp of marginality and to see its wide application, these are the sorts of things she is thinking about.

But this list does not offer clear direction, either for students or instructor. We need an operational statement of the goal. What might students do to show that they can use the notion of marginality analytically? One answer goes like this: students should be able to do in class discussion, on papers, and in tests the sorts of things the teacher does in class. The teacher defines, describes, explains; and students do the same. Yet Jones wants students to do more than repeat what she does in class; she wants them to use the concept in original ways, to build intellectual bridges to groups and situations not treated in class. How can she convey this goal and plan for measuring its achievement? Operational statements of "having an analytic grasp" and "seeing wide application" will help. For example:

1. Given a familiar social situation not discussed in class, the student will state whether any category is marginal and, if so, what traits make for marginality.

2. Asked to explore the possibility of marginal categories among class members, the student will identify at least three of the following possibilities: women, blacks, other minority group members, the very poor, the very rich, transients (students from transient families), foreign students; the student will identify the traits that make for marginality; and the student will specify at least one advantage and one disadvantage of marginality, both for the group and for those in marginal positions.

Instructors cannot safely assume that stated goals, such as ability to generalize, are automatically clear to students. Such clarity comes only when the instructor helps students put the words to work. If Jones wants students to extend the notion of marginality to new groups and settings (i.e., to generalize), then she had better show students how to do it. For doing something is the only verifiable measure of achievement we have. Doing generalizing entails: (1) identifying a class of persons who are marginal; (2) analyzing the traits that confer marginality—strangeness, transiency, lack of common skills (including language), powerlessness, stereotypic labels of inferiority; and (3) locating other classes of persons exhibiting such traits. In particular, the instructor will wish to cultivate the habit of extending ideas to one's own personal experience. Have any of the students themselves been in a marginal position? With what consequences? First generation college students? the student who is also a member of a minority group? the military veteran or older-than-average student?

Putting goals in operational terms not only clarifies matters for the student (and instructor). It clarifies the measure of achievement. Nor is that all. Being a statement of behavior, the operationally stated goal also points to the instructor's behavior, the teaching procedures needed to exemplify the ways that students will ultimately show their mastery.

Understanding Social Distance: Clarifying Goal Statements

Consider one final feature of operational goal statements. They reflect the same desire for precision, testing, and refutability that characterize the specification of variables in research. To be able to work with ideas of social structure, such as boundary permeability or marginality, we must do precisely what Durkheim (1893:64) prescribes for dealing with an abstract concept in research: "we must substitute for this internal fact which escapes us, an external index which symbolizes it and study the former in the light of the latter." This is our only recourse if we are to pursue such goals as understanding the notion of marginality.

And so it is—to take a last ex-ample—with the idea of social distance. Social structures vary in their tightness or integration, in the frequency with which people deal with one another, the closeness or distance they feel between one another. But social distance, or solidarity, or group identification are very abstract notions. Nonetheless, we can substitute for such imputed internal states, an external fact, the fact of physical distance. Physical distance both reflects and affects social patterns.

Students can explore the nature of social (and physical) distance by studying such different groups as juries (Strodtbeck and Hook, 1961) and restaurant employees (Whyte, 1949). In urban studies, students might investigate social distance and differentiation within and between housing projects, neighborhoods, and cities (see, for example, Hawley, 1971; Gist and Fava, 1974; Michelson, 1976; Moos, 1976; Proshansky, Ittelson, and Rivlin, 1970). In both small and large groups, space or social distance is at work, affecting and affected by patterns of communication and social differentiation.

The concept of social structure and such dimensions as space or distance are quite abstract, so much so that we must wonder how the idea can touch a student's choices or interests. Yet we know that effective teaching requires us to link current with past experience, course problems with students' worlds. How, indeed, does physical space affect their lives, their friends, and their families?

Perhaps the instructor will ask students how well they know people sitting next to them, in contrast to those sitting farther away; how friendly their families are with neighbors next door, across the street, or across the hall, in contrast with those more distant; how well they know other students in various locations in a dormitory. Data could be tabulated and analyzed, and the findings could then be compared with those of larger empirical studies and with the predictions of theory.[12] (On propinquity in college classrooms, see Byrne, 1960.) Depending on time available, the instructor might have students create hypotheses to be tested in familiar situations.

Policy implications can be drawn from readings or from in-class exercises. Dormitories, apartment houses, housing developments—these are designed, and their designs have implications for social interaction. If students were designing a dorm, what physical layout would they choose? And why? What patterns of interaction (and, implicitly, what values) would they be seeking to maximize? Why do architects design as they do? What accounts for the design of their classrooms? their dorms? Are older dormitories differently designed than those more recently built? With what likely consequences? By considering such questions as these, students can relate the general sociological issue—space as it affects one aspect of social structure—to their own experiences through a process that actively engages them.

☙

Throughout this chapter, we have been thinking about goals of sociology instruction, goals peculiar to the field. These goals necessarily derive from the distinctive nature of sociology. What is distinctive about sociology is not its methods, nor its purpose (extending knowledge), nor its efforts to develop abstract explanations that we call theory, nor its notion of applying knowledge to practical problems. The field is distinct because of its focus of inquiry—social structure (i.e., nonrandom patterns of social relationships). At the same time that this focus of inquiry separates sociology from other scholarly enterprises, it transcends all of sociology's subfields. The arrangement of social parts—and changes in that arrangement—are at issue no matter which of the forty-plus subfields of sociology we are working in.

Now, this being the substance of sociology, field-related goals can be specified; they will be aspects or dimensions of social structure. And so we have invoked, as examples, size or numbers, social boundaries, the permeability of group boundaries, marginality, social and physical distance–closeness. And throughout the discussion, we have stressed four outcomes of goal setting. First, goals clarify teaching and learning aims for instructor and student. Second, when goals are expressed precisely and publicly as operational statements, they can be discussed, their validity assessed, and the aims revised. (When goals are left as vague aspirations, this process is impossible.) Third, when properly expressed, goals permit us to measure extent of student achievement and, also, degree of instructor success. Fourth and finally, such goal statements provide leads to the behaviors the instructor must exemplify if students are to know how to approach each goal.

The goals we have used as illustrations bear on the special substance of sociology; they are substantive goals. We have others that we share with most if not all other fields. These we will call, for lack of a better term, nonsubstantive goals. As examples, we have chosen three: cultivating a habit of inquiry, extending knowledge and insights to different populations and situations, and developing skill in the methods of inquiry. The first of these three nonsubstantive goals is the subject of chapter 5.

Notes

1. The ASA *Directory* of members (1976) lists thirty-six areas of competence; the ASA *Guide to Graduate Departments of Sociology* (1976) lists forty-seven subfields.

2. An extensive discussion of these features is found in Wilson (1975).

3. This paragraph was derived from Wilson (1975); see also Wilson (1971a:20–22).

4. Marx made the point well: "Men make their own history, but they do not make it just as they please; they do not make it under circumstances chosen by themselves, but under circumstances directly encountered, given and transmitted from the past. The tradition of all the past generations weighs like a mountain on the brain of the living" (Marx, 1852:247). Other fine statements of this central sociological position are found in Berger (1963:176) and Mills (1959:5–8, preface).

5. In constructing this chart we have made use of the books listed below. They discuss the elements of structure we employ (though not always using the terms we use) and review much empirical evidence bearing on these elements. On college classes, see Schmuck and Schmuck (1975), Mann (1970); on industrial organizations, see Haas and Drabek (1973); on cities, see Hawley (1971), Gist and Fava (1974), and Schwirian (1974).

6. The data presented in table 4.2, from Elgin et al. (1974), were gathered during a 1971 survey conducted by the Commission on Population Growth and the American Future. These findings are supported by a number of independent studies also cited in Elgin. The question answered by respondents in the commission survey was: "Where would you *prefer* to live?" The question was apparently an open-ended one. Coding was as follows: "Rural or small town" included farm, open country, or small town responses. "Small urban" represented small city or medium-size city and suburb responses. "Large urban" included responses identifying a large city or its suburbs.

7. Two major articles by sociologists on optimum city size are Duncan (1957) and Ogburn and Duncan (1963). See also Elgin et al. (1974).

8. This conclusion is supported by the analyses in references cited in the preceding note and in Hawley (1971:138).

9. In the first draft of this chapter, we used "an army post for basic training" as an example of a total institution having both voluntary and involuntary participants. But this example was incorrect after 1971, when military conscription ended—and before 1946, when the United States first initiated universal military service. Teachers of sociology must continually work to keep their examples accurate and, whenever possible, relevant to student experience or awareness. During the 1950s and (especially) the 1960s, college students (not just males) were very much aware of the draft. A good example—one that is accurate, meaningful, and memorable—is to be valued.

10. Simpson and Yinger (1972:185–191) discuss marginality of black Americans and Native Americans. Articles in Pavalko (1972:chapter 2) treat "professional marginality: problems of status and identity," dealing with chiropractors, pharmacists, and clergywomen.

11. The link between marginality and status inconsistency is discussed in Simpson and Yinger (1972:186–187). A useful overview of status consistency and crystallization is found in Matras (1975:128ff). Debates among sociologists on the utility of marginality can be found in Simpson and Yinger (1972:185–191) and Rose (1974:164–172). The term *marginality* was first used by Park (1928), although earlier discussions of the same phenomenon are found in the work of DuBois (1897:164) and in Simmel's (1950:402–408) discussion of "The Stranger," referred to by Park (1928:888).

12. In addition to sources cited above, see Sommer (1969).

CHAPTER 5
GOALS TRANSCENDING SOCIOLOGICAL CONTENT: CRITICAL THINKING

Deliberation has its beginning in troubled activity and its conclusion in choice of a course of action which straightens it out.

John Dewey (1922:199)

In undergraduate education, many of the sociologists' instructional goals will not be peculiar to sociology; they will be ends shared with other disciplines. Two such common ends of education are these: learning names for the world's objects and developing problem-solving skills. Insofar as students achieve such ends, they can assimilate novel events to a preexisting framework of thought or alter that framework so as to understand what was previously obscure.

The former goal is descriptive. We build taxonomies and fit empirical reality to our mental map. It is critical thinking insofar as the cognitive crisis precipitated by an anomalous event requires one to locate that event in his intellectual scheme and, having done so, to excite the satisfied response, "Aha, that's where it fits." One might ask, for example, why in the antebellum South there was such harmony between two classes with opposing interests, the rich planters and the poor yeomen or subsistence farmers. The planters deforested and sowed the better land, multiplied their gains with slave labor, bought and sold in England and in the North rather than stimulating mutually profitable exchange with local farmers and artisans (see Cash, 1969:40). With the notion of Simmel's triad in our conceptual lexicon we can assign this perplexing event to the class of propositions asserting that the relationship between two actors is a function of their relationship to a third. Thus the religious say that the brotherhood of man derives from the fatherhood of God. In our case, the harmony and mutual respect of rich and poor was a function of the infinite superiority both enjoyed over a third party, the black slave. Similarly, if the concept of latent function is part of our conceptual apparatus, we may see excessive maternal solicitude as hostility or classify a trial as the ritual occasion for reaffirming the tribal credo.

Beyond useful description (taxonomies) there is another aspect of critical thinking that teachers hope to nurture. This is enhanced skill in solving problems, in explaining the connections between things. Take this example. The set of immediately germane traits describing the student entering a course in Race, Politics, and Poverty consists in a set of knowings. Among these are knowings as to the reasons for, the results of, and the appropriate responses to poverty. Should that student encounter challenges to these convictions and consider them thoughtfully, he may emerge from the course experience with a changed intellectual framework for explaining poverty. Table 5.1 presents one possible summary of these initial knowings, challenges (discrepant data), and revised knowings.

Table 5.1 Changes Induced in the Student's Intellectual Framework for Explaining Poverty

Student's Initial Knowings	Instructor's Challenges	Student's Revised Knowings
People are created unequal in mind and body.	People are pretty much equal (see Hobbes's *Leviathan,* 1651). Few are so unable by nature that they cannot, with the appropriate tools or weapons, match or overcome another.	Genetic differences aren't the differences that make the difference. For example, the legacy of family, class, and race are crucial (nongenetic) sources of poverty or well-being.
People are motivated to work and achieve by threat of pain and promise of pleasure.	We discover that the deprived handle poverty by a familial security system that enables them to be irregular in work habits (see Davis, 1946).	Threat is an inadequate incentive when the structure of opportunity forecloses any possibility of achieving values celebrated in a given group.
Everything, as Professor Pangloss reassured himself, works out for the best in the best of all possible worlds. Or, each person, as Adam Smith put it, pursuing his own ends, promotes, as though guided by an invisible hand, the general welfare.	There are many instances of the social cost of avarice. Pursuit of personal desires (such as wealth through thievery) may produce certain social goods (such as employment for police, courts, lock manufacturers, and insurance companies). But there are also social costs.	There is an inordinate social loss in the failure to redistribute wealth (through taxation) to provide the opportunities that would maximize each person's potential. Things do not work out for the best, especially when individual advantage is the only criterion for determining a course of action.
When male breadwinners become unemployed, low morale, loss of self-esteem, and family strain result.	This is not always the case. In Greece, no; in Trinidad, yes; in Guatemala, true for low-income Ladinos, but not true for low-income Indians. In the United States and many other countries, there is wide variation in the degree to which this is true. There is also variation over time in many countries (see Rodman, 1971: 177–79, 187–88).	Extent of strain induced by unemployment will vary depending on the way manhood is defined (whether male role is dominant and male is seen as the breadwinner) and whether unemployment is seen as a personal failure or a systemic problem.
Poverty is harmful to those who are poor and to the nation as a whole. That is, poverty is dysfunctional.	The poor help to subsidize the national economy and, by their existence, have aided the upward mobility of the nonpoor and helped create jobs for others. Poverty can be functional (see Gans, 1972).	The existence of poverty and the poor is functional for some people and subgroups, and dysfunctional for others. And for the same person or group poverty can be both functional and dysfunctional in different ways.
Saving money is a way of building a secure future. The poor are typically impulsive, incapable of planning and delaying gratification. Rather than bank part of a paycheck, they will give money away or spend it on others.	In the ghetto, giving money away can help insure a more secure future. By helping friends in their time of need, one builds a reservoir of potential aid for himself (see Herzog, 1967:4; Liebow, 1967).	With few economic resources and frequent crises, traditional saving may not be the best way to provide for the future. What constitutes good planning and concern about the future varies with conditions.
Welfare payments destroy the fabric of society.	Higher levels and wider provision of welfare by those in authority are often used to restore social harmony following outbreaks of riots or to prevent rioting (see Piven and Cloward, 1971).	The effects of welfare payments on the social fabric are complex, and the function of welfare depends on its level and societal condition.

Thus the challenge presented by the anomalous finding or discrepant datum sets the stage for altering one's intellectual map of social reality. Insofar as instructors arrange these challenges as conditions for stimulating analytical thought, they are *benign disrupters*.

This touches a second matter: the means by which these goals are achieved. For the first goal, that of identifying and labelling the objects of our worlds, we typically invoke the authority of the elders to transmit traditional lore. The second goal, that of developing skill in problem solving, requires a quite different strategy. To this end, the instructor becomes a troublemaker. But troublemaking is a delicate business both in its potential for discouraging inquiry and in its possible effect on a teacher-student relationship that requires mutual trust. These matters warrant attention.

Finally, we will offer some examples of ways of stimulating critical thought—both in the service of assimilating the novel to the familiar and in thinking through to a new way of apprehending reality.

Developing Critical Thinking by Confronting Problems: The Rarer Pattern

Now to return to the beginning. We can think of college or university education as having, for its principal aims, the transmission of the past and the improvement of the future. Both are more than legitimate aims: each is essential. And they are linked; the latter is impossible without the former. But our impression is that, although the ratio of the one to the other should diminish through time (i.e., acquiring facts should be increasingly subordinate to problem solving and inven-

tion), this is often not the case. Genuine inquiry—poking about in the realm where answers are not provided in tradition—seems to be rare even at the college level where, if anywhere, it should be prominent.[1] Often higher education becomes a matter of the instructor delivering the higher truth, under a series of topical headings, to students whose mastery is indexed by their short-term memory (i.e., remembering to the end of quarter or semester). Becker, Geer, and Hughes (1968) document the point in *Making the Grade*.

Doubtless teaching and learning patterns are infinitely variable. And the simple dichotomy we suggest—doing something *to* the student (delivering facts) and doing something *with* the student (tackling questions whose answers must be negotiated through reason and empirical inquiry)—overlooks an intermediate pattern common in biophysical laboratory work: arranging *for* the student (providing a set of questions whose answers are known and are recaptured as the student follows stipulated laboratory procedures). These points along a scale from authoritative indoctrination to collaborative inquiry are oversimplified. Still, some such scheme as that provided in table 5.2, exaggerated though the extremes may be, can help in the analysis.

We do find occasional examples of instruction that stress doing things with the student (Type 3 in table 5.2). One such is offered by Toby (1972) who tries to "*develop* [with his students] the research problem consensually as well as to *explore* it through a consensual process." Other accounts of sociologists employing collaborative inquiry as the design for instruction can be found in Hiller (1975), Silvers (1973), Sokol (1968), and Wilson (1970). Such problem-oriented schemes of instruction clearly increase the chances of

Table 5.2 Three Designs for Instruction: The Teacher's Role Stresses Doing Things To, For, or With the Student

	(Type 1) To the Student	(Type 2) For the Student	(Type 3) With the Student
Instructor	Reports and inculcates the truth about reality.	Arranges a set of problems whose answers are known.	Presents new problems or methods, or new materials with which to check and revise old answers.
Student	Memorizes and recapitulates.	Follows stipulated procedures to arrive at known answers.	Gathers and confronts the data needed to test the tentative answers given in theory and stated as a target for testing in hypotheses.
Methods	Involve traditional exposition of parental and elementary education, and of adult apprentice training. Especially appropriate for skill training where time and instructors are abundant.	Involve lab work and programmed instruction. More efficient than the Type 1 Design. Goals and methods are operationally defined. Imaginative solutions tend to be limited. Applicable when answers are known. In operation, this design places ceiling on learning. Requires artful construction of autodidactic materials.	Involve methods such as those used in chapters 4, 5, and 6.
Result	Authoritative indoctrination		Collaborative inquiry

sharpening students' skill in analytical thinking. One might assume that this formal goal would be favored by any teaching sociologist. If this is the case, one wonders why the first pattern (Type 1) persists—indeed, often seems to prevail—at the college and university level. Is it because the minimal skills needed for a reasonable adaptation to American society cannot be mastered at the secondary level? Or are there, as we suspect, more fundamental reasons for our reluctance to go beyond traditional transmission?

Resistance to Teaching Skills of Critical Thinking

Why is the transmission of the known past easier than the exploration of un-solved present problems? Why the drift toward conventional didactic patterns in which the instructor reveals what is true and the student memorizes and recapitulates it? One obvious, if superficial, reason is that many students have had at least twelve years of training in a passive, truth-receiving role. But this is to beg the question. The fact that this has been the case drives us to ask: why so?

Perhaps a basic reason for preferring the straight transmission of traditional lore is the anxiety and loss of control entailed in indeterminate situations—including, of course, the teaching-learning situations of interest to us. Blumstein (1973:17) asserts that it is *un*familiarity that breeds contempt. He finds that we make "negative moral judgments [of events] perceived as unlikely, no matter what the reason for the unlikeliness." If this is so, then unfamiliar instructional patterns at the university level will be resisted. But again, why?

High probability events, those regularly recurring, have implications underlying the positive moral evaluation attached to them. If what is, is right, it may well be because unfamiliar sequences are seriously disconcerting. (We know what happened to Pavlov's animals when the stimulus-response sequence was unpredictably altered.) We can infer, then, some association between the recurrent and a sense of control: when there is a high probability of covariance (and only then), we have some control over our fates. Perhaps we have a deep-rooted feeling of impotence in the face of unanticipated consequences. Hence we evaluate the likely with approval and shy away from the unknown.

Also discouraging exploration (and favoring pipeline transmission of the traditional) is the deeply rooted requirement of the common that is implied in communication. Language itself stresses transmission of the traditional. It constrains us to see the world as others see and have seen it. Under the tutelage of the elders we come to attach commonly shared descriptive labels to things. Further, there are few if any desired ends that one can gain without collaborating with others. And collaboration entails communication. Finally, both the tutelage of the elders and intercourse with our peers require us to share that which we hold in common and to suppress that which is unique (by definition, uncommunicable) or problematic in each person's experience.

Tradition and language are more narrowly defined by class. Sociologists scarcely need be reminded of the narrow provincialism of class. A significant result is that middle-class background and aspirations lead many students to stress what

is relevant for achieving some middle-class occupation in teaching, law, medicine, business, and the like—which suggests that routine training in relevant skills for middle-class occupations supersedes exploration of the unknown. This is especially so at private colleges and universities where self-selection and admissions policies reduce variance in student traits. Public universities and distribution requirements commonly make for more heterogeneous classes, although this is obviously a matter of degree.

Even so, it is worth noting that through the course prerequisites we impose, we seek to achieve a certain homogeneity in background (preparation) that is more consistent with a recapitulation of traditional skills than it is with the generation of new ideas. Newcomers are selected, so we hope, with those attributes that, when catalyzed by proper classroom influences, will produce the traits their predecessors bore. And this implies a training routine not unlike what an immigrant goes through to learn the language of the host country: it is not exploratory learning, but rather an essentially adaptive technique.

There is also adaptive efficiency in learning the customary. The authoritative indoctrination of certain behaviors reduces to the triviality of routine what would otherwise be paralyzingly problematic. Survival demands certain minimal skills. Having mastered these, we are released to choose among and engage in a wider range of activities. We are indeed constrained to learn reading and writing. But having done so, a wide range of new options opens up, including the use of symbols to challenge those who taught their use.

The adaptive efficiency of the customary is unwittingly acknowledged when we institutionalize certain processes, such as formal education, to induct newcomers into the secrets of society. Our social institutions have the effect of sustaining the familiar and predictable. The traditional is typically viewed as necessary and good. Any operational definition of the good lies in the past: the Magna Charta, the Declaration of Independence, the Gettysburg address, the Horatio Alger myth. These traditions tell us what is good and true and beautiful. It is significant that our past is that of a westward-moving frontier, of fishing and farming and forestry with a small, privileged minority entering the law, the church, and the military. Life under adverse conditions doubtless made for the authoritarian transmission of survival skills. And these, embedded in our past, we continue to celebrate.

In sum, we argue that the Type 1 instruction pattern in table 5.2 is the conventional mode of instruction for several reasons. Education leans toward the transmission of traditional truth because the familiar is the good and the good is embedded in tradition. The tendency to avoid the unknown may be anchored in neurological disruption. At any rate, the problematic seems to induce anxiety; and unfamiliar or erratic sequences strip us of our sense of control over events. Language itself moves human interchange toward the routinized familiar. Influences of social class, and of college and course admissions, make for like backgrounds, like aspirations, and routinized training to lead from the one to the other. Such a pattern of education would be an efficient means in meeting problems of survival in an unchanging social order, were there any such. When formalized, these routine procedures are social institutions through which the good and the means of its achievement are defined. Past-preserving as they are, they promote training in skills needed by the person to meet the condi-

tions of social existence. For such reasons as these, we find resistance to patterns of instruction that stress critical thinking.

The Limits of Routinized Training

We have used words with bad overtones to describe a familiar pattern of instruction: authoritative, routinized, memorizing, training. But we do not fling such terms about as pejoratives. There is a need for authoritative instruction, especially through those long years of dependency when a child's welfare demands imperative intervention. Facing a threatening environment (for example, his vast vulnerability if he cannot speak the language), the child exists in a situation of crisis. And crises invariably entail authoritative rule. Such indoctrination is obviously needed in every field.

But if there is a need for authoritative instruction, there is also, perhaps increasingly, a need for critical thinking. This is because tradition becomes more maladaptive as the rate of change, physical and social, increases. Beyond the fact that ignorance of history condemns us to repeat it, there is the continual playback of novel circumstances in each moment of the present. To work out solutions to pressing problems requires a reflective analysis of historical parallels and critical thinking about the *un*paralleled present.

If this is so, then the early and necessary transmission of skills must give way to instruction stressing analysis of unsolved problems. The two modes are reciprocally related: the higher the value of the former, the less the emphasis on the latter. A liberal arts education is one that capitalizes on custom and habit to liberate us from inadequate, customary solutions. Habits, inculcated early on, have dual effects. They make for efficiency. But, as

Dewey pointed out (1922:172–3), they can serve as "blinders that confine the eyes of the mind . . . [but fortunately] success in achieving a ruthless and dull efficiency of action is thwarted by untoward circumstance. *The most skillful aptitude bumps at times into the unexpected, and so gets into trouble from which only observation and invention extricate it*" (emphasis added).

Benign Disruption and Learning

We accept Dewey's general position on habits, and from it we infer that a chief task of the professor, perhaps especially in the field of sociology, is to get students into trouble, arranging those circumstances through which they bump into the unexpected. We see the instructor as a benign disrupter. This implies that our courses should consist of a set of problems, some without known answers. One might describe a course as a search for solutions, however tentative, over a period of a semester. This is the collaborative inquiry suggested in the Type 3 instruction pattern in table 5.2. Our impression is that courses ordinarily do not present a model of inquiry; they approximate the Type 1 instruction pattern, the expository mode. Syllabi present a list of topics, together with appropriate readings. The task of the student, in a quite quiescent role, is to ingest the truth transmitted by books and instructor.

While there are occasions when instructors can offer information not elsewhere available to the student, we suggest that more of their role might be cast in the interrogative form, less in the declaratory form. The classroom experience should not be a simple extension of the familiar, but an encounter with the new and different. Thus Newcomb (1961:3) cites Kurt Lewin: "If you want to improve your understand-ing of something you will observe it as it changes [i.e., as differences emerge] and preferably as it changes under conditions that you yourself have created."

Differences can be seen as a condition of perception.[2] White and black depend on each other for perception and definition. Masculinity depends on the benchmark of femininity for recognition and definition. To see a status as elevated, we must observe or have in mind a status with lesser clout. Elements of an undifferentiated mass are not perceived.

The perception of differences is a condition for cognition. Knowing requires both the *description* of a perceived difference and an *explanation* of why it is that way rather than some other way. Examples of the first requirement for knowing are the systematic classification of biological differences by Linnaeus (phylum, family, genus, species), the Periodic Table, and population pyramids. Such classificatory schemes display differences in some comprehensible way. On the other hand, we have to explain differences if we are to predict or induce desired outcomes. Thus if we want to produce a different (lower) level of fertility, we have to know how differing social arrangements are related to high and low levels of reproduction.

Without differences there are no problems.[3] Without problems there can be no answers. Without answers there is no learning. Differences—their discovery and explanation—are fundamental for critical thinking. *A prime trait of good teachers is their ability to help students confront ideas and data that differ from those of their familiar (and necessarily restricted) world.* They elicit incompatible views, present discrepant data. And they always raise the questions, Which is the more accurate? and, How would you find out?

Now, questions are impediments, and the better the question, the less likely that one's previous intellectual position can remain unaltered. (A prior position may, of course, be dramatically reinforced with a new perception of the range and depth of its implication.) This puts teachers in the position of arranging roadblocks, problems that must be solved somehow, if one is to go on his way. It is only when the smooth, ongoing tenor of our lives is interrupted that thought and emotion emerge. Along with thought and emotion, values emerge. "Value arises," Simmel points out (1971:57), "in the interval which obstacles, renunciations and sacrifices interpose between desire and its satisfaction." We can use the logic of the controlled experiment to check this assertion. What would happen under other circumstances—in the absence of the alleged causal influence? Dewey's answer is plausible. Were it not for such impediments, were every need fulfilled automatically, every question answered before it was posed, we would be reduced intellectually to the condition of vegetables. Without some tension, even some anxiety, our psychic muscles would atrophy.

A new observation exerts pressure to make sense of things by assimilating it to some classificatory scheme. This may mean, as Adam Ferguson (1819) once put it, finding "general rules applicable to a variety of cases that seemed to have nothing in common [or discovering] important distinctions between subjects which the vulgar are apt to confound." Thus the issue of fluoridation raises this question: is water so treated to be classified as dangerous or as a preserver of tooth enamel? Or regarding the birth control pill: shall we classify it with other inventions that improve the quality of life by investing more in fewer, or shall we classify it with other means of evading responsibility and making Godlike decisions with little sense of moral consequences? Problems exert

pressure to seek solutions—that is, to learn.

A common effect of novel or discrepant data is a refinement of our classificatory schemes. Simple-minded dichotomies give way to more complex schemes and nominal scales are superseded by ordinal or interval scales. Thus the statement, "Black families are matricentric," divides all black families into two types, those that are and are not matricentric. This yin-yang dichotomizing of the world is a common, crude first approximation to reality. For the naive, it remains the final sort of classificatory scheme.

But data indicate that some white families are matricentric and some black families are patricentric or equalitarian. And these categories may, in turn, be crosscut by the condition, on welfare or not on welfare. And these categories may, in turn, be crosscut by urban and rural residence, or by type and degree of religious commitments, and the like. An important effect of disruptive data, then, is to help us move toward a more accurate picture of the complex social reality.

Social reality cannot be understood by students whose ability at causal analysis is limited to such queries as this: is Y related to X? Novel or anomalous data can prompt us to go further to specify the conditions under which a relationship between Y and X holds. The introduction of new variables—multivariate analysis—is thus an important tool of the benign disrupter.

Let us return to the example of race and family type. To keep the central point clear, we use fictional data in the form of dichotomized variables. Assume a class was presented with table 5.3, which shows that black families are disproportionately matricentric.

How can we account for this finding? Why are black families disproportion-

Table 5.3 Family Type, by Race (fictional data)

| Race | Family Type | | |
	Patri-centric	Matri-centric	Totals
White	70%	30%	100% (500)
Black	50%	50%	100% (500)

ately matricentric?[4] A cultural explanation would hold that as a result of slavery and subsequent socialization patterns, the black family structure had become matriarchal; historically, black males played a secondary and marginal role.[5] Another explanation would hinge on income: the strains of a marginal family economy have given the black mother more power and thus have produced a matricentric family.[6] And the data (still fictional) support this economic explanation in table 5.4.

Table 5.4 Family Type, by Income (fictional data)

| Income | Family Type | | |
	Patri-centric	Matri-centric	Totals
High	80%	20%	100% (600)
Low	30%	70%	100% (400)

But the percentage differences in table 5.4 are greater than those in table 5.3 (50 versus 20 percentage points). Does this close the case? Is the issue income and not race? No, not if blacks are disproportionately of low income as table 5.5 shows them to be.

Thus our class has found that race is related to family type, income is related to family type, and race is related to income. The problem remains: is it race (cultural factors associated with race) or income (through stress on family roles) that makes

Table 5.5 Family Income, by Race (fictional data)

| Race | Family Income | | |
	High	Low	Totals
White	80%	20%	100% (500)
Black	40%	60%	100% (500)

for disproportionately high matricentricity among blacks? How is the issue to be resolved?

Note here that the instructor has at least two aims: to help students learn something of the *substance* of sociology (characteristics of black and white families) and to present the uses of multivariate analysis as an aid in *analytical* (*critical*) *thinking*. Such a teacher might proceed with this question: if we suppose the racial-cultural explanation is the correct one, then how would family type vary among black (and white) families at different income levels? Students will answer that if income didn't make the difference, there would be no difference. The teacher might then ask how the data would fall if the factor most associated with family type was income? Table 5.6 shows how the data might distribute themselves.

Table 5.6 Family Income, by Race and Family Type (fictional data)

| Race | High Family Income | | | Low Family Income | | |
	Pa-tri-cen-tric	Ma-tri-cen-tric		Pa-tri-cen-tric	Ma-tri-cen-tric	
White	80%	20%	(400)	30%	70%	(100)
Black	80%	20%	(200)	30%	70%	(300)

Throughout the preceding example, our class refined a too-simple classificatory scheme and discovered a tool—multivariate analysis—that allows us to tackle causality at a more sophisticated level. To be sure, our example was a simple one: we worked with only three variables and did not even discuss partial effects. But such discussions could be next steps—the logic remains the same. The important point here is that *competing explanations have led to critical thinking* supported by refined tools of analysis.[7]

The benign disrupter is concerned that students develop critical thinking skills, what we have called a nonsubstantive goal of learning sociology. Hence such a teacher would not have answered the initial question, How can we explain the link between family type and race? by immediately trotting out a multivariate table such as table 5.6.

Effective instructors find in daily experience the useful disruptions of novel and unanticipated sequences. We are sure that poverty and ignorance lead to crime. But then we are confronted with anomalous data (the I.T.&T., Mr. Vesco, the laundering of campaign checks, criminal activities of White House personnel) that suggest that education, wealth, and political power may lead to crime of enormous dimensions. Or, we are sure that the most economically depressed blacks must be the most militant in seeking equity and despising "whitey." But then we see that Gary Marx's data (1969) indicate otherwise: that it is, rather, the well-educated and reasonably well-to-do blacks who are the most militant and who, nonetheless, are more tolerant of whites. Novel data challenge the customary conviction about causal sequences.

The economy of customary convictions about appropriate classes of reality and sequences of events is that they can be taken for granted. But what is taken for granted is precisely that which is not understood. To seek understanding, we have

to interrupt familiar sequences. Adam Smith noted in 1795 that curiosity is incited when "customary connection be interrupted" (1967:31–2); more recently, in Festinger's (1957) theory of cognitive dissonance, we find positions that support and add new dimensions to this notion. Dissonance (or discrepant data) creates a drive to reduce or resolve apparently incompatible knowings. Often such a resolution is achieved by retreating from the problem. Thus Lazarsfeld, Berelson, and Gaudet (1948) found that people simply deferred a voting decision when caught between the cross pressures of family and friends who favored opposing presidential candidates. And experienced teachers know how some students, when confronted with disturbing views or data, stop hearing.

Yet teachers have on their side two important features that enable them to create the conditions of reflective thought. First, more than anyone else, a teacher can orchestrate the events of a course so that *students must confront anomalous events.* (Better, incidentally, that it should be the event or datum, not the teacher, who is directly presenting the challenge.) Second, to return to our general theme, we think it accurate to postulate a basic need to achieve a fairly high level of predictability in dealing with one's world. It is on this feature of human nature, the drive to resolve or reconcile discrepant data, that the teacher can build in creating situations that challenge old certainties, customary sequences.

Benign Disruption and the Teacher-Student Relationship

But we must be warned. If, as one would suppose, all problems are in some degree anxiety-inducing, there is the matter of estimating the range of anxiety (from the cerebral itch to horror, paralysis, and flight) and determining where in that range the anxiety load is best suited to effective instruction. The problem for the benign disrupter is sustaining the drive and tension needed to resolve intellectually and morally significant problems while providing the support and demonstrating the confidence that obviate paralysis and withdrawal.

Uncertainty and assurance are the dilemma at the operating edge. But this dilemma is the tip of the iceberg. Its larger meaning lies in apparently contradictory elements of the instructor's role. If it is to be articulated with others, it must entail predictable performances. But we ask the benign intruder to make trouble, to create unpredictable happenings.[8]

As with every human relationship, that between student and teacher depends on shared expectations. This means that within a given range of tolerance, the action of one party triggers an anticipated reaction on the part of the other. Were it not so, were reactions from coitus to combat to be drawn from a table of random numbers, we would be reduced to utter incoherence. Both personal and social existence—in this case, the existence of the classroom group—would be literally intolerable. This no new insight. Max Weber (1947:118, 125) emphasized that human relationships depend for their very existence on predictable connections between ends and means.

But there is a paradox here. On the one hand, we acknowledge that an adequate student-teacher relationship rests on the confidence that the act is followed by a predictable re-act: teacher tells the truth, student repeats it, or some such familiar sequence. But, on the other hand, we advocate the teacher's posing problems to which the answers are, or appear to be,

unknown. Thus a predictable reaction is lost. Or we propose that the teacher present incompatible or contradictory propositions that disrupt the act-predictable-react sequence. Are these not quite inconsistent positions? Does not the use of this technique for educational purposes threaten the trusting relationship that is essential if learning is to occur?

Clearly the student-teacher relationship must be one of mutual trust. If learning is to be properly motivated and enduring, the teacher must not be seen as a grand inquisitor, or as a tricky adversary to be bested. Students must be persuaded that the teacher is an ally in learning whose aim is to sharpen skills, extend knowledge, and nourish wisdom. With such a conviction, students will be willing to assume that the challenges introduced by their instructors are in the service of their learning.

The connection between the teacher-student relationship and dissonant cognitions is complex. It seems likely that there *is* a relationship, that cognition, and sentiment, are some function of an instructor's relationship to student. We might suggest that difference of fact or opinion will be more troubling the more favorably the student (S) feels toward the teacher (T). Or, to tease out a further implication, the drive toward resolution will be greater the more friendly the relationship between T and S.

This implies, probably incorrectly, a linear relationship, as illustrated in figure 5.1(a). Actually, it might be expected that as the relationship approaches either antipathy or adulation (− and +, respectively, on the X axis), critical analysis would be the victim. If this is so, there is no drive for learning or problem solving at either the lower *or* higher values on the X axis. A likelier conclusion then would be that the relationship between variables

(a)

(b)

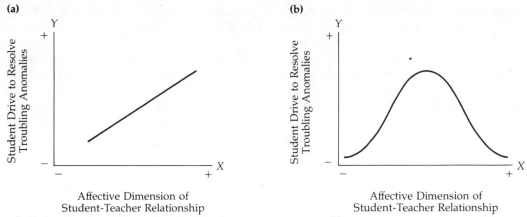

Figure 5.1(a) and (b) Classroom Affectivity and Student's Drive to Engage in Analytical Thinking.

would be curvilinear, as illustrated in figure 5.1(b).

The same might be said for the cognitive realm. If the teacher is omniscient (or ignorant), there can be no development of problem-solving skills. At high X values, recording and memorizing become the appropriate student activities. One must wonder, then, if providing written materials—lectures, texts, programmed materials—is not the appropriate teacher's activity and if classroom activities could not be eliminated. But at a point intermediate between ignorance and omniscience we have the teacher who is competent but recognizes critical problems. In raising questions and presenting discrepant data, students are brought to see realms of extension and application about which we have not yet generalized, and circumstances in which findings might refute or revise existing generalizations. Figure 5.2 represents this teaching-learning situation.

One obvious problem in playing the role of benign disrupter is that more time (money) is required to orchestrate a set of experiences that challenge stereotypes and presuppositions, and so generate critical

thought. Support for research on teaching is harder to come by than funds for other social science research.

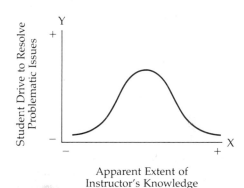

Figure 5.2 Suggested Relationship Between Instructor's Use of Knowledge and Student's Drive to Engage in Analytical Thinking.

The Benign Disrupter at Work

Common Sense versus the Data

We return to this matter of common sense versus the data in chapter 8. There we will see, in Paul Lazarsfeld's propositions (1949) about the adjustment of GIs in World War II, findings that are directly contrary to what is readily established as the commonsense position. As in the Lazarsfeld essay, a common ploy is to establish the plausibility of the commonsense view and then confront that view with the contradicting evidence. For example, a commonsense view of retired people holds that giving up the work role must have disruptive effects on health, economic security, and psychological well-being. Not so: see Streib and Schneider (1971). Or, as another reasonable, commonsense proposition suggests, the more people go to church, the more they absorb religious doctrine, the more they will be tolerant of blacks and other minority groups. Not so: see Marx (1969).

Policy Statements Deduced from Premises at Odds with Research Findings

A related way of exploiting discrepant data is to ask: what are the policy implications of such statements as these?

1. The intellectual sophistication of the graduating senior is chiefly due to the direct influence of highly trained faculty members.

2. By dropping out of high school, students suffer both financially and emotionally.

3. The significance of race in our troubled society stems from the biological traits that enable people to discriminate between blacks and whites.

4. The surest way of protecting the public, rehabilitating criminals, and deterring others from crime is to sentence offenders to serve stiff terms in our prisons.

Accepting these more or less commonsensical statements, we would: (1) fix on faculty members as agents of universal education, investing much in them and holding them responsible for outcomes; (2) do everything possible to prevent high school dropouts; (3) resign ourselves to biologically determined racial differentials; and (4) strengthen our prison system, making such punishment harsher when crime rates go up. But if such decisions are based on premises that sociologists' findings have discredited—*and that is the case*—then the derived policy statements are challenged. And students can be encouraged to derive action prescriptions from the contrary propositions and compare the results.

Individual Aging or Cohort Experience: Competing Explanations

We are in your course on Social Movements and Collective Behavior. You want to help students see that different generations experience different sorts of political, economic, and social events at formative periods of their lives; and that, especially in societies such as ours where for a century social change has been rapid and generational experiences discontinuous, people of different ages may well respond differently to events and issues. (We leave aside for the moment such complexities as the effect of different social strata on people's experiences and perceptions.)

Now you as instructor might simply make such assertions, cite studies, discuss the adequacy of the data and their analyses. That is the conventional mode of instruction. But since this mode does nothing to move us toward the goal of sharpened skills in critical thinking, you elect to attack the instructional problem differently, by a series of questions and a sequence of data.

You put the fictional data shown in

table 5.7 on the board, and you ask the class: "What do we make of these data? What does the table tell us?"

The obvious answer is: "Older people are less favorable to socialism." Very well, you say, but what does that mean? Does it mean that increasing age is associated with conservatism? You pause, then go on: "Do you mean that as people grow older they become more conservative?"

Table 5.7 Percentage of Population Favoring Socialism, by Age, 1970 (fictional data)

Age in 1970	Percentage Favorable to Socialism
18–24	55%
25–34	35
35–44	30
45–54	25
55–64	19
65–74	3
75+	1

Clearly the available data in table 5.7 do not support the last two assertions. For, as someone may point out, the older people represented in this table may have been equally conservative when they were young—*may* have been—though we can't know from the data. Is there another, equally plausible explanation of the data?

Perhaps you get the correct answer. But if not, you add another column to the table so it looks like table 5.8. The additional column will give some students the clue to another possible explanation. It does not change the original information, but provides another, historical dimension, pointing to a different interpretation.

You make the point about generational or cohort differences—*if* no student makes it. Chances are they themselves will discover that the attitudes that people hold toward socialism (and other objects) may

Table 5.8 Percentage of Population Favoring Socialism, by Period in which Respondents Were Age 15, and by Age in 1970

Period in which Respondents Were Age 15	Age in 1970	Percentage Favorable to Socialism
1967–1961	18–24	55%
1960–1951	25–34	35
1950–1941	35–44	30
1940–1931	45–54	25
1930–1921	55–64	19
1920–1911	65–74	3
1910 and earlier	75+	1

well be products of their experiences shared with others of like age at formative points in their growth. Of course these data do not demonstrate the generational explanation, just as they do not prove the earlier aging-conservatism explanation. This must be made clear. Hence the logical next question will be: what sort of studies would be necessary to settle the issue?

Is there any evidence that this challenge-response, question-data-analysis-answer technique is more successful in helping students sharpen their analytic skills? It seems likely that *without* such techniques, these skills will not be cultivated. And we do have some supporting evidence as to what happens *with* their use.* Furthermore, our impression based on conversations with students, and on the level of attentiveness and activity in class, persuades us that such devices can move us toward this nonsubstantive goal.

In concluding this example, we note several possible outcomes. One relates to the objectives of a course in social movements: students learn that the generational notion often helps to explain differential participation and involvement in such movements.[9] Another outcome is the useful tapping of students' knowledge of U.S.

* See chapter 12.

history to promote understanding of cohort-linked experiences and so build bridges between two academic experiences. Another, of course, is the analysis entailed in trying to adjudicate the conflicting claims of two explanations. But still another outcome extends beyond this important goal to a concern that students learn to ask questions about the data they confront in newspapers and other ordinary sources. Asking questions of data is a complex skill but one worth cultivating. For our answers are only as good as the quality of analysis we employ in seeking them.

Provincial Views and Public Reality: The Discrepancy Between Sample and Population

Each of us views the social world through the unique lenses of unduplicated personal experience. Benign disruption will, therefore, often take the form of pitting public against private, social realities against the inevitably partial experience peculiar to the individual.

In the following exercise, we will watch a sociology instructor at work, with three ends in view: setting students to memorize essential data, demonstrating the distortions of personal experience, and finally, revealing the general social-psychological principle that asserts that views and values are socially shaped. The course is one in Urban Sociology at the University of North Carolina.

Introduction. "If you are to think effectively about problems of urban life, you will need to know certain facts—how many people, of what sorts, live in communities of what size. Lacking such facts, you may not even know what to make of certain information.

"For example, this week you will read that 111 million Americans live within fifty miles of a coastal shoreline. Is that a large figure? or a small one? Your answer depends on knowing how many Americans there are—200, 300, 500 million? So the total U.S. population is a figure you must memorize. That figure is 211 million (1974). With that information, you now know that just over half of the U.S. population lives within fifty miles of the Atlantic Ocean, the Pacific Ocean, the Great Lakes, or the Gulf of Mexico. [10] Now you are better able to pursue this question: why do so many live in such a narrow band bordering our shorelines?"

Stage 1: Data from students. "In a few minutes I'll give out a list of twenty-five items of social data that you will memorize as a basis for analyzing urban problems. But now I shall ask you to take a piece of blank paper from your notebook and write the answers to four questions. (I shan't collect the papers. Don't write your names on them.) Please tell me the percent of the U.S. population that is: (1) black; (2) Catholic; (3) Jewish; (4) urban (where *urban* is defined as a place with 2,500 or more persons)."

After the students had made their estimates, the instructor asked them to write on the reverse side of their sheets their place of permanent residence—i.e., where their parents lived. Then papers were passed among students, shuffled several times so that none knew the author of the answers in his hand and reading the answers aloud would cause no embarrassment. Tallying the data, the instructor put table 5.9 on the chalkboard.

Stage 2: Exploiting the data. Now the teacher asked: "Where can we turn to get the actual data? Some information we can rely on?" Some students suggested publi-

Table 5.9 Student Estimates of Four U.S. Population Parameters, 1974

Population Category	Student Responses		
		Range	
	Mode	Maximum	Minimum
1. Black	25%	50%	10%
2. Catholic	5	50	1
3. Jewish	10	25	1
4. Urban	60	90	20

cations of the census, and the instructor was able, then, to fill in a fourth column with the correct answers drawn from the *Statistical Abstract of the United States.* Table 5.10 compares student responses with United States census figures.

Table 5.10 Student Estimates of Four U.S. Population Parameters Compared with Census Figures, 1974

Population Category	Student Responses			
		Range		
	Mode	Maximum	Minimum	U.S. Figures[11]
1. Black	25%	50%	10%	11%
2. Catholic	5	50	1	24
3. Jewish	10	25	1	3
4. Urban	60	90	20	74

At this point, the teacher asked why the estimates had been so far off—especially why the number of blacks had been overstated, while the numbers of Catholics and urban dwellers had been understated? (One student wailed, to the teacher's satisfaction, "How could I have been so wrong?") A few students recalled that they had been requested to write their place of residence on the sheet and suggested that residence might have something to do with the pattern of class responses. "How so?" the teacher asked.

One student mentioned that he had read that the percentage of blacks in North Carolina was about double the overall percentage of blacks in the United States; so being from North Carolina might have influenced the responses. "Maybe," said the teacher, pointing out that under state law, 85 percent of all undergraduates at the university had to be from North Carolina. A quick survey of hands tallied the places of residence: more than three-fourths of the class were state residents.

If the place of residence is likely to affect one's perception of social reality, then figures for the state should more closely approximate the modal responses of the class than those from the census. The teacher changed the headings on the chalkboard table and added a final column. Table 5.11 reflects these revisions.

Table 5.11 Student Estimates of Four U.S. Population Parameters Compared with Census Figures and North Carolina Figures, 1974

Population Category	Student Responses				
		Range		U.S. Figures	North Carolina Figures[12]
	Mode	Maximum	Minimum		
1. Black	25%	50%	10%	11%	22%
2. Catholic	5	50	1	24	5
3. Jewish	10	25	1	3	2
4. Urban	60	90	20	74	45

The class agreed that their own experiences had influenced their estimates. A few minutes of discussion generated hypotheses such as: "Students from North Carolina are more likely to overestimate the percentage of blacks in the U.S. population than students from outside the state."

But the state has distinctive regions, and if these represent differing experiences, then estimates of the percentage of blacks in the U.S. population should vary by region. Students agreed that, on the basis of their first findings, this was a plausible inference. So the teacher advanced a new hypothesis: "Students living in the western (Mountain) region of North Carolina are most likely to understate the percentage of blacks in the U.S. population, whereas students from eastern (Tidewater and Coastal Plain) areas of the state are most likely to overestimate." A quick tally of student responses confirmed this hypothesis. The class discussed the probable explanation, which seemed quite plausible when the instructor put the following new data on the chalkboard.[13]

Percent black (1960)

Tidewater	33%
Upper Coastal Plain	36%
Piedmont	20%
Mountain	5%
Total North Carolina	25%

Reflections on this use of discrepant data. In this exercise, students began to get an intuitive sense of the problem of sampling. Often our view of the whole is shaped by our experience with a part. North Carolina is not the United States in microcosm, and the Tidewater counties are not North Carolina in microcosm. One student observed that this conclusion was hardly surprising since the state had such a small population compared to the nation. That observation enabled the teacher to develop two points.

First, it really was surprising for many students who in the first part of the exercise had, in fact, assumed that the familiar was what generally obtained. But their assumption was hardly surprising, since the familiar is the only basis we have for assessing the unknown—until we recognize our provincialisms and try to transcend them by exploiting new data and doing fresh analyses. Second, the instructor noted that the size of a sample is not what determines whether it is representative. He explained how, although North Carolina has 2.5 percent of the population of the United States, it was a much poorer representation of the whole country than a much smaller, properly drawn sample would be.[14]

There are other features of this exercise that warrant underlining. Beyond the problem of sampling, the exercise moved toward two substantive goals: the memorization of social facts (whose importance was demonstrated) and some understanding of the social psychological proposition that attitudes and opinions develop through experience with others. These outcomes were achieved through a teaching pattern in which a serious question was posed (questions before answers) and in which students actively collaborated, drawing on their own experiences.[15] Such a device differs sharply from a teaching scheme that dispenses with a sequence of questions, data, and tentative answers by simply providing students with data and enjoining them not to overgeneralize from unrepresentative, personal experience.[16] Pressures of time seem sometimes to require such a teaching strategy. But such an approach suffers these defects. It does not tell the student why the required learnings are worthwhile, why the student should invest time in their mastery. It offers only vague injunctions, such as "Don't over-generalize," without demonstrating why this practice is dangerous. It does not give students the chance to explore the extent to which their knowings and preferences are shaped by others. It gives students little or no opportunity for active participation and much less chance to raise questions of their own. Finally, it tends to be a unilateral exchange, with little instructive response from students to instructor.

But two objections will come to mind. First, wasn't the preceding exercise an example of manipulation, and didn't the teacher set up the students for a fall? And second, wasn't the exercise overly time-consuming? As for the first issue, we answer: yes, of course it is literally manipulative to create a laboratory session in which students must arrive at a predesignated destination. But this, we think, is acceptable if there are trust and rapport in the student-teacher relationship, if instructors tell their students what they are about, if they take steps to avoid embarrassing their students (as the instructor in this instance took care to shuffle the papers among students so that no students reported their own responses), and if students are encouraged to introduce explanations, interpretations, and criticisms that enrich the analysis.

Whether this is an inefficient, lumbering process depends on whether instructors can achieve the same ends by simply presenting facts and delivering injunctions. We doubt they can. The approach just exemplified is probably the more effective in approaching multiple goals: conveying information, developing analytic skills, and inducing abstract explanations. Again, it is worth emphasizing that there is some evidence that learning is positively related to level of participation. There is also some evidence

that data presented in context, and related to a genuine problem and to other data, gain in meaning and retention.[17]

But it does require time and ingenuity to prepare such a script, and teachers must balance costs against gains. We cannot always do what we would like to do. Yet, if time rules out one option, others may be available. For example, in this instance, the instructor might have started by placing table 5.11 on the chalkboard, as summarizing data collected in the same course in another semester, then asking students to react to it. While this abbreviation of the process sacrifices some personal involvement of current class members, the strategy of the benign disrupter would still have been employed.

Finally, let us note an implicit moral issue that is embedded in this example, a factor that is probably related to the learning process. One student reacted with the distressed query: "How could I have been so wrong?" But the frustrated desire to be right is not the only source of distress. Students may also be dismayed to discover that the views and values they hold are not theirs alone, but are socially influenced. This assault on personal independence and integrity is a subtle liability in sociology instruction. The antidote is found in our own legacy, especially in the social behaviorism of George Herbert Mead who has led us to the realization that social reality is a collaborative creation. The person is not a pawn but an active negotiator in the construction of reality.[18]

Benign Disruption through Status Incongruities

In one final illustration, we use cognitive dissonance generated by currently incongruous statuses. We have in mind a discussion of social norms, both in the statistical and evaluative sense, and of common status clusters as they link with the division of labor and societal integration. The instructor has devised a fictional situation. The data come from class members themselves.

In a scripted conversation between two people, a series of questions reveals a number of statuses, some of which may be expected, others not. As two students read the script, others in the class write two reactions: (1) immediately after a question is asked, students write the answer they expect; and (2) after the answer is given, students write down the extent to which they were surprised by the answer. Extent of surprise is to be indicated by writing the appropriate number: 1 = altogether unexpected; 2 = surprised; 3 = seems possible, it could be; 4 = I had a hunch, or I would have expected it; and 5 = I predicted it.

The situation takes place during a plane flight on December 22, and students are told that the person sitting next to them is an attractive woman with an infant on her lap. Her age is about thirty. The students are represented by Q, the questioner; the fellow traveller is represented by A. In the following conversation, Q and A pause after each question or answer to give the students time to write their reactions on the answer forms they have received.

Q.1   Going home for Christmas?

A.1   No. Home, but not for Christmas.

Q.2   Oh. You celebrate Chanukah, instead?

A.2   Oh no. We're not Jewish. We're Zoroastrians.

Q.3   Zoroastrians! Is that your husband's faith, too?

A.3   I don't have a husband.

Q.4   Oh. I misunderstood. I thought that was your baby.

A.4   It is.

Q.5   I'm sorry. I didn't mean to pry.

A.5   Quite all right. The best plans sometimes go awry.

Q.6   Hmmm. So . . . do you often fly home?

A.6   Well, yes. I fly all the time, but seldom to my parents' home.

Q.7   Oh, you must fly on business, then?

A.7   I always fly on business. That is to say, my business takes me flying.

Q.8   May I ask: what is your business?

A.8   I'm a navigator with Eastern Airlines.

A tally of the data on five of the degree-of-surprise items might look like table 5.12 for a class of thirty students. The instructor notes what was observed—a female about age thirty, a mother, single or not wed, a Zoroastrian, and an airline navigator—and students' reactions as summarized in the tally. Now the question is: Why did we respond to these observations as we did and what can we learn from this fictional experience?

Table 5.12 Tally of Student Responses to Script Revealing Status Incongruities

Item Number	Altogether Unexpected	Surprised	Seems Possible	Had a Hunch	Predicted It
A.1	4	24	2	—	—
A.2	15	10	5	—	—
A.3	15	15	—	—	—
A.4	5	20	5	—	—
A.8	20	10	—	—	—

We conclude, first, that the statuses revealed by A don't hook together, at least not often in our experience. Mothers usually have husbands. Women are not often plane navigators. Zoroastrians we seldom meet in church. We would not have reacted the same way if this woman had been joining her husband and her parents for a Christmas celebration, including perhaps a midnight Mass on Christmas eve or a religious celebration in some Protestant church, if she had been a housewife, and if she had a nontechnical education stressing the humanities rather than mathematics and engineering.

We might also conclude that statuses, normally, *do* hook together. We might identify other status clusters. For example, a seventeen-year-old boy can be expected to be in the eleventh or twelfth grade, single, not in the full-time labor market, unable to vote, not subject to adult criminal processes if he commits a felony, unable to make a contract. . . .

We have also teased out the connotations of the term *norm*. When we use that word, we refer to: (1) familiar and recurrent behaviors tied to certain social positions, and (2) an implication of *oughtness* ("that woman ought to have had a husband . . . it's too bad she would not be celebrating Christmas . . .").

We note that clusters of statuses define differentiated positions in society, along with differing behaviors, including occupations. Thus the notion of the division of labor takes on added meaning. And we raise these questions: What difference would it make if statuses did *not* cluster in this fashion? Suppose they were to vary randomly? Here the link between stability (or instability and change) and status integration might surface. The instructor might then wish to raise the questions posed by Gibbs and Martin (1958) in their test of the relationship between status integration and suicide. Thus a classroom exercise, employing a mildly

disruptive technique and engaging every student in the process, can lead to some fundamental understandings about social structure, social differentiation, and social change.

In this chapter, we have stressed the goal of analytical (or critical or reflective) thinking, a goal that transcends any particular course content. It can be achieved as instructors cast themselves in the role of benign disrupter. In doing so, they stress differences—differences between the familiar and the strange, between the part and the whole, between contrary or incompatible observations and explanations. The creation of such dissonance exerts a strain to resolve, somehow, the differing views or discrepant data. We can summarize some of these ideas and examples in table 5.13.

Sociologists instructing undergraduates are likely to have other goals that transcend the particular contents of the courses they are teaching. Two such goals we deem important are treated in the next chapter. The first is the ability to extend an idea or proposition to another population or situation. The second nonsubstantive goal is the ability to apply general ideas to concrete situations.

Notes

1. Reading introductory texts and instructors' manuals supports this impression. "Questions for Study," "Suggested Discussion Topics," test items, and the like typically ask students to recognize or recall material read or, sometimes, to elaborate what has already been revealed. A discussion with the next publisher's field representative to visit you will convince you that these materials found in instructors' manuals and texts are widely relied upon.

Table 5.13 Modes of Benign Disruption: Arranging Intellectual Roadblocks that Require Analytic Thinking if They Are to be Surmounted

Differing observations: The teacher presents two differing observations or discrepant data and works with students toward resolution; or, the teacher presents one observation that conflicts with the likely expectations of students and works with them toward resolution.

Observation(s)	Problems Incited	Potential Yield
1. Black matricentric families and white patricentric families	Is the distinction true? If so, how can we explain it?	Students discriminate between covariance and cause, learn something about differing family structures, about multivariate analysis.
2. Common sense vs. research findings	Which is accurate? If common sense errs, how did it go wrong?	Students learn that truth is not determined by majority vote, and that common sense typically fails to specify the conditions under which an alleged relationship holds.
3. Personal view (estimate) vs. social reality	Am I wrong? Is my error attributable to certain social influences?	Students learn certain facts, become aware of sampling problems, grasp the principle that attitudes and views are developed through experience with others.
4. Observations in a given case (husbandless mother who is Zoroastrian and a navigator) at odds with expectations	Do certain statuses cluster? Why do certain combinations of statuses jar one's consciousness? Why do certain statuses cohere?	Students learn that, normally, certain statuses hang together, learn what a norm is, gain some intuitive sense of what may happen in the absence of integrated status patterns.

Differing explanations: The teacher presents fact(s) and two differing explanations, asking students to determine which explanation is more satisfactory and how that can be determined; or, the teacher presents fact(s) and one explanation, inviting students to evaluate that explanation and generate others.

Explanation(s)	Problems Incited	Potential Yield
1. Premise vs. premise, or assumption vs. inconsistent assumption	Which of two or more basic assumptions about social life is more accurate?	Students learn that false premises, at odds with those supported by research, lead to ineffective policy decisions.
2. Two explanations for attitudes toward an object—for example, socialism. Conservatism is a result of aging, or a result of the history-linked experiences of a cohort.	Which is the better explanation? Is there any way they can be conceived as complementary? Are there other and better explanations?	Students learn that the facts don't speak for themselves but are susceptible to different (and sometimes incompatible) explanations. (A biological explanation is opposed to a social explanation here.)

2. The significance of differences enters sociological work at many points. (The very phrase echoes common statistical treatments.) For Durkheim, perceived differences were a crucial condition of agreement. Thus the social importance of criminal activity lies in the occasions provided to celebrate the contrary. Homicide and war and dishonesty prompt reaffirmations of the sacredness of life, the desirability of peace, and the need for trust in human affairs.

Again, the difference between what one does and what one might have done is a measure of value. The measure of a woman's investment in family and housework is earnings forgone. Renunciation or sacrifice can be seen as a condition and measure of exchange value. In sociology, as in other fields, the discovery of differences sets the stage for trying to explain their sources and their consequences.

3. But differences are not always apparent, and one of the tasks and opportunities of the teacher as benign disrupter is to create situations in which students will see them.

Consider the case of illiteracy in the United States. In recent years, illiteracy rates have been very low and steadily decreasing (from 2.9 percent in 1940 to 1.0 percent in 1969). Steady decline of already low rates; apparently little of interest here. But the significance of a low rate only emerges as we ponder *different* rates, contrasts in time and space. For example, in 1969 the illiteracy rate for white females, age sixty-five and over, was 22.4 percent. For their male counterparts the rate was 2.1 percent. In the same year, the rate for blacks was more than five times the rate for whites. Again, in 1969, the rate for Iran was 77.0 percent. (These data come from the U.S. Bureau of the Census, 1975a:382; 1976a:125, 874–5.) As instructors confront their students with such differences, they are making trouble, for differences exert a strain for explanation.

4. The term *matricentric* is sometimes applied to families in which only a mother is present. By this definition, in 1970, about 9 percent of white and 27 percent of black families were matricentric (U.S. Bureau of the Census, 1972:278–80). More often matricentric describes a mother-centered (or mother-dominant) family. Adequate data on gender-linked dominance, by race, are hard to come by. Some studies have found significant differences between whites and blacks (Centers and Raven, 1971). Analysis of several national surveys led Hyman and Reed (1969) to conclude that there was little difference between intact black and white families. Another study that found small differences between black and white families has been reported by Schulz (1968). For a general discussion of this issue see Simpson and Yinger (1972:166, 464–73).

5. This form of cultural explanation was *one* of the factors cited in the report of the National Advisory Commission on Civil Disorders (1968: chapter 2). Frazier (1948) also made use of this theme in his pioneering work on the black family.

6. Such an analysis is indirectly supported by Scanzoni (1972) and by part of the findings of the National Advisory Commission on Civil Disorders (1968: chapter 2).

7. Excellent and detailed treatments of causal analysis are found in several introductory methods and statistics books. See, for example, Cole (1976: chapters 2, 6) and Malec (1977: chapter 11).

8. Most sociologists have run into anomalous findings, contradictions, inconsistencies—the puzzles that make sociological inquiry so fascinating and difficult. There may be occasions when teachers will want to draw upon their own or other sociologists' personal experiences to show how one person confronted and dealt with such issues. Beyond personal experience, there are many resources for teachers to exploit. Durkheim's *Suicide* (1897) is well suited to such uses, and there are several volumes in which contemporary sociologists discuss the puzzling and anomalous findings that emerged in their own work (for example, Golden, 1976; Hammond, 1967; Vidich, Bensman, and Stein, 1964).

9. For a specific example of the use of generational hypotheses, see Zeitlin (1966). The classic statement is Mannheim's "The Problem of Generations" (1952). For an excellent analytic article and extensive citation to pertinent literature, see Ryder (1965).

10. Data are from the U.S. Bureau of the Census (1976: table 7).

11. Data are from U.S. Bureau of the Census (1976a: tables 16, 24, 65). Racial composition and urban/rural residence are from the 1970 decennial census; the religion data are reported in a document issued by the National Council of Churches of Christ. The data on Catholics and Jews correspond rather closely to the only survey ever made by the Census Bureau that asked about religious affiliation. See U.S. Bureau of the Census, *Current Population Reports,* Series P–20, No. 79, "Religion Reported by the Civilian Population of the United States, March, 1957," summarized in U.S. Bureau of the Census (1974).

12. For percentage of blacks in North Carolina, see U.S. Bureau of the Census (1976: table 37). For urbanization rates, see U.S. Bureau of the Census (1973: table T.1). State-specific data on religious affiliation are not readily available. In the example presented here, the teacher obtained a listing of Archdioceses and Dioceses in the United States from DeLury (1973); according to 1972 data reported there, the two dioceses in North Carolina had a combined Catholic population of less than 70,000. The teacher contrasted this to the state of Indiana, which had a roughly equivalent total population and archdioceses and dioceses with a combined Catholic population of over 700,000.

13. Data are derived from Table 20 in Zopf (n.d.:142).

14. The Current Population Survey of the Bureau of the Census regularly employs multistage samples of 50,000 to 60,000 homes—less than .1 percent of all U.S. homes.

15. It should be stressed that these are instructional objectives and not learning objectives. The former relate to teacher intentions and behaviors. The latter specify what students will be able to do after a specified unit of instruction.

16. Devices somewhat similar to those discussed here are found in Marwell (1966) and Toby (1955).

17. See Ericksen (1974: chapters 4, 8, 9), Cross (1976: section II), and McKeachie (1969: chapters 20, 6, 5). See also chapter 11 in this book.

18. Peter L. Berger echoes Mead in *Invitation to Sociology,* a book widely used in introductory courses. In his concluding paragraph, Berger uses the image of the puppet theater. Like puppets dancing on a stage, we are pulled by strings; we play out our parts. "We locate ourselves in society and thus recognize our own position as we hang from its subtle strings. . . . But then we grasp a decisive difference between the puppet theater and our own drama. Unlike the puppets, we have the possibility of stopping in our movements, looking up and perceiving the machinery by which we have been moved. In this act lies the first step towards freedom. And in this same act we find the conclusive justification of sociology as a humanistic discipline" (Berger, 1963:176).

CHAPTER 6
MORE GOALS TRANSCENDING SOCIOLOGICAL CONTENT: SKILLS IN GAINING AND EXTENDING KNOWLEDGE

Our field-related goals in sociology are necessarily connected with the substance peculiar to the field—social arrangements or structures, and changes in those structures. With undergraduates, for whom emphasis is not on professional but on general education, nonsubstantive goals become prominent. And so in chapter 5 we emphasized an initial step in inquiry, an awareness of differences that want explaining. One task of the sociology instructor is to get students into the habit of using space and time to reveal differences that generate why-wondering. We contrast *then* with *now*, or *here* with *there*. But instructors also wish students to gain a heightened awareness of subsequent aspects of inquiry: translating whys into more precise questions, developing the tentative answers we call theory (explanations), walking theories down the abstraction ladder to the point where we can state testable hypotheses, imagining and creating useful indexes of the central variables in our theories. Thus another nonsubstantive goal would be that students gain some understanding of and skill in the process of inquiry.

A related part of this process is achieving solutions that extend beyond the knowledge gained. Indeed, we might wish our students to cultivate the skill of mobilizing past, unorganized knowledge

to make plausible estimates of social situations for which data are lacking.

In this chapter, then, we reflect on two nonsubstantive goals for our students: learning something of the general strategy of inquiry, and developing skills in extending knowledge—beyond the findings of a particular inquiry or to an unknown realm on the basis of past knowledge. Although we offer them as illustrations, it may be that such goals will seem arbitrary, odd, or both. Obviously they reflect our judgments; we see them as significant aims for undergraduate instruction. Quite as obviously, they do not exhaust the list of possible nonsubstantive goals. (That list might include, as further examples, the ability to apply sociological insights to one's own life, the ability to demonstrate the misleading nature of common sense and mundane adages, the ability to articulate the substance and skills of sociological analysis with one's other academic experiences in the humanities and biophysical sciences, the ability to apply sociological principles and suggest solutions to social problems, and so on.) Such a roster of nonsubstantive goals would be long. We speak to two we deem important.

But first, one other preliminary. By definition, nonsubstantive goals cannot be peculiar to sociology. Instructors in other fields will have like aims. But that they are shared makes such aims no less important for the sociology instructor.

Gaining Knowledge: Enhanced Skills in Inquiry

Our knowledge is only as sure as the means used to achieve it.

In the United States, a course in methods of research is commonly a required part of the undergraduate sociology major. And since 1945, it has become increasingly a part of the curriculum in other social sciences. Why so?

Learning Methods of Research: The Importance of This Nonsubstantive Goal

One reason the social sciences are requiring undergraduates to learn research methods is this: problem-solving skills are generic needs. They are invoked in every field and subfield in the social sciences. For social science is a process, an incessant seeking for more accurate understanding of the social worlds we build. The process is endless because the strong undertow of change continually throws up new events not wholly understood by invoking the propositions of extant science or tradition.

The same is true of everyday experience. The kaleidoscope of daily life continuously confronts us with new problems of choice and survival. Mounting crime rates are reported in the daily news. Does the death penalty deter the criminal? Yes? No? Or does it make no difference? And if it does, under what conditions? Do we change others' behaviors as, apparently, we think we do? Does the teacher teach? Or does the student learn chiefly from peers, mass media, and parents? Do

priest, minister, and rabbi make people moral? What would happen in their absence? A CBS newscast suggests that ten years of warning from the surgeon general's office and three years without television advertising have had no effect in reducing cigarette smoking. Is it true? Has it made no difference?

These are questions of cause and effect in daily life, such questions as Spencer (1891:chapter 1) stressed. They are questions about our social worlds, often too simply posed (as we have posed them here) and often too simply answered. And each poses the further question: how can we best solve the problem? For example, there is always the problem of defining terms so clearly and precisely that we can put our tentative answers to the test. There is the problem of sampling, since most of our observations *are* samples of all possible instances of the observed behavior. There is the problem of imputing causal influence and of assessing that influence while other possible causes are controlled. There are always problems of measurement and questions as to how well our indicators represent the thing indicated—the question of validity. And always there is the question whether our measure will serve as well tomorrow as it did today, and whether it will serve in other hands, as well as in ours—the question of reliability.

So one answer to the question, Why is a course in methods so commonly a part of the social science curriculum? is this: the problem of gaining reliable knowledge is generic; it touches what we know and believe in everyday life as well as the inquiries of social scientists. Such matters are important because they are pervasive. But their importance increases with the significance of that inquired into. The crucial part of nature is what we call human nature. And the crucial part of human nature is that behavior peculiar to human beings by virtue of the fact that they live in groups. Thus the extraordinary significance of social phenomena, *and the methods used to inquire into them.* That is why, in every course in the social sciences, every instructor must be sure that students acquire some of the methods they will need to determine whether empirical reality fits the ideational map.

The Process of Inquiry

Inquiry is a complex process. The disposition to monopolize class time with expository teaching (which is often *not* teaching, but talking students into a coma) makes it necessary to remind ourselves that *inquiry begins with a question.* And questions arise from the sort of problematic situations we have mentioned. Something transpires that is extraordinary. Things apparently similar turn out to be different. Or we make the ordinary into the problematic. We ask: Why should it be this way, rather than some other way? Why are things different now than they were then? For example: How can we account for the emergence of capitalism? What explains a decline in political participation? Or, we ask: How can we explain the difference between there and here? For example: Do socialist countries differ from nonsocialist countries in the prestige accorded various occupations? How does a group whose members are treated one way differ from a group whose members are not so treated? This last question typifies the experimentation done with small groups in which we induce differences (between experimental and control groups) to determine whether a hypothesized condition has the outcomes our theory led us to anticipate.

Our experience is that students find it very hard to ask questions, perhaps be-

cause their curiosity becomes dulled as their lives become routinized. If we take as a goal helping students become more effective inquirers, then we must contrive ways to sharpen their sense of interesting differences. Various ways of doing this come to mind. We can ask what difference something made. Or we can point to the future and ask what difference it *would* make. Or we can introduce a moral component and ask if it would not be better (or worse) if . . . ? The first question is the historians' as they reconstruct the past to assess the influence of a dominant character or event. The second question can be put in scores of ways. What differences would it make were workers to share certain decision-making power with management?[1] The question, Would it not be better if . . . ? introduces the matter of preference and value. Such questions are the sort that evaluation research should help us answer—inquiries that identify the range and depth of consequences resulting from one course of action rather than another. Would it not be better if medical insurance covered all persons in the United States for all illnesses?

A questioning mind, then, is one that is conscious of differences. This suggests—as we said in chapter 5—that the instructor's role must often be that of a benign disrupter. Students will describe and explain their worlds inadequately unless they learn to see—and try to explain—differing behaviors. They need to learn, as we all do, that the exception tests the rule; and that one exception is enough to torpedo a generalization. Welfare for the impoverished destroys the incentive to work. There is the self-evident proposition. Are some of the impoverished different? Do some persist in working—or behave quite as they would in the absence of welfare? Chances are they do: for most welfare recipients are dependent children and oldsters who could not work in any case. How about the others, those eligible to work? Do they work, despite welfare? Some evidence suggests that even a guaranteed annual wage (a negative income tax) does not diminish the incentive to work (Wright, 1975). In such a case as this, the instructor's task is to help students discover that the population covered by a proposition is not homogeneous and, since there are differences, we are constrained to alter the proposition advanced on the false assumption of homogeneity.

To speak of a proposition is to point to the building block of theory, a set of logically linked propositions that purport to explain a class behavior. The observed differences that puzzle us call for the tentative answer that we call a theory. Sometimes we build our theory to explain how differences in the independent variable may be expected to have differing effects. Thus we ask: what are the different outcomes, for children, of different allocations of power between parents—father dominant, mother dominant, and equalitarian? But sometimes we start at the other end and, noting different outcomes, try to find an answer that will explain such differences. For example, why are some young people rebels while others are conformists? Whether looking at different influences or conditions, or at differing outcomes, we try through theory to develop a tentative answer that identifies correlates or links causes with consequences.

So far, then, we have a problematic situation that creates a question in students' minds and for which we seek a tentative answer by developing a theory that explains what differing outcomes are to be expected from differing antecedent conditions.

Students, like others, will have the habit of offering cavalier explanations picked up through chance associations (ini-

tially determined by the accident of birth). Their theories will often be crude, pieced together from personal observation, authority, parochial exposures, and many unidentified sources. The instructor must help the student develop a tightly argued (i.e., logical) explanation *and* one that can be walked down the abstraction ladder to a precise operational statement that asserts, as a target for testing, a determinate relationship between variables under specified conditions. These steps are the critical first stages in the pursuit of answers. Let us give the student a skeletal example.

A classic example.   After reviewing unsatisfactory explanations of suicide, Durkheim (1897) reports observed differences between different categories in the incidence of suicide: men more than women, Protestants more than Catholics, officers more than enlisted personnel. The observed differences lead to this question: how can we account for the differing rates—those, say, between Protestants and Catholics? The question prompts us to review various answers drawn from our own experiences, from traditional lore, from the wisdom literature, from empirical research. Some answers we will have to discard promptly. For example, one might hear it said that people commit suicide because they are disturbed or mad or melancholy. Students will come to see at least two defects in such an explanation. First, it dodges the question by rewording it. But the question still remains, only reworded: why are some people disturbed, mad, or melancholy, while others are not? A second difficulty with this explanation lies in its offering as an answer a personal, psychic state when a *rate* of suicide seems to point to the social arrangements (that generate the psychic states) that lead to suicide.

In any case, we do try to develop a theory that explains why categories of people differ in their propensity for suicide. In table 6.1, we represent this theory as an inverted pyramid, starting with broad and general statements, but slowly narrowing as we close in on the tentative answer and converging, finally, on testable hypotheses. Here we follow, roughly, Durkheim's (1897) argument.

Now we face the problem of designing some way of testing the hypotheses we have presented in table 6.1. If we are seeking answers to differing suicide rates, clearly we cannot manipulate conditions so as to check whether certain ones increase suicide rates while their absence depresses the rate. But we can simulate the classical design by trying to make the two groups—the better educated and the less well educated, for example—about the same in all other ways that might conceivably have an effect on the suicide rate. On other sorts of problems we can assign persons randomly to experimental and control groups, and then impose on the former the influence indicated by our theory to be determinative in producing a given outcome.

So far we have noted four aspects of

Table 6.1 A Theory Represented as an Inverted Pyramid, from General Statements to Testable Hypotheses

---

When we consider explanations commonly offered to account for suicide rates, we find that climate, race, and mental instability are unsatisfactory. For persons of the same race and those living under similar climatic conditions yet may have quite different suicide rates. And groups or categories known to have high rates of psychoneurotic disorders—e.g., Jews and women—yet have lower rates of suicide than do Protestants or men. We must therefore rule out such common theories that falsely purport to explain differentials in suicide rates. Consider differences between religious categories, Protestants and Catholics. Why are Catholics' rates consistently lower? A distinctive feature of Catholicism (in contrast to Protestantism) is its reliance on the authority of tradition, mediated by priest through rite and communion, making for a tightly integrated body of believers. The Protestant, to a much greater extent, is left to his own devices to achieve the moral life and secure salvation. The explanation, then, would seem to lie in the extent to which people stand alone, left to their own devices to win through. If this is so, then it should clearly   follow   that:

Hypothesis: Suicide rates should be higher among the better educated than among those less well educated (since the latter rely more on traditional patterns, while the former are likely to arrive at new and often disturbing answers).

Hypothesis: Suicide rates should be higher among officers than among enlisted men, for the same reason.

---

the process of inquiry: (1) noting the emergence of a problem, (2) formulating the question, (3) providing a tentative answer that we call *theory*, and (4) designing a plan of research that will help us test the hypothesis derived from the theory. (Of course, such a sequence should be taken as a model from which practice often departs. Solving problems is seldom a tidy matter following a clean, logical sequence.)

These four aspects are early and essential acts of much disciplined inquiry. They imply the need, or the development, of several rare attributes: a sensitivity to problematic situations (especially where others take things for granted); a disciplined imagination that can conjure up and weigh, revise, and select among competing explanations of observed differences; and the logic and ingenuity to devise a research scheme that will adequately test the hypotheses derived from the tentative explanation (theory).

These four aspects have to do with the strategy of inquiry. The ensuing work calls for tactical skills to carry through the tests of hypotheses. These tactical skills include such things as knowledge of probability sampling (as well as the reasons for it) and methods of gathering, reducing, and analyzing data through the use of descriptive measures, tables, measures of association, and the like. The distinction between strategy and tactics is not so clear as this division would imply. Tactical skills may also entail ingenuity and imagination. But we make the distinction here to clarify our emphasis on generic matters of strategy. We stress such matters because we think these abilities are both critical and less attended to than training in the more familiar tools. Furthermore, they present tougher pedagogical problems than, say, learning to calculate measures of central tendency, or Pearson and Spearman measures of correlation. We do

not minimize such skills; they are needed by the literate adult to cope with results of the polls, or to adjust newspaper reports on income to take inflation (buying power) into account, or to understand such indexes as GNP. We hope that no instructor would disregard instruction in the essential tools of social analysis. But in the following paragraphs, we have simply chosen to fix on the strategy or logic of inquiry—a matter which, although less concrete than the tools, yet figures in everyday life.

A classroom example. We start with an observed difference. January 1974 marked the end of three years during which cigarette commercials had been barred from radio and television. It was also the tenth year since the surgeon general announced the finding: cigarette smoking may be harmful to your health.

Does advertising work? Does it make a difference in the volume of a product sold? Does lack of advertising reduce the sale of a product? Those in business answer yes to these questions and, in that confidence, spend billions annually for advertising. Thus we must infer that a difference in cigarette advertising (its ban from radio and television) must have made a difference, reducing, perhaps sharply, the number of smokers. How could it be otherwise?

Here the teacher, acting as benign disrupter, introduces a dissonant datum. In January of 1974, a CBS newscast reported these figures:

Number of Smokers

1963	50 million
1973	52 million

The reporter, while noting some decline in smoking among certain subgroups, drew the obvious conclusion that, overall, there was an increase, not a decrease, in smoking.

Was the conclusion warranted? Note that, so far, we have asked two questions about cigarette smoking in 1963 and 1973: Is there a difference? If so, in what direction is the difference? For the second question we have contradictory answers: smoking both declined and increased. The answers to these questions *describe* reality. We have not yet moved to *explanation*.

Has the number of smokers increased? Let us accept the figures offered in the newscast. The number has increased. There are now two million more smokers than there were in 1963. But here are two different questions: Has smoking increased? How shall we measure amount of smoking? As some students will suggest, it might be measured by cigarettes smoked per unit time—number of packs per day, for example. Or smoking might be measured by the part of a population that smokes—all, half, three-fourths. Is it possible that smoking, in this latter sense, might decline although number of smokers increased? Students may say that this is possible, paradoxical though it sounds.

How could that be? Well, someone will point out—*and better the student should do it than the teacher*—that the number of persons smoking might increase but the total number of persons might increase even more. At this point we are required to seek the data to test this supposition. And this is what we find:

	U.S. Population	Number of Smokers
1963	188 million	50 million
1973	210 million	52 million
Difference in numbers	22 million	2 million
Difference in percentages	12%	4%

Thus we might conclude that smoking has not kept pace with the increase in population. Smoking, in contrast to smokers, has declined.

But, someone might point out, these newcomers to the overall population are nonsmoking infants and children. It's not right to consider them nonsmokers since they aren't the population at risk. We should consider only those, say, above age fourteen. So we must seek more data to check whether use of the total population has led us to a false conclusion. Here are the data:

Population Age 14 and Over	
1960	127 million
1970	151 million

Thus we find that persons over age fourteen increased by 24 million, or about 19 percent. This makes the case for the relative decline in smoking even stronger, for the population has increased twelve times as much as the number of smokers.

Thus we can *describe* this small (but important) sector of social reality by saying: (1) smokers have increased, and (2) smoking has declined, relative to the population at risk.

But how shall we *explain* this finding which is, let us recall, quite different from the message delivered over television. Is it because radio and television no longer push smoking through their advertising? What is the answer—the theory—that would explain such a decline in smoking rates? Is it owing to the ban on advertising? What other changes have occurred over the decade that might explain the decline? Suppose one were to argue that the decline results not from the producer's failure to push his product, but from the consumer's failure to pull—i.e., to buy. But this is to rephrase the question. Why, then, should the public refuse to buy cigarettes? Because, a student says, cigarettes are known to be carcinogenic. Known? Who knows? The better educated? And are there now more of the better educated than there were ten years ago? Let us suppose there are. Hence it might be that an advance in general level of education, with its concomitant knowledge of carcinogens, accounts for consumer resistance and a lower level of smoking. In that case, it is not lack of advertising but a heightened awareness of the hazards of smoking that accounts for the declining rate.

But are we then so ready to give up our first conviction that advertising does make a difference? Are the businessmen so wrong after all? Is there no way to salvage the advertising industry?

How shall we know? How can we untangle the influence of two presumed causal influences? How can we separate the influence of higher levels of education from the influence of a decline in advertising? Now our discussion will lead students to recognize that we can control the possible causal influence of education by analyzing changes in smoking, between 1963 and 1973, among those who have achieved the same level of education. Thus students learn how to control the possible influence of one variable in order to assess the influence of another. They will see that education is but one of a number of variables that might conceivably be linked to changes in smoking rates. Changes in national tensions and trauma (the Vietnam war, for example), in per capita income, in the religious commitment to health and simplicity—these and other ideas might figure in a multicausal theory of the decline in rate of smoking. Thus we would be led to the construction, use, and interpretation of multivariate tables such as this:

Percentage of Smokers, by Level of Education and Income for Selected Dates

	Education					
	8th Grade or Less		9th to 12th		1 Year or More of College	
	Income		Income		Income	
Year	High	Low	High	Low	High	Low
1953						
1963						
1973						

Let us review, very briefly, significant aspects of this example.

1. We were dealing with a familiar practice (smoking) and a familiar medium (a network television newscast). Since students will continue to hear and read the news, anything learned about careless or unsophisticated reporting will sharpen their sifting of evidence in future.

2. Let us note that we are dealing not only with a sociological problem, but also with a social problem, a matter of social policy, a matter of health and sickness, a matter of life and death. There are moral issues at stake when a sizeable sector of the economy (14.8 billion dollars spent by consumers on tobacco in 1975), supported by taxpayers, profits from practices that degrade consumers' health.

3. We have tackled two jobs that characterize disciplined inquiry—description and explanation.

4. The description that generated a question in our minds did so because it revealed a difference between then and now. (The CBS reporter erroneously implied that smoking had increased—number of smokers had, indeed—despite the ban on television advertising.)

5. The instructor worked toward the introduction of a challenging datum—the concomitant growth in population over the decade. Thus the instructor introduced an element of dissonance (the obvious increase in smokers might not mean, as students thought, an increase in smoking).

6. Students had a chance to develop an index somewhat more sophisticated than a simple enumeration of smokers. This index was number of smokers *related to* the population-at-risk.

7. Questions preceded answers. This is a mandatory sequence if students are to get a sense of inquiry as a process, initiated with a significant problem and unfolding like a detective story: question, tentative answer, data and new leads, revised answer.

As for the seventh aspect of this example, it should be noted that putting questions before answers may mean temporarily withholding data. However, a contrary procedure, perhaps more common, is for the instructor to provide all the data and promptly achieve (it is hoped) a substantive goal: knowledge of a declining rate of smoking. But to do so is to forgo achievement of the nonsubstantive goal: heightened awareness of the strategy of inquiry and enhanced skills in problem solution. (It should also be noted that although fixing on a substantive goal and delivering the truth sacrifice the nonsubstantive objective, the reverse is not true.)

Our example could be extended. The instructor should be sure that students know the source of the data on population and smoking. For an important goal of instruction in the social sciences is to acquaint students with sources of data that will serve them throughout their lives.

Finally, we might stress the usefulness of current and publicly available statements about social behavior, both descriptive (smoking rates have declined) and explanatory (they have declined because of the ban on cigarette advertising on television). Such statements have the virtue of being current, of being pertinent

to students' concerns, and above all, of offering material whose critical analysis can develop useful skills of inquiry. (During my administration, the politician says, per capita income has gone up, more miles of highway have been built, welfare costs have gone down, and the threat of war has diminished. And the implication is that all of this is due to his administration.) Such statements are grist for careful grinding in the service of enhanced skills of inquiry. This is not to forsake the academic content of the course, but to convey it more powerfully.

How much do we know after we have described accurately a decline in the rate of smoking and have explained the decline by discovering its correlates in reduced advertising, higher levels of education, religious commitments, and the like? We suggest, and would try to show our students, that we may know more than we suspected. This is especially the case when we can find another social situation, similar in form but different in content, to which our knowledge may be tentatively extended. For example, is it possible to say that drinking may be hazardous to your health? And if so, might the rate of consumption of spirits (hard liquor) be declining, and for reasons much like those used to explain a decline in the rate of smoking? If we can answer yes to these questions, then we know a great deal more than we thought we did, some of it quite certainly as in the case of tobacco and some much less certainly, but nonetheless suggestively, pointing to subsequent inquiries. Under such circumstances, general findings can be extended to a much larger range of behaviors and are, therefore, much more powerful. One goal, then, would be to help students see the power and the beauty of extending the findings from one piece of research to other situations or populations.

There is another type of extension—and a related nonsubstantive goal. Sometimes we know more than we think we do, yet fail to exploit that knowledge to get better estimates of the unknown. These are the matters to which we turn in the next section.

Extending Knowledge

One can think of intelligence as the capacity to see beyond one's nose. This means we can extend past experience to new circumstances that, despite their novelty, share some critical feature with the known. When one can take past experience (or findings) and extend it to a wider range of situations, the mind has extended its reach, enlarged its control. This is what Adam Ferguson (1819:49) had in mind when he wrote that sagacity was to be measured by the extent to which a person can find "general rules applicable to a variety of cases [especially those that seem] to have nothing in common." When a proposition need not be restricted to blacks, but can embrace women, chicanos, overseas Chinese, and Catholics, it is a much more powerful statement. Similarly, the extension of ideas about socialization from, say, Marine Corps boot camp to induction into the Coast Guard, to entering a convent, to the rearing of a child, to the quarantine period for newly admitted prisoners, to starting work on an assembly line or in a law firm—such an extension greatly increases our grasp of a class of social phenomena. We recognize the importance of extension in research. A given inquiry is far more telling when it brackets the instant research with other inquiries into analytically parallel situations across different populations.

The idea of extension is an old one in education. One of the beauties of mathe-matics is that a command of certain problem-solving processes can be applied to ships *or* sealing wax *or* kings. In teaching sociology, too, extension might well be prominent among the instructor's nonsubstantive goals. Let us take an example of an instructor who uses a piece of research to help students move from a single case to a more abstract statement of conditions and consequences—and then, moving in the opposite direction (from general to specific, deductively) helps those students *discover a quite different situation to which the same propositions might apply.* The course is one in Deviance and Delinquency. And the research is that by three anthropologists, Whiting, Kluckhohn, and Anthony (1958).[2]

Extending Findings to New Populations or Situations

Our instructor in this example presents her students with a three-page handout. On the first page (1a), she presents a question raised by Whiting, Kluckhohn, and Anthony, and she leaves space for students' attempts at explaining observed differences. On the back of the first page (1b), the instructor offers the theory, the tentative answer given by the researchers, together with the hypothesis the students are to test. On the second page (2a), two blank tables appear with titles and stubs labelled, but lacking data. Students are asked in which cells the data will fall, disproportionately. On the back of the second page (2b), the actual findings are reported. On the third page (3a), students are asked to extend these findings to contemporary U.S. society. On the back of the third page (3b), the extension offered by Whiting, Kluckhohn, and Anthony is reported. We will illustrate the sequence of events.

Page 1a. *Why, these investigators asked, do we find initiation rites for young men—emphatic, dramatic, sometimes sanguinary—in some groups while others lack such ceremonies? What is the social function served by initiation rites? Under what conditions is this social function necessary? Or unnecessary? Many groups have transition-to-adulthood rites. Can you give examples from our own society? (Young upper-class ladies have coming-out parties, or debuts. At age eighteen, one can vote and, at twenty-one, enter into legal contracts. Young Jewish boys have a special transitional ceremony called Bar Mitzvah. Catholics and some Protestants have a parallel ceremony called Confirmation.) What is your answer to the question posed by the investigators? Why do we find initiation rites in some tribes, not in others? What conditions would seem to lead to initiation-to-adulthood rites for young men?*

After working on this puzzle—perhaps in groups of two or three—students are asked to turn the page to find there (and to compare with their answers) the answer given by the researchers.

Page 1b. *As the investigators worked out their interpretation of this observed difference in patterns of behavior, their theoretical statement took the following form. Where boys are particularly dependent upon mothers and hostile toward fathers, some sort of initiation rites are necessary to: (1) put a final stop to the boy's wish to return to his mother's arms and lap; (2) prevent an open revolt by the boy against his father who has displaced him from his mother's bed; and (3) ensure identification with the adult males of the society. The general hypothesis that follows is this: a protracted period of intimacy and dependence of male children upon their mothers will be associated with dramatic and sometimes violent initiation rites at puberty. Contrariwise, in societies that do not emphasize the dependence of male infants upon mothers and where the father exercises considerable authority, such initiation rites will be missing or extremely mild.*

What the investigators needed, then, were measures on two variables: (1) some index of the male infant's intimacy with and dependence on the mother, and (2) some measure, for the dependent variable, of the existence and extent of initiation rites. Their data came from studies of fifty-five tribes selected for geographic distribution, diversity of cultures, and adequacy of information on puberty rites. The dependent variable, existence of puberty rites, was simply recorded as being present or absent. The intimacy and dependency of male children were recorded as lasting for a long or a short period of sleeping with the mother (a year or longer, or less than a year), and as entailing a postpartum sex taboo for a long period (at least a year) or a shorter period. Thus we have four possible combinations on the independent variable: long periods of both mother-son sleeping and postpartum sex taboo, short periods for both, and the in-between combinations (long-short and short-long). We will simplify the table students would find on page 2a by calling the long-long combination the condition of *maximum* mother-son intimacy and dependence, the short-short combination the condition of *minimum* intimacy and dependence and the other two combinations simply *intermediate*. The table, then, would look like this, after students have, as requested, marked in those cells in which, if the hypothesis is supported, a disproportionate number of the cases will fall:

Extent of Mother-Son Intimacy/ Dependence	Initiation Rites for Adolescent Males:	
	Absent	Present
Maximum		XXXXX
Intermediate		
Minimum	XXXXX	

Now that they have anticipated the findings, students can turn to page 2b where they will find a display of the actual data, the findings. When they look at this table (see table 6.2), students will discover that the hypothesis is supported: initiation rites for male adolescents seem to be found particularly in tribes in which there is an extended period of intimacy and dependency of male child upon mother.[3] But is there any way of extending this finding, of teasing out its possible implications for other groups—especially for a better understanding of the society we know best (or think we know best), our own?

Page 3a is headed: "Extending Findings on Violent Initiation Rites from 55 Tribes to U.S. Society." And we follow this heading with a question: "Are there comparable situations or behaviors in our society?" To answer this question, students must be clear about the essential features of our present knowledge (about the 55 tribes). They need to distill the findings at a sufficiently high level of abstraction so that they can raise and answer appropriate questions about their own society. It might ease the job if the instructor suggested some such scheme as that presented in table 6.3 for thinking about the question.

After students have made every effort to extend the findings of the study, to tease out possible implications for our own society, they can turn to page 3b and read about the investigators' attempt at extension (Wilson, 1971a:307–8).

Where, in our society, the investigators ask, do we find virtually ritualized violence among adolescent males? The answer: this occurs, if anywhere, among delinquent juveniles with their gangs, their rumbles, their rebellious defiance of authority, their anxious demonstration of virility. This isn't true, clearly, of all juveniles, just

as it is not true that all tribes have initiation ceremonies for adolescent males. A critical distinction between the delinquent and the nondelinquent may well be that the former must rip himself, metaphorically speaking, from an enveloping female world, asserting himself as an adult and finding his role as a male. And so Whiting, Kluckhohn and Anthony suggest (1958:370) that ". . . insofar as there has been an increase in juvenile delinquency in our society, it should be accompanied by an increase in the exclusiveness of mother-child relationships and/or a decrease in the authority of the father. It is not unreasonable [to suppose] that industrialization and urbanization have done just this."

"[If so] . . . then it can be countered either by decreasing the exclusiveness of the early mother-child relationship, increasing the authority of the father during childhood, or instituting a formal means of coping with adolescent boys functionally equivalent to those described in this paper" (i.e., puberty rites, avuncular residence, moving to a "men's house," etc.).

How, then, can we help students develop the skill of extending what is known to illuminate what is unknown, to see connections between things apparently dissimilar? Instead of telling them (i.e., providing the extension), we can write the script that helps students work their way through to possible answers. A first step is to be clear about what is being extended. Second, we need to put our knowledge at a level of abstraction that liberates it from its immediate context. We might shift from mother-son relationships to any relationship of protracted dependence. Similarly, puberty rites are but one case of initiation rites. We may move from a study population of blacks to the more abstract notion of minorities, so embracing women in our generalizations. (That is what Hacker, 1951, did.) Since gender-based inequality often entails conflicts of interest, we might then bracket such relationships with oth-

Table 6.2 Relationship Between Extent of Mother-Son Intimacy/Dependency and the Presence or Absence of Initiation Rites for Adolescent Males in 55 Tribes

| Extent of Mother-Son Intimacy/Dependency | Adolescent Initiation Rites | | | | Totals | |
| | Absent | | Present | | | |
	Number	Percent	Number	Percent	Number	Percent
Maximum	6	32	13	68	19	100
Intermediate	7	64	4	36	11	100
Minimum	23	92	2	8	25	100
	36		19		55	

$X^2 = 69.5 - 55 = 14.5$, d/f = 2, and p < .001

Source: Whiting, Kluckhohn, and Anthony (1958), as appearing in Wilson (1971a:306–7).

Table 6.3 Extending Findings on Violent Initiation Rites from 55 Tribes to U.S. Society

Present Knowledge (Findings on Link Between Dependence of Male Child on Mother & Later Initiation Rites)	Questions to Ask About Our Own Society	Answers that Might Point to Comparable Phenomena in U.S. Society
1. Sex Role Differentiation: One infers that sex roles must have been sharply differentiated in many of the tribes studied.	In what groups are sex roles most sharply differentiated in U.S. society? blue-collar or white-collar? rich or poor? others?	The need for initiation rites will be greater where sex roles are more sharply differentiationed (i.e., among blue-collar workers, the poor, etc.).
2. Early Socialization: Because the early socialization of boys is undertaken by the opposite-sex parent (rather than by the father or other males), preparation is inadequate for male performance in a highly sex-differentiated society.	In what groups in our society do we find the most exposure of young males to the socializing influence of females?	In public school classes, where the young are predominantly exposed to female teachers (in contrast to private schools where men are better represented); in poor families for whom higher male mortality is exacerbated by industrial hazards that leave widows and children; among the poor, especially blacks whose deprivation in the past (aggravated by welfare policies barring aid to mothers and children with a husband present) has led to mother-centered families, etc.
3. Items 1 and 2 Combined: Where these two situations are combined, the male child's association with and extended dependency on females in groups whose adults perform in sex-differentiated roles, we find, at adolescence, ceremony (often violent) to assert identity, obligations, and rights as male.	In what groups do we find these two features in U.S. society? Do the urban, the poor, and blue-collar workers, and blacks engage in any activities in which they seem to assert their manhood? virility?	These two features might be expected chiefly among the poor, the blue-collar, the urban (since among the rural, the male child is likely to be trained in male work from early age), and blacks. ?

ers characterized by conflict of interest and by subordinate-dominant relationships (as did Collins, 1971). Simmel (1950) was a master of such a strategy by shifting from content to forms of social interaction.

Moving to higher levels of abstraction is easier if we define carefully what we mean by the key terms we are using. What do we mean by dependence? by initiation rites? (Here the etymology of words, as well as their technical and everyday usage, can be helpful. [4])

A third step would prompt us to ask: In what sectors of society, among what groups or categories are we likely to find these abstract characteristics exemplified? Among whom is boy-child dependence on females common? Among whom is violence ritualized or institutionalized? And with the answers to those questions, students are on their way to broader, deeper understanding. On rare occasions they may experience the exhilaration of an "Aha" moment. (Even Archimedes said "Eureka" only once.)

If such an ability to extend ideas is an important nonsubstantive goal, teachers may wish to build into their courses several exercises such as this. The talent of extension is too little cultivated through conventional modes of instruction. It is a talent that separates technician from scientist. For the scientist is, as Donald Hall once said of poets, both craftsman and madman. It is in such imaginative sorties (together with their disciplined assessment) that students can get some sense of the way sociology can illuminate our mundane activities.

The skill of extending is not only an intrinsic part of scientific work. It has very practical implications. It is probably especially important in rapidly changing societies. New situations engender new problems. Old knowledge may be inadequate, and the development of new knowledge may fall yet further behind what is desired and needed. Alvin Toffler, in *Future Shock* (1970), has suggested that in times when knowledge is quickly outdated, there is a premium on learning skills useful in meeting novel situations. We think it important that we help students develop and sharpen skills that will stand them in good stead long after the final grades are in. Our students will be faced, as we are, with the need for new facts or with new situations they wish to explain. Often they will have to reach conclusions, even render judgments, despite a lack of adequate information. Extension then becomes a critical intellectual skill. One useful form of extension is estimating.

Estimating: Extending What We Know to What We Don't Know

Estimating is a form of extending knowledge from the more surely to the less surely known. In our classroom experience with estimating, students discover that they know more than they thought they knew. Often the capacity for extending available knowledge has gone unused. Yet it is a skill that merits development. Practice in estimating is a way of making students' talents salient for them and a way of honing them for future use. Because it can strengthen students' self-image, estimating carries educationally useful rewards. Furthermore, it involves students actively in an unfolding detective story as additional bits of forgotten knowledge are invoked to help them move to a better answer.

The impetus to estimate often comes from someone's assertion, or from something read, that seems untenable. But if we are disposed to challenge, we are simultaneously deterred for lack of persuasive data. Now we mobilize skills of estimating to provide tentative answers and to evaluate the accuracy of the information at hand. Let us offer, now, four examples of this process, attempts to achieve a significant nonsubstantive goal.

An example of estimating: extent of unionization in North Carolina. During a class, the instructor had occasion to note the low rate of unionization in the South, compared to other regions in the United States, and added that in North Carolina there were very few union members. A student found this surprising: "I thought North Carolina had a large number of union members; in fact, I think I read that there were two million unionized workers in the state." The instructor did not know the numbers or rates for the state, but felt sure that two million was very far from the mark—and said so, gently. Let us see, the instructor suggested, whether we can make an intelligent estimate of number of union members in the state and whether that estimate comes close to two million. The discussion went something like this.

The population of North Carolina is about five million persons. Few people under age eighteen or over seventy are in the work force. Although we do not know the age distribution of the North Carolina population, we can estimate that 50 percent of the population is not age-eligible. So we have a probable upper-limit of 2.5 million unionized workers. Are all of the 2.5 million actually in the labor force? No. Housewives work, of course, but they are not part of the labor force as that term is currently used. Furthermore, there are others who, for one reason or another, do not seek paid work. We might estimate that perhaps a third of the age-eligible population of 2.5 million are outside the labor force. Hence we are left with about 1.7 million potential union members.

Noting that estimates had already dropped the figure below the initial contention that there were two million unionized workers in the state, the instructor asked students if they were now satisfied with the 1.7 million figure. Of course not, they answered: not all paid workers are union members. Who is not unionized? Students from the eastern part of the state didn't think any farmers in their region were unionized. Some from the Piedmont (central) section of the state said the same was true of textile mill, cigarette and furniture factory workers. Then the questions: Are these economic enterprises important in North Carolina? Do they employ many workers? The class believed this to be the case, and one student supplied a figure: about half of North Carolina's workers were in agricultural pursuits.

Other than farm, factory, and mill workers, are all others unionized? No responses. Other occupations or professions? Doctors aren't unionized, one student suggested. Other occupations were quickly added—teachers, merchants, garage and gas station owners, and so on. The class then reached agreement that perhaps four-fifths of paid workers in the state were nonunionized. This reduced the 1.7 million potential union members to 340,000—a far cry from the original figure of two million. Bureau of Labor Statistics data indicate that, in 1972, North Carolina had about 139,000 unionized workers.[5]

Starting with a known statistic, the approximate state population, the class exploited knowledge of the state, its population and economic base, together with some knowledge of U.S. society in general (for example, the sex ratio and who is typically in the labor force). It is true that the estimate was two-and-a-half times too large; yet it was much closer to the mark than the initial figure, which was fourteen times too great. (At the end of the exercise, students knew where to turn for an accurate answer.)

Obviously the product of such a procedure is not the true figure, and this reservation must be clear. Furthermore, students must be reminded that the accuracy of the estimate depends on the pertinence of the questions asked and the adequacy of the class's collective social knowledge. And knowledge of methods. Had the class considered only the Piedmont area, the location of the university, the estimate would have been farther off the mark than it was. For unionized occupations and firms are disproportionately in the Piedmont. Students did not know that, nor did they need to. But it was necessary for them to consider occupations found in all areas of the state. To do otherwise would have been overgeneralizing—extending from a part to the whole without knowing whether the case was representative. There was a sampling problem at issue. Overgeneralization is one of the potential pitfalls of estimating and extension, as well as of everyday thought.

After helping the class work through this estimate of union membership, the instructor went back over the process, making explicit what they had done and how it was done, identifying pitfalls and ways of avoiding them. Properly done, estimating is much more than guessing. Students are more likely to develop the skill if they review the process afterward, self-consciously and explicitly.

Using estimation in population research. Estimation is not only a lay skill; it is used in social science research. Here is an example, which we enter parenthetically. In their study *3000 Years of Urban Growth,* Chandler and Fox (1974) needed population data for as many 1,000+ cities as they could manage, and

this for the period 800 to 1850 A.D. But the desired urban population counts were available for only some of the cities of interest at various periods. Nonetheless, much else was known about the cities. For example, in many instances parish churches had been enumerated. Where the urban population was also known, there appeared to be a fairly constant relationship between churches and population. That ratio—say, 3,000 persons per church—could then be used to estimate city size where investigators knew only the number of churches.[6]

The usefulness of such a procedure stems from the fact that although population censuses have been rare, censuses or other records of militia members, priests, taxpaying units (hearth taxes), buildings, and the like are more common; and for some cities, such data, together with population size, are available. Accordingly, ratios can be generated and applied to produce population estimates.

Were one interested in illustrating the estimating procedure as employed by social scientists, one might present students with the problem, provide some raw data from which the solution could be constructed, and help students themselves to discover the estimating procedure. One would wish, also, to encourage students to think about limits to such a procedure. Could the multiplier of persons per parish be used in any time or place? If, instead of churches, we used the ratio of forts to population, or merchants, or graineries, would these be indefinitely useful? Students, of course, will see that the adequacy of an estimation procedure is time- and place-bound.

How many black physicians are there in the United States?: one method of estimation. In a class discussion of race differentials in health and health care, a student asked about the number of black physicians in the United States. The teacher's reply was: "I don't know; but I do know that the number of all physicians in the country is about one-third of a million. Perhaps we can make an estimate. Let me ask each of you to write down a specific figure—they won't be collected—stating the number of black doctors you think there are in the United States."[7] (It is useful to ask students to commit themselves on paper, even privately, for it extends their participation and their stake in the project. And it may increase the motivation to arrive at an estimate. The assumption is that motivation is, in part, a positive function of the level of participation. Motivation will also be enhanced because of seeing a clear reason for learning something.)

Then the teacher asked someone to volunteer an estimate and a reason for it, or a suggestion as to how to go about making an estimate. One student suggested that the number would be about 10 percent of the total number of physicians since roughly that percentage of Americans is black. The teacher wrote 33,000 on the chalkboard and asked if the class was content with that estimate. A second student said: "Well, blacks are discriminated against; the number will be lower than 33,000."

Teacher: How much lower?

Student 2: I'm not sure.

Teacher: Neither am I. Anyone else want to estimate how much lower? (No takers.)

Teacher: Okay—I doubt we can attach any numbers to discrimination until we specify the kinds of discrimination that would affect the creation, so to speak, of black doctors. What kinds of discrimination are of interest here?

Student 3: Medical schools that discriminate against blacks.

Student 4: Poor education in schools in black neighborhoods.

A minute's discussion generated the following list of factors affecting the production of physicians where racial discrimination might be present:

1. *Adverse home and neighborhood environments* can affect occupational choices, preparation for schooling, and support for various choices.

2. *Poor quality primary and secondary education* can reduce learning, create cumulative inequalities in learning, and perhaps result in less science education.

3. *Channeling in high schools* can turn black students away from higher education and professions, and lower their expectations.

4. *At the college level,* black students can be affected by channeling, lack of support, differential access to college (because of the need to earn money), and differential college performance (due to need to hold job while in school).

5. *Black students applying to medical school* can be affected by differential admissions policies and financial support availability.

The teacher then asked if anyone had empirical evidence that would allow assignment of a numerical value to these forms of discrimination and the degree to which they might reduce the number of black physicians in the United States. No one had such data, including the teacher. Discussion led students to agree that each form or stage of discrimination might make it twice as hard for a black youth to filter through to the next stage. The teacher reminded the class that such statements were, necessarily, highly speculative.

The class finally concluded that blacks would be underrepresented among physicians by a factor of 5; that is, that there would be one-fifth as many black M.D.s as there are white M.D.s, *after* taking the racial composition of the United States population into account. Twenty percent of 33,000 yielded 6,600, the class estimate of the number of black physicians in the nation.

At the teacher's request, a student brought to the next class session a recent edition of *Statistical Abstract of the United States*, which recorded the number of black physicians (in 1969) as 5,789.[8] Although the class estimate was 14 percent too high, it was reasonably close and certainly a far better datum than anyone had possessed when the question was first raised. During this second class, when the accurate figure was reported, the teacher asked whether the estimates of discrimination used by the class had been confirmed by the fact that the estimated number of doctors was rather close to the mark. Some students felt that this was the case. The instructor then asked whether it was possible that the numerical factors assigned to the impact of *some* forms of discrimination could be wrong and yet the final estimate of black physicians be correct. A few students quickly saw the point: if one factor had been overstated by 2 and one understated in the same amount, the answer could still be correct. The conclusion was quickly drawn that the final estimate did not validate the specific steps along the way because internal errors could cancel one another.

The teacher then pointed out that making estimates by employing an explicitly specified set of assumptions about society, and then checking for the accurate data *for each step*, allows us to find out where our perceptions or beliefs about that society are faulty and where they are accurate.

How many black physicians are there in the United States?: another method of estimation. In this case, the teacher asked the class to try to estimate the number of black physicians, but without knowledge of the total number of physicians in the United States. Using the same question-and-answer, challenge-and-response approach illustrated in the foregoing examples, the class arrived at an estimate of 6,300 black physicians. Table 6.4 lists the steps and calculations used in producing the estimate.

As we have seen, the *Statistical Abstract* (1975) put the correct figure of black physicians at 5,789. The estimate was, then, rather close—off by 9 percent. But why, students wanted to know, should the estimate be off? Here was a chance to help students discover several common sources of error.

First, we had rounded our figures to the nearest million and nearest whole percentage point. A few examples showed how large an error could be introduced by such rounding:

1. 39 percent of 23 million = 9 million (rounding off); but

2. 39.4 percent of 23.8 million = 9.4 million, a difference of 400,000.

Second, when students examined census tables, they found that some reported data for "Negroes" and others for "Negroes and other nonwhites." Third, although some tables were based on the population aged twenty-five to sixty-four, others reported data for persons sixteen and older. Finally, even if the data had been correct, the reasoning behind the categories and their order of introduction (column I,

Table 6.4 Steps Followed to Estimate the Number of Black Physicians in the United States

Step	Item	Class Estimate	Running Total
(1)	Total U.S. population	210 million	210 million
(2)	Black percentage of U.S. population	11%	23 million
(3)	Percentage of black population that is age-eligible to be an M.D. (defined as 25 to 64 years)	50%	11.5 million
(4)	Percentage of age-eligible black population in labor force	60%	6.9 million
(5)	Percentage of black labor force employed	91%	6.3 million
(6)	Percentage of blacks employed in professional and technical occupations	10%	630,000
(7)	Percentage of blacks in professional and technical occupations who are M.D.s	1%	6,300

"Step") could have been faulty. For example, the employment rate should have been that for physicians or at least for professional and technical workers (step 5).

So students learned something about the uses—and misuses—of data. They were pleased with most of their estimates, but were keenly aware of certain pitfalls: errors introduced by rounding; the larger the base, the larger the mistake generated by a small percentage error; and at least one judgment about U.S. society that was much off the mark—the percent of the black population between ages twenty-five and sixty-four, as revealed in the *Statistical Abstract*, was 39 percent rather than 50 percent.

Preparing an estimate of a social datum, making explicit the assumptions and calculations on which it is based, comparing these to the correct data, analyzing the sources of error—such a procedure helps students learn something of the shape of society. But it also works toward a nonsubstantive goal: the ability to exploit one's own knowledge, extending it to the realm of the unknown. In the process, students learn that they can do more with the data in their heads than they might have thought.

Reprise and Rationale

Nonsubstantive goals are critical in teaching sociology as part of a liberal arts education for undergraduates. For many sociology instructors, one such goal is enhanced skill in problem solving—i.e., in methods. Hence our aim in this chapter has been to raise questions and suggest options for teaching two aspects of methods, processes of *gaining* and *extending* knowledge.

We can help students sharpen their skills of inquiry by analyzing such a classic example as Durkheim's study of suicide; or by pursuing a current, garden-variety sort of question: Is advertising useless, as might be suggested by the alleged increase in smoking despite the ban on television ads? As they reflect on such experiences, students will be able to identify major aspects of the strategy of inquiry: perceiving the existence of a problem posed by differences in time or space, putting precise questions, developing tentative answers (theory), and contriving a scheme to test the adequacy of those answers. In the process, students can learn something about the multiplicity of causal influences, the need to control some variables while evaluating the influence of a suspected cause, the habit of checking first-blush inferences (two million more smokers means an increase in smoking), and the need to invent adequate indexes (smokers/population-at-risk).

We suspect that ability to extend knowledge is a skill too little cultivated in our classrooms. For to extend research findings to different populations or situations (from tribal initiation rites to rumbles in Manhattan), or to ransack unexploited knowledge to get a grip on the unknown—these processes extend the power of students' minds and gratify them in the process. Such enhanced skill is, for us, a compelling nonsubstantive goal. For all their lives our students will encounter assertions of alleged fact and causal imputations. From the editor's column, the politician's lectern, the cleric's pulpit, the bureaucrat's desk, and by friends and kin, they will be told this is the case, that is the cause, and this is what needs to be done. How will they handle these assertions, pertinent to their decisions as voters, employees, spouses, parents, taxpayers?

We hope that students' instruction in sociology will help them to react critically, intelligently. This they can better do if they are able to understand the process of inquiry, if they are able to extrapolate from past experience, if they can extend research findings, if they can tap their own considerable resources to invade the unknown, getting a better purchase on social reality.

Notes

1. Much of the research stimulated by Kurt Lewin, Ronald Lippitt, and Ralph White—the group-dynamics school of social psychology—posed similar questions about the democratization of decision-making processes. For one example, see Coch and French (1948); for citation to other work in that tradition, see Hare (1976:293ff).

2. The description of the Whiting, Kluckhohn, and Anthony (1958) research is adapted from Wilson (1971a:304–308, *passim*).

3. It would be well to raise these questions: How much can we rely on these findings? To what extent can we accept the theory, even if the findings are accurate? This would lead to the conclusion that different explanations may be compatible with the same findings. It's conceivable, for example, that mother-child dependency is a function of illness and that tribes having initiation rites are those in which nutrition is poor or sex-linked disease is high, resulting both in extended periods of mother-child intimacy and, having been isolated from ordinary male life (owing to illness), a quick catch-up induction called initiation.

In addition, the instructor can use such an example of social research to stress the sociologist's constant sense of sources of error. Thus the question, What are possible sources of error in this piece of research? would be an appropriate query. Students might recognize that data from the Human Relations Area Files are uneven in accuracy and wealth of detail, and that coding such data always involves the chance of error—as does every step in research procedure. (The HRAF, developed over the years at Yale, is an extensive and intricately coded collection of data from anthropologists' and others' reports on more than 250 tribes and societies around the world.)

4. Using etymology provides a possible link between the students' experience in your sociology class and what is happening in their English or foreign language courses.

5. In 1972, there were 139,000 union members in North Carolina; this was 7.5 percent of nonagricultural employment in the state. North Carolina ranked lowest among the states in unionized employment (the U.S. aver-

age was 27.2 percent in 1972). For the period under consideration, North Carolina had about one-half million agricultural workers. While the number of unionized agricultural workers for the states was not readily available, the *U.S. total* of unionized farm workers was about 39,000. North Carolina has a right-to-work law. These data were obtained from U.S. Bureau of the Census (1975b:tables 573, 605, 608).

6. It should be noted that the procedures employed by Chandler and Fox have been used by many other and earlier historical demographers.

7. At the end of 1973, there were 338,111 "active M.D.s" in the United States (not including more than 15,000 doctors of osteopathy). There were an additional 28,000 nonactive physicians. See U.S. Bureau of the Census (1975b:table 112).

8. The latest data reported in the *Statistical Abstract of the United States* (U.S. Bureau of the Census, 1975b:76) were for "Negro Physicians: 1969," and represented the membership of the National Medical Association (= 4,805). A headnote to the table indicates ". . . coverage estimated at 83 percent of total number of Negro Physicians." Hence the figure of 5,789 Negro physicians. According to the 1970 Census of Population, 2.0 percent of the 256,000 physicians in the United States were Negro; this equals just over 5,100 Negro physicians (U.S. Bureau of the Census, 1975b:361). This figure includes both medical and osteopathic doctors. The *Statistical Abstract* for 1978 does not present data on Negro or black physicians. It does note that Current Population Surveys for 1977 indicate that 9.2 percent of all medical and osteopathic physicians (N = 403,000) were "black or other" (U.S. Bureau of the Census, 1978:419). "Black or other refers to races other than white," and therefore includes Oriental and Hispanic physicians.

PART III
WHAT ARE THE MEANS
WE USE?

Stating goals clearly is a first step, a necessary one, if we are to achieve our ends. The second step is to devise means appropriate to the goals.

Wittingly or not, we all employ some means of instruction. Why do we use the methods we do? For most of us, most of the time, the answer probably lies in our experience as students. Later, under the considerable pressures of academic life, it is not surprising that we simply repeat familiar patterns.

Doubtless our experiences as students differed in degree. And we seem to differ, too, in the instructional modes we find most comfortable. One teacher savors the lively interaction of the small class; another is uneasy with it—indeed, may find it threatening. As Reece McGee (1974:219) writes:

> Even after 17 years of college teaching . . . I find myself incapable of handling well a small group. Other experienced academics . . . find themselves terrified to face my thousand-member classes and incapable of doing so effectively.

Once we find a pattern we are comfortable with, one we think effective, we stick with it. On occasion, changes in class size, or the teaching load, or the nature of the student population may prompt some modification of teaching pattern. Yet our investment in the style we have developed, together with the obstacles to altering that style, make for persistence in the model of the familiar past.

There *are* obstacles to change. In some schools, there is no reward for improved instructional design. In some, the effects may be punitive. Few faculty members can get released time or funding for course development. In their national survey, Bradshaw and McPherron (1977) found that only 4 percent of responding departments reported grants, released time, or other resources for developing the first course in sociology. (There was little variation by school type and size.)

Yet any change from past patterns is costly in time and effort. Under pressure of our current load, we sometimes must select, too hastily, important tools of instruction for next semester. Done appropriately, this would require a lengthy review of texts, reserve readings, offprints, and suitable journal pieces; reviews of films and videotapes; and a reconsideration of the format—lecture, discussion, exercises, demonstrations, fieldwork, laboratory work, and the like.

Although such constraints are very real and the fallback to traditional lecture-discussion (with teacher-talk dominating both) is understandable, this limited solution is not dictated. There is a growing literature on college instruction that suggests a rich range of instructional options appropriate to various conditions—including very large classes (see, for example, Davis, Goldsmid, and Perry, 1977; and Goldsmid and Goldsmid, 1979). By mid-1979, more than fifty articles had been published in easily available sources on techniques of teaching Introductory Sociology. Among these, for example, there were two articles describing tested methods that enable teachers to provide frequent, prompt, and *individualized* reactions to all students in large lecture classes—and at low cost (see our discussion of TIPS in chapters 12 and 13). Despite constraints, we sociology teachers have more options available to us than we often suppose.

Once we know the options, what then? Clearly, we must choose those means that best promise to help students reach our instructional goals. Even those limiting conditions that set bounds to the means we can employ—we discuss such bounds in chapter 7—will, in themselves, point to what we *can* do, as well as to what we can't do.

Conditions of instruction are set at many levels: current social conditions, legislation (state and federal), university and department patterns. And of course, some conditions impose themselves closer to the classroom. In chapter 8, we point to several common problems of instruction, some peculiar to the teaching of sociology, others quite general, but all affecting the means we use.

In chapter 9, we ask how we might more effectively employ two commonly used instructional tools—the syllabus and the text. We fix on these tools because of their importance and pervasive use. The syllabus is a blueprint for a course, an early and continuous communication to students. Other than the spoken word, the textbook is the most widely employed teaching tool in the sociologist's kit.

In chapter 10, we examine three course patterns: lectures, discussion, and personalized systems of instruction (PSI). We choose them because they contrast old and new, embody different patterns of communication (teacher-student, student-student), and vary in their effectiveness,

depending on the goal in view. Chapter 11 explores two means of vivifying the class session: examples and audiovisual aids.

With such a variety of means at our disposal, one might fear the onset of pedagogical indigestion. We must stress, therefore, the need for enlightened choice, the appropriate means for a given end. Furthermore, one may detect a general method that underlies all the means we will consider. That general method, which begins to be an operational statement of the persuasions recounted in chapter 3, entails such elements as the following:

1. Identify a problem whose solution promises to move the class toward achievement of the goal. Its source may be a student, the teacher, campus newspaper, other media, or text. Frame the problem as a researchable question.

2. Resist the temptation to provide the answer. Exposition can sometimes get in the way of learning.

3. Specify the personal and social significance of the problem and enable students to answer the question: Why should I care about this problem and its solution?

4. Specify the problem in operational (i.e., clearly defined) terms.

5. Determine what knowledge is available and what technical skills are needed to move toward a solution. What do students know or need to know, what can they do or need be able to do, to help solve the problem?

6. Involve students in the process of finding a solution: discussion, open commitment to the task, data gathering, and analysis. Tap the knowledge and skills students have. They know more than they realize, but less than is needed.

7. Use raw data when available—cases and documents, as well as statistical data.

8. Exploit other sociological resources—concepts, theories, findings from related studies, etc.

9. Evaluate the adequacy of the solution: How good is the evidence? What remains unclear or unknown? What do the deviant cases tell us?

10. Consider whether the findings can be extended to other populations and situations.

11. Draw parallels and provide practice with similar cases or problems and respond to students, evaluating their efforts.

12. Encourage reflection on the process, as well as the product—i.e., on the form of the inquiry, as well as the solution arrived at. The process may involve comparing attributes of groups or categories, searching for causal linkages, analyzing deviant cases, searching for data that would allow a test of a proposition, testing hypotheses deduced from a proposition, and the like.

Obviously, such a teaching strategy must be adapted to particular situations. Time available will affect the balance of teacher and student contributions, and the extent to which inquiry can unfold through Socratic interchange. And the weight accorded any one of these injunctions will differ, depending on the teaching goal. (We would disregard element 2 if the goal is command of twenty-five facts. Then we might simply rely on the text, or provide flash cards, or issue a dittoed handout with the matters to be memorized.)

It may be well to keep in mind such a general strategy as we discuss specific methods, the tactics of teaching, in chapters 9 through 11. We reserve to chapter 12 a review of the evidence on their differing effectiveness. Beyond the pertinent empirical research, this chapter also presents a theory of learning that can aid us in selecting and using various methods of instruction. It also sketches the contribution of sociological research to our knowledge of effective instruction, and compares sociology and other subject matters as to what we know about teaching.

These are the issues treated in part III, the means we use and their outcomes in student learning.

CHAPTER 7
CONSTRAINTS ON THE MEANS

Cultural legacy and social circumstance limit all forms of behavior. Teaching is no exception. There is no social system, such as that of the classroom, that is not embedded in another or intersected by others. More than most people, social scientists are sensitive to the nesting and intersection of social systems that shape the structure and activities of such a small, embedded system as a classroom group.* In chapter 1 we noted the effect of the post–World War II baby boom, the war in Vietnam, and the access of federal funding of sociological research. What goes on in the classroom is affected by actions of legislatures, state and federal, and, from the past, by the school's mission, dictated by its peculiar tradition. The means and ends of classroom conduct are shaped, too, by the school's administration, by faculty legislation, by the field in which faculty are trained, and by the nature of the student body.

These are some of the influences, both restricting and enabling, that we need to take into account in understanding what we can and can't do in the classroom. Yet the stress should not be wholly on constraint. If freedom is the space formed by bounding walls, the walls themselves define our options, point to the possibilities. So in this chapter we remind ourselves of the typical conditions that bound our teaching task—and the choices indicated by those boundaries.

* See, for example, Dreeben (1970), Lortie (1973, 1975), and Schlechty (1976).

The Bounding Walls: Influences on Sociology Instruction

Circles of Influence, Events in Space

One might suppose that the outermost set of forces shaping sociology instruction would be defined by national boundaries. Not so, of course. We need only recall Russia's Sputnik or the aberration in Vietnam to sharpen our sense of the global impact on our classrooms. External threat engenders internal adjustments. When Sputnik went into orbit, schools at every level across the country were enjoined to sharpen their efforts at technical education. Later, with Vietnam, professors faced some students for whom campus was a sanctuary from conscription in an evil cause and others for whom campus was chiefly a base for political action. Warfare on the far side of the globe altered the composition of sociology classrooms and, therefore, altered problems of instruction.

National Influences

Sociologists enjoyed a sellers' market between 1945 and 1970. In this yeasty period, higher education was a growth industry in the United States. In 1930, 1960, and 1972, college and university enrollments were 1.1, 3.2, and 7.8 million, respectively. At the same time, government grew and foundations flourished, amplifying the effect of growing enrollments by providing employment and consulting opportunities for sociologists. Faculty became remarkably mobile, sociologists more than most. Academic teams bought and traded players (see Caplow and McGee, 1958). There were two principal organizational effects: the spread of common patterns (standardization) and the internal proliferation of programs (education conglomerates). With a free osmotic flow through organizational membranes, identifying boundaries were no longer so clear. And with institutes, centers, and projects of a dozen varieties, it was sometimes hard to know what this beast was. Indeed, each of the blind men from Hindustan would be right: the creature became a rope, a snake, a wall, a tree—more than it was elephant (see Wilson, 1968:135–6).

These societal influences had contrary effects for sociologists. On the one hand, they created alternate—for some, preferred—routes to reputation and rewards. The effect was to depreciate the teacher's role. Keeping the shop at home, the teacher was a local. The teacher's consulting, leave-taking colleague was the cosmopolitan who touched base in the classroom when more telling duties permitted.* Effective teaching was also compromised to the extent that mobile sociologists failed to adapt to, or exploit, the experiences of differing student populations. A third likelihood is that the conglomerate aspect of the larger campuses separated fields from one another and worked against the mutually fructifying liberal arts experience that characterized the smaller, traditional colleges.

On the other hand, the growth and spread of sociology during these years doubtless helped to raise standards of instruction where performance had been parochially protected at inadequate levels.

* Here we borrow terms from Merton (1957:chapter X).

The Influence of the Field on Its Practitioners

Another of the broader influences on sociology instruction is that of the discipline itself. It tells us what class of phenomena we investigate, what sorts of problems we pose, and what kinds of solutions we seek. Instructors are not free to run encounter groups or to push utopian schemes. Their field constrains sociologists to try to describe accurately various social arrangements and to explain their sources and consequences. This is the domain they have been trained to explore. Outside that realm, the sociologist is to some degree a pretender and cannot claim the right to guide students or exact of them compliance to personal demands. Students are protected, presumably, by the accurately defined boundaries of the sociologist's competence.

For a sociologist, the role of instructor is also constrained insofar as we believe our own doctrine. Sociologists study professions. Such studies apply equally to the professing of sociology. The professorial role may vary along several dimensions, and certain values on each of those dimensions point to ways that we *should* act.*

One such dimension describes behavior that ranges from the treatment of another as a unique and special person to actions that treat that person as a member of a category. When an instructor shies away from having a son or daughter in class, the choice is to emphasize the universal rather than the particularistic elements of the teacher-student relationship. One would not wish others to infer favoritism. Universal standards must be set to ensure correct assessment of performance and to rule out any special treat-

* Here Parsons (1951) is our guide.

ment. Hence, as an example, the anonymous grading of papers.

A related scale of conduct is that which ranges from instructor reactions based solely on students' demonstrated achievements to reactions prompted by attributes ascribed to students because of sex or race or religion. Sociology instructors are constrained to react in accordance with the achievements of their charges, disregarding inherited and adventitious traits irrelevant, in themselves, to mastery of course material.

Again, we are limited largely to the matter at hand: instruction in sociology. We have no call to *intrude* in the broad range of interests, activities, and convictions that describe each student. Our proper concern is with the student as explorer in sociology, not as lover, or political ally, or serf in the service of our research. The relationship is a specific one, not diffuse.

Nor is the relationship to be heavily invested with emotion. This is a difficult constraint. For if love and hate must impede the proper job of instruction, a deep concern for the student's intellectual development is an essential part of our relationship. In this, as in the other dimensions of the instructor's role, we sometimes walk a tightrope with an abyss on either side.

The Influence of Different Student Populations

Scribing a smaller circle, we come to the campus where student populations, differing in backgrounds and probable destinations, set conditions for effective instruction. We wrote in chapter 3 that "we do not know what we are saying to students unless we can respond to our utterances as they will. But we cannot know how others will respond except as we know something of the experiences that have shaped their lives and will shape their responses." It makes a difference to teach in a school where almost all the students are from within the state. (For example, University of North Carolina–Chapel Hill gets 85 percent of its students from North Carolina. Oberlin College gets 85 percent from outside Ohio.) It makes a difference whether the student population is urban, suburban, rural, or small town. Here is an assistant professor of sociology speaking at the Montreal ASA meetings: "Most of the students in my classes come from farms or ranches. Central Washington State is located in the middle of vast wheat fields—and I teach urban sociology. Now what do I do?" It makes a difference whether students come from white- or blue-collar families, whether they have had military experience, whether they are married or single, older or younger, predominantly male or female.

Ignorance of the attributes peculiar to a student population both reduces an instructor's ability to communicate and precludes the use of local data that would heighten interest and motivation. Thus we widen the gulf between instructor and student only to find, *mirabile dictu*, that students do not respond. We then conclude that they are inept or retarded. One of our graduate student instructors wrote to this point in his final paper for a course on Problems of Instruction in Sociology.

> I realized that the role of the social scientist, as commonly practiced in the U.S. today, is in many ways one of the roles farthest away from that of a North Carolina 20 year old. We are in the same position as The Ugly American at an embassy or corporation in southeast Asia. We speak a different language, have a generally disdainful view of the local population; feel they need to be enlightened, but, when this fails, we readily revert to biological explanations such as low I.Q. . . . We are ignorant of [their] local

history and even geography. . . . And what is worse, there does not seem to be much in the structure of our situation that would encourage us to break the vicious circle. An especially disturbing thing for me is the degree to which we as sociologists fail to analyze our own situation sociologically. When it comes to our experiences, we are just as naive as the silent majority: we psychoanalyze.[1]

Different student populations pose different problems, problems of effective communication and pedagogy. This is so not only because of background and preparation. It is also so because of different destinations. For example, a 1971 study of 21,000 college students, reported by the Educational Testing Service, found that a larger proportion of black than white seniors planned on working toward a doctorate. (The figures were 18 and 14 percent, respectively. See *New York Times,* 1973:16.) Sex differentials persist, the ETS study found. Women of the senior class did not plan to go to graduate or professional schools to the same extent as did men of the senior class. Among women who did expect to do graduate work, a third were planning on going into education. And about 10 percent fewer women than men planned to go into law or medicine. Yet women made better academic records. (The *Times* article, 1973:16, reported that "almost as many men with C+ or lower grade averages planned to pursue doctorates as women with B+ or A averages.") The ETS report speculated that women have less self-confidence than men and get less encouragement from friends and relatives to do advanced work. Such encouragement appeared to be the greatest influence on a senior's plans for graduate work. (As to religion, the *Times,* 1973:16, reported: "Jews were more likely than seniors of any other religious group to be planning on graduate studies, and a

Jewish senior was more likely to be entering law or medical school than was a Protestant or Roman Catholic student.")

Such evidence suggests that the makeup of a student population makes a difference in performance and in aspiration, qualities that effective instructors take into account. For if professionalism requires adherence to the criterion of achievement, competent instructors must nonetheless take into account the ascriptive stereotypes imposed on some of their students. Thus, on the basis of such data, instructors will make special efforts to encourage senior women to rule out no option indicated by superior performance. And they will capitalize on the drive or motivation of any group spurred by discrimination to compensatory achievement. Student populations requiring special planning and performance are those found in the community college. (This is the setting in which 35 percent of all students taking elementary sociology are taught.) Their enrollments, according to Lombardi (1972:8–11) mounted to 2.4 million. Among eighteen- and nineteen-year-olds, he predicted that 70 percent would be attending such schools by 1980 (the figure is now more than half). Such colleges offer the first two years of the baccalaureate. Some students then transfer to four-year colleges. Others take a terminal two-year degree. And others are older people served by the community college's adult education program. Diverse goals and a heterogeneous student population, often from backgrounds quite different from the instructor's, make instructional problems quite different from those of the conventional four-year college. The teacher must build bridges to varied and unfamiliar backgrounds, become a participant, observe in the community, invoke new examples, devise new exercises, select new readings.

The Influence of Role Requirements

Constraints are inevitably imposed by the sociology instructor's counter-demanding roles. Three such roles are research, teaching, and service. These are the conventional demands placed on the teacher, those in which one's performance is expected to meet certain poorly measured standards if one is to be promoted. (Actually, research is often evaluated with some precision. But adequacy of teaching and significance of service are often very poorly assessed.)* Clearly, the demands of research (or teaching, or service) may devour the time available for the other two activities. (It is equally clear that one could reduce the tension of these counter-demanding roles by increasing their overlap.)

Each of these roles has its peculiar requirements. For example, as to service, the professor is expected to be a good citizen in the department and in the larger arena of the college or university. But service does not stop there. One is expected to support and promote the work of the American Sociological Association, or the American Population Association, or the Society for the Scientific Study of Religion or. . . .

Research, it is assumed, is a continuing activity whose product is to be seen in two to four publications a year, preferably in refereed journals, the referees' judgments serving as one guarantee of the quality of the work. Furthermore, journals are ranked; one acquires more merit by publishing in *American Sociological Review, American Journal of Sociology,* or *Social Forces* than in certain other journals. Books or monographs may be the equivalent of, say, eight journal papers. These will be the role requirements at major uni-

versity departments of sociology, precious of their prestige. Although such requirements are not common at most schools, there is a tendency to stress some evidence of scholarship as one sign of competent instruction.

Teaching is circumscribed in many ways, including regulations imposed on the role by faculty themselves. Here are some examples of faculty-imposed rules within which the sociologists at one school must work:

1. A final examination is required, administered according to a schedule posted by an administrative officer. This is a faculty regulation devised to ensure that students are treated fairly.

2. Within one week (five class days) preceding the regular final examination period, no instructor shall give a quiz or assign a paper that is not part or the equivalent of a current daily recitation.

3. Regular class attendance is a student obligation. . . . Instructors will keep attendance records in all cases. If a student misses three consecutive class meetings, or misses more classes than the instructor deems advisable, the instructor will report the facts to the student's academic dean for appropriate action.

4. Responsibilities of the faculty in relation to the Honor Code [are] . . . to inform students at the beginning of each course and at other appropriate times that the Honor Code . . . is in effect . . . to identify clearly in advance of any examination or other graded work, the books, notes or other materials which may (alone) be used. . . . to require each student to sign a pledge, when appropriate, that the student has neither given nor received unauthorized aid . . . etc.

These are but a few examples of rules that stipulate how sociology instructors (and their colleagues) must conduct themselves. In addition, there are extensive rules governing the organization of the faculty and

* See chapter 14.

the procedures for writing the rules themselves.

This is, of course, a minimum statement of the constraints entailed by the sociology instructor's role set. Further constraints are imposed as spouse and parent, as communicant, as citizen in the wider community. And they are imposed with special force on the young teacher. It is one of the ironies of academic life that the most is often required of those who have the least—heavier teaching loads, more committee work, the expectation of significant research, and all at the time of lowest income, least experience, and, often, heavy family obligations.

Students, too, have competing demands; and these set serious limits on the time, interest, and commitment that instructors can exact of their students. Often teachers are unaware of such countervailing influences that condition students' work in a given class. This is a pity; for to know of them is not only to recognize the limits imposed on one's work, but also to identify circumstances that can lend pertinence and immediacy to the teaching of sociology.

What influences typically affect students' work and therefore, indirectly, qualify the teacher's effectiveness? To answer that question we asked students what striking things had occurred in their lives during the preceding three months. (Our questionnaire acknowledged that we knew little about important events in our students' lives and suggested that we could be better teachers if, sometimes, we could bring our work to bear on matters that meant much to them.)

We asked 326 students at eight schools to list the important things (not course-connected) that had happened to them, things that had taken their time and attention and concern over the preceding three months. The instrument used appears here as exhibit 7.1. The frequency (percent) with which students listed certain types of concerns is reported in table 7.1.

For these students, it seems clear that our questionnaire items 1, 2, 5, and, to a lesser extent, 4 and 3, picked up experiences that were salient and often gripping. These items relate to the immediate network of students' relationships, and to

Table 7.1 Percent of 326 College and University Students Reporting a Preoccupying Concern in Their Lives Occurring in the Preceding Three Months

Item* Number	State University A (N = 112)	Community College A (N = 21)	State University B (N = 32)	Private Liberal Arts College A (N = 40)	Community College B (N = 11)	Private Liberal Arts College B (N = 52)	Private Liberal Arts College C (N = 23)	State College (N = 35)	Total (N = 326)
1.	72%	95%	91%	87%	100%	75%	87%	83%	75%
2.	87	86	84	95	100	81	91	83	82
3.	57	71	53	38	45	27	43	57	44
4.	32	71	75	45	91	40	48	60	43
5.	53	81	81	67	73	71	87	69	62
6.	12	24	34	25	27	23	30	31	21
7.	42	43	66	47	54	35	43	31	30
8.	26	48	41	20	64	36	43	23	29
9.	11	86	63	60	73	35	70	63	37

* For the wording of the items, see the questionnaire, reproduced as exhibit 7.1.

problems of faith and work. The following responses point to circumstances that must have affected students' academic work. (Here we ignore the variation among schools in responses to different items. Given that we used a sample of convenience, these data can only be suggestive.)

Responding to Item 1—*Family-related experiences* (*with parents, brothers, sisters,*

Exhibit 7.1 Nonacademic Experiences Affecting the College/University Student

To the student:

We need your help as we try to improve college and university instruction. One way of doing this is to know better the persons being taught. Students can be known, in part, by what's important to them. What preoccupies them? What's on their minds—and in their hearts?

And so we are asking you to list the important things (NOT course-connected) that have happened to you, things that have taken your time and attention and concern, over the course of the *last three months.*

List only those experiences that have made major claims on your time, thoughts, feelings, and concerns.

To jog your memory we have listed a few relationships that might have moved you, significantly, some time during this period. Just a phrase or a sentence will be enough to describe the event or circumstance. For example: "My mother died." Or: "I broke off a love relationship with my boyfriend."

Responses are anonymous, of course. Your experiences will be grouped with those of all others to get a picture of nonacademic experiences that figure significantly in students' lives.

We thank you for your help.
—Professors Charles A. Goldsmid and
Everett K. Wilson

*   *   *   *   *

1. Family-related experiences (with parents, brothers, sisters, relatives): marriages, deaths, births, quarrels, conflicts _____

2. Experiences with friends and lovers, euphoric and disturbing _____

3. Experiences with employers and fellow workers _____

   a. (If you have a job, how many hours/week do you spend on the job?)_____
   b. (If you have a job, what's the nature of the work?) _____

4. Religious experiences/ideas _____

5. Experiences with roommates, fellow students, close friends _____

6. Political action or other causes _____

7. Experiences with drugs, including alcohol _____

8. Illnesses, accidents _____

9. Other_____
   (Please use reverse side of sheet for additional comments.)

relatives): *marriages, deaths, births, quarrels, conflicts*—these are examples of some moving experiences:

> Separation considered by my parents. . . .
> Parents learned brother smoked pot very regularly. . . . Parents considered divorce, father is alcoholic, sister unhappy in school. . . . Financial crisis—my father went bankrupt. . . . My mother has an alcohol problem. . . . God healed my father of terminal cancer. . . . Money quarrels with parents. . . . I was divorced in the last three months. . . . Separation from husband. . . . Problems with child support, and paying bills in general. . . . Wife filed for divorce, demands custody of both children. . . . There have been quarrels between my family and I (sic) particularly with my father. He disowned me again. I'm wondering when he'll grow up. . . . Coping with 3 children by myself—bigger they get, the bigger the problem, skipping school while I'm in classes. . . . My brother threw me against the wall yesterday. . . . Reconciliation with husband after two year separation. . . .

Along with Item 1, Item 2— *Experiences with friends and lovers, euphoric and disturbing*—most often elicited a response from these students. Except for the community college students, many of whom were older and married, responses to this item turned on friendships, chiefly boy-girl. Between 15 and 25 percent reported the breaking of relationships. Obviously these dyads were quite fragile. Here are some examples:

> Still in love with the same guy. (Last semester I had an abortion: This is still being kept from my parents and friends.) . . . My roommate's boyfriend moved in with us. . . . I fell in love with Jesus Christ and I spent a lot of time with Him. . . . My boyfriend and I have been having some hard times. . . . Was dumped by the girl I was dating for a high school sweetheart. . . . Huge fight with a very close and dear friend. I wrote him a nasty note as a result.

> . . . Just started dating a girl at home 200 miles away. Go home often. . . . Lied to a friend and now she's not talking to me. . . . My roommate has had an abortion. . . . Have begun a new love relationship in past 2 months—takes a lot of time and feeling. . . . Living in the ♀ collective—taken much time and been euphoric. . . . Returned to husband after 11 year separation. . . . I broke off with a loved boyfriend which took up 75% of my time in depression, sadness now anger. . . . My friend is mentally ill and I had to deal with her. . . . My husband and I reconciled and are trying to make our marriage work. . . .

Item 5 asked about experiences with roommates, close friends, and other students. Students responded with remarks such as these:

> Conflict with roommate, not speaking to her at all. . . . I've had a chance to share Christian experiences with three friends. . . . One of my roommates was pregnant and miscarried. . . . One roommate eats all my food. . . . Every now and then I reach a peak from pressure of living with many people, then things cool off again. . . . Mistrust of roommate, things of mine missing. . . .

Relationships with parents and peers, especially opposite-sex peers, seem to dominate students' affective concerns. Events in other institutional spheres, beyond the family, are less preoccupying. About four out of ten reported events bearing on work; and the same was true of religion. But political matters or causes seem to have involved only two in ten. A crude first guess at extent of impact, by institutional sphere, would put family-related events, religion and economy, then politics at eight, four, and two (students out of ten), respectively. As table 7.1 indicates, the weight of influence of these spheres differs by type of school. The following responses give an impression of matters economic, religious, and political that contend, for attention, with affairs of the classroom:

> I'm having no luck in finding a job. . . . I work approximately 25 hours/week Juvenile Detention, as child care worker. . . . Had a fight at the bank I worked at, quit the job. . . . One of my fellow workers writes music and he got me very interested in it. . . . Work with the fire department, really enjoy the people. . . . Joyful, fulfilling (student cook). . . . My food service boss is an ass, but my fellow worker and I have become good friends. . . . Watched fellow worker be abusive to a retarded person. . . .

> Have become closer to God since the death of my father (which occurred this semester). . . . I'm trying to find inner peace with myself and get closer to God. . . . I have found that a lot of the pressures of school have brought me closer to my church. . . . Have doubts. . . . Became very religious for short time, aroused much dissonance with life style I formally (sic) lived. . . . I do not believe in religion. . . . My faith is important to me, but I feel I'm not doing the proper things. . . . I have changed from a devout Catholic to an Agnostic. . . . I am a Zionist—will work at a Zionist youth camp this summer. . . . Probably the biggest of my learning experiences is that I have accepted Christ during my freshman year. . . .

> The demonstration here last week; save the whales, environmental concern. . . . Racial upheaval on campus. . . . Very upset about paraquat spraying of marihuana. . . . I don't fool around with politics. . . . Heavily involved in Bill Fitzgerald for governor campaign. . . . Government belongs to the rich and powerful (I am neither). . . . Assisted in campaigns for Mayor and Congressman. . . . Increased interest in feminist issues. . . . Wrote an appeal letter for Amnesty International. . . . The college's investments in S. Africa have been a big concern with me. . . . Uptight about possibility of Jesse Helms winning again. . . .

We report these examples of students' responses to convey some sense of the preoccupations that affect their learning. It is important to remind ourselves that a course in sociology is but one experience, often a minor one, in those intersecting circles that define a student's life. These other concerns compete with sociology for attention. They shape—sometimes distort—the meaning of the student's work in sociology. But when we recognize these possible constraints, we can exploit them in the service of instruction, sharpening the impact of ideas and promoting retention. Let us put these matters as a set of propositions:

1. A course experience always occurs in a context that affects learning.

2. To be unaware of the texture of student life is to impose serious limits on our teaching.

   a. For we communicate less effectively when we are oblivious of the fact that the ideas we offer are filtered through the mesh of student experience, an experience that may not admit or may distort the proffered ideas. Thus, for example, the student's rural, Republican, privileged, and Protestant background may lead to an overly individualistic view that rejects the likelihood of structural influences.

   b. And we miss the possibility of exploiting salient, extraclass experience in the service of instruction. Thus students from nursing school or those with military service can provide experience with a sharply etched pattern of rank, prestige, and pay differentials useful in treating problems of stratification.

3. Failure to exploit salient events in students' lives prevents those students from linking the new and abstract with the familiar and concrete. Students fail to discover, then, how to use their own social realities as springboards to other social patterns and thus achieve tentative generalizations that illuminate a wider range of social life.

The picture we offer is a field of action in which the sociology instructor's role is affected by successive circles of influence—society-wide or national influences, the influence of the field itself, the influences of different student populations, the role requirements that tug at professors' lives, and student concerns that challenge academic priorities.

Sequences of Influences: Events in Time

Differences in time, as well as space, generate problems and solutions that affect sociology instruction. Publishers now enjoin sociologists writing texts to devote a number of pages to the women's liberation movement and gender roles. So movements, changing through time, affect sociology instruction.

The civil rights movement is a case in point. It brought with it belated efforts to equalize educational opportunities for blacks. Open admission programs in the City University of New York entailed deep disruption for instructors. Customary teaching patterns suited to highly motivated whites enjoying easy access to the professions were inappropriate for blacks with poor secondary school training, low motivation, and profound skepticism about their prospects under whitey's domination. Poor preparation shifted pedagogy from substance to elementary skills. The change was emotionally as well as intellectually unsettling to the extent that some teachers felt their careers were shattered. To a much lesser extent, the women's movement has altered some traditional, segregated campus patterns. In sociology this movement, as in the case of the civil rights movement, has opened the curriculum to new minority studies.[2]

But aside from movements and changing times, there are two other temporal influences on sociology instruction that are recurrent and serious. Both serve to render instruction less adequate. One is the increasing gap between instructors and developments in their field generated by younger colleagues. The other is the increasing gap between instructors' experiences (and the language in which they are expressed) and those of their students.

We have long known that the growth of culture is virtually limitless. It is also almost immortal; and the larger its base, the greater its potential growth. One instance of its growth is seen in the exponential development of sociology and its sundry subfields. In human ecology and demography, in urban studies, in the sociology of medical organization, of religion, and of education, in the sociology of science, of deviance, stratification, and power, in methodology and other branches—in all of these areas developments are so rapid and so highly technical that one's knowledge at the time of the Ph.D. is obsolete in fifteen or fewer years.

Time puts distance, and impediments to communication, between instructors and their successive cohorts of students. As we will note in the next chapter, the experience and examples that relate propositions to empirical reality change through time. Sociologists still at work knew the novelty of radio, hunger in the depression, the impact of December 7, 1941, McCarthyism in the fifties, and man-made satellites first lofted into space. None of these experiences, so vivid to older teachers, can mean as much to their students.

The gap between generations is always there, of course. But the more rapid the rate of change and the more vivid the experience of one party, not shared by the other, the greater the pedagogical problem. We *can* experience vicariously, if new data and ideas are not so strange as to preclude a link with analogous past experience. But effective teaching requires communication; and in the end, *communication* rests on some *community* of experience.

Some Options Suggested by the Constraints

Walls that bound define the space to move in. Sometimes constraints stimulate inventions (sometimes circumventions). Consider certain possibilities linked to the constraints we have just sketched.

Options Related to the Impact of International and National Events on Education

If Israel, Vietnam, and Iran affect research and teaching, or if Senator Proxmire and his Golden Fleece Award[3] and national funding for HEW, NIH, DOT, and the census affect our work, then surely these are linkages that help students learn the meaning of a social system. A chief aim of undergraduate sociology instruction is to help students discover hidden connections among classes of social phenomena. Thus these constraining influences need to be uncovered. We can raise questions about the meaning to the military establishment of an alleged external threat, of the military to the labor force and the economy, of the economy on the status of women, blacks, and other minorities— and we can raise questions about the effects of all this on the classroom where we do our work. A study of OPEC and the network of influence spread by these countries' investments, or of UNESCO, or of the International Monetary Fund, or of the investments of Chase Manhattan and the

ripple of their influence to students' communities, families, and the classroom door, turn the existence of networks of influence into tools of instruction.

The expansion of higher education in past decades, federal agencies' need and support of sociological inquiry, the seller's market in sociology—these developments both spread the faith and cheapened its transmission. Yet both of these outcomes exerted a strain for better sociology instruction, eventuating in such efforts as those of the ASA's Section on Undergraduate Education and the ASA Projects on Teaching Undergraduate Sociology.[4] What needed to be done stemmed directly from limitations imposed by sociology's success in the undergraduate curriculum. Class sizes soared to the hundreds. Students' heterogeneity of background posed vexing problems. Both problems led to a range of solutions. For the problem of size, solutions involved more careful planning, more paper work, more objective (i.e., machine scored) tests with test items tested for level of difficulty and discriminating power, more use of student aides, more devices such as the Teaching Information Processing System (TIPS),* more taped lectures, more self-instructional units, more closed-circuit television, and the like.

Problems of heterogeneity were attacked by running parallel courses differentiated by students' pretest scores, by academic major (business administration, nursing, premed, and the like), or vocational destination. Sometimes students in a large course would meet together, once or twice a week, for lectures on generic issues, but meet in differentiated and more homogeneous sections for other work. Sometimes a class would be broken into parts, with each part homogeneous on

---

* TIPS is discussed in chapter 13.

some relevant trait and rotating between in-class time and out-of-class assignments. Possibilities included such variations on the theme as those represented in table 7.2. Each design reduces the size of the working group and increases its homogeneity. Each requires careful and imaginative planning. But each design holds the potential for a more varied set of experiences and a more active role in learning.

Options Related to the Constraints Imposed by Professionalism

We spoke earlier of the implications of Parsons's pattern variables for performance as sociology instructors. To agree with such a definition of the role is to accept restrictions that must sometimes seem severe. We must wonder what concrete procedures would enable one to achieve the balance between a warm heart and a hard head; between taking account of ascribed traits, but evaluating on the basis of achievement; between a profes-

sional task-orientation and a human concern for other matters; between the impersonal application of universal standards and the particular aspects of some teacher-student relationships.

The constraints themselves suggest some answers. It is better that course goals and tasks lie outside the teacher-student relationship. They are specified in the syllabus, before the relationship is formed; and both student and instructor are bound to work toward those ends. It is better that assignments be imposed by the nature of the task, the problems to be solved, than be imposed (as it might seem) by the whim of the instructor. It is better that the instructor work as collaborator with the student in winning through to a solution than perform as taskmaster, monitoring the student's awkward fumbling toward solutions. It is better that successes and failures be dictated by the nature of the task and that the final evaluation of performance be in the hands of someone other than the instructor—an outside examiner, ETS, or a departmental testing office assessing performance in all departmentally required courses. These are some solutions

Table 7.2 Scheme for Handling Large, Heterogeneous Classes through Subdivided, More Homogeneous Work Groups

	A Class Divided into Three Sections								
	M	W	F	M	W	F	M	W	F
In-class Session	1			2			3		
Differentiated Laboratory or Fieldwork		2	3		1	3		1	2
	A Class Divided into Two Sections								
	M	W	F	M	W	F	M	W	F
In-class Session	1	2	1	2	1	2	1 . . .		
Differentiated Laboratory or Fieldwork	2	1	2	1	2	1	2 .	1 . . .	

for the limitations imposed when the instructor's role is defined by recourse to the pattern variables. (If the surrounding walls are built by Parsons, the space for movement within them is revealed by Simmel!)

Options Related to Differing Student Populations

Means of effective communication will vary from one student group to another depending on where they come from and where they are going. Hence the injunction: get acquainted, and do so in such a systematic way that issues and data bearing on students' backgrounds and aspirations can be exploited in the service of their learning sociology.

We think it well to get such data in two or more stages. During the first week, a questionnaire should gather data largely descriptive: sex, size and place of residence, previous places of residence (if, at some point, migration is to be a variable), number of siblings, religious identification, parental occupation, and the like. Summaries of the aggregated data returned to the class and compared with comparable findings for community, state, or nation will show how such findings can be used to yield more knowledge and advance our understanding.

Later, more sensitive data can be garnered, not only for description but also for explanation. Such data will allow, for example, testing of the null hypothesis that religious fundamentalism is not associated with antiunion attitudes. After the initial reassurance, students will be more amenable to providing information that might, for example, link parental income or occupation with students' vocational aspirations.

Options Related to Boundaries Imposed by the Role Set

Our experience with constraints imposed by college faculty legislation—most regulations are faculty-imposed, rather than administration-imposed—suggests that the rules are badly understood, indifferently obeyed, yet constitute a nebulous set of prohibitions thought to prevent departures from conventional patterns of instruction. But almost everywhere there is great latitude for new departures in teaching. True, conventional patterns may pose problems. For example, the instructor setting aside a reading period must take care lest the time released from class be swallowed up in work for colleagues' classes. (One solution is to ask students to create some product, preferably by successive increments, throughout the reading period.)

We suspect that it is chiefly our experience and imagination that set needless limits. There are possibilities of participant-observation and other sorts of fieldwork. Small exercises in survey research are possible. If the instructor thinks a summer session schedule of five long meetings each week is trying for all concerned, there is nothing to prevent such a schedule as this: lecture on Monday, laboratory exercises on Tuesday, lecture on Wednesday, seminar for half the class on Thursday and for the other half on Friday. (Released class time is, of course, devoted to other class-related work.) Nothing stands in the way of a unit of self-paced self-instruction except the time to prepare it and the ingenuity to do it well. Trade-offs among instructors enable each instructor to add a change of face and pace to the instructional diet. Part or all of the course may be fitted to modules, each under the direction of a different teacher. Some classes might be devoted to a single research problem—for any inquiry, however narrow in its initial conception, can reach out to span a world of social implications. A course in Methods might join another course, such as the Sociology of Education, to collaborate in significant research (which is precisely what Arlie Hochschild and David Nasatir did at the University of California at Berkeley). Or, a course may be built to do a consultant's job, searching out answers to aid the work of a state or city agency (which is precisely how one or more of Vaughn Grisham's courses were designed at the University of Mississippi).

This bears on the matter of the teacher's role set with its competing demands of teaching, research, and service, each pressing its claim on mind and time. In the rare situation in which the same activity can meet all three demands, we have the best of all worlds. But the rarity of such a scheme does not stem from intrinsically insuperable odds. There is no reason why, for instructor as well as students, a course should not reflect the knowledge-seeking, knowledge-building nature of the field of sociology. We see no reason why a course should not include both descriptive findings and explanatory sorties touching matters of public welfare. Nor do we believe that the instructor's research interests or the course's policy implications need stand in the way of students' learning. Quite the contrary. We shall do our job better when the three principal aspects of the professional role set are made more overlapping, complementing one another and so strengthening the process of instruction. (And instruction will be bettered, too, when students' counter-demanding roles are recognized and their cohort-linked experiences drawn into the substance of the course.)

Options Related to Time-linked Influences on Teaching: Movements, the Generation Gap, and Obsolescence

Speaking at a University of Chicago commencement, President Hutchins once urged students to speak and do boldly, saying: "You are freer now than you will be, ever again, in your lives." And being freer than adults of the demands that can compromise good impulses, students often wish to right the wrongs of our society. They attach themselves to various movements. Their activism in the sixties and early seventies often threatened customary patterns of instruction. We often described them as disruptive. Yet these students' impulses—and we shift to present tense, since they are recurrently with us—signal teaching opportunities. For the sociologist, any movement raises questions about its genesis and efficacy. Such questions are fair game for our class inquiries.

Pressures exerted by social movements have sometimes led to lamentable outcomes for sociology instruction—popular but trivial course content, grade inflation, deflated degrees. On the other hand, such pressures may have generated some pedagogical benefits. In some instances they prompted us to define learning goals more sharply and to devise self-teaching, self-paced means of achieving those ends: flash cards for definitions, for basic factual information, and for minimal sets of propositions; more frequent instructor reaction or peer review; various forms of programmed instruction, self-correcting or invoking the aid of peers. Such occurrences as the open-door admissions policy may, then, have given us a stronger armory of instructional devices.

But beyond the sociologically relevant uses of movements, beyond the attention to tools of teaching, there is a more general point to make about students' recurrent impulses to social reform. Student activism points to a degree of moral sensitivity that can be enlisted in support of the discipline. Sociology can supply the perspective and the tools for informed action in support of students' ideals. This doesn't mean that sociology instructors will lead their students to the barricades. It does mean that the fit between map and terrain can often be appraised by sociological analysis: What would be the effect of acting in this way rather than that? Is the analysis of an inequitable situation correct in the first place? Are the contributing influences properly identified and weighed? What are the unanticipated consequences of virtuous action?

The moral of the story is that morals have a place. They are motivational engines of inquiry. To avoid such issues is to invite accusations of irrelevance. But worse, to avoid them is to neglect a great resource for effective instruction. About most major matters in a course we need to raise questions about implications for practice. What does it mean (for your children) that we are social creations? What's implied by the doctrine of differential association in Sutherland's explanation of criminal conduct? Or by labelling theory or the notion of secondary deviance? Is any action suggested when we find that, in relating children's vocational aspirations to their families' class positions, lower-class kids are disproportionately undecided? What are the practical implications of findings that conventional religious behavior has often been found to be related to expressions of racial prejudice?

In short, we believe that, for the undergraduate and for an adequate liberal arts education to which sociology can so distinctively contribute, matters of the true should not be handled independent of the good—and the beautiful.

Currents of change—black liberation, women's liberation, Vietnam—may require periodic adaptations in sociology instruction. These are episodic constraints. But two aspects of time persist to influence, critically, our work as teachers of sociology: cohort (generational) differences and intellectual obsolescence in a fast-growing field. Still, if limits are imposed by the time and experience gap between young and old, we are alerted to compensatory action. We can survey the class early on, exploiting aggregated student responses at various appropriate points throughout the course. Thus political preference might be related to religious beliefs or estimated family income—and to the national distribution of political preference. We might also be impelled to tap student experiences, such as those we have just reported, to identify gripping, extra-academic influences. These would then become points of inquiry and pertinent examples for a whole series of issues that surface in a sociology course.

One might suppose that there is little one can do about the threat to adequate teaching of obsolescence in one's field. But to recognize the limits imposed by the exponential development of sociology is to move us toward at least two solutions. One solution is to shift from the pretensions of Renaissance scholar to the more modest claim of competence in a restricted field. That is, the instructor keeps abreast in a more narrowly defined realm and moves away from the most difficult teaching assignments, such as the introductory course. The second solution—one we should more often invoke—is to enlist one or more colleagues in the fields of their specialties. Thus the design of a course consisting of three to five or six modules would include as many instructors. (A good model of such a course is reported by Marwell, 1973.)

&

We started this chapter by noting the bounds and limits that hedge the sociology instructor's role. There are circles within circles of influence. Yet we found it worthwhile to explore the area formed by those bounding walls. When we go beyond the question, What limits are imposed? to the second query, What options are available? we find a number of suggestive answers.

That there are far-reaching influences on sociology instruction reminds us of an aim as central as any other in teaching sociology: the task of detecting remote connections. Discovering these connections, manifest and latent, can help students grasp the meaning of a social system. Societal changes—the postwar demographic boom, for example—have prompted various innovations. The limits imposed by our profession are probably very much like those circumscribing performance in most professional roles. If so, then we have clues to concrete action. We accept as likely Parsons's portrayal of the professional role and point out the implications for improving the teaching of sociology. Stressing universalism, achievement, specificity of task, and some emotional distance, we turned to Simmel for advice in walking the tightrope between personal concern and professional commitment. The role sets of both faculty and students pose serious problems. On the other hand, to recognize such issues may move us to reduce the counter-demanding claims of teaching and research, and to exploit differences in student populations and in students'

immediate experiences, to strengthen our teaching of sociology.

Recurrent movements that sweep up students in the cause of social reform may be usefully studied, as movements. And these movements have, as in the case of New York City's open-admission policy, virtually required the development of new instructional techniques. In any case, we believe that concern for the better is a useful supplement to a concern for the truer. As to the inevitability of the generation gap between instructor and student, and the probability of obsolescence in a burgeoning field, these restrictions on our teaching will yield to various solutions, some of which we have mentioned.

These are not all the limits imposed on us as sociology instructors. Others will be broached at appropriate points later. For example, we will discuss the requirement that grades follow a normal curve and the (sometimes imposed) requirement that standards be lowered to increase the head count to which budget is tied. There are, of course, scores of constraints. Yet, in devising our courses, in professing sociology, the possibilities of improved instruction are limited not so much by organizational or faculty constraints as by the poverty of our imaginations. We ourselves are not so much alarmed by the inevitable constraints that bound the role of professor as we are dismayed at the docile acceptance of traditional patterns of pedagogy.

Such patterns, old and new, are the matters of chapters 9 and 10. But before we introduce that spate of positive thinking, we will continue with the irritants and roadblocks. Chapter 8 treats some common problems of instruction in sociology.

Notes

1. We thank Professor Lars Bjorn (University of Michigan at Dearborn) for this sug-

gestive parallel between the superior alien, diplomat, or businessman and the sociology instructor.

2. One piece of evidence lies in an advertisement run by The New School for Social Research in the *New York Times,* August 23, 1973. Under the heading "Consciousness Raising at the New School," seventeen courses touching gender roles (and two of uncertain bearing) were offered.

3. This award was the senator's sarcastic jibe at government-supported research that, in his view, was so trivial as to constitute a fleecing of the taxpayer. One experimental psychologist sued Senator Proxmire for so maligning him. The libel and slander suit went to the U.S. Supreme Court in the spring of 1979. See "Golden Fleece . . . ," 1979. Proxmire lost.

4. For information on the ASA Projects on Teaching Undergraduate Sociology, write the ASA office at 1722 N Street, N.W., Washington, D. C. 20036. The project embraces the work of three task groups: Group A, curricular organization affecting sociology instruction; Group B, teacher training and development; and Group C, the effects of institutional context on the teaching of sociology.

CHAPTER 8
COMMON PROBLEMS OF SOCIOLOGY INSTRUCTION

Various influences circumscribe our work. They drive us to circumvention—i.e., to innovation. Or rather, they can, if we are imaginative. Now, from the outer circles of influence and constraint, we move to the inner circle of the classroom. What are the common difficulties that confront us here?

They are legion, of course: how to admit or, having admitted, how to sort out backgrounds, interests, and goals so that expectations will not be frustrated; how to deal with passivity in the classroom; how to create a set of experiences that have, for the student, a sensible sequence and unity; how to communicate effectively; how to dispel the threat sociology sometimes poses to the student who sees himself as master of his fate, captain of his soul; how to show the limitations of common sense—i.e., the advantage of controlled over casual observation; how to show the link between desired ends and the more intelligent means that sociological skills can provide; how to overcome the tendency to analyze social problems by imputing psychic states; and how to overcome the problem of parochialism and the tendency to extrapolate from personal experience to global social realities. These are some of the problems we encounter in the classroom. We shall not attend to them all in this chapter. We touch on several elsewhere. But it will be useful to tackle some of them, to exemplify the diagnosis and treatment of a few common instructional problems.

Some difficulties are common to all undergraduate instruction. Some are peculiar, in kind or degree, to the teaching of sociology. The problems peculiar to sociology stem from the nature of the field (see Bierstedt, 1963:12–27 and our discussion in chapter 4). Some result from students' earlier experience. Almost all high school students do work in U.S. history and English. Most do some work in mathematics, physical science, and world history. But few study sociology (Ehman, Mehlinger, and Patrick, 1974:20–25). Not only is there little exposure to sociology at the high school level, but students may have developed unfavorable attitudes toward the social studies (see Ehman, Mehlinger, and Patrick, 1974:4–5, 33). One group of college-bound seniors with demonstrated interest in social studies (they were attending a conference in Washington, D. C.) rated such courses low on new information learned compared to new learning in science, mathematics, and literature (Remy, 1972). (But the evidence is mixed. Berryman [1977] found that high school students in sociology courses expressed satisfaction in the subject matter and saw the material as mostly new to them. Sociology, science, and mathematics ranked higher on new learning than English grammar, U.S. history, and world history.)

These differences—in the nature of the field and in the expectations of students—must have consequences for sociology instruction. Let us consider a few problems that emerge: sociology as a threat to the student, sociology as an advocate of moral indifference, sociology's language as garbage, sociology as a pretentious obfuscation of common sense knowledge, and difficulties in sociology instruction related to the course cycle.

Sociology as a Threat to Students

"You have learnt something. That always feels at first as if you had lost something." So George Bernard Shaw's character in *Major Barbara* (1931:316) echoes the ironic lesson of the Garden of Eden: a gain in knowledge is a loss of innocence, the grasp of complexity is a loss of simplicity, the growth of the self means a diminution of self importance, a greater learning (about social reality) destroys old verities, induces uncertainty. Learning about the social world can be a threat.

Sociology is questioning and critical. It takes the customary and the common-sensical only tentatively, as matters to be inquired into. From such a posture, students sometimes infer that sociology would subvert their values. They become suspicious of the field and its practitioners (see Leslie, Larson, and Gorman, 1976:4).

Because sociology stresses objective analysis, because it exploits aggregate data, because the data and their manipulation are often quantitative, students sometimes feel that sociology sacrifices immediate, personal concerns for the impersonal, the cold, and the collective. Not only is it cold; it is demeaning. For the student learns that social patterns and his own mode of life are largely shaped by others, at other times and other places. Hence, he loses the sense of making his own way, of participating in his own fate. This is another threat to the inbred individualism generated in our culture. One

resents learning that challenges the conviction of unqualified self-determination.

Moreover, sociological analysis is hard and slow. If it does not paralyze us, it at least puts the brakes on social action. Yet many students coming to sociology are socially concerned; they hope to lessen social ills. But courses in sociology may raise more questions than they answer. For students who want absolute answers and immediate solutions, the probabilistic statements of the sociologist will be disappointing if not contemptible. However politically active sociologists may be—and sociologists are certainly no less active than the general population—their students may not understand the separation of roles, the seeker and the doer; nor may they understand how one can, must, use what is known as a basis for action, yet recognize that the action is clouded by ignorance.

The typical introductory sociology course treats issues that students feel strongly about. Minority-majority relationships (race, gender, age, religion), parent-child relationships, attachment to community, wealth, poverty, class—these are matters that sociologists probe. But what they know about these relationships, their causes and outcomes, sometimes flies in the face of the down-home truths students bring with them to college. And students are unlikely to learn unless the teacher takes such sensibilities into account.

On such matters especially, one must take great care lest the offering of an unpalatable truth create hostility inhospitable to learning. Statements about the South, about blacks, about illegitimacy or level of education achieved, or about fundamentalist religion, however accurate they may be, may carry dangerous side effects. So it becomes prudent to distinguish sharply between description and explanation. To describe a sorry state of affairs is not to explain how it came into being. Students should learn how others, including the instructor, have had misconceptions of the social world. They must learn that even though sociology may contradict assumptions about the social world, this is not an attack on underlying values. Thus, coming from a family whose beliefs are those of a nineteenth-century liberal, a student may believe that people have total control over their occupational destinies. Sociologists know that this inference is false. But this is not the same as a rejection of individualism as a philosophy. Sociologists may find higher rates of female-headed households and higher rates of illegitimacy among blacks. But this in no way challenges the value of equality—in the market place, before the law, in opportunity, in humanity. Especially when treating such threatening matters, sociology instructors need to shift to a triadic pattern, confronting the outside data, which themselves pose the problem of accurate analysis and interpretation.

Such threats do not always surface in a course—which does not mean that they are not there. But sometimes they do surface, as in a course where we used John Scanzoni's *Sexual Bargaining: Power Politics in the American Marriage* (1972). Scanzoni applies social exchange theory in the analysis of marital roles: husbands and wives give to each other, and continue to do so, because they receive or expect to receive. Students read, listened, discussed, analyzed. But a few students cornered the teacher one day and a conversation something like this ensued.

Student A: Do you really believe this Scanzoni?

Teacher: I'm not sure I know what you mean.

Student A: Marriages stick together because of love, *not* this give and take stuff.

Student B: Yeah, he's so rational. That's not what marriage should be like. My parents love each other; they feel for each other.

Teacher: I see what you mean.

Student A: I'm sure there's tit for tat and all that, but Scanzoni's view of marriage is so calculating. Whooo—gives me shivers to think it's like that.

Student C: You're married [this, to the teacher]. Is that what your marriage is like?

Student B: Is Scanzoni married?

We did see what the students meant and could hear their real pain and anger. To some extent they had misread Scanzoni, and to some extent they were pointing to portions of his analysis not clearly spelled out. But also embedded in their questions were issues about the analytic nature of sociology, and about the fact that some approaches, following Durkheim's dictum to explain social facts with social facts, eliminate feelings, sentiments, preferences (except, perhaps, as intervening variables). In the next class session we discussed these issues. Some students found, on second reading, that Scanzoni's analysis was not quite what their first, emotion-clouded reading had suggested. But the discussion did not satisfy all the students; some could not examine the marital relationship analytically. Perhaps this was a failure in our teaching. Perhaps the principles of exchange theory might better have emerged from students' analysis of concrete cases.

Sociology as a Failure of Nerve: Analysis over Action

Like some of their uninformed elders, students may misconstrue sociology as a collection of techniques for social manipulation, as socialism or social work or social reform, a latter-day holy writ enjoining tolerant and humane relationships.* Sociology is—or should be—related to social change; but the two are not equivalent. How can we show (not simply tell) students how knowledge of facts, of relations between facts and predicted relations, are related to action? (See Douglas, 1973:4.) If, as is likely, some students bring false expectations to their first class in sociology, this becomes a serious problem for the instructor. Unanswered, the question of social action will confound confusion. Poorly answered, it may be disenchanting.

However, we can clarify both the distinction and the connection between knowledge and action by: (1) invoking instances of application in connection with the content of the course as designed; (2) demonstrating the usefulness of sociology in action; and (3) clarifying the roles of sociologist and activist and the skills needed by both, while revealing the differing views on the connection between sociology and social change.

Applying Sociology:
Course-relevant Examples

There are many links between sociological knowledge and action. Sometimes ideas and research findings define, inform, explain, and predict events, such as criminal or delinquent behavior, that are seen as practical problems. Sometimes practitioner or sociologist draws on extant work in sociology to understand a practical problem more fully. Let us take the latter instance at the point in a course when students are exploring the social shaping of people's roles. Here we can profit from Robert A. Scott's *The Making of Blind Men* (1969). Scott uses social exchange theory and symbolic interaction theory to illuminate the way sighted people and agencies create a blind role, and one not necessarily determined by the fact of blindness. Agencies for the blind "create for blind people the experiences of being blind" (Scott, 1969:121). His book is very much applied sociology and loaded with implications for action. (The executive director of the New York Association for the Blind said that it would probably "shock 'blind agencies' out of their lethargic, accommodative approaches and toward a new outlook. . . .") In an appendix, Scott discusses the roles of scientist and practitioner, "scientific theory and practice theory," and the relation between them. Workers with the blind need to contrive and control learning situations to help their charges adapt successfully to a world geared to the sighted. But to contrive and control require knowledge. The practitioner is chiefly concerned with control, the sociologist with the knowledge that can improve that control.

There is much work in all fields of sociology that can be analyzed and used in like fashion. There are hundreds of articles on the applications of sociology to social problems and social action. The cumulative indexes of *Social Problems* and other journals, and of some social problems texts can help the instructor locate pertinent material. During the mid sixties, several anthologies of such articles were

* Several authors of introductory sociology textbooks make similar observations. See, for example, Olsen (1968:8); Leslie, Larson, and Gorman (1976:3–4); Lowry and Rankin (1977:5); DeFleur, D'Antonio, and DeFleur (1973:2); Lenski (1970:5); and Wilson (1971a:589–93).

published. Two in particular show how the issue of application, or action, can be treated in tandem with the substance of almost any course. These are Valdes and Dean's *Sociology in Use: Selected Readings for the Introductory Course* (1965) and Shostak's *Sociology in Action: Case Studies in Social Problems and Directed Social Change* (1966).

The table of contents in the Dean and Valdes book resembles that in most introductory texts, with chapters on culture, roles, socialization, stratification, social organization, social and cultural change, and the like. But the fifty articles organized under such headings were chosen because "they demonstrate the actual use of sociological knowledge [and] illustrate for the beginning sociology student what Merton has called the 'visibly practical accomplishments of the discipline' " (Valdes and Dean, 1965:v). Among the articles are ones treating contributions of sociology to public health workers, physicians, public housing officials, ministers, newspaper editors, community organizers, religious organizations, labor unions, airlines, and other businesses. Shostak's volume is organized around social problems of the 1960s and has a similar scope.

Demonstrating the Usefulness of Sociology in Action

"It is not enough to do good; one must do it the right way" (Morley, 1901:58). If students are to appreciate the usefulness of sociology, the instructor must show how sociology helps us achieve desirable ends by means that do it the right way. Scott's work on the blind is a case in point, although the effects of doing it the right way are demonstrated in reason rather than results. Selections in the Shostak and the Valdes and Dean books show how sociology is used to do good the right way.

In the course of doing good, controversy is generated, positions harden, and arguments of reformers and resisters are inflated with hyperbole. Sociology, then, offers a mode of analysis to help sort fact from fiction.

Stephen Cole (1976) provides further examples of sociological analysis that advances social action by correcting and refining views of proponents and opponents. One of his case studies is that of the More Effective Schools (MES) program in New York City. Good public schools are important, perhaps especially to low income families who have no alternative. Yet studies had shown that schools in low income areas got lower funding, fewer resources, and higher teacher-student ratios. Clearly this situation is wrong, perhaps illegal. If low income schools could get not only equal resources, but compensatory resources, the children of low income families would learn more. Would such additional resources be the difference that made the difference? Cole discusses a study by David Fox of the MES Program that reveals that MES did not produce all the gains its partisans claimed for it; the existing program had little or no influence on student learning or on students' attitudes toward school. (The research did produce suggestions as to how compensatory programs could make a difference.) Thus sociological inquiry can refine and make more effective social action aimed at improving our lot.[1]

Different Roles, Varying Views[2]

The pertinence of knowledge to action and the distinction between the two can be clarified by helping students grasp the implications of sociologists' differing roles: scientist (researcher), teacher, advocate, technician, activist, consultant. (Sussman, 1966, once identified six consulting roles!) Doubtless sociological knowledge is used in all these roles—but to what extent? in what way? to what ends? for what audiences? These are complex questions, and their answers carry important consequences.

Among such questions and issues, which is most important for the undergraduate student? It is the recognition that as a sociologist one has a role that differs from other roles; groping for sociological knowledge is a particular form of activity characterized by a particular form of objectivity. Sociologists may disagree on many matters and enact different roles in which they use knowledge in the service of diverse ends. But that fact should not deceive students as to the sociologist's role as sociologist, the gaining of reliable knowledge about a class of phenomena we call social. Such knowledge does not consist in the sociologist's preferences or wishes or hopes. It consists in asking questions that can be answered yes, or no, or something in between, that can be falsified or confirmed by independent observers, that can be linked with the evidence of reason and the results of empirical testing. In the words of Becker (1973:198):

Given a question and a method of reaching an answer, any scientist, whatever his political or other values, should arrive at . . . an answer given by the world of recalcitrant fact that is "out there" whatever we think about it.

Some take the position that sociologists (and sociology) have a special responsibility to fight unfounded inequalities and other social ills. Kloss, Roberts, and Dorn write (1976:3):

The new sociology, radical sociology, or humanistic sociology is a movement within the larger discipline to make moral judgments about the institutions . . . in a given society.

Other sociologists doubt that sociology can or should take such positions. None, of course, would deny that values inform and affect the production of knowledge. Merton's views (1976:25) represent most sociologists': values condition the problems we select and differing problems selected make for differing effects on different sectors of society. Thus there is always a moral choice, more often implicit than explicit, in the selection of problems. Science itself has its own set of values and standards such as the attempt to achieve a useful objectivity.

There are, of course, different interests, different values, different assumptions, theories, and methods. A modest exposure to such professional issues may be useful for the student. Without a yeasty ferment any field of inquiry would lose its *raison d'être*. But students should not miss the point of agreement, the nature of the mission. It is knowledge, not action—reliable knowledge gained through reason and experience, and so formulated as to permit its proof by one's peers. On this, sociologists as different as Merton and Anderson agree (see Anderson, 1971:356). Seeking surer knowledge is not a substitute for acting; we must always act, despite our ignorance. Yet clearly the more informed the action, the more effective it can be. And in the division of labor, as between biologist and physician, some will emphasize the one over the other.

Seeking knowledge invariably entails abstraction; and sociology's abstract terms—role, status, culture, stratification—pose common and often serious problems of instruction. They warrant some attention.

Talking in Tongues: The Academic Tower of Babel

An instructor who is oblivious to problems of language, and whose students are too docile to question terms (or think, erroneously, that they understand the terms), may blunder in ways such as these. (The examples are actual ones.)

• The setting is an orientation session on sociology, a presentation to freshmen the week before classes are to begin. Illustrating the research process, the sociologist refers to "putting your data on tape" and "working with SMSAs as the unit of analysis," but gives no elaboration, no explanation of terms.

• In an after-class conversation, a graduate instructor in an elementary course discusses hypotheses, speaks of "the parameters of concern" and, in connecting points in a scattergram he had placed on the board, refers to "drawing your least squares line."

• In an introductory course, a faculty member discussing internal differentiation of cities speaks of "the process of segregation" as natural and inevitable. The human ecologist's special meaning of segregation was not explained.

All academic fields (indeed, all occupational groups) are marked by their technical terms. These words encode complex and sometimes subtle meanings. They may be rich in content, but only for those made privy to them. What, if anything, the uninitiated student understands by such words may depart wildly from the instructor's intent. Sources of misunderstanding may lie in the gap between technical and everyday usage,[3] in their novelty, the sheer unfamiliarity of technical terms; in the value implications that sociologists attach to them (the insistence that propositions be susceptible to refutation, for example); and in terms, such as *critical* or *analytic*, that describe an attitude toward and a process of exploring social realities.

Terms with Technical and Everyday Meanings

Words such as *role, institution, function, reliable, theory,* and *hypothesis* have common meanings that confound their technical use. In sociology, an hypothesis is not a guess, or a hunch, or something we think is true, but the statement of a determinate relationship between two operationally defined variables under specified conditions. But unless the teacher ensures that students know and employ the word in its technical sense, they will almost certainly use it incorrectly. Not only must the teacher provide clear definitions, illustrations, and applications; the teacher also must provide opportunities for students to determine whether they understand the terms. Hence, self-study examples, self-tests, and the like.

Above all, the *teacher* must not confound the technical and vulgar use of sociological terms. One can understand why students must be confused when the author of an introductory textbook writes: "Moving on to the subject of innovation, we speak at one point about the role chance has played." For teaching sociologists to use the term *role* to mean part, share, or province must confuse the student who elsewhere has been taught that a role is a commonly held set of expectations about the way a person occupying a given position in a social system may be expected to perform. We want to teach students that the word *valid* means to sociologists the degree to which a measure or an index does in fact represent what it says it does. Thus we would not say, "It is not valid to interpret these findings as showing . . ." when in fact we mean the interpretation would be incorrect. The measures involved might be quite valid, but the conclusion, for other reasons, might be incorrect. Sociologists sometimes use the adjective *sociological* when they mean social, thus helping to confuse the student on the distinction between things pertaining to the discipline (sociological) and the nature of the phenomena and data (social) studied by the discipline.

Unfamiliar Technical Terms

Unfamiliar technical terms are of two sorts: those common to scholarly discourse (*empirical, variable, heuristic, sample, paradigm,* etc.); and those peculiar to sociology (*status inconsistency, anomie, structural-functionalism, mechanical solidarity, symbolic interaction, Standard Metropolitan Statistical Area,* etc.).[4] Teachers sometimes forget how hard it can be for students to master technical terms. Our daily use of them makes them so familiar that we easily forget the rich load of connotations they encode. Some words are totally new to our students; *anomie* is a likely case in point. Other terms such as *social system* or *mechanical and organic solidarity* are made of words that students use in different contexts and with different meanings.

New technical terms pose problems for another reason: they refer to things not visible or palpable. We cannot touch, see, taste, or smell a relationship, class position, conflict, amity, cooperation, cohesiveness, social distance, alienation, contingencies of reinforcement—all of which are inferences and constructs. As Komarovsky observed (1951:253), "It takes patient training of the sociological sight to enable [students] to perceive the invisible social structure."

What would "patient training of the sociological sight" entail? How can teachers help students understand terms that have no direct empirical referents? They can help, first, by exemplifying the precise use of terms and, second, by showing how they infer and abstract in their private lives. It is instructive to ask students to report their observations of a small slice of social interaction. Invariably they will report what they could not have seen, what they inferred, using such words as *angry, friendly, frustrated, hostile.* In reflecting on what they have done, students will readily recognize the distinction between perceptions and conceptions—and the inevitable use of such abstractions in everyday life. Third, instructors can point to practices in other fields, preferably those in which the student is concurrently studying. Historians speak of the Renaissance and the Reformation: these are complex and technical abstractions. We find in other fields inferences represented in technical terms that have no direct reference to realities our senses can pick up—for example, *force fields, light waves,* and H_2O (which does not appear in nature, although water does). (See Warriner [1962], who provides the example of H_2O in a paper that merits close reading.)

A fourth and most important mode of "patient training" is to demonstrate, through the process of inquiry, the uses of sociological concepts. Students analyze a cause-effect assertion in an editorial in the local newspaper. They try to explain differing life spans as revealed by tombstones in a very old cemetery and one with recent settlers. On maps of the local community they mark out the costly residential areas, those where the poor live, and the intermediate areas in a study of the ecology of class. In such inquiries they must employ ideas represented by class, spurious correlation, controls, sampling. Through such activities they must learn, if they are encouraged to reflect on it, how technical terms, although lacking direct empirical reference, yet enable us to understand the concrete realities of human experience.

Terms Carrying Unfamiliar Values

Some of sociology's words express values that may be strange, even alien to the student. Empirical evidence is good—not simply one form of evidence, but a desired form. Propositions and hypotheses derived from them must ultimately be testable, both by the investigator and by other scientists. This is not an option; the word *testable* denotes a desired activity. There are many forms of evidence, but they are not equally acceptable. Some forms of evidence, reasoning, and procedure are thought to be better than others. This is not to deprecate insight, intuition, casual observation, or authority. We mean only to point out that terms like *refutability, empirical evidence,* and *response rate* convey a sense of the better or the worse for sociological work.

Sociologists sometimes use the insights of novelists, philosophers, poets, or journalists. This may incorrectly suggest to students that a passage from Kafka, *Newsweek,* Tolstoi, or Vonnegut is acceptable evidence. But of course there is a real difference between a useful idea and a tested fact. Some of sociology's value-laden words point to that difference. It is a difference students need to be clear about. And teachers have an obligation to make clear that sociologists value some forms of evidence and procedure over others, and that they have reasons for those preferences. Some years ago, C. Wright Mills (1961:79) wrote that teachers have special responsibilities

> *to show how one man [the instructor] thinks— and at the same time reveal what a fine feeling he gets when he does it well. The teacher ought, then, it seems to me, to make very explicit the assumptions, the facts, the methods, the judgments.*

The judgments are implicit in the words (and probably in the inflection with which we use them). We suggest that they should be made explicit, be explained and justified as one approach to social reality.

Words Used to Direct Student Inquiry

Some words carry no precise technical meanings but are used by sociologists (and other teachers) in directing students' work. Consider these directions for term papers.

Teacher (speaking to class): As you know, midterm and final exams in this course each count for 25 percent of the final grade. The rest of the grade comes from your performance on a term paper. Now I want you to write a really good paper—it should be a serious piece of work, carefully done, making use of what you've learned in this course. I want a really solid job.[5] The paper can deal with any topic so long as it is centrally related to sociology. Papers are due. . . .

The students listen to these directions and think to themselves (all *sub voce*):

Student A: Well, I guess Jones wants a long paper. This is going to be a tough one.

Student B: Oh God, that makes three term papers this semester and I've got to pour on the footnotes in this one.

Student C: I'm dropping this course.

Student D: What does she mean, "I want a really good paper . . . I want a solid job"? Whose paper is this?

Student E: So what's a "really good paper"? And what's "centrally related to sociology"? What's a "serious piece of work"?

Some teachers do give such vague, hence useless, instructions to their students (foreshadowing equally vague and unhelpful comments when grading the finished paper). But perhaps most instructors give students such directions as these:

Teacher: I want your term papers to be analytic: I'll look for papers that go beyond description and focus on analysis. What do I mean by an analytic paper? One that is the product of serious thought and critical thinking. A paper that synthesizes what you have learned. And I don't want you to present just any evidence; I want you to evaluate the evidence you find and make judgments on what to use.

Are those terms—*analysis, critical thinking, synthesis, evaluation*—clearer than those in the first example? To our students, we suspect not. Injunctions to be analytic and not descriptive may mean something to sociologists. (Take the argument and evidence apart, examine the elements, reveal their connections, and evaluate those connections on the basis of the evidence.) But lacking our experience, students will have no intimation of the meanings that invest such words.

Even the ordinary verb *to read* may be ambiguous, as this (actual) exchange between faculty members suggests.

Teacher A: What's the right number of pages of reading to assign a class during one semester?

Teacher B: Well, it really depends on what type of reading it is— how technical or how tough; and also on what level of mastery you wish students to get. What is your goal? That students be familiar with the articles and book? Is it enough if they know the central ideas? Do you want them to have a full understanding of the work and understand the assumptions, methodology, and the like? Do you have an estimate of their reading speed and the hours available for their work? How much of students' time will be taken up with non-reading work, exercises, lab work, field sorties, and things like that?

Teacher A: God! Of course. Those are good points. I never really thought about them.

What do students do when they get an assignment that uses terms they do not understand in the way the teacher understands them? They write bad papers and examinations. And what do teachers do when they receive such papers and exams? They give students low grades and comment on the lack of analytic thinking. There has been little communication, little useful evaluation, little learning—and much waste of time and energy for all parties. Especially in larger classes with few opportunities for instructor reaction (a midterm, a final, and a paper—the last two at the end of the term), this is a serious problem.

What is the solution? The solution is to talk and write in operational (hence clear) terms that carry meaning for students. This requires of the instructor a very clear vision of the experiences being devised for student learning. What does it mean to ask students "to evaluate the evidence you find and make judgments on what to use"? How will students know they are evaluating adequately? They will know only if the teacher helps them see that evaluation requires judgments based on some yardstick, some external set of criteria. Such criteria can be worked out with students, resulting in such a set of guidelines as these. About the evidence at hand:

1. Does it specify the population (or universe) about which a generalization is made?

2. Is sampling at issue? If so, does it appear to have tapped all elements of the population?

3. If the evidence is based on a sample, was the response rate satisfactory—let us say 60 percent or above? And is there any indication that nonrespondents do not differ systematically from those who did respond?

4. Is the proposition a fertile one? Does it suggest other situations or populations to which it might be extended?

5. Are the measures used apparently valid? Was the matter of validity considered? Ditto with reliability.

6. Is the question clearly put? Is it well crafted, with the evidence marshalled and organized in such a way as to enable the reader to make a sound judgment about the conclusions?

7. Are negative cases—cases that fall in the wrong cells or far from the line of LMSs—taken into account? Or are they overlooked?

Furthermore, does the instructor want students to develop their own evaluation criteria? to state and justify their selection of criteria? Will all student-generated criteria be equally acceptable? The student should be informed.

This discussion of evaluation took many more words than the initial injunction. But such careful specification of what an assignment is about will warrant the care it takes—will enhance learning, save time for students and teacher, reduce anxiety, allow for more pointed and useful responses from the instructor on the written work, and not least important, make the grading less onerous. And it will help the troubled conscience of such a teacher as A in the following (actual) conversation. Two teachers, A and B, are talking informally over dinner during final examination period. Both are fatigued from grading.

Teacher A: Grading papers is such a terrible business. I'm always so unsure; it brings out all my insecurities.

Teacher B: Know what you mean, especially the borderline case problem. You find students misunderstanding points made in a book—or ones you made in class—that you thought were crystal clear; you find some students raising problems you didn't see, and the whole problem of grading itself. . . .

Teacher A: Yes—but for me the tough part is simply assigning grades to the papers, trying to be fair.

Teacher B: Do you give your students a list of criteria you will use in grading—criteria by which you judge a paper?

Teacher A: (long pause) No. (pause) I guess maybe that's why some of them bring me two or three course papers—I assign several—and say they can't see at all why I graded one higher and one lower.

Analysis, synthesis, rigorous evaluation of evidence—these are good words. They point to useful skills. But unless we spell them out operationally, they are little more than noises honeyed over with virtuous overtones. If students do not understand them, if the teacher fails to help students work out their connotations, the words are thrown away; the teacher is talking garbage.*

Sociologists should be particularly sensitive to the outcomes of talking garbage; for many subfields in sociology touch problems of language and communication. Studies of occupational subcultures, of cross-cultural communication and work in symbolic interaction warn us against verbal garbage. In a discussion of occupational argots, Dubin (1958:340) writes:

> The meanings attached to symbols of communication are a consequence of social experience. A particular word, phrase or even an entire idea may have special meaning because of the particular interpretation given to it in a limited social setting.

For decades, anthropologists, sociologists, and public health workers have understood the problems engendered when western physicians use their concepts of pain and disease in working with non-western peoples (see, for example, Adair and Deuschle, 1958; and Adams, 1955). Any fairly enduring group of people, Strauss notes (1959), develops a special language that identifies and connects things held important by its members.

The meanings of words differ, by field and by group. It behooves us, as sociologists, to attend to the evidence on effective communication and, as teachers, to be precious of the symbols that are our stock-in-trade. It is a necessary skill for effective instruction in sociology.

Sociology and Common Sense

Some common problems of instruction stem from convictions and modes of thought that students bring from their past—the wisdom of parents and peers, employers, clerics, and others. One could not survive to the point of entering the sociology classroom without having absorbed some notions about the nature of human nature, what men and women are like, and farmers and teachers and politicians, and blacks, Catholics, Jews, and others. Not only do students establish such categories; they also learn something about connections between things: how decisions should be made, how to win friends and make enemies, what's right and true and beautiful. So much is this a part of newcomers to sociology that convictions have become transformed into social laws. One need not be surprised, then, to encounter this question: why study sociology when common sense will give you adequate answers without the pseudoscientific hocus pocus?

Some Implications of Common Sense

Common sense is indubitably useful in our daily lives—so useful, so economical as a guide to action that ethnomethodologists fix on such ordinary grammars of conduct to increase our understanding of human behavior. (See

---

* In chapter 4 we showed how teachers can operationalize the skills of analysis, understanding, and application.

Garfinkel's discussion [1967] of the routine grounds of social action.)

Not only is common sense useful, it is good; for the normative, in an evaluative sense, is defined by the normative in a statistical sense. What's familiar is comfortable, is good. What happens most often is what we generally approve. Indeed, this is part of the logic behind Gibbs and Martin's index of status integration (1958, 1959), which they saw as inversely related to suicide rates. We may even prefer that bad persons continue to act as such, rather than violating our expectations (see Blumstein, 1973). Advertisements clearly imply that what most people buy and use must be good for you, too. Common sense endows frequency with virtue.

Common sense is not only good—it is simple. We are people of action. It is annoying to be told that things aren't as simple as they seem. The complexities of the social world may seem irrelevant to our daily experience. Douglas (1973:7) reminds us that, "In almost all situations of everyday life, we restrict our interest in understanding the situation to those details we see as important in 'getting the job done' at the time. . . . A business man may say that 'You can't trust anyone because it's human nature to take all you can get,' but his concern is not with human nature in general, but, rather, with the application of such an idea to his dealings with customers."

Common sense is obvious. But obviousness, too, depends on what we have been taught as incontrovertible. Often it is obvious because the range of our experience is so limited as never to have revealed a challenge to the familiar. It is obvious that heavier bodies fall faster than lighter ones. And yet ever since a classic experiment performed by Galileo in the late six-

teenth century, this has been known to be false.

But common sense, although often useful, is typically too simple, too situationally limited, too enveloped by a sense of the good to invite the questioning mind required by science. Cohen (1931:102, 106, 172) describes common sense as "ordinary, pre-scientific . . . disconnected, fragmentary and chaotic or illogical." He says that sciences "differ from common sense to the extent that they utilize rigidly demonstrative reasoning."

Thus sociology and its teachers are likely to be in the position of challenging the obvious, the simple, and the good—what students have been taught by people they trust. For sociologists know that personal experience is often a poor basis for understanding the social world and that many commonly held beliefs and explanations are erroneous. Indeed, it is probably true to say that common sense is invariably wrong. This is not to suggest that students are always wrong, but that common sense as a form of reasoning is incomplete, leading to wrong answers because the conditions-under-which are not specified; or leading to right answers for the wrong reasons; or if right, failing in their limited, local application to embrace experience in wider contexts.

Nonetheless, one asks a lot in asking students to open themselves to new knowledge—especially to new criteria for judging the adequacy of knowledge. The effective teacher takes into account and has respect for students and the thought processes by which they form their opinions and change their minds. And such a teacher will probably convey, by indirection, rather than through a frontal attack, the important point that sociology differs from or refines common sense.[6] But how to do it? Here are some examples.

*Beyond Common Sense: Sociology's
Utility*

When a student makes a common-sense observation, the teacher will do well to invite him to clarify, to be specific. Precision in language often mirrors precision in thought. Nonthreatening probes are indicated: "Could you expand on that and give us an example of what you mean?" Consider the student who asserts that:

When you move to a new community, you have trouble making friends. People who move about a lot have fewer friendships than people who aren't mobile.

Asked by the teacher to elaborate, the student continues:

I'd say that if a person lived in a community for, say, one year, he is likely to have far fewer friends than someone who has lived there for twenty years.

The teacher pauses; a half-dozen variables affecting friendships and their formation come to mind. The teacher is tempted to ask immediately if the student doesn't want to add "all other things being equal." But the student's assertion is a plausible idea; the teacher acknowledges that and, setting aside the definition of friendship, invites the class to explore the statement. Is it likely to be equally true for people in all occupations? In the case of moves to all sorts of communities? Students are led to explore friendship probabilities of assembly-line workers, college teachers, store clerks, small entrepreneurs, and military personnel. They speculate on differences in friendship formation in a college town, a community with a military base, a small town, a neighborhood of high-rise apartments in a large city.

As ideas crystalize, some student might offer this hypothesis: When a person moves to a community where many people have similar life experiences, similar daily rounds, and common concerns, friendships are more easily made. Then differences between relative newcomers and old-timers may be attenuated or washed out. The student who made the initial observation about mobility and friendlessness may note that he was really thinking of his own town. The teacher is now in a position to make some general points: from our own limited experience, we must generalize with caution; hypotheses must be precisely stated and include some specification of the conditions-under-which; casual observation may be a useful beginning, but it is likely to be a bad stopping point. The instructor did not raise the issue of common sense, but did draw on students' experience to spring them from the trap set by common sense.

Another common tactic is to confront students with contradictory statements or situations, one of which is commonsensical while the other, its antithesis, turns out to be true. For example, Jackson Toby (1955) challenges personal experience and common sense in the situation where one is waiting for a bus. One assumes (is it not obvious?) that there ought to be as many buses going in one direction (that of the person waiting) as there are going the opposite way. Yet, in reality, when a person is waiting for a bus, there appear to be more of them going in the opposite (i.e., the wrong) direction. Is it true what this personal experience tells one?

Another tactic is to get students to answer one or more questions, develop a plausible argument for having answered as they did, after which they discover data indicating that their commonsense guesses were wrong. Do the poor pay more than the well-to-do for their stoves and refrigerators? (Obviously not.) Are most of the poor in our country blacks? Do the poor spend a larger part of their income in taxes than the wealthy? Do most of the poor live in the slums of big cities? Does our system of public, free education mean that the children of poor people have about the same chance to make good as the children of middle- and upper-income families?

As a third example, consider Marwell's (1966) "Social Awareness" test. His aim was to generate interest *and* to foster a healthy skepticism of commonsense knowledge among students in the introductory sociology class. On the first day of class, he asks students for the answers to nine true-false statements. On the first question, about 88 percent get the right answer. Now they are confident. (And the confidence helps promote participation in discussing the substance of the question.) On the remaining questions, Marwell typically gets correct answers ranging from 67 through 16 percent. This is one way to get students to think twice about what everyone knows. (Marwell provides sources of the correct answers in the sociology literature.)

One of the best examples of seduction by the obvious—i.e., by common sense—and correction by sociology was offered by Paul Lazarsfeld (1949).[7] He starts with a question: why spend time and money to learn what common sense would tell us? Then he asks us to consider certain propositions emerging from a study of servicemen's adjustment to military life in World War II: (1) the better educated showed more psychoneurotic symptoms; (2) men from rural backgrounds adjusted better; (3) those from the South were better able to stand tropical climates; (4) white privates were more eager to become non-commissioned officers than black privates;

(5) southern blacks preferred white to black officers; and (6) as long as the fighting went on, GIs were more eager to get back to the States than they were after the German surrender.

But each of these statements, Lazarsfeld then reveals, is the exact opposite of what was actually found. He then concludes (1949:280):

> If we had mentioned the actual results of the investigation first, the reader would have labelled these "obvious" also. Obviously something is wrong with the entire argument of "obviousness." It should really be turned on its head. Since every kind of human action is conceivable, it is of great importance to know which reactions actually occur most frequently and under what conditions; only then will a more advanced social science develop.

Consider a fifth example, this one stimulated by news accounts of Negro militance in the United States. Clearly you can push blacks—or any depressed group—only so far before they fight back. The history of black revolts in the South demonstrates the truth of this fairly obvious fact of human nature.

So, what can we derive from this? Well, this proposition leads to some other obvious ones. Table 8.1 provides some examples.

One could put the five propositions offered as obvious facts in the left-hand column of this table in more persuasive fashion, so setting up common sense for more dramatic destruction. This is not a matter of conning the student. It demonstrates that most of us, including professors, are cursed with enough sophistic dexterity to develop quite plausible propositions that may be demonstrably false.

One must, of course, take care lest such devices be seen as tricky. One can acknowledge them as part of a script devised to promote learning. In any case, one

Table 8.1 Obvious Facts vs. Accurate Statements Regarding Black Militancy

Obvious Fact of Human Nature	The Accurate Statement*
1. Among black Americans, those most deprived (those who are from any objective standpoint worst off) are much more likely to be militant than those who are better off.	1. Protest has grown as the standard of living has risen (not fallen). . . . Among Negro Americans, those who have experienced the most improvement and are least subject to objective deprivation are much more likely to be militant than those worse off.
2. The deprived are likely to be the less well-educated. Hence, the less educated a person is, the more likely he is to be militant.	2. The more education an individual has, the more likely he is to be militant.
3. The lower the prestige of his occupation (being relegated to jobs such as manual laborer, janitor, garbage man), the more likely the person is to be militant.	3. The higher the prestige of his occupation . . . the more likely the person is to be militant.
4. The poorer the person is, the more likely he is to be militant. (Well-to-do people have been co-opted: they have too much of a stake in the establishment to be militant.)	4. The greater his income, the more likely [the individual] is to be militant (even when the effect of education on each of these other variables is controlled).
5. There is more militance in the South, where living standards are lower and social justice is more compromised.	5. Centers of militance are in the urban North.

* Statements in this column are quotations from Gary Marx (1969:66).

must be sensitive to the possibility of embarrassing students. If such techniques entail too great a risk of embarrassment, one can resort to fictitious cases.

Commonsense propositions lead students astray because they are oversimple and because they pretend to the whole truth when they are very partial. They also mislead because, relating as they often do to personal experience, they are put in terms of psychic variables. Thus Indian resistance to an imported English system of education is explained by the Indian's sloth, or his ignorance, or his commitment to tradition. It is much less likely that the man in the street, or the student with little exposure to sociology, will invoke caste, religion, and agrarianism as explanations for the failure of English education to take hold (see Davis, 1951). In the following scheme, the commonsense disposition is to explain by invoking psychic states

rather than by antecedent social variables that engender both the psychic condition and the concurrent or subsequent social condition.

I	II	III
Aspects of Social Structure	Psychic State/ Psychic Variables	Social Structure/ Social Variables

The inadequacy of psychological explanations of social phenomena is a central theme in Durkheim's study of suicide (see also Cole, 1976:2–10). In an article in *Science*, Amos Hawley (1973:1197) makes the point.

Everyone knows, from long experience as an initiator of action, that it is the individual who wills things to be done and it is the aggregate of willing that produces social phenomena. People act alike in a given situation, so goes the reason-

ing, because they have common values, a term that probably is translatable as common motives. But . . . the proposition merely begs the question, for it leaves unanswered the question of how commonality of values or motives comes into being. . . . Individuals may expound at length on the reasons for their having a given number of children, for migrating from one place to another, or for engaging in any other kind of activity, but only a few are perceptive enough to recognize that the degrees of freedom in their decision-making are fixed in the structure of society.

Explaining What Is Contrary to Common Sense

Common sense has two aspects: false assertions and faulty reasoning in support of them. To stop with the statement that common sense needs the corrective of disciplined inquiry is not enough. Good teaching requires us to put the question: How do we explain what seems so contrary to common sense? On this matter of elementary theory-building, let us return to the statements in table 8.1 by Gary Marx (1969) on militance among blacks.

After students have had a go at it and we have built upon their contributions, we might invoke reference group theory and, as a facet of the theory, the notion of relative deprivation. One is deprived relative to others and only relative to others. On this point, Karl Marx (Marx and Engels, 1955:I, 94) has a nice statement. (Here we tie into history, politics, stratification; and by linking race with poverty, we demonstrate the increased power of an explanation that goes beyond one class of phenomena to bracket two large and significant categories.)

Thus, although the enjoyments of the workers have risen, the social satisfaction that [increased wages] give has fallen in comparison with the increased enjoyments of the capitalist. . . . Our desires and pleasures spring from society; we measure them, therefore, by society and not by the objects which serve for their satisfaction. Because they are of a social nature, they are of a relative nature.

A sense of relative deprivation can result from comparing now with then, or here with there. By comparison with some past time, we may be dissatisfied with what we have not got and discontent with the inequitable little that we have got. Marx stresses the latter; de Tocqueville emphasizes the former. In *The Old Regime and the French Revolution*, de Tocqueville wrote (1856:214):

So it would appear that the French found their condition the more unsupportable in proportion to its improvement. Revolutions are not always brought about by a gradual decline from bad to worse. Nations that have endured patiently and almost unconsciously the most overwhelming oppression often burst into rebellion against the yoke the moment it begins to grow lighter.

Evils which are patiently endured when they seem inevitable become intolerable when once the idea of escape from them is suggested [emphasis added].

Or, in comparing here and there, we may see various groups whose members' conditions give us a benchmark for measuring and appraising our own condition. And quite contrary to common sense, we may find that the objectively well-off are at the same time the most discontent, the most disposed to rebel.

For example, take the study of servicemen's morale, research done by a number of sociologists during World War II (see Stouffer, 1949). These sociologists got into this research because the way group members evaluate their situation—whether they are content or much dissatisfied—probably has something to do with the effectiveness with which their organization (in this case, the army) pursues its goals. One part of this study compared morale among MPs with that among members of the newly formed Army Air Force. A summary of objective conditions in the two branches would look something like this.

Point of Comparison	Military Police	Army Air Force
Rank:	mostly low	higher (many new sorts of technical ratings)
Promotions:	few and infrequent	many and frequent
Living conditions:	rough; standard GI	clean, comfortable, often at newly built air stations
Public image:	unflattering	very favorable; high repute

Now the question: which category registered the higher morale? (The teacher will ask students to respond to this question.) Certainly common sense would tell us that those who are objectively worse off will have the lower morale. Hence we would conclude that spirits are lower, morale is poorer among the MPs than among air force personnel. But in truth, the reverse was found. Why so? (This is the point, again, for the teacher to encourage students to exercise their imaginations in devising a plausible explanation.)

As it turned out, the MPs were a homogeneously depressed lot. Everyone was in the same boat. Everyone to whom one might compare himself had about the same duties, rewards, and prospects. Not so with the air force people. Here it was very easy for a serviceman to compare himself with others who were moving faster in rank, had higher pay, or received more attractive assignments. Furthermore,

air force men on the whole had higher education, which placed them in the same category as many who had gotten deferments to perform in civilian roles deemed necessary to the national welfare. So the air force people, to a greater extent than the MPs, could locate others who enjoyed a style of life (civilian) and immunities (from threat of death) denied to them.

Thus students can help build an explanation for observed behavior that flies in the face of common sense—in this case, instances in which the objectively well-off (among air force personnel or urban blacks) are, at the same time, the most discontent, the most disposed to rebel.

Common sense, being oversimple, is invariably wrong, no matter what the kernel of truth. Yet in the realm of social phenomena, the student, being a member of the species *Homo sapiens,* is likely to deem himself an expert. A common problem confronting the instructor, then, is to show how personal experience and common sense can mislead. This entails: (1) confronting the allegations of common sense with those challenges that reveal the complexities of social life, and (2) using the unexpected realities as occasions for devising tentative explanations.

The Course Cycle: Periodic Difficulties

Learning and teaching are time-bound activities—and this despite the fact that the thirty-week academic year, semesters, quarters, and half-term modules do not rest on theories of learning. With few exceptions, courses have rigid time boundaries, and teachers must work within them. (A few schools have tried to develop flexible calendars. They cannot avoid time limits altogether, but have experimented with alternatives to the traditional situation in which all students, regardless of learning styles, must fit into one mold. Alverno College in Milwaukee is one such school.) Standard time units typically bound teaching regardless of the method of instruction employed.[8] So courses have predictable beginnings, middles, and ends. Do these different segments have special needs? problems to be surmounted? opportunities to be seized?

Beginnings: The First Class Meeting and Before

Every semester, instructors face new classes for the first time. In larger schools and larger classes, both the people and the subject matter are strangers to one another. Strangers in a strange land, an uncertain circumstance generating special problems for teacher and student. Listen to some faculty members:[9]

- *It was the first meeting of the first class I taught. I was prepared, Lord knows. I walked to the front of the room, smiled, glanced at my notes, opened my mouth—and not a sound came out. I froze. It was thirty seconds before I could force a sentence out of myself. I've never quite forgotten that.*

- *I've been teaching for ten years; first class meetings still get me nervous.*

- *I've heard some colleagues say they are nervous about first class meetings. Not me. I view it as a straightforward proposition: I come in, introduce myself, hand out the reading list and assignments, tell the class to buy the texts and come prepared next meeting to discuss topic #1.*

- *I'm not nervous, either; but for a different reason. I come in, hop up on the desk, say hello, remind them we have a course in stratification, or whatever, and ask them what they want from the course. I listen to their ideas,*

hand out the syllabus and reading list, review course requirements, and then some more small talk. I want to relax my students, give them a chance to air their feelings, and see me as relaxed.

- *You know I'm teaching Social Statistics this semester. I haven't taught it in I don't know how long. Well, today I was honest with my class. I told them I was filling in for Johnson who was on leave, that I hardly ever taught Stat, and that they would have to bear with me; it isn't my area but we'll muddle on through.*

- *I'm using Pophockenhagen's text in Introductory this semester. Best book I could find, but, man, does it have problems. I told my class that the text omits some crucial perspectives—that it's really off the beam on culture and socialization and some other topics. But we'd do the best we could with it.*

If, despite knowledge of the subject matter and ensuing course events, the instructor is nonetheless a mite anxious, how much more so must his students be? (Parallel reactions from students would be instructive.) The first class—perhaps the first two or three classes—are critical in reducing uncertainty, clarifying reciprocal expectations, helping students plan their investment in the course (whether to drop or, if remaining, how much time their interest will warrant), and marshalling resources to be exploited in future sessions.

To clarify expectations is to reduce uncertainty and to enable students to make intelligent choices. (One such choice is to drop a course, when it becomes apparent that instructor's and student's aims differ markedly, and the earlier the better for both.) Clarity is in part a function of structure, the arrangement of parts in a course. McKeachie writes (1969:11) that, other things equal, *behavior is more consistent and more nearly predictable in situations where stimulus events are clear and unambiguous. The Gestalt psychologists say that the variability of behavior bears an inverse relation to the degree of struc-*ture *in a situation.*

On the teacher's side, then, the first class is the time to convey a panoramic prospect of the course: its purpose, content, and organization; the instructor's expectations and hopes for students' learning; factual information on office hours, attendance policy, and grading scheme; and ways and extent to which the instructor will be able to help. Such a sketch, together with an adequate syllabus (and perhaps an expanded outline of the course available in the department office and at registration) will help students decide whether to drop the course and substitute another.

A review of the syllabus is obviously one good way of handling the question, What is this course about? Barring some unusual circumstance, the first class meeting is the time to do this. It provides the occasion, too, to explain the connection between the text and other assigned readings—and the classroom operation. Do lectures expand upon the text? Supplement it? or not? Must students read certain material before a given class session? and why? What parts of the text will be omitted? and why? Corrected? and why? In his discussion of "situation structuring" during the opening class, McKeachie (1969:12–13) speaks about the possible

disagreement between the textbook and the materials you intend to present in your lectures. Unfortunately this is a matter which cannot always be solved simply by judicious selection of text materials. In some cases, there is simply no book available which presents certain material as one would like to have it presented. In others, the textbook is decided upon by someone other

than the instructor who has to make the best of it. In the case where disagreement is inevitable, the student has a right to know which version to accept as TRUTH and what he is supposed to do about such discrepancies on examinations.
. . .

To be avoided is the tirade against the author. This may serve as an emotional catharsis for the instructor. But for the student, any severe criticism you raise may generalize to the textbook as a whole. Or, if the student is not convinced by your argument, it may generalize to much of what you have to say.

There is one other, imperative matter. Students should learn, early on, why this sociology course merits the time they are asked to spend on it. This means that the instructor must provide a persuasive case for sociology. Justifying the course is not a defensive strategy. Nor does it mean exaggerated claims, the impossible promise to be all things to all people. It implies only that the teacher should be able to make a case that mastery of certain ideas, skills, and information contributes to some desirable (and publicly stated) goals. Students should know not only where they are going, but why the trip is worthwhile; and they should choose to go there when they elect a sociology course. Otherwise, the aims and values of instructor and student being incompatible, frustration and disenchantment must ensue. And less learning.

The first class, then, is a time for sketching the terms of the contract for the semester. It is also a time to learn something about the partners to the contract. Students want to know what their instructor is like.

From the student's side, the first class, or an early one, is a good time to reveal the range of resources represented in student backgrounds, academic majors, and career plans. The instructor with clear and justifiable aims in mind, can use a questionnaire to get basic information about students. The diversity of interests and backgrounds thus uncovered can lead to some adaptation of course work to tap these interests. Furthermore, such a technique provides a set of data that can later be exploited at appropriate points in the course. These are aggregate data, of course; yet they are personal data in which students have some investment.

A course starts long before the first class meeting. But beyond preparation, planned and unwitting, provided by antecedent experience, there are useful things to do before the first class meeting. The teacher can visit the assigned classroom, check on book orders, discover what equipment is available or needed. And on the day of the first class, the teacher can come early to enable casual conversation with students as they arrive.

An anticipatory visit to the assigned classroom will tell you what needs to be done to create an adequate setting for teaching. Can you control the temperature so that the room will be neither too hot nor too cold? Is it a light, bright, sensorily stimulating setting? If the class is large and the room a narrow rectangle with the instructor far removed from the last row of seats, is it possible to move down the aisles or rearrange the seating pattern so as to reduce physical and social distance between instructor and student? (When the teacher leaves the lectern, seat of protection and symbol of authority, students attend more closely. Physical immediacy can be a means of commanding attention, having some of the effect of calling a person by name.) Do the windows have shades so that films can be shown? Are there appropriately located electric outlets for the film projector or for an overhead projector? Are there enough chalkboards, appropriately located? (If not, the instructor will have to rely more on ditto masters or transparen-

cies for graphs, charts, tables, and outlines.) How large will the instructor's writing have to be? How loud the instructor's voice, to reach the remoter rows? Would it be best to ask that the class be assigned to another room better suited to the tasks that lie ahead? (An instructor might well wish to request different sorts of classrooms for each of two or three courses, rooms differing in size, having fixed or movable desks, with resources such as reference books or calculators, and facilities for audiovisual aids and the like.)

Well ahead of the first class it is important to check with the bookstore and library to see that orders and requests made months earlier have been carried out. All this scouting of resources for instruction may seem tedious. Yet those with some experience will know of the avoidable blunders that can occur: the tardy discovery that students were unable to do their first assignment because the book never arrived; or the late revelation that the instructor's blackboard writing was invisible or illegible to students in the farther reaches of the room; or the frustration of being unable to show a scheduled film because the extension cords were three-prong and the wall socket two-prong.

Students pick up cues about the nature of a course and its instructor early on. Does the teacher arrive on time? or well ahead of the class, to allow time for informal conversation and banter? or late? Is the first class session well organized? Is it tight with heavy detail about requirements? Does the instructor relate matters of local interest to the substance of the first class session? How does the instructor address students? (Names designate unique persons. To use them may indicate a personal interest in students' learning and a claim on the person for conscientious performance.) [10] Does the teacher listen to students' concerns and queries sympathetically? Does the teacher exploit a question without embarrassing the asker, in order to reveal facts and generate ideas? To questions and needs expressed in an early class, does the teacher respond by bringing appropriate materials to subsequent sessions? Does the teacher listen to student interests with care, so as to incorporate them, when appropriate, in the structure of the course? Does the teacher get into the substance of the course in such a way as to establish a mood and relationships that are congenial and, for the student, supportive?

The instructor will doubtless wish to convey the notion, early on, that sociology is a rigorously disciplined way of looking at human relationships, and that the sociologist's inquiries can bear, usefully, on students' concerns, present and future. But it is doubtful that simple assertion will be adequate: telling is not teaching. Such goals may be more effectively met if the teacher develops these points in the substance of the course. And that can be begun on the first day.

As an example, take the instructor in an introductory course. The students are strangers—to one another, to the teacher, to the subject matter. How do they feel in a strange situation? What past experiences would help or hinder them in feeling at home in such a strange setting? Students respond, we assume, setting the stage for the question, What other sorts of persons are strangers? What situations create strangeness? Thus an extension from being new to college to making new beginnings more generally: the migrant, the immigrant, the new employee, the infant, the military recruit. What, then, must be done in all these instances? Rearing, teaching, training, retraining—in short, socialization. This might move the class to see

the need to institutionalize certain social patterns and lead students to some recognition of major social institutions. It is not inconceivable that, beginning with the situation of strangeness in a new course, one could proceed, through student-teacher dialogue, to frame the whole course. And in doing so, the teacher would have recognized the genuine feelings of uncertainty and apprehension felt by some—and would have linked these feelings, constructively, with parallel circumstances, so enabling students to take a more objective look at their own situation. Indeed, the instructor would have made a start on introducing students to the sociological perspective.

The beginnings of a course build impressions that shape the student-teacher relationship. An instructor may be over-anxious, trying to do too much, blocking out student queries and responses, filling the first class until it overflows the brim. Mistakes at the beginning need not doom the course; they can be rectified. Yet because some imprinting probably does occur during the first few classes, a change in direction had better be handled explicitly. For example:

I've been thinking over our first few classes and realize that I didn't convey at the outset how much I would appreciate your participation in class. I said I wanted your questions, but only mentioned it in passing. In thinking this over, it occurred to me that some of you may not be sure what kinds of questions I mean. That's reasonable: I never told you. I have some types in mind, but I'd like to hear from you: What kinds of questions have occurred to you? [Then, after some discussion] Now I want to ask that, before next Wednesday's class, each of us write down at least one question and bring it to class. Then maybe we can put them in a hat and I'll draw a few for us to deal with.

Beginnings are important, but it may be that there are other points in a course

equally if not more critical. One such is
midterm.

The Middle: A Slump in a Zest-Apathy Cycle?

A graduate teaching assistant (now
Professor Dwight Billings, University of
Kentucky) once came to us at midsemester
with a problem:

> *My course isn't going well. Students aren't
> reading . . . aren't keeping up with their work.
> Interest and participation have dropped. What
> really bothers me is that the course started so
> well. The first few weeks we had good discus-
> sions, kids were reading, discussions were good.
> Questions, too. My approach isn't any different
> now—same class, material isn't any harder. But
> things aren't going so well. Do you have any
> ideas?*

We had heard such reactions before
and experienced them ourselves—a good
start, initial enthusiasm, and then a falling
off of interest. Reflection on the problem
persuaded us that there were good reasons
for a midsemester slump. We concluded
that, had we the data, they would follow
the curve of the solid line in figure 8.1.
Interest in the course and commitment to
the work are high at the beginning and at
the end of a course, but for different reasons. Toward the end, the day of judgment
approaches, and some work can be post-
poned no longer. The desire for good
grades becomes increasingly salient. At
semester's start, there is a degree of eager
anticipation; students are optimistic about
the course and generous in their attitude
toward the teacher. The students' slates
are clean, and the instructor's is, too, as yet
unmarred by discouraging performances.

But in the middle of the course, some
saturation effects surface; another day, another chore. The same old faces, the same

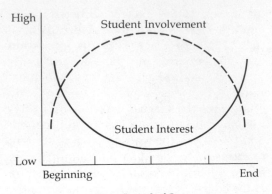

Time Period of Semester

Figure 8.1 A Zest-Apathy Cycle?

instructional pattern. By now some student work has been rated as poor or
mediocre. (Even the teacher's omniscience
may have come into question!) Furthermore, other interests and obligations will
have increased as the semester has advanced, possibly peaking in the middle.
The curve for such counter-demanding activities is shown in the dashed line of
figure 8.1, the inverse of the interest-and-
commitment curve.

Certainly this is too crude a representation of the reality that is complicated
by class and age of students, whether the
course is required or optional, the instructor's load, the congruence of course material with research interests, committee
assignments, and the like. Yet in our experience, the midsemester slump is a real
tendency, both for students and for instructor. If this is indeed the case, two
things seem indicated: the teacher must be
alert to the possibility (and perhaps take
soundings to determine what is happening), and the teacher must take remedial
action.

As a check, a teacher might pay attention especially to changes in attendance
and participation. Talks with students can
reveal flagging interest and counter-
demanding pressures. If action is indi-

cated, the teacher can try to break the repetitive pattern that has characterized the course to that point. Various options are available: laboratory sessions, demonstrations, field sorties, buzz groups, guest speakers, panel discussions or debates, a unit of self-directed study and self-testing—any arrangements that heighten student activity and participation. It may be useful, too, to take into account the typical demands of other courses, altering the timing of special work in the sociology course to dovetail, rather than coincide, with other requirements.

It will also be helpful to recognize that groups move through developmental stages requiring somewhat modified roles. Thus, for example, Schmuck and Schmuck (1975:177–87) discuss four stages: inclusion and membership, establishment of shared influence and collaborative decision making, pursuit of individual and academic goals, and self-renewal (adapting to changes). Instructors who are sensitive to such identifiable stages will wish to meet the needs of one stage and prepare for the next—for example, meeting promptly the need to establish group membership and the legitimacy of sharing common concerns so that the class can move ahead to work toward the academic goals of the course.

And the End: Another Unit? A Retrospective, Integrating View? A Launching Pad?

The end of the term poses special problems. Teachers are often concerned about covering the material, getting through the last topic in the syllabus. Students are concerned about final examinations. The instructor must decide whether to continue, simply, with another link in the chain; to conclude with efforts

to synthesize and integrate; or (perhaps, and) to stress the bearing of the course experience on probable future experiences at work, worship, play, reading, subsequent courses, and the like. The instructor's strategy will vary depending on the nature of the course (whether introductory or advanced) and on students' standing (whether they are majors, whether they are freshmen or seniors, and the like).

In some texts, the last chapter is another link in a sausagelike chain of topics. Instructors following such a text simply wind up with the last topic. Contrast such a windup with the final chapter of Lenski and Lenski, entitled "Retrospect and Prospect" (in *Human Societies*, 1974:460).

The study of societal evolution is much like the study of a giant mural. In both cases, we are easily overwhelmed by the many small details. If we hope to grasp the picture as a whole and develop some feeling for it, we have to step back from time to time and look at it in its entirety . . . [to see] the overarching patterns. This time, however, we will try to discover the extent to which technological progress has been accompanied by progress toward man's other goals—freedom, justice, morality and happiness.

There are persuasive reasons, especially when teaching once-only students in introductory courses, for making the last classes a culmination, for integrating past work and aiming toward the future. For most students, this will be their last direct experience with sociology. Much of what they have studied is new, and the range of exposure has been great. So many trees, so few views of the forest. Students, if not their instructors, probably feel some need for closure. Furthermore, it is a good occasion on which to check on extent of achievement of the course's goals, both those transcending particular sociological content and those specific to the course (see chapters 4 and 5). Such a review can be gratifying to students who discover how much knowledge, how many skills they have acquired. Of course, this retrospective assessment will be useful as well to teachers in evaluating their own performance; for measurable student achievement is the ultimate test of the adequacy of instruction.

Such a retrospective summary, in the final classes, may fix on concrete content or on analytic dimensions. Where the emphasis shall lie merits the teacher's attention. Shall it be on child-rearing in the family? or on socialization processes in families, factories, and the military? Shall it be on women's roles and the liabilities imposed by institutionalized discrimination? or on discrimination, bracketing blacks and women and Puerto Ricans and others? Shall it be on the women's movement as an agency of social change? or on the features of movements in general, including the civil rights movement, the conservation movement, the right-to-life movement as well? In each case, the latter choice makes for the larger view, since it brackets more concrete instances. The purpose of integration is, therefore, better served if the instructor moves from concrete cases to the analytic dimensions that describe various instances of the same class of phenomena.

This association, in students' minds, of quite different manifestations of the same, underlying social features should enhance the prospects for applying sociological views in the future. For example, if students see that many categories exemplify the traits of minorities, they may be better prepared to apply the concept to, say, inner city dwelling WASPs in the future.

In this sense, instructors must hope that the course never ends. But as a transient social organization, it must, of course, end and often before we are ready for the final class. Is this a bad thing?

One must regard it so, if the syllabus was offered as a contract and if the course was tightly structured around desired objectives with reasons, time, and methods spelled out in detail. Not getting through the syllabus will, presumably, deprive students of what might have been. It appears to be a default of contract.

Therefore, instructors need to make early and periodic checks that will help them identify whatever adjustments are necessary to meet desired goals. Indeed, one reason to have a syllabus with exact or approximate dates for the sequence of problems to be tackled is because it is a continuing reminder to the instructor (and students) to keep on track and on schedule—or make adjustments.

There may often be good reason for building flexibility into a course. Clearly, no single course will treat effectively the forty subfields of sociology. One might not even treat all of the major institutions. Choices have to be made, depending on the teacher's judgment of importance, on available time, and on the interests of students. The last two may not be clear until the course is under way. Hence, the choice may be deferred. If students are so advised at the outset, the instructor's responsibility is met—and there is a gain in flexibility.

Assigned work for students can help them toward a culminating integration of the course experience. This would imply less conventional ingestion and more effort at synthesis on the part of students. The teacher can encourage synthesis by way of the final examination, or a final paper, or a series of very short papers, each of which aims at some guided integration of a sector of the course experience. By the word *guided* we mean a synthesis framed by a set of questions that offer pegs for students to hang their thoughts on. Thus, for example, in reviewing stratification, one might ask that the integrating statement include answers to such questions as these:

(Observation and Description)

1. What categories or circumstances reveal stratification? (Answers would include race, gender, nationality, place of residence, and the like.)

(Explanation and Theory)

2. What explanations are available to help us understand such observations? (Answers would include inherited power and privilege, rarity of skills or knowledge possessed, social needs, and the like.)

3. Which explanations seem to you most persuasive?

(Method)

4. How has (or might) this explanation be tested?

(Application)

5. What outcomes, intended or unanticipated, stem from such differences in wealth, power, education, occupational standing, and the like? Are any of these outcomes undesirable? If so, how might they be mitigated or eliminated?

Some may object that any effort at integration is lost unless it is embodied in the final examination. To the extent that this is so, and if indeed such a broad and integrated view is a central aim of the course, then, certainly, the final examination (or paper) should be designed with this purpose in mind. A final exam is not simply a device to enhance motivation (although it does that). It is one means of tapping central course goals. Furthermore, when students know from the outset that an understanding of the whole, as well as its parts, is important, they have some reason for making repeated efforts to set the part in the larger gestalt.

Beginnings, middles, ends—they occur predictably, and they present special problems. If the instructor anticipates such problems, the chances are better for exploiting their special features and for offsetting the impediments to learning that they may entail.

These, then, are some of the difficulties confronting the sociology instructor: the discipline may be seen as oblivious to the person, and its efforts at objectivity may be seen as a threat to personal values; sociology may be viewed as a failure of nerve, putting analysis over action; sociology may appear as gibberish; sociology may seem to be a needless revelation of knowledge embodied in common sense; and sociology instruction must face different problems at the beginnings, middles, and ends of courses. Although these are matters we have chosen to stress, quite clearly they do not exhaust our common problems.

A Final Miscellany of Problems

Our task is made more difficult by the vast range of social data and sociological specialties, by the appearance of a field that is fragmented and conceptually chaotic, and by an unresolved eclecticism that embraces everything. Problems arise because students have direct experience with the social world, the sociologist's raw data. Some may be convinced that they already have the answers. And, like other mortals, students suffer from ethnocentricity and related centricities. They may listen, yet not hear, filtering out what is incompatible with their predispositions. Perhaps more than in the biophysical sciences, selective perception and retention may compete with text and teacher. Teachers, too, may bring to the classroom predispositions that get in the way of effective instruction: defensive proclaiming of sociology's status as a science, or repeated assertions about its value. (On some campuses, perhaps owing to ignorance of contemporary work, sociology is viewed as second-rate, intellectually anemic, the heart supplanting the head.) We suspect that protestation is futile, and that the point is better made by the careful analysis and telling insights of actual research.

Some teachers, probably as a carry-over from graduate school, invest a good deal of teaching time in recapitulating professional debates and demonstrating the superiority of their positions. The criticism of functionalism, as functionalism (rather than its application in a specific work), is a case in point. Such issues are more significant to the teacher than the student. In our large, general education classes, the superiority of Skinner's behaviorism over Mead's social behaviorism (symbolic interaction theory), of exchange theory over normative theory, of conflict or interest group theory over functionalism needs to be considered, probably without the labels, *only in concrete cases* where one seeks the better explanation. At the general level of contending theoretical explanations, such matters are better left for later courses in theory and for graduate students.

Readers will certainly note another common problem of sociology instruction that we have not discussed. Pointing to this problem, Mirra Komarovsky (1951:253–54) wrote:

> Students come to sociology . . . with a very "psychological" and "individualistic" view of human nature. They think of individuals in a pre-Cooley and pre-George Mead fashion, as isolated, separate, autonomous beings, each enclosed in his own cell of consciousness, now and then communicating with others, but essentially independent of society. . . . Students are much more aware of individual variations from some norm than of the norm itself . . . re-lated to their insensitivity to social structure, I find students inclined towards a strictly psychological interpretation of social life and social problems. . . . When students think of social problems, from family to war, it is usually in terms of "aggression," "insecurities," "neurosis," and so on.

McGee (1977:x–xi), in a "Letter to the Student," speaks to the sources of this disposition. He writes:

> Our society has a strongly individualistic flavor. . . . Our culture is strongly psychologistic; it looks to individuals for explanations of behavior. (What is the explanation for murder? Study murderers obviously.) . . . But a great deal of human behavior cannot be adequately explained by . . . individual characteristics. . . . Further, it is simply impossible to explain or interpret the characteristics and behavior of human groups on an individualistic-psychologistic basis. (Why do all modern armies organize their combat forces into units of approximately the same sizes?)

How can the sociology teacher convey the usefulness of *social* variables in explaining changes or differences among aggregates, categories, and groups? We think it better to demonstrate the plausibility of social explanations rather than attacking, directly, individualistic forms of explanation. Durkheim's work in *Suicide* (1897) continues to stand as a good model as attested by the number of books that cite and use it (see, for example, Cole, 1976:2–10). Certainly it is not appropriate to convey the impression that the teacher is attacking psychology as a worthless field, or that the individual's thoughts and feelings do not count.

❧

The problems in sociology instruction are many. Yet the means for dealing with them are at hand. We have suggested some. In the next chapter we begin to think about two of the conventional means used in sociology and other instruction: the syllabus and the textbook.

Notes

1. Cole's other cases deal with consumer practices of low-income people (using Caplovitz's *The Poor Pay More*) and the relationship between black family structure and social pathology (using the Moynihan report, *The Negro Family: The Case for National Action*). Cole reanalyzes data in the three cases, sometimes showing how the conclusions reached by the researcher were not supported by the evidence at hand. Another volume teachers may find useful is Tufte's *The Quantitative Analysis of Social Problems* (1970).

2. The issues we raise here have often been discussed by sociologists. See, for example, various articles in Reynolds and Reynolds (1970). Cole's (1976) introductory-level volume has a useful, short discussion that takes a reasonable position (pp. 221–27 and chapter 6, *passim*). Also valuable is Merton's introductory chapter, "The Sociology of Social Problems," in Merton and Nisbet (1976).

3. Some of the ideas in these paragraphs come from Professor Peter Filene (Department of History, University of North Carolina at Chapel Hill).

4. The distinction between terms used by academics in many fields and those used within a specific discipline was stimulated by our reading of Dubin's (1958:342) distinction between industrial language and occupational argot. The former cuts across occupations within a given industry; the latter is occupation-specific.

5. The instructor's statement, "I want . . ." is unfortunate, suggesting, as it does, that students are to please the instructor. Indeed, students will sometimes write on the title page of a term paper, "For Professor Jones." We need to convey to our students that it is *their* education that is at stake, that they are working for themselves. Judgments rendered should reflect independently stated standards that the teacher is striving to help the student meet. (Thus, outside examiners, clearly stated learning goals, and clear and explicit criteria for evaluating work help reduce student-teacher friction.) Grading systems along with ambiguous course requirements reduce the student to guessing what the teacher wants and learning all the devices of academic gamesmanship. Students bring to a course years of experience with such a lamentable system. The only recourse for instructors is to make learning goals and methods absolutely clear and independent of personal whim, then cast themselves as allies in achieving those goals.

6. Several contemporary introductory sociology texts do raise the question, sometimes in the opening pages of the first chapter: cf. McGee (1977:6–7), Broom and Selznick (1977:2), *Society Today* (1973:6), Douglas (1973:3, 6–13, 22–23), and Wilson (1971a:591–93).

7. Various introductory sociology books reprint or report Lazarsfeld's device: e.g., Wilson (1971:591–93), Bart and Frankel (1971:8–9). Discussions following the same approach with their own lists of commonsense statements can be found in McGee (1977:6–7) and *Society Today* (1973:6).

8. Some instructional methods are more suited than others to flexible time arrangements. Forms of personalized instruction can allow not only for self-pacing *within* a semester, but for flexibility in the total time allowed for completion of a course or module. However, many who use PSI note that open-ended time is not always in the students' interest, especially when they are taking other courses which have rigid time requirements. See the discussion in Johnson and Ruskin (1977:chapter 5).

9. This section draws on several sources: Ericksen (1974:241–42), Goldsmid (1972), McKeachie (1978:chapters 2,3), Schmuck and Schmuck (1975:chapter 9), and Shulman (1971).

10. Seating charts will be useful in learning names (and necessary in larger classes). Eble (1976:40) suggests that the seating chart is "too mechanical: its small gain in identifying is

offset by the reminder of mass education it reinforces." But the mechanistic suggestion can be offset by explaining why the chart is being used, making it after the students have chosen their own seats, allowing students to change seats so long as they inform you, making it clear that the chart is not being used to take attendance (unless it is and then this should be said), and indicating that it is a temporary measure.

For classes of up to thirty, we have followed a procedure suggested by Professor Paula Goldsmid of Oberlin College. During the first class, we ask students in turn to introduce themselves, give their major and year in school, and make a few comments about themselves or their reason for taking the course, or anything else of interest to them. As each student speaks, we write down his or her name and a few notes on a file card, keeping the cards in order. Later in the class, while students are reading the syllabus, we review the cards and make a seating plan. During the remainder of the first class, we take care to refer to students by name—using the plan and cards as needed. Between the first and second class, we review the cards several times, trying to connect the name, face, and some salient fact about each student. We shuffle the cards and again try to connect names and people. When we lose a connection, we refer to the seating chart, which often helps. Students are not asked to keep their same seats. During the second class—and this is a crucial step—we take pains to call each student by name. If we forget, we either use the cards, the seating plan, or ask the student to help out. At a few points in the first two or three classes, we try to name all students in the class. Throughout a semester, students will tend to sit in the same part of the room, if not in the same seats. This makes it easier to learn their names.

Professor Reece McGee notes that at the beginning of each semester, his colleague, Purdue University botanist Sam Postlethwait, takes Polaroid pictures of each student in his large lecture class and memorizes the names and faces at a rate of six to ten a day.

CHAPTER 9
THE USES OF TWO COMMON TOOLS: SYLLABI AND TEXTS

The course syllabus and textbook are central in the teaching-learning process. The syllabus is the course plan: it embodies the teacher's decisions about the content, structure, and process of the course. Despite its importance, the syllabus is rarely discussed in the literature on the teaching of sociology. The textbook is the teaching-learning tool most widely used by teachers of sociology.

These two tools crosscut all patterns and techniques of instruction and all subject matter divisions. The ways in which the teacher develops and uses these two tools have far-reaching consequences that we explore in this chapter.

The Course Syllabus

In the United States, the practice of using a course syllabus is very common. Some schools require their faculty to distribute them to students and, also, to file them with the department chairperson or dean. In some cases, administrative approval of a syllabus is required before a course can be offered. Other schools strongly suggest that a syllabus be used.

Why are they so often used? And for whose benefit? What are the different ways in which syllabi can be used? Are they needed in all types of courses? How detailed should syllabi be? What are the consequences of not using one? What kinds of things can be included in a course syllabus? Are detailed syllabi really worth the teacher's valuable time?

The Usual Content and Use of a Syllabus

The typical syllabus for a sociology course includes the course title and number, the instructor's name, a listing of the required texts and readings, the course requirements (exams, papers, etc.), and topics to be covered. These items were identified by Ballantine (1977:5–6) in a content analysis of 100 syllabi for Introductory Sociology collected from a variety of types of schools.[1] Our informal review of several hundred other syllabi supports her findings.[2] Ballantine found these items in one-third to one-half of the syllabi reviewed: statement of office hours; description of the course, its focus, format, and methods of instruction (including required projects, labs, and learning aids); lists of learning objectives and collateral readings; sample exam questions and study guides. Some syllabi also included advice to the student on studying, active listening in lectures, seminar participation, and note-taking; statements of the teacher's (or school's) policies on attendance, plagiarism, and cheating; discussion of major course readings with indications of how they fit into the course pattern; and statements introducing each major section of the course.

The syllabus provided as exhibit 9.1 is typical of many used in sociology. To determine the adequacy of a syllabus we need to consider the purposes a course syllabus is intended to serve for different audiences.

Exhibit 9.1 Typical Course Syllabus

SOCIOLOGY 41: U.S. RACE RELATIONS

Instructor: Dr. Johnson (SSB 501)
Assistants: Ms. Smith (SSB 580)
Mr. Elliot (SSB 580)

Required Readings:
James Vander Zanden. *American Minority Relations.*
Autobiography of Malcolm X.
Peter Goldman. *Report from Black America.*
Larry King. *Confessions of a White Racist.*
Louis Knowles and Kenneth Prewitt. *Institutional Racism in America.*
Kerner Commission *Report of the National Advisory Commission on Civil Disorders.*
Sterling Tucker. *For Blacks Only.*

Dates	*Topics*	*Readings*
Sept. 6	Course Introduction	Vander Zanden: Ch. 1, 10
8	Dominant-Minority Relations: Overview	
13	Race in Intergroup Relations	Vander Zanden: Ch. 2 Kerner: Ch. 9
15, 20, 22, 27	Historical Background of Black-White Relations in United States	Kerner: Ch. 5, 6
29 Oct. 4, 6	Sociological and Social-Psychological Dimensions of Dominance and Subordination: The Dominators	Vander Zanden: Ch. 3–6 King: whole book
11, 13 18	Sociological and Social-Psychological Dimensions of Dominance and Subordination: The Dominated	Vander Zanden: Ch. 11–15 Malcolm X: whole book
20	Midterm exam	
25–27	Race Relations in Institutions	Kerner: Ch. 7, 8
Nov. 1, 3, 8, 10	Economy, Education, Religion, Politics, Family, and Other (e.g., Public Accomodations)	Knowles and Prewitt: Ch. 1–8, Appendix
15, 17	Separatism vs. Integration and Other Forms of Power Relations	Kerner: Ch. 16, 17 Goldman: Ch. 6
24–29 Dec. 1	Means for Effecting Changes	Kerner: Ch. 2 Goldman: Ch. 2–4 Tucker: whole book Knowles and Prewitt: Epilogue
6–8	The Future of Black-White Relations	Goldman: Epilogue

Components of Course Grade: Midterm Exam: 30%   Paper: 10%
Section Grade: 20%   Final Exam: 40%

Class Meeting Schedule and Locations: Lectures each M and W in Social Science Building Room 100 at 9:00 A.M.; Section Meetings:

41:1	2	TH	SSB 412	Ms. Smith		41:4	3	TH	SSB 410	Mr. Elliot
:2	2	F	SSB 412	Ms. Smith		:5	4	TH	SSB 410	Mr. Elliot
:3	4	F	Horton 208	Ms. Smith		:6	3	F	Cobb 128	Mr. Elliot

The Purposes and Audiences of a Syllabus

A course syllabus can serve one or more purposes; it can: (1) provide an *overview* of a course—its content, requirements, and scheduling; (2) serve as a *guide*, advising students how elements of the course can be handled, how students might approach readings or term papers; and (3) be a *sourcebook*—a compendium of basic information about the field of study covered in the course. Syllabi can be useful for several audiences: students in a course; students considering taking a course; the course instructor; other instructors; and chairpersons and administrators.

The student and the syllabus.

Course syllabi are organizational devices that provide some protection to students and serve to answer their sometimes unarticulated questions. In our discussion of the first class meeting (chapter 8), we noted that in the early days of a course, a contract is drawn, implicitly or explicitly, between students and teacher. Students, like teachers, deserve to start a course with certainty about its key elements. Students typically take between three and five courses a term, and they need to be able to plan their work throughout that period. Careful time budgeting and effective study skills will not insure good student work if the student does not know in advance what the course requirements are and when they are due. More generally, students deserve

to know what a course involves. Teachers are granted by their departments or schools certain rights in controlling the scope and content of a course; the responsible exercise of these rights requires that instructors inform students of their plans and expectations. College and university catalogs typically provide little information about the scope of a course and rarely list its requirements. Since these descriptions typically employ code words to describe the course (". . . both ecological and sociocultural factors are stressed throughout. . . ."), they are often little more than Rorschach Tests. Especially in larger schools where the informal student information network may be less complete, it is the syllabus (and the first day of class) that provides the student with basic information about the course. If teachers believe that students should take an elective course on the basis of informed choice, it is necessary to provide an overview of the course content, structure, and requirements. This can be handled in the syllabus.

Students usually arrive in a first class meeting with two unarticulated questions about the course: "What's it all about?" and, once that is known, "What's the point of it?" While it is true that complete answers to these questions must come from experiencing the course, the syllabus can provide partial answers.

What's it all about?

1. What questions are being raised in this course? Are they questions to which I'm expected to get answers? What are the big questions?

2. How do those questions differ from (or complement) those raised in other courses I'm taking?

3. How will these questions be dealt with throughout the semester? By what methods? How will they be staged during the semester?

4. How will the instructor evaluate my answers to the questions posed in this course? Through tests? papers? participation? And when will the instructor evaluate my answers?

5. What resources, aside from the instructor, will I have available to help me get answers?

6. What skills am I expected to pick up in this course?

7. What kind of person is the instructor? Is the instructor fair in grading, interested in helping me learn, accessible to me for help?

What's the point of it?
1. Has the course any payoff for me in understanding myself and preparing me for future roles—work, familial, civic, etc.?

2. Will the course help me in my other courses?

3. Can I shape any parts of the course in a way to make them pertinent to my own interests and needs as I define them?

In short, students enter courses needing and deserving but lacking something the teacher already has—a cognitive map.

How many of these questions should be answered in the syllabus, how many handled orally, and how many handled in both ways? We suggest four guidelines. First, anything that forms part of the contract between teacher and student belongs in writing. Such contractual matters include course requirements, load (amount, type, timing of reading, papers, labs), attendance and grading policies, and the

basic orientation of the course. All courses have some defined scope: some things are included or includable, others not. If an urban sociology course will deal only tangentially with contemporary urban social problems and solutions, students should know that. If a teacher requires term paper topics be drawn from a provided list, students should know that.

Second, to the extent that course content or procedures cut against the grain of past student experiences or expectations, it is important that the syllabus discuss these course elements. This suggests greater need for specificity and clarity in syllabi for classes composed chiefly of first-year students, for courses that are typically the first upper-level sociology course taken, and for courses employing a novel instructional pattern. For students accustomed to lecture classes, the seminar presents special demands they should be made aware of. Courses in schools that have a high percentage of first-generation college students are also those in which student and teacher expectations should be handled in both written and oral fashion.

Third, the agenda for the first one or two class meetings can be a long one. While many things in a syllabus bear discussion, syllabi reduce the need to say everything. They also allow the student to read and ponder the course after the first class meeting. Finally, the utility of having basic course information written in the syllabus is underlined by the fact that some significant portion of students in a class will not be present on the first day, sometimes for reasons not of their own making. For them especially, the course contract and housekeeping matters (e.g., teacher's office location and hours) need to be in writing.

The syllabus is useful beyond the opening class. Containing a time schedule, it tells students when to expect what, and it aids them in planning and meshing various course requirements and coordinating work in their several courses and their nonacademic responsibilities. For all students, but especially for those many students who have part- or full-time employment (or family responsibilities), the written time schedule is necessary for rational planning.

If, from prior experience, the teacher knows that some students will have trouble analyzing tables or graphs, he or she can include in the syllabus both examples and suggested sources for help. Such sources might include pages in the text where the author explains the use of tabled data, or pages in an elementary methods book available through library reserve. And if such sources prove inadequate, the syllabus then might indicate that students should see the teacher during office hours or make a special appointment. Since different students may encounter this difficulty at different points in the course, addressing the concern within the syllabus makes sense. Thus, the syllabus can be an aid to students throughout the course.

Syllabi can be useful to students after the completion of a given course. This would be true when syllabi cite books or articles that the student may want to read after the course, names of journals that typically publish work in the course area, names of major indexes that catalog work in the field, and major data sources. One useful way to organize such material is by the occupational field in which students may employ it. Since many students will have nonprofessional interests in a field after their college work exposure, teachers might suggest some journals, articles, or books that contain nontechnical but sound treatments. Such source material is most useful when it is not simply an alphabetical list of citations but is organized under headings (such as those suggested

above) and when brief annotations are provided. Sociology has much to offer citizens, policymakers, and those in a great variety of occupational roles. Thus the learning and application of sociology can extend beyond the period of formal education. One way to give substance to such possibilities is to provide students with source materials useful *after* the course.

Syllabi can also help students who are considering taking a course in a subsequent semester. It is often the case that neither students nor their academic advisers are familiar with a course, and catalogs typically are of little help. Advisers often counsel students planning their next semester's courses to consult the listed faculty members for further information. Such students are well served when they can review a syllabus from a prior offering of the course and are told that while the current course will differ in some aspects, this syllabus provides a general idea of the scope of the course. An even better situation for the student obtains when a department maintains a syllabus file. Such strategies may have payoffs for teachers as well as students: in the long run, teachers save time and may also attract a higher percentage of students eager to start a course in which the aims and requirements are known in advance.

The instructor and the syllabus. Course syllabi can be viewed as organizational devices that aid the teacher in course planning, provide some checks on the progress of the course, and offer protection for the teacher by stating, clearly, course policies. To the extent that the syllabus serves as a student guide or reference, the syllabus may enhance student learning—a benefit to the teacher as well as the student. The syllabus embodies the teacher's goals and objectives, instructional arrangements, and also the means by which learning will be assessed. Courses have fixed beginnings and endings: films, statistics labs, simulation game materials, and the like must be reserved in advance for specified dates. Thus the time schedule is a basic part of a syllabus, and teachers must allocate either exact or approximate numbers of class meetings for different topical portions of the course and exact or approximate dates for class activities.

When the syllabus contains a time schedule, the instructor is forced to recognize how much—or how little—time can be devoted to the several issues treated in a course. The time schedule also allows the teacher to check on the progress of the course. If it becomes desirable to change the time devoted to a topic or activity, the teacher knows the extent to which other changes in the initial plan of the course will be necessary.

When the syllabus contains written statements of course policies, it provides protection for the teacher as well as the student. Matters of assessment of student learning and grading, late papers, missed exams (and make-up opportunities), attendance, expected class participation, criteria on which term papers will be judged, and optional versus required assignments are often misunderstood. Teachers who commit to writing policies on such matters are more likely to give careful thought to them and, also, to have clear guidelines for handling student questions and complaints.

Another benefit syllabi provide to the teacher relates to job market concerns. If a department considers teaching in promotion, salary, and tenure review, it is useful to the teacher to have tangible indicators of the care taken in construction of a course. Course syllabi can be used in this way—along with sample handouts, exams, assignments, memos to students, student or peer evaluations of teaching, and various assessments of student learning. Such material can also be used in a job search: departments seriously interested in recruiting effective teachers will welcome tangible forms of evidence (see Ewens, 1976a, 1976b).

Colleagues and the syllabus. There are persuasive reasons why information about courses needs to be shared within a department. Most departments have some structure of prerequisites; often the introductory sociology course (or one in a set of entry-level courses) is a prerequisite for some or all other courses. In most departments, more than one person teaches the introductory or entry-level courses. (In large departments, in one year, a dozen or more faculty and graduate students may be so involved.) If teachers of higher level courses are to build upon the courses stipulated as prerequisites, they must know something about the content of those prior courses. The well-prepared syllabus contains such information, and a departmental syllabus file is an economical way of sharing it. Departments in larger colleges and universities frequently offer elementary and advanced courses in the same subject area. Over a three- or four-year period—a span affecting several cohorts of undergraduates—several different faculty members will teach *one* of these courses. To know what the distinction is, or should be, between an elementary and an advanced course, or what learnings are prerequisites for an advanced course, teachers obviously need to know what students are learning. Our impression is that this rarely happens; sharing well-developed course syllabi would help.

There are some types of courses in which department faculties have a corporate stake. For these, it is imperative that information be widely available. Thus, a department has a special interest in courses required of majors. Presumably, the department is requiring more than a course label: it plans—or hopes—that students will acquire specific sorts of information and skills no matter who offers the course (or a section of the course). Sharing course syllabi provides a basis for discussion about just what information and skills the department wishes to have all majors (or some other category of students) achieve. To the degree that courses are related, and to the degree that teachers and their department wish to foster cumulative learning (prerequisites and sequencing) and rational curriculum planning, faculty colleagues can gain from sharing information in course syllabi.

Independent of such concerns, many chairpersons and deans see review of course syllabi as a useful or necessary quality control mechanism. There are potential abuses of such an orientation— imposition of orthodoxy among them. But our central point is that rational curriculum and course planning require shared information and the syllabus is a way of accomplishing this. Whether the context is collegial or managerial is important but does not vitiate this point.

The Relation of Content and Construction of Syllabi to Course Planning

The course syllabus is the result of the teacher's course planning. As such, the syllabus is the *end* of a process that starts with the instructor's choice of course goals. Once these goals are chosen and stated in measurable form, the teacher can select those means of teaching best suited to helping students attain the goals and objectives. "The choice of text, the selection of the type and order of assignments, the choice of teaching techniques, and all decisions involved in course planning should derive from your objectives" (McKeachie, 1978:5). Following (1) identification of goals and objectives, and (2) selection of instructional arrangements, the teacher plans (3) a series of assessments to reveal to both student and teacher whether the goals of the course are being met. Assessment has two basic purposes: most importantly, for learning and as a basis for diagnosing student and teacher progress; secondarily, for purposes of grading and certification (see chapter 13).

Various important factors come into play at each of these steps: the characteristics of students, the preferences of the teacher, the resources available to student and teacher (e.g., library, computer, audiovisual, teaching assistants), and the constraints on the teacher's time and preferences.

But exactly what information should be included in a course syllabus? We think the answer depends, in part, on the style of the individual instructor and, to some extent, on the size of the class. Some teachers distribute detailed memoranda for each segment of the course and/or for each course assignment. For students of such teachers, it may be useful to receive on the first day of class a syllabus that catalogs the segments and assignments of the course, together with the first of the detailed memos to be used. In larger courses and those with a complex design, the need for a detailed syllabus is probably greater.

In exhibit 9.2 we offer a checklist that a teacher might use in planning a course and in constructing and reviewing its syllabus. We think those items in the checklist that embody the contractual elements of the course (goals, scope, requirements, and ground rules) are minimum essential ingredients for syllabi. We are convinced that the checklist includes

Exhibit 9.2 A Checklist for Constructing and Reviewing Syllabi

1. *The Syllabus as a Message to the Student:*
   a. Is the substantive framework of the course gotten across?
   b. Is the calendar of events clear?
   c. Are requirements clear?
      (1) tests?
      (2) readings: required and desired?
      (3) exercises? assigned papers?
      (4) attendance?
      (5) due dates for various assignments?
      (6) conditions justifying exceptions and not?
   d. Are course goals and objectives stated? (see item 2 below)
   e. Are course prerequisites—formal and informal—stated?

2. *Course Goals and Objectives:*
   a. Does the syllabus contain a statement of general goals for student learning?
   b. Are the general course goals translated into operational statements? Or are they left as murky, equivocal, general though virtuous statements?
   c. Are the operational statements of objectives such that the student will know the extent to which they are achieved?
   d. Can the instructor explain: (1) how the instructional activities of the course will help the student achieve the course goals, and (2) how extent to which goals are achieved will be measured?

3. *Instructional Activities:*
   a. Is there a clear link to course goals?
   b. Is the need for variation provided for? (see item 4c below)
   c. Are the instructional activities appropriate to the skills and abilities required to master subject matter?

4. *Student Load:*
   a. *Quantity?* too much? too little? Using reading as an example: estimating 42 sessions in 14 weeks and 3 class hours each week, and assuming 2 hours of outside work for each hour in class, we get 84 hours. This would be the equivalent, at 20pp/hour of three 560-page books, minus the time needed for writing papers, doing labs and exercises, and the like. Difficulty of material, teacher goals, and student background obviously need to be taken into account.
   b. *Distribution through the semester?* Is it well staged?
   c. *Variation?* Is there some change of pace/interest through the offering of different sorts of assignments and different class activities? Lab exercises, quizzes, book reviews, essays, field work, library exploration, seeing and reviewing films or tapes, tapping current events and other media, computer-assisted instruction, simulations, analysis of raw data, etc.?

5. *Teacher Load:* Is the teacher trying to do too much in one course, in terms of his or her own time constraints? Is quantity likely to diminish quality? Thus, given a relatively fixed amount of time, could the teacher provide significantly more guidance and assistance to students and provide them with better and quicker feedback on papers, if 2 rather than 3 were assigned?

6. *Assessment of Testing:*
   a. Is there any consideration of two uses of testing:

    (1) for learning, stimulating discussion, as a basis for diagnosing strengths and weaknesses?

    (2) for grading/certification?

  b. Any indication of the type of test to be used? Realistic appraisal of the time needed to devise the test? and to evaluate it, including useful feedback to the student? Take-home? open book? multiple-choice? essay? other?

  c. Source of test items: Will students be asked/encouraged to contribute questions/problems/test items?

  d. Are the course goals indicated in a set of questions/problems stated at the outset? perhaps in the syllabus itself? Is the link to testing clear?

  e. Will the instructor test on:

    (1) knowledge of sources of relevant data?

    (2) knowledge as to how data are handled to improve the chances that our propositions are dependable?

  f. Is there any consideration of use of outside examiners?

  g. Staging of tests: When will they be given? How early does the instructor think he or she needs to get some feedback to the student?

  h. Are there plans for review, sessions with borderline people, preparation for exams?

7. *Assessment of Paper Assignments:*
  a. Number? scope? goals? due dates? format?
  b. Range of acceptable topics or questions for papers?
  c. Criteria to be used in assessing papers?

8. *The Course as an Element in the Student's Life Space:* Is there any indication that the instructor has considered the problem of
  a. Tying the material of this course to the student's major, or probable major, field? to the student's other concerns?
  b. To current social issues?
  c. To other courses the student may be taking concurrently? In short, does the syllabus leave room for adaptation to special interests of individuals and subgroups within the class?

9. *Active vs. Passive Teaching-Learning* (see item 4c above):
  a. Are there devices available for students to modify the agenda, help to reshape the syllabus?
  b. Are there various points in the course, as planned, at which the student can become actively engaged in the pursuit of problems bearing on course content?

10. *The Course as Part of the General Framework of Sociology:*
  a. Is there some indication that students will be able to see this particular course in the general framework of sociology? An intellectual setting in which the material of this course forms an understandable part?
  b. Do social issues override sociological problems?

11. *Office Hours:*
  a. Does the syllabus offer any encouragement for conferences with the instructor?
  b. Are teacher-student conferences required? requested? encouraged?
  c. Are appropriate matters for discussion suggested?

12. *Preparation and Follow-up of Audiovisual aids:* If films or other aids are to be used, are they treated seriously rather than as entertaining interludes?

13. *Classroom operations:* What alternatives to conventional lecture-discussion procedures have been considered?
    a. Lab periods?
    b. Seminar sessions with students presenting and defending a thesis to whole group or some part of it?
    c. Role playing? sociodrama?
    d. Demonstrations of one sort or another?

14. *Flexibility:*
    a. If the teacher intends to have some, is this indicated?
    b. If there are boundaries to that flexibility, are they specified?
    c. Would examples of student initiative (and teacher response) taken in the past be useful?

15. *Utility of the Syllabus as a Sourcebook and Guide:*
    a. Does the syllabus provide students with sources useful in work on assignments (term papers, etc.)?
    b. Does the syllabus identify common stumbling blocks in the course and places students can find assistance?
    c. Will the syllabus be useful to the student *after* the course?
       (1) Does it list books or articles a student might want to read after the course?
       (2) Does it list sources (e.g., journals) that will carry future work in the field?
       (3) Is this information organized in a useful way?

16. *Structuring the Syllabus around Questions:* Does the syllabus reveal a course structured around questions worth asking and the pursuit of answers to them?

17. *Clarity, Organization, and Structure:*
    a. Does the syllabus provide explanations of those technical terms used in the syllabus and course that are likely to cause confusion (e.g., those technical terms that also have everyday meanings such as *role, theory, hypothesis, evidence*)?
    b. Is the syllabus organized such that it is easily usable? If long, does it contain a table of contents? Are major topics flagged by special headings, etc.?
    c. Does the syllabus reveal a course introduction too long or complex or so stressing theoretical and conceptual issues that you may lose the student?

important issues that should be faced in course planning. The degree to which these items are represented in syllabi will depend, in part, on how much teachers believe they can handle orally or in other written communications to their classes. Finally, it is well to remember the words of our colleague, Reece McGee, who reminded us that "a syllabus is neither a magic wand nor a freight wagon."

Several of the items in the exhibit 9.2 checklist require some explanation.

Checklist item 1e: Course prerequisites. If a course has formal prerequisites (specific prior courses or class standing), these should be stated in the syllabus. In some cases, students can lose credit if they take a course out of sequence or take a course without having fulfilled a prior requirement. Even where this is not the case, if prerequisites have any meaning at all, students who take a course without them may learn less than they otherwise could have learned. While students should read the school catalog and check for prerequisites (and while advisers are often mandated to catch problems), teachers demonstrate their concern for students when formal prerequisites are stated in the syllabus. Following the first class, a teacher can meet with students who do not meet a formal prerequisite to see if there is basis for a waiver. We do not think that "caveat emptor" is an appropriate position for a teacher: the matter of prerequisites should be addressed.

If there are no formal prerequisites for a course, this should be stated in the syllabus, since this fact is a crucial part of the implicit contract between teacher and student. If there are no prerequisites, teachers cannot legitimately hold students responsible for any specific material. If there are prerequisites, what assumptions can teachers make about what their students already know? In large schools, prerequisites may be the only piece of information teachers have about students. Teachers should disclose to students at the outset of the course what types and levels of prior knowledge and skills they have assumed in constructing the course and hope to build upon. Even where formal prerequisites for a given course do not exist, teachers make assumptions about prior general knowledge and skill. These, too, should be disclosed to students.

Checklist item 14: Flexibility. The written syllabus can be a cognitive map, contract, reference, and organizational tool to assist the student and teacher; it embodies the course. But the written syllabus need not foreclose flexibility. Consider the course calendar. During the semester, a teacher may decide to change the details to be covered or the approach to be used before a particular topic is due for discussion. Student interest can be an important variable affecting the optimal pace and structure of a course; the teacher may feel that continued work on an issue exciting student interest is warranted. To accommodate such unplanned situations, the teacher may wish to avoid a very high level of specificity in attaching dates to the coverage of each of the course's subtopics.

However, leaving a course plan open to some modification is not an argument for doing away with a syllabus nor for a teacher failing to reveal course goals and plans. In fact, when students perceive a teacher as nondirective, they often see that teacher as uninterested in the class (Mann, 1970, cited by McKeachie, 1978:12).

We assume that all teachers have their own agendas and that these were not arrived at lightly. On an agenda will be some goals the teacher believes essential to the course. Likewise, the teacher may be convinced that certain goals and instructional approaches—and perhaps some specific assignments—may be open for negotiation. The teacher can so specify. The course calendar can provide blocks of time for new topics or expanded treatment of included topics, and the schedule itself can be modified as the course goes along. But we think it is the student's right to know at the outset of the course, the scope and basic outlines of the course and the dates on which major assignments are due and exams given.

Here is how we tried to build some flexibility into exam and paper requirements in one course. The syllabus, handed out on the first day of classes, included the following statement.

> *Course Requirements:* There will be at least two one-hour exams and two short papers in addition to the comprehensive final given during the regularly scheduled exam period.
> I will not decide on course requirements, other than the final, until the second

or third class meeting. I want to get your preferences, and your reactions to my initial proposal which is this: (a) two exams, evenly spaced during the semester, covering course readings, lectures, and discussion; multiple choice items, and some essays stressing application of concepts and theories to cases; (b) four short papers—each about five pages and each prepared prior to a specifically designated class discussion session and relating to the topic of those sessions. Page 3 of this syllabus describes the type of paper I will ask you to prepare and my reasons behind that choice. I think course topics #s 3, 5, 8, 11, and 12 would provide us interesting topics, but I am open to papers (at least two) on any of our fourteen topics.

Please come to Wednesday's class meeting prepared to discuss your preferences for exams (number of) and papers (number, topics).

In the first class, we asked students to read this statement and answered questions about the nature and scope of the papers. In the second session, we provided for about fifteen minutes of discussion and took a few straw votes. We brought to the third class meeting a handout with the final requirements—including due dates and details.

Thus we built some flexibility and student choice into selection of course requirements. But we had thought through, in advance of the course, what requirements we defined as nonnegotiable (the minimum number and type of exams and papers, etc.). We did not raise false expectations. Discussion with the class indicated they were anxious about papers of the type we wanted—they asked for few papers. And so the course requirements included the minimum number of papers initially specified (two). And students had some definite preferences for paper topics and these were accommodated. While this particular handling of the flexibility-on-

course-requirements issue can no doubt be improved upon, it is clearly preferable to an open-ended query, in the first class, about what students' druthers are, then finding their suggestions unacceptable, and then arriving in the second class meeting with a set of requirements markedly different from student choices.

But what of courses that employ seminar discussion of student papers, or treat student-selected topics, or topics that emerge as the course develops? What is the task of the syllabus in these cases? The syllabus should still serve some of the same basic purposes—indicating course goals, suggesting sources and aids, describing any aspects of the course that the instructor defines as fixed, and so on. Thus, in a seminar on stratification where class sessions after the first two weeks will focus on student papers, will the teacher welcome any paper on any aspect of stratification, however defined? Does the teacher want papers to make cross-national comparisons? Is this optional, suggested, very desirable, or required? We think the teacher should pose and answer such questions. This should be done in writing so students working on papers six or eight weeks hence will be able to refer back to guidelines as they prepare their papers.

Parallel considerations apply to discussion topics and courses based on emergent issues. Does the teacher define anything as out of bounds? If the teacher plans on having students contribute to the development of the course outline, will the teacher insist on any procedures or boundaries? If so—and if these procedures or boundaries are not made explicit to students—the teacher will be placed in the position of either covertly manipulating students or bringing down a heavy hand after suggesting a wholly open situation. A course syllabus can encourage student creativity and participation by defining it, providing examples of how in prior semesters student contributions have helped shape the course, and by providing models, sources, or exercises designed to stimulate creativity. Since instructor and course flexibility are not often available in college (and less often a feature of undergraduates' high school experiences), teachers may find it useful to provide illustrations of flexibility in past offerings of the course in question or, lacking past experience, to use hypothetical cases. Such examples may lend credibility to the claim of flexibility and encourage students to suggest new directions.

Checklist item 4: Student load.   What we wish to emphasize here is that there are no *a priori* answers to the question whether any given reading load is too great or too small. Some colleges and some teachers speak of a certain load as appropriate for any course—thus, "students should read about 100 pages a week in a three hour course." Such norms do not consider: (1) other elements in student work load (labs, exercises, simulations, etc.), (2) student characteristics that the teacher may want or need to consider, (3) the nature of the reading material, and (4) the teacher's goals in assigning the reading. There is nothing intrinsically rigorous, rewarding, educational, or virtuous about the course with a lengthy list of assigned books and articles. Some books are more complex than others; some treat matters totally new to students. Such issues make page-limit targets less meaningful. And what does the teacher want students to do with an assigned book? Is it to be closely read and mastered, or only skimmed for the major points? Does it contain exercises, problems, or issues at the conclusion of each chapter, and does the teacher want students to work with them? Does the teacher want students to construct a hypothesis inventory for an assigned book? Does the teacher want students to consider each assigned book or article on its own merits or to make comparisons (systematic or informal) between it and other readings? Does the teacher want students to study each assigned article for what it says about each of a dozen larger issues? Questions such as these suggest that the appropriate reading load depends on various factors, most of which are derived from the instructor's course goals.

Checklist item 16: Structuring the syllabus around questions.   Does the syllabus reveal a course structured around questions worth asking and the pursuit of answers to them? We ask this because most courses (and syllabi, and textbooks) are organized around topics. In contrast, phrasing something as a question suggests that there is something to be explained, that one is looking for an answer—and presumably that is what education is about.

Consider this example. Most urban sociology courses examine the effects on primary and secondary social relationships, and personality, of living in large cities. Louis Wirth's "Urbanism as a Way of Life" (1938) is a classic theoretical statement of the issues involved. In a syllabus, the concerns addressed by Wirth and others might appear under topical labels such as:

The Theory of Urban Anomie, or
Social Relations and Community Scale, or
The Simmel-Park-Wirth Thesis Explored.

We think students' interest might be raised and their attention more usefully focused if such topical labels were replaced with questions such as:

Does City Living Affect Social Life Adversely? or
What Does Living in Big Cities Do to Family, Friendship, and Mental Health?

Here we have questions that are not about sociology but about the social world. We think that in undergraduate education, courses, especially introductory courses, should be organized around questions about society (its structures and processes) and human social relationships, and seldom about sociology. Sociology should be used both to frame the questions and to move us toward answers. The topical labels given above suffer other defects as well: they prematurely introduce terms such as *anomie* and *community scale*, which may mean nothing to students, and they do not touch the world as students know it.

Another way to build questions into syllabi is to organize a course around topics and provide subsidiary questions for each topic. For example, the syllabus we used in a graduate course on the teaching of sociology included the following section:

III—EVALUATING STUDENT ACHIEVEMENT OF COURSE GOALS

November 19:
What are the purposes of testing? Are they compatible? What are the advantages and disadvantages of different modes of examination? How shall I grade? On a curve? Otherwise?

Assignment: *Please read. . . .*

Checklist item 11: Office hours.   Among the many factors influencing student use of a teacher's office hours are: the backgrounds of students in the class, the level of difficulty of course material and the clarity with which it is presented, whether the course is required and for what, the types of assignments given, and whether office visits are required. The timing of office hours is also a factor: teachers who post hours of 5:00 to 6:30 P.M. on Wednesday and Friday are not likely to have many visitors. The volume of visits will also be affected by the written and oral invitations teachers extend. If teachers really want students to come in during office hours, they will find it is useful to say so in the syllabus and to say why they view such discussions as important. No matter when the teacher sets office hours, some students will not be free at those times and the syllabus can note "other times by appointment." Posting hours on the chalkboard during the opening classes and repeating announcements will also convey to students the teacher's interest in conversation with them. Some teachers are reluctant to announce office hours in the first class (or place them in the syllabus) since their schedule of committee assignments may not yet be set. But the teacher's early performance can set a pattern of student expectations (the opening classes can be viewed as pedagogical imprinting). At least two paths are open to the teacher. First, the teacher can set office hours in advance and hold them as religiously as class hours; second, the teacher can announce temporary office hours to be replaced later by well-publicized permanent hours.

Checklist item 17c: Introduction to the course.   A course in Industrial Sociology might start with a review of changing definitions and boundaries of the field. The teacher might trace the diverse roots of the field in industrial psychology, management and personnel studies, labor economics, public administration, group dynamics, sociometry, and social exchange and conflict theory. Marx, Weber, Veblen, Taylor, Mayo, Roethlisberger, Dickson, Gulick, Lippitt, Barnard, Simon, Whyte,

Gouldner, Blau, Crozier . . . ah, what a beginning! Logical, comprehensive, developmental. But also one that might result in students losing sight of the subject matter and the questions that the field of industrial sociology seeks to answer.

It may be logical to begin a course with conceptual, theoretical, and historical matters, but logic is not a sufficient yardstick. Students may not be able to benefit from such an approach. The student—everyone—needs pegs on which to hang new ideas and information. And we think the most useful pegs are questions and issues that tap student experience and concerns. A long introduction at a high level of abstraction will be lost on most students.

Contrast the opening chapters of the two editions of Turner and Killian's *Collective Behavior* (1957, 1972). In both editions, the opening chapter is titled "The Field of Collective Behavior," and the authors discuss the definition of the field and recurring issues in it. The first edition opens with an essay on the development of the field: the student reads of the contributions of Spencer, Durkheim, Tarde, Le Bon, McDougall, and dozens of other social scientists, political philosophers, and political activists. This introduction is densely packed and connected with little that undergraduates can have any grasp of. The second edition opens with brief extracts dealing with an eleventh-century crusade and with a mid-1960s civil rights march. Explanation of those two events and the class of phenomena they represent is kept in the fore in succeeding discussion. The approach in the first edition is useful for the graduate student who brings to the course a knowledge of the basic questions being asked, a knowledge of the phenomena under study, and a prior interest in the field; but not for the undergraduate.

So it is that the course organization and syllabus for graduate and undergraduate courses ought to be markedly different (even if the same sociological tools are used to study the same social phenomena). Many teachers, especially new teachers, rely heavily on syllabi from their graduate courses as they plan their undergraduate courses. This is understandable but lamentable: the notion that an undergraduate course can be effective when modeled on a graduate course seems to us to fly in the face of what a rudimentary sociological analysis suggests about the two types of classes.

The syllabus serves many audiences in diverse ways. It is a tool and only one tool. But as it is the first and most extensive written communication from teacher to student, and because it embodies the course plan, the syllabus is vitally important in teaching and learning.

Textbooks and Other Written Materials*

The revolution in teaching media has not been the advent of television, teaching machines, or computers, but rather the readier availability of printed materials. (McKeachie, 1978:7)

Other than oral communication, the textbook and other written resources are used more widely in the teaching of sociology than any other teaching-learning tool or method. What types of readings are available, and how do teachers use them?

* Throughout this chapter we cite many textbooks in use during the mid- and late-1970s. We cite specific books to illustrate general points; however, such citation does not imply that these are the best or only works to follow a particular model or use a particular approach. Some readers may wish to examine these books to further explore the category they typify. Teachers selecting course texts will naturally want to explore the full range of works available; portions of this section discuss methods of text selection.

How can texts be used in the teaching-learning process, and what do students learn from them? What are some of the criteria for using or not using reading materials of different types? In answering these questions we focus on introductory textbooks since textbooks are widely used and since close to 50 percent of all sociology enrollments are in the introductory course.[3] Nonetheless, many of the issues we raise are applicable to anthologies and other written forms.

What Texts Are Available and How Are They Used?

In 1895, George Vincent and Albion W. Small published what Howard Odum (1951:103–104) called "perhaps the first elementary textbook in sociology prepared for popular use as a college text." In 1959, there were twenty-four textbooks in Introductory Sociology (Van Valey, 1975:24),[4] and by 1974/75, the number in print had grown to sixty to sixty-six texts augmented by more than forty anthologies and dozens of workbooks and manuals (Van Valey, 1975; Brown, 1976). Thus teachers of Introductory Sociology have a large number of texts from which to choose, not to mention other monographs and articles. To what extent are texts and other books used?

A national sample survey conducted by the ASA Projects on Teaching Undergraduate Sociology in 1976 (Bradshaw and McPherron, 1977)[5] revealed that books are by far the most frequently used teaching-learning tool in the introductory and other sociology courses. Textbooks are used extensively (versus occasionally, or not at all) in 90 percent of introductory and 75 percent of other sociology courses. The corresponding figures for books other than texts are 35 and 55 percent. There is little variation in these figures by size and type of school. No other teaching tool or technique (e.g., film, simulation and games, computer-assisted instruction) approaches this level of use. Ballantine's (1977) analysis of course syllabi for 100 nonsystematically selected introductory courses supports the Bradshaw and McPherron findings: 82 percent of the courses used a textbook and 43 percent employed an anthology or other books.[6]

The scores of available texts vary along many different dimensions. There is the traditional, full-sized text and the compact model. Some are organized around a single theoretical perspective; others are eclectic. Some introductory books are designed for independent student use; others assume classroom elaboration. And texts are produced in different ways. There is the traditional author-controlled volume, the author-assisted textbook, and the managed text. There are instant texts produced on demand by a publisher with content selected by the instructor from existing articles and/or material prepared by the teacher.[7] Furthermore, the content of texts varies widely as do the forms of organization and modes of presentation. Given this welter of materials, what should the teacher use? The answer should come from the instructor's goals and the composition of the class.

How Teachers Can Learn What Texts Are Available

At least four sources are available to assist teachers in locating and assessing texts, anthologies, and other books. A first and very important source is the teacher's colleagues. Scanning colleagues' bookshelves and asking them for their experiences with different texts (and the reactions of their students) can yield useful information. A sociologist located at a smaller school, where he or she may be the only sociologist or the only sociologist with a given specialty, might write or call nearby sociologists for advice.

Students represent a second source of information about textbooks. In addition to direct conversation with students, teachers can sometimes obtain student opinion from colleagues who have gathered student evaluations of course readings.

A third source of information is journal advertisements, advertising flyers, and examination copies sent by publishers. Publishing houses maintain (or purchase from commercial sources) mailing lists of sociologists with different teaching specialties (including both Introductory Sociology and Social Problems). Teachers who believe they are not on such lists can write publishers and ask to be placed on their lists. At publishers' displays at national and regional sociology meetings, teachers can scan books in print, pick up catalogs, and sign up to receive complimentary desk copies (not to be sold) of texts suited to their courses.

A fourth source of information on books is reviews appearing in journals. Many specialized journals carry reviews on new books in their field, and those that do not carry reviews frequently list "publications received." Reviews of introductory and other sociology texts regularly appear in *Teaching Sociology* (TS), *Contemporary Sociology* (CS), and *Sociology: Review of New Books* (SRNB). But many texts are not reviewed, and only a small portion of all texts are reviewed in more than one journal. In 1975, there were in print approximately sixty-five introductory texts, forty anthologies, and dozens of workbooks (Van Valey, 1975; Brown, 1976).[8] According to a study by Young

(1975), during 1965/75 a total of seventy-one different introductory textbooks were reviewed in one of the following journals: *CS* (or prior to 1972, *The American Sociological Review* [ASR]), *Social Forces* (SF), and *The American Journal of Sociology* (AJS). Three-fourths of the seventy-one texts received only one review. The seventy-one texts received a total of eighty-nine reviews; just under 80 percent of the eighty-nine reviews appeared in *CS*. During 1978, the numbers of texts and readers (in all course areas) reviewed in *TS* and *CS* were thirty-nine and sixty, respectively.

Reviews in *TS* deserve special mention since they are written by sociologists who have used the books in their classrooms. Starting with the third issue (October 1974), the fourteen issues of *TS* published through January 1979 carried reviews of 132 textbooks applicable to the following courses:

Course	Texts Reviewed
Introductory	21
Methods; Statistics	18
Criminology; Deviance	13
Stratification	13
Social Problems	10
Theory	8
Marriage and Family	7
Minority Groups	6
Medical	4
Gender Roles	3
Urban	3
All other courses	26

What information is contained in reviews of introductory texts? Young's analysis of all such reviews appearing in *CS* (or *ASR*), *SF*, and *AJS* between 1965 and 1975 indicates only four types of reviewer comments present in more than a third of the reviews. His analysis, summarized in table 9.1, also shows that many aspects of texts teachers are likely to consider important are dealt with in only a small percentage of reviews. It is our impression that higher percentages of reviews appearing in *TS* devote attention to the Type II and Type III categories listed in table 9.1.

Table 9.1 Reviewer Comments on Introductory Texts, Selected Journals, 1965–1975

Type of Reviewer Comment	Percentage of Reviews with Comments of This Type	Rank
I. Content Categories		
A. Coverage	75%	1
B. Content Areas		
1. Definition of Sociology	29	6
2. Empirical Research	15	15
3. Methodology Problems	21	10
4. Theory	18	12.5
C. Accuracy[a]	14	16
D. Bias or Orientation[b]	52	2
II. Presentation Categories		
A. Organization	49	3
B. Integration[c]	33	5
C. Readability	47	4
D. Difficulty	25	8
E. Physical Format	20	11
III. Other Categories		
A. Distinction[d]	16	14
B. Limitations[e]	25	8
C. Student Interest	25	8
D. Provocation of Thought	18	12.5

Notes:
(a) The reviewer questions the accuracy of some data or interpretation of them as presented in the book reviewed; does not include typographical or editorial errors such as where the reviewer feels the author is making a statement of fact, not opinion, that the reviewer believes to be incorrect.

(b) Includes comments indicating or decrying a particular theoretical or ideological orientation or bias in the presentation or selection of materials; no distinction is made here between theory and ideology since reviewers have different definitions of the terms.

(c) The reviewer considers whether the book presents a

From time to time, sociology journal articles or reviews provide comparative information on texts. For example, Brown (1976), in *CS*, presents detailed information on thirty-two introductory texts published during a two-year period; Van Valey (1975), in *TS*, indicates the level of treatment of research methods in 113 introductory texts and anthologies; and Spanier and Stump (1978) review the use of substantive research findings in eighteen marriage and family texts.

Thus, sociologists have available a number of sources from which they can learn what texts are available and something about their content. It seems apparent, though, that there is no good substitute for detailed review of competing texts for a given course. We will argue shortly that such a review is worth the effort since available research suggests that the textbook is a major influence on what students learn. In later sections, we discuss criteria for selecting course texts and other reading materials. One important criterion is the degree of congruence between the text and the instructor's course goals.

Learning Goals and Textbook Selection

College textbooks contain the *results* of the author's thinking; they represent what one writer called "the finished products of inquiry" (Phenix, 1975:27). Introductory texts usually seek to present

coherent whole, and whether it brings all parts of sociology together.

(d) Includes comments on any features that the reviewer believes set the book apart from its competitors.

(e) Includes comments suggesting circumstances under which the book can be most fruitfully used; includes such factors as type of student and potential coupling of the book to other teaching-learning resources of various types.

Source: Young (1975). For journals reviewed, see text discussion.

sociology "within an integrated and systematic framework," or to be "determinedly and thoroughly comprehensive," making an effort to "explain and exemplify every major concept normally treated in the first course in sociology, to describe and explain the dominant theoretical positions in the field—and the quarrels associated with them—the classical studies, and to begin at least, to indicate the kinds of qualifications, hesitations, objections and uncertainties associated with *any* statement that claims to say 'this is what sociology is.'"

If the transmission of information is the teacher's sole instructional goal, conventional textbooks will be appropriate and efficient teaching tools. But many teachers and departments have additional goals, such as helping students understand everyday social life and developing critical thinking skills (see evidence cited by Bradshaw and McPherron, 1977). And most texts are not prepared or organized to meet such ends. Stressing synthesis, exposition, and integration, texts provide answers—not the steps that one takes to arrive at answers. Most texts provide basic information but do not help the student learn to identify problems, formulate questions, or develop solutions or answers. They do not actively involve the student in doing sociology. They seldom show how sociology is done. They do not help the student to learn and apply the skills of induction and deduction or to recognize inconsistencies. As Sanders (1966:106) notes:

In a classroom that centers on memorization of the textbook, students do not encounter illogical thinking because it is carefully screened out.

Transmission of information is one very important purpose of education. But if teachers have additional instructional goals, tools to supplement the conventional textbook will be needed. Of course, some textbooks and some other reading materials are structured to meet some of these other instructional goals. Thus, Vander Zanden (1970:v–vi) expresses an interest in helping "the student begin 'thinking like a sociologist.'"

Much of modern sociological research is highly technical and relatively uncomprehensible to the neophyte. As a result, it is easy to slip into the habit of merely telling *students that "sociologists have found" this or that to be true or that "studies have been done" which reveal this or that about a particular phenomenon. Yet we certainly do not want to contribute to the production of robots who mechanically recite facts with little or no insight or creativity. To do so is to belie the ethos of science—a spirit characterized by rationality and skepticism. For this reason,* Research Studies *have been included throughout the text at appropriate intervals. Each study is related to the subject matter of its respective chapter and is divided step-by-step into problem, hypothesis, method, findings, and conclusions. The aim is to examine a significant piece of research with the student and to give him a "feel" for sociology and what sociologists do. The instructor may also wish to have his students outline a number of other sociological papers, using a somewhat similar format: problem, hypothesis, method, findings, and conclusions.*

Many texts contain "selected readings." However, we cite Vander Zanden because his text is one of those that does not simply provide a synopsis of what was studied and learned, but lays out the logical (if not temporal) steps in sociological research. Vander Zanden's statement is also useful because it suggests that teachers can have students work with and use readings and not simply read and memorize their content.

Of course, reading materials are not the only vehicle for meeting instructional goals. Lectures, class discussions, exercises, assignments, tools such as simulation games, and the way the text and other readings are used can help meet instructional goals beyond the transmission of information. But some written materials are more useful than others in helping achieve these goals. Some books are designed to have students confront problems; they pose important and unresolved issues about the study of the social world and provide students either with alternative answers or the raw materials with which to construct answers. Such books help the instructor in the role of benign disrupter (see chapter 5).

In some sociology courses, students read Weber's *Protestant Ethic and the Spirit of Capitalism* (1904–1905). The relationship suggested by the title is by no means a settled question. A teacher wishing students to confront Weber's thesis might use a volume such as Green's *Protestantism and Capitalism: The Weber Thesis and Its Critics* (1959). This book opens with an essay by Weber, a summary of Weber's argument, and an essay by Troeltsch supporting the Weber thesis. The rest of the book includes various critical analyses of Weber along with other explanations for the rise of capitalism. Or consider Benton's *Town Origins: The Evidence from Medieval England* (1968). What accounts for the origins of towns and cities? Answers to this question variously focus on markets, mercantilists, clergy, associations and guilds, the military, and so on. Benton's volume provides the reader with three types of material. First, brief statements of three general theories (those of Pirenne, Mumford, and Ennen); second, four competing analyses of town origins in medieval England; and third, "a sample of evidence," raw materials students can analyze as they build an explanation for the rise of towns. Included are lists of place-names and their origins,

extracts from the Domesday Book, court records, exchequer records, town charters, tax lists, laws, and the like.

We know of few textbooks for Introductory Sociology (or other courses) that are structured around questions or that involve the student in learning in active ways. Brown's (1976:124) systematic comparison of thirty-two introductory texts published in 1974/75 finds that "most are 'eclectic' attempting to present all points of view. . . . Four books are more serious about their eclecticism. Light-Keller, Kenkel-Voland, Wright, and Lasswell mention the competing models at the beginning of the book, and refer to them throughout." Brown found five texts with a specific, single theoretical orientation (conflict, functionalism, or symbolic interactionism). Of the twenty-seven eclectic texts, only four confront the student with competing explanations for social phenomena.

Some introductory textbooks do include review questions, controversies, or suggested research projects. Thus each chapter of McGee (1977) contains summary questions and four or five activities that invite the student to apply the information in the text through a variety of student exercises variously involving census data, popular magazines, and student-conducted research projects. Perrucci, Knudsen, and Hamby (1977) open each of their twenty chapters with a "number of questions that will give the reader a quick glimpse of some of the ideas which will be discussed . . . followed by a Controversy section in the form of two brief, divergent statements on a particular topic. These controversies are designed to acquaint the reader with some broader, unresolved sociological and social issues and to indicate the relevance of a sociological perspective in contemporary society" (pp. vi–vii). Most chapters of Kloss, Roberts, and Dorn

(1976) end with a student project devised to meet a stated purpose and problem. It indicates the research setting, suggests appropriate procedures, and provides a report form. Many of these projects allow the teacher to cumulate the findings of individual students or groups of students. This same text contains twenty-three extracts from popular magazines. The narrative portion of the text raises but does not usually answer questions about the content of these vignettes, which thus become raw material the student can analyze.

An example of an introductory textbook that moves beyond traditional exposition is one designed for high school students, *Inquiries in Sociology* (Hughes, 1978). It includes twenty-eight exercises that ask students to answer questions based on tabled data, charts, photographs, and narratives. These exercises are noteworthy because they attempt to develop students' analytic skills. Some exercises involve categorization, comparison, specification of relationships between variables, discovery of links between attitudes and behaviors, development of hypotheses, and specification of needed data and modes of testing.

Exercises such as those just mentioned are rarely found in textbooks, but are sometimes included in instructor's manuals. Teachers can certainly devise them. There are several workbooks that offer students the opportunity to analyze data, apply concepts, replicate studies, and otherwise use or do sociology—e.g., Dean and Valdes (1976), Larsen and Catton (1971), Richard and Mann (1973), Sokol (1970), Straus and Nelson (1968), and a few others that accompany major texts.

Books and other teaching tools should serve one or more instructional goals and, insofar as possible, not be an obstacle to the achievement of other goals.

According to Sanders (1966:158):

> *Textbooks create a major problem for teachers concerned with composing good questions. Although many are attractive, accurate, readable, and understandable, they are also one of the biggest deterrents to thinking in the classroom, because the writers assume that students learn best by studying a polished product. The key function of the writer is to explain, and a good explanation is interesting, orderly, accurate and complete. The vocabulary suits the level of the student and complex ideas are clarified by dissection, integration, example and visual images. Thus, the textbook is weak in that it offers little opportunity for any mental activity except remembering. If there is an inference to be drawn, the author draws it, and if there is a significant relationship to be noted, the author points it out. There are no loose ends or incomplete analyses. The textbook is highly refined and as near perfection as a human mind is capable of making it—but the author does the thinking. The book never gives a clue that the author pondered (maybe even agonized) over hundreds of decisions. The result is that the creative process and the controversy of competing ideas are hidden from the students.*

Thus, the traditional textbook (and most are) is an excellent source for conveying information—an important goal in most courses—but is not well suited for other educational goals.

The Importance of Books in Teaching and Learning

Much research suggests that textbooks and reading materials are a major influence in what students learn in college courses. So powerful may be the effect of assigned reading that it is believed by some to explain the "no difference" findings of many comparative studies of teaching methods.*

* These studies are discussed in chapter 12.

All researchers have been inclined to overlook what is, perhaps, the outstanding commonality among teaching methods compared in a given study. This is the textbook(s) utilized. As Professor [Ernest R.] Hilgard so perceptively stated:

> *Most studies have relied very heavily on a common textbook in all courses, and in order to be "fair" most of the examination questions are based on that book. I can't help but believe that more careful exposition goes into a good textbook than a lecturer can put into a lecture. . . . Hence I believe we are often measuring what the student learned from his textbook. . . . [Textbooks] may be so powerful as to override differences in teaching. (Dubin and Taveggia, 1968:47, quoting Hilgard, Personal Communication.)*

In many (especially large, introductory) courses, examinations form a major part of the student's grade and are based in important part upon the textbook. Judging from what we have observed and been told by publishers' representatives, the test-item manuals and files geared to the text are the source of many examinations in such courses. There is good reason to think that students are well aware of this grade-test-text linkage (see, for example, discussion throughout Becker, Geer, and Hughes, 1968).

While there are sound, research-based reasons to think that teacher activity and interaction with students can be important factors in student learning (see chapter 12), there is little doubt that reading assignments are important determinants of what students learn. Hence they merit careful attention to both the criteria for selecting some readings over others and the way readings are introduced and exploited in class. McKeachie (1978:103–104) cites studies that find that:

1. Students read more efficiently when they are given questions to answer on the material.

2. Active questioning and recitation is more effective than passive reading.

3. Having students keep reading logs on which teachers give periodic feedback and having students spend a major portion of their time in reading of their own choice results in marked improvement in critical and integrative ability.

4. While study questions do not automatically guarantee learning gains, the types of questions teachers ask and when the students are given the questions can affect learning gains.

There are at least four other ways in which assigned readings are very important in teaching and learning. First, the selection of reading assignments communicates much to students about how the teacher defines the scope of the course and its desired outcomes. Second, "perhaps the most effective way to change teaching strategies and objectives will be to change the starting place for most instruction, the materials for students" (Fenton, 1967:60). The teacher who wishes to shift the emphasis in an introductory course from presentation of sociology as a theoretically eclectic discipline and focus on a structuralist orientation will do well to select a text with such an emphasis. Third, the selection of reading material touches the matter of course integration. The parts or dimensions of a course can be meshed by the text or the instructor—it is rare when undergraduates can do it. Class time is limited and teachers may want to rely on the text to be the integrating mechanism, thus freeing some class time for other pursuits. Or the teacher may want to assign a collection of readings and make integration the work of class meetings. Or a middle path may be chosen. These are matters of personal preference, but it is clear that the choice and handling of reading material affects whether students come to view their course and its subject matter holistically or as a succession of apparently unrelated topics.

Finally, assigned reading may set patterns for students' future reading and use of sociology. There is some evidence that, during their college years, students read little beyond that which is required for their courses. We suspect that course reading constitutes a large part, if not all, of what most students ever read in sociology. But many teachers want to encourage their students' reading and use of the sociological perspective beyond the period of formal education. This is probably accomplished to the degree that teachers reveal sociology as providing the student with tools useful in understanding their experiences and place in the evolving social world. Assigned course reading probably plays a large part in this. If a text is about "the academic discipline of sociology, not about society and how it works," if the "content disproportionately consists of highfalutin but vague concepts, wars between academic armies mostly consisting of one soldier each, [and] glittering generalities," it is likely that students will be closed to future reading or application of sociology.[9]

There are several ways to avoid this outcome. Rather than assume or assert the utility of sociology, teachers can demonstrate it, model it, and provide students with opportunities to practice it. Lectures, discussions, exercises, assignments, and examinations can be devised in which students apply the concepts, theories, methods, and substantive materials of the text in tackling actual problems and issues in their own lives and social settings. Individual student assignments involving application of textbook knowledge may be especially important since they model an activity students can engage in on their own after college. After college, we know

many of our students will read newspapers and news magazines and listen to and watch news broadcasts. Much of their knowledge about the social world will derive from such sources. Exercises that call for application of textbook knowledge to such material may be especially useful in fostering long-term use of sociology.

There are several small ways in which teachers can encourage independent student reading. Providing summer reading lists at the end of the spring term, including suggested readings for the future in a syllabus, bringing to class collateral books which students can borrow, and maintaining a shelf of lending books in the teacher's office are all ways the instructor can tell students that their lives will be enriched by reading beyond that which is required for the course. We borrowed the last two suggestions from Kenneth E. Eble who concludes his own discussion of texts with the following observation (1976:90):

> *Textbooks are academic. Their impact on learning beyond the academy may well be negative. Since so much textbook reading is done under duress, reading either seriously or casually may be one of the casualties of a college education. The enormous resale and turnover of textbooks suggest the lack of permanent value that students attach to them. Few texts become permanent parts of a student's library. . . . The teacher's highest aims in respect to the use of texts may be those of not turning students away from reading, of illuminating the range of experience and pleasure that can come from the written word, and of keeping alive curiosity and a willingness to learn by whatever means the real world offers.*

Selecting Texts and Other Reading Materials

At least five general considerations need be taken into account when the instructor selects textbooks and other reading materials.

1. *Instructional goals and objectives:* Reading assignments (and all instructional tools and techniques) are chosen to accomplish particular goals.

2. *Course attributes:* The teacher must consider how size, type, and level of a course will affect instruction; whether there are prerequisites; what instructional format and techniques to use; and what resources are available.

3. *Student attributes:* The teacher must consider how much exposure students will have had to sociology and the problems to be treated in the course.

4. *Constraints on the teacher:* Twenty-nine percent of all sociology departments require the use of a specific text in all sections of Introductory Sociology; about 15 percent of all departments give a common exam in all sections of that course (and about the same percentage of departments require use of a common syllabus). These practices are reported by Bradshaw and McPherron (1977). How many courses and different preparations will a teacher have—how many new preparations? Such load factors may lead teachers to assign materials previously adopted or materials that have extensive auxiliary resources geared to them—test files, workbooks, manuals, etc.

5. *Availability:* Earlier we described the large number and wide range of textbooks available for Introductory Sociology. Exhibit 9.3 gives examples of types of written materials available and their sources.

Methods of Text Selection

Ruth Esther Brown (1976), in her *Contemporary Sociology* report on models used in introductory texts, presents data on thirty-two texts published during 1974 and 1975. Readers may find her category system useful:

Basic information
  Author, title, publisher, date, edition, pages, chapters, price.

Type text
  Comprehensive and eclectic *vs.* a shorter, core-type text.
Auxiliary books
  Teacher's manual? student workbook? Do text or auxiliary books contain classroom activities, bibliography, glossary, inserts, key terms, lecture suggestions, media resources, outlines, projects, study questions, readings, summaries?
Accessibility
  Reading level, layout, illustrations, writing, organization, study aids.
Content
  The text contains chapters on which institutions? what social problems? which sociological research methods? what other topics?
Other
  Does the text have a consistent theoretical orientation or is it eclectic? What types of data does it use (e.g., historical, cross-national)? What other author emphases can be identified?

Some teachers may want to consider how texts treat specific topics. Sociologists interested in research methods may want to look at Van Valey's (1975) examination of how 113 texts and other introductory course materials treat the teaching of methods. Those interested in examining how women are treated in introductory texts might look at Kirschner (1973). And sociologists might pay special attention to the opening chapter of each text they review. Kurtz and Maiolo found that most of the twenty-one introductory texts they reviewed devoted excessive attention to defending sociology as a science; compared to texts in other disciplines, "sociology stands out in its lengthy attempt to defend its place in the world of science" (Kurtz and Maiolo, 1968:40).

Reed Geertsen (1977) provides an easy-to-use, five-step test for text selection. He reports that in his "own experience, student response and willingness to read textbooks is highly correlated with

Exhibit 9.3 Examples of Types and Sources of Reading Material

Textbooks

Full Size:

Comprehensive:	Broom and Selznick; Light and Keller; McGee; Robertson
Selective:	Smelser, ed.
Focused:	Lenski and Lenski; Berger and Berger; Baldridge

Intermediate:

Core Type:	DeFleur, D'Antonio, and DeFleur (Brief edition)
Focused:	Anderson

Compact:

Core Type:	Cole; Chinoy; Hewitt; McNall
Focused:	Jensen

Modular: Prentice-Hall "Foundations" series; Random House Short Studies; Wm. C. Brown Co. "Elements of Sociology: Series of Introductions"

Workbooks and Manuals: Text-associated

Study Guide/Manuals:	Lowry and Rankin's *Study Guide;* Perrucci, Knudsen, and Hamby's *Study Guide;* Popenoe's *Study Guide and Access Workbook* (Include key terms and concepts, self-study questions, minor projects, chapter outlines, objectives, etc.)
Exercises and Projects:	Wilson's *Student Supplement;* DeFleur, D'Antonio, and DeFleur's Study Guide; *Research and Review* (Contain extended exercises or projects)
Coordinated Readings and Questions:	Light and Keller's *Readings and Review*
Programmed Auxiliary Books:	Dorsey Press Plaid Series: *Programmed Auxiliary Text in Sociology*

Workbooks and Manuals: Independent

Richard and Mann's *Exploring Social Space* (Lab Manual: short exercises and questions based on provided readings)

Larsen and Catton's *Conceptual Sociology* (Self-teaching exercises based on analysis of specimens—news reports, photographs, excerpts from articles, cartoons, etc.)

Sokol, *Laboratory Manual . . . A Data Card Approach* (Designed to allow students to test hypotheses with provided data cards; uses existing studies)

Faulkner and Warland's *Exercises in Sociology* (Exercises using data on class members and other sources designed to teach skills of analysis)

Dean and Valdes's *Experiments in Sociology* (Similar to Sokol)

Wiseman and Aron's *Field Projects for Sociology Students* (Manual designed to give students experience with field-based research methods)

Straus and Nelson's *Sociological Analysis* (Assignments based on replications of sociological studies)

Anthologies

Coordinated with Texts: Anderson

Comprehensive: McNall's *The Sociological Perspective*

Focused: Valdes and Dean's *Sociology in Use* (Uses applied sociology throughout)

Coser's *Sociology Through Literature*

Data-based Books

Compendia of Data: U.S. Bureau of the Census's *Pocket Data Book*

U.S. Bureau of the Census's *Statistical Abstract of the United States*

Case Studies and Ethnographies: Blythe's *Akenfield;* Winslow and Winslow's *Deviant Reality: Alternative World Views* (Social problems from the point of view of the deviant)

Monographs: Gans's *Urban Villagers*

Vidich and Bensman's *Small Town in Mass Society*

Lipset, Trow, and Coleman's, *Union Democracy*

Chirot's *Social Change in the Twentieth Century*

Other Auxiliary Books

Berger's *Invitation to Sociology: A Humanistic Perspective*

Cole's *The Sociological Method*

Bart and Frankel's *The Student Sociologist's Handbook*

Becker and Gustafson's *Encounter with Sociology: The Term Paper*

Other Print Media

Sociology Journal Articles: American Journal of Sociology, Social Forces, American Sociological Review (via library reserve, library assignments, reprint series).

Other Academic Journals: Public Opinion Quarterly, Administrative Science Quarterly, Social Psychology Quarterly, Public Administration Review, Journal of Personality and Social Psychology

Occupation-related Journals and Magazines: Resident and Intern

Government Documents: Census, government commission reports (federal, state, and local)

United Nations Documents: Demographic Yearbook, etc.

Semipopular Journals: Society, Social Policy, The Public Interest

Popular Magazines: Newsweek, Time

Semipopular Magazines: National Review, Nation, New Republic

National Newspapers: New York Times, Washington Post, Christian Science Monitor

State and Local Newspapers

five important factors: appeal, coverage, interest, difficulty, and salesmanship. Together they form a simple, yet basic ACIDS test for evaluating a textbook." Geertsen's five factors are defined below; his article includes a "textbook rating form":

Appeal
"Basic attractiveness and appeal, that is, one's impression of a textbook after leafing through it . . . page layout, size and type of print, use of headings, subheadings, and italicized words, variety in color, use of charts, figures, pictures, and so forth."

Content
". . . how well the textbook covers or handles the concepts, theoretic perspectives, and substantive areas which the teacher feels are important."

Interest
". . . Style and interest with which concepts are elaborated . . . the proportion of the written material about a particular concept which is devoted to concrete, personalized examples, and illustration. . . ."

Difficulty
"Probably the most important single factor in whether or not a student will read and understand a textbook is its difficulty . . . [is the text material] just plain too hard or complicated. . . . [And consider that:] textbooks which try to present too many ideas on a single page do so at the expense of providing interesting, detailed, personalized examples."

Salesmanship
". . . the book's ability to sell itself to the student. More specifically, does the book motivate the student to continue after reading the first four or five pages?"

While Geertsen and Brown touch on important issues, we suggest three additional categories that derive from our persuasions regarding effective instruction.

Organization of textbooks.   There are introductory textbooks with more than two dozen chapters grouped in half a dozen noncoordinated categories; there are texts with two dozen chapters presented seriatim with no clustering and no discernible order. Books are more comprehensible when they have a simple structure and sequence—a progression that builds on what has gone before and prepares for what comes after. Simplicity and progression can take many forms; consider three cases. Each edition of Broom and Selznick's *Sociology* contains two basic parts: "Part One: Elements of Sociological Analysis" (e.g., culture, socialization, stratification, associations, population) and "Part Two: Analysis of Specific Areas" (e.g., family, religion, education, minorities). Each of the chapters in part two is discussed in terms of each of the part one elements ("We bring sociological analysis to bear on specialized areas of interest"). Broom and Selznick note that their part two topics could have been extended (for example, to include a chapter on the military), and they suggest that "it would be a challenging project for the student or class to apply the pattern of Part Two chapters to a field not included in this book" (Broom and Selznick, 1963:8; see also, Broom and Selznick, 1977:14–15).

Wilson's *Sociology* (1971a) is organized into three major parts: building, sustaining, and changing human groups. The chapters in each of these major sections are crosscut by rules, roles, and relationships. Rules constitute a cultural heritage; they help to define our roles—the building blocks of social structure. Roles are related to form groups and other units of social structure.

Lenski and Lenski's *Human Societies* (1974) is organized historically around evolving societal types. The basic concepts and processes (discussed in part one of their book) are applied or examined in each of the major societal types, which are treated sequentially (in parts two and three).

There are many other important aspects of text organization. For example, the teacher who finds theory and research to be important might search for a text in which these tools crosscut all chapters (rather than receive limited treatment only in an introductory chapter).

Uses of sociology in textbooks. Some teachers believe that sociology can and should inform social action, that the amelioration of societal ills will be more effective and humane if we have reliable knowledge about the structure and processes of society. The teacher who wishes to convey such a view to students might look for a textbook in which social policy implications or applications crosscut the subject matter of the book. In like manner, the teacher who believes that sociology can inform individual biography will value texts to the degree that they contain clear and repeated linkages between larger societal structures and the settings in which daily life is enacted.

Pedagogical concerns of textbooks. Teachers might look for texts written in an interrogative rather than expository mode. Chapters of such texts may be structured as responses to questions: they may be shot through with instances of benign disruption (see chapter 5). An inquiry-based text will offer the student some raw data on which to work. The author of such a text will not simply present findings and conclusions of studies but will often reveal to the reader the *process* that the researcher went through in arriving at the answer. Teachers can look for texts with powerful

examples (see chapter 11). And they can choose books that demonstrate the skills of extension of knowledge to new populations or settings (see chapter 6).

Textbooks are widely used and powerful influences on student learning. The text and other reading materials used by the teacher convey to students not only the content of sociology but messages about its use in their lives and the way in which the teacher defines the learning experience. We agree with sociologist Richard L. Means (1966:101), who says that "textbooks represent to the future generation the best and the worst of our profession."

Notes

1. Ballantine's (1977) content analysis was performed on 100 syllabi from almost as many different departments (or schools). The syllabi were collected by the ASA Section on Undergraduate Education and ASA Projects on Teaching Undergraduate Sociology; they were solicited from sociologists active in the two groups and sociologists attending round-table discussions on the introductory course at ASA meetings. The 100 syllabi are not a systematic sample. They were prepared between 1974 and early 1977 and came from: junior and community colleges (15 percent), private colleges and universities (22 percent), public colleges and universities (34 percent), branch campuses of public universities (8 percent), and institutions not identified in the syllabus (21 percent).

2. We estimate that during the past ten years we have read in excess of 900 sociology course syllabi from about 200 different institutions. Four hundred fifty of these were collected as part of the work of the ASA Section on Undergraduate Education and ASA Projects on Teaching Undergraduate Sociology; an additional 120 came from sociologists attending Chautauqua-type Short Courses sponsored by the American Association for the Advancement

of Science; about 150 were prepared by faculty and graduate students at the University of North Carolina–Chapel Hill; 9 syllabi from courses in The Sociology of Education are found in Persell, Hammack, and Thielens (1978); 7 syllabi in Urban and Community Sociology in Olson, Aucoin, and Fort (1976); and 12 syllabi from Social Problems courses in Weston (1979).

3. The aggregate enrollment in 1974 of the ten most frequently offered sociology courses was estimated at 1.8 million, of whom 50 percent were enrolled in the introductory course ("Undergraduate Sociology," 1975:4).

4. Van Valey (1975:24) here cites Inkeles (1964:8), "who in turn credits an unpublished study by Hornell Hart—the Project for Comparative Analysis of Recent Introductory Sociology Textbooks, Florida Southern College, 1959."

5. For details on the sampling procedures used, see note 2 to chapter 10.

6. See note 1 (above).

7. For example, Xerox Individualized Publishing (191 Spring Street, Lexington, Massachusetts 02173) has over 200 articles from which to choose (and instructors can use their own materials) for a do-it-yourself textbook/reader.

8. Van Valey (1975) sought to compile "a complete listing of introductory materials" as of November 1974. He wrote to eighty-five publishing houses (receiving forty-seven replies), asking for a listing of all materials; he augmented this search by scanning his colleagues' shelves. His search yielded a total of 113 publications geared to the introductory course—including about sixty textbooks and forty anthologies. Not included were books of exercises, simulation games, modular materials prepared for use in the introductory course, or study guides, books of test items, and instructor manuals accompanying some texts.

Brown (1976) identified introductory *texts* listed in *Books in Print;* she listed the number of new texts and revisions published as follows: in 1975, twelve new and five revisions; in 1974, seven and seven; in 1973, six and six; for years prior to 1973, a total of twenty-three texts still in print. Thus, a grand total of sixty-six introductory textbooks (including revised editions) appeared from 1973 through 1975 or were still in print from prior years.

9. Quoted material is from James A. Davis (1978:236), speaking here about "most sociology courses (demography aside)." Davis adds that most students leave most courses with "little or no empirical information about the topic covered."

CHAPTER 10
THREE COURSE PATTERNS:
LECTURE, DISCUSSION,
AND PSI

Three patterns of teaching are discussed in this chapter: lecture, discussion, and PSI—the personalized system of instruction also known as The Keller Plan. PSI differs markedly from conventional instructional methods; it stresses student self-pacing, the written word, mastery of course materials, and the use of advanced students as tutors.

Lecture, discussion, and PSI are usually thought of as distinct *formats* for an entire course. But each can be viewed as a *technique*, as one of several modes of instruction that can be used in a single course.

There are, of course, many more than three course patterns. Two reasons for choosing these were the extent of their use in sociological instruction and their vintage—how long they have been in use. Lecture and discussion are not only venerable methods but are the most widely used in sociology. PSI falls at the opposite extreme: it was first employed in the early 1960s; and although it is used extensively in some other disciplines, notably psychology, this is not the case in sociology. A third reason for focusing on these three course patterns is that they illustrate different relationships between the teacher and student. With some simplification, the *lecture* is teacher-focused, and communication is chiefly one-way; *discussion* emphasizes teacher-student and student-student exchanges; and *PSI* stresses the student-subject matter relationship, me-

diated by the teacher and student assistants.

To select is to omit. We do not discuss such methods as simulation and gaming, project methods and varieties of independent study, field and experience-based methods, computer-assisted instruction, contract learning, role playing, and team teaching. For readers interested in these and other methods not discussed, we describe, in appendix 1, seven widely available books on instructional methods. Audiovisual techniques are discussed in chapter 11.

To what extent are different instructional formats and techniques used in sociology? Two research studies provide partial answers. Baker (1976) conducted a survey of graduate departments of sociology and those in public and private universities and colleges with a minimum enrollment of 10,000.[1] In eighty-four departments, he identified 229 sociology courses, each of which enrolled at least 100 students. Baker reports the frequency of use of different instructional methods in these 229 mass classes. Bradshaw and McPherron (1977) conducted a national sample survey of all departments of sociology, asking respondents how often different instructional techniques were used in their department's Introductory Sociology courses.[2] Their study, together with Baker's, indicates that: (1) the lecture and lecture-discussion classes are dominant in sociology instruction, (2) the printed word is the most widely used teaching aid, (3) among other listed teaching aids, only film and motion pictures are often used, and (4) a wide variety of other methods and tools is occasionally used. (But the data do not tell us about overlapping uses in a course.) Although schools that vary in type and size also differ in the extent to which they use various techniques, this does not alter the general conclusions (see tables 10.1, 10.2, and 10.3).

Throughout this chapter, we try to illustrate the uses in sociology instruction of various teaching patterns. We have also used examples from sociology classes in explaining the generic advantages and limitations of each. Finally, while every

Table 10.1 Frequency with which Specified Methods Were Used in Mass Classes in Sociology[a]

Technique	N	%
Classroom Lecture	156	68%
Films	97	42
Discussion Sessions	94	41
Graduate Student Teaching Assistant	60	26
Slides	29	13
Videotapes	24	10
Undergraduate Teaching Assistant	17	7
Field Experience	15	7
Independent Study	10	4
Simulation and Gaming	7	3
Self-paced Study (within classroom)	7	3
Self-paced Study (outside classroom)	6	3
Audiotapes	6	3
Computer Data Analysis	6	3
Telephone Network	3	1
Replication Studies	3	1
Sociodrama	3	1
Integrated Use of Multimedia	2	—[b]
Internships	2	—
Television	1	—
Radio	0	0

Notes:
(a) Total possible classes was 229.
(b) Less than 1 percent.
Source: Baker (1976:11); reprinted by permission of Sage Publications, Inc. and Paul Baker; percentages supplied by authors.

method has its gains and losses, effectiveness of instruction depends heavily on how well a method or technique is used. (This is one of the great unmeasured, but not unmeasurable, variables in research in education.) Not only can a method be used well or poorly, but teachers develop preferences for one or another mode of instruction. These facts led to our decision to treat in a separate chapter the question whether the choice and use of given instructional methods make any difference in what students learn (see chapter 12). While such research should have a part in the selection of methods used to achieve particular instructional ends, we know that teachers like ourselves are sometimes constrained to use a particular method and that they have their own preferences. Whatever method is used for whatever reason, it should be used to fullest advantage.

Lecture

Lecturing may be "more or less uninterrupted talk from a teacher" (Bligh, 1972:10) during part of a class. It *can* be the dominant means used for a whole class session, or through a whole course. The imagery associated with the lecture usually involves a large class and virtually no give-and-take. Lectures are variously viewed as occasions of boredom, inspiration, or entertainment. They are lamented as wasteful, given the widespread availability of the written word. Lectures can be a dull happening in which "the notes of the professor become the notes of the student without going through the minds of either" (Walker and McKeachie, 1967:13–14). On the other hand, at its best, the lecture is a virtuoso performance—a stimulating discourse that organizes complex or diverse materials in new and useful ways.

Despite the likely hazards of lectures and the rarity of stunning performances, lecturing is the most widely employed teaching mode in all types of classes. The link between lecturing and the mass class is not forged in iron. While many teachers argue that once you have fifty to sixty students (let alone 150 to 500) you have no choice but to lecture, some teachers lecture for a whole semester to classes with five students. And a small but significant proportion of sociologists teaching large classes forgo lecture techniques (Baker, 1976). Notwithstanding variations across schools of different sizes and types, the lecture, especially when combined with discussion, is the modal form of instruction. Eble (1972:8) is correct when he observes: "The professor's training, the reward structure and the conflicting claims on his time make the lecture the most common mode of instruction at any given time for almost any teacher."

One frequent goal of lecturing is to convey information. Other aims are to explain, integrate, or assess information students gain from books or other sources. Some teachers see lectures as a means of stimulating student interest, and some systems of instruction, such as PSI, use lectures as a reward for students who have mastered specified bodies of information or skills.

Courses can be wholly and purely lecture-based, or lectures can be combined with discussion sessions, or both modes can be used within a single course or class. Some lectures are formal and delivered without audiovisual aids. Jacques Barzun argues the case for such lectures when he

Table 10.2 Instructional Format of Introductory Sociology Courses[a]

	Weighted Total	Percentages of Colleges/Universities Responding					
		Small University	Large University	Small 4-Year College	Large 4-Year College	Small Community College	Large Community College
Large Lecture/Small Discussion Sections	6%	21%	18%	3%	3%	3%	5%
Large Lecture/No Discussion Sections	6	16	25	2	8	2	2
Lecture-Discussion Class	81	56	38	87	87	88	85
Seminar	—[b]	0	0	0	0	0	2
No Class: Individualized Instruction	—	0	0	0	0	2	0
Other	3	2	6	5	3	0	2
No Response	4	6	13	3	0	5	5
Totals	100%	101%	100%	100%	101%	100%	101%
(N)	(443)						

Notes:
(a) The question asked was: "What is the general format of your department's first course?" The title of the first course in 90 percent of responding departments was Introduction to Sociology or Principles of Sociology. Details on sampling for this study are provided in note 2 to this chapter.
(b) Less than 1%.
Source: Bradshaw and McPherron (1977). Reprinted by permission.

writes:

> The lecture room is the place where drama may properly become theater. This usually means a fluent speaker, no notes and no shyness about "effects." In some teachers a large class filling a sloped-up amphitheater brings out a wonderful power of emphasis, timing and organization. . . . The "effects" are not laid on, they are the meaningful stress which constitutes, most literally, the truth of the matter. This meaning as against fact is the one thing to be indelibly stamped on the mind, and it is this that the printed book cannot give. That is why their hearers never forgot Huxley lecturing, nor Michelet, nor William James. Plenty of facts can be conveyed too—the more highly organized the better; but in the hands of a great lecturer it is the feeling and principles that illuminate the soul as does a perfect play or concert. (Barzun, 1944:38, quoted in Brown and Thornton, 1971:83)

Other teachers supplement their lectures with films, videotapes, amplified telephone interviews, the use of transparencies, and other audiovisual techniques. Some teachers build into their lectures student buzz-groups or debates. Most lec-

Table 10.3 Use of Different Instructional Methods in Introductory Sociology Courses[a]

| | Percentage of Departments Indicating Use | | | |
	Extensive	Occasional	None	No Answer
Textbooks	90%	8%	2%	—%[b]
Other Books	36	57	5	3
Term Papers	15	54	27	4
Objective Exams	60	32	5	2
Essay or Oral Exams	25	61	11	3
College Level Entrance Program (CLEP)	—	37	53	9
Audiotapes	3	59	33	6
Computer-assisted Instruction	—	18	74	8
Experiential Learning Exercises (role playing, sociodrama, etc.)	7	63	24	6
Field Experience	6	66	25	3
Films	19	76	3	2
Independent Study and Research	6	63	27	4
Integrated Use of Multimedia	5	44	44	8
Televised Presentations	1	33	59	7
Modules	3	21	67	9
Programmed Learning	—	21	72	7
Self-paced Study	2	22	69	7
Simulation and Gaming	3	53	39	5
Undergraduate Student Teaching Assistants	1	11	79	8
Other Innovative Teaching Techniques	3	21	25	51

Notes:
(a) The question asked was: "Indicate to the best of your knowledge the extent each of these techniques is currently used by teachers of your department's *first course*." Percentage figures are weighted totals; see note 2 to this chapter for explanation.
(b) Less than 1 percent.
Source: Bradshaw and McPherron (1977). Reprinted by permission.

tures are delivered in person, some by television. And finally, lectures are used in classes both large and small.

Need lectures be dominated by teacher talk? Must they be exercises in exposition, or can they be occasions for inquiry? What are different patterns of lecture organization and how can the teacher choose among them? Are there principles of effective lecturing common to different lecture patterns? In the following section, we discuss these four important issues in detail and, more briefly, three other matters: preparation and delivery of lectures, means of handling content in them, and ways to check on their effectiveness.

Major Issues About Lecturing

Need lectures be instructor-dominated and marked by limited communication? This problem is very real, especially in large classes, since the larger the group, the less time is available per group member for overt communication during a meeting of any given length. Further, research tells us that with increasing group size, participation is increasingly inhibited and "the gap between the top participator and the others tends to grow proportionately greater as size increases" (Hare, 1976:231). Nonetheless, communication in lecture

classes, even very large ones, need not be dominated solely by the teacher and marked by one-way communication.

Figure 10.1 presents four patterns of communication: the basic lecture pattern is that represented by Pattern A—communication flow in one direction, from the teacher to each of the students. Yet even where this pattern obtains, the communicator need not be the instructor: it could be a student, a panel of students debating an issue, representatives of some small groups of students reporting on their work, or the like. Pattern B (we call it the Ping-Pong model) represents a sequence of exchanges between teacher and a series of individual students. That most communication still originates from the teacher is represented by the size of the arrowheads in the figure 10.1 illustration of Pattern B. An example of this pattern is a practice that some teachers find they can carry out even in large classes: answering a limited number of questions from students. One way of handling questions of concern to large numbers of students is used by Robert K. Merton. He asks students to write their questions on slips of paper that are collected and sorted by a teaching assistant who selects a few that represent common queries. He then responds to these questions. No one would confuse this technique with a seminar dis-

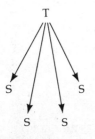
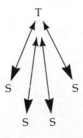
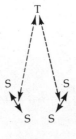

Pattern A   Pattern B   Pattern C   Pattern D

Figure 10.1 Four Patterns of Classroom Communication.

cussion or office hour conversation, but it does take the class a step away from the purely one-way communication pattern.

Another way to achieve Pattern B classroom communication is for the teacher to ask one or more questions and request that students respond by writing down their answers or making some other form of response (e.g., raising hands). One example of using this pattern is Marwell's (1966) "social awareness test," which he uses in his large, introductory classes. On the first day of class, Marwell distributes a short quiz that asks students to respond, true or false, to a series of statements about presumed social facts. Common sense provides correct answers to the first few questions, but not to later questions. As Marwell provides the answers, he asks students to raise their hands to indicate when they have the correct response. Student confidence builds early on, only later to fall. (It is important to note that Marwell's classes are large enough that this technique does not embarrass any individual student; and raising hands is a voluntary act.)

In another example of Pattern B communication, students can respond through a process that Earl Babbie (1977a) calls "body learning": students move to positions in the room representing categories, attributes, or answers. In small classes, all students can move; in large lectures, such as Babbie has, a sampling of thirty or forty students can participate. A colleague of ours, Margaret Gulick, used this technique during a late November class meeting devoted to gender roles and stratification. She asked students who had helped clear the Thanksgiving table to go to one side of the room and those who did not do so to go to the other side. Then she asked for a separation by gender with females in both groups moving to the back of the room and males to the front. At this

point, the class had distributed itself in the cells of a 2×2 table, and Ms. Gulick recorded the Ns on the blackboard. If she had wished to introduce a third variable (say, religiosity of a student's family or whether a student's mother has a career), students in each of the four cell-groups could have sat or remained standing to represent the values of the third variable.

Pattern C of figure 10.1 represents another communication pattern that can be used in lecture classes. The teacher asks students to form face-to-face groups of four to deal with one or more questions posed by the teacher. After five or ten minutes of work, group representatives are polled or asked to report to the whole class. Since students can remain at their seats, shifting around to face their fellows, such a device can be employed even in very large classes. In addition, Greenblat has devised a number of simple games and exercises designed to be carried out during very short periods in large sociology classes in buzz groups (see Dukes and Greenblat, 1979).

Pattern D represented in figure 10.1, where all students and the teacher participate and communicate with one another, probably cannot be achieved in a very large class and is incompatible with the lecture scheme, except in small classes. But, as we have seen, there are available to the teacher several options that fall between the poles of open exchange and straight lecture. These variants relieve the monotony of the fifty- or seventy-five-minute lecture. Student response informs the teacher, and the heightened student participation can enhance learning (see chapter 12).

Need lectures be exercises in exposition? The traditional lecture—indeed, much teaching—is telling, rather than exemplifying the process of inquiry. The traditional lecture is structured around a number of major topics or points, each of which is bolstered by the report of findings of five or six major studies ("he found . . . she found . . ."), and then given a conclusion. Teachers should only use lectures for conveying such information if it cannot be effectively communicated by other means—and even then the question remains as to whether the lecture should be solely expository. We contrast exposition to inquiry that fixes on questions rather than on topics, and develops answers rather than reveals them. Even in large lecture classes, students can be brought into the process of inquiry in a meaningful, if limited, way.

A teacher's outline for lectures on stratification might look like this:

> *Stratification Defined* (contrast to differentiation)
> *Review of Ranked Groupings*—ethnic, racial, income, gender, age, education
> *Class, Status, and Power* (three analytic concepts)
> *Major Theories of Stratification—*
> > Functional (Davis and Moore)
> > Economic (Marx)
> > Power and Conflict (Mills, Dahrendorf)
> > Distributive Laws (Lenski)
> *Stratification and Institutional Dynamics* (use education as an example)
> *Stratification and Symbol System—* "culture," dress, speech
> *Summary*

Such material *could* be organized around big questions. Thus, given a definition of stratification, we ask whether ranked statuses and roles are ubiquitous? Are they found in all societies? and over historical time? Or, as Dahrendorf asks: "Why is there inequality among men? Where do its causes lie? Can it be reduced, or even abolished altogether? Or do we have to accept it as a necessary element in the structure of human society?" (Dahrendorf, 1970:4, quoted in Matras, 1975:63). Such questions can also be framed in terms of student life chances.

Rather than simply revealing the *answers* that sociologists have provided to such questions, the teacher can show (or better, help students discover for themselves) how theorists and researchers developed their questions and how they pursued answers to them. Unless students are exposed to the process by which questions are formed and answers sought, they will become intellectual blotters unable either to understand where findings come from or how to move beyond them. (Ideally, of course, students should have practice actively engaging in the process of inquiry.) Teachers can also reveal to students the process of their own thinking. Students need to understand that issues dealt with in a class are chosen for reasons, and that some questions are more important than others and hence dealt with. They need to discover by what standards questions are deemed important, what would be lost by not asking them, and by what logic the question can be pursued.

Lecturers can move beyond the expository by putting questions (sometimes rhetorical, sometimes not) to students, and by asking students (alone or in concert with their peers) to respond then and there (on paper). Rhetorical questions are unlikely to have any effect if they are posed in a vacuum; students will have neither interest nor information on the point at issue. Further, teachers must ensure that asking such questions is not an empty gesture; they must not immediately provide answers to the questions they pose. Students need time to consider a question before they can join the teacher in pursuit of an answer. The teacher can ask students to jot down their answers to a question and can indicate that, should they come up with different answers, this will become an agenda item for the class. One of the easiest ways in which to build questions into a lecture is through the use of contingency tables. The teacher can present students with the table's framework—column and row headings and marginals—and ask the class, given a certain theory, how they would expect the data to fall.

Handouts can be used as a basis for active student work during a class—turning the lecture into an exercise or a demonstration. Returning to the example of a class studying stratification, let us assume that the teacher had assigned and discussed the Davis and Moore functional theory of stratification and the NORC studies of occupational prestige. The teacher might now ask how the occupational prestige scales and the functional explanation are related. Davis and Moore would predict that those occupations requiring high levels of ability and training,

those that provide services essential to the welfare of a society, would be those with high prestige rankings. As individuals or in buzz groups, students might be asked to examine the NORC data (North-Hatt and Hodge-Siegel-Rossi) and reach their own conclusion.

An additional step would be to ask whether the respondents to the NORC surveys (a sample of the adult U.S. population) actually used the Davis-Moore factors as they ranked occupations. The teacher might distribute such a table as that shown in exhibit 10.1. Students could be asked to write, in column A, the percentages of the adult U.S. population they think chose each response category. The teacher could then ask students to place, in column B, a check mark next to each item they believe central to the Davis-Moore theory, and a different mark for nonessential items. Later, students can record, in column C, the answers actually given by respondents in the NORC sample (and provided by the teacher).[3] Such an exer-

---

Exhibit 10.1 Attributes of Jobs with Excellent Standing

"When you say certain jobs have 'excellent standing,' what do you think is the one main thing about such jobs that gives this standing?"

The Job:	A	B	C
1. Pays well	___	___	___
2. Is pleasant, safe, and easy	___	___	___
3. Has a good future; the field is not overcrowded	___	___	___
4. Carries social prestige	___	___	___
5. Serves humanity; it is an essential job	___	___	___
6. Affords maximum chance for initiative and freedom	___	___	___
7. Provides security and steady work	___	___	___
8. Requires preparation: much education, hard work, and money	___	___	___
9. Requires intelligence and ability	___	___	___
10. Requires high moral standards, honesty, responsibility	___	___	___
11. Miscellaneous answers: don't know, no answer	10%	10%	10%
	100%	100%	100%

cise, which is feasible in a large lecture class and does not consume an inordinate amount of time, *allows students to actively apply what they have read.* To make their column B predictions accurately, they need to understand the Davis-Moore thesis. The exercise also provides practice in relating theory and research, and in relating two readings.*

What principles undergird effective lecturing?

While there are many useful ways to organize a lecture, a number of principles cut across different modes of lecture organization. First, lectures must not simply be organized in the mind or notes of the teacher; students must perceive the organization. In this, the teacher has both a stake and responsibility. Donald A. Bligh (1972:101–103) has identified a number of ways of making lecture organization clear to students:

State the organization at the beginning
    After stating the lecture goals and objectives or the problems at hand, the lecturer explains the procedure to be followed. This is especially important with difficult subject matter. If the teacher believes that beginning with a summary will detract from a desired developmental approach, the teacher can stress the *logic* of the lecture's organization.
Itemize each point
    "First, each item provides a peg on which detail may be hung. Detail is best remembered by association and the item provides this." Second, when the lecturer is moving to a new point, this should be explicitly indicated. Third, itemization lets the student know if he has lost a point and helps him to "pick up" at a later point.
Use a blackboard buildup
    "The organization of itemized points will be clearer if they are written on the board im-

* Other inquiry-based exercises have been provided in chapters 4, 5, and 6.

mediately after being mentioned." Or, the teacher can provide students with a handout with major points presented. Such buildups are more important when the structure of the lecture or the subject is complex.
Take stock and summarize
    Summaries at the beginning and end of a lecture are recommended. "The technique of 'taking stock' which consists of reviewing what has been said up to that time, is valuable for setting the next point in its context. It aids learning by showing how the parts are related to the whole."

Second, if a lecture is too densely packed with new information, students will have trouble following its structure and understanding particular points. Ericksen (1978:4) illustrates this principle by constrasting the student in the lecture course with the student reading a book. In the latter case,

the student is in control; she determines the sequence of information and the rate and frequency with which it is reviewed and evaluated. . . . When reading, the student moves forward at her own rate . . . tests herself, speculates and wonders . . . [in the lecture context, by contrast,] it is unlikely that students will understand topic B if they are still trying to grasp the meaning of topic A. It is important therefore, that students have an opportunity to "catch up" with the speaker. Repetition, redundancy, and even silence serve this purpose. The use of frequent examples, anecdotes and personal speculations may stimulate similar kinds of "bridging" on the part of the students. If the substantive information is presented too fast, the students have difficulty organizing in their heads or in their notes. . . .

Teachers are often so familiar with the basic points they are developing in a lecture that the need for such pacing is not evident. Teachers who are unsure whether they are meeting this need have several ways of finding out. They can ask students during or after the lecture period. They can request written responses from students. They can ask some students to show them their lecture notes. Teachers can try to sense, vicariously, the student's plight in a class that ventures into unfamiliar terrain. (Playing a racquet sport with your other hand will remind you of the irritation and consternation that can result in trying something new.)

We offer a third principle—less grand but, we suspect, often overlooked: to open a lecture with an historical or a philosophical prologue, heavy in definitions and concepts, may be a good way to lose one's students. Effective communication depends on knowing one's students and starting with issues that grip them. Some teachers view this as a sign of weakness— the acquiesence of a teacher to the interests and aims of a student. But as Ericksen (1978:3) notes:

> *This defensive position misstates the instructional problem. The teacher is part of the motivational picture whether he likes it or not. Effective learning in the classroom—lecture course or otherwise—depends on the teacher's ability to transform resistance to support and to maintain the interest that brought students to his course in the first place. . . .*

Issues that grip students are those that are relevant to students' concerns as they define them. This may seem obvious, but our practice often belies its obviousness. Especially during the 1960s, many teachers of sociology worked to be sure their courses were relevant, by which they meant touching the major issues of the day—or the issues that they as sociologists knew affected the life chances of their students. Civil rights, Vietnam, institutional racism, the politics of pollution and its control, trade union militancy, the bureaucratization of the professions were

favorite subjects. Two problems arose. First, in some cases, these issues were treated without use of sociology—a pity since sociology has much to say about such trends and events. The problem was not intrinsic to these issues but to the ways in which they were handled. Second, some teachers found that despite their own deep concern with such issues and their importance to society, students did not get excited by them. Some students, in different schools and at different times, are concerned with such issues, and there are often good reasons for teachers of sociology to bring such matters into their courses. But there is another meaning of relevance—that of locating oneself in time and space.

Factors that touch the biography of students, their relationships to their peers and parents, their hopes, expectations, and fears are likely to grip them. In chapter 7, we presented evidence of the drama in the personal life of students, events that grip them and are useful takeoff points in teaching. First-year college students are often experiencing major shifts in their lives—leaving the family, entering dorm life, facing new freedoms and choices, and coping with new anxieties. And most students have had more direct experience with the social world than teachers sometimes realize. Consider a lecture on political participation. Planning to touch on studies of political apathy and alienation, the teacher wonders how to relate such matters to the students' lives and experience: few of the students have yet voted, fewer still have any involvement in partisan politics or pressure groups. Are there any points of linkage between political participation and student experience and concerns? Yes. During their senior year in high school some of these students took a trip to the state capital where a guide let them sit in their senator's chair, told them how high the ceilings were, and showed them the tattered flag carried at Gettysburg. Other students took a government course that was nine-tenths civics with politics strangely missing. And many students participated in elections for the high school or college student council or, more likely, refused to participate out of cynicism. These actions or nonactions *are* relevant and usable experiences. Students who say that college student senate elections are a waste of time offer the teacher a point of entry into the discussion of broader issues of political participation.[4]

A fourth principle cutting across different forms of lecture organization is this: both teacher and student need frequent evaluative response (feedback) on their performances. For without such response, one cannot tell what one is doing or saying to others. Testing is the usual mode of getting a message from student to teacher. Especially in larger courses, such information comes infrequently and late in the term. It

has the added disadvantage of not telling the teacher how and why students are having difficulty with an aspect of the course. In earlier sections, we have described some other ways in which teachers can get information from students. In chapter 13, we will describe the Teaching Information Processing System (TIPS), an economical tool for providing rapid response (and individualized learning suggestions for students) in mass classes.

What are different patterns of lecture organization? The content of a lecture should be organized in the way that best suits the instructional goals and nature of the subject matter, respects the students' information, skills, and motivation, and is comfortable to the teacher.

Our discussion of lecture organization draws heavily on a fine book by Donald A. Bligh, *What's the Use of Lectures?* (1972). Bligh reminds readers that lecturing is a linear process since it moves,

---

Exhibit 10.2 Linear or Chronological Lecture Organization

Lecture Topic: What Is Sociology?

I. Subject Matter of Sociology	(1)
A. Human social interaction	(2)
1. differences from other social sciences	(3)
2. differences from humanities and natural sciences	(4)
B. Central questions about order and change	(5)
II. Methods of Sociological Inquiry	(6)
A. Scientific method	(7)
1. validity	(8)
2. reliability	(9)
B. Types of data	(10)
III. Theory in Sociology	(11)
A. Definitions	(12)
B. Major theories	(13)
1. classical	(14)
IV. Applications of Sociology	(15)

Note: Numbers in parentheses indicate the order in which points are made.

minute by minute, through a fixed period. However, since the logical structure of the lecture may not be linear, the teacher must enable students to understand that structure or to derive it. All lectures are delivered in a chronological sequence. This can be illustrated by the lecture outline in exhibit 10.2. Readers should note that the exhibit and three figures used here to illustrate different modes of lecture organization have been markedly abbreviated and simplified for purposes of clarity. The form but not the content of exhibit 10.2 and figures 10.2, 10.3, and 10.4 comes (with permission) from Bligh (1972).

The outline shown in exhibit 10.2 is clear enough and presents no problems. Or does it? The neophyte freshman student may not be easily able to make connections and see the differences as the teacher moves from one level of hierarchy to another. The ordering of the fifteen points requires jumps—as when the teacher moves from point 10 to point 11. Here students can become lost, unless the teacher provides a map of the larger terrain to be covered during the lecture. This can be done orally and through use of a blackboard outline similar to that shown

in exhibit 10.2. The graphic representation of the lecture's hierarchical organization appears clearly in figure 10.2, which reminds us that, even in this simple illustration, lectures often make conceptual jumps of one or two levels.

Bligh has usefully classified lecture organization as follows:

Hierarchic Forms—
    Classification hierarchy
    Problem-centered lecture
Chaining
Variations and More Complex Forms—
    Comparison
    Thesis
    Logical dichotomy
    Network

We have already illustrated the classification hierarchy in exhibit 10.2 and figure 10.2. Here different points of information are grouped together with a unifying feature as a heading. This frequently used organization is simple in structure, and contains few points of linkage (each point linked to only one other point). Thus content is easy to remember by fixing on the four key themes. The teacher can readily accelerate or slow down a lecture or-

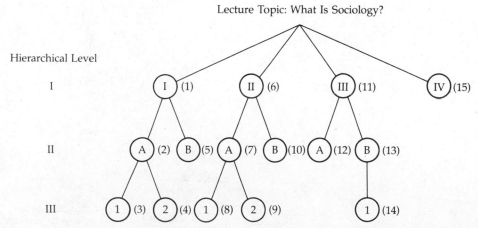

Figure 10.2 Lecture Scheme I: Classification Hierarchy. *Note:* Numbers in parentheses indicate the order in which points are made.

ganized in this pattern; it is probably the easiest form for the inexperienced lecturer. Simple in structure, this form is well suited to presentation of facts and to surveys of general areas of knowledge.

"When using the problem-centered form the lecturer asks a question or presents a problem, and thereafter gives information, arguments and hypotheses as possible solutions so that everything focuses on the initial problem. For example, the approach may be a telescoped presentation of a scientific investigation" (Bligh, 1972:87). The problem-centered lecture, illustrated in figure 10.3, has a hierarchical structure, but the relationship between the lecture's units is not one of classification; rather, it involves a process of reasoning. "This difference is important. . . . Although they only demand limited patterns of thought, problem-centered lectures will be appropriate for promoting thought in those circumstances in which it is not pos-

sible to give the problem to the students directly in discussion. It is also suitable for stimulating students' interest if the problem can be made to arouse their curiosity" (Bligh, 1972:87–88). In problem-centered lectures, it is essential that the problem be understood at the outset; all else hinges on that. Since the reasoning involved may be complex, it is useful for the teacher to take stock each time an item of evidence has been applied to each of the possible solutions to the central problem. "More than other forms of lecture, the problem-centered approach makes assumptions about the students' previous knowledge and their ability to handle new concepts" (Bligh, 1972:89–90). We expect it would be a mistake to use in an introductory undergraduate course the problem-centered form to handle the lecture illustrated in figure 10.3. Students would probably get lost as the teacher had to detail each classic study; such a form would be more appro-

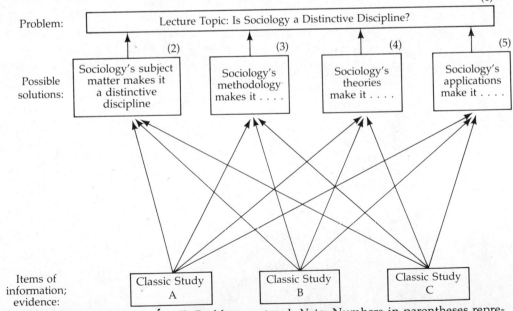

Figure 10.3 Lecture Scheme II: Problem-centered. *Note:* Numbers in parentheses represent the order of points in the lecture; lines represent inferences—application of the studies to the four possible solutions to the problem posed.

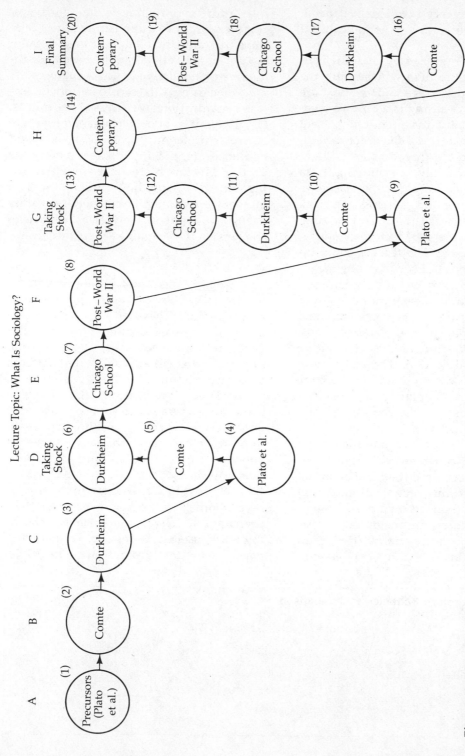

Figure 10.4 Lecture Scheme III: Chaining. *Note:* Numbers in parentheses represent the order of points in the lecture. This chain-organized lecture has nine major segments, three of which are devoted to taking stock and summarizing (D, G, I). Usually taking stock is done with increasing frequency during a lecture; however, successive instances of taking stock are progressively more compressed. In this illustration, for each of the substantive elements in the chain (A, B, C, E, F, H), the teacher would explore sociology's subject matter, method, theory, and application.

priate for an advanced course. In general, the problem-centered form is difficult but rewarding.

A lecture organized by chaining is illustrated in figure 10.4. "Assuming the links between one stage and the next are easy to follow, chaining is a form of organization that maintains attention . . . but if attention is lost, it is difficult for the student to pick up the thread again" (Bligh, 1972:90). Accordingly, in moving from step to step, it is useful for the teacher to indicate the move and perhaps take stock by tracking backwards and summarizing.

Another pattern of lecture organization is comparison. The teacher could introduce the subject of sociology by means of a systematic comparison between sociology and two other disciplines using four dimensions: subject matter, method, theory, and application. A blackboard outline provided to students in such a lecture appears as exhibit 10.3. The comparison could be by row or column. This lecture would end with a summary of differences and similarities among the disciplines, emphasizing attributes (singly or in combination) that uniquely define sociology.

Bligh and other writers (e.g., Hart, 1973b:19–20) have described and analyzed other forms of lecture organization. For example, lectures can be organized around logical dichotomies, chronological or spatial relationships and patterns. Topics can be arranged in an ascending or a descend-ing order (of importance, familiarity, or complexity), or to demonstrate causal relationships and their implications. Finally, lecture organization can be based on inductive or deductive logical structures.

In closing this consideration of lecture organization, we stress three points: (1) different modes of organization are suited to different pedagogical tasks and audiences, (2) making linkages among the parts of a lecture is crucial to student learning, and (3) providing students with a map of the terrain to be covered is not only useful to students but also helpful to teachers as they organize their thinking.

~

Lectures need not be dominated by teacher talk. They can use inquiry as well as exposition. They can be organized in different ways, each suitable to particular goals and audiences. We explored several principles that cut across different patterns of lecture organization: the student's need to perceive organization, the teacher's need for evaluative response from students, the dangers of packing too much into a lecture, and the advantages of knowing one's students and the issues that grip them.

We now turn to discuss, more briefly, several other issues about lectures: their preparation, delivery, and means of checking on their effectiveness. In the following pages, we draw from Beard (1970:107–

Exhibit 10.3 Lecture Scheme IV: Comparison			
Lecture: What is Sociology?			
	Sociology	History	Chemistry
1. Subject Matter	1.	1.	1.
2. Method	2.	2.	2.
3. Theory	3.	3.	3.
4. Applications	4.	4.	4.

109), Bligh (1972:103ff, 122ff), Brown and Thornton (1971:84,92–93), Eble (1976:52ff), Hart (1973a:11–12; 1973b:10,18), Verner and Dickinson (1967:94), and Wilson and Wood (1974).

Preparing Lectures

What are the teacher's instructional goals?   Teachers must ask themselves what they want students to be able to do as a result of the lecture being planned. What implications does this have for the lecture organization, and for the use of examples or student activities during the lecture?

What is the subject matter?   What aspects of the subject matter will best be conveyed by lectures? Could some things be handled more efficiently through readings or another learning mode? Does the subject matter itself suggest a particular form of lecture organization?

What is the audience?   What prior knowledge, concerns, interests, experiences, and attitudes do students have on which the teacher can draw, relating them to the content of the lecture? How can the teacher establish common ground between student experience and lecture content, especially in the opening of the lecture?

What resources are needed?   What audiovisual materials and handouts need to be ordered or prepared, arranged for, and checked before the lecture?

What examples are possible?   Teachers must seek hard and unrelentingly for precise examples. Examples should be planned in advance just as one plans other parts of a lecture (see chapter 11).

How should lecture notes be handled?
It is often useful to prepare notes in outline form—they are easier to refer to, supplement, and revise.

Handling Lecture Content

Lecture content and readings.   Avoid duplicating the text. Instead, regard the lecture as an opportunity to synthesize, evaluate, clarify, develop, and compare ideas and facts. Teachers need to relate the lecture to readings and other out-of-class assignments.

Scope.   Narrow the lecture to essential points and their development rather than make a superficial survey of more than can be grasped in a single lecture.

Things to be avoided.   Avoid: excessive qualifications of concepts; arcane terms; private quarrels with authorities over esoteric points; learned quotations that are lengthy or complex; preoccupation with the academic history of a concept or an issue to the neglect of the instructional goals at hand; and lectures that fail to link contemporary contexts and broader issues to the lecture's subject matter.

Making a point during a lecture.   Bligh (1972:103ff) suggests the following form: (1) concise statement of the basic point; (2) use of the chalkboard or transparencies to display the point and fit it into the progressive outline of the lecture; (3) restatement of the point in different terms; (4) elaboration with detail, explanation, supporting evidence, and the use of examples that are concise, familiar, and concrete; (5) obtaining some response from students—to whatever degree possible, and; (6) recapitulation and restatement.

Delivering Lectures

Voice, gesture, and movement. "Develop and use a range of voice, gestures, and physical movement that is appropriate to your style, to the material, and to the occasion, and that reinforces content, fixes attention, and stimulates the audience . . . root out mannerisms and affectations" (Eble, 1976:53). Teacher behaviors which are fixed or repetitive are monotonous and diminish the students' ability to identify central points and issues. Periodically leaving the podium (and the front of the lecture room) heightens student attention.

Sound and sight.   Can students hear or see the lecturer, board illustrations, films, transparencies?*

Rapport between the lecturer and students.   Sarcasm about the course, textbook, students, or the material at hand, or any attempt at humor at the expense of students can diminish student receptivity. Rapport is also diminished when the teacher asks for student response in a routine way or does not make use of it. Rapport and student interest are enhanced when teachers are able to communicate their enthusiasm for the subject matter and their concern that students learn. It is usually a mistake to stress the depth of one's ignorance (or gaps in a body of knowledge), especially at the beginning of a course. This is not to be confused with appropriate modesty about self or discipline, nor is this a suggestion to fake mastery.

Improvisational ability. Lecture classes are living audiences, not tape recorders. It is useful for teachers to develop an ability to improvise and adapt when un-

* See chapter 8 for pertinent suggestions.

anticipated questions or issues arise in class or in the teacher's mind. One way to develop this ability is to think through, in advance, the categories of attack one can use in such a situation. Such a list might include: "specifying the problem, analysis, alternative solutions, decision criteria, data search, resolution"; or "pertinent theory, pertinent research, levels of analysis," etc.

Checking the Effectiveness of Lectures

Checking during the lecture.   Pay attention to nonverbal forms of student behavior: observe student reactions—perhaps focusing on a few students seated at different places in the lecture room; note attendance patterns; watch student note-taking behavior or whether students are actually watching a film. To the degree feasible, use student verbal or written responses as a guide—including the answers to questions, and whether students ask questions when invited. Make this invitation to students: "Raise your hands if you don't understand a point, or if I am moving too quickly." Plan in advance to solicit student response at crucial stages in your lecture.

Making delayed checks.   See note 25 to chapter 14 for various ways that teachers can determine student response to lectures after a class is completed.

Resources: The Literature on Lecturing

Baker (1976) provides an overview of the use of mass classes (defined as a classroom enrollment of 100 or more students) in sociology. In addition to discussing the problem of mass classes, reporting on a national survey of departments using them, and cataloging the use of different teaching methods in large sociology classes, Baker briefly describes five alternatives to mass instruction. These techniques can replace the mass class or supplement conventional large-class instruction; included are PSI and TIPS (discussed later in this chapter and in chapter 14), modular instruction, multiple option formats, and a lecture-tutorial course developed by Reece McGee.

The use of TIPS in sociology is discussed in detail in two articles by Bassis and Allen (1976, 1977); applications of PSI in large sociology classes are described by Clark (1974), Francis (1974a), Johnson and Walsh (1978), Malec (1975), MacDaniel (1974), Ludwig (1975), and Rogers, Satariano, and Rogers (1977). The literature on the teaching of sociology includes many articles that describe the use of other instructional devices and techniques in large lecture classes. Exhibit 10.4 lists a number of examples of articles that de-

scribe devices and techniques that can be used in large classes. We know of no articles that deal with the lecture form *per se* in sociology.

However, the literature on lecturing in general (as opposed to its use in sociology specifically) is large and well developed. The most comprehensive work available is Bligh's *What's the Use of Lectures?* (1972). It contains the best available review of the literature on student achievement of different instructional objectives through the lecture compared to other techniques, and the best available treatment of lecture organization, preparation, and evaluation. Firmly grounded in research and theory on learning and communications, it is one of the best written books in the field of teaching and learning.

The best short work available on lectures is Ericksen's "The Lecture" (1978), which is richly rewarding for the short time it takes to read it. Another useful work that includes a review of research on lecturing is McKeachie's *Teaching Tips*

Exhibit 10.4 Articles Describing the Use of Selected Devices or Techniques in Large Lecture Classes

Device/Technique	Course Size	References
Films	200	Smith (1973)
Experiential/Improvisational Techniques	Large	Conover (1974)
Team Teaching	120	Pape and Miller (1967)
Undergraduate Teaching Assistants	40+	Wallace (1974), Moxley (1974), Rice (1978)
Peer Teaching	400	McNall (1975), Pape and Miller (1967)
Applying Symbolic Interactionism in Classroom	100	Petras and Hayes (1973)
Practice with Research	225	Clifton (1976)
Device to Deal with Common Sense and Increase Student Interest in Sociology	Large	Marwell (1966)
Using Novels and Other Fiction	350	Jones (1975)
Modularized Instruction	50–100	Dukes (1975)
Small-group Alternatives within Large Classes	50+	Wallis (1973)

(1978, 7th ed.). Beard (1970) treats styles of lecturing, forms of lectures, and the preparation, presentation, and evaluation of lectures.

Several books on teaching offer useful suggestions on lecturing—for example, Eble (1976) and Brown and Thornton (1971). A useful short review of theories of learning undergirding lectures is found in Davis (1976:39–58). A fine volume contrasting the didactic and evocative modes of instruction is Axelrod (1973). Wolford and Smith's *Large-Course Instruction* (1977) is a collection of four papers prepared for a conference on the large course; these papers treat the use of audiovisual techniques and PSI, and the evaluation of teaching effectiveness and student achievement in large courses.

Discussion

The student who learns in discussions sees learning as it really goes: fitfully, haltingly, speedily with one set of things, stumblingly with another, now following logical pathways, now connecting at unlikely points. Viewed in this way, both truth and learning seem less forbidding. The pursuit of truth is anyone's game, a game with very old rules and penalties for setting those rules aside altogether, but a game that gives room for error, scope for the imagination, and many different rewards and satisfactions. (Eble, 1976:66)

Discussion is purposeful conversation in a relatively small group. Although teachers can build some active student involvement and exchange into a lecture course, these elements define discussion. Compared to lectures, discussions have the following characteristics (paraphrased from Thompson, 1974a:19–22): (1) opportunities for all participants to speak; (2) intimacy—size and seating arrangements that encourage participation; (3) pooling

of resources—all are expected to share information and develop their ideas and skills through interaction with others; (4) peer feedback—direct and immediate response among participants; and (5) teacher contribution to group process—the teacher guides the group, handling disagreement, keeping the conversation on track, encouraging participation, modeling careful listening, and the like.

Some mix of discussion and lecture is the common mode of instruction in sociology. Even in large classes (100 students or more) we know that discussion is widely used (see table 10.1). But discussion may take many forms (and there are dozens of techniques that can be used to generate and guide discussion). Some of these forms are:

Type of Activity	Example
Case Study Method	Goal-directed discussion of a printed case study
Buzz Session (in groups of two to six)	Small groups briefly discussing a problem, then reporting outcomes to the class
Role Playing (by two or more)	Members acting out a situation or incident (using a script with minimal instructions or guidelines), then analysis by the class
Debate	Pro and con presentations on an unsettled issue
Public Interview	"Meet the Press" format, followed by class discussion
General Group Discussion	Discussion following a fixed or flexible agenda

This brief list suggests some of the differences among discussion methods. They vary in degree of structure, preparation, and the nature of student and instructor roles. Some methods are useful for particular goals. For example, buzz sessions ensure wide participation, while role playing may develop empathy and produce insights. Research reviewed in chapter 12 tells us that discussion methods *can* be more effective than lectures in promoting thought and helping students develop skills at analysis, application, and problem solving. We now turn to a number of basic issues that crosscut different discussion methods.

Major Issues about Discussions

Fixing on the problem, the procedures, and the outcomes. What will be discussed? how? and to what end? Except in unusual circumstances, the answers to such *procedural* questions need to be shared before discussion begins (and preferably in print—on the chalkboard or in a handout). This is necessary because of an endemic problem of discussions: they tend to wander. Some searching activity is useful in a discussion, but unless it is focused within some bounds it will probably not be productive. Topics make notoriously poor foci for discussion; effective discussion classes fix on an issue or problem that needs exploration or solution. As opposed to topics, questions provide an orientation: the search for an answer. In our experience, one of the more frequently used points of discussion—a particular book—often makes a poor basis for discussion *unless* students know what aspects of the book will be discussed. How will the discussion work? Will the teacher ask questions and the students answer them? Can anyone talk at any point? Will the fifty- or seventy-five-minute class be divided in any fashion? How much time will be spent clarifying the question? summarizing? Such questions require answers. And given a problem and procedure, what outcomes does the teacher have in mind? What does the teacher want students to be able to do as a result of a discussion class?

Student and teacher preparation for discussion. It is easy for teachers to underprepare for a discussion class. The teacher is usually quite familiar with the material under consideration and has a repertoire of questions to be asked: what did X say about Y? what do you think is meant by Z? and so on. Such questions can be useful, but teachers are likely to have better discussion classes if they carefully plan for the role of discussion leader. There is some parallel here in sociological research to the questionnaire and the interview protocol. In such forms of data collection, as in the classroom, time is limited and success depends on using it well. Our research instruments are carefully thought out: we anticipate responses (and thus precode some questions), we pay careful attention to the type and sequence of our questions (variously designed to tap awareness, general and specific information, reasoning behind a choice, salience, etc.). When preparing a protocol for a depth interview, we devise probes we can use as follow-ups to questions. We consider in advance what alternative questioning modes we may need to keep in reserve, depending on how the interview proceeds.

Similarly, teachers of discussion classes need to anticipate student responses and plan ways to stimulate, react to, and assist students in developing their responses. This is true even in those classes where the teacher wants to foster student creativity. Again, there is a research parallel—the unstructured interview or observation that is not wholly spontaneous and unplanned. In such a class, students and teachers need to share a vision of the task: What does creativity look like? How will we know when we are being creative? (Unless we know where we are going, we will not know if and when we have arrived there.) Would a new hypothesis—one not found in readings or already used in class—be a creative product? If the student or class generates a model of stratification that rests on assumptions different from those used in theories already reviewed, is that creativity? Or is applying an hypothesis or concept to a class of people or behavior creative? Can the teacher provide an instance of his or her own creativity, showing how an idea was developed?

Students, too, need to prepare for effective discussion participation. And for this, they need a more explicit focus on questions than one finds in a typical injunction from teachers: "Read text chapters 4 through 6 and the Davis and Moore article, and come prepared to discuss the materials." An alternative form of preparation question would begin:

> *The problem for our discussion on Wednesday is this: Do we rank some people higher than others and reward them more because they make necessary contributions to society and because there aren't very many such people?*

Exhibit 10.5 presents a handout distributed by a teacher in advance of a discussion class in an urban sociology course. The first question treats an issue that will give some students trouble, as the experienced teacher knows. The second question refers to a paper students had completed the week before, in which they were asked to search for empirical data bearing on whether an optimal city size could be identified for a particular variable of their choice (e.g., low risk of illness, access to classical music and the arts, low taxes, good public schools).

How discussion involves learned skills. "Classes don't automatically carry on effective discussions. To a large extent students have to learn how to learn from discussions just as they have to learn how to

learn from reading" (McKeachie, 1978:47). One thing that is learned during discussions is how to listen to others. Another is how to work within group norms, and another might be how to be effective in a leadership role. All teaching involves matters of process as well as content, but as teachers move away from expository modes of instruction, these process concerns are increasingly important. There is a connection between the process and the yield of classes. This is not simply a matter of philosophy: social science research (Lewin, Bales, Mills, Strodtbeck, and others)[5] tells us that the structure and process of a group affect outcomes both for individuals and for the group itself.

Effective discussions require that all participants try to act in certain ways: keeping a sharp focus on the issue at hand; respecting the process by which people change their minds; being sensitive to others' feelings and open to their contributions. These are group norms and teachers have an opportunity in discussion classes for reflexive analysis of group process, using the class as an example.

Teachers of discussion groups need certain skills—ability to start discussion, deal with nonparticipants and monopolizers, handle arguments, and perhaps above all, fasten people's attention to the problem at hand. Teachers may deal with these problems by imposing a relatively rigid structure on the discussion and playing a highly directive role. Such an approach will miss out on some of the goals of a discussion class: active participation and taking some responsibility for one's own learning. On the other hand, the teacher who provides virtually no direction and guidance will also subvert the class as a discussion group. For students do not enter classes with needed discussion skills, and classes need to establish norms for effective participation and work. Thus, the teacher must take the middle ground—having patience and trying to be a leader rather than a rigid commander. Two sets of techniques may be helpful.

First, the teacher needs to be sure that the entire class is clear about the prob-

lems, procedures, and desired outcomes of discussion. The teacher may follow the pattern of developmental discussion in which the class goes through a four-step process: formulating a problem, suggesting hypotheses, getting relevant data, and

---

Exhibit 10.5 Sample Handout Distributed in Advance of a Discussion Class in an Urban Sociology Course

Questions for Discussion Class: Thursday, April 14th

Assigned Reading: Chapters 4–5 in text;
Duncan's "Optimum Size of Cities";
Ogburn and Duncan's "City Size as a Sociological Variable"

1. In his article, Duncan makes a set of explicit statements distinguishing between the *normative* and the *empirical* elements in the optimum size issue. As part of this discussion, he writes about the "empirical validation of a criterion." Normative issues, he notes, are not at stake in the validation of a criterion. A value regarding a criterion is assumed, the empirical validation goes beyond that and does not involve normative concerns or investigation (see p. 759 especially).

   Do you have any problems with Duncan's distinction between the normative and the empirical aspect of the optimum size question? First, any difficulty seeing Duncan's point? Second, once seeing the point, do you agree or disagree, and on what grounds?

   Suppose that city planner Jones believed control of city size was essential to achieve a certain planning objective; and that city planner Smith believed city size was irrelevant to whether or not the same objective was achieved. Which planner(s) would want empirical validation of the criterion (i.e., the objective)?

   a. Jones (size is important)   and why
   b. Smith (size is unimportant)   and why
   c. Both   and why
   d. Neither   and why

2. Your paper was a response to the question, "Is there an optimum city size in the United States in regard to X?" You wrote the paper with reference to the contemporary period in the United States. You may have wondered how this optimality might have changed over time, though the assignment did not specifically request that. Let's do that now. Consider your X:

   a. Do you think that the optimum city size you identified for X (or the lack of one) would have been the same 50, 100, 150, 200 years ago in the United States? Why—why specifically? What types of evidence would indicate if you are correct? Do you think such evidence is available? or could be obtained now? How?

   b. Do you think that the optimum city size you identified for X (or the lack of one) is: (1) a *necessary* result of industrialization; (2) a result of something about the social, economic, or political structure in the United States (think about readings in Warner for some possible leads here); (3) related to Warren's "Great Change" thesis; (4) related to, or more intelligible in terms of, the ecological perspective?

3. What reasons (if any) might you personally have for asking questions about optimum city size?

evaluating alternative solutions. At each stage, all members of the class are asked to work on the same step. For as McKeachie says (1978:37): "One of the reasons discussion often seems ineffective and disorganized is that different members of the group are working on different aspects of the problem and are thus often frustrated by what they perceive as irrelevant comments by other students. In developmental discussions the teacher tries to keep the students aware of the step of discussion that is the current focus."[6] It is the teacher's responsibility to ensure that there are group norms and that all members of the group are aware of them.

A second set of techniques that teachers can use to make discussion more effective is to prevent drifting and monopolizing of class time by one or more students *or by themselves.* One way to accomplish this is to build on what small groups research has told us: groups develop and need role specialization. Appointing or inviting one member of the group to serve as a clarifier or summarizer and another to serve as a discussion leader can be very useful. Such roles need not always be performed by the same persons. They can rotate on a weekly basis, or one speaker can select the next speaker. But teachers need to remember that "discussion leader" is a learned social role; if students are to be effective in this role, they may need some assistance from the teacher in developing their role skills. This assistance might be conveyed in class, in writing, or in office conversations with students as they anticipate their work as discussion leaders. And at least equally important, students will probably use the teacher's in-class behavior as a role model. Other techniques of handling monopolizers include raising the issue with the class (in such a way as to avoid embarrassing

particular students) and talking outside of class with monopolizing students.

The importance of questions in discussions. First, questions can help improve communication within the group as is the case with questions designed to clarify the goals of discussion or the meaning intended by a previous speaker. Second, questions about procedures help improve group process—e.g., "What would be a useful way to divide our remaining time?" or "What information do we need before we can evaluate these solutions?" Third, questions can be used to motivate and to focus attention and work; this is one purpose of beginning a discussion with a major question.

A fourth reason to use questions is that they guide learning. Consider questions of the following type:

1. Do all societies have some form of stratification system?

2. How do sociologists define stratification?

3. Can anyone tell us three or four bases of stratification in the United States?

4. What is the difference between intra- and inter-generational social mobility?

5. Does stratification exist on the Israeli kibbutz?

6. What does Talmon say about sex-role stratification on the kibbutz?

7. What do Lenski and Lenski say about the possibilities for economic inequality in horticultural societies, in contrast to hunting and gathering societies?

Each of these questions taps an important concept or issue in social stratification, and questions such as these are the stock-in-trade of most teachers. The form of these questions should also be familiar to teachers who either use or read test-item manuals for textbooks. To what type of learning are such questions directed? To answer these questions, students would have to recall or recognize information. Whether this is a worthy educational goal (the ability to recall or recognize) depends on the material at hand and its utility. But recall and recognition of information are not the only educational goals teachers may hold. We often say that we want our students to be able not only to know (recall or recognize) information, but to be able to use it: to compare, to analyze, to apply, and to extend knowledge (see chapters 5 and 6).

Different types of questions call forth different types of answers. Different types of questions depend on different intellectual skills for their answers. The memory questions about stratification posed above will not be sufficient for the teacher who hopes to help students develop skills of application, analysis, and extension. Consider these questions:

1. Can you take the text's definition of social stratification and restate it in your own words?

2. What is, or would be, an example of stratification within an organization—other than schools and prisons, the examples that were used in Monday's lecture?

3. What are the basic assumptions of the Davis and Moore thesis?

4. What type of evidence would be needed to test Davis and Moore's explanation of inequality?

5. Based on the article we read describing the kibbutz in the early 1970s, what do you think the prospects are for a mjaor change in its stratification in twenty years?

Each of these questions moves the student beyond the level of memory and information. To answer the first two questions, students must know the text definition of social stratification; but the questions call for them to demonstrate comprehension by rephrasing the definition in their own words and by providing an original illustration of it. Question 3 requires skills of analysis—breaking down the Davis and Moore thesis into assumptions, concepts, hypotheses, and other elements. Of course, if an article has explicitly stated assumptions, asking students for them does not require the skill of analysis. Questions 4 and 5 depend on, but move well beyond, the information provided. Question 4 assumes that students understand what sociologists accept as empirical evidence and that they know the Davis and Moore theory. Since Davis and Moore do not adduce or discuss evidence bearing on their thesis, to answer question 4 students must understand the theory, be able to break it into its component parts, and determine what types of evidence would shed light on the assumptions and hypotheses in Davis and Moore. To answer question 5, students must extend what they know about the kibbutz in the 1970s.

One way to build questions into discussion classes is by resisting the understandable temptation to assign *for a given discussion class* all relevant reading on a topic. Thus, in an introductory-level course, it may be useful to assign Davis and Moore's "Some Principles of Stratification" (1945) but *not*, at the same time, the Tumin (1953) reply and subsequent exchange among these authors. This may offer the teacher a better opportunity to work with students on skills of analysis, application, and critical thinking. It may make it easier to construct questions, classroom exercises, and activities in which students confront a theory on its own grounds, using and developing their own skills. Such discovery-based teaching strategies take time, and few teachers could accomplish what they want by using this strategy for *all* meetings of each class. But this does not mean it cannot be used judiciously and as an example of how one goes about analyzing and evaluating. Some teachers may object that it is unfair to students to give them only half the debate on sources of inequality; some may feel it is deceptive or artificial. While learning may, in some sense, be natural, education rarely is: teaching is a purposive activity designed to enhance learning. As teachers must select some issues and books and not others, and fit them into a fifty-minute class or fifteen-week unit, teaching is surely artificial. But it need not be deceptive. There is no reason why the teacher assigning Davis-Moore alone cannot tell the class there are criticisms of Davis-Moore and *why* these criticisms are not being assigned *now*. This approach is not simply intended to give the teacher a ploy; rather, it is intended to help students develop their skills of reasoning. Finally, the teacher who assigns Tumin with Davis-Moore may be omitting to assign Stinchchombe's or Wesolowski's work on the inequality debate. Or, if Stinchchombe and Wesolowski are assigned, the teacher may have decided to omit the contributions of Wrong, Buckley, Simpson, and Lenski.

Using data in discussions.   Using raw data as the point of discussion is an especially useful technique. Students can often work together analyzing and drawing inferences from the data provided. (By raw data, we mean tables and figures, independent of an article that summarizes and analyzes them for the reader.) Throughout this book (especially in chapters 4 through 6), we have provided examples of the use of raw data. Here are two more illustrations of the use of raw data in discussion classes.

Early in an advanced undergraduate course on collective behavior and social movements, we wanted to give students a chance to work with real data and to develop and test hypotheses. We distributed to each member of this class a table listing individually every known vigilante movement in the United States (from Brown, 1969). For each movement, the following data were provided: name of the movement, state and county of occurrence, approximate size and importance, number of members, dates of existence, and number of victims killed, if any. The listing was organized by state; the dates of the 326 known movements extended from the late eighteenth to the early twentieth century. We asked students to come to the next class, a discussion session, prepared to advance and support hypotheses as to why vigilante movements occurred in the United States when they did and where they did. Since the data on the movements were in list form, students had to construct categories for grouping the movements.

We opened our next class by asking whether students had any difficulty with the assignment. A few minor problems were dealt with. We then indicated that we wanted to try to explain the distribution of movements in time and that a first step would be to summarize the raw data. A student offered his frequency count of movements over time. Another student indicated that she had used different cutting points in dividing time and clustering movements. We compared the differences in frequency counts using the two systems and discussed their implications. At this point we turned to hypotheses that would explain the distribution in time of vigilante movements. Students had different explanations for the same data, and this led to discussion of how we might decide between competing hypotheses. After about two-thirds of the class time had passed, we provided students with some of the explanations developed by the compiler of the list, historian Richard Maxwell Brown. They were dissatisfied with some of Brown's explanations and felt they could challenge his views.

A second and rather different use of raw data is to present students with only part of a statistical table or chart and to ask them to use other information they have to fill in the blanks. Teachers of research methods and statistics often use a version of this technique when they provide students with a table having only some marginals and ask them to derive the other marginals and cell values. But here our concern is not with the logic of contingency tables but with substantive issues. To estimate the missing data, students need to apply what they know about the issue at hand. Another version of this technique is to give students a graph and indicate the variables but omit the values, as in figure 10.5.[7]

We asked students to provide the dates for which the data on civilian employees of the federal government would apply. The underlying question was this: What events in U.S. history would have led to changes in the *growth rate* of the federal establishment? We used this question in a class where federal domestic pol-

icy was under discussion. In the spirit of the classroom exercise, we will leave it to our readers to fill in the dates on the X-axis of figure 10.5, or to consult U.S. Bureau of the Census (1975a:1102–3; 1976:249).

Resources: The Literature on Discussion

Many articles in the literature on the teaching of sociology describe techniques that can be used in discussion classes; they are cataloged in bibliographies and review articles cited in appendix 1. In our earlier discussion of lectures, we listed a number of articles describing teaching techniques compatible with the lecture class. Many of these techniques were developed for use in, or are pertinent to, small-group instruction.

Rice (1978:259) describes his use in an Introductory Sociology course of "a structured technique for processing cognitive content in a small group format." His technique rests on small-group theory and research. Students prepare for each discussion class by answering a series of questions about readings and lectures. In their discussion group, these answers become the materials for preparing a "group cognitive map," the agenda the group will follow. The map consists of eight prespecified steps (e.g., definition of concepts and terms, main themes and subtopics, time allocation for discussion of themes and topics, and evaluation of readings). Teaching in a four-year college, Rice uses advanced undergraduate sociology students as discussion leaders; they receive precourse training and meet weekly with the professor. Rice's technique is a modified version of the learning-through-discussion method developed by William F. Hill (1969). In Hill's method, group norms and individual roles in groups re-

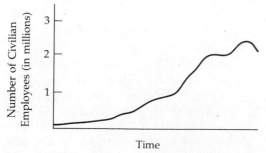

Figure 10.5 Civilian Employees of the U.S. Government over Time.

ceive explicit attention. Hill's basic technique and Rice's adaptation of it for his sociology courses are well developed and deserve careful attention by teachers who believe that discussion groups can be useful instruments of learning.

Four other articles on the teaching of sociology may be especially useful. Dunphy (1967) describes the placement of students from a large lecture class into small "self-analytic groups" that are laboratories for reflexive study as well as learning contexts. Silvers (1973) discusses the factors involved in the shift from a teacher-centered to a student-centered class, the latter based on discussion. Pape and Miller (1967) describe the use of undergraduate discussion leaders. Finally, Rosenfeld (1978) has written a useful article on ways to reduce the student anxiety that has been found to block learning. Since anxiety about participation often surfaces in discussion classes, the issues and procedures this article treats are worth attention.

The general literature on discussion and small-group learning formats is large and well developed. Perhaps the best single treatment is McKeachie (1978:chapter 5), which reviews research on discussion classes (including student-versus teacher-centered instruction) and considers formats, problems, and skills in discussion classes. He deals chiefly with the problem-solving discussion. Other short treatments of discussion are Beard (1970:chapter 5), Eble (1976:chapter 6), Milton (1978:chapter 3), and Watson, Pardo, and Tomovic (1978). While none of these treatments contains extensive reviews of research, all address basic issues facing teachers of discussion classes and provide much useful advice on techniques of promoting learning in small groups.

Although it offers little in the way of detailed advice, Olmstead's *Small-Group Instruction* (1974) presents succinct and well-organized descriptions of nine small-group teaching techniques and a review of research bearing on each. The methods reviewed include several case study techniques (including the Harvard Case Method), buzz sessions, role playing, and topical discussions.

Teachers interested in developing their skills at asking different forms of questions to assist students in achieving different learning outcomes will find Sander's *Classroom Questions: What Kinds?* (1966) highly useful. This volume is based on Bloom's taxonomy of cognitive educational objectives and, although designed for secondary school teachers, is clearly applicable to the college classroom. A rationale for concern with questions in the classroom is provided by Thompson (1969).

There are several excellent handbooks on discussion techniques that rest on research in small-group dynamics and communications. A good example is Brilhart's *Effective Group Discussion* (1974). The theoretical and research basis for much of the writing cited above is summarized and discussed in volumes such as Hare (1976) and Schmuck and Schmuck (1975).

Personalized System of Instruction

In the early 1960s, psychologist Fred S. Keller developed a personalized system of instruction (PSI), sometimes referred to as The Keller Plan. PSI and its many variants are now used in thousands of college courses in dozens of disciplines. By 1977, PSI was the subject of more than 300 articles and papers. PSI was one of the first, and is the best known, of several methods that apply principles of behavior to instruction and seek to individualize the process of learning.

In his best known article, Keller (1968:83) identifies distinctive features of PSI:

1. *Student self-pacing:* A student moves through the units of the course at a pace "commensurate with his ability and other demands on his time."

2. *Unit-perfection requirement:* The student moves on to new material only when he has demonstrated mastery of that which preceded.

3. *Lectures used for motivation:* Lectures and demonstrations are used as "vehicles for motivation, rather than sources of critical information."

4. *Stress on the written word:* A textbook, other assigned literature from the field, and a teacher-prepared set of guidelines and instruction form the core of teacher-student interaction.

5. *Use of proctors:* Peer tutors are used to provide "repeated testing, immediate scoring, almost unavoidable tutoring and a marked enhancement of the personal-social aspect of the educational process."

PSI courses differ markedly from courses using any combination of lecture and discussion. They are divided into a series of relatively small units (perhaps ten in a semester). For each unit, students are provided with an explicit statement of learning objectives and a detailed study guide geared to assigned readings. When a student believes he has mastered the material for that unit, he takes a quiz covering the unit. The quiz is taken in a special room where proctors or TAs (usually advanced undergraduates or graduate students) immediately grade and return it. The proctor discusses the quiz with the student to find and eliminate any sources of misunderstanding. If the student has achieved unit mastery (often defined as a quiz score of 90 percent or better), he moves on to the next course unit. If he has not mastered the unit, he does more independent study, consulting with proctors and assistants, if necessary, and then takes a different quiz covering the first unit material. Within some limits, a student moves through a PSI course at his or her own pace. Typically, a PSI course does not have any required class meetings. Students' grades are usually based on a combination of unit quizzes (number passed and grades achieved on the last quiz taken in a unit) and a cumulative final exam. Grading is on an absolute, not relative, basis; each student is evaluated by the degree to which he has mastered the course's material (information and skills). Grading norms or curves are not employed: everyone can get an A; everyone can get an F.

The instructor's responsibilities in a PSI course include: (1) determination of course goals; (2) preparation of statements of learning objectives, study guides, and other communications to the student; (3) selection of course materials, designing of work units; (4) construction of exams and the series of quizzes for each unit; (5) final assessment of each student's work; (6) selection, training, and supervision of proctors and assistants; (7) monitoring the course and students' progress within it, watching for and dealing with problems; (8) giving any special lectures or discussion groups; (9) being available to proctors and, on a limited basis, to students in the class; and (10) course assessment and revision.

Student proctors have already demonstrated mastery of the material in the PSI course and have usually done advanced work in the field of study; they should have maturity of judgment and understand the problems of the beginning student.

Although PSI will not be the method of choice for all teachers or all teaching-learning situations, there are several reasons for being familiar with the method. First, it is one of the most widely adopted and influential developments in teaching in several decades. Second, the effectiveness of PSI has been well established: there is now no question that within specifiable limits, PSI is more effective in enhancing some types of student learning than conventionally structured courses.* Third, many of the principles and some of the specific elements of PSI can be used to advantage in more traditional instructional formats, including lecture classes. Fourth, PSI raises fundamental questions about the proper bases of grading, modes of student learning, the role of the teacher, and student-teacher and student-student interaction.

Finally, PSI is one of the few instructional methods that has an explicit theoretical base.[8] Ruskin (1975:6) provides a synopsis of some of the "principles of psychology learning research" that have been shown to enhance learning and that undergird PSI and related techniques:

> Learning is more efficient if the student is presented material in small, logically related amounts; students perform (learn) appreciably better if they are constantly made aware of exactly what is important for them to know (thus eliminating student guessing games at exam time); students perform at a higher level and with less anxiety if they receive immediate feedback on their progress and performance in the educational system; and, punishment is usually detrimental to the learning process.

Types and Uses of PSI

PSI shares with some other instructional methods a number of principles and

procedures. The mastery principle is sometimes used in nonbehavioral approaches to traditionally organized courses. Self-pacing is present in various forms of supervised individual study, and specification of objectives and a fitting of evaluation procedures to objectives can characterize any instructional method. But PSI most resembles a number of other behavioral methods of instruction; interested readers can consult Johnson and Ruskin (1977:chapter 2).

Few PSI courses follow Keller's original plan without some modification. For example, research and experience have shown that it is useful to place some limits on PSI's self-pacing feature. This helps counter the tendency of some students to procrastinate or give in to the more regular pressures of other courses, and also takes advantage of the fact that learning is enhanced if it is spaced rather than massed at one or a few points during a semester. Figure 10.6 illustrates two of the many variants of PSI.

Teachers who do not use PSI as a method might still consider building into their courses some of the elements of PSI, such as frequent checks and rapid response, a limited amount of self-pacing, or the opportunity for students to take repeated tests on the same unit of subject matter until they achieve a given performance level. The research literature on PSI is useful to such teachers, since many studies test the contribution to student learning of given components of PSI.* One student of PSI, James A. Kulik, has concluded that available evidence supports the view that "continuous feedback of individual performance toward unit mastery is the most important single feature" of PSI (Ericksen and Kulik, 1975:5). Frequent

---

* We review the pertinent research in chapter 12.

* For a review of these studies, see Johnson and Ruskin, 1977:chapter 5.

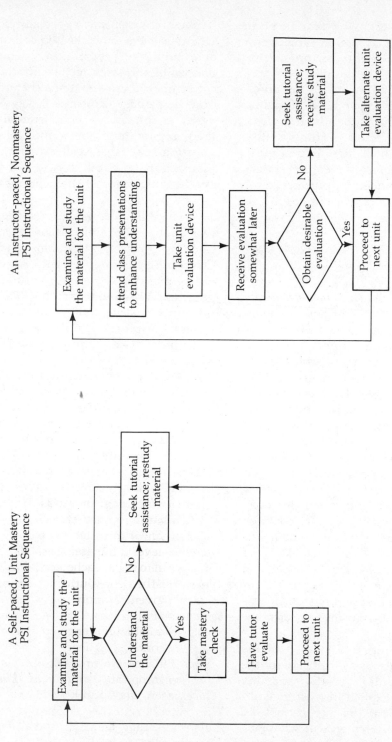

Figure 10.6 Two Variants of PSI. *Source:* George Watson and Dickson McGaw, "Personalizing Instruction in Political Science," in *PSI and Political Science,* edited by Ralph B. Earle, Jr. (Washington D. C.: American Political Science Association, 1975), p. 32 (figure 2) and p. 34 (figure 3). Reprinted by permission.

quizzing and feedback, which can be built into many course patterns, are thus considered especially useful in promoting student learning.

PSI is probably best suited for large, introductory courses that have students of widely varying backgrounds. It is clear that an effective PSI course requires a substantial instructor investment in planning and preparation before the course starts. That time, plus the need for proctors, may restrict the adoption rate of PSI or limit it to schools with large enrollment classes.

Major Issues about PSI

Does PSI promote only the memorization of simple facts?   It is sometimes suggested that PSI is useful in helping students learn information but not analytic skills, elementary but not complex information, and what one sociologist (Baker, 1976:24) has called the "rhetoric of conclusions," in contrast to learning intellectual skills and developing creative abilities. Some observers charge that, to the degree teachers specify learning outcomes for their students, the learnings will be rudimentary or even trivial. It is undoubtedly true that it is easier to specify learning objectives for elementary than complex materials, and to ask students to define or recall than to analyze or synthesize. While some PSI courses may surely be vulnerable to this charge, there is nothing in PSI (or any other method) that requires that learning objectives and outcomes be elementary.

Just as it is easy to stick with the elementary, it is also easy to stick with the vague. One advantage of PSI (and any method that uses explicit instructional objectives) is that the teacher cannot be vague. Nebulous statements of what students are expected to learn are real dangers in most courses and especially common when teachers have heavy course loads and multiple preparations. Thus, the teacher of the large lecture class finds it convenient to use test items that often tap only elementary learnings. Likewise, it is easier to construct a poor true-false item than a good one, or a multiple-choice question that taps recall rather than one that taps analytic ability. And it is easier to specify simpler rather than complex objectives.

There is evidence from six comparative studies that PSI can be effective in teaching complex information and skills. One carefully designed study shows that PSI is effective in teaching students "to apply concepts and principles to examples not in the instructional materials [and] to generate original examples of concepts or principles" (see Johnson and Ruskin, 1977:73–75).

The danger of trivialization is real but *not intrinsic* to PSI or to other teaching methods. By avoiding specification of learning outcomes, teachers may derive a false sense of security as to what they are teaching. A study by Logan (1976) using pretest and post-test comparisons of students (in Introductory Sociology through graduate courses) reminds us that the "widespread claim that sociology teaches students how to think more critically and scientifically about social issues" is often not matched by what students actually learn. The only class in which Logan found gains in critical thinking was one that made such thinking an *explicit* course goal and devised active means to achieve it.

Does PSI assume that learning is simply the mastery of a body of knowledge specified by the teacher?   We hope none of our colleagues would disagree with the assertion that learning social facts and empirically tested relationships has an important place in any sociology course (see James A. Davis, 1978:235–41, for a pertinent statement). But some sociologists charge that PSI courses accomplish no more than this, that they teach the student to internalize facts in such a way as "to enable a proper text-response" (Francis, 1974a:161). Baker (1976:24) argues that in PSI courses "all worthwhile knowledge is predetermined and explicit, giving teachers and students no opportunity to explore something genuinely new in classroom interaction." He holds that "on occasion the teacher should deliberately structure ambiguity in order to allow for creativity. Such ambiguity," Baker concludes, "is eschewed in the Keller Plan."

Most PSI courses do prespecify a body of knowledge to be mastered, and it is true that such courses allow little room for emergent concerns and issues. While we endorse the importance of knowledge, we also lament a course that does not help students develop intellectual skills to apply and extend that knowledge, and that fails to accommodate and encourage emergent issues.

But as we suggested in the preceding section, intellectual skills *can* be taught in introductory-level courses using PSI. To say this can happen does not mean it often does; but this may be no less true for courses taught by methods other than PSI. In a response to Francis, Malec (1975:216) takes this view, saying that any course can be "structured to promote rote learning and regurgitative feedback . . . [while] well-constructed courses, PSI or any other, can and do encourage critical thinking and intellectual growth. Poorly constructed courses, PSI or any other, can and do stifle." And we fully agree with Baker about the value of structuring some ambiguity into all courses in order to foster creative thinking; indeed, this is a

central concern of chapters 5 and 6 in this volume.

It appears that in most PSI courses, opportunity for flexibility in instruction and responding to student initiatives is severely limited. Such opportunity may not, however, be impossible to create. While one can envision a PSI course that encourages and builds on such initiatives, it would not be an easy course to design or teach. It seems clear, though, that if the PSI teacher does not build student initiative and creativity into the course, these qualities are not likely to emerge, or, if they do, they are likely to go undeveloped.

Is PSI really personalized or individualized? both? or neither?   Some observers have suggested that PSI is not so much *personalized* as it is *individualized* (see, for example, Francis, 1974a:160). Our dictionaries do not make a clear distinction between the terms; both refer to unique human beings. But there is the view that PSI is impersonal because course content is largely or wholly predetermined and not selected or presented to meet the needs of particular students, and because traditional face-to-face interaction between the professor and the student is largely or wholly absent. We agree with Malec (1975:215–16) that PSI is personalized or individualized

in at least two ways. First, it proceeds, within limits, at a rate that is comfortable to the individual person taking it. The student can work when he wants and as fast or slow as he wants. Second, it is personal in the sense that a strong interpersonal relationship can build up between teacher (tutor) and student. With tutor:student ratios of about 1 : 8, the tutor can respond more easily to the student as a person, a person with his or her own problems. . . . I . . . concede that the professor's relationship to the students is not always personal, for he is often one step removed from them.

On the other hand, it would appear that PSI courses do have a certain amount of built-in rigidity. Study guides and assignments must be prepared in final forms well in advance of the beginning of the course. To be sure, some flexibility and options could be included in the course design, but once the course has begun, opportunities for adjusting the content and process of the course would seem quite limited. Since PSI tends to be used in larger classes in larger schools, the likelihood of heterogeneity in the enrollment is high. This would seem to increase the need for diverse types of examples in the study guides, careful selection of alternative readings designed to deal with the same body of content or skills from different vantage points, and perhaps alternative assignments. These tasks are both difficult and demanding on the teacher's time; probably they are rarely done.

PSI appears to us to preclude major gear-shifting or adjustment during the course. There is no intrinsic virtue in such shifting, but often early calculations and plans for a course seem to require flexibility. We realize that PSI-users, like their colleagues, often develop and modify their courses with successive offerings. Perhaps, too, the losses in within-course flexibility are offset by other aspects of PSI. We do not know. In any event, because of the frequent evaluation in PSI courses, teachers get quicker feedback on student performance and this more quickly reveals needs for modification.

Finally, the degree to which PSI is impersonal depends on what it is compared to.

Good-bye, teacher? good-bye, peer learning?
PSI uses student proctors who teach, although they are not professors. Some observers are displeased with PSI because it does away with the teacher as

role model. It is useful for students to see teachers go through the process of problem definition and solution. PSI courses seem to break the subject matter down into parts and handle it in such a way that the student may not see the teacher-as-sociologist at work. In this sense, we agree that the loss of the teacher as role model is worth worrying about. It may be that the optional lectures and other meetings that are part of some PSI courses fill this need. But if what the teacher is exemplifying in these sessions is worth understanding, presumably PSI teachers would require their students to participate in these sessions and build such learnings into their course objectives and quizzes.

The PSI literature establishes the tutor-student relationship as contributing to student (and tutor) learning. But this seems to be the only interaction among students in PSI courses. While this may be better than the traditional large lecture situation, we would think that methods that lead students to exchange ideas—and thereby test them—are desirable.

We expect that PSI can be modified to retain the teacher-as-role-model and peer learning. Some student work could be self-paced and done alone, some done in teams, and the class could meet periodically with the professor.

To what types of courses is PSI best suited?
It is probably true that courses or portions of courses that place a premium on learning factual material (but not necessarily learning to analyze, apply, or synthesize it) are most readily suited to PSI. However, as we noted earlier, there is some indication in the literature that what are sometimes called "higher cognitive learnings" can be taught through PSI. One nonsystematic survey of PSI users and former users (Smith, 1977:44) suggests that open-ended and exploratory courses, often

Exhibit 10.6 PSI: Bits of Wisdom from Those Who Have Learned the Hard Way

1. Don't try PSI if you are looking for an easier way to teach.
2. Do try PSI if you want to know more definitely what your students are learning.
3. Don't change to a PSI format if you have good reasons to believe that your lecture course is effective and successful.
4. Do provide plenty of preparation time if you plan to give a PSI course.
5. Don't get involved in a PSI course unless you have a real sense of commitment regarding it.
6. Do plan on giving a PSI course, not one, but two or three times—it will take that long to perfect the course.
7. Don't expect, at least initially, to find enthusiastic support for your PSI efforts from colleagues and deans.
8. Do expect to find a substantial drop-out rate from your PSI course.
9. Don't try the PSI approach until you have worked out a detailed specification of the objectives of your course.
10. Do learn how to specify behavioral/learning objectives.
11. Don't give a PSI course until you know definitely about the availability of proctors/tutors.
12. Do try some aspects of PSI even if you cannot for some reason or reasons implement a full course.
13. Don't be reluctant to use at least some course materials prepared by others. The preparation of materials from zero is a major burden of a PSI course.
14. Do investigate the instructional and technological aids available to you before embarking upon the design of a PSI course.
15. Don't expect all students to like the PSI approach. More likely than not, it will be a love-hate thing; some students will think it's great, others will think otherwise.
16. Do expect that the grade distribution in your PSI course will be different than in one of your standard courses. It may not be, but it probably will be.
17. Don't invest your time and effort in developing a PSI course unless the course will serve a substantial number of students (over 30 or 40, at least, and preferably more).
18. Do expect some "flack" from your immediate colleagues if you are the only PSI user in your department or program.
19. Don't embark upon a PSI course unless you are assured of special financial support for materials, tutors, etc.
20. Unless one or more of the above tells you "No," try PSI: you might like it!

Note: These "bits of wisdom" were collected by means of telephone interviews with a nonsystematic sample of PSI users and former users.

Source: William M. Smith, "The Use of PSI in Large-Course Instruction," pp. 40–53 in *Large Course Instruction,* edited by George L. Wolford and William M. Smith (Hanover, New Hampshire: Dartmouth College, 1977), pp. 49–50. Reprinted by permission.

advanced undergraduate seminars, may not be readily amenable to PSI since "precise, pre-specified course objectives . . . [are] clearly inappropriate."

Is it true that in a PSI course all students might get the grade of A?　　Yes. Just as it is possible for all to get an F. PSI courses publicly specify at the outset the information and skills to be mastered. This does not mean that students are provided in advance with the test questions and answers, except in those cases where recognition or recall of specific information is a course objective. Student achievement is measured by assessing the degree to which a student masters the course objectives. If all students meet all the objectives, all get A's. Teachers in PSI courses must make judgments about what levels of performance constitute what grades. PSI uses an absolute grading system; each student's performance is measured against the standard embodied in the course objectives and achievement criteria set by the teacher. The performance or grade of one student does not affect that of other students; grading on a curve or the use of grading norms rest on completely different assumptions.

　　The grade in a PSI course usually depends heavily on student performances in the unit examinations—which students can and often must take until they achieve either unit perfection (100 percent) or, more commonly, some other specified minimum achievement level (e.g., 80 percent). Many PSI courses also use achievement on a midterm or final examination in arriving at the final student evaluation, and some courses use term papers or other assignments.

　　Grade distributions in PSI courses are generally markedly skewed toward higher grades with a substantial proportion of students earning A's. The distribu-

tions are often bimodal, the second mode (an F or withdrawal) being quite small. PSI grade distributions can be explained, in part, by the use of absolute (or criterion-referenced) rather than relative (or norm-referenced) standards and, in part, by the PSI method itself. But does the grade of A in a PSI course reflect the same achievement level as in a conventional course? Leaving aside the issue of absolute versus relative grading, the answer depends not on the *method* of instruction, but on the teacher's selection of objectives and materials and on the construction of the tests. There is no reason why the A in PSI cannot describe the same achievement as an A in a conventionally taught course. (Note that the studies comparing PSI with other methods generally employ common tests.) Research on PSI indicates that the high rates of student withdrawal or grades of Incomplete are avoidable and, in any event, do not explain away the higher grade distribution in PSI (see Johnson and Ruskin, 1977:50–59).

Resources: The Literature on PSI

　　Six articles, listed in exhibit 10.7, discuss the use of variants of PSI in sociology courses. All report learning gains by students, and four of the papers base this conclusion on comparative studies. The magnitude of these gains is between one-half and one and a half letter grades (in mean class grades: see chapter 12 for further discussion). The papers by Clark (1974) and MacDaniel (1974) in exhibit 10.7 contain useful descriptions of their courses as well as assessment of learning gains. An unannotated forty-item bibliography on PSI was published in *Teaching Sociology* (1974a). Several of the articles cited in exhibit 10.7 contain advice for potential PSI users; two articles appearing in the journal, *Teaching Sociology*, that include some severe criticisms (though some praise) of PSI are Francis (1974a) and Baker (1976). Malec (1975) has published a reply to some of Francis's criticisms.

The general literature on PSI and other forms of behavioral instruction is very large and continues to grow. According to Johnson and Ruskin (1977:3), by 1975 there were more than 500 papers discussing such courses in some fifty disciplines. By 1977, there were well over 300 articles on PSI, with an annotated bibliography appearing annually in the *Journal of Personalized Instruction*, published since 1976 (see, for example, Bono et al., 1977). The quarterly *Journal*, along with a bimonthly *PSI Newsletter*, is published by the Center for Personalized Instruction, 29 Loyola Hall, Georgetown Univeristy, Washington, D. C. 20007. The Center sponsors an annual PSI conference and workshops held throughout the United States. A publications list and other brochures are available.

The most comprehensive review of theory and research on PSI and other behavioral methods is Johnson and Ruskin's *Behavioral Instruction: An Evaluative Review* (1977). The chapter on "component analysis of behavioral instruction" reviews theory and research on mastery learning, self-pacing, unit size, frequency of quizzing, proctors, and more than a dozen other components. Another chapter reviews studies comparing behavioral and conventional instruction (including exam performance, retention of learning, and transfer of learning to new situations). Another extended treatment of PSI is Keller and Sherman's *The Keller Plan Handbook* (1974).

Useful short discussions of PSI are found in Ericksen and Kulik (1975) and McKeachie (1978). A brief review of research literature is provided in Cross (1976:9–110). Medium-length treatments of PSI are found in Milton (1978), Ryan (1974), and Ruskin (1974, 1975).

Discussions of problems associated with PSI courses are found throughout Johnson and Ruskin (1977) and the other sources cited above. Other works treating PSI problems are Smith (1977b), Green (1972), and Sherman (1972). Consideration of PSI's utility in a single discipline— political science—is found in Earle (1975); attention is given to curriculum and departmental implications of the use of PSI.

Exhibit 10.7 Articles on the Use of PSI in Sociology

Course	Approximate Number of Students	Type of Institution Course Taught at	Reference
Intro. Sociology	60–70	Large University	Clark (1974)
Intro. Social Science	60–350	Large Community College	Ludwig (1975)
Research Methods	80	Medium-sized University	MacDaniel (1974)
Social Statistics	30–80	Large University	Malec (1975)
Intro. Sociology	60	Medium-sized University	Rogers, Satariano, and Rogers (1977)
Intro. Sociology	150	Large University	Johnson and Walsh (1978)

❧

Lectures, discussions, and PSI schemes represent strategic choices of modes of instruction. They may be mixed and adapted in various ways. But they are large-scale instructional patterns. There are other commonly used means of instruction closer to the tactical level—means commonly used to link abstract ideas with concrete cases, to bring the distant closer to home, to vivify instruction. Two of these methods we discuss in the following chapter: the use of examples and the use of audiovisual aids.

Notes

1. Baker (1976) sent questionnaires to all departments listed in the 1974 *ASA Guide to Graduate Departments of Sociology* and all public and private institutions with total enrollments of 10,000 or more students. This yielded a sample of 287 U.S. and Canadian institutions. One hundred sixty-three (of 287) departmental chairpersons responded, thirteen of whom provided insufficient information. Sixty percent of the respondents reported that some of their courses were taught in classes with 100 or more students. In sum, in eighty-four departments of sociology, 202 instructors taught a total of 229 mass classes. Forty-six percent of the 229 mass classes were in Introductory Sociology

and 12 percent in Social Problems. No other course accounted for more than 10 percent of the total. This information is drawn from Baker (1976:10–11).

2. Bradshaw and McPherron's (1977) sampling frames were provided by the 1975 *ASA Guide to Graduate Departments of Sociology*, an ASA list of all four-year college departments offering sociology, and a list of community colleges from the American Association of Community and Junior Colleges. As table 10.4 shows, the sample yielded responses from 443 departments (an overall response rate of 65 percent). Part of the explanation for the low response rate from community colleges was that for only a portion of 1,190 institutions were Bradshaw and McPherron able to obtain the names of sociology or social science division chairpersons for use in addressing inquiries. Summary data in Bradshaw and McPherron make use of weighted totals based on the sampling percentages (1,5,5).

3. The actual responses from the NORC national sample in 1947 (in the North-Hatt study) were, in percentages: 18, 2, 3, 14, 16, less than 1, 5, 14, 9, 9, and 10; see National Opinion Research Center (1947).

4. This example, and some of the phrases in this paragraph, are borrowed from Macrorie (1970:168ff). It is also useful to recall that the lack of treatment of politics in many secondary school government texts has been the subject of sociological analysis. See, for example, Litt (1963).

5. For a review of small groups and group

Table 10.4 Breakdown of Bradshaw and McPherron (1977) Sample, by Type of School, Percentage and Number Sampled, and Percentage and Number Responding

Type of School	Total Number	Percentage Sampled	Number Sampled	Response Rate	Number of Responses
Graduate	253	100%	253	77%	195
Four-Year	960	20%	192	67%	129
Two-Year	1190	20%	238	50%	119
	2403		683	65%	443

dynamics work as applied to the classroom, see Schmuck and Schmuck (1975): chapter 2 has an historical overview of this literature; the body of the book discusses group process in the classroom under the concepts of cohesion, communication, norms, leadership, sequential stages of development, etc. A comprehensive review of small-group studies is Hare (1976).

6. *Developmental discussion* is a term coined by Norman Maier. We borrowed this discussion from McKeachie (1978:36–37).

7. We learned this from Professor Peter Filene, Department of History, University of North Carolina—Chapel Hill.

8. The following list of PSI principles is from Watson and McGraw (1975:24–26), who discuss the principles in detail: specification of objectives, congruence of evaluation and objectives, active responding, short units of instruction, frequent and immediate feedback, spaced learning, positive conditions and consequences, mastery before advancement, self-pacing, and tutorial instruction. Note that several of these principles can be applied to non-PSI instruction.

CHAPTER 11
VIVIFYING THE CLASS SESSION: EXAMPLES AND AUDIOVISUAL AIDS

Whether a course is discussion- or lecture-based, the instructor needs to vivify the social phenomena and sociological concepts and relationships used in class. Examples contribute toward this end. Most classroom examples are in oral or written form, but the audiovisual media (films, transparencies, chalkboard, and the like) also convey them.

By use of examples, the teacher moves from the map of big ideas to the terrain of specifics (and to the testing of those ideas). There are parallels here between comprehension and apprehension, conception and perception, between Weber's (1921) *verstehen* and *begreifen* and Cooley's (1902) sympathetic and empirical modes of understanding.

Examples

The Power of Examples

Examples are widely used tools of teaching; they can rivet the attention of the student to a larger issue, provide focus, illustrate application, clarify and crystallize. The power of examples is suggested by the fact that when students describe a course they took, examples used in the course often are mentioned:

Yes, I took a population course with Professor Jones. We spent a good deal of time on popula-

tion and economics and on the causes and consequences of the population explosion. I remember she told us that if the population growth rates of the early 1960s were continued for only 600 years that there would be one person for every square foot of land surface on earth, including mountains, deserts, and ice packs.

Or, if a colleague asks us to provide a short summary of the book *Unobtrusive Measures* (Webb et al., 1966), we might write:

The authors argue that interview and questionnaire data need to be "supplemented and cross-validated by measures that do not require the cooperation of the respondent and that do not themselves contaminate the response." They discuss several sources of such data—different kinds of archival records, covert observation, and recording and measurement of various physical traces. For example, "The floor tiles around the hatching-chick exhibit at Chicago's Museum of Science and Industry must be replaced every six weeks. Tiles in other parts of the museum need not be replaced for years. The selective erosion of tiles indexed by the replacement rate, is a measure of the relative popularity of exhibits."

Or, if we are preparing a lecture on "the sociological perspective," we might wish to demonstrate how sociological research and analysis often lead to unexpected findings and that sociologists take nothing about the social world for granted. Then to develop these points, we might give examples of how conflict can lead to cohesion (following Coser, 1956) and how ignorance has positive social functions (following Moore and Tumin, 1949). When later pressed by a student to clarify how empirical data are used in theory development, we turn to Durkheim's explanation of suicide and his development of a theory of social integration. To illustrate the social component in acts that seem thoroughly personal, we may use Barry Schwartz's work (1970) on the sociology of sleep.

Like oatmeal and glue, powerful examples stick to one. Students often remember the teacher's (or author's) examples either as a vehicle for recalling a larger point or in their own right. At their best, examples lead the student to the point of saying "Aha! *Now* I understand it." The power of examples is also suggested when we examine teaching without examples:

> *Role conflict and strain involve dilemmas. Any given role may contain inconsistencies and thus competing expectations or attributes. Further, all people play out different roles which may come into conflict. For a single role or for a cluster of linked roles, obligations and rights come into conflict. Viewed either from the point of view of the individual actor or the social systems in which individuals are embedded, disjunctions occur that must be resolved. There are many mechanisms for doing this. For the individual they include: leaving a role (unless there is an ascriptive element involved), prioritizing, compartmentalizing, compromising, combining role performances and so on. For organized units of society, additional conflict-reducing mechanisms are available: engaging in concerted social action with similarly situated others to find mutual support and protection; and compartmentalizing role performances. Most cultural groups have a variety of prescriptions and proscriptions for behavior that reduce or prevent role conflict and strain.*

Assuming that the teacher has already defined key terms (*role, ascription*, etc.), this

statement is a reasonable and largely non-technical discussion of role conflict and its reduction. But because the discussion is devoid of examples, students are likely to be puzzled and left with many questions. What are these strains and conflicts like? Do strains really inhere in roles, or are they the result of an individual's particular confusions or incompetence? Students listening to an example-free lecture or discussion *may* ask such questions. But many students may find example-free discussions so abstract that they cannot formulate the questions that would bring answers providing clarification. Hence, one reason to use examples is to provide check points to see if students understand a more general point.

What examples might a teacher use to illustrate and clarify role conflict and strain? From the large literature available, the teacher might have picked the military chaplain and the elected public official. Military chaplains "as officers in the armed forces are expected to remain distant from enlisted men and promote military aims," but as "priests, ministers, or pastors, they are expected to be accessible to the men and pursue the path of Christian love" (Vander Zanden, 1970:151, drawing on Burchard, 1954). The role requirements of the chaplain as officer involve discipline, universalism, and distance; the role requirements of the chaplain as minister involve particularism, close personal ties, and interpersonal trust. In similar manner do elected public officials face incompatible expectations from different groups. "Political party loyalty may conflict in letter as well as in spirit with the impartial behavior expected of a judge or administrator" (Vander Zanden, 1970:150–151, drawing on Mitchell, 1958). The elected public official is both party member and administrator of the law.

Chaplain and official: two examples

of occupations with role strain. But why did the teacher choose occupational roles? two roles? those particular roles? Could the teacher have illustrated role conflict more effectively with other examples? What are the characteristics of powerful examples— those that enhance learning? What can we accomplish through the use of examples? Before continuing our discussion of examples of role strains, let us turn to these general issues.

Powerful Examples: Their Characteristics and Outcomes

Examples are tools—means to certain ends rather than ends in themselves. The primary meaning of the word *example* is something that is representative of a larger group or whole—a sample or a specimen of something. Prisons, military camps, and convents are examples of total institutions. To use an example is to provide a case in point.

There are many reasons to use examples. Examples can *clarify*—make a concept or relationship easier to understand. They can help to *crystallize* a complex process. Through examples, teachers can help students *learn to apply a sociological concept to the social world*. Because so many sociological concepts are abstract, examples are important for effective instruction in our discipline.

By exposure to and use of examples, students can *understand the economy and leverage* concepts give us. Concepts that embrace an unexpectedly large number of concrete cases are parsimonious; especially illuminating are those concepts that embrace cases that seem to have nothing in common. Through the analysis of examples, we can better explore the utility of concepts. Sinners and saints are both cases of deviance. If we can characterize the

treatment of French-speaking Canadians as a case of neocolonialism, then from that concept and other examples we have leverage for understanding or predicting various other characteristics. Thus, we will expect French-Canadians to be segregated within the labor force, we will expect their fertility to be higher than that of the dominant group, etc.

Finally, through the careful use of examples, we can increase our ability to discriminate between ostensibly similar things. Consider this example from Lenski and Lenski's *Human Societies* (1974:16). The Lenskis note that human beings are unique among animals in the development of culture as mode and adaptation to physical environment. Central to culture are "symbol systems and all aspects of human life dependent on them." Symbol systems are not equivalent to communication, though it may seem that way at first blush. "All mammals are able to communicate with others of their species, but except for man, they are limited to the use of *signals*. Man, however, uses symbols as well as signals." Signals and symbols share attributes: both transmit information, both can be either vocal or involve gestures, and both can anticipate experience as well as respond to it. But signals are often involuntary, relatively fixed in meaning, and genetically determined. In contrast, symbols are not genetically determined and can have multiple and easily modified meanings. The Lenskis provide an example of human language as symbol system that powerfully demonstrates how signal and symbol are only ostensibly similar:

The genetic independence of symbols can be illustrated in yet another way. When we examine the symbols we currently use, we find that many have a variety of unrelated meanings. For example, consider the sound we designate in our written language by the letter c. *This single sound may refer to the third letter of the alphabet, the act of perceiving, the jurisdiction of a bishop, or a large body of water. To Spanish-speaking people, the sound means "yes," to French-speaking people it means "yes," "if," "whether," or "so." Obviously, there is no logical connection between these meanings, nor is there any genetically determined connection between the meanings and the sound. All of them are simply arbitrary usages that the members of certain societies have adopted. (Lenski and Lenski, 1974:17–18)*

Thus, when we use examples, there are at least five potential payoffs: clarification, crystallization, application, economy and leverage, and discrimination. What are the attributes of examples that will have these payoffs? We think powerful examples are those that: (1) rivet the student's attention to a larger issue and aid concentration (dramatic examples can be useful); (2) provide focus, drawing attention to the distinctiveness of that which is exemplified; (3) are pertinent not only to the larger issue (that is essential), but to the experience of the student, therefore vivifying things (pertinent examples are those that are connected to student experience—directly or indirectly); and (4) are accurate samples of specimens, models, or illustrations of the larger concept or issue being exemplified.

When we first drafted this discussion of examples in the teaching of sociology, we considered opening with this example described by Kenneth E. Eble (1972:46) in *Professors as Teachers*:

One of my most memorable classroom experiences involved watching a college professor bet his brains against the laws of physics. Standing on one side of a cavernous auditorium, he held to his forehead an iron ball attached by a long cable to the ceiling. He let it go and then stood unmoving as the ball swung across the room and back. It did not, as the laws of motion said

it would not, bash his brains out. The students were impressed, relieved, and faintly disappointed.

This classroom demonstration apparently meets all of the defining attributes of a powerful example for a physics class. We decided not to open our discussion with it, since it did not seem pertinent to our audience (colleagues in sociology). We were also afraid that the example would lead readers to think we saw examples as linked only to physical demonstrations.[1] For similar reasons we decided against using another example: the burning match and the rusting nail, though markedly dissimilar phenomena, are both cases of oxidation. This similarity of form (isomorphism), despite difference in content, is an attribute of useful sociological concepts—those that provide leverage in understanding phenomena that are only apparently unlike.[2] We decided not to use these examples, but rather ones that dealt with social phenomena and sociological concepts. Dramatic and clever examples that come quickly to mind may not be sufficiently pertinent either to student experience or the subject matter at hand.

Sometimes there is definite value in using examples drawn from realms other than that in which the teacher is working. For example, in explaining cycles of ecological change in cities (invasion and succession), the teacher may find it useful to give an example of the processes drawn from biological environments (seashores, fields and forest, etc.). In explaining the concept of social system, the teacher may use the analogy of the human body. Examples such as these may be especially useful because they tap experience close to the student and use physical, tangible referents that are easily comprehensible. But if the teacher relies *only* on examples drawn from the nonsocial world, the student may remember only the example and not the sociological point. When using such analogies, it is important to use examples pertinent to the social world as well and to link both types of examples to the sociological concept under consideration.

Let us return now to our discussion of role strain and conflict. Our hypothetical teacher used the military chaplain and the elected public official to illustrate role strain. Both examples are accurate, but were they otherwise powerful? Should the teacher have chosen occupational roles? two occupational roles—or more? and those particular roles? The answers to such questions depend, in part, upon the mix of students in a class. What is pertinent to students in an urban community college class may be different from what is pertinent to a class of small-town students in a four-year college. It is unlikely that most students in any type of school have had contact with military chaplains or elected officials. Keeping to occupational roles, the teacher might have used examples more familiar to some or all students: factory foreman, police officer, waiter, or college professor.

> For example, a role may call for friendship or intimacy but also may require impersonal judgement or command. To the extent that a professor's role leads him to attempt to influence some students deeply, he needs to be on friendly terms with them, to treat them as unique persons, and to develop a sense of mutual loyalty. But the role of professor also requires that the man be a judge, evaluate the work of the student, and make decisions that may affect the latter's entire career. These conflicting aspects of the role may require painful adjustments by both professor and student. (Broom and Selznick, 1963:17)

Some nonoccupational roles and role sets might also have been useful: for role strain, the Little League baseball coach whose child is on the team; for role conflict, the adult role set—parent, spouse, voter, carpenter, parishioner, bowler, sibling, son or daughter, and so on. Such roles—and that of the student—are familiar to our students. It is not surprising that many introductory texts exemplify role strain and conflict with some version of the adult role set, and that several texts (e.g., Vander Zanden, 1970:152–155; Wilson, 1971a:207–209) use Stouffer's study (1949) of students who work as exam proctors and are caught between the incompatible expectations of their fellow college students and the college authorities. The role of student involves other strains and conflicts: students with perceived obligations to academics and athletics (or to journalism or political activism), students in schools with an honor system who observe a friend cheating, etc.

To exemplify role strain and conflict, we have discussed a large number of roles:

military chaplain
elected public official
factory foreman
police officer
college professor
adult (parent, spouse, etc.)
student proctor
student-athlete
Little League parent/coach

Some of these roles are more pertinent to students or certain types of students than others. But not only is there no best example, there is good reason to illustrate a concept like role strain with many different examples. We can convey to students the utility of the concept when we show how it embraces and illuminates roles as diverse as college student exam proctor and elected public official.

Using Examples: Cautionary Notes

Henry Fielding observed that "examples work more forcibly upon the mind than precepts." But the sword provided by examples is double-edged, since incorrect as well as correct examples will work upon the mind. The more frequently and more effectively a teacher uses examples, the more care must be taken to ensure their accuracy and their pertinence to the principles the teacher seeks to illuminate. The teacher must also ensure that the link between an example and the point at hand is clear. Teachers can ask students to adduce examples and to trace the connections to the underlying point.

An example can be an appropriate and accurate illustration of a concept and yet be wanting. Consider the teacher who uses prisons or asylums to illustrate Goffman's concept (1961a) of the total institution. Both examples are accurate, but if the teacher relies on either or both of these examples, students may conclude that residents of total institutions are there on an involuntary basis. This is not always the case. Participation in some total institutions is wholly voluntary (convents and monasteries); in others, there is a mix of voluntary and involuntary participants (old-age homes and sanatoriums). An army basic training post *was* another example of a total institution with both voluntary and involuntary participants. But this example became misleading after mid-1973 when selective service induction ended and the volunteer army was reinstituted. Prior to 1948, there was no selective service system in the United States and so the example would be accurate only for a twenty-five-year period. "The draft" means different things to different student cohorts.

Many students attending sociology classes during the mid- and late 1960s heard their teachers use the 1963 actions of Birmingham, Alabama Police Commissioner Eugene Connor as an example of how *opposition* of certain types can *help* a cause. The example provided by Connor was dramatic and shown on television screens across the nation.

> On Thursday, May 2 large numbers of students joined in the Birmingham [civil rights] marches. The police, who had in most cases until then been relatively restrained in making arrests, began, under orders from Police Commissioner Eugene Connor, to use dogs and high pressure fire hoses against the children . . . high school age and even younger. . . . On May 4, a notable news photograph appeared all over the world, showing a Birmingham police dog leaping at the throat of a Negro schoolboy. If there was any single event or moment at which the 1960s generation of "new Negroes" can be said to have turned into a major social force, the appearance of that photograph was it. Intense pressure upon President John F. Kennedy to initiate federal action began to be applied the moment the photograph appeared, and both financial and political support for all organizations in the civil rights movement multiplied at once. (Waskow, 1967:233–234)

But what of the young Americans starting college in 1980? They were one year old on that day in 1963. References to "Bull Connor" and the civil rights movement of the 1960s will be heard differently by them than by those in earlier cohorts. Exhibit 11.1 further illustrates this basic teaching problem. For a college freshman in 1980 and his or her parents, it provides their ages at the time of certain key historical events in the period of 1929 through 1979. We assumed that the student was born in 1962, entered college at age eighteen, and has parents born in 1934. Our 1980 freshman, then, is likely to have no

Exhibit 11.1 Selected Historical Events (1929–1979) and a Student Cohort

Event	Year	Age of Student (born 1962)	Age of Student's Parents (born 1934)
Three Mile Island nuclear crisis	1979	17	45
Jonestown (Guyana) massacre	1978	16	44
Bakke case argued before U.S. Supreme Court	1977	15	43
Mayor Richard J. Daley dies	1976	14	42
Watergate; Nixon resignations	1973/1974	11–12	39–40
ERA goes to states for ratification; MS magazine founded	1972	10	38
Vietnam War	1961/1973	−1/11	27–39
Eighteen-year-olds gain vote (26th Amendment)	1971	9	37
U.S. landing on moon	1969	7	35
Martin Luther King and Robert F. Kennedy assassinated; Chicago Democratic Convention	1968	6	34
Antiwar, antidraft demonstrations; race riots	1965/1967	3–5	31–33
Black power movement	1966	4	32
War on Poverty	1964	2	30
J. F. Kennedy assassinated; Birmingham marches	1963	1	29
Greensboro, N.C., sit-in	1961	(−1)	27
Sputnik launched	1957	(−5)	23
Montgomery bus boycott	1955	(−7)	21
Brown vs. Board of Education	1954	(−8)	20
Korean armistice	1953	(−9)	19
World War II ends; United Nations founded	1945/1946	(−17/−18)	11–12
New Deal begins; repeal of Prohibition	1933	(−29)	(−1)
Stock market crash	1929	(−33)	(−5)

memory of the civil rights movement, vague awareness of the Vietnam protests, and parents who did not fight in Vietnam, Korea, or World War II. Sociologists know that key generational or cohort experiences are important in the way subsequent events are interpreted and decisions made. Theoretical work by Karl Mannheim (1952) and later empirical and theoretical work support this teaching concern (see Cain, 1964; Elder, 1975; Ryder, 1965; and Zeitlin, 1966).

If there is a payoff in using examples that are pertinent to student experience or awareness, teachers must review their examples and check their currency. This is a continuing task. None of this is to suggest that only contemporary examples are useful and that pertinence to student experience and awareness is a necessary attribute of all examples used.

When we use a case or instance to exemplify a concept, the relationship is usually clear and easy to state. This is the case for the student proctor as an example of role conflict and the prison as an example of a total institution. But often teachers use case studies to illuminate a complex process, set of relationships, or societal trend. While a well-chosen case study often is very useful for such a purpose, one must be especially cautious in this instance. It is often true that the broader the phenomenon the teacher seeks to illustrate, the more likely a single case study will leave many questions unanswered and allow students to draw faulty conclusions about the general phenomenon from the single case. Finally, examples are not the same as conclusive evidence.

We wish to illustrate the use of case studies as examples, and some of the attendant problems, with William F. Cottrell's article entitled "Death by Dieselization" (1951). We have used this often-reprinted article as a vivid example of how technological change can have profound effects throughout the social structure of a community.[3]

Early in the twentieth century, small towns were strung out at 100-mile intervals across the western United States. These towns were founded to service steam locomotives and as places to change operating crews. Especially after World War II and the development of high tensile steel and the diesel engine, train speeds were increased and servicing intervals were increased to 150 miles and then 200 miles. These technological changes were introduced within a very short period of time. What happened to the scores of railroad communities affected by these changes? Cottrell (1951:358–359) focuses on one community he calls Caliente.

Based upon the "certainty" of the railroad's need for Caliente, men built their homes there, frequently of concrete and brick, at the cost, in many cases, of their life savings. The water system was laid in cast iron which will last for centuries. Businessmen erected substantial buildings which could be paid for only by profits gained through many years of business. Four churches . . . a twenty-seven bed hospital . . . school buildings represent the investment of savings guaranteed by bonds and future taxes. . . . All these physical structures are material evidence of the expectations, morally and legally sanctioned and financially funded, of the people of Caliente. This is a normal and rational aspect of all "solid" and "sound" communities.

The residents of Caliente had to pay a price for progress. Railroad exployees were hard hit. Many jobs were lost, and union seniority, being linked to local shops and crafts, was not transferable. Local merchants, homeowners, and those who had helped build a church all paid. Cottrell (1951:361) describes them:

In a word, those pay who are, by traditional American standards, most moral. *Those who have raised children see friendships broken and neighborhoods disintegrated. The childless more freely shake the dust of Caliente from their feet. Those who built their personalities into the structure of the community watch their work destroyed. Those too wise or too selfish to have entangled themselves in community affairs suffer no such qualms. The chain store can pull down its sign, move its equipment and charge the costs off against more profitable and better located units, and against taxes. The local owner has no such alternatives. In short, "good citizens" who assumed family and community responsibility are the greatest losers. Nomads suffer least. The people of Caliente are asked to accept as "normal" this strange inversion of their expectations.*

Efforts at community self-preservation did not work, and sentiment began to change: "In the past, the glib assertion that progress spelled sacrifice could be offered when some distant group was a victim of technological change." But when the distance was removed, the analysis changed. The railroad was charged with "cold-blooded disregard of employees, their families, and the communities which have developed in the good American way through decades of loyal service and good citizenship" (Cottrell, 1951:363, quoting a local newspaper editorial).

The people of Caliente sought to remedy their plight by joining with other communities similarly affected by railroad changes. New and widespread support for unions surfaced. In a short period of time, technological change had profoundly transformed the economic and social structure of the community and the sensibilities, values, and politics of its citizens.

The case of Caliente has most of the attributes of a powerful example, but it remains a single case study touching one

technological development and tracing its effects on only one community (or by extension, a small class of communities). Listening to the example, some students might conclude that all technologically induced change is rapid or has debilitating effects on communities and their residents. Others might not realize that the degree to which external change affects local communities is influenced by attributes of the communities themselves (see articles by Simon and Gagnon, French, and Adams in French, 1969). To avoid these and related problems, the teacher might use additional case studies or studies reporting aggregate data and carefully locate all examples and evidence in a systematic framework.

Types of Examples

Examples can be categorized in different ways. Such classifications do not provide mutually exclusive groupings but are useful in suggesting the range of examples teachers can employ. Different types of examples have more or less distinctive advantages and disadvantages. Our experience leads to this list:

Instances (facts describing a single, usually narrow, case)
Aggregate Data (statistics describing a phenomenon or relationship for a large number of cases)
Contrived Cases (descriptions of a fictional situation)
Case Studies (systematic description and analysis of a single, usually complex, case)
Research Studies (systematic examination of a general problem, using representative cases and controlled analysis)

Instances.   Personal examples are often of this type: "During the 1960s and the civil rights movement period, my neighbors and I . . ." Instances also include examples such as this: "In the 1840s and 1850s, Galena, Illinois was one of the largest and most important cities in the state. In 1970, the total population was just under 4,000 with some 300 Illinois communities being larger. Declines such as this illustrate the fact that . . ."

Aggregate data.   To illustrate a general proposition or a conclusion, teachers often adduce summary data. Aggregate data only become useful in examples (as opposed to evidence) when they meet the criteria for powerful examples discussed earlier (providing focus, riveting attention, having pertinence and accuracy). To illustrate the thesis that the economic growth of a country is affected by its demographic composition, the teacher might contrast the widely varying dependency ratios (nonworking age to working age population) for different countries.

Contrived cases.   In our discussion of role conflict, we reasoned that adults enact several competing roles. We did not present evidence that such conflicts had marked effects on behavior. We simply described the complex of roles enacted by a fictional adult and made a logical argument that they were in conflict.

Case studies.   Cottrell's case study of Caliente provides an example of technological impact on social structure for a single community. Case studies usually have rich descriptive material and thus provide a pool of information that all students can share and on which the teacher can repeatedly draw for specific examples. Case studies may be especially useful in classes with students of heterogeneous backgrounds and, also, whenever the teacher wants the class to work on a social

phenomenon with which they have little familiarity.

Research studies.   Stouffer's study of exam proctors provides an empirical demonstration that role conflict is pervasive among student proctors when they find a friend (as opposed to "an ordinary student") cheating. Stouffer's study not only illustrates role conflict, but documents the extent of its presence in a population under controlled conditions.

Sources of Examples

In our reading or daily interactions we often find good examples. They sometimes emerge during class: a student provides a powerful example or one occurs to the teacher. Since such examples can easily be lost to memory, we make a practice of immediately jotting down new examples and, after class or on return to our office, writing them up and adding them to our lecture notes or discussion outlines. Teachers can increase the frequency with which they happen upon powerful examples. What is needed is an interest in finding (and developing) good examples and a set of criteria that define them. Once sensitized to powerful examples and their uses, teachers are more likely to see them in newspapers, news broadcasts, novels, films, social science journals, concert programs, federal reports, talks with colleagues, special interest group mailings, magazines, television programs, and in the daily round of social interaction.

But often we must find examples quickly—for tomorrow's lecture or for Wednesday's seminar. Where then do we turn? When the phenomenon in question is in our field of specialization, we are likely to be familiar with potential sources for the types of examples we need. Thus, the teacher of criminology and deviance knows that aggregate data are available in the FBI's *Uniform Crime Reports* and the reports of the Law Enforcement Assistance Administration; that reports of presidential and congressional commissions and committees contain data, research summaries, policy recommendations, and quotations from interviews with criminals, police, and judicial representatives; and that various textbooks, anthologies, monographs, and journal articles contain or describe current theory and research. Available too are numerous case studies and descriptions of the lives of criminals or deviants from their own perspectives.

Where do we turn for examples when the phenomenon in question is outside our major field of competence? While all teachers face this problem at times, those who teach Introductory Sociology or other survey-type courses face it frequently. In our own teaching we have found it extremely helpful to have on our shelves certain books that continually provide us with useful examples.

Three statistical publications of the U.S. Bureau of the Census we continually turn to are the *Statistical Abstract of the United States* (published annually), *Historical Statistics of the United States: Colonial Times to 1970*, and *Social Indicators 1976*. Also useful for basic statistical data and historical information is the type of almanac one can buy at most drugstores (e.g., *The World Almanac and Book of Facts*, *The Information Please Almanac, Atlas and Yearbook*).

For nonstatistical examples in fields outside our major areas of competence, we often turn to an Introductory Sociology text or a textbook or anthology in the particular area of concern. We find it helpful to keep near our desks about a dozen introductory texts and one or two texts and anthologies for major subfields in sociology.

In addition, we include, on this shelf, books with the *types* of examples we often want. Thus, when we want an example from fictional literature of a basic social process, we might turn to one of the several "sociology through literature" anthologies.[4] Colleagues with different specializations can often provide specific examples or suggest books that will be sources of examples.

Graphic examples.   Particularly when there is a significant spatial component in the topic under discussion, graphic examples may be employed. To illustrate points made in Strodtbeck and Hook's "Spatial Dimensions of a Twelve-Man Jury Table" (1961) or to present an analysis of urban systems, graphic examples are especially appropriate. Students will probably better understand and remember the concept of gerrymandering if they see a picture, such as the one offered in figure 11.1. Consider this classic case of gerrymandering for racial reasons: Tuskegee, Alabama, in the mid-1950s. Eighty percent of Tuskegee's 6,700 citizens were black, yet the electorate had very few blacks in it. In the early 1950s, efforts to register black voters began to show success. White public officials

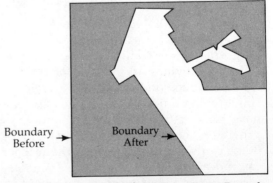

Figure 11.1 A Graphic Example: Town Boundaries of Tuskegee, Alabama before and after Gerrymandering. Reprinted by permission of B. Taper.

reacted by asking the Alabama legislature to redraw the town boundaries with the effect of making the town virtually all white; the legislature complied. Three years later, in November of 1960, the U.S. Supreme Court (in *Gomillion vs. Lightfoot*) struck down local court decisions supporting the Alabama legislature's approval of a redistricting that changed Tuskegee from a four-sided town to one with twenty-eight sides (Taper, 1962; see also figure 11.1).

The mass media as a source of examples. Newspapers (including student newspapers), magazines, and the broadcast media often provide examples. Such examples may have their greatest impact when they deal with local issues and when they are used quickly—since they tap a current issue of which students are likely to be aware. In 1973, as prices for meat were soaring, a national boycott was called. During the boycott, a Thursday evening newscast noted that supermarket meat sales in many cities were lower that week than they had been on the preceding Thursday through Saturday. In class, on the day following the broadcast, we placed figure 11.2 on the blackboard. We repeated the substance of the newscast, along with the announcer's inference that the boycott was effective. Asking the class to accept

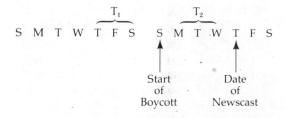

T = Time Period

Figure 11.2 A Revealing Timetable Giving the Start of an Event and the Date of a Newscast Describing Its Effectiveness.

the information as accurate, we asked if they also accepted the conclusion that the boycott was effective. We used this example in a freshman seminar where, in previous class sessions, we had discussed causal inference. We asked the class if the newscaster's assumption of causality was warranted and, later, what additional information they would want before deciding if the boycott was effective.

Another case of a useful example drawn from the mass media of communication is provided in the instructor's manual (Lenski et al., 1974) for Lenski and Lenski's (1974) introductory text. As an example of the fact that chance or serendipity has figured in the emergence of technological and scientific discoveries, they note:

> There is an excellent discussion of this topic in the June 8, 1969 New York Times. In a lengthy article headed "Right Place and Time," Dr. Howard Rusker describes a number of happy accidents in recent decades that led to major medical discoveries. For example, a woman with Parkinson's disease contracted Asian Flu and was given an antiviral agent to counteract it. She and her family noticed that after she had taken the drug for six weeks her rigidity and tremor caused by Parkinson's disease were markedly improved, and this led to the development of the first effective counteragent against this dread disease. Dr. Rusker cited a number of other equally interesting examples. (Lenski et al., 1974:13)

Examples and Evidence

Earlier we noted that teachers must take care to ensure that students do not confuse examples and evidence. Evidence sometimes shows a reasonable example to be an exception to the rule, or simply incorrect. Teachers might present students with two logical examples that stand in contradiction to each other and thus require resolution that will come through empirical testing. (We discussed the rationale for using such an approach in chapter 5.) The following is an instance of teaching in which both examples and evidence are used.

In a course on Community Conflict, it was established that some citizen concerns become public issues and others do not; and that some public policies are implemented and others are not. What accounts for this? And why is this important? It is argued that all organizations and systems operate by certain rules of the game, but that these rules are often unstated. How can we discover them, observe them at work, and learn their consequences? Such questions threaded throughout our course.[5] During a section of the course on mass media and political process, we used a quotation from Gay Talese's *The Kingdom and the Power*, a book about *The New York Times*:

> There was no policy, there was an almost conspicuous lack of policy on so many things within The Times, and this led to assumptions about the paper that were not true, causing some Timesmen to obey rules that did not exist—causing other Timesmen, the less inhibited ones, to operate freely and then suddenly discover rules did exist, hundreds of them, thousands. Every generation of Timesmen was subject to the changing interpretations of the rules and values of the men at the top. (Talese, 1970:74)

> The editor's opinions and tastes were imposed everyday within the news—either by the space they allowed for a certain story or the position they assigned to it, or the headline they ordered for it, and also by the stories they did not print, or printed for only one edition, or edited heavily, or held out for a few days and then printed in the back of a thick Sunday edition. . . . The reporter's ego was also a factor in the news coverage—he wrote what he wrote best . . . he

> wrote sometimes to please the editor . . . he wrote with the hope that he would get a by-line. . . . (Talese, 1970:73)

Here we have one example of how unstated rules of the game can operate on a newspaper. And we may have some cues as to how they can be measured. But it is only one example—one analyst's view of one newspaper, and not a representative newspaper at that. Has Talese provided us with evidence about *The Times*, about newspapers, about organizations? What would such evidence look like? We ask students such questions.

Warren Breed is a sociologist who has shed some light on this matter. Like Talese, he worked as a professional journalist, and in his article "Social Control in the Newsroom" (Breed, 1955), he drew on that experience. But Breed also conducted more than one hundred interviews with newsmen on daily newspapers in the Northwestern United States that had circulations of between 10,000 and 100,000. While he did not employ representative sampling, we have reason to think his data are reasonably representative for middle-sized newspapers.

Sociological research often finds journalistic conclusions wanting. But in this instance, that was not true. Breed's description of how journalists learn policy includes all of the points mentioned by Talese and some others. Breed and Talese agree on why reporters conform to policy: fear of sanction, feelings of obligation and respect for superiors, mobility aspirations, absence of organized support for opposition, among other reasons. Breed also describes several structural situations permitting reporters to deviate from policy. When we discussed Breed's work with our students, we pointed out that his basic concern is socialization—pertinent not only on newspapers, but in all formal and informal organizations, families, college classes, and other groups.

Our point of departure was example and evidence bearing on unstated rules of the game and their effects on the scope of issues in an organization or polity. Talese provides an example; Breed provides some evidence of these dynamics as applied to newspapers. Throughout our course, we used examples and evidence, and we sought to help students realize the difference between the two and also their relationship. When examples are representative, sufficient in number, and collected under controlled or known conditions, we have evidence. When evidence is analyzed according to the rules of logic and causal inference, we can test hypotheses.

Examples and Student-teacher Interaction

Teachers can use examples to increase responses from students and also to provide students with a tool to test their comprehension of the material at hand. We noted earlier that students may find example-free discussions so abstract that they cannot formulate questions, the answers to which would provide clarification. The student who listens to an example-free discussion may be hesitant to ask the teacher for an example and is unlikely to ask, "Can you explain again what you just said?" For many students (and most students in some schools), asking questions is not easy. The student's fear of revealing ignorance ("It is better to be thought a fool than to open one's mouth and prove it"), and anxiety that he or she is the only one in the classroom who does not understand, inhibits question-asking. But when the teacher makes a practice of providing examples, students may find asking for clarification easier. If

students cannot see a connection between the teacher's general statement and an example provided, they can ask for the link to be explained or for additional examples to be provided. To ask such a teacher for another example, is easier than asking an example-free teacher for a first example and easier than asking for a general point to be restated.[6]

Teachers can also ask students to provide examples—during a class, as a diagnostic exercise, or as an assignment. This provides information to the student and also to the teacher. During a class, a teacher can ask students to work in clusters of three or four and generate a list of original examples of a point under discussion. Student clusters can be asked to try to reach consensus on at least two examples and to select one of their number who will report for the group. Such a teaching device has many benefits: it creates an opportunity for students to learn from each other, structures a situation in which examples can be analyzed for accuracy, and asks students to *use* information provided by the teacher (or reading material). It also offers the student an active role in the learning process. When all or some representatives report their groups' examples and rationales, the teacher can draw other students into the analysis. Feedback can be provided. With adaptation, such a device can be used in classes of any size.

Audiovisual Aids (AVAs)

Most, if not all, teachers use audiovisual techniques. Bradshaw and McPherron (1977) offer evidence that sociologists rely heavily on the printed word; and most of our colleagues carry the professional stigmata of chalk dust. Of course, we do not usually think of these mundane tools as audiovisual techniques;

yet they have much in common with film, videotape, overhead projectors, and slides. And they have like purposes: to inform, to excite interest, to develop analytic skills, and to promote understanding. But because audiovisual techniques can provide a useful change of pace, are sometimes more vivid and telling than other tools of instruction, can heighten attention by shutting out competing stimuli, and can unify a class as members are commonly absorbed in a central image or sound, they merit our consideration as tools in the instructor's kit.

The uses of AVAs (audiovisual aids) derive, in part, from their special properties; chief among these properties is that *the media offer reproducible information or events*. The instructor's spoken word is ephemeral, as are any visual images associated with it. But tapes can be replayed, photographs reviewed, transparencies screened for longer or shorter periods—or viewed later in the course. This reproducibility has important implications for instruction. For students, the chance to look or listen, again or longer, fits differences in individual background and speed of learning. For teachers, charts, tapes, transparencies, and films can be long useful additions to their kit of tools, saving time and eliminating duplicated efforts.

Two other properties of many AVAs are *simultaneity and superimposition*. A teacher cannot talk about two different things at the same time. But a pair of slide projectors (or split-screen television, or two charts on a chalkboard) can convey two sets of messages that can be examined by students almost simultaneously. Furthermore, AVAs can be used to overlay one or more pictures atop an original picture in such a way that each picture (or map, or graph) is comprehensible. Consider population pyramids, often used in portraying the age-sex structure of populations and in analyzing the interplay of social and cultural factors with population structure. A series of pyramids can be drawn on the chalkboard, placed on posterboard, or projected by a slide or opaque projector. But through the use of an overhead transparency projector, the teacher can superimpose two or more population pyramids, thus showing more clearly and dramatically any similarities or differences (see figure 11.3).

Or consider Urban Sociology courses where the structure of metropolitan areas is a concern; teachers discuss social, functional, and service areas, changes in them over time, and overlaps among them. Using an overhead projector, the teacher might project on the classroom wall a base map of a metropolitan area and then superimpose over it transparencies showing the influence of the central city on retail sales and patterns of the journey to work, friendship ties, and newspaper circulations. The final projection could look something like figure 11.4. Rather than use the transparencies one at a time, or in superimposition, the teacher could ask students to use information they have to predict what a particular boundary might look like, or what a pattern already projected might look like in twenty years (and to identify conditions likely to cause the situation they predict).

There are many types of AVAs, and they have diverse uses. One useful way of classifying audiovisual materials is according to the means of presentation:

Projected Materials (visual or audiovisual)
    Slides (typically 2 × 2-inch, 35mm)
    Filmstrips (typically 35mm, sometimes 16mm; with or without synchronized audio track)
    Motion pictures (typically 16mm)
    Overhead projectors (for transparencies)
    Opaque projectors

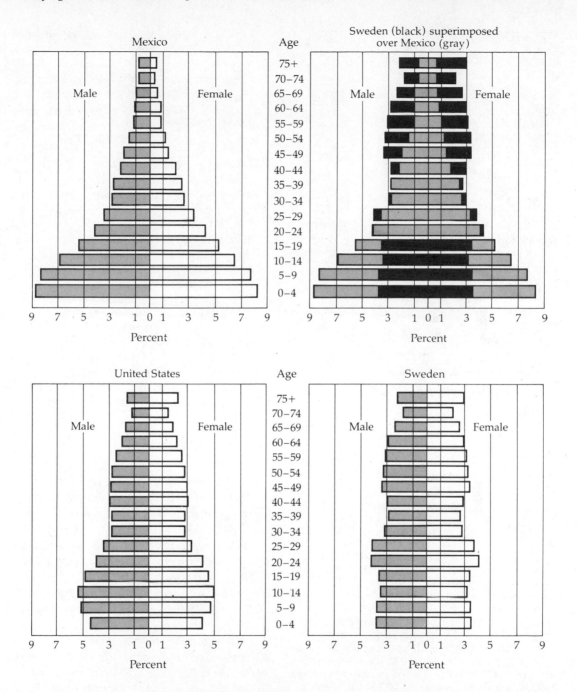

Figure 11.3 Material for Overhead Projection: Population Pyramids. *Source:* U.S. Department of Commerce, *Social Indicators 1976* (Washington, D. C.: U.S. Government Printing Office, 1977), p. 20. Data are for 1970.

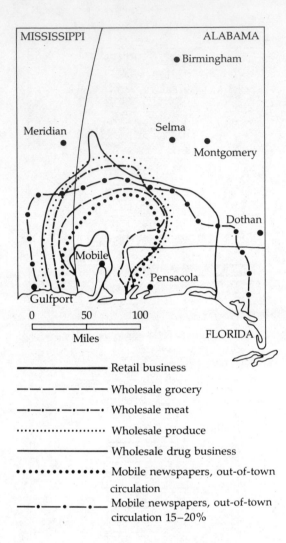

Figure 11.4 Material for Overhead Projection: Map of a Metropolitan Service Area. *Note:* "The figure shows seven different measures of the influence of Mobile, Alabama, over its service area. Each measure contains differing amounts of land area, but the shape remains much the same. Each of the boundaries encloses an area in which 50 percent or more of the transactions are done in Mobile with the exception of the last, which includes an area of 15 to 20 percent of out-of-town newspaper circulation." *Source:* Raymond Murphy, The American City: An Urban Geography (New York: McGraw-Hill Book Company, 1966), p. 56. Reprinted by permission.

Television programs (closed or open circuit; commercial or educational, etc.)
Film loops or cartridges
Microfilm and microfiche
Videotapes and videocassettes
Nonprojected Visual Materials
Books and other printed matter
Photographs
Chalkboards
Flannelboard
Drawings, charts, maps, posters, cartoons, tables, etc.
Models or dioramas
Audio Equipment and Materials
Audiotapes
Radio broadcasts
Speech compression machines
Phonograph records
Dial-Access listening facilities
Amplified telephone hookups
Computer-based Techniques and Tools
Computer-assisted instruction (on line, interactive, using an instructional program)
Computer-managed instruction (e.g., TIPS)
Multimedia
Combinations of two or more of above

There are three major ways in which AVAs can be used to enhance student learning: either instructor or student may use AVAs as instructional tools, or students may produce audiovisual materials just as they might produce a term paper. Table 11.1 elaborates and illustrates these uses; all citations in the figure are to articles on the teaching of sociology (except those in item 2b).

In the rest of this chapter, we will discuss: (1) three problems in the use of AVAs, (2) special uses of AVAs in the teaching of sociology, and (3) four types of AVAs: the chalkboard; the overhead projector; film; and photographs, drawings, cartoons, and other graphic materials. We chose these four categories because they are frequently used (and misused), technically simple, inexpensive, and flexible. A final section briefly reviews the literature on instructional uses of AVAs, especially in sociology. See the appendix to this volume for a guide to locating audiovisual materials.

Problems in the Use of Audiovisual Aids

AVAs: Incidental or integral to the course?

Most affairs in teaching revolve about three basic responsibilities: (1) curricular decisions as

---

Table 11.1 Major Uses of Audiovisual Aids

---

1. *Teacher Use of AVAs:*

    a. as a tool within a class

    e.g., a chart or diagram that helps explain a complex point (cf. Chapin, 1923); transparency or film that illustrates, provides raw data, etc.

    b. as a basis of a course

    e.g., a course taught via a series of twenty-seven films or film excerpts, plus readings and lectures (cf. Smith, 1973).

    c. as a technique to convey an instructional sequence or setting

    e.g., a televised lecture course (cf. Sussman, 1958).

    d. as a means of bringing a slice of social life into the classroom

    e.g., a tape of a speaker or segment of social behavior (cf. Stoll, 1973; Leevy, 1944).

    e. as a means of studying group dynamics and/or improving group dynamics in the classroom

    e.g., classroom interaction taped by the teacher (or students) and used as data to be analyzed (cf. Stoll, 1973).

    f. as a training device

    e.g., using tapes of social interaction to help students learn techniques of participant observation or interviewing (cf. Stoll, 1973).

2. *Student Use of AVAs:*

    a. as a supplement to classroom-based learning

    e.g., viewing film or listening to audiotape in the college/university library or media center.

    b. as a basis of an independent study program

    e.g., Postlethwait's Audiotutorial method, which combines individual study of written materials with a variety of AV media (cf. Postlethwait, 1969; Mintz, 1975).

3. *Student Production of AV Materials:*

    as a means of learning to enhance understanding, of learning to translate (and illustrate) concepts from written words into other media, such as a schematic drawing, videotape, or film.

    e.g., student production of schematics or diagrams translating Weber's theory of action or Durkheim's theory of the division of labor (cf. Bluth, 1975:151–156).

    e.g., student production of a videotape as an alternative to a term paper, but designed to achieve the same types of learning goals (cf. D'Andrea-Burkhart, 1977).

    e.g., student production of an 8 mm film as an alternative to the term paper, again designed to achieve the same types of learning goals, plus experience in role-taking (cf. Francis, 1974b).

    e.g., student projects using still photography (cf. Cheatwood, 1978; Curry and Clarke, 1977).

---

to what students should learn, (2) classroom procedures, and (3) evaluation of student achievement. Good teaching requires coherence and consistency among these three aspects of instruction, and the use of [various AVAs] does not alter this basic paradigm. (Ericksen, 1972:2)

AVAs are used as instructional tools because the teacher believes they will help students learn and because they complement other tools used. To ensure effectiveness, teachers must be able to specify their instructional goals and the intended contribution of media use. Does the instructional goal center on conveying information, understanding concepts or theories, or learning a particular analytic skill? Does the teacher seek a means to illustrate a concept or relationship, point out an application, stimulate interest, orient discussions, or provide raw material for in-class analysis? Once such questions are answered, the teacher can ask whether an AV medium will be useful and whether a particular film, photograph, or chart is available or can be produced to meet the need at hand. The pertinence of AV material must also be clear to students; as Ericksen (1974:189) observes:

Students judge technology in terms of its usefulness for their own learning. They discount a classroom presentation which comes on as an "ersatz" teacher, or as an "enriching learning experience." Unfortunately, many students come to the campus waterlogged by excessive exposure to films as "rainy day" substitutes for an active classroom involvement. On the other hand, they will usually respond favorably to a film, videotape, a recording, or a computer program which they perceive as being really relevant to a principle, or adding clarification to a problem.

How should AVAs be exploited? with or without preparation and follow-up? Experience and research (see chapter 12) suggest that if they are to serve instructional ends, AVAs must be *used* and not simply shown, projected, or played. This requires several types of preparation. Media specialist James L. Booth (1973:19–23) provides a helpful list of factors involved in preparation for media use (we have added the material in parentheses):

Preparation by the teacher:

   1. Plan the integration of the media into your instruction.

   2. Consider how the media can best be used.

(Items 1 and 2 speak to the matter of instructional goals and objectives.)

   3. Procure the media and materials in advance.

   4. Preview the materials to be used.

   5. Edit the material for your purpose. (There is no law that films must be shown in their entirety or started at the beginning.)

Preparation of the students:

   1. Explain why a particular medium is being used.

   2. Direct student attention to important areas. (This can be a matter of raising questions rather than being expository.)

   3. Discuss what they should get from the material. (This need *not* mean that the teacher provides answers students should look for or listen for.)

   4. Define new terms, concepts, principles, etc., that may be unfamiliar to students. (Time-bound references might be explained.)

   5. Describe any follow-up activities.

   6. Do students have background information and skills necessary to understand the AV material and any assignments or follow-up activities? (While very long buildups or introductions to the use of media can be counterproductive, teachers can alert students to important linkages between what they will see or hear and other elements of their course or noncourse experience.)

Preparation of the media and materials:

1. Make certain that all materials are accounted for and in proper order.

2. Check equipment to be certain that all is in working order. (Some media centers provide an extra bulb with a projection device.)

3. Check the physical conditions of the room (proper outlets, screens, light control, ventilation, etc.).

4. Eliminate potential distractions. (Can the student in the corner seat in the back near the window see the screen or board?)

Preparation for follow-up activities:

1. Discuss the presentation in detail. (*What* in a statistical table or film needs clarification before matters of explanation or application are dealt with?)

2. Ask questions that relate directly to the presentation.

3. Allow students to respond freely to the presentation. (Then the teacher—and students—may set an agenda of specific questions to be dealt with unless it has been specified in advance.)

4. Evaluate presentation in terms of objectives.

5. Evaluate presentation in terms of student interest.

6. Make linkages to prior and subsequent course objectives and activities.

7. Discuss any out-of-class assignments that follow from the in-class use of the media.

When to use what?
To answer this question we must clearly distinguish between audiovisual media and audiovisual materials:

Term	Synonyms	Examples
Medium	Equipment/ Hardware	a. motion picture b. overhead projector c. chalkboard
Materials	Software	a. film (e.g., "Lewis Mumford on the City")

    b. transparency (e.g., a population pyramid for the United States, 1980)

    c. hand-drawn contingency table (e.g., $2 \times 2 \times 2$ of religion $\times$ party voting $\times$ income)

Decisions on when to use particular AVAs depend on the attributes of the media and the particular materials that are available. Thus, even though motion pictures may be a useful way to introduce a new topic, the teacher must still obtain a particular film that meets the instructional goals at hand.

Each AV medium has strengths and weaknesses. First, if the teacher wants to provide students with detailed statistical tables for use in a classroom exercise, a blackboard (small class) or handout (large or small class) may be preferable to the use of projection (overhead or opaque), since it is often hard for students to read detailed projected material. If the teacher has access to a large-print typewriter, projected transparencies may be adequate. Second, teachers should decide whether still or moving visual images are needed. Motion pictures and videotapes present moving images (unless they are shown on a projector with a high quality stop-action feature); slides, transparencies, and photographs are still images. In teaching interviewing skills, moving images are useful, since the teacher will want to analyze interviewer-respondent interaction. But for many instructional purposes, media using still images will be preferable since they allow continuing analysis by students. Further, if the teacher uses AVAs to *develop* a complex concept or theory (or to trace a chronological development or set of analytic relationships), a still image that the teacher can build or modify in the class will be highly desirable. In such a case, the chalkboard illustration or use of transparencies in an overhead projector (but not an opaque projector) will meet the needs at hand. Third, whenever motion is extraneous to the instructional task at hand, still images should be used. Fourth, other things being equal, "a sound source . . . does not hold attention as well as does the visual image, especially when the sound waves are not responded to directly as in music, but require cognitive translation as in listening to a lecture. There are [however] instances where the *necessary* element for learning is carried by audio cues" (Ericksen, 1974:177) or partly carried by them as in a film of social interaction. Fifth, especially where a class has heterogeneous learning styles and abilities, printed materials that the students can retain for themselves are especially useful. A handout or article can be read at each student's own pace and reread as necessary. Instructional methods in which students use films or tapes in study carrels provide this stop-start-replay capacity.

One other consideration: a film that poorly illustrates a concept can be harmful. While a teacher may be able to use a poor film as a foil successfully, unless the teacher prepares very carefully, students may learn well some things the teacher wishes they had not.

AVAs and the Teaching of Sociology

AV materials have long been used in reports of sociological research and in instruction. The familiar population pyramid was first used in an 1874 Bureau of the Census publication (Newcomb, 1957:387); the uses of graphic methods in instruction were described more than fifty years ago by F. Stuart Chapin (1923).

In teaching as in research, AVAs, especially graphic methods, are often used in sociology to illustrate, summarize, and clarify; to organize information into categories and to demonstrate relationships and patterns (similarity and difference, trend, causality). Textbooks, monographs, and journal articles are often filled with tables, graphs, photographs, charts, and diagrams designed to meet such ends.

A second use of AVAs in sociology is to extend observation. Students are often asked to study (read articles about, listen to lectures on, discuss, write about) social phenomena with which they have no experience. In some courses and for many students, this can be a block to learning. Lacking contact with big cities, some students in an Urban Sociology course may invoke misleading stereotypes. When these stereotypes are revealed, they become further data for analysis. One way of countering or using the stereotypes is through classroom use of films, slide collections, or videotapes of aspects of cities and city life. Or teachers can ask students to draw maps (another media-related technique) of the city or town in which their college is located, plotting those areas distinctive in function or type of resident. Such maps, along with actual social-base maps, can be the takeoff point for various classroom and nonclassroom activities. There is a rich literature in sociology and related fields that draws on such maps and on perceptions and use of social space (see Michelson, 1976:chapter 2; Lynch, 1960; Lynch and Rodwin, 1970; Strauss, 1961; Schorr, 1963; and Carr, 1967). AVAs can be useful in reducing some of the provincialism we all share and can provide common bodies of information to which students and teachers can refer. This usage of AVAs—to extend observation—is probably most important in courses that deal with aspects of the social world far from student experience. Teachers who employ a comparative approach (cross-cultural, cross-national, or with a wide historical perspective) are well advised to search for appropriate AV materials.

A third use of AVAs is to provide raw material for exercises in analysis. For such purposes, the high level of descriptive information found in many films is useful since it requires or invites analysis. Similarly, films made from a particular point of view are also useful since the teacher can work with the class to uncover the bias and to show how all observers see the world through special lenses. The teacher can work with students to help them develop skills of moving from description to explanation. The teacher can ask students who have seen a film or tape: (1) what general propositions are implicit in the film or derivable from it; (2) whether the film provides acceptable evidence and, if not, how such evidence might be generated; and (3) what implications can be drawn from the film as to how the world might be changed to alleviate a problem, fulfill some need, do something differently. These three questions bear on theory, method, and application—each important in sociology and its instruction.

The abstract nature of sociology suggests a fourth use of AVAs. Many concepts in sociology have no tangible existence (you cannot touch, see, or hold a role, a social system, or conflict). But we use our abstract concepts to organize, classify, and understand real phenomena. Though tapes or films cannot picture norms or roles, students can use these media to practice application of concepts to cases. Often, abstract concepts have tangible indicators, and these can be seen and heard. For an example of an introductory workbook that asks students to apply sociological concepts to photographs, cartoons, and other print materials, see Larsen and Catton (1971); see also Curry and Clark (1977).

Student *production* of films, tapes, photographs, and drawings offers a fifth use of AVAs. For class projects, students can replicate research applications of AVA. For example, students could film or videotape instances of social interaction in various settings among different types of persons. These could be analyzed using Edward T. Hall's work (1966) on proxemics, the spacing between people and body orientation, which we know vary by culture and according to circumstance.[7] Published reports describe sociology students producing films (Francis, 1974b), videotapes (D'Andrea-Burkhart, 1977; Stoll, 1973), and diagrams (Bluth, 1975) to gain insight into the social world, learn sociological concepts, and develop skills of analysis. These authors suggest that in producing AVAs, students confront issues of theoretical perspective, evidence, and hypothesis formation. They call attention to the parallels between the decisions faced in deciding when, where, and what to film (and film editing) and the stages of the research process. Bluth's article on teaching sociological theory as a tool of analysis describes the benefits he believes students gain from translating written theoretical statements into nonverbal schematics.

The Ubiquitous Chalkboard

Rubbing compressed, powdered limestone on dark slate is one of the most widely used AVAs; the use of the chalkboard in education dates at least to the first third of the nineteenth century. We say chalkboard to remind readers that not all blackboards are black and that some research suggests that dark writing on light surfaces may be more effective than the traditional pattern (Beard and Bligh, 1971:31–32). Chalkboards have a number of advantages: they are readily accessible, require little training in use, can be readily erased or corrected, do not require extensive preparation before use, and allow a continuous display of visual information. The fact that most classrooms contain chalkboards is important: we suspect that if classrooms came equipped with overhead projectors more teachers would make use of them.

Instructional uses of the chalkboard.
Perhaps the most frequent use of the chalkboard is for *emphasis or reinforcement;* teachers who wish to highlight the importance of a concept or fact may write it on the board as they discuss it. This use calls to mind a second one: chalkboards can be employed to help *focus student attention.* An anecdote in a nineteenth-century pedagogy text (Trumbull, 1887:144–145) underscores this use:

> *Dr. John H. Vincent has said that one decided gain in the use of the blackboard is its help in calling attention. In illustration of this, he, on one occasion, took a chalk crayon between his thumb and fingers, and turned with it toward a blackboard on the platform, in sight of all the audience. "Just look here!" he said, holding the chalk near the board. Every eye in the room was attent to him. "That is all!" he said, as he dropped his hand at his side, and turned back to his audience. "I only wanted your attention."*

Dr. Vincent had a point; writing on the blackboard, assuming this is a break in the pattern of instruction, can focus attention. Bligh (1972:102) suggests two other reasons why such writing can gain attention and provide emphasis:

> *Students are more likely to note what is written on the board partly because they believe it must be important if the lecturer has taken the trouble, and partly because they have time to write it when the lecturer stops his steady flow of words to do the same.*

This suggests a third use of the blackboard: *to aid the student by reducing the load placed on memory or the race to take notes from the relatively rapid verbal flow of information.* Another use of the chalkboard is to clarify the unfamiliar word with uncertain spelling (*gemeinschaft, ethnocentrism, anomie, heuristic, coefficient, demography, dyad, fecundity*); or the complex relationship between variables in a causal system can be clarified by use of the chalkboard.

A fifth use of the chalkboard is to *record the buildup of a lecture or other presentation.* As major points in a lecture are developed, the teacher can record them on the board in that order, or, if the chronological development of points does not follow their logical sequencing, "they may be written up as they come but suitably spaced for later insertion . . . with most lecture [formats,] numbering, inserting and underlining assist clarity by differentiating points and indicating their relative importance" (Bligh, 1972:200,101–102). Such a blackboard buildup can also be used in a sixth way: *to take stock and to summarize.* At the end of a class and at suitable points during it, the teacher can review with the class how the lecture or discussion has developed, where they have travelled, and where they have yet to go. These two uses of the chalkboard allow both teacher and student to check on the progress of the class.

In a seventh and related way, the chalkboard can be used to provide a public and continuous *display of the agenda for a class session,* along with other information or reminders the teacher wants to emphasize. Some teachers place such information in a corner of the chalkboard. For example:

> November 14th–Wed.
> Agenda: (1) *Question left from Monday's class (differences: role-status)*
> (2) *IV(B): How account for ubiquity of stratification?*
> Friday 16th: *IV (C) and (D) syllabus*
> Reminder: *2nd paper due in class 11/21*
> Weekend Thought: *Fri. 9 P.M., Cobb Hall, address by Sen. James on unemployment/ inflation; Sat. 7:30 P.M., Miller Hall, film: Room at the Top*

In an eighth use, teachers can turn to the chalkboard during a class *to store for later referral* emerging questions or issues that can best be handled at a later time. Such posting decreases the chance the teacher will forget to return as promised to the issue; it also conveys this concern to the student who raises the point and to others in the class. If the point is not treated in that class session, the teacher can take notes on any unfinished agenda items to ensure they don't get lost.

One useful discussion technique reveals a ninth use of the chalkboard: to *list several questions or answers* before discussing any one of them. As mentioned earlier, discussions are often more productive when idea-gathering is separated from and precedes idea-evaluation. Finally, the chalkboard can be used *as a backup medium* when an overhead projector bulb blows and the teacher has no replacement.

Limitations of the chalkboard.   Useful as it is, the chalkboard has its limits. The size, seating arrangements, and lighting of a room affect how well students can see the board; so does the condition of the board

itself. (Old chalkboards may not yield high-contrast images.) It's a useful practice to check these conditions before the first day of class. If necessary, perhaps the room can be changed or, if it cannot, the teacher will know some of the limits he or she faces and can search for alternative media. Another limit is the size and legibility of the teacher's writing. In the precourse visit to the classroom, it is useful for the teacher to place on the board several specimens—a statistical table, handwriting of different sizes, and the like—and then sit in a number of student chairs (including those farthest from the board) to see what is and is not easily visible to students. Two other limits of the chalkboard: it can only be used for static images and, in using the board, the teacher (unless possessed of remarkable dexterity) momentarily loses eye contact with students.

Some tips for using the chalkboard. [8]

1. Some teachers use different parts of the blackboard for different purposes: separating the day's agenda, sequential development of points, key terms, and ad-lib explanations or illustrations minimize student confusion.

2. If the teacher places a long or detailed list on the board, it may be useful to use the natural divisions of the board, or draw vertical lines, to separate the pages of the board material.

3. Especially if the material on the board is sequential, the teacher should try not to stand in front of a filled chalkboard panel while writing new material. In order to avoid blocking what is already there, some teachers start lists on the right-hand panel (from the students' vantage point) and move left.

4. Many teachers have found that if material is on the board when students come into class, they will immediately start copying it down. This encourages witless ingestion. And if copying continues after the start of the class

session, students will be unable to give their full atttention.

5. More generally, one may ask what is to be gained or lost in placing material on the board in advance of class. If the material is detailed (and assuming the teacher has a reason not to provide it in a class handout), the teacher may not want students to take class time for copying a lengthy table or flowchart. Another consideration is that material on the board will attract student attention. To eliminate misplaced concentration, the teacher may want to cover the material until it is used; this is easily done if the room has a pull-down map or movie screen above the board. A large piece of cloth or paper will also do the job.

6. Except for detailed material, it is generally best to place terms and other items on the board as they are introduced in class.

7. If chalkboard material is no longer pertinent to students, it should be erased to avoid needless clutter and confusion. (The teacher may want to ask the class whether they would like an item left on the board, and watch their head-noddings—as important as oral responses—for the answer.

8. If it is desirable to place a statistical table on the board before a class, but also important to have students derive some of the information, the stubs or cell-values or perhaps both might be omitted. Having part of the table on the board will save in-class time for more important matters.

9. Try to use only standard abbreviations or those that have been explained in class. Some teachers use symbols such as the following which, unless explained, may not be meaningful to others:

Rel Bet = relationship between
w/   = with
=   = is
Rs   = respondents
Soc   = sociology (or social)
+/−   = more or less
value   = not a value

10. Talk to the class and not to the board.

11. Consider using colored chalks in a complex chart that will be referred to throughout a class. Keep in mind that some colored chalk is more difficult to erase than conventional chalk.

12. Think through, in advance of a class, which concepts, terms, and tables should be placed on the board and which would be more useful if they were included in a class handout or shown to students by some other medium (e.g., an overhead projector). Some teachers insert in their lecture notes a list of items to be placed on the board.

13. Finally, at the conclusion of a class, erase the board so that the next instructor can start with a clean slate.

The Overhead Projector [9]

It's really a pity that the overhead projector is underused and underappreciated, because this AVA is versatile, economical, easy to use, widely available, comes in portable models, and has most of the instructional uses of the blackboard and some of those of the slide projector.

The size of the image projected can be small or large—easily visible in a teacher's office or a large lecture hall. The visual information projected can be typed, printed, handwritten, or drawn material, statistical tables, cartoons, and some photographs. The original and resulting image can be black and white or in color. The teacher can use materials prepared in advance or written or drawn during class. Transparencies are durable and can be saved and used repeatedly. They can be produced by many office copying machines. Some overhead projectors are equipped with rolls of acetate or thin plastic, which can be rolled across the projection area; the teacher can write or draw notes or tables on them with a felt-tipped pen or crayon. The instructor can place a pencil or other object on the transparency to draw student attention to a particular point.

Overhead projectors are designed for use in fully lighted rooms and are positioned in the front of the classroom. Thus, both the students and the teacher can read or take notes, and the teacher can face the class, maintaining eye contact, observing student reactions, and adjusting the presentation accordingly. Students can observe the teacher and easily shift their attention from teacher to screen (or front wall) to front blackboard, if it is being used. If darkened rooms foster drowsiness and inattention, the overhead has additional value. Finally, teachers can use a sheet of paper to mask portions of the transparency; for example, a mask might be used to reveal progressively items on a list or portions of a flowchart or statistical table.

The overlay and masking features of the overhead projector allow the teacher to alternate presentation of data and discussion, and to withhold information temporarily to enable the gradual unfolding of argument and analysis. Such a teaching pattern encourages students to think through a problem or idea as it is progressively developed. For example, the teacher might start with a problem: Why are fertility rates different here and there, or then and now? A transparency provides the two gross fertility rates, and there follows a discussion aimed at identifying possible reasons for the observed difference. Then the teacher introduces an overlay that shows actual differences between whites and blacks, or urban and rural populations. Another discussion at this point will consider whether these variables explain the differences. And then another overlay will be presented. For other examples of uses of the overhead projector, see figures 11.3 and 11.4 and discussion of them.

Films

After books, films are the most widely used teaching device in introductory courses and mass classes in sociology (see Bradshaw and McPherron, 1977; Baker, 1976). There are good reasons why this should be so; films

are capable of enlarging, slowing down, or speeding-up action, visualizing the otherwise unobservable (through dramatizations or documentary presentations), heightening interest (through various dramatic effects), and juxtaposing experiences (through cutting and editing techniques) for emphasis and clarification. Each of these potentialities has useful applications in college and university teaching. (Brown and Thornton, 1971:146)

Through film, students can witness an historical event; unfamiliar persons, relationships, and social settings can be seen. While few films offer proof of a given principle, some "offer visual demonstrations or illustrations of a principle or the way in which proof was obtained" (McKeachie, 1978:130).

Media specialists point out that not only are films widely used and useful, they are also frequently abused. We can use films effectively and avoid some common failures if we: (1) use only films clearly appropriate for clearly stated instructional goals; (2) introduce the film with appropriate questions and suggestions for things to look for; (3) design follow-up activities; (4) integrate the film with other aspects of the course—readings, lectures, etc.; (5) alert students to the fact that most films have points of view—and then capitalize on that for instructional ends; (6) remember that teachers can show only portions of a film and can rerun, in a subsequent class session, portions of a film that postfilm discussion revealed as problematic;[10] and (7) use the stop-action (hold-a-frame) capability of many projectors. Many abuses of film can be avoided if teachers preview each film and decide for themselves how (or whether) the film bears on the course and how it can best be used.

Research on instructional use of film highlights the importance of the instructor's introduction to and follow-up of a film. A film is more valuable if students understand how it is related to course concerns and what they should be looking for in the film. And as is true with other aspects of teaching and learning, active participation may enhance learning. Students should know that following a film, they will work together to extract sociologically relevant material, generate hypotheses, and explore issues of generalizability of the film's data.

A detailed example of the teacher's introduction and follow-up to a particular film is provided by Wilson (1971c:23–26). The film is *My Childhood*, in which "former Vice President Humphrey and writer James Baldwin recount their boyhood experiences. It gives us two vivid and dramatically contrasting examples of socialization. It shows us differing patterns of father-son, student-teacher, neighbor-neighbor, citizen-official relationships. And it suggests how such relationships depend on the variables of race and place (urban-rural)." To aid students in anticipating the film and its uses, Wilson suggests questions that might be put to the class. For example:

1. *What self-image is this boy picking up? Humphrey? Baldwin? . . .*

3. *What did religion mean to these two boys as they grew up? . . .*

9. *As you watch the film, and reflect on it, try to work out one intriguing hypothesis that bears on the socializing process.*

Wilson's follow-up notes are based on the goal that students see the different subcultures and webs of social relationships in which these boys were reared, and how they differed along the dimensions of race and place. For example:

1. *Self-image. Humphrey's relationship with his father, with the doctor and neighbor who brought him through a case of the flu, with teachers and students (he was valedictorian)— all these created a self-respecting image. For Baldwin, his relationship with his father, with the police, with whites generally, and with fellow Negroes (whom he despised)—these relationships "spelled out to me . . . that I was a worthless human being." He could discover "no acceptable image of who I was."*

The barber shop scene tells us something about one way of reacting to this feeling of worthlessness. One identifies with the majority group. (Students should be able to think of other examples of members of ethnic groups who imitate, or emulate the majority group patterns.) Two other responses Baldwin speaks of are crime and dope addiction. Scenes in the Harlem church illustrate still another solution. Some turn to religion. Perhaps having little hope for improving their lot in this world, religion holds out hope for the next world. But Humphrey's church affirmed good things that were apparent in the here and now. And through his church, the bonds of community were strengthened. There is still a fifth response mentioned in the film: achievement in the white world (while retaining one's identity as a black). Baldwin chooses this alternative, looking to the school, inadequate as it is, to help him. And with his achievement, he becomes a marginal figure—neither a member of the white world nor the Negro ghetto. (In fact, Baldwin now spends much of his time in Europe.)

3. *Religion. Church was a satisfying experience for Humphrey. Furthermore, this was a setting in which his father again played an important role, as did Dr. Sherwood, the family physician. For Baldwin, religion had an altogether different meaning. The church had failed his father (a deacon). His father saw reli-*

gion as a way of getting back at white people; for if one could not himself strike back at whites, God would punish them. But God did not, and one can assume that young Baldwin feels that religion betrays him, as it did his father.

   *9. **Hypotheses.** A significant test of the usefulness of this film in sociology classes is the extent to which general propositions form in students' minds. Stating these as testable hypotheses may be a useful exercise. Perhaps some hypotheses such as these might emerge.*

> *i. There is a positive relationship between ratings of occupational prestige (on the North-Hatt scale) and measures of self-esteem. (This is stimulated by Baldwin's statement that, in a depreciated category, he developed the sense that he "was a worthless human being.")*
>
> *ii. Men from father-absent (in contrast to father-present) families will score higher than their counterparts on a scale measuring degree of deviance from conventional male adult roles.*

There are various ways films can be used in courses. An instructor might use a small number of films as raw data for analysis or to provide information and stimulation for discussion classes or for buzz groups in larger classes. Some teachers have structured entire courses around film. Smith describes (1973) an Introductory Sociology course that uses twenty-seven films and film excerpts (as well as a textbook and collateral reading); the course format combined lecture and discussion. An appendix to Smith's articles lists the films and reading for each of the course's fourteen topics.

Photographs and Other Graphics

Photographs, cartoons, maps, charts, drawings, and other graphics can be used to stimulate interest, introduce a topic, raise questions, suggest hypotheses, illustrate a principle or process, provide a focus for discussion, and serve as raw materials for analysis. In class, graphic material can be screened by means of an overhead or opaque projector, or distributed as handouts. The sources of such materials include textbooks, newspapers, news and other magazines, and postcards. One reason to use such sources is that students come in contact with them throughout their lives.

Figure 11.5, a schematic illustration of roles and statuses, might be used with students to help them derive and apply principles of status inconsistency, role strain, and role conflict. The photographs in figure 11.6 reminds us that the meaning of a particular behavior is culturally defined (the Indian girls are not praying, but saying hello). And finally, figure 11.7 reprints an advertisement that raises more questions than it answers.

Resources: The Literature on Audiovisual Aids

There is a small but informative literature on the use of AVAs in the teaching of sociology:

Film
   Francis (1974b), Pringle (1950), Quinney (1977), Smith (1973), Wilson (1971c:23–26,63,64)
Slides
   Bronson (1975), Cheatwood (1978)
Photographs
   Cheatwood (1978), Cheatwood and Lindquist (1976), Curry and Clarke (1977), Larsen and Catton (1971), *Videosociology* (1972–1974)
Television
   Hoult (1958), Leevy (1955), Schermerhorn (1958), Sussman (1958)

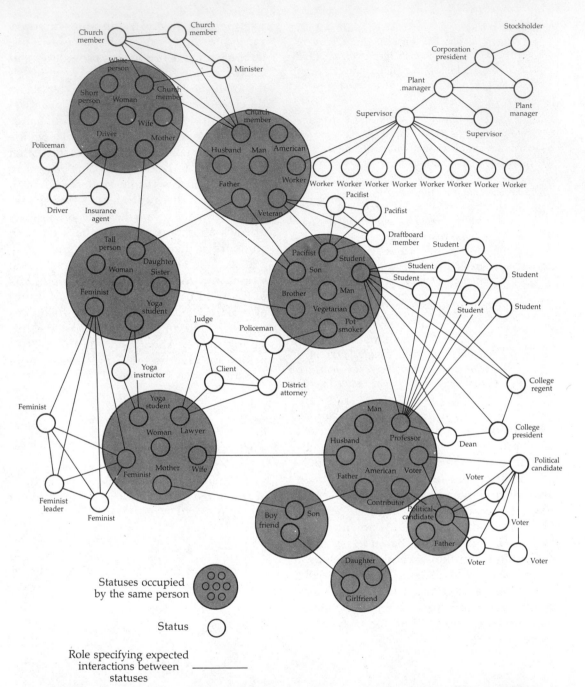

Figure 11.5 Schematic Illustration of Roles and Statuses: A Sociological View of the World. *Note:* This figure portrays statuses and roles for a woman, her husband, their two children, and other actors. *Source:* Earl R. Babbie, *Society by Agreement: An Introduction to Sociology* (Belmont, CA.: Wadsworth Publishing Company, Inc., 1977), p. 110 (figure 5.2). Reprinted by permission.

Figure 11.6 Illustration Showing that the Meaning of Behavior is Defined by Culture. *Source:* Sociological Resources for the Secondary Schools, *Inquiries in Sociology* (Boston, MA.: Allyn and Bacon, Inc., 1972), p. 32 (*photo by:* Leon V. Kofod).

Videotape
  D'Andrea-Burkhart (1977), Stoll (1973), *Videosociology* (1972–1974)
Radio
  Hoult (1958)
Audio recordings
  Leevy (1944)
Schematic drawings
  Bluth (1975:151–156), Chapin (1923)

Several of these articles discuss student projects using one or more media, usually as an alternative to a traditional term paper assignment (cf. Cheatwood, 1978; D'Andrea-Burkhart, 1977; Francis, 1974b; Bluth, 1975; and Schlenker, 1976). Two

studies reporting on the use of AV materials within sociology courses are Bradshaw and McPherron (1977) and Baker (1976). The ASA Projects on Teaching Undergraduate Sociology issued, during late 1979, a film guide that includes an extensive introductory essay by Robert Wolensky (with detailed information on film sources in sociology) and a directory of films used by sociologists (with detailed descriptions). The guide is available from the ASA Teaching Resources Center, 1722 N Street, N. W., Washington, D. C. 20036.

Instructional application of audiovisual media is a large and well-developed field complete with its own or-

Let's declare War on the <u>cause</u> of Poverty

THERE will always be some people mentally, morally, physically unable to earn a living. They should be under expert care or in institutions.

Others don't want to work — living off the working taxpayer is too easy. If "relief" were reduced to necessities, we'd be surprised at how many of these would sprout ambition.

But by far most of the poor don't know how to win their war—and they are the only ones who can win it. They need skill more than money.

The inexorable rule (which all the laws in the world can never change) is that you are paid out of what you produce, so to earn more, produce more. Therefore let's stop telling people we can give them something for nothing. *No one can.* Let's help them understand they must produce more, and then help them do it. Not by cutting the work week "to spread the work". (All that does is spread poverty by raising costs and prices.) Not by emphasizing minimum wages but by emphasizing maximum productive earnings. Not by teaching hatred of the prosperous but by stimulating ambition to join them.

The Hopto® hydraulic backhoe excavates basement at large eastern shopping center.

WARNER & SWASEY
Cleveland
PRECISION MACHINERY SINCE 1880

YOU CAN PRODUCE IT BETTER, FASTER, FOR LESS WITH WARNER & SWASEY MACHINE TOOLS, TEXTILE MACHINERY, CONSTRUCTION EQUIPMENT

ganizations, journals, and directories. A large number of books and articles appear annually reporting research on media effectiveness, new developments in media technology, and newly available materials. The following paragraphs provide an entree to this literature; campus media specialists will be able to provide additional sources.

Extended treatments of instructional uses of AVAs are found in Brown, Lewis, and Harcleroad (1973), and Wittich and Shulder (1973); a partially overlapping volume, which is also an excellent guide to local production of AV materials, is Kemp (1975). Short overviews of instructional AVAs are provided in textbooks on college teaching, such as Brown and Thornton (1971:chapter 5). Sources helpful in locating AV *materials* have been listed above; there are several directories that list, describe, and picture AV *equipment,* including the annually issued *Audiovisual Equipment Directory* and Davidson's *Audiovisual Machines* (1969), which also explains and illustrates the operation of equipment. Scores of books discuss instructional applications of specific media (including local production techniques); two examples are Maynard (1971) on film, and Crow (1977) on television.

Short reviews of research on the instructional effectiveness of various AV techniques are found in McKeachie (1978:chapter 12); Cohen, Rose, and Trent (1973:1023–1028); and Levie and Dickie (1973). Sociologists interested in exploring the long-range impact of instructional technology can turn to sources such as Fraley and Vargas (1975) and the report of the Carnegie Commission on Higher Education (1972).

There are some specialized catalogs listing films and other media materials likely to be of interest to some sociologists—for example, an excellent direc-tory of films useful in teaching anthropology and related areas (Heider, 1977). This catalog describes hundreds of films and is indexed by the cultural group studied or reported on in the film and the substantive topics treated or illustrated in the film (e.g., stratification, education). An excellent source for topics in psychology is Maas (1973). The film guide, available from the ASA Teaching Resources Center in Washington, D. C. (1722 N Street, N.W., 20036), is most useful since its exclusive interest is in films pertinent to sociology instruction.

Finally, we want to call attention to a major resource for sociology teachers, the U.S. Department of Commerce's *Social Indicators, 1976* (1977). It contains close to 500 statistical tables with corresponding color charts that can be used to create transparencies. The book is described in an appendix to this volume.

Notes

1. After he provides this example, Eble (1972:46) goes on to observe: "Such demonstrations are somewhat suspect in the sciences today. Demonstrations get in the way, one physicist told me. Students remember the gimmicks but do not grasp the principles. There is a much older objection, rooted in the attractiveness of the Platonic world, where the sensory is inferior to the abstract, the world of things lower than the world of ideas, mathematics the means by which one rises out of the prison of his sense. These statements are all true, but they are only partial truth as regards transactions between teacher and student. The best witness for the incompleteness of that truth is Socrates himself. It is an important moment when the student realizes that the Socratic dialogues do not talk just about the abstractions—beauty, justice, virtue—but about pipemakers and charioteers, bees and horses, plows and pots, beds and bed-makers. As much as Socrates was concerned with help-

ing the young to perceive truth, he was always drawing upon the particulars of experience and constantly turning to illustration and example."

2. Simmel's (1950) formal sociology is valuable partly because he uncovers so many isomorphisms in the social world.

3. Chapter 4 of Cottrell (1972) updates this 1951 case study through the late 1960s.

4. Lena and London (1979) cite many of these anthologies and much of the literature on sociology through fiction.

5. Specialists in community decision making will recognize that the basic issues here involve what has been called *system bias* or *the mobilization of bias* and *non-decision making*. Because our present concern is with the use of examples, we have omitted many issues and cited none of the pertinent literature. Readers interested in pursuing this field might look at Stone's (1976) case study of urban renewal decision making in Atlanta, or Bachrach and Baratz (1970:part 1), which presents the non-decision-making perspective and cites some of the major critiques of it. See also Debnam (1975) and the reply and rejoinder published with it.

6. We are indebted to Wendy J. Looman for reminding us how difficult it can be for a student to formulate and ask questions of an example-free teacher.

7. We adapted this idea from Collier (1967) who cites a paper by Mead and Byers (1967) that studied proxemics through the use of photography. Collier's volume and other works describing research uses of AV media (e.g., Davis and Ayers, 1975) offer procedures that can be adapted for classroom instructional use, sometimes with only modest effort and resources.

8. We have borrowed some of these chalkboard techniques from Brown and Thornton (1971:156), Committee on the Undergraduate Program (1972:6–7), and Bligh (1972: passim).

9. In writing this section, we have drawn on Daniels (1973:218–222), Brown and Thornton (1971:153–154), and McKeachie (1978:133–134).

10. As Daniels (1973:217) puts it: "There is little reason for showing *all* of any film unless *all* of that film fits into the lesson. If it doesn't, show only the part that does. There is no law that says the entire film must be shown."

CHAPTER 12
RESEARCH FINDINGS ON
THE MEANS WE USE

This chapter reviews empirical evidence, and some theory, bearing on the question, Do the means of instruction used make a difference in what students learn? The answer is *yes* (although others have answered differently). We were not always so sure in answering affirmatively. But our confidence grew as we reviewed the evidence. It is true: there is much *un*known about teaching and learning, especially in higher education. But much is known, and much more is known about teaching than is put to use.

Do the means of instruction make a difference? Dubin and Taveggia (1968:35) say no; and we begin with a review of their argument that "there is no measurable difference among truly distinctive methods of college instruction." We then turn to another sociologist, Reece McGee (1974:210), who asserts that "in one important sense, teaching is irrelevant to learning"—although, he concedes, teachers can make a difference.

We then examine research evidence bearing on the instructional effectiveness of six teaching methods and nine components of teaching—factors common to many teaching methods. Several of these components (such as active learning and the primacy of questions over answers) were first presented in chapter 3 as our persuasions and have entered our discussions throughout the book.

Teaching methods and approaches should rest on a theory of learning. We present, in abbreviated form, one such theory and discuss its implications for teaching. Since this theory of learning, like most, is essentially psychological, we are led to ask what contribution sociology makes to our knowledge of instruction and learning. A final section explores what we know about effective instruction in sociology, in contrast to other subject matters.

Paradox and Perplexity?

Dubin and Taveggia's Paradox: Method Doesn't Matter

> We are able to state decisively that no particular method of college instruction is measurably to be preferred over another, when evaluated by student examination performances.

This is the conclusion Dubin and Taveggia reach (1968:10) in their monograph *The Teaching-Learning Paradox: A Comparative Analysis of College Teaching Methods.* The conclusion rests on the reanalysis of the data from ninety-one comparative studies conducted between 1924 and 1965. These studies compared student performance on final examinations (the dependent variable) in classes taught by different teaching methods (the independent variable). The final exams measured mastery of course content. The teaching methods examined were lecture, discussion, various combinations of lecture and discussion, supervised independent study, self-study, and autonomous small groups. Seventy-four of the ninety-one studies were "comparable with respect to research design and the data presented on student examination performance" (1968:55). In most of these studies, students who had enrolled for the course in question were arbitrarily assigned to experimental and control groups; "in many studies, these groups were tested before the outset of the experiment in order to insure their comparability on such attributes as age, sex, intelligence, aptitude, etc." (1968:55). Average scores (and in some cases, average gain scores and distributions of scores) on a final examination were reported. Since many studies used more than one experimental and control group, the number of comparisons was larger than the number of studies. Sign tests of group differences were calculated, and for fifty-six studies that reported standard deviations as well as mean scores, standardized scores and differences were calculated (see Dubin and Taveggia, 1968:24–26, 53–63, for discussion of methods). Different tests and comparison groups all resulted in findings of no differences in student learning in courses using different teaching methods.

Two major inferences were drawn by Dubin and Taveggia: first, replication of the types of studies they reanalyzed would not produce new conclusions; second, new teaching-learning models are needed. The conventional model is the "Teaching-Learning Black Box" (1968:4) represented in figure 12.1. The box represents the actual classroom performances that link teaching and learning. Dubin and Taveggia argue that what happens in the black box should not be ignored—as it is in most comparative studies of teaching methods. The model is also deficient because it ignores many factors affecting the teaching-learning process. These include instructor attributes, such as subject knowledge, judgment, and analytic skill, and student attributes, such as:

(1) *voluntarism on the part of the student in choosing the subjects of instruction;*

(2) *a knowledge base possessed by the student for making judgments about the content and quality of instruction received, judgments which, in turn, include the voluntary choices made; and*

(3) *the complex of culturally derived expectations and behaviors which comprise what we will loosely summarize as the motivation to learn.* (1968:7)

The authors do not develop a new model, but urge us to focus attention on linkages between teaching and learning and on commonalities among teaching methods. They suggest that the textbook, often overlooked, is the outstanding commonality. In comparative studies, classes usually use the same textbook, and it may be that "the 'no difference' results of comparing teaching methods can be attributed

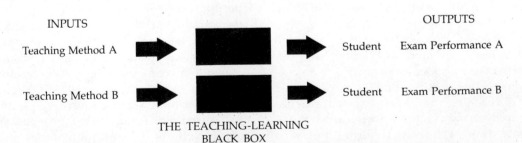

THE TEACHING-LEARNING
BLACK BOX

Figure 12.1 Traditional Representation of Instructor Intervention and Its Effects.

largely to the powerful impact of textbooks which cannot be washed out by any known methods of teaching" (1968:47).

There are important strengths in Dubin and Taveggia. Rather than tot up the conclusions of researchers (as previous summaries have done), they reanalyzed the data reported, and they exercised much care in selecting and analyzing the studies. We think they are correct in urging attention to commonalities among methods and to what happens in the classroom.

Yet there are important problems with Dubin and Taveggia's work. Consider the dependent variable: student final examinations on "subject content" or "course content." What were the hundreds of teachers in the classes studied actually trying to teach? Did they test on the text? Dubin and Taveggia don't say, apparently because the authors of the ninety-one studies do not provide specific answers.

Is it not possible that some teaching methods are more effective for some types of learning than others? Some teachers want students to acquire factual information. Other teachers accept the importance of acquiring information, but want their students to understand this knowledge, apply it, and use it in problem solving. At the time Dubin and Taveggia wrote, such distinctions were well established in the literature and some evidence was accumulating that some teaching methods are better suited than others to some types of educational outcomes.* Dubin and Taveggia do not specify the dependent variable—what learnings were being measured. One can infer from their work (1968:46–47) that acquisition of factual information from textbooks was the only dependent variable.

* This research is reviewed later in this chapter.

And what of the independent variable in the studies reanalyzed by Dubin and Taveggia? Here again, we find inadequate specification, and the fault rests heavily with the authors of the original studies. We don't know what was done in lecture, in contrast to discussion, classes. Ample writing on teaching (including work prior to 1968) tells us that teaching methods can be used in markedly different ways. (For example, discussion classes can be marginally or highly structured.) We don't know what took place in the black box of the classes studied. If there was only low variation in the independent variable (for example, if teacher-talk dominated in most lecture *and* discussion classes), we would expect only marginal differences in the dependent variable. There may be more commonality among teaching methods *as actually practiced* than Dubin and Taveggia expected. It may be that students learn more from teachers who use an instructional method to advantage than from teachers who do not.

There are various unmeasured variables in the studies that Dubin and Taveggia report—teacher preference for instructional method and class composition among them. The possibility of differential effect by student type is also untapped.

In sum, we think that Dubin and Taveggia's conclusions require modification. Our conclusion, based on their work, is that:

Teaching method (lecture, discussion, independent study) is not importantly related to the level of student learning of factual information under the following conditions: the methods are not distinguishable; testing is to the text; the teacher's preference for and skill in using a given method are not considered; student type is not introduced as a variable; and class composition is heterogeneous.

Over the years, many teachers have mentioned Dubin and Taveggia's book to us, suggesting that efforts to understand and improve undergraduate instruction should not be given much time. Of course, we think such an interpretation and conclusion is incorrect. And there is an interesting postscript. Taveggia (1977, 1976) applied the methods used in the 1968 monograph to comparative studies of conventional teaching methods (lecture and discussion) and personalized instruction (PSI). His reanalysis of studies conducted between 1967 and 1974 shows PSI superior to conventional instruction. This finding was foreshadowed in the earlier work, when Dubin and Taveggia (1968:48) noted that "the Skinnerian model and the technology of operant conditioning move in exactly the right direction because in these is a self-conscious concern with the teaching-learning linkages." Later in this chapter, we will see that other theoretical approaches share that concern.

McGee's Perplexity

While teaching does not seem to make much difference to student outcomes, teachers may. (McGee, 1974:214)

This is the central message of "Does Teaching Make Any Difference? A Perplexed Essay" by Reece McGee. He begins by accepting the analysis and conclusions of Dubin and Taveggia, and he states that concern for "teaching, its methods and variations in structure, are largely, or entirely misdirected; that in one important sense, teaching is irrelevant to learning" (1974:210). "To put the matter bluntly, we have very little empirical knowledge which reliably relates teacher inputs to student benefits" (1974:213). Further,

McGee reports that his research at Purdue University suggests that "such common sociological variables as the sex, age, politics, religion, and provenance of either students or instructors" do not make a difference in student learning. On the other hand, he notes that variables shown to make a difference include extent of study by student, class attendance, and teacher experience.

McGee reminds us that students do learn during their college years; the question is why and how. His answer is twofold. First, some students may teach themselves; second, student and teacher goals overlap:

The motives which bring most college students to the classroom do to some extent coincide with those of the instructor. The instructor wants the student to learn and the student also wants to do so—to some degree which seems adequate to him and perhaps for reasons very different from the instructor's. Nevertheless, a coincidence of interest does exist and, within the limits of that coincidence, the student will learn the subject matter of the class, no matter what the instructor does or fails to do. To this extent, then, the instructor is irrelevant. Even if he is miserably prepared, indifferent or even hostile to his students, or possesses some personality defect which prevents any but the most rudimentary communication with them, they learn anyway, and at depressingly similar rates and amounts in most of their classes, because they are, in essence, teaching themselves what they think they need, and want to know. This model of student behavior may be most apropos of the large introductory class. . . . (1974:216)

But some teachers may be able to "excite [student] interest to respond above their normal, voluntaristic level" (1974:218). What types of teachers might these be? Those who like young people, are excited by their subject, and want to communicate this excitement to their students (1974:217–218).

McGee draws six implications from his analysis: (1) to improve teaching, one must focus on teachers, not teaching methods; (2) "superior teachers are born and cannot be made. If faculty members are not themselves particularly excited by the subject matter they are required to teach, or do not enjoy communicating that excitement to the young people they face in the classroom, there is probably no way in which they can be changed to be and to do so"; (3) departments can hire and promote teachers who do have these characteristics; (4) these characteristics can "be developed by experience," and new teachers might be required to try out different teaching styles until they find those with which they are comfortable; (5) as a general principle, "there is probably no 'best' way of teaching anything," though this does not imply "that there are not best ways of organizing particular kinds of classes or handling materials"; and (6) "the model also forces us to confront what for many will be an uncomfortable hypothesis . . . the teachers most popular with the students are the best" (1974:218–220). McGee goes on to cite data that support the use of student evaluation of teaching instruments, noting that some carefully constructed forms have been found to be valid indicators of student learning.

However, McGee's article has important internal inconsistencies. He says that teacher experience is correlated with student learning, but he repeatedly denies the contributions made to learning by the decisions and activities that comprise teaching. He says experience matters, but he understates what that experience can teach the teacher. We think one reason why McGee understates the importance of teaching factors in learning is that he

overgeneralizes from Dubin and Taveggia. As we saw earlier, the research reanalyzed by Dubin and Taveggia did not study teaching (in the broad sense), or teaching styles or activities, but teaching *methods*—narrowly defined, ambiguously described, and (probably) spuriously differentiated. And yet the research discussed later in this chapter shows that some teaching methods are more effective than others in fostering certain types of student learnings. We will also see that some teacher activities common to many instructional methods can enhance learning.

McGee notes that some common sociological variables—the background traits of students and teachers—are not related to student learning. At an aggregate level of measurement, we think this is probably true. But McGee ignores other sociological variables. Classes are social groups; might they not develop norms that help or hinder their members' learning? Cannot teacher behaviors help shape these norms? Might not the patterns of communication and participation (affected by group size and leadership) influence individual learning? While McGee properly stresses the importance of the motivation and knowledge that students bring to class, he underplays the ways in which teachers can build on it to enhance learning.

McGee says that superior teachers are those who are excited by their subject matter and who enjoy communicating that excitement to their students. But in discussing these teacher traits, McGee is again inconsistent. He holds that "superior teachers are born and cannot be made" and that it is doubtful that teachers can be changed to have such traits. However, he then suggests that such traits can be "developed by experience" and that departments can selectively hire and reward persons with those traits. We imagine it was only hyperbole that led McGee to invoke genetics. Nonetheless, McGee understates the degree to which the teacher traits he cites, and many others, can be developed through purposive work.

Despite these inconsistencies, McGee makes a number of valuable points:

1. Method *per se* should not be stressed as we work to improve teaching; using any method to its fullest potential is probably far more important (and feasible).

2. Effective teachers can be identified, selected, and rewarded.

3. Different teachers will find certain instructional methods and techniques more to their liking than others, and they will have more success with those.

4. Teacher experience and initial student motivation contribute to student learning.

Finally, we think McGee is correct in saying that student evaluation of teaching is one useful (if indirect and partial) measure of teaching effectiveness. McGee cites supporting research, and more research has become available since he wrote (see chapter 14).

⨕

Is teaching well described as paradox and perplexity? We think not. We now turn to our review of some of what is known about teaching and learning. This review is neither complete nor thorough. Like other sociologists, we are not specialists in research on college teaching. Hence we have relied heavily on others' research. For each of the six methods discussed, we review available evidence and assess the method's adequacy, present major conclusions and some specific findings about the method, and then review research specifically on sociology classes.

Evidence Bearing on Teaching Methods

Lecture

Available research and its adequacy. Since the mid-1920s, hundreds of studies and dozens of review articles and books have explored the effectiveness of lectures compared to other instructional methods. Depending on the criteria used, between fifty and 100 of the available studies meet rigorous methodological requirements. Many of these studies report two or more independent comparisons between lecturing and another method, employ large samples, and use sophisticated research designs controlling for theoretically relevant variables or assessing their contribution through regression analysis. Several articles review these studies: Bligh (1972:chapter 1), Kulik and Kulik (1979), McKeachie (1978:chapter 4), and Dubin and Taveggia (1968:chapter 3), which cites earlier reviews (chapter 2).

Taken as a whole, the literature has a number of deficiencies that are much less evident in the better studies referred to above. In addition to study-to-study variation in definitions employed, the deficiencies include: inadequate specification of the dependent variable—what it is that students were to learn, the types of knowledge or skills involved; failure to measure what the teacher and students actually do in class; and failure to measure a number of theoretically relevant variables. Only since the early 1960s has the link between student learning style and teaching method been scrutinized.

While many studies do not adequately specify the types of learning intended by the teacher, we can conclude that factual information of the type contained in textbooks is what is usually being measured (see Dubin and Taveggia, 1968:47; Bligh, 1972:20.) However, McKeachie and Bligh have carefully reanalyzed the literature and identified those studies that test the relative effectiveness of the lecture method in helping students learn *different types or levels of information and skills.* Despite some significant gaps, the literature on the effectiveness of lecturing is large, well developed, and accessible to nonspecialists through several high-quality reviews.

Conclusions about lecture.   Three conclusions emerge clearly from the comparative studies. First, lecture is at least as effective as other methods for transmitting information (factual material); the one exception is that varieties of PSI are consistently more effective than lecturing. Second, lecturing is *not* as effective as discussion or other active-learning methods in promoting thought and developing higher order intellectual skills (e.g., analysis, application, problem solving, synthesis).

Table 12.1 The Effectiveness of Lecture Compared with Other Instructional Methods

	McKeachie (1978)	Kulik and Kulik (1979)	Bligh (1972)	Dubin and Taveggia (1968)
Total Number of Studies Reviewed[a]	17	—[c]	91	88
Statistical Criteria Employed[b]	signed differences		signed differences/ significance test	signed differences/standardized differences
Dependent Variable (Type of Learning)				
Factual Knowledge	L > D (16)	L = D	L = other (79)	L = D (36)[d]
Higher Cognitive Skills	L < D (4)	L < D	L < active methods (23)	
Attitudes/Motivation	L < D (6)	L ? D	L ?/< other (24)[e]	

Notes:

* Symbols used:

L   Lecture
D   Discussion
=   Indicated methods are equal in their effects
>   More effective than
<   Less effective than
?   Uncertain relationship
Other   Refers to instructional methods other than lecture, but including discussion (see text for details)

(a) The number of independent comparisons between lecture and one or more other techniques is typically far larger than the number of studies reviewed. Thus, Dubin and Taveggia's thirty-six studies comparing lecture and discussion contain eighty-eight independent comparisons. In many cases, a single study compared performance in a larger number of classes; thus McKeachie's seventeen studies involved seventy-four different classes of students.

(b) Signed differences refers to the direction of the finding of the study. Significance tests are usually at .05 level or are more stringent. The method of standardized differences used by Dubin and Taveggia computed standardized scores from the standard deviations and number of students reported to be involved in given studies to take into account the magnitude of reported differences.

(c) The Kuliks' conclusions are based on twenty articles that review hundreds of empirical studies comparing the effectiveness of different instructional methods.

(d) In comparisons between lecture and some other methods, no differences in effectiveness were found.

(e) These twenty-four studies pertain to changes in student attitude toward the course subject matter. Bligh reviewed eleven studies concerning the popularity of lectures with that of other methods (finding that lectures are less popular) and five studies on effects on personal and social adjustment (finding that most studies report no significant differences).

Third, a weak case can be made that lecturing is less effective than other methods for changing student attitudes, values, and motivation pertaining to the subject matter. Table 12.1 summarizes findings from four major reviews of pertinent work.

There is some evidence that lecturing is most effective in promoting student learning when the lecture is perceived by students as well organized, when students play an active part in organizing the information presented, and when the lecture is structured to promote student attention, motivation, and memory. Several studies suggest the importance of effective use of communications skills in lecturing. One

Table 12.2 Lecture vs. Discussion: McKeachie Review, 1978

Reference	Course	Criteria		
		Factual Exam	Higher Level Cognitive	Attitude, Motivation
Spence (1928)	Educ. Psych	*L		
Remmers (1933)	Elem. Psych	L		
Husband (1951)	Gen. Psych	L (5 classes)		
Lifson et al. (1956)	Gen. Psych	L = D		*D
Ruja (1954)	Gen. Psych	*L (4 classes)		
	Philosophy	D (2 classes)		
Elliott (1951)	Elem. Psych			D
Casey and Weaver (1956)	Human Devel. and Behavior			D
Beach (1960)	Social Psych	D		*D
Hill (1960)	Anthropology (15 classes)	D		D
Bane (1925)	Education (5 experiments)	L (3) D (2)	*D (5)	
Solomon et al. (1964)	Government (24 classes)	L	D	
Gerberich and Warner (1936)	Government	L		
Barnard (1942)	Science (6 classes)	L	*D	*D
Barnard (1936)	(2 classes)	L = D		
Dawson (1956)	Elem. Soil Sci. (6 classes)	L	D	
Lancaster et al. (1961)	Physics	D		
Warren (1954)	Physics	D		

Notes:

L = Lecture Superior

D = Discussion Superior

* = Difference significant at .05 level or better. All other results indicate only the direction of difference in the experiment.

Source: Reprinted by permission of the publisher, from Wilbert J. McKeachie, *Teaching Tips: A Guidebook for the Beginning College Teacher* (Lexington, Mass: D. C. Heath and Company, 1978), p. 28, Table 4.1.

major study concludes that class size is relatively unimportant to student learning in lecture situations (though there is considerable evidence that size has marked effects on classes based on discussion and on classes in which development of complex cognitive skills is a central concern).

Some specific findings: reviews of comparative studies. Here we review the findings of the analyses whose conclusions are reported in table 12.1. Table 12.2 summarizes data reviewed by McKeachie, who examined seventeen studies involving a total of seventy-four classes. He concludes that lectures are somewhat more effective than discussion in conveying factual information and clearly inferior to discussion in developing higher cognitive skills and changing attitudes toward the course subject matter. McKeachie notes that the magnitude of the differences typically is not very large. Table 12.3 summarizes the findings from Bligh's analysis. It supports McKeachie's conclusion that lectures are inferior to active methods (e.g., discussion) in promoting thought (higher cognitive learnings).

Why should students develop higher cognitive skills in discussion classes to a greater degree than in lecture? While we will have more to say about this when we discuss research bearing on discussion, we note here that a number of experiments indicate that such skills are best developed when students are actively rather than passively involved in the learning process and when they have an opportunity to practice use of skills and receive feedback on that practice. Discussion classes (and smaller classes generally) provide more *opportunities* for active involvement and feedback.

Lecturing is at least as effective and is more efficient than most other instructional methods for conveying factual information. Lectures will be more effective if lecturers apply available research on knowledge acquisition. Bligh (1972:chapters 2, 3) devotes more than 100 pages to review of theory and research on student attention, motivation, and memory; the effects of organization; and various communications processes in lectures. For example, on student attention, evidence supports the assertion that teachers are ill

Table 12.3 Lecture vs. Other Instructional Methods: Bligh Analysis, 1972

(1) Type of Learning (Criterion)	(2) Number of Studies	(3) Lecture > Other	(4) No Significant Difference	(5) Lecture < Other	(6) Conclusion
Information	79[a]	24[a]	62	21	L = other
Promoting thought	23	0	5	21	L < active methods
Attitudes toward subject	24	1	9	15	L ? other
Popularity of lectures	11	3	3	9	L < other
Personal and social adjustment	5	0	4	2	L ? other

Note: (a) Column 2 reports the total number of studies examined that compare the effectiveness of lecture versus one or more other instructional methods. The remaining columns report the number of independent comparisons made in these studies; since many studies made more than one independent comparison, figures in columns 3, 4, and 5 should not necessarily add to the total number of studies.

Source: This table summarizes data in tables 1, 3, 4, 5, and 6 in Bligh (1972: chapter 1). Used by permission of the author.

advised to lecture uninterruptedly for fifty or more minutes; decrements in attendance and in acquiring information have been demonstrated. Learning is enhanced if the instructor's presentation is varied and if students are actively involved in some way. It is often useful to break a lecture into segments punctuated by some active student work, audiovisual material, or other change in the mode of participation or presentation.

Implications of the "Dr. Fox" research.   In 1973, some research on lecturing gained brief prominence in the national news. An article in the *Journal of Medical Education* seemed to suggest that students were wholly gullible and that teaching was a matter of histrionics. Ericksen describes the experiment (1978:2):

> *An actor, "Dr. Fox," was introduced to a class as a visiting specialist on the biochemistry of memory. His lecture, however, contained little substance and made considerable use of double talk, neologisms, non sequiturs, and contradictory statements. His presentation included parenthetical humor, and emotional phrases and gestures, but also meaningless references to unrelated topics. This "seductive" lecture received favorable ratings by students on an eight-item questionnaire.*

Yet later studies showed that lecture content, as well as dramatic style, made a difference in student ratings. What can we conclude about this unsettling view of lecturing-as-make-believe? We agree with Ericksen's (1978:2) observation that

> *the important generalization for those of us who lecture is to recognize that enthusiasm (seduction?) is important, but equally significant is the fact that students come to class with the expectation of learning something; they trust their teachers who are, presumably, credible sources*

> *of valid information. We may bluff on occasion but if we lose our credibility, our usefulness as teachers is largely destroyed.*

These points about enthusiasm and credibility are echoed by McKeachie (1978:24) who reminds us that "vocal variety, audibility, and movement are overt cues to [the instructor's] own enthusiasm, and if there is any teacher characteristic related to learning, it is enthusiasm." McKeachie observes that the Dr. Fox studies underline the fact that students usually cannot know whether the instructor is providing accurate information (which points to one limitation of student evaluations of teaching effectiveness). Finally, there is ample research to support the notion that communication skills *are* important in teaching as well as in acting. The original Dr. Fox study is reported in Naftulin, Ware, and Donnelly (1973); subsequent studies are described in Ware and Williams (1975), and Williams and Ware (1976, 1977).

Research on lecture in sociology.   L. D. Zeleney (1927, 1940) compared student learning in sociology classes using lecture or discussion methods. His findings confirm others: as measured by end-of-course examinations, both methods were equally effective in teaching information and concepts. We know of no other comparative studies that deal with the lecture in sociology classes. It is likely, however, that at least some of the hundreds of studies comparing lecture and other methods used sociology classes. In chapter 10, we cited more than a dozen papers in sociology that describe (and sometimes evaluate the effectiveness of) some specific instructional devices and techniques used in lecture classes. It is worth noting that some of the better comparative studies and reviews on the lecture method are by sociologists—for example, Dubin and Taveggia's (1968) review, and studies by Hill (1960) and Solomon, Rosenberg, and Bezdeck (1964). Finally, much of the literature we have cited above studied classes with subject matters not wholly unlike sociology (e.g., anthropology, social psychology, psychology, human development, and government).

Discussion

Available research and its adequacy. The preceding review of research comparing lectures with other instructional methods touched on many studies pertinent to the discussion method. The most frequent experimental comparison is between lecture and discussion. Additionally, there is a substantial literature bearing, directly and indirectly, on small-group discussion. Beyond studies of college learning, there are scores of studies of industrial communication and change, leadership and human relations, all shedding some light on the relative efficacy of discussion under various conditions. Studies are reviewed in a number of sources, including McKeachie (1978:chapters 5, 20), Olmstead (1974:especially part II, chapter 4), and Brilhart (1974:especially chapter 5). While the effectiveness of discussion classes in achieving various instructional goals rests on a firm research base, there are some serious gaps in the literature. According to Olmstead (1974:116–117), "the most glaring example is the case method, which is one of the most widely used of all small-group techniques in both universities and industrial training. No objective evaluation of the effectiveness of case studies was found" by Olmstead as he reviewed the literature on small-group instruction. Most of the limitations of the research on lectures, discussed earlier, apply to research on discussion.

Conclusions about discussion. Compared to lectures, discussion classes are about as effective in teaching factual information, possibly more effective in changing attitudes toward subject matter and motivating students for continued study, and more effective in teaching higher cognitive skills, such as problem solving, application, and synthesis. The superiority of discussion over lecture in teaching higher cognitive skills deserves underlining. While the observed differences are not always large, we know of no comparative study finding discussion inferior to lecture in developing intellectual skills. The scores of comparative studies have all found the discussion class superior in this respect, and many of the studies report statistically significant findings (see McKeachie, 1978:27ff; Bligh, 1972:32ff; Olmstead, 1974:113ff; and Kulik and Kulik, 1979). The literature on discussion provides an empirical base for improving the effectiveness of the method. Research on class size indicates that in discussion courses, but not lectures, smaller classes are useful in developing higher cognitive skills.

Some specific findings on discussion. When instructors wish to convey content and to help students develop intellectual skills, a mix of lecture and discussion seems sensible. But when conveying content is the only instructional goal, the evidence does not support such mixes over the sole use of lecture or discussion (Dubin and Taveggia, 1968:37–38, 66–67). Several studies find that students prefer discussion classes to lectures and that, to a slight degree, they prefer mixed formats over the sole use of either.

Various studies demonstrate the contribution to learning that results from student practice with teacher feedback and from active student participation. These conditions are more easily attained in smaller discussion classes, and this is believed to account for the superiority of discussion over lecture in teaching cognitive skills. One assumption here is that students are more active in discussion classes. Clearly, smaller classes *allow* more participation per student. And there is some indication that in discussion classes, students are more attentive and devote more time to problem solving and other higher cognitive acts than in lecture classes. Bligh (1972:32) describes a study touching on this:

> Bloom re-played tape-recordings of lectures and discussions to students and asked them at intervals to recall the thoughts they had in the original situation (1953). Admittedly, the stimulated student recall was subjective, but the sample is large. It is difficult to suggest a better way of obtaining such data and Siegel et al. have since found the method "reasonably valid" when compared against independent measures of student learning (1963).

Some of Bloom's findings appear in table 12.4;[1] research on student-centered versus

Table 12.4 Student Thinking During Discussion and Lecture Classes

Time Spent In	During Lecture Class	During Discussion Class
Passive thoughts about the subject and thoughts evidencing simple comprehension	37%	20%
Irrelevant thoughts	31%	15%
Attempting to solve problems and to synthesize (interrelate) information	1%	8%

Note: All comparisons between lecture and discussion classes are statistically significant.
Source: Bloom (1953), as found in Bligh (1972:32–33).

instructor-centered teaching patterns lends some support to these lines of analysis (cf. McKeachie, 1978:52–63).

Available research provides guidance to teachers on how to enhance the effectiveness of discussion-based instruction. For example, in discussion classes where the task at hand is problem solving, it is advisable to focus, *in turn,* on: (1) setting goals, procedures, and criteria; (2) specifying the problem; (3) collecting, but *not* discussing, potential solutions; and (4) assessing proposed solutions (cf. Brilhart, 1974:97–104; McKeachie, 1978:44, 46–47). This and other research indicate that agreed-upon structure is important to successful discussion classes.

Some specific findings on class size.   As sociologists, we know that group size affects the form and content of interaction. Larger groups tend to be more heterogeneous and contain more resources, but the resources are more difficult to use. For any given time period, as size increases, communication becomes more difficult; the average member has fewer chances to participate and a lower satisfaction level (cf. Hare, 1976:chapter 10). The effect of class size on learning depends on the teacher's educational goals and instructional methods. McKeachie (1978:chapter 20) concludes that smaller classes are more effective in promoting retention of knowledge, critical thinking, and attitude change, but not more effective in teaching factual information. Attiyeh and Lumsden (1972) found that student achievement was significantly related to the size of tutorial classes, but not significantly related to the size of the lecture class (the classes studied used both techniques). This study is important, since it employed a very large sample and used regression analysis in which a pretest score, student and teacher variables, as well as a number of course characteristics, were used as independent variables. The dependent variable was a final examination stressing skills of application of concepts to problem situations in college economics courses.

Rarely can teachers obtain classes of the size they want, but to the degree they have a choice, they might want to follow Herbert Thelen's (1954:187) "principle of individual challenge in the least-sized group." Thelen declared that to secure maximum motivation and quality performance, we should establish the "smallest group in which it is possible to have represented at a functional level all the social and achievement skills required for the particular required activity" (Thelen quoted by Brilhart, 1974:33).

Research on discussion in sociology. As noted earlier, Zeleney (1927, 1940) found no differences in student learning in sociology classes taught by lecture and discussion. Much of the basic research on small groups has been conducted by sociologists and social psychologists (cf. Hare, 1976; Schmuck and Schmuck, 1975). Only some of this work has had the college classroom as its subject of analysis. In chapter 10 we cited a number of articles reviewing different approaches to the use of discussion in sociology classes; none reports comparative tests.

Personalized System of Instruction (PSI)

Available research and its adequacy. PSI is probably the best studied instructional method. Of the several hundred research papers on PSI, there are at least three dozen highly sophisticated, carefully controlled, comparative studies. Among them are studies that allow one to draw conclusions about which components of PSI have the greatest effect on student learning. The best review of PSI research is Johnson and Ruskin (1977). While many PSI studies have methodological problems, the same flaws or omissions "do not exist for each study in which superiority has been shown. In addition, there have been several studies that are adequate with respect to differential withdrawal rates, introduction of treatment, and equivalence of groups in other respects" (Johnson and Ruskin, 1977:79).

Conclusions about PSI. "It is rare, in educational research, to find such clear findings as those reported in the PSI literature. There is substantial agreement in the research that students learn more [content learning] under PSI approaches than they do in conventional classes, and they like it better." This statement by K. Patricia Cross (1976:94), senior research psychologist with the Educational Testing Service, is echoed by several other students of research on higher education (e.g., McKeachie, 1978:114–117), as well as specialists in behavioral instruction (e.g., Johnson and Ruskin, 1977:chapter 4).

Some specific findings on PSI. (1) Of the scores of experimental studies that compare PSI courses to lecture or lecture-discussion courses, more than 75 percent find statistically significant differences favoring PSI; the typical difference in grade performance is one letter grade (between 9 and 15 percentage-point differences). Studies on which such conclusions are based are only those that are carefully controlled; the dependent variable is usually examination performance in which content learning is stressed. (2) Comparative studies consistently indicate that students in PSI courses prefer this method to conventional modes of instruction; the finding holds regardless of course content. Students most like the self-pacing and the interaction with tutors. (3) Component analysis of PSI and closely related techniques indicates that frequent testing with immediate feedback, together with use of the mastery criterion on small units, contributes most heavily to student learning gains; self-pacing is not a central contributor. (4) Many PSI courses have high withdrawal rates; however, research indicates PSI courses can be designed to reduce withdrawal rates and that learning gains are not a function of selective withdrawal. (5) A small number of studies suggest that PSI courses can be more effective than conventional instruction in introductory-level courses where complex learnings and skills (e.g., application) are a major course goal. (6) All eleven studies comparing retention of learning in PSI with that in conventional courses report statistically significant effects favoring PSI. The studies measured student retention at times between one and fifteen months after completion of the courses. (7) Evidence from four studies suggests that when the subject matter in a curriculum is cumulative and sequential, students taking a PSI course will do better in subsequent courses than those whose initial course was conventionally structured. (8) There is some indication that although all students benefit from PSI-based courses, the effect may be greater for lower ability students.

Research on PSI in sociology.   The six papers on PSI courses in sociology report findings consistent with those in the larger literature. Four are comparative studies and report superior student performance in PSI courses: three in Introductory Sociology (Clark, 1974; Johnson and Walsh, 1978; Rogers, Satariano, and Rogers, 1977)

and one in Social Statistics (Malec, 1975). The other two papers provide noncomparative evidence supporting PSI: MacDaniel (1974) for a research methods course, and Ludwig (1975) for an interdisciplinary social science course. Rogers, Satariano, and Rogers, (1977) employed analysis of variance and covariance techniques and concluded that just under one-fifth of the variance in pretest, posttest improvement by students is accounted for by the instructional technique used (PSI versus lecture) after controlling for the effects of student SAT and high school rank and their interactions. All studies in sociology report student enthusiasm with PSI; the sociologist-authors were generally pleased with their experience, but several provide cautionary notes to future users.

Teaching Information Processing System (TIPS)

TIPS is a computer-based system for rapidly providing students with diagnostic responses and individualized assignments throughout a course. Students take a series of quizzes, which are scored and returned to the student (but not counted toward the course grade); the quizzes are the basis of the assignments. This low-cost system can be used with courses regardless of the instructional format, but it is most useful in large classes. Teachers can use TIPS printouts to improve instruction during the course and in subsequent semesters. TIPS is discussed at length in the appendix to chapter 13.

Available research and its adequacy. The research literature on TIPS is very small but of high quality. TIPS developer Allan C. Kelley (1968, 1970, 1972; see also *Change*, 1977) has conducted a series of carefully controlled studies involving more than 1,000 students in Introductory Economics courses. The studies compare student learning in TIPS with otherwise comparable classes. Kelley's studies test retention of knowledge and the effect of TIPS as a motivational factor in selecting economics as a major. Finally, these studies report extensive information on student and teacher reaction to TIPS. A study by Bassis and Allen (1977) compares the performance of 326 students in an Introductory Sociology class using TIPS with the performance of 166 students in an otherwise comparable class. As was true with Kelley's research, Bassis and Allen made a conscious effort to reduce Hawthorne effects. They report performance on midterm and final examinations of students in the TIPS and non-TIPS classes, and student reaction to TIPS. Other published reports provide information on student and teacher reaction to experience with TIPS and very similar systems (see, for example, *Change*, 1976; Cross, 1976:70–71).

Conclusions about TIPS.   The comparative studies by Kelley and by Bassis and Allen show that TIPS contributes significantly to student achievement. Careful statistical analysis (employing regression techniques) by Kelley clearly supports this conclusion. Students and teachers like TIPS and believe it contributes to the effectiveness of their work.

Some specific findings on TIPS.   (1) TIPS increases student achievement on course examinations by an average of one letter grade (10 percentage points); these differences are statistically significant. (2) Kelley found that the improved exam performance was independent of the type of questions posed—multiple choice; short-answer, applied problem-type questions; and essay questions. (3) However, while student improvement in Kelley's studies averaged about 15 percent, students with lower SAT or ACT scores benefitted more (19 percent) than students with higher scores (13 percent). (4) TIPS students retain knowledge longer than usual, as measured by Kelley two years after the initial course. (5) The proportion of these students who selected economics as a major (two years after TIPS) was 23 percent higher than in the control class. (6) Overwhelming percentages of students in TIPS classes report satisfaction with the technique and recommend its wide use. (7) Some teachers using TIPS believe the system has led to more effective classroom experiences. (8) TIPS engenders better study habits; "students in the TIPS classes have been shown to study and review continuously throughout the semester, allocating a relatively smaller share of their time to preparation for major examinations" (*Change*, 1977:25). This may help account for the learning gains, and especially the retention of knowledge, in TIPS classes, since spread-out studying and periodic review have been found to be positively associated with enhanced learning.

Research on TIPS in sociology.   Bassis and Allen (1977) compared student performance on the same midterm and final examination for students in a TIPS class and a non-TIPS class (both of which had the same instructor, texts, lectures, and study guides). The mean percentage score on the final exam was 11 percentage points higher for the TIPS student (7 points higher on the midterm); midterm-to-final examinations score averages for the class improved 3 points for the TIPS students and 1 point for the control group. Student perception of TIPS was very favorable.

Audiovisual Aids (AVAs)

Available research and its adequacy. The extent of research varies by medium; there is much on television, but fewer studies of radio, the use of photographs, illustrations, and transparencies. The literature on film is sizable, but deals chiefly with the secondary and primary levels. Most research on a given medium was performed during the years that medium was introduced into formal education as an instructional tool. Thus many studies of television were performed in the mid- and late 1950s.

The scope of the literature is suggested by these data on instructional uses of television: Chu and Schram (1967) identified 207 studies that made 421 comparisons between a television course and a control course. Forty-eight percent of the comparisons were in college classes. Dubin and Hedley (1969) read seventy-nine studies of college-level uses of television and selected forty-two as containing almost 200 experimental comparisons. However, there is relatively little research on the use of television (and some other media) as a tool used *occasionally* in a course; most research focuses on "TV courses." Also, there is little available research assessing the effectiveness of instructional television and some other media "used in ways that utilize the unique capabilities of the medium" (Jamison, Suppes, and Wells, 1974:56). Some research is available on student learning differentials according to *how* the teacher uses a particular medium.

Conclusions about AVAs. In general, audiovisual-based instruction does not produce learning outcomes markedly different from those produced by conventional instruction. Nonetheless, it is clear that some media have unique uses that make important contributions to the teaching process. Thus, closed-circuit television can show things to a large number of students with a level of clarity and detail otherwise impossible. The importance of this observation is bolstered by some research showing that television's effectiveness depends partly on how well students can see what is being shown (McKeachie, 1978:123). Research on media use for particular instructional purposes provides some guidance to the classroom teacher.

Some specific findings on television. "Taking into account the results of all research on instruction by television, it seems safe to conclude that (1) television instruction for an entire course is inferior to classroom lectures in communicating information, developing critical thinking, changing attitudes, and arousing interest in a subject, but that (2) this inferiority is probably not great" (McKeachie, 1978:128). Others who have evaluated the research have reached the same view or concluded that television and conventional instruction are little different in shaping learning outcomes (cf. Jamison, Suppes, and Wells, 1974:38; Dubin and Hedley, 1969:chapter 1). Several analysts have pointed out that few comparative studies assess how television is actually used and its potentially unique contributions. Thus, Jamison, Suppes, and Wells (1974:38) note that "it is plausible—though not, to our knowledge, experimentally verified—that attempts to use the distinctive potential of the television medium would result in more systematic findings of significant differences between TV and alternative treatment groups." Unfortunately, there is little research evidence bearing on the use of television as a teaching aid in conventionally organized courses.

Some specific findings on film. There is scattered evidence suggesting that films can be useful in promoting learning of concepts and new attitudes as well as facts. Most research on film is not concerned with college instruction (though much of it deals with adult learners). Among the most useful findings are those showing that the effectiveness of film as an instruction tool depends on how the teacher uses the film. The following guidelines are supported by research (cited by McKeachie, 1978:131; and by Quinney, 1977).

> *1. Participation increases learning: teacher discussion before a film of "things to look for" during the film and class discussion after the film are associated with student learning.*

> *2. Student "note-taking during a film does not increase participation in learning from the film but rather distracts attention from the film. If the instructor stops the film to give students time to take notes, that is a different matter."*

> *3. Students can learn how to learn from films; students with prior experience with instructional films learn more than students without it.*

> *4. Organized activity after an experience with educational films and some prior experience with the subject matter are independently associated with learning benefits from viewing film.*

Some specific findings on transparencies. Few studies are available that provide evidence on learning benefits derived from instructor use of transparencies on an overhead projector. Most of the studies known to us are in fields rather remote from sociology: engineering drawing, foreign languages, geometry, and hydrology. These studies (cited by Beard and Bligh, 1971:32; Brown and Thornton, 1971:152–154; McKeachie, 1978:133–134) suggest that using transparencies, compared to instruction with blackboards, can save instructor time, maintain or enhance student attention (as measured by the number of questions asked), and contribute to student learning.

Research on AVAs in sociology. We do not know of any empirical studies of the effectiveness of AV-based, compared to conventionally based, instruction in sociology. It is very likely, however, that some of the hundreds of comparative studies use sociology classes. There are many descriptive articles that provide a rationale for using various media in sociology instruction, and some of these papers report student evaluation of instruction data (e.g., Smith, 1973, on films).

Computer-assisted Instruction (CAI)

In CAI, the "computer is used to interact tutorially with the student as he or she moves through a self-paced program or courses of instruction" (Cross, 1976:61). The interaction is accomplished through an on-line teletypewriter. The teacher-designed computer program may present information, ask and answer diagnostic questions, store data on which the student can draw, provide the student with drill and practice, solve problems on student demand, and offer reviews of information presented. Entire courses can be conducted with CAI. More commonly, CAI packages augment a conventionally organized course. The term *CAI* sometimes embraces student assignments using a computer's batch processing mode. CAI should be distinguished from computer-*managed* instruction (CMI) in which the computer is used to score diagnostic quizzes and provide individualized feedback and prescriptive assignments to students, as well as maintain individual and class records for instructional use by the teacher. In CMI, the student does not interact with the computer.*

Available research and its adequacy. There are several dozen controlled studies of CAI effectiveness in higher education; judging from secondary reports, many are well designed. A small number of studies shed light on specific aspects of CAI (including its effectiveness with students of differing backgrounds and achievement) and its uses for different instructional purposes.

Conclusions about CAI.   Most studies that compare CAI to conventional instruction find no significant differences in the amount learned by students. But many studies report that students learn the material in a considerably shorter period of time, and some specific CAI systems have been shown to be effective. Research suggests, for example, that student learning is enhanced when CAI and other computer-based approaches are used as a *supplement* to conventional instruction.

Some specific findings on CAI.   (1) Some studies indicate that CAI may be especially effective when used in small doses as a supplement to conventional instruction. (2) There is some agreement that CAI is also useful in those courses (or portions of courses) calling for frequent drill and practice. (3) "Students using CAI for drill express particular pleasure with the patience of CAI. There is no embarrassment, no feeling of delaying the teacher or other students, no awareness of being 'slow' in accomplishing the task. While the com-

puter has been charged with being impersonal, there is no evidence that students feel depersonalized by their practice sessions with the computer" (Cross, 1976:63). (4) Low-achieving students react well to and benefit from CAI; a few studies have found that the use of CAI truncates the lower end of the grade distribution. (5) Several studies have demonstrated that CAI courses can effectively teach complex intellectual skills (problem solving, for example) and subject matters (such as data analysis and research design).

Research on CAI in sociology.   Pratto and Knox (1973) evaluated the utility of a computer-simulation project compared to lecture-based instruction in an undergraduate sociology course. They report that quiz scores for the two groups were about equal; but when students were exposed to *both* the computer-simulations and lectures, test performance was higher than for either the lecture or computer-simulation alone.

Table 12.5 describes empirical findings or teacher impressions of nine computer-assisted sociology courses. It should be stressed that, with the exception of the Pratto and Knox study, the computer was used to supplement, not replace, conventional instruction. While Sokol's (1968) data card approach does not employ a computer, it does have goals and procedures similar to those used in these courses. Sokol compared trials of his method in three colleges. Students using the data card approach used more sociological concepts and propositions in their essay tests and exhibited "tighter thinking" compared to the control group students.

The IMPRESS system developed at Dartmouth College in the late 1960s uses time-sharing computers. IMPRESS, an acronym for Interdisciplinary Machine Pro-

---

* See the chapter 13 discussion of TIPS for an example of CMI.

cessing for Research and Education in the Social Sciences, is described and illustrated with a scenario (Cline and Meyers, 1970) of a student using this system, which includes a sample computer printout of the interactive conversation (see also, Davis, 1971). According to Davis (1978:245), "80 surveys and data files are available in the IMPRESS public library, and users can choose studies, variables within studies, mappings of variables, a wide variety of statistical routines, and obtain results—all during a single brief (half-hour or less) English conversation with the computer." Sociologists who developed applications of IMPRESS report satisfaction with the system (by students and teachers), but Davis notes that it is expensive and would

Table 12.5 Reports of Computer Use in Sociology Courses

Source	Course	Evaluation
Best (1977)	Introductory	TI* of improved skills in causal analysis and analysis of survey data.
Conklin (1976)	Introductory	Among eighty-nine students, a correlation of +.39 between completing computer exercises and single best item; also, students doing exercises more likely to use demographic data in responding to an essay question; TI that computer use was popular among students.
Harper and Selvin (1973)	Freshmen seminar Upper division methods; upper division statistics	TI that computer simulation work helped students learn skills of data analysis and research design, but not questionnaire construction; student enthusiasm.
O'Kane (1976)	Specially designed two-semester course in research methods statistics, computer utilization	TI that students were very interested in and learned more from this course and its particular approach.
Pratto and Knox (1973)	Undergraduate small-groups course	Test performance of students in computer simulation and in lecture class was about equal; but when the two approaches were jointly used, test performance was higher than with either method alone.
St. George (1978)	Research Methods	TI (based on course evaluations and other comments) that students learned from and enjoyed the course; no formal data reported.
Schure, Malamuth, and Johnston (1975)	Research Methods	TI that computer simulation was successful in promoting students' grasp of experimental design.
Sim et al. (1971)	Research Methods	TI that their instant batch turn-about assignments were an effective teaching aid making possible sophisticated analytic exercises for many students at reasonable cost.
Wieting (1975)	Research Methods	Reports comparison between an experimental group that did computer simulation work and a control group (each numbering about twenty); computer group had statistically significant changes in attitudes toward subject and increases in problem solving and research judgment, but not in subject matter content.

* TI = teacher's impression; no systematic data reported.

be impractical for many computer facilities. There are no empirical studies of the effectiveness of IMPRESS as a teaching device. Professor David Millar at Dartmouth now directs the IMPRESS program.

The literature on instructional uses of the computer. A useful short review is found in Cross (1976:60–74). Major research on CAI in higher education is reviewed in Jamison (1974:49–55). An excellent CAI primer is Pool's *Computer-Assisted Instruction in Political Science* (1976), which contains short essays on the theory and practice of CAI and includes much illustrative material. A "Guide to Selected Continuing Sources of Information on CAI" is included as an appendix to Pool.

The rapidly growing literature on instructional applications of the computer in sociology includes a substantial amount of material useful to interested teachers. Anderson's "Bibliography on Social Science Computing" (1974) cites 531 works published between 1960 and 1973; thirty-one citations deal specifically with instructional applications. Four-fifths of Anderson's thirty-one citations appeared in 1970 or thereafter. Halley (1975) describes a package of computer programs specifically designed for small computer installations such as are found at many small colleges. Richardson et al. (1971) stress the need for computer literacy among college students, report on a survey of computer use in sociology, and provide a case study of an attempt to integrate computer training into courses and research at one university. Van Valey (1977) provides teachers with detailed advice on designing and teaching courses using large data sets and batch processing. Falk and Cortese (1974) report on a three-year effort to develop a sociological computer laboratory in a small college and review the steps necessary to achieve

such a resource at low cost. Ericksen and Jacobsen (1973) explore the rationale for making computer skills an integral part of statistical training in sociology and describe and illustrate a procedure for writing programs for test statistics based on the definition of the statistic. Finally, Davis (1978) argues that time-sharing computers are the best way to teach elementary multivariate analysis of social facts and relationships.

Anderson (1975) describes CONDUIT, a mechanism for the discovery, review, and distribution of computer-based undergraduate curriculum materials in the social sciences. CONDUIT publishes a quarterly newsletter, *Pipeline;* the organization is interested in exercise sets, student manuals, computer programs, and other instructional materials. Sociologists can write to CONDUIT, Box 388, Iowa City, Iowa 52240. Starting in 1970, a Conference on Computers in the Undergraduate Curriculum has been held annually; a listing of the *Proceedings* through 1977 appears in St. George (1978).

Conclusions about Teaching Methods

We have seen that some instructional methods have an edge over others in helping students achieve particular learning goals. But what accounts for these differences? Why is PSI superior to all conventional forms of instruction in fostering content learning? How does TIPS raise student achievement levels in lecture courses? What is it about discussion classes, especially smaller discussion classes, that enhances student learning of higher cognitive skills? In different ways, and in varying degrees, each of these methods provides frequent and prompt feedback to students, and actively involves students in the learning process. In the following section we review research showing that these and other factors enhance student learning.

Before examining that evidence, we need to recall that the learning effects among different methods of instruction are not always large and do not apply equally to all students, classes, or schools. This should hardly be surprising since a teaching method is only that—a method. Studies of student achievement in classes taught by different methods typically do not consider the effectiveness of the teacher in using the potential of a given method.[2] They do not ask whether the method was well suited to the instructor's goals, nor do they always inquire about different student learning styles. Unmeasured variables abound and the fact that, for example, TIPS raises student grades by only one letter grade (above non-TIPS students) must be viewed against this larger picture.

Nonetheless, the research evidence suggests that for given instructional goals, some teaching methods are more effective than others. We now turn to ask what components of those methods render them effective.

Evidence Bearing on Components of Effective Teaching and Learning

We review research bearing on nine components: (1) frequent quizzing and practice, (2) prompt feedback, (3) required corrections, (4) active learning, (5) questions before answers, (6) enthusiasm, (7) significance and meaning, (8) operational statements, and (9) benign disruption. The evidence on components one through four is consistent and strong. Components four through eight bear directly on our persuasions, discussed in chapter 3, and compo-

nent nine—benign disruption—was the central point of chapter 5.

These nine components can be part of most, if not all, teaching methods and approaches. Prompt feedback is an integral part of PSI, but it can also be built into large lecture courses (by use of TIPS) and into smaller, discussion courses (through teacher response to student oral and written statements). While several of the components can be used individually, some imply or benefit from pairing with others. For example, while frequent quizzing or other opportunities for students to *use* knowledge and skills (component one) enhances student learning, its effectiveness depends in important part on students getting prompt feedback (component two) on their work.

Each of the components involves student learning processes as well as teacher activities. The student practices, uses feedback, sees materials as significant, and takes an active rather than passive role. We suggest that an instructional method enhances learning to the degree that it makes it easier for teachers to build in the nine components.

Frequent Quizzing and Practice

In both conventional and individualized forms of instruction, learning is enhanced when students move step by step through sequentially organized material with their proficiency tested at each step along the way. Kulik and Kulik (1979) review research establishing that final examination performance is significantly higher in courses in which students have taken frequent quizzes than in courses otherwise similar but with few quizzes. Why should this be so? It is probably true that in the former case, students study more and receive more feedback. We have some research that suggests that studying is associated with learning (cf. Dubin and Taveggia, 1968:26), and we know that practice (such as can occur when students take quizzes) does not make perfect unless it is accompanied by feedback (and some other conditions to be discussed below). But the difference that may make the difference with frequent quizzing is that students distribute their studying during the semester rather than mass it at only one or two points (midterm and final). Research on the frequent unit-quizzing component of PSI clearly demonstrates its contribution to student learning (cf. Johnson and Ruskin, 1977:chapter 5). Kelley (1968:452) believes he has evidence that the same dynamic is at work in the use of TIPS with large lecture classes.

Prompt Feedback

Theorists and researchers agree that students learn more when they know the results of their work. Kulik and Kulik (1979) review research showing that for both individualized and conventional courses prompt feedback on quiz performance is associated with higher achievement levels in a course. In most college courses, feedback is sparse, slow, and, in larger courses, restricted to grades on a midterm and final exam. But feedback can take many forms and only some are associated with exams and grading. For example, teachers can: (1) prepare self-scored student quizzes or use those provided in some textbooks and student manuals; (2) give informal feedback to students during discussion classes ("that's a good point, a linkage between religion and motivation; now perhaps we can apply that to. . . ."); (3) use systems such as TIPS (see chapter 13); (4) give diagnostic quizzes that are promptly scored and returned to students;

(5) build into their lectures questions or problems that students—singly or in buzz groups—can answer or solve and on which they receive feedback; and (6) separate grading from feedback for learning (and the role of the instructor as helper from that of certifier) by means such as the use of outside examiners. (This practice has been used at different times by Colorado, Oberlin, and Swarthmore Colleges and by the University of Chicago.) A useful essay on feedback to students is Carlson (1978). The separation of grading (a certification function) from feedback for learning and other purposes is important because students are often preoccupied with grades (cf. Becker, Geer, and Hughes, 1968).

Feedback, even *prompt* evaluative response, strengthens learning only under particular conditions. McKeachie (1976:824) cites Robert M. Thorndike's conclusion that:

> Knowledge of results facilitates learning and performance when (1) it provides information, (2) the learner is motivated to improve, and (3) the learner has better response alternatives available.

Research suggests that the means by which feedback is provided (orally or in written form, for example) is less important than that it come quickly—preferably immediately following the student's performance. That *prompt* feedback should be effective as an aid to learning may be due to several factors. First, when feedback on examinations is prompt, students "have a chance to correct misunderstandings before errors are consolidated and interfere with new 'learning' " (Kulik and Kulik, 1979:88); errors need correction before they are learned and become encoded in long-term memory. Second, when the feedback comes close to the point of performance (test or otherwise), it is more salient to the learner and more likely to build on what motivation is present. When students prepare for a test, oral presentation, or seminar contribution, they make some investment of time and energy; a prompt response to their work taps this investment. It is also courteous.

Required Corrections

A number of investigators have also demonstrated that student achievement is further enhanced when students are required to restudy and repeat quizzes if they do not reach a defined level of mastery [often defined as 90 percent of a possible score]. . . . a remediation requirement insures that these errors are corrected and that at some point, each student has a chance to respond correctly to each important kind of question asked in a college class. (Kulik and Kulik, 1979:87–88)

Required remediation is a central component of an educational approach labelled *mastery learning,* which holds that "learning must be thorough—one unit must be learned to a high level of competency before the next unit in the sequence is tackled" (Cross, 1976:77). While this approach dates back to the 1920s, it gained impetus in the late 1950s when researchers found that students who learned a unit to a high level of mastery, learned subsequent materials in less time than those who did not. Block (1971:8–9) notes that results from forty major studies, carried out in actual classroom settings, yield the general conclusion that "three-fourths of the students learning under mastery conditions have achieved to the same high standards as the top one-fourth learning under conventional, group-based instructional conditions."[3] The major features of mastery learning and some guidelines for implementing the approach are provided in exhibit 12.1.

Active Learning

According to McKeachie (1976:822), "if there is one thing human learning experts have agreed upon, it is that 'active' learning, in the sense of mental activity at least, is generally better than passive learning." Relatively passive learning acts include listening, reading, memorizing, and observing. Active forms include talking, writing, interacting, and teaching others. Research suggests that when obtaining and storing information is the learning goal, passive observation is adequate and perhaps more efficient than active practice. But when teachers wish to "develop concepts or to teach problem solving skills . . . there is experimental evidence that active participation on the part of the learner is more effective than passive listening or observing" (McKeachie, 1978:26).

One form of active learning occurs when students organize materials themselves. Studies by Katona (1940), Marton and Säljö (1976a, 1976b), and others demonstrate that "learning by organization," in contrast to memorization and other passive techniques, promotes retention and application of knowledge. When students give their own structure to materials (and relate them to their own conceptual framework) they learn more. These are probably some of the reasons why a number of studies find that peer instruction—students teaching students—is effective sometimes for the person tutored but most often for the tutor. To teach others requires one to develop a structure for the material to be taught in order to explain it. McKeachie (1978:94–100) summarizes evidence supporting the efficacy of using students as teachers. Scott McNall (1975) reviews research on applications of peer teaching in sociology classes at two universities. PSI makes use of a form of peer

Exhibit 12.1 Mastery Learning*

The major features of mastery learning include the following: (1) mastery is defined in terms of stated, specific objectives each student is expected to achieve; (2) objectives and instruction are organized into well-defined, sequentially organized units; (3) students are expected to master one unit before proceeding to the next; (4) diagnostic tests (scored and returned to the student) are frequently used to reinforce the student and highlight, for student and teacher, material still to be mastered; and (5) on the basis of these tests—which do *not* count toward the student's "grade" or level of achievement—the student's initial instruction is supplemented or redesigned. Time is used as a variable: in some cases, mastery learning is self-paced; in most cases, the time a student can take to complete a unit or set of units is flexible.

According to a model used by mastery learning proponents (Carroll, 1963), the degree of learning of a student is a function of five factors: time allowed to the student for learning, the student's perseverance, aptitude for the learning task at hand, ability to understand instruction given, and the quality of the instruction. The model proposed a number of trade-offs—notably, if the value of the last three factors was high, the time and effort spent by the student in learning would be low. And students of lesser aptitude could still attain mastery if they had more time and good instruction (assuming perseverance and the ability to understand instruction).

In an influential paper, Benjamin S. Bloom (1968) argued that teachers had come to believe in the normal grading curve, which, he said "describes the outcome of a random process. Since education is a purposeful activity in which we seek to have students learn what we teach, the achievement distribution should be very different from the normal curve if our instruction is effective. In fact, our educational efforts may be said to be *unsuccessful* to the extent that student achievement is normally distributed." Bloom argued that individual differences in aptitude, while existing, need not completely define learning outcomes if mastery learning was used. While the aptitude and achievement levels for a class might be normally distributed under the conditions of uniform instruction, the achievement curve under conditions of mastery learning with some individualization of instruction would be markedly skewed toward higher achievement.

However, mastery learning does not work equally well under all conditions. Block (1971:64–76) suggests that mastery learning: (1) is probably most effective when the student can start learning for mastery in the elementary phase of a subject, since the approach depends on prerequisite learnings; (2) works best with subject matter that can be learned sequentially, that makes maximum use of the idea that complex learning behaviors depend on sequential learning of less complex behavior; (3) demonstrates its potential most clearly in subjects emphasizing convergent rather than divergent thinking, in those subjects for which teachers can define a finite and specifiable set of learnings to be mastered; (4) employs an absolute, as opposed to relative, standard for achievement; (5) uses formative evaluation—short assessment quizzes on which students receive prompt feedback, but which are not counted as part of the course grade or which, in the definition of mastery, are assessed separately; (6) requires that the teacher can design corrective or prescriptive assignments to assist students who have not yet mastered particular materials; and (7) requires that students be oriented to this rather different approach to learning.

* This description draws heavily on material from *Mastery Learning: Theory and Practice,* edited by James H. Block, with selected papers by Peter W. Airasian, Benjamin S. Bloom, and John B. Carroll. Copyright © 1971 by Holt, Rinehart and Winston, Inc. Reprinted (in paraphrase) by permission of Holt, Rinehart and Winston. An excellent short overview of mastery learning and its applications, which summarizes much of the basic material in Block, is Cross (1976:chapter 4).

instruction, and research indicates that PSI proctors benefit from their instructional work (cf. Johnson and Ruskin, 1977:chapter 5). Other techniques that use student peer instruction also have been shown effective in promoting learning; see, for example, McKeachie's (1978:98–99) discussion of "the learning cell" in which students work in pairs, alternately asking and answering questions on materials they have read.

Small discussion classes foster active thought and participation, and evidence reviewed earlier shows that such classes promote learning of higher-order cognitive skills more than larger and lecture classes. On the basis of his research Bloom (1953:168–169)* concludes that

> *the lecture is especially successful in securing the attention of students to what is being said but . . . it evokes primarily those thoughts which are appropriate to the following and comprehending of information, while the discussion is more successful in evoking complex, problem-solving types of thoughts . . . [I]f we consider evaluation, synthesis, and application as representing active types of thinking which are important for the development of problem-solving abilities and skills, four-fifths of the discussions evoke more thoughts of this type than the average lecture.*

Questions before Answers

One way to motivate and promote active student involvement with subject matter is to pose questions that tap student interest, experience, and curiosity. Theory and research support the conclusion that learning is enhanced when college classes are organized around questions, about that which is not known rather than

---

* See table 12.4 and pertinent discussion.

around recitation of fact. Research by Katona (1940) and Berlyne (1960) shows that use of questions that arouse curiosity, a basic motive in learning, is associated with learning.

The type of question asked makes a difference in the type of learning. This may be so because, as some research shows (Howe and Colley, 1976), questions provide the student with a set for approaching or studying subsequent material. Thus, teachers need to match the types of questions they use to their instructional objectives. Solomon, Rosenberg, and Bezdek (1964) found that teachers who used interpretation questions were effective as measured by gains in student comprehension. "Hunkins asked only analytical and evaluative questions of one class and only factual questions of another (1967, 1968). Subsequent tests showed no difference in the groups' abilities in questions requiring knowledge, simple comprehension, application and synthesis of facts, but significant differences in the predicted direction in the students' abilities to analyze and evaluate" (Bligh, 1972:165–166). Recent studies of cognition and learning suggest that rote memory questions (such as, "What are the three main characteristics of stratification systems stated in the text?") produce surface-level processing (short-term memory) of information, while "deep level processing" is induced by questions that require explanation of facts (Marton and Säljö, 1976a, 1976b). While questions can motivate, research by Berlyne suggests that the motivation may be highest in situations of moderate novelty. This leads McKeachie (1978:227) to suggest that "one of the first steps in teaching may be to stimulate doubt about what has previously been taken for granted." Ericksen (1974:163–164) makes much the same point when he suggests that "questions which arouse students' curiosity about novel aspects of things already familiar to them may have significant influence on the development of curiosity. . . . [Furthermore,] such tactics draw students actively into the substance of the lecture and research clearly shows that they learn better when they participate in the learning process than when they passively accept the output of a 'distant' speaker."

Teachers often use rhetorical questions. Bligh (1972:165) notes that, while such questions do not compel student activity, our language and training condition us to try to answer them when they are followed by brief silence. Although some of our students may be conditioned simply to await the teacher's answer to a rhetorical question, some evidence suggests that such questions may raise student attention level and enhance the learning of factual materials (Sime and Boyce, 1969, cited by Bligh, 1972:166; Zillman and Cantor, 1973).[4]

Enthusiasm

A case can be made that students learn more from teachers who show enthusiasm for a course and its subject matter, and who demonstrate concern for student learning, than from teachers who do not. Nine studies reporting experimental comparisons for several scores of classes find teacher enthusiasm significantly correlated with student learning.[5] McKeachie (1978:24) writes that "if there is any teacher characteristic related to learning, it is enthusiasm . . . [and] enthusiasm probably cannot be successfully faked, but it is possible to influence the degree to which your enthusiasm shows. . . ." Bligh agrees: "It is often said that the best way to interest a class is to display interest oneself."

Significance and Meaning of Subject Matter to Students

Research on cognition strongly suggests that a central factor affecting memory is the significance to the learner of what is to be remembered. Significance, here, means how well some information fits or can be fit by students into ideas and frameworks they already possess. If students can see a link between what they are learning and the ideas or facts they already possess (or issues that already concern them), it is reasonable to expect higher levels of learning. McKeachie (1978:29–30) notes that some psychological theories predict that "relatively fresh ideas would be motivating but that experiences too far removed from the student's past experience would produce anxiety. This suggests that the organization of materials should be of great importance in learning." This is consistent with research by Berlyne (1960), which finds that learner motivation is highest in conditions of only moderate novelty.

"In a lecture containing terms that a student does not understand, he is faced with grammatically correct sentences which have no meaning for him. He may take notes with the hope of making sense of them later or he may refuse to write down what appears to lack meaning. Because, as we have seen, meaning is an important factor affecting long-term memory, the latter strategy is unlikely to produce effective learning. The former relies on the accuracy of short-term memory" (Bligh, 1972:59). But, as Bligh points out, short-term memory is typically not very accurate for information the learner does not understand. The implication is that teachers should try to ensure that the content of classes is meaningful to students—is comprehensible, connects with their experience, and is interpretable in terms of knowledge frameworks they already possess.

Operational Statements of Learning Goals*

The goals of learning must be clear and must be made explicit to the learner. . . . One can have clear-cut, measurable objectives that are not worth pursuing, and the blind faith in behavioral objectives as a cure-all for poor instruction has been justifiably taken to task. . . . Nevertheless, both logical analysis and research do support the notion that students . . . will experience greater satisfaction and achievement if they have a clear idea of what is expected of them. (Cross, 1976:52)

There are several reasons for expecting the use of operational statements of goals to enhance student learning. Duchastel and Merrill (1973:64–65) suggest that objectives can provide direction for student learning, organization for subject matter, aid to students as they organize their own time and learning experiences, feedback to students on their progress, and task reinforcement. Each of these possible benefits to the students has an analog for teachers as they prepare courses or specific classes. Specifying the type of learning at hand—knowledge, application of knowledge, problem-solving skills— means that the teacher can better select or develop instructional strategies for achieving the goals. Decisions on whether to try to build small discussion groups into the class, or on what types of questions to use in classes, can be properly made only

* For a review of the use of operational statements in teaching sociology, see articles by Vaughn; by Goldsmid in Baker and Wilson (1979); and by Goldsmid (forthcoming).

when the teacher knows the goals at hand.[6]

Research findings lend only modest support to the notion that use of instructional objectives enhances learning. Perhaps this is not surprising if we remember that objectives are only a tool and not a teaching strategy or method. If they are to advance learning, objectives must be integrated into instruction. Research has been conducted on whether student learning is helped by student possession of objectives, of specific compared to general objectives, and by teacher possession of objectives. The results of these studies are divided between those finding small, statistically significant helping effects and those reporting no significant differences. However, available research suggests that student use of objectives reduces the time necessary to complete a given unit of instruction and that, when coupled to other learning tools, clear statements of objectives can enhance learning. Research on objectives is reviewed by Duchastel and Merrill (1973), Kibler et al. (1974:5–8), and Robin (1976:especially 337–338).

Benign Disruption

In chapter 5, we asserted that a major end of education is ability in problem solving and that this ability is marked by the capacity to fit an anomalous event into a parsimonious intellectual framework and, where necessary, to alter an existing framework or create a new one. We argued that teachers can help students develop this ability by using benign disruption: arranging roadblocks or novel situations that require analytic skills if they are to be surmounted. We spoke of two major types of roadblocks: differing observations (discrepant data about the social world) and differing explanations for a single phenomenon.

A number of theories and some research lend support to the use of benign disruption as a vehicle to promote thought. In our earlier discussion of questions before answers, we saw that questions can motivate the learner by arousing curiosity about that which is unknown. Research by Berlyne and others suggests that a moderate level of uncertainty, novelty, and complexity arouses curiosity and serves as a launching pad for thought. The underlying process here is that perceived conflict in available information heightens learner attention and interest. As Dewey notes somewhere, thinking begins with a felt difficulty.

Contradictions do not in themselves result in resolution; the teacher's job is not only to bring the contradiction to the student's attention, but to aid in the process of resolution. Imbalances can be reduced in many ways, not all of which are conducive to learning. The student might deny the contradiction or ignore it as being unimportant. Hence, the teacher working as benign disrupter needs to identify contradictions that students understand, find meaningful, and realize are consequential.

Theories of Learning—and Teaching

We have asked: "Do the means of instruction make a difference?" We answered yes. Research indicates that particular instructional methods enhance learning of specific types of knowledge and skills. Research on several components of teaching and learning tells us something about *why* these methods work. But the components do not comprise a theory of teaching or learning, nor do they derive from a single theory. We have

not defined this as a problem for several reasons. A comprehensive theory is beyond the scope of this book and beyond our competence. Furthermore, one can find support in very different theories for most, if not all, of the components of effective instruction discussed. For example, the view that feedback is central to effective instruction is held by theorists as diverse as B. F. Skinner, Robert Gagné, Benjamin Bloom, and Jerome Bruner. Zillman and Cantor (1973:172–173) note that their finding that teacher use of rhetorical questions can enhance student learning is predicted both by drive-based theories (e.g., Hull) and behaviorally based theories (e.g., Skinner). Nonetheless, a model that provides a comprehensive view of the learning process can be useful to teachers as they design instruction or assess their classroom practice.

Gagné's Essentials of Learning for Instruction

We find useful the work of learning psychologist Robert M. Gagné. In *Essentials of Learning for Instruction,*[7] Gagné discusses learning "in terms of the information-processing model of learning and memory, a model that underlies many contemporary theories. This model posits a number of internal processes that are subject to the influence of a variety of external events. The arrangement of external events to activate and support the internal processes of learning constitutes what is called instruction" (1974:vii–viii). "Learning is inferred when a change or modification of behavior occurs, which persists over relatively long periods during the life of the individual" (1974:6).

Gagné's model of learning is summarized in table 12.6. He posits eight phases comprising any incident of learning; a set of internal and external events make up each phase. The external events are elements in the instructional process; "these are the readily observable things: the stimulation that reaches the learner and the products (including written and spoken information) that result from his responding" (1974:26). The events that are internal to the learner's brain and central nervous system are referred to as processes of learning and are inferred from observation. Gagné stresses that "the processes and phases . . . result from many years of controlled observations of people who are engaged in learning followed by rational construction of 'what must be going on' " (1974:27).

From consideration of these phases and processes, and from experimental research, Gagné derives a series of instructional strategies to enhance individual learning:[8]

1. *Gain and maintain the learner's attention and motivation.* The teacher needs to create an attitudinal set favorable to the learning at hand—what is to be learned is worth the effort and can be learned.

2. *Inform the learner of expected outcomes.* The teacher needs to tell the student what he or she will know and be able to do as a result of the learning.

3. *Stimulate recall of relevant prerequisite capabilities.* Since most learning builds on prior knowledge and skills, the learner needs to be reminded of the relevant knowledge and skills (and helped to gain them, if they are not possessed).

4. *Present the instructional stimuli inherent in the learning task at hand.* The teacher conveys, illustrates, demonstrates the information and skills comprising the learning at hand.

5. *Offer students guidance for learning.* Usually by verbal cues, the teacher attempts to guide the learner to discovery of the concepts or rules (or other learnings) to be acquired; this often takes the form of questions.

6. *Provide feedback.* The teacher gives the student information on how correctly he or she has learned (implicit is verification or compari-

Table 12.6 Gagné's Model of Learning: The Processes of Learning and the Influence of External Events

Learning Phase	Process	Influencing External Events
Motivation	Expectancy	Communicating the goal to be achieved
		Prior confirmation of expectancy through successful experience
Apprehending	Attention/Selective perception	Change in stimulation to activate attention
		Prior perceptual learning
		Added differential cues for perception
Acquisition	Coding/Storage entry	Suggested schemes for coding
Retention	Storage	Not known
Recall	Retrieval	Suggested schemes for retrieval
		Cues for retrieval
Generalization	Transfer	Variety of contexts for retrieval cueing
Performance	Responding	Instances of the performance ("examples")
Feedback	Reinforcement	Informational feedback providing verification or comparison with a standard

Source: From *Essentials of Learning for Instruction* by Robert M. Gagné. Copyright © 1974 by The Dryden Press, a division of Holt, Rinehart and Winston, Inc. Reprinted by permission of Holt, Rinehart and Winston.

son with a standard). This feedback on student work is for learning, not certification.

7. *Promote performance with appraisal.* The teacher provides opportunities to practice the learned information or skill followed by prompt feedback.

8. *Make provisions for transferability.* To ensure that the student can generalize a newly acquired capability (information or skill), the teacher uses a variety of new and different examples (or cases). The student needs to practice and receive feedback on these extensions of what was initially learned.

9. *Ensure retention.* The teacher must make sure that new learnings are "readily sub-

sumable under previously learned ideas and at the same time distinguishable from them" (Gagné, 1970:319).

Classification of Learning Outcomes

Earlier we saw that some teaching methods and approaches are better suited to some instructional objectives than others. Gagné's strategies (and our nine components) are usefully refined when we consider the *types* of things to be learned. Gagné classifies learning outcomes into five categories that cut across disciplinary lines as well as levels of education (e.g.,

Table 12.7 Types of Learning Objectives: Their Critical Learning Conditions, Instructional Features, and Prerequisite Learnings

Class of Learning Objective	Critical Learning Conditions	Instructional Features	Outcome Question	Possible Prerequisite Learning
Verbal information	1. Activating attention by variations in print or speech 2. Presenting a meaningful context (including imagery) for effective coding	Meaningful context; suggested coding schemes, including tables and diagrams	Will the student be able to *state* the desired information?	Referent meanings of words (i.e., concepts)
Intellectual skill	1. Stimulating the retrieval of previously learned component skills 2. Presenting verbal cues to the ordering of the combination of component skills 3. Scheduling occasions for spaced reviews 4. Using a variety of contexts to promote transfer	Prior learning and recall of prerequisite skills	Will the student be able to *demonstrate* the application of the skill?	Component simpler skills Information specific to the application examples
Cognitive strategy	1. Verbal description of strategy 2. Providing a frequent variety of occasions for the exercise of strategies, by posing novel problems to be solved	Occasions for novel problem solving	Will the student be able to *originate* new problems and their solutions?	Intellectual skills involved in problem solution Information involved in problem solution Masses of organized knowledge

secondary, undergraduate, graduate). His five categories of learning outcomes are presented below (Gagné, 1974:chapter 3; see also, Gagné, 1972), with some illustrations from urban sociology. Table 12.7 presents for each of the five categories: (1) critical learning conditions, (2) key instructional features, (3) the learner outcome expressed as a question, and (4) some possible prerequisite learnings.

Verbal information. Verbal information encompasses knowledge—in either oral or written form. Conventional units of knowledge are facts, names, principles, and generalizations. Verbal information is *knowledge that* something is so. Viewed as a capability, verbal information means that the individual can state what he or she has learned. Verbal information is important (1) in its own right, (2) as a prerequisite for further learning, and (3) as a vehicle for thought. *Examples: Stating* the definition of an urban place according to the U.S. Bureau of the Census. *Stating* the rank-size relationship for cities in developing and developed countries.

Table 12.7 (*Continued*)

Class of Learning Objective	Critical Learning Conditions	Instructional Features	Outcome Question	Possible Prerequisite Learning
Attitude	1. Reminding learner of success experiences following choice of particular action; alternatively, ensuring identification with an admired "human model" 2. Performing the chosen action; or observing its performance by the human model 3. Giving feedback for successful performance; or observing feedback in the human model	Experience of success following the choice of a personal action; or observation of these events in a human model	Will the student *choose* the intended personal action?	Prior success experience following choice of desired personal action Identification with human model Information and skills involved in the personal action
Motor skill	1. Presenting verbal or other guidance to cue the learning of the executive subroutine 2. Arranging repeated practice 3. Furnishing feedback with immediacy and accuracy	Learning of executive routine; practice with informative feedback	Will the student be able to *execute* the motor performance?	Executive routine controlling performance Part-skills or motor chains

Source: From *Essentials of Learning for Instruction* by Robert M. Gagné. Copyright © 1974 by The Dryden Press, a division of Holt, Rinehart and Winston, Inc. Compiled from Tables 4.2, 5.1, and 5.2. Reprinted by permission of Holt, Rinehart and Winston.

Intellectual skill. Intellectual skill involves learnings that enable the student to deal with classes of objects in the world by symbolic means. Intellectual skill involves *knowing* how to distinguish, classify, identify, and demonstrate or generate a rule. *Examples:* Given descriptions of them, *classifying* places as urban areas, cities, or SMSAs. *Demonstrating* that heterogeneity increases with larger population size and density. *Generating* a rule for predicting the physical structure of an urban place, given information about its technology level, population size, geography, and hinterland.

Cognitive strategy. Cognitive strategy includes "internally organized capabilities which the learner makes use of in guiding his own attending, learning, remembering, and thinking" (Gagné, 1974:64). While intellectual skills enable the learner to work with his environment, cognitive strategies govern the learner's mental activity. The learner uses a cognitive strategy to select and categorize (code) what he or she learns or to solve a problem. *Example: Creating* an hypothesis about the relationship between city size and heterogeneity of production bases.

Attitude. Attitude concerns learned capabilities reflecting particular preferences. It is an acquired internal state that influences the choice of personal action toward some class of things, persons, or events. Attitudes vary in strength and direction. *Example: Choosing* to use empirical data in deciding the type of community in which one wishes to reside.

Motor skills. As learned capabilities, motor skills "make possible the precise, smooth, and accurately timed execution of performances involving the use of muscles" (Gagné, 1974:67). Many daily activities and occupations require motor skills (as well as other learned capabilities). *Examples: Using* a keypunch machine or computer terminal. Also, driving a car, typing, performing auto mechanics or brain surgery.

Another classification of educational objectives was developed by Benjamin S. Bloom and his colleagues. Bloom categorized objectives into three major domains:

Cognitive
  Those objectives dealing with acquisition of knowledge, information, verbal skills, and reasoning; what are sometimes called the "intellectual" aspects of education.
Affective
  Those objectives dealing with emotions and attitudes; feelings toward, beliefs about, valuational matters.
Psychomotor
  Those objectives dealing with skills involving the muscles; learnings involving physical acts.

Each of these domains has been the subject of a book detailing the scores of subcategories of learnings in the domain and illustrating the uses of the classification: for the cognitive domain, see Bloom (1956); for the affective domain, see Krathwohl, Bloom, and Masia (1964); for the psychomotor domain, see Simpson (1972). Objectives in the cognitive domain are those of most concern to sociologists; table 12.8 presents, in abridged form, Bloom's classification of cognitive objectives. The first column presents categories of objectives; the second provides terms referring to aspects of the subject matter to be learned, and the third column contains verbs used by the teacher to achieve a more precise statement of the type of learning outcome intended. Objectives in category I refer to knowledge or information; those in categories II through VI refer to intellectual skills and operations done with information. Learning objectives in any of the six categories can be simple or complex, trivial or important. The categories are sequential. While each category of objectives has its unique attributes, it includes some from the prior categories. For example, before one can apply knowledge, it must be comprehended.

The utility of schemes for specifying and classifying learning outcomes can be seen when we examine the course goals and the instructions we give students on assigned papers. We say we want students to grasp the fundamental concepts of sociology—not to parrot definitions, but really to understand their use. In a course in contemporary sociological theory, we say we want students to learn four theoretical perspectives, understand the relation-

Table 12.8 Bloom's Classification of Cognitive Learning Objectives

	(Direct) Objects	Acts (Infinitives)
I. *Knowledge*		
Terminology and specifics (low abstraction)	vocabulary, terminology, definitions, facts, information (sources, names, events), properties	to recall, recognize, define, distinguish, acquire, identify
Ways and means of dealing with knowledge (e.g., conventions, trends, sequences, classifications, criteria, methodology)	forms, conventions, arrangements, procedures, treatments, rules, divisions, classes, causes, criteria, uses	to recall, recognize, identify, acquire
Abstracts and universals of a field	principles, generalizations, propositions, laws, interrelations, theories	to recall, recognize, identify, acquire
II. *Comprehension (understanding)*		
Translation (paraphrase, shift) Interpretation (reorder) Extrapolation (extension)	abstractions, relationships, theories, methods, corollaries, ramifications, effects	to translate, transform, rephrase, illustrate, demonstrate, estimate, conclude, predict
III. *Application*		
Use of appropriate abstractions in particular, concrete situations	principles, laws, procedures, conclusions	to apply, generalize, relate, choose, organize
IV. *Analysis*		
Breakdown of elements, relationships, organization principles	elements, hypotheses, particulars, effects, assumptions, evidence, fallacies	to distinguish, detect, deduce, contrast, compare, analyze
V. *Synthesis*		
Production of a unique communication or of a plan; derivation of a set of abstract relationships	patterns, products, designs, solutions, hypotheses, generalizations	to write, produce, originate, modify, document, propose, specify, synthesize, formulate
VI. *Evaluation*		
Judgment in terms of internal evidence; in terms of external evidence	accuracy, consistency, errors, exactness, efficiency, utilities, theories, standards	to judge, argue, validate, decide, contrast, appraise, standardize

Source: Adapted from Kibler et al. (1974:189–192); based on Bloom (1956).

ship between theory and research, be familiar with basic issues in theory building, and appreciate how knowledge of theory can help us understand the social structures in which we live. In assigning a term paper, we stress that we want an analytic paper, one that goes beyond mere description.

But what do we mean when we say "grasp the fundamentals," "understand their use," "appreciate," "be familiar," "be analytic"? How can our students, as they read and study, know when they "appreciate the utility of theory," or have "the sociological perspective"? What will our students have to do to demonstrate that they understand and can apply a concept or theory?

Answers to such questions can be built by use of such schemes as those offered by Gagné and Bloom. These classifications help us describe different types of learning in language that is more precise and geared to observable student acts (usually written or oral). To Bloom (see table 12.8), one way students demonstrate that they understand or comprehend factual knowledge (say, a concept) is by translating it into a form other than the form employed by the teacher or text. Rephrasing a definition, using new words and providing new examples of a different order, constitutes translation. In chapter 3, we reviewed reasons to state learning goals in operational form; in chapter 4, we provided examples of teacher use of operational statements.

Sociology and Effective Instruction

Gagné's "essentials of learning for instruction" rest on a theory of intrapersonal dynamics. Yet we know that social factors play an important part in learning.

What does sociology tell us about different means of instruction and whether they make a difference in how students learn?

Recall our exploration of lecture and discussion methods. We saw that class size—a social variable—affects type and extent of participation, which in turn is related to how much a student learns. We saw evidence that leadership—one teaching role—can provide structure to discussion classes and that this structure affects learning. When discussing ways in which teachers of large lecture courses can build feedback mechanisms into their classes, we made implicit use of research on communication patterns and their consequences for individual participation and satisfaction, and group productivity. Here and elsewhere, we have seen that social factors and processes shape both individual learning and group-level outcomes (such as group effectiveness in problem solving).

Sociologists and social psychologists have made important contributions to what is known about teaching and learning. Ample testimony is found in Boocock's *An Introduction to the Sociology of Learning* (1972) and in various review articles (e.g., Boocock, 1978; Cohen, 1972). Some of the better studies of teaching and learning, and student culture in higher education, have been done by sociologists (e.g., Solomon, Bezdeck, and Rosenberg, 1963; Solomon, Rosenberg, and Bezdek, 1964; Becker, Geer, and Hughes, 1968; and the work of David Riesman and his colleagues). Many studies by sociologists of communication, leadership, cohesion, attraction, and norms in small groups have contributed importantly to our understanding of what goes on in classrooms (cf. work cited by Schmuck and Schmuck, 1975). Sociological theories have been used to develop instructional procedures and to analyze interaction in sociology class-rooms (see, for example, the work of Karp and Yoels, 1976; Petras and Hayes, 1973; Spector, 1976; Wieting, 1975; and S. R. Wilson, 1973.) Hedley (1978) has shown that what we know about sources and reduction of error in sociological research can be used to improve the grading process. In addition to what these articles tell us about instruction in sociology, they are models of how sociology can be used in the study of teaching and learning.[9]

Despite these contributions, the application of sociology to understanding teaching and learning in *higher education* is an underdeveloped field. Sociologists tell us much more about primary and secondary than about higher education; more about schools as organizations and occupational settings than as contexts of teaching and learning; more about noninstructional factors affecting learning (e.g., family background of students) than about instructional factors; and far too little about the college class as a social group. There are some important exceptions to these generalizations. It is also true that some of the work on primary and secondary education can be usefully extended to higher settings. We think of work by sociologists such as Dreeben (1970, 1973) and Bidwell (1973), and of sociological work by colleagues in schools of education, such as Lortie (1973, 1975) and Schlechty (1976).

We know far less than we need to know about the consequences for student learning of "non-individual factors arising from the formal and informal social structure of the classroom"; we borrow this phrase from Cohen (1972:441), whose review of sociology's contribution to the study of classroom interaction supports the conclusion. From studies conducted at the primary and secondary level, we know that a variety of social factors affect what

goes on in the classroom, including:

Ecological structure and participation
Status of students
Reward structure
Teacher expectations
Role behavior of the teacher
Effects of students on teachers
Existence of class norms and the development of informal normative contracts
Class composition (as a contextual effect)

Few studies using such variables have student learning as a dependent variable. Further, "most research on the classroom is weakened by lack of a model or theory of the classroom as a social system" (Boocock, 1972:170). Those wishing to review research on these social factors may wish to consult Dunkin and Biddle (1974:especially chapters 7, 11), Boocock (1978, 1972:especially chapters 7, 8), Cohen (1972), and Schmuck and Schmuck (1975).

We know little about the effects on student learning of nonindividual factors arising from the formal and informal structure of colleges and universities. Schools have complex normative structures, a culture and subcultures, and selection criteria for the allocation of people to roles. Student and professor are learned social roles; actors in both roles have peer groups and subcultures. Yet we have few studies that explore nonclassroom contextual effects on instruction, student learning, and their links. Some important exceptions are Becker, Geer, and Hughes (1968), Newcomb and Wilson (1966), and R. C. Wilson et al. (1975);[10] see also Bassis (1977) and Davis (1966). Finally, we still have much to learn from Durkheim's writings on education and the work on teaching of sociologists such as Waller (1932) and Cantor (1949, 1950, 1953).

Effective Instruction in Sociology

In earlier sections of this chapter we saw that some instructional methods enhance student learning of sociology more than others. For example, studies find PSI more effective than conventional formats in fostering content learning in sociology. We also saw that teachers can enhance the effectiveness of some instructional methods. Thus, research on social science classes tell us that *how* a film is used affects student learning. Such findings have added significance because they confirm findings in the larger literature on college teaching.

Most of this chapter has reviewed research bearing on college teaching and learning as generic activities that have attributes cutting across different subject matters. Yet at several points in this book, we have argued that in important ways the teaching of sociology is different from instruction in other disciplines. In chapter 8, we reasoned that some common problems of instruction in sociology derive from or are closely related to our subject matter. Thus many of our students are accustomed to using individualistic or psychological variables to explain social phenomena. In chapter 4, we discussed the implications for instruction of a view of sociology as a generalizing discipline; and in chapter 10 and earlier sections of this chapter, we suggested that some instructional methods are more suited to some types of subject matter than others.

Does research confirm this view that subject matter matters? Little is reliably known about the distinctiveness of teaching and learning sociology at the higher education level. We are aware of very few studies that employ comparative designs to tease out disciplinary differences in learning and teaching. There are, however, several bodies of research that lend

support to the notion that teaching and learning are more than generic activities.

Several studies of student evaluation of teaching (SET) in colleges and universities report consistent differences in ratings of teachers of different disciplines (controlling for a variety of other factors). Linsky and Straus (1973) analyzed SET data from sixteen universities and found that among faculty in seven disciplinary areas, sociologists (and psychologists) ranked lowest in student evaluations.[11] They advance five possible explanations for this finding, most of which are related to sociology as a subject matter: (1) large class-size characterizes sociology and leads to student dissatisfaction; (2) the indefiniteness of sociological content renders it less satisfying for some students; (3) student expectations that sociology is a means of bringing about social change are not realized; (4) sociology is not seen as relevant to students' occupational concerns; and (5) selective recruitment draws alienated students into sociology. Linsky and Straus found that, within sociology, teachers of history of theory, statistics, and social psychology received higher ratings than teachers of other courses. They note that "this 'internal comparison' suggests some support for explanation 2, above . . . [since] these courses, especially statistics, have a fairly definite curriculum or more factual materials than most sociology courses" (Linsky and Straus, 1973:110).

Disciplines vary according to the degree of hierarchical structure in their content. Some disciplines have many basic concepts that are prerequisite learnings for advanced work; learning in such fields has more of a sequential and cumulative structure. Walker and McKeachie (1967:6) suggest that psychology is, in this regard, midway between mathematics and history. We expect sociology is similarly located. While there are overlaps in the underlying structure of content in different disciplines, it is clear that there are differences. Cognitive psychologists have described the different structures and hierarchies of various subject matters and suggested implications for instruction and learning (cf. Gagné, 1970:chapter 9).

At the primary and secondary educational level, studies show that several attributes of classes as social systems vary with subject matter. Research cited by Dunkin and Biddle (1974:chapter 7)[12] finds differences between social studies and mathematics classes in classroom structure, communication patterns, participation, teacher use of physical space, teacher role behavior, lesson format, and various types of classroom activity.

There is other, indirect, evidence of disciplinary differences. Caine et al. (1978) demonstrate that the research methods, levels of measurement, sample size, and statistics used by sociologists differ from those employed by psychologists. On this basis, they lament the fact that 73 percent of four-year colleges do *not* offer a statistics course *in the sociology department* (compared with 43 percent for psychology and 6 percent for mathematics departments). R. C. Wilson et al. (1975:chapter 6) report disciplinary differences in teachers' definitions of the purpose of education, their attitudes toward students, and their teaching styles and practices. Kurtz and Maiolo (1968) report that the opening chapters of sociology texts, compared to those in four other disciplines, are marked by a defensive concern with sociology as a science.

Finally, many sociologists believe that our subject matter affects our teaching roles. As noted in chapter 9, authors of many introductory sociology texts note distinctive elements of sociology that lead to both problems and opportunities for teachers (see also Page, 1959; Komarovsky, 1951).

The means of instruction used make a difference in what students learn. Much of importance about teaching and learning is not known, especially in higher education, certainly in sociology. But much is known, some quite reliably, and much more is known than is used.

Research and theory on college teaching generally, and on teaching sociology specifically, provide guidelines for instructors who seek to improve their teaching to create conditions fostering learning. The literature is accessible to teachers through many high-quality review articles, books such as McKeachie's *Teaching Tips*, and annotated bibliographies on the teaching of sociology. The appendix to this volume, "Resources for Teachers of Sociology," and the resource sections found in chapter 10 cite major works touching different aspects of college teaching and the teaching of sociology.

Notes

1. In his study, Bloom used five lecture and twenty-nine discussion classes at the University of Chicago. The classes were predominantly introductory-level courses in the humanities and social sciences; they do not constitute a representative sample. Another study suggesting that Bloom's method is valid is Krauskopf (1960).

2. Chapter 10 and earlier sections of this chapter present evidence that the effectiveness of an instructional method depends on how well it is used. Students learn more from motion pictures when the teacher introduces the film in such a way as to focus class attention on central features or issues and provides, before the showing, ways in which students can be mentally active during the film. The educational value of discussions is enhanced when the teacher and student clearly fix on the prob-

lem at hand before tackling it and when they possess identifiable communication skills. Lectures are more effective when their organization is congruent with the instructor's goal and the nature of the material being presented. The effectiveness of PSI depends, in part, upon the quality of the study guides, the skills of the student proctors, and specific requirements bounding the self-pacing feature.

3. Many, if not most, of these studies were of secondary and elementary school populations.

4. "In a well controlled experiment, Sime and Boyce (1969) inferred that questions raised the level of attention because the learning of concepts about which no questions were asked showed greater improvement in classes with questions than in classes in which students had none to answer" (Bligh, 1972:166). "The findings of the main experiment and the replication support quite clearly the expectation that the use of rhetorical question-and-answer sequences in a lecture enhances the learning of factual materials in an audience that is not otherwise highly motivated to pay close attention" (Zillman and Cantor, 1973:180). In the Zillman and Cantor study, lectures in the experimental and control classes (both artificial classes) were identical except for the use of question-and-answer sequences in the former. Facts later to be tested were given equal exposure in both classes. The lecture content was chiefly anthropological materials.

5. For citation of research bearing on teacher enthusiasm and warmth, see McKeachie (1978:24, 242) and Bligh (1972:80); see also Solomon, Rosenthal, and Bezdeck (1964) and Goldsmid, Gruber, and Wilson (1977). Coats and Smidchens (1966) found that the dynamism (enthusiasm) of speakers was correlated with the extent of student recall in a study of college speech courses. The relationship was significant at the .001 level and 36 percent of the variance in immediate student recall was accounted for by speaker dynamism.

6. Norris Sanders' book *Classroom Questions: What Kinds?* (1966) discusses and illustrates the different types of questions (used in instruction and evaluation of learning) that teachers can employ when working toward different types of instructional objectives. Sanders' work is keyed to Benjamin S. Bloom's *Taxonomy of Educational Objectives: Handbook I, Cognitive Domain* (1956), but is useful regardless of the classification of knowledge used.

7. This volume is a short (164 pages) and very useful monograph that builds on Gagné's more extensive writings. Sociologists should not be put off by that portion of chapter 1 that presents a rather elementary review of research design (validity, reliability, control groups, etc.).

8. These strategies are discussed in the later chapters of Gagné (1974). An extended discussion, from which we have borrowed heavily, is found in Gagné (1970:chapter 11). Here Gagné briefly reviews experimental literature supporting the components of instruction discussed.

9. One of the best applications of sociological analysis to dynamics in the college classroom is by psychologist Richard Mann (1970) and his colleagues.

10. See also the studies reprinted in Feldman (1972) and Sanford (1962). However, few of these studies report evidence on student academic achievement.

11. Sociologists were rated below average as teachers, by students at fourteen of the sixteen colleges and universities in Linsky and Straus's "convenience sample." To allow comparison among the schools, Z scores were used that expressed "the average teaching rating of a department in terms of the number of standard deviations which the department average is above or below the mean for all departments in the college" (Linsky and Straus, 1973:107). Average weighted Z scores for the sixteen schools in the seven academic areas were as follows: Languages (+.25), Humanities (+.13), Social Sciences other than sociology and psychology (+.07), Professional Schools (−.08), Physical and Biological Sciences (−.19), Sociology (−.33), and Psychology (−.38). The unweighted Z scores followed a similar pattern. Linsky and Straus do not name the schools

studied, but do describe them and present data for each. The two schools in which sociology ranked comparatively high were a "high-prestige private-urban undergraduate college within a university" (weighted Z score of +.25) and a "southwestern state university" (+.20). For both of these schools, the average Z scores for psychology were low (−.65 and −.37).

12. See, specifically, the findings involving subject matter under "context-process relationships," cited on pp. 212, 214, 216, 222, 227. While Dunkin and Biddle (1974) here cite several studies, they draw heavily on Adams and Biddle (1970), who studied thirty-two teachers and their pupils in social studies and mathematics classes at grade levels 1, 6, and 11.

PART IV
ARE THE MEANS EFFECTIVE IN GAINING OUR ENDS?

To know how well we have done what we set out to do, we evaluate. To improve on past performances, we evaluate. We assess the level of student achievement (how much was learned) and instructor achievement (how much was taught). Since we define teaching as "intentional activities designed to enhance learning" (recall chapter 3), measures of teaching should be measures of learning. This equation is useful, for it puts the stress where it ought to be—on changes in student performance. Yet the equation is not wholly proper, for teachers have only marginal control over many of the factors that affect student learning. Furthermore, the equation is too simply put. If teachers are to improve the effectiveness of their teaching, they need to know not simply the degree to which students learn, but also what it is in their teaching that has helped or hindered the learning of concretely defined matters. Otherwise we shall be in the lamentable position of St. Augustine who cried: "For so it is, O Lord my God, I measure it; but what it is that I measure I do not know."

Evaluation is central to teaching and learning of all types. Learning by trial and error involves evaluation. Discovery-based, nondirective forms of teaching assume that, in personal exploration or interchange among learners, self-evaluation will take place, at least implicitly. Yet despite its inevitability, evaluation is endlessly debated. Often the controversy hinges on technical issues. Is the instrument valid and reliable? Is it possible to design measures of student learning that take into account various goals and styles of teaching? Such questions are useful, but they may deflect attention from more serious issues. For the technical aspects of assessment can be handled fairly easily once we are clear and agreed on *what* is to be measured and *how* the measurements are to be used.

But research on methods of assessing instructor performance cannot provide answers to three critical questions: What is to be measured? How and by whom are the evaluations to be used? And to what ends? These are the knotty issues, not the technical matters that, although important and not wholly settled, are far more amenable to the same developmental and testing procedures in which sociologists are well trained.

Part IV tackles problems of evaluating student and teacher performance. In chapter 13, we ask about the purposes of evaluation, about the role of the teacher as evaluator, about grading (a special case of evaluation), about the means of evaluation, and about its implications for the student-teacher relationship. In chapter 14, we pose the two obvious questions: Why should instructor performance be evaluated? And by what means is, or might, this evaluation be done?

CHAPTER 13
EVALUATING STUDENT
ACHIEVEMENT

Most sociologists, most of their lifetimes, are required to assess student achievement. Why do we evaluate student work? How do we do it? How might we do it better?

Our discussion of the evaluation of student achievement hinges on five questions that expand the three principal ones just posed. First, what is the point in testing? A second, related query is this: What is implied when we say that part of the teacher's role is to act as certifying agent? Third, what does the grade measure? Does it measure conscientiousness? competence? In what? quantity? quality? attitudes? Fourth, how do we measure? How do we contrive a grade? What are the commonly used instruments for testing, and what are they good (and bad) for? And finally, what are some problems in the teacher-student relationship that arise through conventional testing procedures?

The Purposes of Testing: Why Is It Part of the Teacher's Role?

One use of testing, too little exploited, is to assess the instructor's effectiveness. For example, if most people in a class score low on certain questions, there is a mandatory message for the teacher. Among other things, both ability in constructing examination items and skill in teaching are put in question.

From the students' point of view, adequate testing samples their command of facts, ideas, and skills, telling them how they are doing. Insofar as tests accurately diagnose strengths and weaknesses, students learn where they need to invest their energies. Since tests convey (or withhold) praise, they affect motivation. In summary form, the test grade is a communication to the student comparable, perhaps, to the pay envelope for a piece-rate worker. The tangible coin of the classroom realm is a grade, a compressed symbol of a certain level of achievement. Doubtless, ascribed traits come into play sometimes. But in general, it is assumed that the grade is a measure of actual academic performance.

A third use of testing is as a learning device. Testing hinges on the asking of questions, a talent too little cultivated. Especially if students themselves are encouraged to pose questions, they may learn something about this first stage of inquiry—learn how hard it is, and yet how necessary. As a learning device, tests can also be useful because they substitute, for a quite passive posture in learning, a highly participative learning technique. Students get much involved in tests—often for the wrong reason. But the point is that, confronted with an exam, their level of attending soars. The vagrant mind snaps to attention. Furthermore, test items make good foci for discussing points and unravelling ideas. They are often clearer than the spontaneous oral inquiry: the written question, publicly displayed, can be more readily assessed for triviality or ambiguity. In three ways, testing can promote learning through the chance to review: (1) before the test, as students prepare, (2) during the test, when the order of items may reinforce the structure of experiences the student has been through, and (3) after the test, when the instructor can exploit the test to discuss and illustrate with useful responses taken from student papers.[1]

Examinations, and other evaluations of student achievement, should not always be counted toward the course grade. They can be used for diagnostic purposes, for students to learn how they are progressing, and for the teacher to learn of student difficulties (these suggesting changes in the instructional pattern). The Teaching Information Processing System (TIPS) emphasizes this need for frequent checks and evaluative response—not for grading, but for teaching.*

Above all, we would stress the use of testing to reinforce correct and useful responses, to help the instructor diagnose ailments that need remedies, and to cut short the errors that, once set in motion, carry students increasingly astray.

A fourth reason for testing derives from this fact: whether in public or private schools, teachers are official socializers. Private colleges are chartered by the state and required, through their boards of trustees, to serve the public interest. Public colleges are more directly controlled by state and city legislators. In either case, the enterprise is heavily vested with a public concern. Hence there are stipulated ways of certifying the teacher's competence and controlling curricular offerings. Professional and regional accrediting associations set curricular standards. Standards of performance are set by the admissions office and by faculties. And the teacher is expected to determine the extent to which

standards of performance are met. Teachers serve the public interest by identifying and developing abilities and interests that foster discovery of, and assignment to, appropriate social slots. This requires some sort of testing.

The Teacher as Certifying Agent: What Is Implied?

Testing is not only a communication to the student. The grading aspect of the teaching role requires an instructor to report to some unknown others—a future employer, an admissions officer—about a student's performance. The teacher is saying to whom it may concern: "This person has done work of a given quality."

There is no avoiding this—at least as education, economy, and polity are now organized. One aspect of the rationalization of the modern world is seen in the effort to get ever more precise measures on all traits relevant to adult roles. Business and industry with their personnel managers, the federal civil service, the educational system and we, its operatives—all are engaged in grading as groundwork for role-allocation. This is so for us because education, as it is organized in our society, is preeminently a social thing. It is misleading to think of the teacher's certifying role as directed toward the maximum development of capacities unique to the individual student. This is a romantic illusion. "Far from having as its unique or principal object the individual and his interests, education is above all the means by which society perpetually recreates the conditions of its very existence" (Durkheim, 1922:123).[2]

A central condition of social existence is the continuous restaffing of those roles institutionalized precisely because they assure social survival. The teacher is a

* In chapter 12 we reviewed research on TIPS; in the appendix to this chapter we further describe the system.

chief agent of this restaffing job, an agent of society. In private as well as public schools, the teacher is charged by society with the task of assuring that the needed contributions of one generation will also be contributed by their successors.

Fortunately, this task is never the exclusive prerogative of a single teacher. Students have some degree of grade insurance because each student's grade-fate is a decision made many times by many teachers. This may be a source of relief to the individual teacher: most of us feel uneasy about playing God.

Yet one can't always be certain that independent judgments of achievement (registered in grades) will, among many teachers and different courses, produce a fairly sound judgment of overall performance. For both the expectation and evaluation of performance may be contaminated by judgments passed on from teacher to teacher. One of the great vices of the small department or college, like the small community, is premature and irrevocable branding of a student as his reputation precedes him. One of the incidental virtues of mass education is that student reputations are less readily communicated. Assessment of performance can then be more independent than it might otherwise be.

But the matter is still more complicated. Initial student performances in class may influence the instructor who, in turn, sets a self-fulfilling prophecy in motion. Rosenthal and Jacobson (1968) have shown how low expectations may under certain circumstances generate shoddy performances while high expectations encourage superior work.[3]

From these considerations we can infer certain practical prescriptions.

1. When independence of judgment is in jeopardy, grade papers namelessly.

2. Try to set the self-fulfilling prophecy in motion through initial assignments that have a high probability of success—i.e., assignments that can honestly be graded high. In this and the following statement, we invoke Shaw and Goethe along with Merton. In *Pygmalion*, Shaw has Eliza Doolittle say: ". . . the difference between a lady and a flower girl is not how she behaves, but how she's treated." And to the same point, something from Goethe: "If you treat an individual as he is, he will stay as he is. If you treat him as if he were what he ought to be and could be, he will become what he ought to be and could be."

3. Never convey a doubt about a student's capacity. Better to accompany a low grade with a remark conveying dismay and surprise that the work does not reflect the student's perception, general knowledge, and ability. Which is to say, grading is a process that requires us to look forward as well as backward. Any grade is a communication about past performance; but it also sets the stage for future performance. Future performance will be affected by the grade, and especially by the interpretation put on the grade.

In this connection, a note about failures in college. The very word *failure*, for a red-white-and-blue citizen, seems heretical, blasphemous, and cowardly. Our preference for success is reasonable enough. But failures, some of them, may be inevitable. We had best be ready to acknowledge them as evidence of differences in capacities, readiness, effort, or interest. This assumes, of course, that our teaching has been responsible.* The great crime in our classrooms should not be failure, but indifference.

In sum, the sociology instructor is inevitably a certifying agent. Even if tests are used chiefly for teaching (as we think they ought to be), instructors are usually

---

* See our discussion, in chapter 3, of "the effective and responsible teacher." See also, exhibit 12.1 on mastery learning.

asked to certify, publicly, their students' levels of achievement. In the process, they must walk a tightrope between judicial assessment and pedagogical stimulation. (We will comment later on this dilemma and suggest one way of resolving it.)

The Grade: What Does It Measure?

A grade is a highly compressed symbol. What does it stand for? It is generally assumed by parents, employers, and schools receiving transcripts that it is a measure of competence in a given subject matter. Is it indeed this, and this alone, that a grade describes? How about supporting skills? clarity of thinking? logic? literacy? ability to manipulate symbols—mathematical and verbal? frequency of attendance? punctuality in disposing of chores? Quantity of work, as well as quality? Extent of student effort? And if the grade *does* stand for competence in subject matter, what standard has been used?

Grading and the Craftsman's Skills

The separation between content (or subject matter) and supporting skills seems to us difficult if not spurious. We are teaching sociology, and certainly one aspect of the sociologist's role is some competence as a craftsman (see Mills, 1961: appendix on craftsmanship). Among other things, this means the sociologist should be able to use the language of sociology precisely, parsimoniously, tellingly.

There are special problems here, which we discussed in chapter 8. Let us note one additional difficulty. Words may give us special problems in sociology be-

cause corrective responses usually come from outside the student's immediate, personal experience. Students typically *talk about* science, rather than *do* it. In the laboratory, students in the biophysical sciences can muck about until they discover their errors and correct them. In effect, students substitute, for the manipulation of words, the manipulation of things that symbolize specified elements being investigated. If they "misspell" H_2O and come up with H_2S or H_2SO_4, their noses will correct them. The activity of inquiry carries its own checks and corrections. But when undergraduate students talk *about* sociology, the only check is the vicarious doing of science that they get through the instructor's responses. And the over-familiar words, contaminated with popular usage, lead to confusion.

We are constrained, therefore, to get key terms precisely expressed. Perhaps aside from that, one can argue that clear expression and clean craftsmanship, although generic virtues, are nonetheless to be reinforced in a sociology class. One way of handling this is to couple the requirement of competent craftsmanship (as something simply taken for granted) with an evaluation based exclusively on other criteria, those closer to matters sociological. One might, then, decline to read papers until they were correct in such taken-for-granted details as spelling and grammar.

Grading and Organization

The fine line between content and mode of expression becomes especially obscure when we think about matters of organizing written material. We might argue that organization of student papers should keep in mind the process of inquiry. This process—in logical sequence, not as it actually occurs—can be used as a model for reporting and discussing the process of sociological inquiry.

There is, first, a problem, some sort of cerebral itch to be attended to. Then there is the rumination that leads to a plausible answer. Walking down the abstraction ladder from the general answer (the general interpretation or explanation), we come to the point where we have an hypothesis to test. Then we gather data, order, and analyze them. Finally we determine whether the hypothesis is supported or refuted and how our original explanation (theory) needs to be patched up.

Obviously we are not suggesting that all written work in sociology courses follow such a format. But it does offer a useful framework for organizing one's writing, whether reporting on others' research, reviewing a book in sociology, or writing an essay exam.

Grading and the Ability to Separate Quantity from Quality

If it is hard to separate craft from content in grading, what shall we say about including other matters in the cryptic symbol that is the grade? What of attendance, for example? Or how about completeness of work done?

Conscientious attendance cannot be equated with competent performance. Yet the two are often confounded in a single symbol. A problem perhaps more frequent is the confounding of quantity and quality. It seems likely that grades are commonly taken to be a measure of performance—i.e., quality. But suppose we have little or no evidence on which to base a judgment of quality, the student having failed to submit the required work.

What then? Shall we give that student a low grade, which will doubtless be read as a judgment of incompetence? It is at least conceivable that the student might be a highly able person, erratic but brilliant. Unhappily, our thoughtlessness as teachers and a traditional pattern in registrars' offices lead us too often to report lack of evidence as condemning evidence. The solution, it seems to us, would be a separate symbol—one meaning, simply, that the person had registered for the course, but no evaluation of performance is possible.

We are arguing that the grade, for certifying purposes, should be a symbol as unambiguous as we can manage. Thus we would strip it of confounding connotations—conscientiousness, punctuality, grace of expression (although we favor a standard of minimally acceptable craftsmanship), frequency of attendance, and the like.

It may seem obvious and platitudinous to suggest that symbols better serve their purposes to the extent that they are unidimensional. Yet a keen sensitivity to the principle would much improve academic communication.

But cleaning up the symbol still leaves the problem of arriving at it in the first place. How do we measure performance? How do we arrive at a grade?

The Grade: How Do We Contrive It?

This question leads to a host of others. But we will pose, here, only three general issues: What constitutes the benchmark for determining a student's grade? Why—or why not—grade on a curve? What sorts of instruments can be used to sample students' command of course content?

Performance—Relative to What?

We said that evaluation is required by the elders because it serves an allocative function in society. We said that evaluation is to be desired, because it is an instructor's responsibility to respond with useful evaluations, so helping students improve their performances. (Indeed, we think students should demand evaluation as an essential element of their costly education.)

To achieve these ends, we have to locate a person's competence relative to something. Extent of achievement or degree of competence always requires comparison of two or more values. We may compare current achievement with what a student was able to do at an earlier date. Second, we may use peer performance as a benchmark: Is this student above or below the average for the class? How many standard deviations above or below the mean? Or we can combine the first two measures, asking whether a student's standing, relative to others, has improved, worsened, or remained the same as it was at some earlier time. Fourth, we can use some standards established by the teacher as the benchmark for measuring student achievement. Or, finally, we can use national standards as the benchmark, so that each student is competing with unknown others across the country on an examination prepared by some third outside party. The Educational Testing Service exams are a case in point.

The examination contrived by some outsider or scored on national standards has very real advantages that may be gained if, among different instructors, each agrees to test another's students. The advantage stems from the fact that to act as evaluator compromises a definition of the teacher's role that emphasizes helpfulness, professional concern, and a desire that one's students get the most from their work. We emphasize a point made before: the customary pattern of testing runs the danger that the teacher may be transformed into adversary, prosecutor, and judge. The outside examiner, on the other hand, allows teacher and student to work as collaborators in the solution of problems and in preparation for the judgment of competence. Exploiting this principle in our testing/grading should allow for a more stable teacher-student relationship and more effective learning. At least the teacher-as-judge-and-prosecutor won't get in the way. [4]

One striking advantage of personalized systems of instruction is that the standard of achievement set by the instructor is public, and specified with great clarity. A critical problem—but not, of course, one peculiar to PSI—is what the standard should be and how it may be altered, in type and extent, as circumstances change. The pressing need is for professional societies to publicize several benchmarks for performance in each of several commonly taught courses—as much to stimulate thought and reaction as to provide one set of useful standards.

*Why—or Why Not—Grade on a
Curve?*

The benchmark used in grading has consequences. For example, if the instructor uses students as the base point for assessing performance, the grade distribution, other things equal, will follow a curve—with most students in the middle of the grade range and a few at either extreme.

Now, one of the advantages of grading on a curve is that the teacher need not worry about standards. In effect, the students unwittingly create the standards that determine whether a person gets an A or an F or anything in between. For even with muddy objectives (perhaps because of them), even with an ill-organized course (perhaps because of it), we have a situation in which diverse stimuli are thrown at a fairly heterogeneous group, resulting in a distribution of scores that fall along the curve.

On the other hand, if the competition is not student-student but, in effect, student-instructor (that is, if the teacher rather than fellow students sets the standards), then other consequences follow. For example, the very fact of setting standards implies the need for behaviorally stated objectives, and the announcement and general knowledge of them. This of course is much more demanding. Indeed, we suspect that one reason for the popularity of curve-grading, especially in large classes and at the undergraduate level, is that it is the easiest way out at the same time that it conveys the delusion of professional rigor.[5]

We would not suggest that this is, typically, a conscious default. It is not. And conditions of academic life conspire to make it seem both a necessary and reasonable mode of grading. Sociology instructors often do have very large courses. Few have ever pondered the complexities of assessment. Often new instructors are teaching courses for the first time. (And rarely is it supposed that released time to prepare for a new, next-semester course is a legitimate use of school resources.) The result is inevitable. The means are ready at hand. One does nothing; and competition among students yields a distribution that seems to suggest that the teacher has clearly done good things for a few, that others have failed despite the teacher's admirable efforts, while most students have compromised with counter-interests

and counter-demands, producing the gentleman's C.

Pedagogical naiveté, poor preparation, lack of time and resources are not the only reasons for the common addiction to the curve. Wherever there is grade inflation, some instructors might wish to institute the curve as a standard for distributing evaluations. For grade inflation implies that instructors are evading the tough job of discriminating appraisals. It may suggest not only that evaluation is sloppy but that courses are easy and their content trivial.[6] Hardheaded sociologists will resent these reflections on the discipline—and on themselves as its putative exemplars. Hence the injunction: grade on the curve.

But the penalty falls not only on the instructor. Students suffer from a devalued or inflated currency. As with any other consumers, their efforts buy less. Furthermore, there are serious issues of inequity. One chairman of a sociology department wrote persuasively: "Grades should have as nearly as possible the same meaning in different departments and in different courses within a department. It may seem very generous to give a C student a B for his work . . . but in doing so, we are taking something away from the B student who has truly earned that grade in another course. . . . I see no reason why our department should differ sharply from [the standard suggested by the university-wide distribution of grades]." That distribution was as follows. In the right-hand column is the recommended pattern of

	University X (1970)	MSU (1960)
A	18%	0 to 15%
B	34	20 to 30
C	33	40 to 50
D	11	10 to 20
F	4	0 to 1

grading for several large courses at Michigan State University (Dressel and Nelson, 1961).

We can appreciate, then, the further issues of accuracy and justice that prompt some sociologists to lean on the curve. But there are problems. These have two principal sources: (1) differing subpopulations within the college or university, and (2) sound instructional techniques sacrificed when falling into the pattern of curve-grading.

The first difficulty is clear enough. Does it make sense to distribute performances of a highly selected group of students—graduate students, an honors course—along a curve? Conversely, it might be reasonable to expect that a highly *un*selected group of students, taught indiscriminately, would result in a distribution badly skewed downward. Is the solution, then, to have several different distributions corresponding to several student populations differing in background and prior training? What then is the meaning of the symbols A through F?

This is not so serious a difficulty as the next. For in a vague way we come to accept a distribution of evaluations that differs by student population. More troubling is a pattern of instruction that generates a normal grade curve and, by virtue of that fact, entails certain pedagogical defects. For it suggests a less than satisfactory pattern of instruction (errors of commission) and, at the same time, errors of omission in overlooking promising alternatives. To make the point, let us suggest the sort of instruction that generates a normal grade distribution.

Take a course registering 50 to 500 students. Assemble them from backgrounds that, for any given trait, provide a distribution more or less normal around a mean. This central tendency would be fostered by a common culture and similar

mechanisms of enculturation: predominantly nuclear and monogamous families transmitting elements of the Judeo-Christian tradition, compulsory school systems with common curricula, anticipatory socialization appropriate to a given labor force, and the like. There will, of course, be a dispersion of values on any given trait owing to different birth orders, family size, rural-urban and regional differences, variation in parental education, occupation, income. . . .

The students come together and are exposed to new facts (or ideas, or attitudes, or values). Let us assume that concurrent stimuli outside the course are shared pretty much in common and/or vary randomly.

Then it should follow that a bit (element) of information delivered in the class in conventional didactic fashion will be retained—and returned on an examination—in accordance with its impact (or interaction effect) on a preexisting set of knowledge having, for the class, the mean and variance generated by the conditions we have described. We can think of this as the impact of a stimulus on a normally distributed set of receptors where receptor means the experience-conditioned, relevant trait receiving the impact. Therefore the grade distribution, based on one student's performance relative to others, must approximate a normal distribution around the mean. (The image we have in mind is that of a normal distribution generator used in statistics classes to show how a probability curve can be produced. Steel balls—bits of information—bounce successively and randomly against a series of baffles—differing background traits—resulting, approximately, in a normal curve.)

The error of commission is to accept students' performance as the standard in place of the instructor's. The error of omission is to fail to orchestrate the educational experience to take account of those differing antecedent experiences on which the course must build.

To put it the other way around, the extent to which a normal curve does not describe the distribution of grades will be a function of the extent to which the instructor (rather than the class) clearly sets the standards, and the extent to which the instructor intervenes to enable students of differing backgrounds to achieve those standards of performance. The instructor may intervene by:

1. adjusting the time of learning to variations in student experience and background (as in self-paced learning, programmed learning, or some variant of the Keller method)

2. increasing the clarity of learning objectives (as in the behavioral statement of such goals)

3. bridging the familiar worlds of students with the novel material of the course—a different task for each differing category of student

4. giving diagnostic tests and providing students with evaluative responses including prescriptions for things they can do to enhance their learning (TIPS is one mechanism for doing this)

Thus an upwardly skewed distribution of grades may be taken as an outcome of highly professional and effective instruction.

We recognize, too, that such a skewed distribution of grades may result from ineffective instruction. Everyone moves closer to the grade ceiling when a course is less demanding. Sometimes we find instructors depreciating cognitive content and stressing affective bonds among students, and between students and instructor. This is the case of the indulgent teacher, sometimes the insecure tyro, sometimes the obsolete oldster who depends on students for the psychic income lost through professional incompetence.

In sum, grade-curving may be, and doubtless often is, an index of poor teaching. And highly skewed distributions may be, and doubtless often are, an index of poor instruction. But some skewed distributions resulting from a careful orchestration of learning experiences adapted to differences in student backgrounds may point to superlative instruction. In our view, the pattern of grading on a curve in large, lower division sociology courses points, at best, to mediocre teaching—the kind that fails to touch many students, disenchants some, and ignites interest in too few.[7] We believe the teacher should use standards of performance toward which all students can aim and against which all students are measured.

What Sorts of Instruments Can Be Used?

For most sociologists, the answer to this question seems to be use of multiple-choice (m-c) examinations for very large classes and essay (sometimes oral) examinations for small classes. Since most students taking sociology do so in large classes, we would expect that most will have been graded from scores on m-c—or, as they are sometimes misleadingly called, objective—examinations. The best estimate of the extent of use of the three instruments most often employed to sample students' command of course content comes from a study under the auspices of the ASA's Project on Teaching Undergraduate Sociology. The data are presented in table 13.1. The first course is the one with heavy enrollment and the one in which m-c exams are most heavily used. In data

Table 13.1 Extent of Use of Three Most Common Types of Evaluations Used in the Introductory Course and in Other Undergraduate Sociology Courses, United States, 1976

Type of Evaluative Device	Extent of Use: First Course				
	Extensive	Occasional	None	No Answer	Total
Objective Exams	60%	32%	5%	2%	99%
Essay or Oral Exams	25	61	11	3	100%
Term Papers	15	54	27	4	100%

Type of Evaluative Device	Extent of Use: Other Undergraduate Courses				
	Extensive	Occasional	None	No Answer	Total
Objective exams	40%	47%	5%	8%	100%
Essay or Oral Exams	46	43	2	9	100%
Term Papers	44	43	5	8	100%

Note: Responses are from sociology departments in 443 schools. See chapter 10, note 2 for details.
Source: Bradshaw and McPherron (1977).

not reported here (see Bradshaw and McPherron, 1977), the use of m-c exams was almost equally extensive in universities, four-year schools, and community colleges. In each category, schools with larger enrollments in undergraduate sociology more often resorted to the use of m-c examinations.

Multiple-choice tests

To describe tests as either objective or subjective is to slip into a spurious antithesis. Anyone who has reviewed a multiple-choice test with students, in class, will be acutely aware of the subjectivity of interpretation of an allegedly objective examination. Consider, for example, this very simple multiple-choice question:

Sociologists investigate the way things
  a. are.
  b. should be.

  c. can be.
  d. are destined to be.

The writer gives the correct answer as *a*. Yet one can argue plausibly for each of the other options. Option *b* is a perfectly good response if this is the question: How *should* one draw a sample in such a way as to be confident (within specified limits) that the part represents the whole? Again, *c* might be interpreted as what every probability statement tells us. For example (Meyer, 1968), the probability is very remote (.002) that the greater number of levels of supervision in the data-processing divisions of 254 public departments of finance (greater than in other divisions of bureacratic organizations) is due to chance. Such a difference, then, *can be* attributed to nonchance, which is to say, to a circumstance embodied in a theory of organization that purports to explain such differences. Similarly, *d* can be supported by anyone who takes a position of social determinism: given certain conditions, then predictable outcomes *are destined to be.* Given a slum setting, low parental education, a father-absent, mother-dominated family, uncertain and inadequate income, peers commonly depreciating white bourgeois patterns, there's a high probability that the male adolescent is destined to choose delinquent solutions.

This suggests a use of multiple-choice examinations, not for testing-grading purposes, but for review and teaching purposes. The correct or best answer then becomes unimportant. Each option becomes a pivot for exploring a limited aspect of the field and ways of looking at social phenomena (as in the discussion of option *c* above). There are at least three things to be said for such a teaching use of m-c tests. First, the teaching revolves around questions rather than (as in the usual pattern of expository teaching) assertions, declarative statements, or topics. Implicitly, the emphasis is on inquiry rather than receiving the word and committing it to memory. Second, examinations generate emotion and fix attention as do few other classroom activities. A review of examination items makes for quite general participation, yet focused on a particular point of inquiry. (Doubtless such an effect would be attenuated if examinations were never used for grading purposes.) Third, because they are put together by the teacher, m-c tests can be so devised as to reveal a sequence and structure that reinforce the pattern of the course—the gestalt that lends meaning to an otherwise heterogeneous collection of details.

It has become fashionable with some sociologists to deplore multiple-choice examinations and to celebrate the essay sort of test. The more freewheeling essay examination is supposed to plumb the student's ability to reason, to generate ideas, to interpret. On the contrary, the m-c type of examination is alleged to be a necessary evil when one must test large numbers of students; for, unfortunately, such examinations must, by their nature, lead to the regurgitation of trivial facts. These positions are overdrawn. Probably the commonest sort of examination is the bad one, whether essay or m-c. But it is possible to devise m-c items that transfer learnings to new contexts, that are relevant to daily concerns, and that touch matters of sociological importance. The three items that appear in exhibit 13.1 are pretty fair in touching the logic of inquiry, or research design, and in applying such hoped-for learnings to matters of common, everyday experience.

The following m-c question also requires more than simple return of memorized facts. The student who is not simply guessing must discriminate between group, aggregate, and category.

Which of the following conforms to the sociologist's definition of a group?
a. American college students majoring in mathematics
b. eligible persons not voting in the last election
c. the UNC football team
d. people waiting at Grand Central Station to board the train for Boston

Multiple-choice items can help students practice discriminating between fact and preference statements. Consider these two questions:

White, upper-class Americans make the following statements. Which statement is ethnocentric?
a. There is a disproportionate number of blacks in the lower class.
b. People in the upper class are usually better educated than lower-class people.
c. Americans are more attractive, physically, than other peoples.
d. Our country has a higher per capita income than Russia.

The socialization process:
a. *produces ethnocentric attitudes.*
b. *occurs chiefly in secondary groups.*
c. *is aimed at developing those traits that distinguish the individual human personality.*
d. *is peculiar to complex societies that require specialized recruitment and training.*

These m-c questions are offered not as examples of perfection in objective tests, but to suggest that it *is* possible to tap important sorts of learning—matters other than the memorizing of facts—through this sort of examination.

It requires much thought, and time, to construct a battery of m-c test items that adequately sample a sector of sociology. The preparation of an m-c test on, say, stratification will be much more onerous than devising one or two essay questions.

Exhibit 13.1 Three Examples of Multiple-Choice Items that Do More than Test Memorization of Trivial Facts

Following an article on intellectuals in government published in *Life* magazine, someone wrote a letter to the editors, saying:
"Your fine article on the scholars in government is, unfortunately, praise of a lot of duds. These men are palpably unfit for government service. They are theorists, impractical, far out of touch with reality. Washington is full of economists as a result of whose brilliance: (1) inflation has increased, (2) cost of living has increased, (3) taxes have increased, and (4) the national debt has increased.

Although I am a Republican, let me say that Al Smith could do a better job than all the college boys put together, and he was only a graduate of the Fulton Street Fish Market."
(*Life,* June 30, 1967, p. 19)

1. A cause and its effects are asserted here. Good research design increases our confidence that an alleged cause contributes (in some degree) to a given outcome. In this statement, what element of good research design is missing?
   a. a control situation
   b. a correlation of independent and dependent variables
   c. an independent variable
   d. a before-and-after situation

2. The independent variable implied in this statement is:
   a. number of scholars in Washington, D. C.
   b. proportion of government officials who are economists.
   c. measures of costs of living and of government operations.
   d. level of education achieved by public officials.

3. The *best* reason for being skeptical about such a statement is the following:
   a. it is an emotional statement suggesting lack of objectivity.
   b. even though scholarly, economists are likely to be as economy-minded as most other people.
   c. we can't be sure that the same things would not have happened, under the same conditions, in the absence of economists.
   d. the statement doesn't recognize the returns for these increased costs in armaments, public service, and the like.

Essay questions are often quite spongy; for we can rely on good students to redeem a bad essay examination. On the other hand, to read and evaluate the essay examination requires much more time than to grade the objective type of test. Indeed, this latter sort can be machine scored. For a large number of students or for frequent testing, ease and speed of scoring compensates for the difficulty in construction. (And it allows for prompt return of scored exams, which contributes to learning.) Some of these difficulties—and some of the errors we commonly make in developing m-c examinations—can be avoided by following the very good suggestions offered in various pamphlets and books on m-c test construction. See, for example, McKeachie (1978:157–160), Middleton (1965), Milton (1978:110–120), Milton and Edgerly (1977), and Psychological Corporation (n.d.).

Although good m-c items are very hard to write, we have better procedures for detecting inadequacies and improving items than we have with other sorts of instruments. For example, using electrographic answer sheets which can be optically scanned, we can process the data through a computer program (e.g., TESTAN) and receive much useful information. Very rapidly we can get certain descriptive statistics on the examination: the mean, standard deviation, a measure of test reliability, and frequency distribution of scores with cumulative percentages. For each question, this information is provided: frequency and percent of each response, the point biserial value, a difficulty index, and a discrimination index.

A test item that does not discriminate between top and bottom scorers on the examination may be one we would wish to revise or throw out, so that we improve our examination. Many teachers believe that an item so hard (or so easy)

that none (or all) could answer it should be eliminated. But should it be? Consider a test item correctly answered by eighty percent of a class. Did most get it correct because it was easy? or because the teacher effectively taught the concept tapped by the item? Did the item test an important point? or a trivial one? The answers to these questions must come from the teacher's review of the item itself and the instruction given. But knowing that an item fails to discriminate does not tell why this is the case. And before acting we need to know. If the subject matter is important, the item well designed, and the teacher satisfied with his or her instruction, an outcome of eighty percent correct should be welcomed; the item should be retained.

Instructors can run a test analysis in order to correct an m-c instrument, then rerun it as revised before moving to the grading process. For example, the first analysis will allow the instructor to eliminate items that discriminated *in reverse*. Items missed by, say, two-thirds of the class might be examined to see if the instructor made a mistake on the key or, perhaps, simply wrote a bad item. Perhaps two options turn out to be plausible answers. Then the item might be discarded or both options allowed. Then the key is revised and the examination rerun as the basis for grading. (If the item was not ambiguous, and the key correct, the high failure rate for the item may indicate a lack of student effort or ability, or poor instruction.) Professor Ross Purdy (Corpus Christi State University) notes that this test analysis procedure has several advantages:

1. Time is saved. (The whole process takes less than an hour.)

2. Better tests are created. (By eliminating poor items, each test is improved.)

3. Student complaints are reduced. (Hard data related to item ambiguity are available.)

4. A test file of reliable questions can be compiled.

Another way of protecting oneself from the inevitable shortcomings in writing m-c exams is suggested by Professor David Heise (University of North Carolina) who writes: "I routinely put the instructions below on the face sheet of an objective exam, and I typically drop one or two items from scoring on this basis. Deleted items tend to be either extraordinarily difficult or ambiguous."

> You can vote to have up to five items removed from this exam.
> So if you think an item is ambiguous, write the question numbers (left) and hand in this face sheet along with your answer sheets. If 25% of the class votes against an item, it will not be scored. But answer all items anyway in case they are scored!

The emphasis in the preceding paragraphs has been on the use of m-c examinations for grading. They are probably used more than any other form of testing, in connection with the undifferentiated instruction that leads to grading on a normal curve. We note, again, that this form of examination is not necessarily linked with such uses.

Essay Examinations

Used as a teaching device—as the basis for class discussion or for teacher-student conferences—the student essay can be very effective. It guarantees some prior thinking on the question at issue and some more or less ordered presentation of these thoughts. The essay can be an occasion for a thorough treatment of an issue or problem. The student is invited to integrate diverse materials, make judgments about their pertinence and interdependence, and use several analytic skills.

But used for grading purposes, essay examinations present special problems. Students may not tackle the same problem—or the same aspects of a given problem. Thus there is no common standard for evaluation: a different scale may be applied to each paper. And often the scale, or yardstick, is ill devised to assess the range and depth of students' solutions.

The value of an essay examination depends in part on the clarity, precision, and specification of the question. Questions such as "Discuss (or describe, or tell about) the relationship between X and Y" should be avoided. The words *discuss* and *relationship* convey nothing; the question calls forth no structure and is too broad in scope. Better essay questions result from use of precise nouns and verbs (see table 12.8) and a restricted range of response. Freewheeling essay questions invariably provide students with more than enough rope to hang themselves.

So one way to improve essay examinations is to word the questions carefully. Another is to devise a grading guide for student responses, indicating what matters should be covered, and in what depth, in a perfectly adequate essay (i.e., one that would be graded A). For example, if the essay treats a research problem, one might anticipate this sort of evaluation guide. The student's essay should speak to these questions (and in each case, the instructor will have written a model response):

1. What is the sociological problem? (in contrast to a social problem that might be related to the issue under scrutiny)

2. What is the population studied?

    a. Is it a sample? If so, how was the sampling carried out?

    b. If a sample, to what population can generalizations be extended?

3. What is the independent variable?

    a. What index of the independent variable is to be used?

    b. Is the index a valid indicator of the independent variable?

4. What is the dependent variable? (4a and 4b as above)

5. What are the control variables?

6. What is the hypothesis embodying these variables? Is the student sensitive to the need to make explicit an hypothesis as a target for testing? a statement asserting a determinate relationship between operationally defined variables under specified conditions?

7. What theory establishes a plausible connection among these variables, leading to the specification of the hypothesis to be tested?

8. What were the sources of the data?

9. How were the data analyzed? Were the methods of analysis appropriate to the problem at hand?

10. What were the findings? How do they alter the theory from which the hypothesis was deduced?

11. What are the social implications of the findings? What do they imply for the mundane operations of a community? for our society?

We wrote in chapter 2 about the peculiar standardlessness of teaching in contrast to research. The illustration just offered points to the way a social scientist would anticipate the findings of a carefully contrived inquiry. In research one would have answers to all the questions we have raised here—tentative answers, of course. (And the strength of the researcher's convictions would depend on antecedent research and the power of the theoretical position he or she takes.) Yet we suspect it is common for an instructor to tackle a set of essays without having analyzed, in careful detail, the process of asking and answering. This, then, is another instance in which double standards betray the instructor, the sociologist, and the discipline.

The instructional value of essay examinations can be increased by careful use of marginal comments on the returned paper. We do not refer to comments such as "huh?" "how come?" "good," "awkward," or "use readings." Rather, we refer to teacher statements or questions that raise issues clearly, reveal faulty connections, show how a conclusion could have been extended, convey praise specifically, or indicate *how* an assigned article would have corrected or enriched a point. (A way to do this for larger classes is described in note one to this chapter.) One study has shown that marginal comments on an essay exam can enhance student creativity on subsequent tests (McKeachie, 1978: 241–242, see also p. 156).

We have offered some observations on just two types of tests. They are among those most commonly used (Milton, 1978:106). But many other means of evaluating student achievement are available: written tests (true-false, sentence completion, and matching questions), other written productions (book reviews and comparative book reviews, student journals, laboratory exercises, and term papers), and oral evaluations (oral exams and class participation). Much of what we said about m-c and essay examinations applies to these other means of evaluation. But some of them have special characteristics. For example, oral evaluations, conducted in the teacher's office, reduce ambiguity of measurement through the opportunity afforded for clarification.

But the possible range of test instruments goes far beyond these conventional types. This is especially the case when tests are used for teaching. Consider these examples.

1. The campus newspaper makes a causal assertion. Students are asked to write out the central propositions of a theory that would make that assertion plausible. And to counter that with a better explanation of the conduct in question. They are to work, first, as individuals, then in work groups of three or four to revise and polish, then to report and assess in a committee of the whole.

2. Students are given data on family incomes—data drawn from themselves, their state, and the nation. They are then asked: (a) to account for differences in the distributions, and (b) to determine whether these distributions accord with American values.

3. After studying Weber on bureaucracy and having interviewed university personnel at each level of the college or university, students are asked to identify rules and procedures that hinder (and help) in the educational process.

These three examples, then, are a caveat to underline the obvious: we have not exhausted the means by which evaluation, especially for teaching purposes, can be made a useful part of instruction in sociology. Now, finally, we turn to an extremely important issue.

What Do Testing and Grading Mean for the Teacher–Student Relationship?

Much is made to hang on the compressed evaluative symbol that is a grade. Hence grading often generates excessive anxiety, which can reduce learning for some students.[8] So, also, a grade may supersede learning as the goal of a course. Beyond this, the instructor may be seen as a person who stands in the way of a good grade, as an obstacle to be circumvented.

Which is to say that grading may corrupt the ends and means of education, while compromising the relationship between teacher and student (see Becker, Geer, and Hughes, 1968). So we need to find a mode of evaluation that threatens as little as possible, one that strengthens rather than diminishes the student.

Some Guidelines for the Tester's Role

Finding a mode of evaluation that is nonthreatening and strengthening for the student means a number of things. First, it is desirable to follow through on a test, using it as a means of review, as a diagnostic instrument, and as a tool for filling lacunae and remedying deficiencies. This implies a slower pace. Our impression— perhaps a matter of projection—is that we teach introductory courses in a superficial sweep, sacrificing depth and application to what we misconceive as coverage. If we are to raise questions, as we do in examinations, they had better be worthwhile ones. And if they are, in fact, worthwhile, then they merit dwelling on.

Second, we need to stress, throughout a course, the goal and the means of achieving it. The goal is reliable knowledge about the social world, sought by the best methods available. The stress, that is to say, is on seeking, not on absorbing. We seek answers, however tentative. Answers imply questions. Questions are what testing is about.

Third, we need to demonstrate that the teacher's role is that of ally rather than inquisitor—despite the fact that we ask questions! As we have contended before, we need to shift from a dyadic to the triadic relationship shown in figure 13.1, in which both teacher and student focus on the problem at hand. This implies a posture largely instrumental, universalistic,

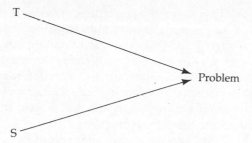

Figure 13.1 Teacher and Student in a Triadic Relationship.

achievement-oriented, and focusing specifically on the complexities of the social order. Whether the professional role is also affectively neutral is perhaps more debatable. Certainly it is not a matter of indifference whether one's student succeeds or fails. But this affectivity is properly a reaction to the way the student deals with the question. It is *not* a reaction to the student. As figure 13.2 schematically reveals, the primary orientation is to *A* (mode of action), not *S*—not the student, but the way the student handles a problem.

But it is all too easy to shift into a personal, particularistic orientation and so undercut the teacher-student relationship. Students themselves promote this. Their question sometimes is not whether a grade is an accurate evaluation but whether it is fair, where fairness is contingent on circumstances peculiar to themselves. When we evaluate a person, it is a moral ques-

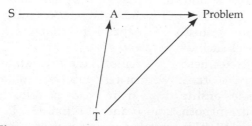

Figure 13.2 The Teacher Reacts to the Student's Actions rather than to the Student.

tion. When we evaluate performance, it is a pedagogical question and an easier one. Here we're on safer ground. We doubt we ever need to do the former, although some would argue that to avoid moral evaluation in the classroom is to dodge the duties of a conscientious teacher. But let us take the sort of case that we must face from time to time.

The Issue of Honesty in Test Performance

Dishonesty in testing takes two principal forms: cheating (who is being cheated is not always transparently clear) and snowing, or pretending. Cheating will occur whenever the ends of education are confused and grade-anxiety is high. One victim is the student. Students who cheat successfully reinforce an unscrupulous, totalitarian morality: the ends justify the means. And they reinforce a misconception of education that sees the end as a good grade. Teachers, too, are victims. For they receive a false message about the efficacy of their own work.

To cheat is an error of commission. To pretend is to cover an omission. In either case, we must not slip into particularistic role performance. We must not shift from an impersonal concern over intellectual performance to a personal concern over moral dereliction. This means that we do not need to impugn a student's honesty. Suppose, for example, the student has taken an essay examination consisting of a critical review of a book. And suppose that the instructor is unsure whether the student has, in fact, read the book. A four-fold table reveals the possibilities, where + means the student has indeed done the work and − means that he or she has not.

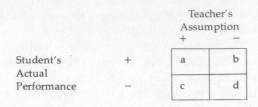

In cells *a* and *d*, there's no problem: teacher's inference and student's behavior agree. In the first case (*a*), expectations have been fulfilled, the assignment carried out. This is not true in cell *d*, but the teacher's assumption is accurate: the job has not been done. It might be argued that failure to do an assigned task merits a flunking grade. But this is so, we suggest, only if the teacher is willing to take on the role of preceptor and to make clear that it is conscientiousness, not quality of performance, that is being graded. So far as the intellectual quality of the task is concerned, failure to read the book simply means that the teacher must withhold a grade for lack of evidence.

However, if the situation is the one described in cell *b*—that is, the teacher assumes the book has not been read, when in fact it has—the outcomes are disastrous. First, the teacher does the student a grave personal injustice. Furthermore, by fixing on a moral failure, the teacher is deflected from a primary concern with an intellectual failure and the reasons for it. Finally, the instructor will most certainly lose the student who, understandably enough, will convert the T-S relationship into an adversary relationship and read himself out of the course.

Thus, in cells *a*, *b*, and *d*, we have situations that can best be handled without recourse to moral, personal, and particularistic judgments. Cell *c* is a tougher problem—that of pretense, or "the snow job." If the student hasn't read the book but the teacher assumes he or she has, the instructor is snowed. The best way to

guard against such an erroneous judgment and to protect the student's learning is to do what good teaching would dictate (and what we do too seldom): follow through on such an examination with a conference. It is unlikely that most students can sustain such a snow job in oral exchange with a knowledgeable instructor.

But there is no impregnable defense against the situation represented in cell *c*. Confused purpose and poor background on the part of the student; defensive or punitive or uncertain teaching strategies on the instructor's side—these can readily lead to technically efficient and educationally useless means of getting a good grade. This is the innovative solution suggested by Merton (1957) in his renowned essay on "Social Structure and Anomie," a solution to the gap between culturally specified goals and institutionally unavailable means: there is no satisfactory solution except competent teaching. And this involves continual reinforcement of the learning goal and staying close enough to the student to provide necessary means for that learning.

Resources: Statements and Studies on Assessing Student Achievement

This chapter falls far short of treating the technicalities or resolving the issues that surround testing and grading. But there are useful resources ready at hand for the professor of sociology who takes teaching seriously. Two excellent chapters in McKeachie's *Teaching Tips* (1978:151–173) discuss test construction, administration, and scoring; when to test; teacher-student roles and testing; grade changes; and returning tests and papers. Milton and Edgerly (1977) review conventional practices in measurement and evaluation of learning. (They also touch on a number of important social and legal issues affecting teachers.) Two other short treatments of testing and grading are found in Ericksen (1974: chapter 12) and Milton (1978: chapter 4). Scholl and Inglis (1977) include eight papers on testing and grading, discussions of essay tests, contract grading, test design, grading versus evaluation, criterion-referenced testing, and statistics for testing. Payne (1974) is an example of the many useful educational measurement texts.

Testing and grading in sociology have been discussed in more than a dozen published articles cited in Davis, Goldsmid, and Perry (1977:70–72) and in review articles appearing in each April issue of *Teaching Sociology*. For example, Stasz (1976) discusses a contract grading system. Hedley (1978) shows how what we know about error measurement in social research can be used to improve grading practices. Michaels (1976) argues that grading on a curve weakens student performance and has other negative effects; and, in another paper, Michaels (1977) examines research relating classroom reward structures to academic performance. Data on the use of term papers and different forms of examinations are found in Bradshaw and McPherron (1977).

These are useful resources. Time in faculty meetings could be (has been?) more poorly invested than in reporting on and reviewing such studies of testing and grading.

∂⌐

To recount, we have pointed to several purposes of testing. Students' performance bears some relationship to teacher competence: the former may be an index of the latter. Certainly students deserve frequent, accurate communications about their rates of progress. In addition, tests

can teach. And inevitably, the teacher is a social agent serving as a recruiting officer.

As a certifying agent, the teacher confronts a dilemma. For the role of judge (and sometimes prosecutor) is incompatible with that of concerned and able instructor. That is why a shift from dyad to triad may be desirable.

Evaluation, we have seen, is a complex business, and sometimes the symbols used are needlessly confounded. Evaluative symbols are better to the extent that they represent a point on a single dimension.

Evaluation is complex not only because several attributes are at issue (and may confound a grade's meaning), but also because the measurement process is complicated. We must decide what the benchmark of measurement is to be; whether a normal distribution is a reasonable assumption (and how it bears on the style of instruction); whether a skewed distribution of grades is an index of soft-headedness; and what sorts of measuring instruments to use—and why.

Finally, we have stressed the close connection between testing and the nature of the teacher-student relationship. The hazards of this connection are reduced to the extent that: we stress reflective inquiry rather than a furious, fact-regurgitating coverage of material; we use outside examiners; we fix on each student's problem-solving performance rather than on his or her person; we apply universalistic criteria and eschew personal moral judgments.

This is but a beginning, not a final definitive statement about the problems of assessing student performance. (We urge the reader to tap the resources just mentioned.) But it does highlight some crucial issues and offers, as targets for discussion and revision, a few solutions that emerge from some decades of teaching and the lore in the field taught.

Student performance alone is not at issue. For us, current and prospective professors, the evaluation of our own performance is critical. This is the matter to which we turn, after a final look, in the appendix to this chapter, at TIPS as a system of testing for teaching.

Chapter 13 Appendix

TIPS: A Response System

TIPS, an acronym for Teaching Information Processing System, is "designed to give an instructor the capacity, on a regular and continuing basis, to monitor both individual and class performance, to diagnose individual students' strengths and weaknesses, and to provide individualized assignments and suggestions for students with different demonstrated performance patterns" (Bassis and Allen, 1977:142). By using the computer, TIPS can provide such evaluative responses to students and the teacher within hours after students take a diagnostic quiz. The system is inexpensive and does not require extra staffing. TIPS was designed by Allen C. Kelley, an economics professor, for use in large lecture courses, but the system can be used in classes of any size, taught by any method.

Students in a TIPS course are provided with study guides that highlight the information and skills central to each unit of the course. Six to ten times during a term, students take a "survey," a ten-minute diagnostic quiz designed to assess student achievement of the content in one or more sections of the study guide. Each student receives a computer printout containing his or her score on the survey, correct answers for all items, an indication of

general strengths and weaknesses (as revealed by the pattern of responses), and prescribed learning activities based on performance on the survey. These learning activities may include suggestions that the student reread specific pages in the text; that the student get in touch with the instructor, a teaching assistant, or join a special discussion group; that the student tackle additional questions provided in the printout. The learning activities are recommendations to the student; TIPS is not part of the grading process.

At the same time students receive their progress reports, the instructor receives computer-generated summaries of class achievement as well as copies of the individual progress reports. Thus, the teacher gains information that can be used in developing class activities and in modifying course plans and procedures. TIPS can store students' survey results and print out a composite score with prescriptions. This cumulative feature can be very valuable both to student and instructor.

TIPS is implemented through use of a computer program that Bassis and Allen (1976:187) describe as developed in four steps. First, the course is divided into units that typically correspond to a one- or two-week period. Then the questions for the student surveys are prepared, each survey corresponding to one or more units. Third, decision rules are formulated based on possible student response patterns on the surveys, and the assignments or learning prescriptions created. Fourth, by means of a "simple, cookbook-style program," the material described above is programmed. Bassis and Allen estimate that up to a month's time is necessary for the instructor to prepare a TIPS system for a course. During the semester, the time required to use TIPS is minimal.

For very large classes, rapid, detailed,

and individualized feedback is made possible through use of the batch-processing computer. But as McKeachie (1978:118) notes, the computer is not essential to the system. (It should be stressed, however, that a very modest computer facility can handle TIPS.)[9]

Bassis and Allen (1977) report a controlled experiment on learning differentials between two Introductory Sociology classes, one of which used TIPS. Their findings confirmed those of TIPS developer Allen C. Kelley (1968): the system works. Student exam scores in classes using TIPS run about 9 to 15 percent higher than in control classes taking the same exam (and having the same readings, lectures, assignments, etc.). Further discussion of research on TIPS appears in chapter 12.

Major Issues about TIPS

TIPS can be used as part of any course. According to Bassis and Allen (1976:187), "the instructor is free to use almost any teaching style or pedagogical technique he deems appropriate. In fact, TIPS in no way dictates or interferes with course design. . . ." TIPS was developed for use in large lecture courses but can be used in connection with PSI-based courses, discussion-based courses, or off-campus correspondence or television courses.

TIPS can be used for parts of any course. Some teachers believe that they cannot design short-answer questions for some of their instructional goals and objectives. In this instance, TIPS can be used for those goals that can be assessed by limited-choice items. This partial use of TIPS may alleviate a problem that goes with more extensive use. As teachers change their instructional goals, text-books, or examples, the content- or skill-specific TIPS program must be revised (at least in part).[10] While not all changes will be very time-consuming, the teacher who wants to reuse a program over a given period of time might select for TIPS those portions of the course that remain relatively unchanged. Thus, a teacher of Introductory Sociology might design a TIPS program covering an introduction to research methods, elementary statistical concepts and techniques, basic sociological concepts, or basic social facts about the United States. A TIPS program covering such a content or skill area might be prepared by a pair of teachers who alternate teaching a given course. Partial uses of TIPS may not produce the same learning benefits as the fuller version, which provides repeated feedback with cumulation of information and prescriptions.

TIPS rests on three assumptions that must be realized if the system is to work.[11] TIPS assumes that objectives can be specified, translated into test items, and that test ("survey") results can serve as a valid basis for diagnosing student difficulties. Second, TIPS assumes that the teacher can create useful learning prescriptions for students with different types of difficulties. Presumably, the use of the prescriptions can be improved if information on the individual student's background and learning style is built into the system. Cross (1976:73) uses the analogy of the physician who determines a course of treatment based not only on the patient's symptoms, but also on his or her other characteristics—height, weight, general health, etc. Thus, the more the teacher knows about a student, the more help TIPS (and any response system) can be. Third, TIPS assumes that instructors—as well as individual students—will use the information provided. Experimental evidence suggests that students do make good use of the TIPS guides, surveys, and prescriptions.

Practice, with response, is important to learning: TIPS provides one way of achieving it. In chapter 12, we saw that research on learning supports the desirability of giving students practice in using information and skills and of giving them prompt evaluative response on their progress. TIPS works toward these ends.

Resources: The Literature on TIPS

The first use of TIPS in sociology was in 1975–1976 at the University of Rhode Island (in an introductory course with more than 300 students). This application was reported in two articles in *Teaching Sociology* by Bassis and Allen (1976, 1977). The first article presents a brief overview of TIPS and a summary of findings from research on his economics classes by TIPS developer Allen C. Kelley (1968). The second article further discusses the rationale and procedures for TIPS, reports the authors' own study of TIPS' effectiveness, and reprints a study guide, diagnostic survey, and three progress reports from one unit of their TIPS course.

Other descriptive and evaluative reports on applications of TIPS are: in economics, Kelley (1970, 1972), Hansen, Kelley, and Weisbrod (1970), and Henry and Ramsett (1978); and in chemistry, *Change* (1976). Additional information and materials on TIPS are available from the Education Systems Project, P. O. Box 4747, Duke Station, Duke University, Durham, North Carolina 27706.

TIPS and other systems of computer-managed instruction (CMI) are briefly discussed in Cross (1976:70–74). Brudner (1968) explores the range of possible applications of CMI in education.

Notes

1. In some classes, when we return examinations, we distribute a handout that: (a) provides correct answers for multiple-choice or other short answer items, (b) reprints, namelessly and with our comments, student responses to some essay items, (c) reproduces other student responses without comment—for use in post-exam class discussion, and (d) reminds students about particular readings or lectures they can review to clarify a point or remove a misperception.

2. Perhaps our statement is too strong. There are doubtless occasions when the unique constellation of social experiences that make a person become useful and relevant in building that person's education. Durkheim (1922:51) allowed for uniquely individual aspects of education, simply saying that these were not the primary objective. "Education does not restrict itself to developing the individual in accordance with his genetic nature, teasing out those hidden capacities that lie there, dormant, asking only to be revealed. It creates a new being." Nonetheless, educational criteria of achievement are universalistic, transcending personal idiosyncracies. Which is to say, standards are social, and the teacher is the guardian of those standards. Whether the standards are appropriate, good, or desirable is another issue.

3. Since 1968, more than a dozen studies have explored "expectancy effects." While some have confirmed the Rosenthal and Jacobson findings, few have found consistent, significant differences. It is clear that grade level and many student attributes (including race and socioeconomic status) affect teacher expectations and their consequences. It seems clear, however, that teacher expectations do, under some circumstances, influence patterns of teacher-student interaction and teacher evaluations of student work. Specialists conclude that more research is needed to tease out relation-

ships and the conditions under which they hold. For citation of the pertinent literature, see Boocock (1978:7–9; 1972:113) and Dunkin and Biddle (1974:128–130).

4. Not that this scheme is without hazards. One is a deflection of the teaching process so that the allies are preoccupied with getting correct answers rather than the importance of the questions, with hot pursuit rather than fruitful exploratory dalliance, with product rather than process. But it's worth asking: Is this bad? Or, if to a degree undesirable, is it necessary?

5. On the advantages and disadvantages, the uses and misuses of grading on a curve, grading by percent mastery, and blanket grading (all students receiving the same grade), see Michaels (1976). Readers of Michaels's article should note the apparent error in the second sentence of the abstract. Compare the first clause of that sentence to the discussions on page 200 and page 203 of the article.

6. Some of the permutations describing a course can be represented by the crosscutting of two dimensions: softness of assessment and importance of content. Thus:

	Effort with which a Good Grade is Gotten	
Triviality of Material	*Very Little*	*A Great Deal*
Mickey Mouse	easy	hard
	trivial	trivial
Non-Mickey Mouse	easy	hard
	significant	significant

7. A friend and very able sociologist moved to a distinguished West Coast university. Shortly after his first semester of teaching there, he wrote that, to his surprise, his distribution of grades in a very large course was almost exactly the same as that in the course he had previously taught in the East. His surprise was a symptom of his ingenuousness. An elitist posture in pedagogy provides for the like-minded, right-thinking few. Failing to take account of different categories of students, much less individual variance, he could not help but have generated a normal distribution—and that for the reasons we have noted in this section.

8. One way to reduce anxiety is to allow students to write comments on their tests, especially m-c tests, explaining their answers. For discussion of anxiety and testing, see McKeachie (1978:249–251) and Rosenfeld (1978).

9. Teachers might substitute for the computer, the use of a simple paper-and-pencil survey (quiz) that could be scored with the same type of "mask" many instructors use to grade multiple-choice tests. The student reports could consist of a form response sheet providing correct answers, on which the teacher checks off those survey items the student missed and adds observations and learning prescriptions (suggested assignments) pertinent to each student's pattern of response. However, by using the computer, the teacher ensures that students get more detailed reports and that, for large classes, turn-around time will be quicker.

10. This is, of course, true for non-TIPS courses as well. Whenever teachers revise or update a course it is necessary to similarly modify the materials used for that course (including the syllabus, assignments, handouts, and exams). If TIPS is used, there is more material to update. We are indebted to Professor Michael S. Bassis for reminding us of the generic nature of the need for revision.

11. These three assumptions and many of the points in this paragraph are from Cross (1976:72–74), who discusses computer-managed instruction (CMI) generally and not just TIPS.

CHAPTER 14
EVALUATING INSTRUCTOR ACHIEVEMENT

There are at least four reasons for systematic appraisals of instructor performance: instructors need them, students need them, administrators need them, and life itself requires them. Student evaluation of teaching merits special attention both because it is widely used in sociology departments and because it is the means of assessing instructor and course effectiveness most thoroughly investigated. Here we return to a theme developed earlier in chapter 3: ultimately, teacher effectiveness is indexed by student achievement. This relationship is neither straightforward nor easy to assess, yet teachers can get some measure of course-generated student changes. This chapter discusses only the evaluation role and means of improving it that involve evaluation. Scholarship, service, and student advising,[1] as well as important faculty activities, receive only passing consideration.

Why Evaluate Instructors?

The Ubiquity and Persistence of Evaluation

"Thank God I no longer have to face examinations." So spoke a colleague after a trying session at which we were reviewing the work of graduate students on written Ph.D. examinations. This remark reveals a narrow and misleading view of examinations. Our colleague is not free of tests. She never will be. She faces an exam-

ination whenever she submits a paper to a professional journal. If her article is rejected, it may be accompanied by comments from referees more acerbic than anything she has ever written on student papers. In faculty and committee meetings, her contributions will be heard and weighed, yielding assessments that will come into play whenever rewards and responsibilities are to be assigned. Her students will evaluate her in every class. She will be judged when considered for promotion and tenure, and when she applies for a sabbatical, fellowship, released time, research support, or a new position. Always and everywhere, people's deeds, misdeeds, and undeeds are recorded and assessed—to various ends and by a vast variety of means, many of them, one suspects, quite inadequate.

But to assert that a pattern of behavior obtains is not to explain its being. One explanation is that people inevitably differ—in interests, in background, in training. So, likewise, organizations differ. It follows that the degree of compatibility between individual and organizational traits must differ. Testing of some sort is the device by which we determine, for ourselves and others, the degree of fit, so minimizing unproductive mismatches. Whether this is done formally or informally, accurately or otherwise is not the issue here. We simply note that the ubiquity and persistence of evaluation is rooted in the social and psychic nature of things.

Beyond this root source of assessment, there are three other reasons for the pattern of evaluation in academic life. First, we owe students the experience of evaluating. A second reason: department heads, other administrators, and some faculty, especially the younger, increasingly want evidence of competence in teaching sociology to enter into decisions on promotion and tenure. Finally, and above all, instructors owe it to themselves.

Students Need to Become Proficient in Evaluating

How so? In the last chapter we contended that students should take, as a right, the thoughtful appraisal of their work by their instructors. Here we assert that the instructor should give students the chance for a reflective assessment of the experiences to which we have subjected them. On what grounds?

Certainly, a liberal education means an extended knowledge of the world—physical, organic, and social. But as a concomitant of this extended range of knowing, we learn that not all objects are equally useful in the service of all ends. Among stones, not all will serve equally well as the stylus in one's hi-fi pickup. In the organic realm, not all points in the food chain will serve equally well in providing both nutrition and the conservation of resources. In the social realm, not all modes of defining women's roles—or those of blacks, or Catholics or Jews—will best use human resources or be compatible with the ideals of our tradition. With a greater range of knowing comes a greater range of choice. Choice implies evaluation. The experience of discriminating between the better and the worse is a critical element of a liberal arts education because it is the inevitable corollary of extended cognition. (We might well have cited such enhanced

skill in moral reasoning as a major non-substantive goal in sociology instruction in chapters 5 and 6.) The capacity for reasoned discrimination between the better and the worse can best be developed in those situations that immediately engage students, such as the courses contrived for and required of them. Thus, one pertinent means for working toward a nonsubstantive goal—enhanced acuity in the reasoning that supports a moral choice—lies in the chance to make a careful assessment of the instructor's work.

This implies, we should note, that the experience of evaluating should itself be evaluated. We need to ask what evaluative skills, what criteria for effective evaluation, we are developing—skills and criteria that transcend the immediate situation, that will serve in the future, elsewhere, throughout the student's life. And our instruments of assessment must be examined as well. Do they touch the critical components of that composition we call a course? Are the more important elements more heavily weighted? Do they enable the student to discover generic dimensions for assessing any work situation: clarity of role definitions? specification of goals and the congruence of student-teacher, worker-employer goals? suitability of means to ends? sufficient resources to do the job? whether efficiency was enhanced by occasional, sanctioned regression to less demanding roles? (See Cottrell, 1942.) Was the product adequate? How much did students learn: information? skills? the logic of inquiry? a new perspective that enables them to see social reality as a social construction? a sharpened tendency to ask about the unintended consequences of an observed pattern of behavior (such as pink for girl babies, blue for boys)? Or, in later years, in military service or employment with GM, the effect of bureaucratic edicts in prompting patterned circumvention? If, as we contend, evaluation is a needed, generic skill, then appraisal of the course experience is one obvious means to that end.

Quality Control: Effective Teaching as a Condition of Promotion

Quality control has unlovely associations with time-motion studies and the effort to exact work, in unconscionable volume, from defenseless laborers. There is, indeed, an aura of toughness about the term; and we think that appropriate. We believe that the standards for assessing performance in teaching should be as rigorous as those by which we appraise research. Of course, this requires definitions and indicators of effective teaching, and opportunities and encouragement for the development of effectiveness. These can and should be provided. And once provided, we believe that the response to ineffective teaching should be dismissal or redefinition of role in such a way as to protect the student, the discipline, the department, and the school.[2]

As we suggested in chapter 2, this is simply an application of a standard that we employ in research; we must guard against the harming of human subjects. The extent of harm is to be assessed not so much by acts of commission. This is a lesser problem; no sociologists we know are commonly malign in deed or intent. Instead, the question is one of omission, ineffectual performance due to ignorance, oversight, or incapacity.[3] We ask the question, what *might* these students have learned had the instruction been all that it could be? This is a question that must be answered by a good sociologist and a knowledgeable teacher. Useful as student evaluations may be, they must necessarily speak to acts of commission, not omission.

For students lack the experience that enables the elder to answer the question, What might have been?

These are significant uses and purposes—to help students sharpen their skills in discriminating between the better and the worse, and to provide more reliable evidence than we usually employ to inform critical decisions on promotion and retention. But the last reason is the most important one: we evaluate in order to know what we're doing and to know, in part, who we are. Beyond that, impelled by the Protestant ethic and the disposition to build better mouse traps, we evaluate to pick up cues for bettering our performances.

Quality Control: Instructors' Need to Know What They Are Doing

Underlying reasoned conduct is always this assumption: if we do thus and so, there's a high probability that others will respond in expected ways. This is implicit in Weber's (1903–17:118) conception of human relationships. This assumption is exemplified daily in our own lives; it informs economic and political life, the exchanges we regularly make of goods, money, power, and favors. Lacking such predictable outcomes, our lives would be pointless: we could not institute certain means with the assurance that they would achieve the ends we desire. To cite Weber (1903–17:124–125) again: "The characteristic of 'incalculability' [i.e., unpredictability] . . . is the privilege of—the insane." To arrange a sequence of events by a table of random numbers would be the essence of unreason. Reason, by contrast, allows us to act in ways that elicit a predictable re-act.

But knowledge is partial; predictions are bound to time and place. Because of this—and because some efforts to produce desired outcomes are new (for example, the effort to persuade Americans to conserve energy)—sociologists are often employed by agencies dedicated to changing people's behavior. Somehow lacking or needy or uninformed, these clients are treated in ways thought to change beliefs and behavior. The task of the sociologist is to find out whether, and to what extent, the treatment works. Are the hoped-for goals achieved? What unanticipated outcomes result from the use of inappropriate means?

Yet there are sociologists who seem unaware of the professional standards that guide evaluation research. For there is a great gap between profession and practice. The sociologists of whom we speak often fail to state outcome variables in operational terms. They can, therefore, have only the foggiest idea about the effect of intervention. They may do their work unaware of the contingent or intervening variables that affect outcomes. Usually they have no measures of population attributes at time-1. And they measure outcomes with an instrument not pretested or revised after field trials. Since they typically lack time-1 measures, they cannot assess the effects of intervention. Often they have no assurance that the post-test measures adequately sample the population of traits thought to be changed among the clients. Almost invariably, post-measures are gotten so soon after program impact that these sociologists have no conception of the persistence of change. And equally often, they lack a theory that would guide them in manipulating conditions to alter clients' behavior more effectively.

Who are these sociologists? They are you—and we, and most of us. We are the change-inducing agents representing the sociology department, the discipline, and the academic community. What is the outcome of our intervention? We assume that when we enact the conventional teacher's role, students will respond, as a result, with displays of desired learning. It is sad that this self-deception dominates our professional lives. For it is surely incontestable that, by the standards we would apply to our research, in teaching we simply do not know what we are doing.

How do we know that the outcomes, whatever they may be, are owing to our stimulating intervention? When the plant flourishes, are we taking credit for what sunshine and a fruitful soil have brought about? Is the learning demonstrated on a final exam attributable to peers? to other instructors? to texts? to parents? to a high school teacher? to an employer? or to the impact of television or other media?

What do we know about the achievement of subtle and significant goals such as enhanced ability in critical thinking? What do we know about adverse outcomes: a dulling of interest? a reinforced allergy to quantification? a conviction that, in its cold treatment of aggregated traits, sociology breeds insensitivity to the individual's needs and hopes? We are trained to ferret out unanticipated consequences. Do we know about the vicious outcomes of virtuous intent in teaching? Can we answer the questions, What difference did this course make? or, How different would my students be had they never taken my course? or, What might I have done to enhance my students' learnings?

The answer must be that we do not know. Yet we persistently deceive ourselves by assuming that we do know, that what we do has effects, and that those effects are good. We need evaluation, then, to learn what we are doing—and what we aren't—and to enhance our effectiveness.

One way of learning what we do (and don't do) is to discover what others contribute to our students' performance. Such a study as that done by Wilson (1966) provides some clues to educational influences that we can disregard only at the peril of falsely inflating our own. Wilson found that, in contrast to the combined effects of maturation, job experiences, and the impact of informal relationships with faculty and fellow students (as well as many other influences), the impact of courses was seen as quite modest. Although we don't know the validity of these findings, it seems a sensible inference that learning deemed important by students comes from many sources. Sociology instructors especially need to be aware of events and persons that can strengthen their hand in promoting learning.

That we need to know better what we are doing is further suggested by studies that ask, How is learning affected when we vary teacher-student contact? or, Is the conventional performance of the instructor indispensable for student achievement? Studies reviewed in chapter 12 reveal no difference in student learning of factual material in lecture as compared to discussion courses, and but small (though definite) differences in learning of higher cognitive skills in the two class formats. Some studies (e.g., Churchill, 1957, cited in Wilson, 1966:84–85), report that reducing teacher-student contact by as much as 60 to 80 percent results in virtually no difference in student learning.[4]

Such findings should induce a salutary humility. They suggest that we may be accomplishing less than we think. But overall, the research cited in chapter 12 tells us that teachers can (and sometimes do) make a difference. This occurs when we do not equate teaching with telling, when we specify types of learning goals and select instructional strategies likely to maximize the desired goals, and when we take full advantage of whatever instructional strategy we use. We also need to re-

member that the indirect instruction a teacher contrives can be so effective as to mask direct teacher influences. Thus, as we pointed out in chapter 12, Dubin and Taveggia (1968:47) note that the no-difference finding of many comparative studies of teaching methods may result from the powerful impact of the textbooks used. It may be, too, that many findings of no-difference result from the method used to measure gains in learning. Using the students themselves as benchmarks for grading one another in large heterogeneous classes, will yield a normal curve for grades no matter how much the whole class has moved up—or down—the ladder. (This is true, except for those cases in which the instructional method can take account of differences in student learning style and pace.) And using grading norms (fixed proportions of As, Bs, and so on) will ensure that student learning, as indexed by grades, will appear unaffected by teacher acts. Thus, since student learning is one indicator of instructor achievement, we need to know more than we do about that learning and the conditions that affect it.

For various purposes, students, teachers, departments, and schools need to assess the effectiveness of instruction. As it is, we know too little and assume too much about our effectiveness as teachers. Of course, college teaching is evaluated, and we should ask two questions: How is it done: and, How might it be better done?

How Do—or Might—We Evaluate Instructors?

Evidence on Current Practice

Modes of teacher evaluation vary in type and extent of use. Table 14.1 provides information on evaluation for samples of all colleges and universities in 1966 (column 1), for liberal arts colleges in 1966 and 1973 (columns 2 and 3), and for sociology departments in liberal arts colleges in 1975 (column 4; see note b).

The list of modes of evaluation in table 14.1 does not exhaust the range of possibilities. Yet, even when given a chance to do so (in the Ewens and Emling survey in sociology), only between three and six percent of departments in different types of schools reported use of "other methods of evaluation."

At least two things are worth noting. First, the commonest forms of evaluation are those done secondhand or requiring

Table 14.1 Frequency of Use of Various Sources of Information in the Evaluation of Teaching Effectiveness[a]

| | "Used in All or Most Departments in" | "Always Used in" | | "Routinely Used in Sociology Departments in" |
| | All Colleges and Universities | Liberal Arts Colleges | | Liberal Arts Colleges[c] |
	1966 (1)	1966 (2)	1973 (3)	1975 (4)
Chairman evaluation	85%	82%[b]	85%	88%
Dean evaluation	82	84[b]	85	69
Colleagues' opinions	49	51	40	82
Scholarly research and publication	44	37	20	66
Informal student opinion	41	47	18	72
Grade distributions	28	36	2	21
Course syllabi and examinations	26	29	11	47
Committee evaluation	25	29	42	51
Student examination performance	20	25	4	20
Self-evaluation or report	16	15[b]	20	48
Classroom visits	14	10	5	28
Systematic student ratings	12	11	29	87[d]
Enrollment in elective courses	11	14	3	33
Long-term follow-up of students	10	10	2	19
Alumni opinions	10	11	2	19

Notes:

(a) Data reported in column (1) are from academic deans at 1,110 colleges and universities (of all sizes and types); column (2) from academic deans at 484 liberal arts colleges; column (3) from academic deans at 410 liberal arts colleges. In all cases, the unit of analysis is the school. In column (4), data reported are from 111 departments of sociology in four-year colleges; chairpersons usually filled out the questionnaire.

(b) With the *exception* of these items, all 1966–1973 differences for the two liberal arts college samples are significant beyond the .01 level (using a t test); as reported in Seldin (1975:50–51).

(c) Ewens and Emling (1977) also provide data on university and community college departments. University and liberal arts college rankings were similar (rho = .91). Evaluation by deans, course syllabi and exams, and student examination performance, however, were used far less (15 percentage points or more difference) in universities than in liberal arts schools. Two-year departments differed markedly from those in universities (rho = .48). They were more like liberal arts schools (rho = .68). Evaluation procedures used far less in two-year schools were chairpersons, colleague, and committee evaluation, informal student opinion, and enrollment data; class visits were used to a far greater degree in two-year schools. The rank order correlation coefficients were calculated by Goldsmid and Wilson.

(d) Comparable figures for sociology departments in universities and two-year schools were 86 percent and 79 percent. In both cases, systematic student ratings were the top-ranked evaluation method.

Source: For data in columns (1) and (2), Astin and Lee (1967:298, 300); for column (3), Seldin (1975:48); and for column (4), Ewens and Emling (1976: table 12).

large inferential leaps. In each of the three surveys, and for all types of schools, the assessments of chairpersons, deans, colleagues, and their committees, informally gathered student opinion, and scholarly publication top the lists. (The only exception, to be discussed shortly, is the heavy use in sociology departments of systematic student ratings.) Chairs and deans probably rely on others' opinions and on secondhand, unverified evidence. This may apply to colleague opinion as well— note the separate and much lower ranking of classroom visits.

Second, as to the teacher's actual impact on students, "it is unfortunate that those sources of information most likely to yield information about this influence are least likely to be used" (Astin and Lee, 1967:364, speaking of their data reported in columns 1 and 2 of table 14.1). Table 14.1 shows that, in the mid-1970s, systematic student ratings were used very widely (79

to 87 percent) in all types of sociology departments, and that their use in liberal arts colleges increased from 11 to 29 percent between 1966 and 1973. Since student ratings can provide useful information for teacher improvement, this is a gratifying exception to the general reliance on secondhand and indirect measures. And, as we shall see, there are many student rating forms with high inter-item reliability and at least moderately high validity. But not all forms are well analyzed. What can be said of those used in sociology departments? We don't know. But we suspect that many forms have not been developed with the same care that sociologists invest in the instruments they use in real research.

In the 1966 survey, less than 1 percent of the liberal arts colleges report any research on their instruments. For no type of school does the figure exceed 5 percent (see Gustad, 1967:271).

There is other, more direct evidence

Table 14.2 Information Used in Tenure Reviews to Evaluate the Teaching Ability of Sociology Faculty, 1977[a]

	Most Relied On Source	Second Most Relied On Source	Third Most Relied On Source	N
Observing classes in progress	13%	7%	12%	245
Written evaluations by students	44	26	10	245
Personal conferences with individual faculty members	16	16	14	245
Informal input from students	12	22	24	245
Informal input from colleagues	10	20	23	245
"Drop rate" of enrollment in individual courses	1	2	6	245
Grade distribution in individual courses	2	5	13	245
Other[b]	—	—	—	—
No specific evaluation of teaching in tenure decision[c]	—	—	—	—

Notes:

(a) This table reports the responses of 276 sociology chairpersons to this question: "Rank the *three* sources of information you rely on most heavily to evaluate the teaching ability of the faculty in decisions to grant tenure."
A separate survey asked the same question of a sample of 171 faculty members; the rankings and levels of responses were very similar (see Bowker, 1978:53).

(b) Twenty-six chairpersons specified other factors.

(c) Thirteen chairs said there was no specific evaluation of teaching in tenure decisions.

Source: Bowker (1978:33). Reprinted by permission.

suggesting that evaluation of sociologists' teaching effectiveness leaves much to be desired. Evaluation should rest on explicit written criteria, yet in 1975 less than a quarter of all types of sociology departments reported having such criteria. And this is not because they are able to use criteria provided by their schools: only one-third of all sociology departments (with little variation by type) reported that their schools had written criteria (see Ewens and Emling, 1975:table 13). When sociology departments hire a new faculty member or review a current member for tenure, the means by which teaching is evaluated are indirect and probably not very reliable (see tables 14.2 and 14.3).

We suspect that evaluation of teaching performance is increasing, and will continue to do so, perhaps as an extension of what Crozier (1964) called "the bureaucratic phenomenon"—an extension of the rationalization of human relationships from business and industry to the service occupations. Less global factors may also be at work. The rising costs of education,

increasing tax rates, and other trends in the economy of the 1970s have led to increased demands for accountability in education. These demands press persons in certain roles—legislators and administrators, for example—to initiate or imitate means of quality control. The consumers themselves have begun to take legal action in cases where they claim to have suffered incompetent instruction (Semas, 1975).[5] And with constriction of the academic job market, instructors seem to have become more sensitive to the need for reactions that will help them better their performances—if for no other reason than to assemble evidence that level of competence in teaching need not prevent their retention and promotion. Colleges are growing selective in recruiting newly minted Ph.D.s, requiring a dissertation in hand, perhaps a publication on its way, and in some cases, evidence of demonstrated teaching ability (or its promise).[6]

Finally, any increased emphasis on evaluation in sociology may be traced, in part, to a belated concern[7] on the part of

Table 14.3 Evidence on Teaching Ability Used by Sociology Departments in Hiring a New Faculty Member, 1977[a]

	Required	Optional	Not Used	Total (%)	N
Written references	92%	6%	1%	99%	263
Written evaluations by students	7	55	38	100	248
Candidate teaches a class as part of interview procedure:					
undergraduate class	9	16	75	100	236
graduate class	4	9	87	100	227
Candidate presents a lecture to the faculty	34	12	55	101	236
Other[b]	—	—	—	—	—

Notes:

(a) This table reports the response of 276 sociology chairpersons to this question: "What evidence of teaching ability does your department consider when recruiting a new faculty member? Note whether the evidence is required or optional for appointment."

(b) Fifty-five chairpersons specified other factors.

Source: Bowker (1978:32). Reprinted by permission.

the American Sociological Association, manifested in the ASA Projects on Teaching Undergraduate Sociology. Sociologists are properly concerned lest the image of the field conveyed annually to hundreds of thousands of students be a distorted one. The profession clearly has an interest in the public conception of sociology as the disciplined inquiry into the causes and consequences of changing social patterns—especially the views held by our congressional representatives, who are sometimes reduced to apoplectic stutters (and adverse votes) owing to misunderstood research projects. The profession also has a stake in its perception by all who may commission and use (or ignore) sociological research.

Certainly, if adequacy of instruction is to be taken as one criterion in hiring, promotion, and tenure decisions, and if teaching is to be as effective as it can be, we need better data than have been available in the past. And from the student's perspective, scuttlebutt or fraternity and sorority files are certainly less satisfactory than thoughtfully contrived evaluations, especially those that offer bases for comparison. The increased resort to various forms of evaluation is justified not only by our ignorance and our need to know. It is also indicated by what we do know: sociologists are sometimes held in low esteem, even on their own campuses. (For a closely related point, see Komarovsky, 1951.) This condition of low esteem is not necessarily the result of a reputation for poor teaching, although sociology courses are sometimes known as "slide courses."[8] But reputedly poor teaching may be a part of the picture. In chapter 12, we reviewed research by Linsky and Straus (1973) indicating that sociology shares with psychology the lowest student ratings on all but a few of the sixteen campuses for which data were available.

Modes of Evaluating Instruction and Their Use

In table 14.4, we estimate the validity of thirteen modes of evaluating three aspects of instruction: the teacher's command of subject matter, and the means of instruction used and their effects on learning. The list of evaluation modes is not exhaustive and is subject to several qualifications set down in notes to the table. Our estimates of validity are derived from reflection on our experience and observations and are informed by some empirical research cited later in this chapter. The three aspects of instruction have implications for one another. Thus, the means themselves convey content to students. Instructors transmit a message when they do not hear or respond to their students' questions, or when they structure classroom relationships around power based on rank rather than authority based on knowledge (see Ewens, 1976a:307ff).

Table 14.4 suggests that there is no single means of evaluating instruction that meets all needs. This is, indeed, the case. Different aspects of the instructional role require different means of evaluation. Further, evaluation needs to take account of differing teaching styles and practices. One instructor's lecture notes might provide an index of his or her subject matter mastery. But not all teachers use or need the detailed notes that would be required for a reliable assessment. And reliance on notes alone would be less helpful in evaluating mastery of a subject area in which the teacher has only a discussion-based course. Scholarly publications reflect competence, but only for a restricted range of subject matter. Since no one type of evidence is likely to be adequate for all instructors in each of their courses, multiple indicators must be used. And evaluators must be careful not to confuse a form of

Type of Evidence Sought	Source of Evidence	Estimated Validity as an Index of Teaching Effectiveness for:[b]		
		Content of Intervention (Mastery of Subject Matter)	Process of Intervention (Means of Teaching)	Effects of Intervention (Student Learning)
(1) Competence in field; scholarship	Publications and other noncourse written material	F/G		
(2) Course materials	Syllabi, exams, handouts, etc.	L/F	G	
Observations:				
(3) Classroom visits	Written reports by peers	L/F	G	
(4) Classroom visits	Written reports by teaching specialists		G/E	L
(5) Videotapes of class session(s)	Tapes and written analysis[c]	F	E	
(6) Audiotapes of class session(s)	Tapes and written analysis[c]	L/F	G	
Subjective Estimates:				
(7) From students	Informal reports		U/L	
(8) From students	Formal, systematic reports	L	G/E	F/L
(9) From alumni	Formal, systematic reports	L	G	L/F
(10) From instructor	Written self-evaluation	U	F/L	L/F
(11) From colleagues	Written reports	U	L	L
Objective Estimates:				
(12) Student performance	Class grade distributions		L	L
(13) Student performance	Individual performance on exams, taking T_2-T_1 differences into account	U	U	F to E[d]

Notes:

(a) Omitted from this table are evaluations made by deans, chairpersons, and committees. Such evaluations are typically based on the sources of evidence reviewed in the table. Of course, chairpersons are colleagues and can do classroom observation, review systematic student ratings, etc. We also omit use of course enrollment data, since this evidence seems open to widely varying interpretations (and is affected by numerous, rapidly changing variables).

(b) Key: U = Uncertain; L = Low; F = Fair; G = Good; and E = Excellent. A blank space indicates our belief that it is inappropriate to use this mode of evaluation for the purpose indicated.

Most modes of evaluation provide only partial evidence on the area being evaluated. Note, too, that the validity of each mode of evaluation is assessed independently. The validity of each measure typically depends on: (1) matters of sampling (e.g., the number and distribution of classroom visits), (2) the evaluator's knowledge of the subject area and/or teaching and learning dynamics, (3) the criteria with which data are examined, and (4) the care with which the data are used.

(c) See note b2 above.

(d) This range reflects the adequacy of controls used in analyzing the data.

evidence with what they think it measures. Competence in one's field may be indexed by publications. But, in the assessment of teaching, the absence of publications means the absence of a source of evidence, not necessarily of competence. Other indicators may be available (e.g., unpublished work) or can be contrived (e.g., interviews with the faculty member under review by external evaluators whose competence in a field is accepted).

Effective evaluation starts with and requires specification of what is to be evaluated. Once such specifications are in writing, teachers can offer their evaluators (peers, chairpersons, deans, instructional development specialists, *and* themselves) the most valid sources of evidence bearing on their individual practices.

Information from one or all of the sources listed in table 14.4 will not be sufficient for evaluation, for teaching is affected by factors over which a teacher may have but marginal control—class size, course load, and initial student interest, to name but three. These factors need to be considered in evaluation. So must the knowledge and skills being taught.

Evaluating the instructor's goals and command of subject matter. Some things are easier to teach and learn than others. And some knowledge and skills are worth more than others (for given purposes). It is usually appropriate that teaching improvement efforts take teachers' instructional goals as given: the emphasis here is on the development of teaching skills. But when teachers examine their own work, and when that work is assessed by a department, judgments need be made about goals.

Periodically, instructors should examine their goals and ask such questions as these: Am I helping my students learn the best that my field has to offer persons at their educational level? Am I remembering that few of my undergraduate students will take another course in sociology? Am I helping my students develop skills and exposing them to resources that will be useful in their postcollege life?

Departments have to inquire about what is being taught because corporate stakes are involved (a teacher's work affects that of his or her colleagues, present and future) and because departments have responsibilities to ensure quality and protect human subjects (students). The responsible exercise of such evaluation requires that departments specify expectations of its teachers: the retroactive imposition of criteria (especially vague ones) must be avoided. And, of course, departments must be wary of fostering uniformity that would ill-serve the teachers, the students, and the departments themselves. The generation, by departments, of minimum or core learnings (or goals) for given courses—especially those that are entry-level prerequisities or required of majors—seems an appropriate solution. Finally, deans (and faculty educational policy committees) need to remind departments that their undergraduate courses must serve the liberal arts.

Obviously, subject matter competence—command of one's field—is part of instruction. But what is meant by those terms? Is command synonymous with knowledge of the established and current work in a particular field? Or are developments in related fields to be considered? Is it important that each teacher reach his or her own synthesis of the field? and that this be reflected in a course? Is command to be equated with contributions to the discipline of newly discovered knowledge? Professor Norman F. MacLean (1974:12) says that *a teacher must have a wider range of discovery than this. A teacher must forever be making discoveries to himself. . . . And then he must have . . . the power to lead students to the power of self-discovery . . . and must have . . . command of the best that is known among his colleagues.*

Whoever evaluates teaching must specify what is meant by *command over subject matter;* otherwise, the means used to assess command will define poorly what is being looked for.

Many students set much store by the apparent command of field revealed by the teacher. Several studies reporting student evaluations of teaching (including one in sociology: Wimberly, 1978:especially 12, 18) find teacher command important in student assessment of teaching.[9]

Willy-nilly, the sociologist represents a department and a discipline. Each presents himself or herself as a sociologist—as a person with a particular perspective, knowledgeable where others are not. The presentation of self is constrained by this identity. How can one judge the propriety of this claim to be a sociologist, a scholar (i.e., a learned person)?

One obvious source of evidence is a teacher's writing, whether or not published. In such an assessment, published work has this advantage: it tells us that certain peers, those best equipped to judge, have found his or her scholarship good. Over past years, various efforts to assess departments of sociology offer clues to more systematic appraisal of a sociologist's scholarship. See, for example, Knudsen and Vaughan (1969), Glenn and Villemez (1970), and Sturgis and Clemente (1973). Unpublished writing merits the same careful appraisal as writing that has appeared in print. Which is to say, in sum, that we must profess *something,* must have command over that which we profess and,

one would hope, could profess our special lore with clarity and grace. The extent of our ability to do so is seen in our writing.

But the range of one's writing seldom matches the range of one's teaching. And the absence of publications cannot, in any event, be equated with lack of command. Further, there is no evidence that a track record of publication (or citation to one's published works) is correlated with effective teaching (typically indexed by student ratings); see, for example, Harry and Goldner (1972) and Linsky and Straus (1975).[10] Were publications a reliable indicator of teaching effectiveness they would still have limited utility, since many academics publish very little during their professional careers.[11]

Command of subject matter, then, must be carefully specified and measured by multiple indicators. Publications, unpublished papers, lecture notes, syllabi and other course materials, and interviews with an external examiner can all provide information on command over subject matter.

Finally, command over subject matter, like other aspects of instruction, must be assessed with the instructor's situation taken into account. While the point will be painfully obvious to some, sociology instructors are often expected to teach in subfields in which they have little background. This is especially the case in smaller schools where during a two-year cycle, an instructor may teach eight or ten quite different courses. Such a pattern has its benefits, but one cannot ignore its costs to the teacher, students, institution, and discipline, and its implications for assessing teacher command of subject matter.

Evaluating the instructor by changes in student performance. The critical test of the teacher's intervention is what students can do after the course experience that they could not do at the beginning. (When we say "do," we mean to include, of course, demonstrable thought processes such as framing a testable hypothesis, explaining by a single theory apparently disparate patterns of conduct, or extending a proposition to different populations or circumstances.)

This poses tough problems of experimental design. One requires a base point with which to compare measured outcomes and clear-cut statements of aims whose degree of achievement can be appraised. And one must have some means of eliminating the influence of factors other than the instructor's intervention in order to evaluate the effect of the intervention. Such other factors include students' initial motivation, effort extended, and precourse knowledge and abilities, as well as nonclassroom factors contributing to student learning and various attributes of the *course* over which the teacher may have little or no control.

The simplest way of visualizing this design problem and welter of variables is to call on the classical model of research with experimental and control groups and measures, before and after intervention, of behaviors presumed to be affected by intervention. Statistical techniques such as partial correlation and regression may serve to effect controls when we lack an actual comparison group. Often, the conditions of instruction, including time and resources, prevent our use of the optimal design. But whatever the approximation of the ideal, it is most desirable to get some measure of change in skills, knowledge, and attitudes pertinent to the course.

Falling between the optimal design and doing nothing are these options: (1) pre- and postcourse comparisons; (2) postcourse assessment with use of student class rank, grade point average, or standardized test score in lieu of a precourse measure; and (3) comparison of student achievement during the progress of the course. Faced with time constraints, a teacher might consider using one of these techniques in only one course or for only some of the goals for a given course.

Course grade distributions (aggregate, postcourse-only measures) by themselves do not allow us to draw conclusions about the distance traveled by students. Another method sometimes suggested, that of comparing individual student performance across different courses taken in the same semester, is fraught with methodological problems.

Student achievement as an index of teacher effectiveness has this major limitation: while teachers may learn the extent to which their students have learned, they may not be able to discover what it was that they did to promote the change. Even though the change may be correctly attributed to their intervention, instructors may not know what particular aspects of a course were responsible for which gains. Although well-designed evaluation instruments can provide clues to specific features of instruction, one must still be cautious in interpreting results. There is a judgment to be made about the value of what was taught. Typically, we lack the information needed to compare the effectiveness of two teachers on the basis of student achievement measures.

Ericksen and Kulik (1974:4) suggest that "unless extensive norms have been developed, only instructors giving the same course can ordinarily be compared, and then, only when these instructors agree about the content to be covered in their courses." (In required courses, these problems would be eased were the minimum core of desired learnings specified by a third party—the department or some other third party stipulating the course as requisite.) These design problems are the greater when we remember that some subjects are more difficult to teach than others. Nonetheless, one might hope that sociologists would take the lead in developing objective measures of the degree to which they are achieving their aims, even when such aims are, in first formulation, modes of thought and perspectives hard to specify. On matters of factual information and skills, there is less difficulty.

What evidence do we need? and which evidence is more (and less) important? What we look for in evaluation depends, in part, on the use to which the evaluation will be put. If teachers seek only to learn how effective their students believe them to be, a few questions will probably provide an adequate answer. But if the aim is to improve instruction, teachers will need far more detailed information. Consider this one aspect of instruction: the teacher's use of questions in the classroom.

One might inquire about: (1) the mechanics of teacher questioning—too many or too few questions? timing of their use? time provided for student response? clarification if a question is not understood?; (2) the content of questions—general or specific? relating subject matter to student experience? tapping information only or the student's ability to use information?; (3) the use of questions—to frame issues? to test student preparedness or comprehension? to help develop analytic skills? to help the teacher avoid premature closure of a topic?; and (4) the handling of student responses—use of praise? demonstrated respect for the student as a person? use of student answers in subsequent class segments? This brief list only begins to tap the range of issues pertinent to questioning, which is in itself but a single dimension of instruction. A roster of such dimensions, each specified in de-

tail, is needed if instructors are to improve their performances.

In this connection, checklists such as those in chapter 9 for reviewing a course syllabus and selecting a textbook provide useful guidelines. Checklists for assessing different aspects of instruction can be found in many books on teaching, obtained from instructional development centers, or constructed by teachers, using their own goals and judgments, those of colleagues, and available material.*

Beyond checklists on aspects of instruction, we need to weigh the evidence we collect. Depending on the instructor's aims, some of the evidence will bear on matters more important than others. The evidence from students that the course load is heavy may be less significant to the instructor than the evidence about the bearing of course content on students' lives. The determination of significance must rest with the instructor as he or she interprets the mission of the school, the department, the discipline, and the course.

We now turn to examine, in some detail, two modes of assessing instruction: student evaluation of teaching and peer observation. When designed and used with care, these methods can provide guidance for improving instructional effectiveness.

Student Evaluation of Teaching

A teacher has no choice as to whether he wishes to be judged by students, he only can exercise some control over the procedure itself and its usefulness in terms of his own teaching. (H. H. Remmers, as paraphrased by Miller, 1974:208)

Students' ratings of courses and instructors are widely used in sociology (see

* See note 25 of this chapter.

table 14.1). Rating forms used vary from those that have been thrown together in an afternoon's work to those that have been carefully developed, pretested, revised, and subjected to research spanning several decades. There is marked variation, too, in the matters rated.

Students can provide us with their perceptions of many aspects of the courses they take with us, including:

1. the effectiveness of the *instructor* as lecturer and discussion leader

2 . the ease or difficulty, the readability and stimulation offered by texts and other *written materials*

3. the interest and learning generated by laboratory *exercises and projects*

4. the clarity and appropriateness of course *goals*

5. the adequacy of the *planning and organization* of the course and of individual class sessions

6. the usefulness of films and other *audiovisual aids*

7. the *examinations*—their adequacy and pertinence and accuracy in reflecting student achievement

8. the estimated *gains in knowledge*—information and ideas

9. the interest in and *respect for the student*

10. the level of *difficulty and volume of work*—whether appropriate, too much or too little

Obviously these ten items do not exhaust the matters on which student perceptions can help us review and revise aspects of our teaching.

But how reliable and valid is the information obtained through student ratings of courses and instructors? What attributes of students, courses, and teachers affect student ratings? What do ratings tell us about student perceptions of superior instruction? We now review studies that treat such questions, particularly those that employ the more satisfactory evaluation forms developed at a number of universities around the country and by organizations such as the Educational Testing Service. While the conclusions do not apply equally to all student rating forms, several conclusions have a broad enough research base to allow generalization for a specifiable range of questions, forms, or populations.

Research on Student Evaluation of Teaching (SET)

Reliability of student ratings.   Major student rating forms are internally consistent and stable. High interitem correlations for questions designed to tap a given characteristic are reported by virtually all major studies; coefficients of .8 to .9 are typical (Doyle, 1975:35–37; Costin, Greenough, and Menges, 1971). Several studies demonstrate test-retest reliability for periods of time ranging from one day to ten years. Drucker and Remmers (1951) report coefficients of .40 through .68 for ten-year intervals; Centra (1973) reports an average coefficient of .75 for a five-year interval (see also Costin, Greenough, and Menges, 1971; and Doyle, 1975:chapter 3).

Validity of student ratings.   Most well-designed studies comparing student ratings and how much students actually learn report moderate to low positive correlations. These studies employ before-after tests of student learning or introduce as control variables intelligence test scores or grade point averages. While the studies employ different measures, and thus cannot be compared directly, the following table illustrates findings of well-designed studies on objective validation.

Study	Courses	Correlations Between SET and Learning
Bolton et al. (1979)	Psychology	.21 to .71
Centra (1977)	Various	.63 to .87
Frey (1973)	Calculus	.84 to .90
Doyle and Whitely (1974)	French	.18 to .54
Gessner (1973)	Medicine	.69 to .77
McKeachie et al. (1971)	Economics	.43 to .44
Solomon et al. (1963)	Government	.46 to .57 (factual) .11 to .21 (comprehension)

A study receiving much national attention found that "students rate most highly instructors from whom they learn least" (Rodin and Rodin, 1972:1164). The Rodins found a correlation of $-.75$ between examination scores and student ratings. This study has serious problems in design, analysis, and interpretation (see Rodin and Rodin, 1972; Doyle, 1975:58–59; Centra, 1972b; Ericksen and Kulik, 1974:5; Frey, 1973; and also Rodin, 1973).[12]

Kulik and Kulik (1974:55) point out that the extent of teacher experience may affect the correlation between rating and learning. "Sullivan and Skanes (1974) found that student ratings and achievement were highly related for a group of experienced instructors, but only trivially related for a group of teaching assistants . . . results like those of Rodin and Rodin may be more typical of inexperienced teachers. . . ."

A few studies report modest positive correlations between student ratings of instructor and instructor self-ratings and ratings of instructors by colleagues and by administrators.

Student characteristics affecting their ratings of instructors. Most demographic and academic attributes of students have very weak and inconsistent relationships to ratings of instructors. These attributes include: age, gender, veteran status, grade point average, course grade, expected course grade, and year in school for undergraduates (graduate students tend to give more favorable evaluations).[13] There is some evidence suggesting that students who elect to take a course and who have high expectations for the course and the instructor give more favorable ratings. Ratings by majors do not differ from those of nonmajors.

Instructor characteristics affecting student ratings. Instructor gender, research ability, and severity of grading have virtually no relationship to overall student ratings, though this last factor should not be confused with fairness in grading. Teacher personality traits are not consistently related to student ratings. However, a few studies do report that teacher enthusiasm is positively related to both student ratings and student learning (see, for example, Williams and Ware, 1976; and studies cited by McKeachie, 1978:24). Student liking for a teacher as a person is not related to ratings of the teacher's general ability, though it does correlate with responses on some more specific rating scales.

There is some evidence that more experienced instructors receive somewhat higher ratings than their colleagues. The finding for experience is bolstered by several studies showing that training in teaching (for graduate student instructors and faculty) raises teacher ratings over time (see, for example, Carroll, 1977; Costin, 1968; and Erickson and Erickson, 1979a, 1979b). One study compared teacher ratings by students with independent measures of the teacher's knowledge of subject matter (chemistry). "For the laboratory instructors, the correlation was a positive but nonsignificant .30; for the recitation instructors, the correlation was a positive significant .40" (Doyle, 1975:53–54).[14]

Course characteristics related to student ratings. Most studies report a small negative correlation between class size and student rating of the instructor. Crittenden, Norr, and LeBailly (1975) report that the negative relationship remained after other variables known or believed to influence ratings were held constant. Wood, Linsky, and Straus (1974) reported a curvilinear relationship between size and rating: teachers of classes with between 60 and 290 students obtained lower than average ratings. Since several studies compared classes of under and over 20 or 30 students, the Wood finding is not inconsistent with the broader literature. There is good evidence that ratings vary by discipline. Recall the Linsky and Straus (1974) study that found wide variations, with sociology and psychology rated below several other fields. This same study reported differences in the average ratings for teachers of different sociology courses. In general, we have little evidence about the effect of the content of specific courses on student ratings.

Teacher improvement and student ratings. Most recent research reports that providing teachers with student ratings does not result in improved ratings in subsequent semesters. This should not be surprising. Change occurs only when three conditions are met: (1) information is provided, (2) the learner is motivated to change, and (3) the learner has better response alternatives available. Providing teachers with ratings meets only the first

condition. When teachers work to improve their teaching and when counsel and guidance are available to them, their ratings *do* improve. Erickson and Erickson (1979a, 1979b) report a controlled study showing that ratings significantly improved for University of Rhode Island faculty participating in a teacher consultation process. In this process, the student ratings are used by the consultants and are not simply indicators of student perceptions. Several studies report that student ratings are higher for teaching assistants who took a seminar in teaching than for their colleagues who did not (see Costin, 1968; Carroll, 1977).

Further, when the information provided by student rating forms is *new to instructors*, the instructors are more likely to modify their teaching behavior. Some rating procedures call for teacher self-rating and teacher prediction of student ratings, as well as the conventional rating by students. Some revealed discrepancies appear to provide motivation for change. For example, research shows that when the teacher self-rating is higher than student ratings, improvement occurs after receipt of this information. When teacher self-rating is equivalent to or lower than student ratings, change is less likely. Using regression analysis with data from 400 teachers in five colleges, Centra (1973) found that the greater the discrepancy (self-rating higher than student rating), the greater the likelihood of change. He notes that at least two semesters of experience with student evaluations may be necessary before change is noticeable.

It seems likely that teacher motivation to change will be increased if the evaluation instruments used reflect the teacher's own course objectives and if the teacher has been able to contribute questions to the instrument. (There are, of course, other extrinsic motivators such as reward and sanction for given ratings.) Finally, student rating forms are more useful in promoting teacher change when the questions are specific and tap potential change areas.

Studies bearing on the use of rating in teacher improvement are cited and/or discussed in Doyle (1975:83–85), Kulik and Kulik (1974:55–56), McKeachie (1978:269–270), and Miller (1974:64–65).

Student perceptions of superior teachers. Based on a review of dozens of studies, Feldman (1976) concludes that students consistently report the following as attributes of superior teachers:

1. stimulation of interest
2. clarity
3. knowledge of subject matter
4. preparation
5. enthusiasm
6. friendliness
7. helpfulness
8. openness to other's opinions

These and closely related components are reported in studies conducted since the 1940s using different instruments, modes of analysis, and student populations. Support for such components is reported in Doyle's (1975:49–53) review of ten factor-analytic studies and in Miller's (1974:31–33) review of eight studies in which students were asked to rank order different teacher attributes. Almost all of these studies presented students with forced-choice questions. However, the categories or factors listed above are very similar to those discovered inductively in a content analysis of student statements nominating instructors for superior teaching awards (Goldsmid, Gruber, and Wilson, 1977).

There is some evidence that sociology students conceive superior teaching in terms such as those just sketched. Wimberly, Faulkner, and Moxley (1978) report a study of more than 4,300 students in 167 classes in a sociology-anthropology department.[15] Students were asked to rate their teachers on forty items using a five-point scale. Factor analysis and cluster analysis yielded similar patterns. Wimberly and his colleagues conclude that highly evaluated teachers are those who: are seen as capable, devoted to teaching, and at ease with course material; are responsive to students in several ways; respect students and their views; provide encouragement; and are perceived by students as enhancing student development or attainment. Such findings lend support to an interpretation made by Goldsmid, Gruber, and Wilson (1977:429), of their own data, that perceived excellence in teaching is embodied in two general traits: *"competence* (in command and handling of subject matter), and *conscientiousness* (reflecting a concern for student's achievement).

In an earlier section we noted that some course characteristics affect student ratings. One study allows us to assess the impact of course versus teacher on dimensions of teaching effectiveness discussed in this section. Kulik and Kulik (1974) identified four dimensions of teaching that they found common to nine factor-analytic studies of student rating forms. The first three of these four dimensions—teacher skill, rapport, course structure, and difficulty—overlap the dimensions identified by Feldman (discussed above).[16] Kulik and Kulik reanalyze data from a study by Hogan (1973) and partial out some of the influences on ratings of teacher versus course. Scores on the skill dimensions were strongly influenced by teacher characteristics (51 percent of the variance); for rapport, structure, and difficulty, the corresponding figures were 24, 42, and 7 percent. Attributes of courses account for 55 percent of the variance on the difficulty dimensions and just over a quarter of the variance for skill and rapport (error terms range between 26 and 50 percent).[17]

As Kulik and Kulik note, Hogan is only one study and it uses small samples in only one institution. But the data suggest that student ratings on different dimensions of teaching are differentially affected by teacher and course characteristics. Accordingly, "student ratings do not provide a common yardstick for measuring the excellence of teachers in varying disciplines with varying course assignments. Teachers of different courses cannot be compared easily because the various influences on an individual teacher's ratings cannot be disentangled at the present time" (1974:53–54).

This cautionary note seems warranted. Our conclusion—here we echo Doyle and others—is that student ratings can be useful and should be used for instructional improvement, but that heavy reliance on them in personnel decisions generally is not warranted. Of course, their usefulness for either purpose depends on the quality of the form used and the research done on it.

Research on Self, Colleague, and Administrator Ratings

Very little research has systematically examined faculty self-ratings, or colleague or administrator ratings, of teacher effectiveness. Little is known about their reliability, validity, generalizability, and correlates. Doyle (1975:67) is aware of no study that has compared any of these types of ratings with any measure of student learning.

Faculty self-ratings. A few studies report modest correlations between self-ratings and student ratings. The best available research, Centra (1973a), studied 343 classes in five colleges. The median correlation for student and self-rating on seventeen items was .21. However, the rank-order correlation between the two rating groups for the items was .77—reflecting agreement on the pattern but not the level of instructor strengths and weaknesses. Centra found differences by discipline as well as by item-type. Although "self-ratings are sometimes more severe than student ratings, the general tendency is for instructors to rate themselves more favorably than students do" (Doyle, 1975:71). Correlations between self- and colleague (and administrator) ratings are also typically slight.

Colleague and administrator ratings. Students and colleagues (and administrators) have high agreement on who are the best and worst teachers. However, while student ratings are based on direct and extended experience in the classroom, colleague and administrator ratings are typically "inferences about classroom activities based on their experiences with the instructor in other settings" (Doyle, 1975:72). Centra's (1975) study employed ratings on a large number of specific rating items and found positive correlations that were low to moderate at best (though often statistically significant). In Centra's study, the colleague raters visited the classroom before they made their ratings. Centra also examined the reliability of colleague ratings where fifty-four teachers were rated twice by the same three raters. Correlations between first and second visits/ratings were high (.55, .69, .77, and .88). However, correlations among the three raters averaged .26 and exhibited a wide range.

*Selecting or Constructing a Student
Rating Form*

The best student rating form is one that provides the needed information, is consistent with the uses to which it will be put, and fits available resources. The teacher must first decide on what is wanted from student responses. If course goals have been specified, he or she will want questions pertinent to these goals (tapping student perception of gains in specific knowledge, skills, attitudes, and perhaps the arousal of curiosity and interest). If the teacher is concerned about the organization of lectures or the perceived level of difficulty of textbooks, items on the student rating form should touch these matters directly. If the teacher is concerned about the effectiveness of the teaching assistants, he or she will need items that tap the work of these TAs as distinct from his or her own.

Student ratings can be used to assist the teacher to improve instruction, to provide information for promotion or salary reviews, or to furnish students with information useful in course selection. Different uses have implications for the content of an evaluation form. For example, if the form is to be used for course improvement purposes, questions must be directed to the specific, modifiable elements of the course. If the form is to be used for personnel decisions or to compare a teacher to other teachers in other fields, it is important that norms exist for the items selected and that the items tap some aspects of instruction that are not discipline-specific. A form used for student benefit should inquire about the perceived level of course difficulty, teacher clarity, and accessibility, since research shows that these are matters that concern students. If the form is to be administered early in the course as a guide to useful

modifications during the term, an easily and quickly analyzed form will be needed.

Resources enter the picture in several ways. Does the teacher have the time to prepare a carefully constructed form? How will the form be analyzed? and by whom? Can the teacher resort to a well-researched institutional rating form? and does that form meet most of the teacher's needs?

Most student evaluation-of-teaching forms are developed in an ad hoc manner with little care. Most teachers and departments start from scratch, failing to make use of existing forms and research. There are good reasons for teachers and departments to construct their own forms; such forms are more likely to meet their needs and the investment in the use of these forms will be greater. On the other hand, newly prepared forms will have unknown reliability and validity and no comparison group data. There are three solutions to this dilemma. Teachers (or their departments) can create a form that borrows some questions from well-researched, existing forms, adding other questions devised to assess certain features peculiar to a given course; or they can use a standardized form that includes space for the insertion of teacher-prepared questions. As a third option, teachers can use a "cafeteria form" that allows them to select items from a large pool or catalogue of pretested questions as well as add their own specially designed questions. We discuss these options in the following section.

Drawing, in whole or in part, on existing, well-researched forms makes sense. Sociologists are well aware of the difficulty in constructing a good measuring instrument. Since assessing student reactions to instruction deserves to be done carefully, completely new forms require a large investment of time. Teachers constructing assessment forms will find useful Doyle's (1975) chapter on "instrumentation." He discusses question content and format, scale type, means of error reduction, and related topics. (See also McKeachie, 1978:268–272.)

Well-designed forms. There are many excellent rating forms on which teachers can draw. Table 14.5 lists ten forms that are well researched, allow for teacher-inserted questions, and for which comparative data are available. Most of these forms were developed in the early 1970s; those who prepared them drew on research and earlier forms used in their schools or organizations for periods of ten to forty years. Table 14.5 is not an exhaustive list; other schools with useful forms include Grinnell College, Northwestern University, Miami University, the University of Wisconsin at Green Bay, and the University of Washing-

ton (which has been using standardized forms since 1925).

In table 14.5, the forms numbered 1, 2, and 5 are cafeteria forms. Thus teachers can select thirty questions from a catalog of 145, add some of their own specially developed questions, and have the form specially printed. Comparative data on all questions in the catalog (as well as five core, or required, questions) are available for the University of Michigan form. Forms 3, 6, 7, 8, and 10 include between seven and fifty-six core or required items, plus space for teachers to add as many as eleven teacher-prepared questions. Several of the organizations that offer these forms provide computer scoring and analysis on a fee-for-service basis. Forms 4 and 5 are part of larger instructional improvement systems (employing, in the case of TABS, vid-

---

Table 14.5 Information on Selected Student Evaluation-of-Teaching Forms

Name of Form	School or Agency[a]	Description of Form[b]	Forms, Norms, and Research[c]
1. Instructor-designed Questionnaires	*University of Michigan* Center for Research on Learning and Teaching 109 E. Madison Ann Arbor, MI. 48109	5 core; 3 open; catalog 145 (choose 30)	(F) Kulik (1976) (N) Michigan (R) Yes, write CRLT/UM
2. Cafeteria (Purdue Instructor and Course Appraisal)	*Purdue University* Office Instructional Service ENAD, Room 402 West Lafayette, IN. 47907	5 core; some open; catalog 200+ (choose 40)	(F) Doyle (1975:112) (N) Extensive (R) Yes, write Purdue
3. Cornell Inventory for Student Appraisal of Teaching and Courses	*Cornell University*[d] Cornell General Stores Ithaca, NY. 14853 (James B. Maas, Dept. of Psychology)	56 core; 11 open; 8 optional essay	(N) Cornell (R) ?, write Maas
4. TABS (Teaching Analysis by Students)	*University of Massachusetts*[e] Clinic to Improve University Teaching Amherst, MA. 01002	Several forms (8 to 50 core) for students and teacher	(F) Bergquist and Phillips (1977:chapter 5) (N) ?, write clinic (R) Erickson and Erickson (1979a, 1979b); write clinic

Table 14.5 (*Continued*)

Name of Form	School or Agency[a]	Description of Form[b]	Forms, Norms, and Research[c]	
5. IDEA (Instructional Development and Effectiveness Assessment System)	*Kansas State University*[f] Center for Faculty Evaluation and Development 1627 Anderson Avenue Manhattan, KS. 66502	39 core; catalog of 150+ (choose 25); plus teacher forms	(F)	Miller (1974:37–40) for a very early version
			(N)	Extensive
			(R)	Yes, write CFED
6. SIR (Student Instructional Report)	*Educational Testing Service*[g] ETS College & University Programs Box 2813 Princeton, NJ. .08540	39 core; 10 open	(F)	Miller (1974:37–40)
			(N)	Extensive
			(R)	Centra (1973a, 1973b, 1973c, 1975) and write ETS
7. Student Opinion Survey	*University of Minnesota* Measurement Services Center 9 Clarence Avenue, S.E. Minneapolis, MN. 55414	Basic form; 23 core; 8 open; auxiliary forms available	(F)	Doyle (1975:100–109)
			(N)	Minnesota
			(R)	Doyle and Whitely (1974) and write Minnesota
8. SIRS (Student Instructional Rating System)	*Michigan State University* Office of Evaluation Services East Lansing, MI. 48824	21 core; 3 open	(F)	Miller (1974:41–42)
			(N)	MSU
			(R)	Yes, write to MSU
9. Course Evaluation Questionnaires	*University of Illinois* Measurement & Research Division 307 Engineering Hall Urbana, IL. 61801	25 core; essay questions	(F)	Miller (1974:57–59)
			(N)	Extensive
			(R)	Spencer and Aleamoni (1970) and write UI
10. Student Description of Teachers	*University of California* Center for Research & Development in Higher Education Berkeley, CA. 94720	Short form: 7 core, plus open Long form: 38 core, plus open	(F)	Miller (1974:43–47)
			(N)	California
			(R)	Hildebrand et al. (1971) and write UC

Notes:

(a) In all cases, except form #5, add the university name to the address.

(b) *Core:* standard questions printed on the form; *Open:* spaces provided for insertion of instructor-designed questions; *Catalog:* a bank or catalog of questions from which instructor can select; all forms include several background questions (e.g., student major, year in school, grade point average); almost all core and catalog questions are forced-choice using a five-point scale.

(c) (F) = Book or article in which the form is reprinted. (R) = Research available on the form. (N) = Comparison norms. (?) = we do not know if forms or research for the forms exist. Most of these forms and related materials are copyrighted.

(d) The Cornell Inventory was developed in the early 1970s by James B. Maas as part of his work with the Center for Improvement of Undergraduate Education. The center no longer exists. Copies of the form and an excellent instruction manual are available from the Cornell General Stores.

(e) The TABS system is described in detail, with copies of all forms included, in a 56-page chapter in Bergquist and Phillips. TABS is part of an instructional improvement system.

(f) The IDEA system of instructional improvement (based on student appraisals) is available on a fee-for-service basis to institutions and departments; service includes consultations. A packet of detailed information is available on request.

(g) Individuals or organizations can purchase from ETS the SIR forms and, if desired, computer analysis service. A packet of descriptive and research information is available for a small charge.

eotape analysis, consultation, and teacher as well as student rating forms). Several forms (e.g., 3, 4, 5, and 8) have accompanying manuals to help teachers interpret their ratings.

The last column of table 14.5 lists books or articles in which the complete rating from (or a sample form, in the case of the Purdue Cafeteria) is reprinted; in some cases, new editions of these rating forms have become available. Teachers may want to borrow or adapt some questions from these forms (note that almost all of the forms themselves are copyrighted). The last column in the table also indicates the availability of research and comparison norms for the ten forms.

Research on several of these forms is extensive. The ETS form has been the subject of more than a dozen published reports.[18] Periodically, ETS publishes "comparative data guides" summarizing student responses. In 1974, 472,000 students in 21,000 classes in 118 schools used ETS's rating form (SIR: Student Instructional Report). For each of the thirty-nine items on the form, summary data are presented by school type (university, four-year college, two-year college), course level (freshman-sophomore, junior-senior), instructional format (lecture, discussion, laboratory, and their combinations), and subject matter (thirty-one different disciplines). Frequency and percentile distributions, means, medians, and standard deviations are presented for the aggregated student responses in each category. The 1977 data guide covers four-year colleges only; for sociology, it provides data from almost 7,000 students in 273 sociology classes.

Norms for student ratings.[19]   To interpret student ratings for a given teacher, we need some base of comparison. Several are

available. Teachers might compare their ratings: across several semesters or courses; against a personal standard of achievement ("I should get a mean rating of 4.0 or better on items tapping . . . because. . . ."), or with those of other teachers. But how valid are such comparisons? And can they be generalized? We have seen that class composition and some attributes of courses can affect ratings. We know there are differences across disciplines. And ample research demonstrates variation in student response patterns to different items and types of items on rating scales. We must, then, interpret teacher evaluations with some care, taking into account these sources of variation, including the evaluation instrument itself.[20]

Adequate evaluation of teacher performance requires the use of several types of measures as well as information about the teaching context and research on student assessment of teaching. For example, factors affecting some rating items will, for a given course or in general, be more or less beyond the control of a teacher. And reliance on percentile distributions alone obscures the fact that, by definition, half of all teachers must fall below the median percentile—even if all teachers do a very creditable job.

Selecting questions.   Sociologists know about questionnaire design and scale construction, and much of that knowledge is applicable to student assessment of teaching forms. Yet, the following comments may be useful:

1. Select or design questions with their specific use in mind; this point was illustrated earlier.

2. The form used should be detailed enough to provide the needed information, but not so complex that you haven't the time or resources to analyze and use it.

3. Consider a variety of questions and question types; if you use rating scales, it is advisable to use the same number and direction of response categories.

4. Although general rating items (e.g., "Compared with other courses I've taken, I would rate the overall value of this course to me as . . .") can provide convenient summary data, specific questions will be more useful for instructional improvement.[21]

5. Follow the canons on question construction (e.g., questions should not inquire about a composite of independent traits).

6. Use questions that are linked to specific behaviors of the teacher or student or to the results of behaviors.

7. Consider questions that tap student selection of and preparation for courses, including precourse interest in the subject, reasons for taking the course (e.g., the course was required for the student's major, etc.), how students learned about the course, adequacy of the college or university catalog description, and the adequacy of the course prerequisites. Such items should supplement the more conventional background questions (class, major, grade point average, gender, etc.).

8. Questions should tap all facets of the course that are of concern to the teacher—readings, written assignments, teaching assistants, the syllabus, lectures, discussion groups, and particular aspects of instruction (e.g., teacher use of examples and illustrations).

9. Consider including questions about matters that research reveals as important to most students (see discussion above of student perceptions of superior teachers).

10. Many forms inquire about the degree of effort students put into a course. McKeachie (1978:294–295) suggests additional questions on student responsibility: "I attended class regularly," "I try to make a tie-in between what I am learning through the course and my own experience," and "I utilize all the learning opportunities provided in the course."

The issues of clarity, specificity, and the behavioral dimensions of questions may be sharpened by contrasting these four questions about student effort:

(a) *I worked hard in this course.*
    (*response categories: very true . . . [through] not at all true*)
(b) *I spent much out-of-class time working on this course.*
    (*accurate . . . not at all accurate*)
(c) *Compared with other courses you have taken, how much time did you spend on this course?*
    (*much more . . . much less*)
(d) *On the average, how much time per week do you estimate that you spent on this course outside of class?*
    (*one hour or less . . . nine hours or more*)

Using Student Ratings to Improve Instruction[22]

Seven steps are suggested for teachers who use student ratings to improve their teaching:

1. Select a reasonably specific aspect of your instructional work on which you plan to work (e.g., questioning skills in discussion sections). The job should be so narrowly and specifically defined as to be manageable in the available time. Prior evaluation responses can help in selecting the problem.

2. Determine what resources are available to assist you—a colleague whom you trust and believe effective in the teaching technique at issue, a staff member from a local instructional development center, and articles and books on the teaching skill in question. When possible, use materials from the literature on the teaching of sociology. (See the appendix and pertinent resources sections of this book for suggestions.)

3. Design a student evaluation-of-teaching form with specific questions that tap this aspect of teaching.

4. Augment this information with other forms of feedback from students and colleagues.[23]

5. With a trusted colleague or instructional development specialist, analyze your data and select alternative ways of teaching; then adapt them to your needs and proclivities and try them out.

6. Gather some new data on the effectiveness of the new approaches you have tried. Make your own judgments about the results and determine your next steps.

7. Finally, document and share the process you have gone through. It may be helpful to your colleagues and may benefit you in salary and promotion reviews.

Student Evaluation of Instruction: A Summary

Student evaluations of teaching can provide information to the teacher valuable in improving instruction; reliance on them for personnel decisions does not seem warranted, although they can be of assistance. There are a number of carefully prepared forms and research on these shows that student ratings can be highly reliable (internally and on test-retest measures) and valid (with moderate to low positive correlations with student learning). Few attributes of teachers or students have consistent or strong effects on ratings; exceptions are students' initial interest and expectations, and teacher experience, which are positively correlated with student ratings. Some course attributes affect ratings: there is a small negative correlation with size, and teachers in some disciplines, including sociology, tend to get lower ratings. More than a dozen factor-analytic studies of student rating forms yield relatively consistent factors, many of which hinge on perceived teacher competence and concern for students and their

learning. Information from student ratings helps teachers be more effective only when they are motivated to change and have the option of other teaching patterns (and help in using them). Teachers have substantial resources available to them in constructing their own forms. The well-researched forms provide useful comparison data and often allow inclusion of teacher-selected and teacher-designed questions. Helpful as they can be, student evaluations have limitations and cannot provide the range of information needed in assessment of instruction. Students lack the breadth of experience to enable them to know what might have taken place in a course, and they are not prepared to judge the teacher's subject matter competence.

Some of these limitations of student evaluation of teaching are removed in the method of assessing instruction we next turn to: peer observation and evaluation.

Peer Observation and Evaluation

It is easier to conceive a different way of teaching if one has the help of a perceptive classroom observer. Such an observer provides the reactions that, in Mead's theory, transform subject into object. Thus the teacher can recreate his or her conceptions of self-as-instructor. For who that person is as instructor, and how efficacious, can only be known through others' responses. The same end might be served by students' questions and comments, by their answers on examinations, and by their ratings of our work. But in the classroom session the instructor often preempts the fifty-minute hour, so losing the chance for self-defining responses from the clients. As for examinations, we are often so preoccupied with our students' test scores that we seldom fix on their achievement as a means of assessing our performance. Using student performances to improve our own may be a little-used approach to self-knowledge because of the way we choose to interpret student work: for gratifying achievement, the instructor is responsible; for poor performance, the student. Even when we are not so facile, student achievement is affected by factors over which we have no control, and knowledge of student achievement does not always provide guidelines for altering our instructional pattern.

Through observation of our classes, review of our course material, and purposeful discussion, our colleagues can provide us with reactions we can use to improve our instruction. In certain ways, our colleagues are especially suited to the task: they share with us a discipline and an understanding of the problems and opportunities peculiar to instruction in it. They labor under similar conditions (with like resources and constraints) and know, firsthand, the ego-involving work that teaching can be. More than others, our colleagues share with us a set of goals, a universe of discourse, and a vested interest in our teaching. As sociologists, their reputations in the academic community are enhanced or diminished by our own.

Of course, our colleagues vary in their definitions of and commitment to effective instruction, and we find ourselves more comfortable with some than others. But a peer with whom we have much in common and whom we trust can be especially helpful.[24]

Classroom observations can be used to provide information about ourselves as teachers for tenure and promotion reviews or to help us improve our instructional effectiveness. We speak here solely to the second use. But note that an observed teacher is not the only beneficiary of observation. The observer, too, can learn, and discussions following the observation can help us develop categories for more systematic evaluation, starting us on the road to a reasoned conception of effective instruction. A program of voluntary visits and discussions can also serve as a stimulus for departmental consideration of teaching and curriculum issues.

We noted, earlier, the paucity of research available on colleague ratings of instruction. We have little information about peer observation in the service of instruction improvement. The most useful and easily available material is found in Bergquist and Phillips (1975:chapters 4, 5).

In the following pages, we discuss the process, analysis, and use of observations, and then provide some excerpts from letters we wrote to graduate student instructors whose teaching we observed.

The Process of Observation

Planning the observation. What is to be observed? Observation may fix on a particular aspect of instruction—for example, the clarity and organization of a lecture or the teacher's use of questioning and method of responding to student questions—or it can remain open-ended. In any event, the teacher being observed needs to define the situation and indicate what he or she wants reactions on. The open-ended approach may be useful to a teacher with no information about his or her teaching and no readily available way of getting it. But if the teacher, perhaps using student evaluations, can specify some points of focus, this seems the better course. Bergquist and Phillips (1975:88) suggest that the teacher may want to select for observation an aspect of instruction about which he or she feels moderately confident. "Such selectivity is productive, for areas which are highly threatening are probably also areas in which little initial learning [by the teacher] will actually take place. Once an instructor has received and made use of information in less threatening areas, he will perhaps be inclined to accept information which may be potentially more threatening."

A talk before the class visit can help to focus the observation and enhance its use for the teacher. During this talk, the teacher can describe the general approach to the course and instruction, inform the observer about what has happened in immediately preceding class sessions, and provide the observer with a copy of the course syllabus and any other pertinent course material.

A talk should be scheduled as soon as possible after the observation. A long lag between the observed class and initial feedback may result in lost information and needlessly heightened anxiety for the teacher. If the teacher believes that the observed class did not provide an adequate specimen of the aspect of instruction on which advice was requested, a second visit can be planned. The colleague's advance agreement to this possibility can help reduce the teacher's apprehension. In any event, it is well to remember that no one class provides a representative sample of a teacher's work.

It is useful to think of these initial arrangements as a process of contracting. Both the teacher and the colleague-observer need to be clear about the situation and their obligations. The teacher who is uncomfortable with the process is likely to dismiss or resist the information it provides. Both need to agree on the claims that the process will make on the observer's time and on what, if anything, the observer is free to say to third parties about the class observed or the discussion following it. Finally, it may be useful at this stage for the teacher to think about how to use the feedback the process pro-

vides. This, too, is a matter of contract—a personal one.

The observation and the feedback on it. These two steps have an important link. The observer who hopes to provide useful reactions will need to anticipate the kinds of information that must be collected during the observation. It is useful to prepare a checklist of points for observation. An excellent set of checklists for analyzing lectures, discussion and other small groups, questions and questioning, motivating and supportive teacher behaviors, and introductions and endings of classes is provided by Kindsvatter and Wilensky (in Scholl and Inglis, 1977:307–332).[25] Clearly reactions to a teacher should respond to concerns the teacher has identified. Beyond this, what can be said about the focus of the observation and the feedback on it? If the observer's reactions are to be heard and used by the teacher, they will need to be descriptive, specific, and based on observed behaviors. There are implications for the observation itself. For example, the observer will need to record instances in the class when he or she lost the thread of the teacher's lecture or found the teacher's examples particularly valuable in clarifying an abstract point.

Constructive feedback speaks directly to the class and course in question, the subject matter and skills dealt with, and the instructional approach used by the teacher. Additionally, this feedback must be delivered in a supportive and nonthreatening manner. Colleague observations usually work well when the observer's primary tasks are to describe what was seen and heard, and to provide reactions to these events. Yet the requirements of evaluation, judgment, criticism, and inferences about motivation may be hazards in this relationship. To bring it off effectively, Bergquist and Phillips (1975:223–225) list fourteen features of constructive feedback. Useful evaluative response is, first of all, solicited, not imposed. The observer describes what was seen, heard, and done (without imputing motives) and describes his or her own reactions. This approach is specific, fixing on the behavior rather than the person—and especially on behavior the teacher can do something about. It is a process that should help both parties, entailing an exchange (without an overload) of information. It occurs very shortly after the observation, when memory is fresh. In this postobservation review, the threatening aspect of the visit and evaluation is reduced when the teacher, rather than the observer, opens with his or her own assessment. The message is checked with the teacher (and with others, if they are involved) to be sure what is sent is being received—without distortion. With a mutual concern for improving their work, both observer and teacher move toward a relationship of openness and trust, laying the groundwork for continuing exchange in the service of improved instruction.

There is a tendency, in postobservation discussion, for a colleague to open with a series of vaguely stated positive points and then move quickly to far more specifically phrased reactions about problems. For example:

> *I really liked your lecture organization and the handout. But about two-thirds of the way through the class, when you were applying Smelser's value-added model to the women's movement, I felt that the examples—especially of the first two components—were not clear. Maybe it's me, I haven't done the readings assigned for the class, but I couldn't see the connections between. . . .*

The second part of this particular observer's reaction was sufficiently specific (and constructively phrased) to be useful to the teacher. But when the observer said

she liked the lecture organization and the associated handout, she said too little. What was it about the organization and the handout that she liked? How were they useful to her? What attributes did they have that could have been identified, praised, and reinforced and that the teacher could have extended to other classes and courses? Most colleague-observers are sensitive to the need for positive reinforcement; however, like this observer, they often forget that positive feedback must be specific if it is to be useful.

Videotapes of classes can be extremely valuable in peer observation. A tape can be made in lieu of the actual observation (with the observer reviewing the tape after class, first alone and then with the teacher) or the tape can be made with the reviewer present. The latter option will provide more information. Videotapes have the advantage of providing a repeatable record (and they can be erased by the teacher). Just as coaches review a football game with their players, examining each play on videotape, so the instructor and observer can isolate instructional acts and raise the question, How might the outcome have differed had the act been otherwise performed? Tapes are also useful correctives, since the teacher and observer will remember the class through their selective filters. Albert and Hipp (1976) describe the use of videotape in a teacher development course for graduate students of sociology. Much of what they say has application to the colleague observation process, and they provide a useful bibliography as well (see also Fuller and Manning, 1973).

A useful variation of the observation process involves a third person whose role is to keep the teacher and colleague on their agreed-upon agenda, indicate when the discussion is moving beyond the evidence, keep track of time, and finally, help summarize the general points that emerged in the discussion.

Using colleague observations. Once the observation and follow-up discussion(s) are completed, the teacher must decide what use to make of the assessment. It helps to select one specific aspect of teaching for developmental work. The teacher must decide whether more observations or data are needed (e.g., a special student evaluating form to gather data on the teaching problems of concern to that instructor). With this information, the teacher can turn for assistance to books, colleagues, or instructional development personnel for help in working out alternative teaching patterns. These, in turn, must be assessed. The teacher should share with the colleague-observer the results of this larger process. And the teacher and colleague may want to share with their department a description of the process they went through and its results.

Statements from Observations

In the following pages, we present excerpts from five letters written to doctoral students in sociology (at the University of North Carolina-Chapel Hill) after they were observed as they taught. Most of these graduate student instructors were about midway through their first stint at independent teaching. Their classrooms were filled largely with first-year undergraduates in an Introductory Sociology or Social Problems course.[26] In past semesters, the graduate student instructors had served as teaching assistants, and they were taking our seminar-practicum on the teaching of sociology.[27] Immediately following our observation of each instructor, we talked briefly with them about their class session. The letters were written within two or three days of the observation and were followed by another, longer, talk in which we discussed the class observation as well as the written material for the course and student evaluations. After presenting the excerpts, we will review the points of observation illustrated, and comment on our approach to the observations.

Excerpt 1

It was good to outline, as you did, the class work for the day by putting those topics on the board; it helps to tie ideas together. To do so, confers on a class session both an intelligible sequence and a degree of integrity (unity). It also has another benefit: it frees one to wander afield since there's a clear structure to return to, to help students—and teacher—recall the central issues. A technique I've found useful is to frame the agenda as questions—especially questions that have meaning to my students. Tillich says, somewhere, that teachers often throw answers like rocks at the heads of students who have not yet asked the questions.[28] I take the aim of education as getting answers, however tentative, to questions that have some significance for most students. Logic suggests that questions should precede answers. Hence the importance of an agenda stated as a set of, say, three to five questions.

Excerpt 2

Your agenda for the day was stated as three topics or matters to be covered: (1) shortcomings of certain sociological research on the family, (2) patterns of deference in the family, and (3) changes in the family under conditions of change from agrarian to industrial society. I'm glad you suggested [in a postobservation discussion] that those topics would have been better put as questions. Too much of education (classes, courses, and curricula) is a link-sausage of topics. And we deliver truth about topics; we transmit truth (answers) before it has any demonstrable bearing on questions worth posing (and so perceived by our students).

It was quite clear in the discussion of deference in the family that you were tapping a matter on which students had vivid experience. For that, and a more important reason, I wondered why you chose the ordering of the three topics as you did. When you discussed (first) the adequacy of some research on the family, you provided some well-prepared examples. But why didn't you use the deference research for your examples? And discuss the methodological issues (all important and well chosen) second and within the context of the deference work. In that sequence they might have had more power; students might have understood better the need for concern about methodology.

Your mini-lecture on family and history, focusing on technological changes was, I thought, nicely done. Good use of Linton, Zimmerman, and Goode: your competence and preparation showed. The points emerged clearly: changes in family type, structure, role, and function; changes in romantic love as a marriage basis; generation gaps and so on. The link to technology, your key independent variable, was always clear to me and, as best I could judge (from students' questions, comments, and facial expressions), to your students. You might have used that little lecture as an opportunity to extend the technology-family link. Take the generation gap you spoke of. Gaps and lags—in general, not just in the family. Ogburn wrote on the family and technology; he was concerned about culture lag generically. The power of the basic concept lies partly in its broad applicability. Effects on family patterning is only one case.

Excerpt 3

Two students asked you what you expected in the book review assignment. And I gather they were not the only ones to do so. Your answer to them was quite clear. And I was a bit surprised at the question itself since I found the book review assignment, as given in the syllabus and elaborated in the handout, specific and coherent. I thought, as you no doubt did, that the assignment was clear. I gather we were wrong. Reflecting on this, I wonder how many of your

students have ever read a book review—one in, say The New York Times, The New York Review of Books, *or in any journal. Perhaps none. Hence, your carefully prepared words may have been read by students with no instances to relate them to. I recall that Professor Smith used to provide her Sociology 52 classes with a sample book review (or maybe she put it on library reserve), along with explicit guidelines and criteria. Incidentally, you might ask Smith about the comparative book review assignment she uses in her 121 course. I've found it useful (I've learned a lot from her assignment).*

Excerpt 4

At several points during the class, you asked if others heard what a student was saying. (I was glad you did that: it told me, told all in class, that you wanted each to hear, and that student contributions mattered.) That some could not hear is some evidence of the difficulties imposed on us by sheer physical distance. To get around this, you might consider changing the seating pattern. Any arrangement that reduces the average distance between teacher and students (and among students) will enhance eye contact and heighten the level of attending. I think it's plausible that, in any rectangular classroom, the distant right and left corners plus the rearmost seats are those where students who've read themselves out of the operation are likely to sit. I'd bet that one could predict high and low grades on the basis of seating location with much better than average success. [29] *[For example, see figure 14.1.] In any event, when one has a classroom with movable seats (and when one has, as you did, blackboards on the long and short walls), alternative seating patterns are possible. Zest, control, attentiveness, and participation are functions of propinquity. You*

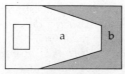

$\bar{X}_a > \bar{X}_b$ and p < .01
(Mean grade among a's is significantly higher than mean grade among b's.)

Figure 14.1 Estimated Classroom Location of Students Who Are Higher and Lower in Participation and in Grades Achieved.

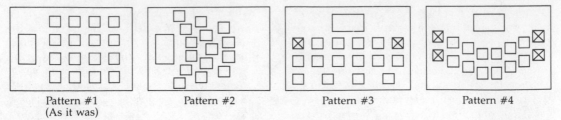

Figure 14.2 Four Classroom Seating Arrangements that Affect Propinquity, Participation, and Involvement.

might have shifted from pattern #1 [see figure 14.2] to #2 or #3 or at least to #4. The three other patterns reduce average student distance from the teacher and the front blackboard. Such patterns have limitations: if you show a film or use the extreme ends of the blackboards, students in the seats I've marked with X's will have difficulty seeing.

You're lucky your room has movable seats; most rooms in Dey Hall have fixed seats arranged as in pattern #1. In their inscrutable wisdom, the classroom architects have minimized propinquity.

Excerpt 5

I wasn't able to get any sense of continuity—of the articulation of the session with earlier parts of the course . . . or any sense of how today's sessions would tie into future work in the course. This is especially important in getting students to look for similarities of form between situations apparently different in context. You talked about differentiation and inequality. In discussing urban blacks and whites, you spoke about causes and consequences of differentiation and inequality. Can a link be made to Irish Catholics and Protestants in Boston (or Ireland), or orientals on the West Coast, or . . .? If one can see the themes running throughout the course, it lends a desirable integrity to the whole enterprise (and, of course, demonstrates the utility of the theme—in this case, the concepts of differentiation and inequality).

Now perhaps you've done this, in one way or another, at other times. I'm only indicating that I didn't find it apparent in this one session. Relatedly, your syllabus indicates a film coming up next week. How will you link . . .

Points of observation. In these excerpts from letters to graduate instructors, we identified six points of observation:

1. *The Physical Setting*
How do physical conditions—space, light, heat, and time—affect reciprocal influence? (See excerpt 4.)

2. *Setting the Agenda*
What are the problems posed, the answers sought? (See excerpts 1 and 2.)

3. *Questions*
How central are they to the presentation? how salient in students' minds? How significant are they demonstrated to be? (See excerpts 1 and 2.)

4. *The Integrity of the Class and the Course*
Do things hang together sensibly? Are sociological themes carried throughout the course? (See excerpts 1, 2, and 5.)

5. *Communication*
How can the teacher fulfill the need to provide instances and examples to ensure comprehension? (See excerpts 2 and 3.)

6. *Resources*
Does the teacher know of colleagues (or written materials) who can provide assistance pertinent to something observed? (See excerpt 3.)

These points provide a summary of the elements identified in portions of five observations. We hope that our discussions and letters, based on the observations, provided a useful mirror of sorts for our young colleagues and helped them think about their teaching. These (and many other) points of observation also allow us to identify areas for more systematic consideration and attention. And they can start us—teacher and observer—on the road to seeking out research that will enhance our effectiveness. A specific example: our observations sensitized us to the possible effects on student learning of different seating patterns. We found pertinent research justified our concern, and provided some cues for altering our classroom practice (even where we can't alter seating arrangements).

The nature of the feedback.   Our five excerpts illustrate some of the elements of constructive feedback described earlier, as well as some other points about the nature of feedback.

We tried to: (1) accent positive elements in the teaching observed—as in excerpts 1, 2, and 4; (2) be specific in our reactions—excerpt 2 is perhaps the best example; (3) provide the reasons we found something particularly useful or problematic—excerpts 1 and 2; (4) remember that we were observing a *sociology* class and respond on substantive points—as in excerpts 2 and 5; (5) describe our own reactions and acknowledge that our impressions were based on partial evidence and could be ill founded—see excerpt 5, for example; (6) report the observed basis for our reactions and justify our suggestions—excerpts 1 and 2; and (7) remember that we, too, share with those we observe, our colleagues, problems and opportunities—see excerpt 3.

Because our observations were made in connection with a graduate course on teaching, our evaluative response was more directive than it might otherwise have been. And certainly we made mis-

takes in the nature of our feedback. We hope, though, that these excerpts and the analysis of them illustrate the benefits that can accrue from peer observation.

Resources: Literature on Evaluating Instructor Achievement

We find evidence on different modes of evaluation of teaching used in colleges and universities in Astin and Lee (1967) and Seldin (1975). Parallel data for sociology departments appear in Ewens and Emling (1975) and Bowker (1978).

A convenient collection of some of the better writing on evaluation appears in Scholl and Inglis (1977:section IV). Two short treatments are Eble (1972:chapter 4) and Landers (1978).

Miller (1972) proposes a system of evaluation of teaching, research, and seven other sorts of faculty work. He provides a series of appraisal forms for each of these areas and a 120-item annotated bibliography of works published since 1960. While his procedures are rudimentary, they provide workable starting points. Another, more useful, volume by Miller (1974) discusses the development of institution-wide faculty evaluation programs; included is a detailed case study, a chapter on student evaluation of teaching, a 285-item annotated bibliography (two-thirds of the citations are works published since 1965), and sixteen rating forms—ten of them, well-known SET instruments. Dressel (1976:chapter 15) contains a short, useful overview of issues on evaluation of faculty in teaching and other roles.

Grasha's (1977) excellent little book discusses sources of resistance to faculty evaluation, means of overcoming them, and principles and models for the assessment and development of instructional ability. He includes a training simulation of faculty assessment based on case studies provided.

The most extensive review and rigorous analysis of the literature on student evaluation of teaching (SET) is Doyle (1975); a short review is found in McKeachie (1978:chapter 26). Among the better articles reviewing empirical research on SET are Costin, Greenough, and Menges (1971), Kulik and Kulik (1974), and Kulik and McKeachie (1975). Several dozen papers reporting use of SET in sociology courses are available; these are cited in Davis, Goldsmid, and Perry (1977:65–69) and in literature reviews appearing in each April issue of *Teaching Sociology* since 1976. Beyond the work on SET and the scores of articles evaluating the use of specific instructional methods in sociology (see chapter 12), there is little available on the assessment of teaching in sociology.

The meager literature relating to faculty self-evaluation, and colleague and administrator evaluation through classroom observation and other methods, is briefly discussed in Doyle (1975:37–38, 45, 67, 71–72, 81), Miller (1974:20–29), and Seldin (1975:18–23). Although many sociologists have written about the professorial role and diverse aspects of higher education,[30] few of our colleagues have closely examined assessment of instructor achievement. One notable exception is the attempt by Hind, Dornbusch, and Scott (1974) to develop a theory of evaluation applied to a university faculty.

Finally, problems of research in the evaluation of teaching are discussed in many articles and in books on teaching; one brief, easily available treatment is McKeachie (1978:257–263). Bozeman (1976) has described how one might apply to the assessment of college teaching various evaluation research designs. Doyle (1975:*passim*) is also worth consulting.

ॐ

We need to evaluate for many reasons—among them, to learn how well we have done what we set out to do and to get cues as to how we might do it better.

Many means of evaluation are available but each mode is not equally useful in assessing the teacher's command of field, use of the means of instruction, and extent to which students have learned from the course. Generally speaking, the means most commonly used to assess teaching are indirect, removed from the classroom, and of unknown reliability and validity. One exception, at least for many sociology departments, is the wide use of student evaluations of teaching. When well designed, such ratings can provide the teacher with valuable information of known reliability, validity, and pertinence.

While there are persuasive reasons to use student evaluations, we need to compensate for their limitations by also using other methods of assessment. These include colleague observation, examination of the teacher's writings (including course materials), and evaluation by changes in student performance.

Ample resources are available to assist sociologists in the crucial task of evaluating, and improving, their effectiveness as teachers.

Notes

1. The advising role is sufficiently important and, often enough, unassessed to warrant this note. For many years, Antioch College asked students to rate their advisers. The Testing Office provided instructors with a summary of advisee ratings and comments (noting variation by student type and comparison to other

advisers). Students were asked if their faculty adviser: "(a) is genuinely interested in you and your problems, (b) is readily available, for example, keeps office hours, saves time for advising, keeps in touch with you, (c) is friendly, makes you feel at ease and free to talk, (d) sees problems from your point of view, (e) talks over your problems, offers suggestions, but leaves decisions up to you, and (f) knows Antioch thoroughly, for example, courses, requirements, fields, etc." Brief, useful discussions of advising can be found in Eble (1976:72–75) and Bordin (1969). Wilson et al. (1975) includes some pertinent research.

2. Redefining the teacher's role may mean shifting the balance of teaching, research, and administrative work, and of different types and levels of teaching. It can be temporary or permanent and aided by sabbaticals or grants to attend in-service workshops and institutes. Pertinent issues are discussed in Eble's *Career Development of the Effective College Teacher* (1971b).

3 . Incapacity is sometimes generated or reinforced by circumstances beyond the teacher's immediate control. Examples are extremely heavy teaching loads, a variety of professional and personal cross-pressures, a department's or college's failure to define, encourage, measure, and reward effective teaching, an institution's failure to offer programs of instructional improvement, and the failure of graduate departments to provide purposive training in the teaching role. The low visibility of teaching compared to research, while not necessary, no doubt fosters a lack of attention to teaching. On this last point, see Hind, Dornbusch, and Scott (1974:121–124).

4. This one study takes on added importance because of its use of: a controlled experimental design; student samples matched on a variety of attributes, including initial knowledge of subject matter; a variety of types of learning gain (direct, anticipatory, accumulated, and overall); test instruments checked for reliability and validity; and measurement by several types of instruments (including multiple-choice tests, essay exams, attitude scales, and outside reading records). However, we are not aware of the exact nature of the learning measured, whether factual, skills in analysis, problem solving, and the like. In an unrelated study, R. C. Wilson et al. (1975) report that the extent of student-teacher interaction *outside the classroom* is a significant factor affecting perceived student changes.

5. This article in *The Chronicle of Higher Education* reports on a lawsuit brought by a student to recover costs of books and tuition in a course at the University of Bridgeport she described as worthless. She charged that she learned nothing except how to use an overhead projector and that (Semas, 1975:1) "the only requirement was to write a book report and that all the students in the course received A's." Other suits against schools and instructors are reported in this article and, periodically, in the *Chronicle*.

6. While we detect in sociology no massive trend toward increased concern with instruction, it is our impression that an increasing (if modest) proportion of job announcements in the *ASA Employment Bulletin* explicitly indicate an interest in demonstrated teaching competence. And we know that the number of graduate departments of sociology that offer courses or workshops for graduate students in the teaching of sociology has increased during the 1970s (see Goldsmid, 1976a:230–231).

7. We call this concern belated because the ASA delayed action in support of improving sociology instruction long after other professional societies—economics, psychology, history, biology, mathematics, and others— had moved to set standards and improve instruction. This was sometimes justified by the contention that the sole concern of a professional society must be to advance knowledge. We think it myopic to disregard the conditions for advancing knowledge that include protecting our publicly exposed flanks and improving our induction procedures. Both conditions entail a concern for the adequacy of undergraduate instruction in sociology. Since 1974, the ASA Council has strongly

supported the ASA Projects on Teaching Undergraduate Sociology.

8. In an issue of the campus newspaper at the University of North Carolina at Chapel Hill, the editors discussed the frustrations of registration, students trying to gain admission to thirteen very popular courses. Two of these courses were in sociology: Crime and Delinquency and Family and Society. (Others were in astronomy, botany, drama, music, physical education, physics, psychology, and radio-television-motion pictures.) They then wrote: "It is remarkable how closely this list approximates the list of 'slide' or 'gut' courses on campus . . . [and] students who get closed out of these thirteen courses should not be terribly disappointed because in many cases they have only been spared some of the worst courses at UNC" (*The Daily Tar Heel*, Editorial, October 29, 1975).

9. One study conducted at the University of Iowa in 1948 reported that students felt less confident in their ability to assess the instructor's knowledge of subject (57 percent did feel competent) than they did the teacher's clarity in explaining points (95 percent), interest in class progress (81 percent), friendliness and cooperativeness (94 percent), enthusiasm for subject (88 percent), and fairness in examinations (68 percent). This study by Stuit and Ebel (1952) is summarized in Miller (1974:226). The student modesty regarding rating of instructor knowledge is, we think, appropriate, since students cannot know what the teacher is not teaching.

10. We know of no study that reports a significant negative correlation between teaching and research. Most studies report either no significant relationship or significant correlations under +.25. The studies employ a variety of measures of research productivity, including publications (books, articles, both), citation in the work of others, primary (versus secondary) authorship, journal reputation, etc.

11. Recent data on this well-documented fact come from the 1977 Lipset-Ladd survey of the American Professoriate (Ladd, 1979). Forty-three percent of all academics had published four or fewer articles and no books; 24 percent had no publications at all. Ladd documents variations by age, discipline, and type of school. But substantial proportions of academics in all categories have few publications.

12. The Rodin and Rodin conclusion is suspect because: (1) the rating accorded the teacher (eleven teaching assistants) may have been confounded indeterminately with the satisfaction with the course and the professor in charge; (2) we lack information about the reliability of the measures used (mean grades and mean instructor ratings) in discriminating among instructors; (3) the student rating was a single general question—"What grade would you assign to his total teaching performance?"; (4) within-section variation was not examined; (5) the variance in class grades was severely constricted and section-to-section differences may be accounted for by error; and (6) the sampling error of the correlation coefficients is large. Centra and Doyle have each presented reasonable interpretations of the Rodin and Rodin findings that suggest that their ratings should be used as a *negative* index.

13. The relationship between student ability and teacher ratings is open to several interpretations (see Doyle, 1975:74–75).

14. The study described by Doyle is Elliott (1950). Elliott also "found that the correlations between tested instructor knowledge of chemistry and student achievement (test scores adjusted for initial ability) ranged from −.01 through −.56. That is, he found a tendency for students to learn less in freshman chemistry from recitation and laboratory instructors who knew more about chemistry, especially freshman chemistry." Although this result might be explained by differences in instructors' motivation to teach, it merits further study (Doyle, 1975:54, note c).

15. Data for this study were from "questionnaires administered to students attending class during the last week of the fall semester, preceding finals, for two consecutive years. Each instructor received uniform instructions on administering the forms and having them anonymously returned from classes" (Wimberly et al., 1978:6). About 80 percent of the

instructors and classes were in sociology; an additional 15 percent were in anthropology and the rest were in social work. In the factor analysis, the forty-two factor loadings (twenty-one items, two years) ranged between .30 and .66; twenty were .45 or higher and an additional ten were between .35 and .44. Of the forty cosine levels reported (in the cluster analysis) thirty were .9, seven were .8, and three were less than .7. (See Wimberly, Faulkner, and Moxley, 1978:9–17.)

16. Kulik and Kulik's four dimensions appear to have the following equivalence to the Feldman categories: *skill*—Feldman categories 1 and 5; *rapport*—6, 7, and 8; *structure*—2 and 4; *difficulty*—no clearly appropriate category.

17. Using Hogan's data, Kulik and Kulik calculated correlations for the four teaching dimensions (skill, rapport, structure, and difficulty) for these situations: same course, same instructor (N = 30 pairs); same instructor, two different courses (N = 45 pairs); and two different instructors, same course (N = 39 pairs). These correlations were used to parcel out contributions to the variance in student rating scores for the course and the instructor. Path coefficients were used to track the influences on ratings. The variance in the four rating scales contributed by teacher, course, their covariance, and the error term were calculated. *Kulik and Kulik are careful to note important limitations of Hogan's data and their reanalysis.*

18. Research on ETS's Student Instructional Report touches: item reliability, validity, correlates, and factor structure; comparisons of student ratings with those by colleagues, with those of the same students five years after taking the course, and with the self-ratings of the teacher; and many other factors. Because ETS has such a large N available, it is able to perform extremely detailed analyses using sophisticated designs and statistical analyses. Throughout this chapter, we have drawn on some of the ETS research; see, especially, citations to work by John A. Centra. For a small charge ($5.00 in mid-1979), ETS will provide a packet of materials on the SIR form. It includes sample forms, copies of some published articles, and in-house bulletins reporting research

on SIR, a list of colleges using SIR, and a schedule of fees for ETS services.

19. Normative data for rating forms are usually not statistical norms in the strict sense. Although such data are based on very large numbers and diverse types of students and teachers, usually they do not precisely represent the populations of concern. ETS, for example, notes that since institutions using their SIR form are not proportionately representative of the types of American, higher education institutions and since local definitions of classifications (e.g., course level) are used, their data guides present comparative rather than normative data.

20. While there is clear variation in student response patterns to different rating scales, research suggests that a halo effect is sometimes present. However, this effect "is not so powerful that stable factor structures cannot emerge" in analysis of forms (see Doyle, 1975:24, 41). Some evidence suggesting that students discriminate in answering different rating items can be found by examining normative data collected for various evaluation forms. Consider these data on 12,000 students who rated their teachers using the Cornell Inventory (Maas and Owen, 1973). The median ratings for six 5-point, one-directional scale items tapping different aspects of discussion sections were: 3.1, 3.3, 3.9, 4.3, 4.6, and 4.8. For three questions on assigned papers, the median ratings were 2.9, 3.7, and 3.8. And for eight questions on examinations, the range of medians was 3.0 to 4.4. The mean ratings exhibited similar range, and the standard deviations for all items was about 1.1. Because these data aggregate responses from several hundred courses, they are clearly not the best evidence and are only suggestive.

21. Teachers interested in developing their skills as lecturers might consider questions about the organization of the lectures; the pacing of their speech, enunciation, and interfering mannerisms; the use of audiovisual materials; the ability to tell whether students could follow a set of points; the use of examples to clarify; whether they made clear how a given topic fit into the larger course pattern; their ability to help students see links between lecture material and course reading; the use of summaries to promote student retention; the level of detail; whether it would have been easier (and just as effective) for students to read, rather than listen to, a certain lecture or set of lectures, etc.

22. For a detailed description of how one student rating form, TABS, is used as part of an instructional improvement process, see Bergquist and Phillips (1977:69–123). See, also, Grasha (1977).

23. Wilson and Wood (1974) provide a useful description of ten "faculty-initiated methods for getting feedback for improving instruction." Each of these methods can be used in the early portions of a course in time to allow use of information gained; some methods are particularly useful in large class situations: (1) *student liaison committee*—weekly meetings with a three- to five-student committee, the membership of which can be rotated or fixed, but is known to the entire class; (2) *student lecture notes*—especially useful when you suspect your organization and clarity of presentation is not all it should be (the teacher borrows and reviews some notes); (3) *audiotapes and analysis*—do you wait after asking students a question? fail to answer questions? ask certain types of questions? know the relative proportions of class time devoted to exposition, questioning, student talk?; (4) *videotaping and analysis*—reviewing the tape with a colleague or teaching specialist to help overcome selective perception; (5) *colleague observation*—which often happens when teachers trade guest lectures (but let your colleague know in advance of the visitation what you want commented on); (6) *telephone tape-answering machine*—to record student queries and reactions, (an economically feasible possibility in a department or school with many large classes); (7) *focused questionnaires*—very short and designed to elicit comment on a single, specific aspect of your teaching (sampling can be employed in large classes and it is important to keep the process simple enough to give yourself immediate feedback); (8) *early student ratings and self-ratings*—student evaluation or self-

evaluation of teaching form used early in semester and repeated later (watch for large discrepancies in student response patterns or between student and self-ratings); (9) *student characteristics and course objectives*—design a short instrument to provide you with information on your class (background attributes and learning styles, for example) and consider ways in which instruction can take advantage of what you learn; and (10) *course impact*—before and after tests and student self-assessments of their learnings.

24. Persons outside one's department (e.g., a trusted faculty member in another department or a skilled and trusted campus instructional development specialist) can often be effective in the observer role and, indeed, can bring special resources and perspectives to the task.

25. Most of the books on college teaching described in the appendix to this book provide checklists or will be useful in their construction. In addition, see Bergquist and Phillips (1977:206–207), on active or effective listening skills, and Bergquist and Phillips (1975:chapters 4,6) for checklists on teacher presentation skills, questioning skills, ability to increase student participation, student and teacher verbal interaction patterns, discussion groups, and paraphrasing and other interaction skills. Finally, many student evaluation-of-teaching forms (especially those that have a large catalog of rating items) are useful in constructing checklists (see the appendix to this chapter for several forms).

26. As we noted earlier, because we consider introductory-level and survey courses the hardest to teach, we think it unfortunate that they are so often relegated to those with least experience in the discipline and in the classroom.

27. For a description and commentary on this seminar-practicum, see Wilson (1976). The full syllabus for the course is part of a set of materials on such teacher development courses available for purchase from the American Sociological Association's Teaching Resources Center, 1722 N Street, N. W., Washington, D. C. 20036.

28. The exact quotation, which appears in Brown (1971:15), is "what Paul Tillich has called the fatal pedagogical error—'To throw answers like stones at the heads of those who have not yet asked the questions.' "

29. A number of studies have found that students who sit in the central section of a classroom (and especially those who sit close to the teacher), participate more than those who do not. And at least one study reports that teachers *initiate* more exchanges with those

students. See Dunkin and Biddle (1974:227, 391) and Schmuck and Schmuck (1975:147–149). While the causal influence here is not necessarily one-way, teachers wanting class participation are well advised to make special efforts to foster the involvement of students at the fringes of the room.

30. The work of David Riesman and his colleagues is noteworthy; see, also, Caplow and McGee (1958) and papers in Anderson and Murray (1971).

Chapter 14 Appendix: Selected Student Evaluation of Teaching Forms

---

Exhibit 14.1 University of Michigan

CATALOG OF ITEMS FOR
INSTRUCTOR-DESIGNED QUESTIONNAIRES

Student Development

Knowledge and Skills

1. I learned a good deal of factual material in this course.
2. I gained a good understanding of concepts and principles in this field.
3. I learned to apply principles from this course to new situations.
4. I learned to identify main points and central issues in this field.
5. I learned to identify formal characteristics of works of art.
6. I developed the ability to solve real problems in this field.
7. I developed creative ability in this field.
8. I developed the ability to communicate clearly about this subject.
9. I developed the ability to carry out original research in this area.
10. I developed an ability to evaluate new work in this field.
11. I learned to recognize the quality of works of art in this field.

Interests and Curiosity

12. I deepened my interest in the subject matter of this course.
13. I developed enthusiasm about the course material.
14. I was stimulated to do outside reading about the course material.
15. I was stimulated to discuss related topics outside of class.

16. I developed plans to take additional related courses.
17. I developed a set of overall values in this field.

Social Skills and Attitudes

18. I participated actively in class discussion.
19. I developed leadership skills in this class.
20. I developed new friendships in this class.
21. I developed greater awareness of societal problems.
22. I became interested in community projects related to the course.
23. I learned to value new viewpoints.
24. I reconsidered many of my former attitudes.

Self-concept

25. I gained a better understanding of myself through this course.
26. I gained an understanding of some of my personal problems.
27. I developed a greater sense of personal responsibility.
28. I increased my awareness of my own interests and talents.
29. I developed more confidence in myself.

Vocational Skills and Attitudes

30. I developed skills needed by professionals in this field.
31. I learned about career opportunities.
32. I developed a clearer sense of professional identity.

Instructor Ratings

Instructor Skill

33. The instructor gives clear explanations.
34. The instructor makes good use of examples and illustrations.
35. The instructor stresses important points in lectures or discussions.
36. The instructor is enthusiastic.
37. The instructor puts material across in an interesting way.
38. The instructor seems to enjoy teaching.
39. The instructor appears to have a thorough knowledge of the subject of the course.
40. The instructor seems knowledgeable in many areas.
41. The instructor is not confused by unexpected questions.
42. The instructor is skillful in observing student reactions.
44. The instructor teaches near the class level.

Rapport

45. The instructor is friendly.
46. The instructor is permissive and flexible.
47. The instructor maintains an atmosphere of good feeling in the class.
48. The instructor acknowledges all questions to the best of his or her ability.
49. The instructor treats students with respect.
50. The instructor encourages constructive criticism.
51. The instructor is willing to meet with and help students outside class.
52. The instructor gives individual attention to students in this course.

Interaction

53. Students frequently volunteer their own opinions.
54. One real strength of this course is the classroom discussion.
55. Students in this course are free to disagree and ask questions.

Feedback

56. The instructor suggests specific ways students can improve.
57. The instructor tells students when they have done particularly well.
58. The instructor keeps students informed of their progress.

Organization

59. The instructor has everything going according to schedule.
60. The instructor follows an outline closely.
61. The instructor uses class time well.
62. The instructor seems well prepared for each class.

63. The objectives of the course were clearly explained.
64. Work requirements and grading system were clear from the beginning.

Difficulty

65. The amount of work required is appropriate for the credit received.
66. The amount of material covered in the course is reasonable.
67. The instructor sets high standards for students.
68. The instructor has made the course sufficiently difficult to be stimulating.

Course Elements

Teaching Assistant

69. My TA gives clear and understandable explanations.
70. My TA is enthusiastic.
71. My TA appears to have a thorough knowledge of the subject of the course.
72. My TA is skillful in observing student reactions.
73. My TA is friendly.
74. In my TA's section, students volunteer their own opinions.
75. My TA tells students when they have done a particularly good job.
76. My TA plans class activities in detail.
77. My TA asks for more than students can get done in the time available.
78. My TA sets high standards for students.
79. My TA grades papers (exams, homework) fairly.

Recitation Section

80. The recitation section is a valuable part of this course.
81. The recitation section is a great help to learning.
82. There is ample opportunity to ask questions in the recitation section.
83. The recitation section clarifies lecture material.
84. The recitation section extends the coverage of topics presented in lectures.
85. Students get individual attention in the recitation section.

Written Assignments

86. Written assignments (papers, problem sets) seem carefully chosen.
87. Written assignments are interesting and stimulating.
88. Written assignments make students think.
89. Directions for written assignments are clear and specific.
90. Written assignments require a reasonable amount of time and effort.
91. Written assignments are relevant to what is presented in class.
92. Written assignments are graded fairly.
93. Written assignments are returned promptly.

Reading Assignments

94. Reading assignments seem carefully chosen.
95. Reading assignments are interesting and stimulating.
96. Reading assignments make students think.
97. Reading assignments require a reasonable amount of time and effort.
98. Reading assignments are relevant to what is presented in class.

Laboratory Assignments

99. The laboratory was a valuable part of this course.
100. Laboratory assignments seem carefully chosen.
101. Laboratory assignments are interesting and stimulating.
102. Laboratory assignments make students think.
103. Directions for laboratory assignments are clear and specific.
104. Laboratory assignments require a reasonable amount of time and effort.
105. Laboratory assignments are relevant to what is presented in class.
106. Laboratory reports are graded fairly.
107. Laboratory reports are returned promptly.

Textbook

108. The textbook makes a valuable contribution to the course.
109. The textbook is easy to read and understand.
110. The textbook presents various sides of issues.
111. The textbook is accurate.

Media

112. Films are a valuable part of this course.
113. Films used in this course are interesting and stimulating.
114. Films used in this course are a great help to learning.
115. Videotapes are a valuable part of this course.
116. Videotapes used in this course are interesting and stimulating.
117. Videotapes used in this course are a great help to learning.
118. Slides are a valuable part of this course.
119. Slides used in this course are interesting and stimulating.
120. Slides used in this course are a great help to learning.
121. Audiotapes are a valuable part of this course.
122. Audiotapes used in this course are interesting and stimulating.
123. Audiotapes used in this course are a great help to learning.

Exams

124. Examinations cover the important aspects of the course.
125. The exams cover the reading assignments well.
126. The exams cover the lecture material well.
127. Exams are creative and require original thought.
128. Exams are reasonable in length and difficulty.
129. Examination items are clearly worded.
130. The exams are returned in a reasonable amount of time.
131. The examinations are graded very carefully and fairly.
132. The test items are adequately explained after a test is given.

Grading

133. Grades are assigned fairly and impartially.
134. The grading system was clearly explained.
135. The instructor has a realistic definition of good performance.

Instructor-Written Items

136. — Instructor-written —
137. — Instructor-written —
138. — Instructor-written —

Open-Ended Questions

139. Comment on the quality of instruction in this course.
140. How can the instructor improve the teaching of this course?
141. Which aspects of the course did you like best?
142. Which aspects of the course did you like least?
143. What changes would you make in the lectures?
144. What changes would you make in the readings?
145. What changes would you make in the discussion sections?
146. What changes would you make in the examinations?
147. Which aspects of the course were most valuable?
148. Which aspects of the course were least valuable?

University Core Items

149. I would recommend this course to others.
150. I would recommend the instructor for this course to a fellow student.
151. The instructor motivates me to do my best work.
152. I feel that I am performing up to my potential in this course.
153. I had a strong desire to take this course.

Exhibit 14.2 Educational Testing Service

STUDENT INSTRUCTIONAL REPORT

SIR Report Number

This questionnaire gives you an opportunity to express anonymously your views of this course and the way it has been taught. Indicate the response closest to your view by blackening the appropriate oval. Use a soft lead pencil (preferably No. 2) for all responses to the questionnaire. Do not use an ink or ball point pen.

SECTION I Items 1-20. Blacken one response number for each question.

NA (0) = <u>Not Applicable or don't know</u>. The statement does not apply to this course or instructor, or you simply are not able to give a knowledgeable response.

SA (4) = <u>Strongly Agree</u>. You strongly agree with the statement as it applies to this course or instructor.

A (3) = <u>Agree</u>. You agree more than you disagree with the statement as it applies to this course or instructor.

D (2) = <u>Disagree</u>. You disagree more than you agree with the statement as it applies to this course or instructor.

SD (1) = <u>Strongly Disagree</u>. You strongly disagree with the statement as it applies to this course or instructor.

		NA	SA	A	D	SD
1.	The instructor's objectives for the course have been made clear..	⓪	④	③	②	①
2.	There was considerable agreement between the announced objectives of the course and					
	what was actually taught..	⓪	④	③	②	①
3.	The instructor used class time well...	⓪	④	③	②	①
4.	The instructor was readily available for consultation with students...................................	⓪	④	③	②	①
5.	The instructor seemed to know when students didn't understand the material............................	⓪	④	③	②	①
6.	Lectures were too repetitive of what was in the textbook(s)..	⓪	④	③	②	①
7.	The instructor encouraged students to think for themselves..	⓪	④	③	②	①
8.	The instructor seemed genuinely concerned with students' progress and was actively					
	helpful..	⓪	④	③	②	①
9.	The instructor made helpful comments on papers or exams..	⓪	④	③	②	①
10.	The instructor raised challenging questions or problems for discussion................................	⓪	④	③	②	①
11.	In this class I felt free to ask questions or express my opinions.....................................	⓪	④	③	②	①
12.	The instructor was well-prepared for each class..	⓪	④	③	②	①
13.	The instructor told students how they would be evaluated in the course...............................	⓪	④	③	②	①
14.	The instructor summarized or emphasized major points in lectures or discussions......................	⓪	④	③	②	①
15.	My interest in the subject area has been stimulated by this course...................................	⓪	④	③	②	①
16.	The scope of the course has been too limited; not enough material has been covered...................	⓪	④	③	②	①
17.	Examinations reflected the important aspects of the course...	⓪	④	③	②	①
18.	I have been putting a good deal of effort into this course...	⓪	④	③	②	①
19.	The instructor was open to other viewpoints..	⓪	④	③	②	①
20.	In my opinion, the instructor has accomplished (is accomplishing) his or her objectives					
	for the course...	⓪	④	③	②	①

SECTION II Items 21-31. Blacken one response number for each question.

21. For my preparation and ability, the level of difficulty of this course was:
    1. Very elementary   4. Somewhat difficult
    2. Somewhat elementary   5. Very difficult
    3. About right

22. The work load for this course in relation to other courses of equal credit was:
    1. Much lighter   4. Heavier
    2. Lighter   5. Much heavier
    3. About the same

23. For me, the pace at which the instructor covered the material during the term was:
    1. Very slow   4. Somewhat fast
    2. Somewhat slow   5. Very fast
    3. Just about right

24. To what extent did the instructor use examples or illustrations to help clarify the material?
    4. Frequently   2. Seldom
    3. Occasionally   1. Never

Questionnaire continued on the other side.

572MRC103P200

25. Was class size satisfactory for the method of conducting the class?

- ① Yes, most of the time
- ② No, class was too large
- ③ No, class was too small
- ④ It didn't make any difference one way or the other

26. Which one of the following best describes this course for you?

- ① Major requirement or elective within major field
- ② Minor requirement or required elective outside major field
- ③ College requirement but not part of my major or minor field
- ④ Elective not required in any way
- ⑤ Other

27. Which one of the following was your most important reason for selecting this course?

- ① Friend(s) recommended it
- ② Faculty advisor's recommendation
- ③ Teacher's excellent reputation
- ④ Thought I could make a good grade
- ⑤ Could use pass/no credit option
- ⑥ It was required
- ⑦ Subject was of interest
- ⑧ Other

28. What grade do you expect to receive in this course?

- ① A
- ② B
- ③ C
- ④ D
- ⑤ Fail
- ⑥ Pass
- ⑦ No credit
- ⑧ Other

29. What is your approximate cumulative grade-point average?

- ① 3.50-4.00
- ② 3.00-3.49
- ③ 2.50-2.99
- ④ 2.00-2.49
- ⑤ 1.50-1.99
- ⑥ 1.00-1.49
- ⑦ Less than 1.00
- ⑧ None yet--freshman or transfer

30. What is your class level?

- ① Freshman
- ② Sophomore
- ③ Junior
- ④ Senior
- ⑤ Graduate
- ⑥ Other

31. Sex:

- ① Female
- ② Male

SECTION III Items 32-39. Blacken one response number for each question.

	Not applicable, don't know, or there were none.	Excellent	Good	Satisfactory	Fair	Poor
32. Overall, I would rate the textbook(s)......................	⓪	⑤	④	③	②	①
33. Overall, I would rate the supplementary readings............	⓪	⑤	④	③	②	①
34. Overall, I would rate the quality of the exams..............	⓪	⑤	④	③	②	①
35. I would rate the general quality of the lectures...........	⓪	⑤	④	③	②	①
36. I would rate the overall value of class discussions........	⓪	⑤	④	③	②	①
37. Overall, I would rate the laboratories....................	⓪	⑤	④	③	②	①
38. I would rate the overall value of this course to me as.....	⓪	⑤	④	③	②	①

39. Compared to other instructors you have had (secondary school and college), how effective has the instructor been in this course? (Blacken one response number.)

One of the most effective (among the top 10%)	More effective than most (among the top 30%)	About average	Not as effective as most (in the lowest 30%)	One of the least effective (in the lowest 10%)
⑤	④	③	②	①

SECTION IV Items 40-49. If the instructor provided supplementary questions and response options, use this section for responding. Blacken only one response number for each question.

	NA												NA									
40.	⓪	①	②	③	④	⑤	⑥	⑦	⑧	⑨		45.	⓪	①	②	③	④	⑤	⑥	⑦	⑧	⑨
41.	⓪	①	②	③	④	⑤	⑥	⑦	⑧	⑨		46.	⓪	①	②	③	④	⑤	⑥	⑦	⑧	⑨
42.	⓪	①	②	③	④	⑤	⑥	⑦	⑧	⑨		47.	⓪	①	②	③	④	⑤	⑥	⑦	⑧	⑨
43.	⓪	①	②	③	④	⑤	⑥	⑦	⑧	⑨		48.	⓪	①	②	③	④	⑤	⑥	⑦	⑧	⑨
44.	⓪	①	②	③	④	⑤	⑥	⑦	⑧	⑨		49.	⓪	①	②	③	④	⑤	⑥	⑦	⑧	⑨

If you would like to make additional comments about the course or instruction, use a separate sheet of paper. You might elaborate on the particular aspects you liked most as well as those you liked least. Also, how can the course or the way it was taught be improved? PLEASE GIVE THESE COMMENTS TO THE INSTRUCTOR.

If you have any comments or suggestions about this questionnaire (for example, the content or responses available), please send them to: Student Instructional Report, Educational Testing Service, Princeton, New Jersey 08540.

Reprinted by permission.

Exhibit 14.3 University of Minnesota: Student Opinion Survey (SOS)

STUDENT OPINION SURVEY

This questionnaire gives you the opportunity to share your views about certain aspects of this course with your instructor. For each item below, please indicate the response closest to your opinion by circling the appropriate number. Please circle only one number for each item.

Thank you for your help.

GENERAL

Course _____

Instructor _____

Quarter & Year _____

measurement services center

9 clarence avenue s e minneapolis, minnesota 55414

	Very Strongly Disagree	Strongly Disagree	Disagree	Agree	Strongly Agree	Very Strongly Agree	Most Strongly Agree
The INSTRUCTOR:							
1. clearly presented the subject matter.	1	2	3	4	5	6	7
2. was approachable.	1	2	3	4	5	6	7
3. got me interested in her/his subject.	1	2	3	4	5	6	7
4. raised challenging questions.	1	2	3	4	5	6	7
5. when appropriate, related course material to other areas of knowledge.	1	2	3	4	5	6	7
The READING MATERIAL--including the textbook:							
6. held my attention easily.	1	2	3	4	5	6	7
7. was clearly written.	1	2	3	4	5	6	7
8. served well the purpose for which it was intended.	1	2	3	4	5	6	7
The TESTS:							
9. concentrated on the important points and topics in the subject matter.	1	2	3	4	5	6	7
10. seemed to have been carefully and conscientiously prepared.	1	2	3	4	5	6	7
11. were about the right length.	1	2	3	4	5	6	7
12. were clearly worded.	1	2	3	4	5	6	7
13. seemed to be good measures of my knowledge and understanding.	1	2	3	4	5	6	7
In GENERAL:							
14. procedures for determining grades were appropriate for this course.	1	2	3	4	5	6	7
15. the amount of work required was appropriate for the number of credits offered.	1	2	3	4	5	6	7
16. adequate information about how well I was doing was readily available.	1	2	3	4	5	6	7
17. adequate help was available when I needed it.	1	2	3	4	5	6	7
18. my responsibilities in the course were clearly defined.	1	2	3	4	5	6	7

Please continue on the other side. ⟶

19. How much did you like the SUBJECT MATTER of the course, forgetting about the instructor?

1	2	3	4	5	6	7
Disliked Intensely	Disliked Greatly	Disliked Somewhat	Liked Somewhat	Liked A Lot	Liked Very Much	Liked Exceptionally Well

20. How much did you like this instructor AS A PERSON?

1	2	3	4	5	6	7
Disliked Intensely	Disliked Considerably	Disliked Somewhat	Liked Somewhat	Liked A Lot	Liked Very Much	Liked Exceptionally Well

21. How would you rate this instructor's OVERALL TEACHING ABILITY?

1	2	3	4	5	6	7
Very Poor	Poor	Fair	Good	Very Good	Excellent	Exceptionally Good

22. How much would you say you LEARNED from this instructor?

1	2	3	4	5	6	7
Almost Nothing	Very Little	Little	A Fair Amount	Much	Very Much	An Exceptional Amount

23. How much EFFORT did you put into this course?

1	2	3	4	5	6	7
Almost None	Very Little	Little	A Fair Amount	Much	Very Much	An Exceptional Amount

24. In which YEAR in school are you?

1	2	3	4	5	6
Freshman	Sophomore	Junior	Senior	Graduate	Adult Special

25. Was this specific course REQUIRED of you?

1	2
Yes	No

26. What is your overall cumulative GRADE-POINT AVERAGE at the University of Minnesota?

1	2	3	4	5
2.0 or Below	2.1-2.5	2.6-3.0	3.1-3.5	3.6-4.0

27. Which SEX are you?

1	2
Female	Male

Your instructor may provide some additional questions. If so, please use this section to answer them. If not, please leave this section blank.

28.   1   2   3   4   5   6   7   32.   1   2   3   4   5   6   7

29.   1   2   3   4   5   6   7   33.   1   2   3   4   5   6   7

30.   1   2   3   4   5   6   7   34.   1   2   3   4   5   6   7

31.   1   2   3   4   5   6   7   35   1   2   3   4   5   6   7

Exhibit 14.4 Center for Faculty Evaluation and Development in Higher Education: Instructional Development and Effectiveness Assessment System (IDEA)

 SURVEY FORM -- STUDENT REACTIONS TO INSTRUCTION AND COURSES

Your thoughtful answers to these questions will provide helpful information to your instructor.

● Describe the frequency of your instructor's teaching procedures, using the following code:

1 — Hardly Ever	3 — Sometimes	
2 — Occasionally	4 — Frequently	5 — Almost Always

The Instructor:

1. Promoted teacher-student discussion (as opposed to mere responses to questions).
2. Found ways to help students answer their own questions.
3. Encouraged students to express themselves freely and openly.
4. Seemed enthusiastic about the subject matter.
5. Changed approaches to meet new situations.
6. Gave examinations which stressed unnecessary memorization.
7. Spoke with expressiveness and variety in tone of voice.
8. Demonstrated the importance and significance of the subject matter.
9. Made presentations which were dry and dull.
10. Made it clear how each topic fit into the course.
11. Explained the reasons for criticisms of students' academic performance.
12. Gave examination questions which were unclear.
13. Encouraged student comments even when they turned out to be incorrect or irrelevant.
14. Summarized material in a manner which aided retention.
15. Stimulated students to intellectual effort beyond that required by most courses.
16. Clearly stated the objectives of the course.
17. Explained course material clearly, and explanations were to the point.
18. Related course material to real life situations.
19. Gave examination questions which were unreasonably detailed (picky).
20. Introduced stimulating ideas about the subject.

● On each of the objectives listed below, rate the progress you have made in this course compared with that made in other courses you have taken at this college or university. In this course my progress was:

1 — Low (lowest 10 per cent of courses I have taken here)
2 — Low Average (next 20 per cent of courses)
3 — Average (middle 40 per cent of courses)
4 — High Average (next 20 percent of courses)
5 — High (highest 10 per cent of courses)

Progress on:

21. Gaining factual knowledge (terminology, classifications, methods, trends).
22. Learning fundamental principles, generalizations, or theories.
23. Learning to apply course material to improve rational thinking, problem-solving and decision making.
24. Developing specific skills, competencies and points of view needed by professionals in the field most closely related to this course.
25. Learning how professionals in this field go about the process of gaining new knowledge.
26. Developing creative capacities.
27. Developing a sense of personal responsibility (self-reliance, self-discipline).
28. Gaining a broader understanding and appreciation of intellectual-cultural activity (music, science, literature, etc.).
29. Developing skill in expressing myself orally or in writing.
30. Discovering the implications of the course material for understanding myself (interests, talents, values, etc.).

● On the next four questions, compare this course with others you have taken at this institution, using the following code:

1 — Much Less than Most Courses
2 — Less than Most
3 — About Average
4 — More than Most
5 — Much More than Most

The Course:

31. Amount of reading
32. Amount of work in other (non-reading) assignments
33. Difficulty of subject matter
34. Degree to which the course hung together (various topics and class activities were related to each other)

● Describe your attitudes toward and behavior in this course, using the following code:

1 — Definitely False	
2 — More False than True	4 — More True than False
3 — In Between	5 — Definitely True

Self-rating:

35. I worked harder on this course than on most courses I have taken.
36. I had a strong desire to take this course.
37. I would like to take another course from this instructor.
38. As a result of taking this course, I have more positive feelings toward this field of study.
39. I have given thoughtful consideration to the questions on this form.

● Describe your status on the following by blackening the appropriate space on the Response Card.

A. To which sex-age group do you belong?

1 — Female, under 25	3 — Female, 25 or over
2 — Male, under 25	4 — Male, 25 or over

B. Do you consider yourself to be a full-time or a part-time student?

1 — Full-time
2 — Part-time

C. Counting the present term, for how many terms have you attended this college or university?

1 — 1 term	3 — 4 or 5
2 — 2 or 3	4 — 6 or more

D. What grade do you expect to receive in this course?

1 — A	3 — C	
2 — B	4 — D or F	5 — Other

E. What is your classification?

1 — Freshman	3 — Junior or Senior	
2 — Sophomore	4 — Graduate	5 — Other

F. For how many courses have you filled out this form during the present term?

1 — This is the first course	
2 — 2 or 3 courses	3 — 4 or more courses

G. How well did the questions on this form permit you to describe your impressions of this instructor and course?

1 — Very well	3 — Not very well
2 — Quite well	4 — Poorly

If your instructor has extra questions, answer them in the space designated on the Response Card.

Your comments are invited on how the instructor might improve this course or teaching procedures. Use the back of the Response Card (unless otherwise directed).

Reprinted by permission.

AFTERWORD

Looking back after so many years of work on this book, we ask, as we would with any course we taught: What difference will it make? As with much of our teaching, we can only guess at the answer. Perhaps this volume will stimulate some bit-by-bit, incremental efforts, successively refined—more imaginative and more precise operationalization of instructional goals, or a cumulative file of regularly revised test items along with measures of their adequacy, or a collection of more powerful examples.

Some things we have proposed are readily done; others are more difficult. The clarity and meaning of a syllabus might be improved with but a slight investment—especially if one followed, systematically, research practice and did pilot runs on the instrument. Third-party testing might be readily effected. Single-shot field sorties, a laboratory exercise, or a demonstration can be honed to a fine edge, so enhancing the yield in information, explanation, and application. Time, imagination, and a drive to better the product are obviously needed; yet the job is manageable. Other undertakings require a longer commitment: converting a course to PSI or to TIPS; or devising the course as a research project with the instructor in the role of senior investigator; or exploiting students' background experiences to create sections with different aims, a venture achieved by tapping different, if overlapping, sectors of sociology; or creating laboratory or field experiences to engage students actively in the pursuit of problems in every major aspect of the course.

What difference will it make? The answer is complicated, too, by the confounding effects of program influence (this book) and self-selection. It is conceivable that many who read our book will be untouched by it because they already have a heightened self-consciousness that raises questions of instructional adequacy and constantly spurs them to better their teaching. Others may not be touched because effort invested in improved instruction is little rewarded; or because they regard teaching as an unteachable art; or because they are persuaded that command of the field suffices for effective instruction. Some would ask the question put rhetorically in Matthew 6:27: "And which of you by being anxious can add one cubit to his span of life?" That is the revised standard version. The St. James version asks: "Which of you by taking thought can add one cubit unto his stature?"

It is quite clear to us that a little anxiety about the quality of one's teaching is a needed first step in adding a cubit to the span of life—i.e., in extending the time one's influence is felt. When the anxiety leads to taking thought, and acting on the thinking, one can enhance one's stature as a teacher. Indeed, the contrary position is so implausibly anti-intellectual it is hard to conceive that a teaching sociologist would accept it.

About what, then, should one take thought? And how should one act on it? We have suggested a simple framework for thinking about teaching: ends, means, and weighing the worth of the means in achieving the ends. If sociologists are to act sensibly to actualize their thoughts on teaching, they will try, and try again, to state their teaching aims with utmost clarity—in the service of their students, of course; but above all, for themselves as teachers, so that they know what they are trying to do and can, as otherwise they could not, discover the extent of their success.

To add a cubit to their stature (and extend their impact beyond the mortal bounds of a class), instructors need to choose means appropriate to their ends. Such a choice entails learning about the range of available options—and others' experience in using those means. Others' experience, reported both orally and in scholarly papers, favors certain general means to be used regardless of course format or specific teaching device: changes of pace (variations in teaching techniques); high levels of student participation in tackling problems that are personally and professionally significant; frequent evaluative response; sensitivity to pedagogical problems posed by the inquisitor's role; an interplay between substantive information, theory, methods, and applications; priority given to questions that, answered differently, carry significantly differing implications for students' lives. (These general means we have discussed in chapter 12 and throughout the book.) Much of what we need to know about teaching remains in the realm of hunches born of idiosyncratic experience. But much, as we have stressed, is known quite reliably, and more is known than instructors put to use. Throughout the book, we have called attention to the wealth of resources available to improve the means of sociology instruction.

Whatever the means, the instructor, like a good sociologist, will raise serious questions about the effects of intervention. (We teachers do not escape the implicit claims of evaluation research: to forgo such assessment means that we will not know what we are doing.) Instructors will anticipate *un*anticipated outcomes. They will take soundings to discover unwanted as well as desired effects. And they will see objective, third-party measures of changed student behaviors as imperative supplements to subjective estimates of teacher performance.

Like all scientific efforts, sociology is both craft and art. It entails the craft of manipulating symbols precisely, tellingly. It enlists the imagination of the artist in detecting patterns in the tangled, crisscrossing web of social relations. ("Inspiration plays no less a role in science than it does in the realm of art," said Weber, 1922:136.) The art, the craft, the content, and the perspective of sociology—to teach these, and to do so better, is more than an evening's work. In the preface we said that improving instruction is an ongoing task that captures a whole teaching career. To say as much suggests that such a large and enduring task must be justified by the importance of the mission. Its importance is defined both by insiders and outsiders. The outsiders will see the field as important if sociologists can provide an occasional insight— for example, the streets are dirty because the pay of trash collectors is too high and their status is above that of those they serve (Kemper, 1979)—or if they can predict accurately (rates of recidivism, the size of the cohort entering the 8th grade in 1985, etc.). But the worth of the mission is most visible in the work most sociologists do most of the time. That is teaching. If that teaching is done with the rigor we require of a research discipline, if it capitalizes on sociology's position between the humanities and the biophysical sciences, if hardheadedness is joined with warm heartedness, competence with conscientiousness, if we tap the wisdom of the field for clues to better teaching strategies*—then, if we teach in these

---

* In chapter 3 and elsewhere, we have given examples of ways in which the lore of sociology can be exploited to improve teaching.

ways, sociology will merit the esteem of both insiders and outsiders: students, administrators, colleagues, and the public.

There is, of course, the insider's view of the rewards intrinsic to sociology. It is this view, after all, that must ultimately justify our efforts to improve instruction, "doing something that in reality never comes, and never can come, to an end" (Weber, 1922:138). Among all the contrivances and artifacts people have built across the ages, the creations most touching their fates and fortunes are the constructions we call human groups. Sociologists, then, enjoy the enviable position of helping students use their greatest talent—that of reason—to explore our greatest creations, human groups. Nor do we employ sociology only to help students

get closer to the truth. There is an aesthetic quality in the kaleidoscopic variations of social arrangements and in the lean precision we aspire to in describing and explaining these patterns. So, too, sociologists' teaching is informed with a moral component: not all organizational means are equally effective in achieving good ends. We must know how to do good in the right way. We justify the field as it gets us a little closer to the good, the true, and the beautiful features of the critical class of phenomena we call social. We justify the commitment to teaching by the significance of the field.

Hence this book. We hope it will induce some disposition to make fair good and good better, so adding cubits to the sociology instructor's influence.

Appendix : Resources for Teachers of Sociology

Throughout this book we have pointed to useful resources available to sociology teachers. Two such resources, which we have not discussed elsewhere, merit some thought: people and instructional development centers. We seldom think of teachers as their own resources, with the result that we close off valuable options. For example, teachers can act as more careful gatekeepers; preselection (prerequisites) and allocation can help bring students' aims and talents in line with those embodied in a course. Teachers can get out of the center stage position and orchestrate a set of experiences to provide a varied, stimulating, and artfully integrated intellectual adventure. They can encourage peer learning, devising means for students to work in teams—so releasing time for personal evaluation and help. Especially in larger classes, teachers may wish to consider another option: with out-of-class work well defined, they can divide the class in half and work more closely with each half on alternate class days or weeks. Another option is to set aside a reading period (but with specific tasks to be completed during that time). This arrangement allows teachers to meet with class members individually or in pairs or triplets to check on progress and adapt course material to students' backgrounds and concurrent experiences. Research projects conducted by clusters of class members are a related option.

Some teachers share syllabi, exchange guest lectures, and loan specially prepared charts or transparencies. There are other, more rarely employed opportunities for teachers to draw on their colleagues. Some of our most exciting classes have been conducted by teachers hundreds of miles away using telelecture equipment. After our students finished reading Gerhard Lenski's *The Religious Factor*, they had much to say and ask about it. So we made arrangements to borrow from a campus office a speaker-phone and amplifier, and for the price of a long-distance phone call, our students and Professor Lenski were able to talk with one another. The conversation was animated and fruitful. We used this technique in larger classes where we asked groups of students, in advance of the phone call, to discuss pertinent issues and concerns, formulate questions for the author, and select one of their number to talk with the interviewee. Both Professor Lenski and Professor John Scanzoni (with whom we also employed this technique) found the experience enjoyable and stimulating. Second, our colleagues (departmental and those nearby) can serve as outside examiners; many advantages accrue from separating the roles of teacher and inquisitor. Third, since we often assign papers in which students assess a piece of research by a sociologist, why not have the students relay their reactions and appraisals to that sociologist? In our experience, these colleagues have been pleased to respond to the thoughtful reactions of undergraduates. In the process, students learn in a vivid way what is meant by the pursuit of ideas. Finally, teachers can draw systematically on their colleagues at home and at nearby schools through a committee of correspondence, the members of which trade notes on teaching.

Each teacher prepares a brief but careful description of an instructional device. These are circulated within the committee (and, if possible, discussed at a department, state, or regional sociology meeting), which works to improve both the quality of the device and the utility of its statement. In each of the departments represented by the collaborating sociologists, these statements will build into a library of instructional devices available to all members of the department. As they accumulate, the statements can be filed and cross-filed under various subfields of sociology for easy retrieval by teachers seeking instructional ideas for their courses. For some ideas about what the statements about teaching might look like, see Geertsen (1979).

Students are another resource too seldom used to benefit instruction. We have already mentioned team assignments, which set the stage for mutual aid and peer instruction. Students can also be a great resource as preceptors. In some instances of self-paced instruction, advanced students can serve as consultants and instructors to other students. Not only can they multiply the instructor's strength, but they themselves are put in the best position for learning. Similarly, advanced undergraduates have been used with some success in the role of teaching assistant. For pertinent literature in sociology, see Moxley (1974), Wallace (1974), and Rice (1978) on undergraduate teaching assistants; and McNall (1975) and Pape (1967) on peer teaching.

Teachers can draw on the resources of the more than two hundred instructional and faculty development programs and centers on college and university campuses around the country. Such centers are listed in Jerry G. Gaff's *Toward Faculty Renewal* (1975). A slightly shorter version of Gaff's list is in William Bergquist and Stephen Phillips's *A Handbook for Faculty Development,* Volume 1 (1975). Finally, audiovisual media centers, found on most campuses, sometimes have people who can help teachers locate a variety of off-campus instructional resources. (They can also help in designing instructional units.)

Now, in the following pages, we identify further resources of four sorts: (1) those dealing with college teaching generally; (2) those bearing specifically on the teaching of sociology; (3) sources of useful data about the social world; and (4) sources helpful in locating appropriate audiovisual materials. In a final section we suggest which of these and other resources might be made available through the college or university, in the department's office or library, or on the instructor's own bookshelf.

Resources: On College Teaching

For this section, we have selected seven books that are recent, readily available, of high quality, and touch several strategies and techniques of teaching. The *Change* (1978) volume illustrates practical applications of a variety of teaching techniques. Each of the other books contains, in addition to material on application, general overviews and leads to pertinent research and related literature. After providing brief descriptions of the books, we offer table A.1, which lists thirty-three teaching strategies, techniques, and issues and indicates their treatment in the seven volumes. *Passing on Sociology* treats about three-fourths of the listed strategies and techniques. Thus table A.1 supplements treatments in this volume and provides leads to the reader for topics we have omitted. (The reader should note that the prices listed for each of the following seven

Table A.1 Sourcebooks (with page references) for Sociology Teachers, by Topic

Teaching Techniques, Formats, and Tools

	Change (1978)	Cross (1976)	Eble (1976)	Ericksen (1974)	McKeachie (1978)	Milton (1978)	Scholl and Inglis (1977)	Goldsmid and Wilson (1980)
Audiovisual techniques	108–121	50, 54, 83–89	79–82	172–178	120–135		115–123	251–269, 286–287
Autotutorial techniques	89–91, 102–104, 113	50, 54, 83–89			134			
Case studies	80–85				149	258–285	138–140	245–247
Computer-assisted instruction	26–44	60–70		178–184	109–111	184–211		287–290
Contract learning					118	212–235	155–163, 224–229	
* Discussion; seminars			54–72	164–165	35–67	62–100	109–114	218–226, 277–283
Field experience	124–145					314–339	143	59
Independent study				169–171	86–92		144–154	
Laboratory methods				166	83–85		140–142	
* Lecture	8–23		42–53	162–164	22–34	34–61	97–102	201–218, 276–283
* PSI; self-pacing	88–106	90–110	76–79	37, 108	112–119	153–183	103–108	226–235, 283–284
Role playing					136–141		124–128	
Simulation; gaming	46–61			144–147	146–150	286–313	129–137	
Textbooks; reading			85–90		12, 31, 101–104		44–46	185–198
* TIPS; CMI	30–37	70–74			117–118			330–332

Assessing Teaching and Learning

	Change (1978)	Cross (1976)	Eble (1976)	Ericksen (1974)	McKeachie (1978)	Milton (1978)	Scholl and Inglis (1977)	Goldsmid and Wilson (1980)
Evaluating students; testing; grading		80–81, 101–102, 132	101–119	194–218	151–186	101–124	185–250	311–333
Evaluating teaching					264–272	355–375	251–332	334–378
Feedback to students					26, 53, 117, 230–231, 275–276	125–152		204–205, 291–293, *passim*

Components of Teaching and Learning

	Change (1978)	Cross (1976)	Eble (1976)	Ericksen (1974)	McKeachie (1978)	Milton (1978)	Scholl and Inglis (1977)	Goldsmid and Wilson (1980)
Instructional objectives; competency; mastery		75–83		26–42		8–33, 236–257	194–207, 242–250	293–294, 297, 51
Interpersonal skills; learning		201–231						220–222
Learning; cognition; motivation		*passim*		1–149	221–243		16–43, 194–207	291–304
Peer teaching; students as teachers	64–78				93–100			293, 295, 383
Student attributes		49, 55, 111–133		1–11, 80, 97, *passim*	244–256			55–56, 127–128, 130–134
Teacher–student interaction			25–32	152–159	68–82		69–93	326–328

Table A.1 (*Continued*)

	Miscellaneous							
	Change (1978)	Cross (1976)	Eble (1976)	Ericksen (1974)	McKeachie (1978)	Milton (1978)	Scholl and Inglis (1977)	Goldsmid and Wilson (1980)
Advising; counseling			72–75		196–201			366–367
Assignments			91–100		142–144			*Chs.* 4–7, 10
Course design					5–21		44–49, 164–181	159–167, 171–185
Critical thinking; problem solving	148–159			131–149	*passim*			*Chs.* 5, 6, 295–298
Ethical issues					218–220			41, 51–52, 138–139
Large classes					202–214			201–218, 282–283
Students and research	162–174							34–36, *Ch* 6
Teacher development; TA training			137–162	219–244	273–279		333–396	42–44, *Ch* 14
Environments of teaching							50–68	*Chs* 1, 7

books represent the approximate costs in mid-1979.)

(*Editors of*) Change. Guide to Effective
1978 Teaching. *New York: Change Magazine Press. (Council on Learning, NBW Tower, New Rochelle, NY. 10801; $6.95; $5.95 each for ten or more; 175 pp.)*

The *Guide to Effective Teaching* reports teaching strategies employed by eighty-one college teachers (six of them sociologists) in more than a dozen disciplines. The reports are organized in ten chapters: lecture, computers, simulations, peer teaching, case studies, self-pacing and modules, multimedia, field study, problem solving, and undergraduate research courses. The reports are brief and well written. These eighty-one reports are half of those that have appeared in six special issues of *Change* magazine focused on teaching and published from 1976 through 1978. Material in the *Guide* is not copyrighted. Each report typically includes a description of the teacher's strategy, notes about its development, and in many cases, evidence bearing on its effectiveness.

Cross, K. Patricia. Accent on Learning:
1976 Improving Instruction and Reshaping the Curriculum. *San Francisco: Jossey-Bass, Inc., Publishers. (433 California Street, San Francisco, CA. 94104; $11.95; 291 pp.)*

In contrast to other works, *Accent on Learning* limits itself to careful reviews of instructional and curricular programs of promise in aiding "the new students," those who have come to higher education through open admissions policies. These students often are low performers in traditional educational environments. Cross's book, however, will also be useful to teachers in schools without large proportions of "new students." In part, this is because *Accent on Learning* is exceptionally well grounded in empirical research studies of the programs described. The chapters on individualizing instruction, mastery learning and self-paced modules, and student cognitive styles are excellent treatments containing extensive references to the research literature. The chapters on curriculum treat programs and courses designed to teach interpersonal and life-long cognitive skills as well as subject matter. Few books touch these important subjects. At the time *Accent on Learning* was published, Cross was Senior Research Psychologist at the Educational Testing Service and associated with a higher education research center at the University of California at Berkeley.

> *Eble, Kenneth E.* The Craft of Teaching: A
> 1976   Guide to Mastering the Professor's Art. *San Francisco: Jossey-Bass, Inc., Publishers. (433 California Street, San Francisco, CA. 94104; $10.95; 179 pp.)*

From 1969 to 1971, Kenneth Eble, a Professor of English at the University of Utah, directed the Project to Improve College Teaching (sponsored by the Association of American Colleges and the American Association of University Professors). Eble's experience with that project informs this book, which offers advice to new and experienced teachers. *The Craft of Teaching* makes only passing use of (or reference to) research and theory on teaching and learning. The index is brief, and its entries are chiefly proper nouns. Eble's chapters on learning to teach are among the better statements on this subject.

> *Ericksen, Stanford C.* Motivation for Learn-
> 1974   ing: A Guide for the Teacher of the Young Adult. *Ann Arbor: University of Michigan Press. (615 East University, Ann Arbor, MI. 48106; $10.50; 259 pp.)*

Ericksen's preface well describes his book as "an account of how students learn and what can be done to improve the conditions for acquiring knowledge and form-

ing new attitudes and values. It is not a how-to-do-it manual nor a super-synthesis of different theories of learning. What I want to do is describe the main ideas about motivation and learning that are prerequisite for good teaching in most content-specific courses. . . . I have tried, therefore, to transform the findings and principles from research and theory on motivation, learning, thinking, social psychology, and personality development into the practical procedures of teaching a course" (1974:vi). Although Ericksen treats lectures, seminars, audiovisual aids, grading, and the like, his book is organized around chapter headings such as: "The Theory of the Learner," "Transfer of Learning," "Attitudes and Values Students Study By," "Learning How to Learn and Remember," and "Interaction in the Classroom." While not a how-to book, Ericksen is never more than a step from the classroom and the opportunities and problems students and teachers face there. Ericksen is Professor of Psychology and Senior Research Scientist at the Center for Research on Learning and Teaching at the University of Michigan; for eleven years, he directed the center.

> *McKeachie, Wilbert J.* Teaching Tips: A
> 1978   Guidebook for the Beginning College Teacher. *7th ed. Lexington, MA.: D. C. Heath and Company. (125 Spring Street, Lexington, MA. 02173; $5.95; 338 pp.)*

We think *Teaching Tips* is the best single book available on college teaching. The subtitle is somewhat misleading, since experienced teachers will also find *Teaching Tips* useful. Its twenty-eight chapters are fine introductions to various teaching methods, problems, and strategies. Among the longer chapters are ones dealing with lecture, discussion, examinations, grades, cognition and motivation, the roles of teacher, and audiovisual techniques. Among the other chapters are treatments of meeting a class for the first time, ethical standards in teaching, doing research on teaching, class size, and large classes. Each chapter contains tips (especially useful to new teachers), a review of alternative approaches, and excellent reviews of theory and research. The book includes a detailed index and extensive references to literature. This seventh edition contains more material on theory and research on teaching than past editions. McKeachie is Director of the Center for Research on Learning and Teaching and Professor of Psychology (and former department chair) at the University of Michigan. He is past president of the American Psychological Association and the American Association for Higher Education.

Milton, Ohmer, and Associates. On College
1978   Teaching: A Guide to Contemporary Practices. *San Francisco: Jossey-Bass, Inc., Publishers. (433 California Street, San Francisco, CA. 94104; $13.95; 404 pp.)*

This volume contains fourteen chapters, each treating one instructional technique; they are bracketed by two short essays by Milton (who also contributed a chapter on classroom testing). Each chapter is an extensive, competent essay on an instructional method (e.g., lecturing, simulation games) or process (e.g., providing feedback to students). Most of the chapters cite earlier studies and give examples of actual applications of a method or process in the classroom. The index is brief and entries are chiefly proper nouns. Milton is Professor of Psychology and Director of the Learning Research Center at the University of Tennessee. He is the author of several books on teaching.

Scholl, Stephen C., and Sandra Cheldelin
1977   Inglis, eds. Teaching in Higher Education: Readings for Faculty. *Columbus: The Ohio Board of Regents. (30 East Broad Street, Columbus, OH.; $6.50; 400 pp.)*

This volume reprints thirty-three articles, essays, and guides grouped under four major categories: theory and design of instruction; alternative modes of instruction; testing and grading; and faculty development. Four of the entries are previously unpublished; the rest appeared in journals or books unlikely to cross the desks of sociologists. The book includes a twenty-six-page article that presents a systematic procedure that teachers can use to analyze their own teaching, especially their skills in lecture and discussion. Scholl is Dean of Educational Development at Ohio Wesleyan University; Inglis is an assistant dean at Ohio University.

Resources: On the Teaching of Sociology

There are about 700 published articles on the teaching of sociology. Work began to appear early in the life of our profession. Articles on curriculum appeared as early as 1895; articles on specific teaching techniques and on teacher development in sociology began to appear in the early 1920s. By 1935, there were dozens of published papers in sociology journals on such topics as fieldwork, discussion methods, the use of audiovisual materials, and the teaching of specific courses. By 1955, there were articles on student evaluation of instruction and the use of literature, film, radio, and television in the teaching of sociology. Publication on the teaching of sociology expanded considerably with the appearance, in 1973, of the journal *Teaching Sociology*. A selected bibliography on the teaching of sociology (Davis, Goldsmid, and Perry, 1979), reporting on work published since the mid-1960s, contains 470 references. Between 1975 and 1978, inclusive, about seventy-five articles of direct interest to teachers of sociology appeared annually; 45 percent of these articles were published in sociology journals, and about 55 percent of the articles dealt specifically with the teaching of sociology. These articles appeared in fourteen sociology journals and dozens of other social science and higher education journals.

In this section, we briefly describe some of the major sources that teachers of sociology can use to locate this large literature and keep abreast of newly appearing materials.

Journals, Newsletters, Organizations

Teaching Sociology (TS). Published since the fall of 1973, *TS* has appeared quarterly since the 1976/77 volume. By the end of 1979, more than 125 articles and an equal number of textbook reviews had appeared in its pages. A typical issue carries seven articles and a dozen reviews. *TS* articles often deal with course-level teaching strategies or specific techniques used within a class session. An increasing number of articles report empirical tests. Some articles have reported surveys of teaching practices. Some reviewed teacher or departmental experience with efforts to improve instruction. Two special issues have been published: one on preparing sociologists to teach (April 1976), and a second devoted to sociology curricula (October 1977). *Teaching Sociology* is published by Sage Publications, Inc. For information on individual or institutional

subscriptions, write to: Sage, 275 South Beverly Drive, Beverly Hills, CA. 90212. The current editor is Richard J. Gelles, Department of Sociology, University of Rhode Island, Kingston, RI. 02881.

ASA Teaching Resource Center (TRC). Through the TRC, interested sociologists can: (1) purchase teaching resource material; (2) obtain some free material; (3) arrange to have a "literature table" of teaching and curricular materials sent to a state, regional, or national sociology or social science association meeting; and (4) get answers or leads to answers about questions on teaching and curriculum in sociology. The TRC has a listing of sale materials, "Teaching Resources Available." The early 1979 edition of that list includes more than forty items, which are about equally divided between specifically sociological materials and materials on generic aspects of college and university teaching. The TRC was created and operated for two years as part of the ASA Projects on Teaching Undergraduate Sociology; since August 1978, the TRC has been a regular function of the American Sociological Association. Sociologists wishing to obtain a copy of "Teaching Resources Available" or to use other services of the TRC should write to: ASA Teaching Resource Center, American Sociological Association, 1722 N Street, N. W., Washington, D. C. 20036.

ASA Teaching Newsletter. Since early 1976, the ASA Projects on Teaching have published the bimonthly *ASA Teaching Newsletter*. Each sixteen-page issue carries dozens of articles and notes on classroom teaching techniques; instructional and curricular issues facing teachers, departments, and the professor; reader-contributed essays; announcements of workshops, publications, and grants related to the teaching of sociology; and news notes about the activities of the ASA Projects. Information on annual subscriptions to the *Newsletter* can be obtained by writing to: *ASA Teaching Newsletter*, 1722 N Street, N. W., Washington, D. C. 20036. One need not be a member of the ASA to subscribe. The current editor is Lawrence J. Rhoades, ASA Executive Associate.

ASA Projects on Teaching Undergraduate Sociology.

The ASA Projects are developing resources to assist sociologists in their teaching role. More than 150 sociologists from four-year college, two-year college, and university departments of sociology have worked on diverse aspects of curriculum, teacher development (of faculty and graduate students), and the institutional contexts in which teaching is done. In existence since the fall of 1974, the ASA Projects have sponsored dozens of workshops on teaching and curriculum, worked cooperatively with state and regional sociological and social science associations, sponsored the publication of dozens of documents, founded the *ASA Teaching Newsletter* and ASA Teaching Resources Center (both described above), and currently operate a Teaching Resources Group (TRG). The TRG is a network of sociologists who serve as resource persons to departments of sociology (and state and regional associations) that request their services. The ASA Projects received grants from the Fund for the Improvement of Postsecondary Education (HEW) in 1974 and 1977, and from the Lilly Endowment, Inc. in 1976 and 1978. Those who wish to obtain more information about the ASA Projects on Teaching and its services can write to the director: Hans O. Mauksch, ASA Projects on Teaching, TD3-W Medical Center, University of Missouri, Columbia, MO. 65201.

ASA Section on Undergraduate Education.

Founded in 1972, the ASA Section is an important forum for concerns about teaching within our profession. Through the ASA Section, a full day of sessions on undergraduate education is part of the program of the ASA's annual meeting. Members of the section receive a quarterly *Newsletter* and periodic papers on issues in undergraduate education. The section has a syllabus project that, by early 1979, issued sets of syllabi and related materials for the Introductory Sociology and the Social Problems courses; these materials are more fully described below. Membership in the section is open to all ASA members. Annual section dues are $7.00; those interested in joining can send a check to the ASA, payable to the section. Officers of the section come from four-year college, two-year college, and university departments. For additional information, write to: Charlotte Vaughan, Chairperson, Department of Sociology, Cornell College, Mt. Vernon, IA. 52314.

Community College Social Science Journal (CCSSJ).

This triannual publication of the Community College Social Science Association has been published since 1970. *CCSSJ* carries articles on teaching as well as substantive topics in all of the social sciences. For information about membership and subscriptions, write to: Gerald Baydo, Editor, *CCSSJ*, Grossmont College, El Cajon, CA. 92020.

Population Reference Bureau, Inc. (PRB).

Sociologists teaching courses or sections of courses on population and demography may wish to join the PRB or otherwise obtain *Interchange* (a quarterly population education newsletter); *Population Bulletin* (a bimonthly monograph on a special topic in population); *Intercom* (a monthly newsletter); the annual "World

Population Data Sheet," and the several instructional modules and other reports issued by the PRB each year. For further information, write to: Population Reference Bureau, 1337 Connecticut Avenue, N. W., Washington, D. C. 20036.

ASA Publications.   *ASA Footnotes,* a newspaper issued monthly (except in June, July, and September) regularly carries articles and notes about teaching. Issued quarterly, *The American Sociologist* (*TAS*) occasionally carries articles of interest to sociologists in their teaching role. *Footnotes* is distributed to all ASA members; *TAS* is available to members as a journal choice or at a reduced rate; both are available by subscription to nonmembers.

Supplementary Empirical Teaching Units in Political Science (SETUPS).   The American Political Science Association produced a series of "computer related instructional materials whereby students learn methods of analysis." Each SETUPS is a "module that can be taught in one to two weeks . . . designed to supplement instruction in introductory courses." SETUPS are comprised of a student monograph and a data set available for use with SPSS, OSIRIS, or as a card image. Several SETUPS are of direct interest to sociologists teaching political sociology, research methods, or policy-related courses (e.g., "Political Socialization Across the Generations," "Comparative Voting Behavior," "The Fear of Crime," and "U.S. Energy, Environment and Economic Problems: A Public Policy Simulation." For further information, write to: ASA Teaching Resource Center (or directly to the American Political Science Association), 1527 New Hampshire Avenue, N. W., Washington, D. C. 20036.

Bibliographic and Other Key Resources*

Teaching Sociology: An Annotated Bibliography, 3rd ed. (1979).   This 168-page book contains 470 different annotated references specifically on the teaching of sociology. Major categories include Introductory Sociology (forty-seven citations), Teaching Research Methods, Statistics, and Using the Computer in Teaching (fifty-four citations), Approaches to Course Formats (forty-two citations), Sociology Curriculum (twenty-seven citations), Sociology and General Education, Simulation and Gaming, Audiovisuals and Sociology, Fieldwork, Assessment of Student Learning, and ten others. The volume was compiled by Ethelyn C. Davis, Charles A. Goldsmid, and Wilhelmina Perry for the ASA Projects on Teaching.

Eighty-One Techniques for Teaching Sociological Concepts (1979).   This volume is a collection of teaching techniques developed by more than sixty teachers, each technique designed to help students learn about and use one or more sociological concepts. Each of the techniques is presented in a standard format, listing the concept(s), courses in which the technique might be used, any necessary materials, description of the techniques, special uses or limitations, and related references. Among the concepts included in the volume are: authority, bureaucracy as an ideal type, communities as cognitive maps, deviance, ethnocentrism and cultural relativity, group structure, hypothesis formation, norms and their emergence,

* All resources cited in this section, except for the annual reviews, can be purchased from the ASA Teaching Resource Center, 1722 N Street, N. W., Washington, D. C. 20036. Write for the price list, "Teaching Resources Available."

the normal curve, role expectations, rumor, sex roles, and social control; a number of techniques treat aspects of social structure, stratification, sex roles, and socialization. This document was edited by Reed Geertsen for the ASA Projects on Teaching Undergraduate Sociology.

Introductory Sociology: A Set of Syllabi (1977). This set of sixteen syllabi also includes sample handouts, assignments, exercises, reading lists, and other materials for the Introductory Sociology course. The courses represented are taught at a variety of types of schools and were chosen to represent a variety of substantive approaches to the course as well as diverse instructional strategies and techniques. The set was edited by Charles A. Goldsmid for the ASA Section on Undergraduate Education's syllabus project.

Social Problems: A Set of Syllabi (1979). The twelve syllabi and related materials that comprise this set were selected to illustrate diverse approaches to the Social Problems course. The preface includes a bibiliography on teaching Social Problems. The set was edited by Louise C. Weston for the ASA Section on Undergraduate Education's syllabus project.

Issues and Resources in Undergraduate Sociology Curriculum (1977) and *Data Report (1977).* This sourcebook consists of a report and presentation of marginals from a representative sample survey of universities, community colleges, and four-year colleges (N=438). Among the topics treated are: course offerings and how departments determine them; means by which sociological concepts are presented; instructional techniques employed in sociology courses; the nature of the first (introductory) course in sociology; ways courses are fit together to form a curriculum; and the use by departments and individual faculty members of teaching objectives. The two documents are twenty-one and forty-five pages, respectively. They were prepared by Sharon McPherron and Ted Bradshaw for the ASA Projects on Teaching.

The Sociology Curriculum (1977). This special, 120-page issue of the journal *Teaching Sociology* (5:1; October 1977) contains six major articles that treat: (1) the first course in sociology (models from the natural sciences); (2) experimenting with curricular designs; (3) sociology as viewed from the community college; (4) uses of goals and objectives in curriculum review; (5) a primer on the evaluation of innovations in teaching methods; and (6) an easy-to-use method for assessing and selecting textbooks that fit teacher goals and student characteristics. The issue was edited by Sharon McPherron for the ASA Projects.

Preparing Sociologists to Teach (1976). This special, 153-page issue of the journal *Teaching Sociology* (3:3; April 1976) includes seven articles and an extensive resource section. Three of the articles describe teacher preparation courses at the University of North Carolina-Chapel Hill, the University of Connecticut, and California State University at Sacramento; other articles treat videotape as a teacher development tool, theoretical issues in teacher development, teacher development for current faculty, and professional socialization of teachers of sociology. The issue was edited by Charles A. Goldsmid for the ASA Projects.

Data Book on the Institutional Context of the Teaching of Undergraduate Sociology (1978). This document provides basic data from surveys conducted in 1977 of samples of deans, chairpersons, and faculty in more than 200 institutions. Only aggregate data are presented; future reports will provide comparisons among the four- and two-year colleges and universities sampled. Approximately fifty tables are presented for each sample; comparisons among types of respondent can be made through use of the detailed index. Among the topics explored are: accreditation, evaluation procedures, faculty work load, resources available in support of teaching, salary, sabbatical, tenure, hiring practices, role of the chairperson, quality of teaching, and the reputation of sociology. This data book was edited by Lee H. Bowker for the ASA Projects on Teaching.

Annual Reviews and Bibliography on the Teaching of Sociology.   Starting in 1976, annual review articles and annotated bibliographies have appeared in the April issue of *Teaching Sociology.* For example, the 1979 review is based on a search of seventy-three journals, primarily in sociology, secondarily in other social sciences, and finally from the field of higher education. This search uncovered seventy-two articles of direct interest to teachers of sociology. The annotated citations in these reviews are indexed according to twenty-one subject categories. Each review article describes major patterns found in the literature reviewed, highlights strengths and weaknesses reflected in the year's work, and discusses problems and prospects for the teaching of sociology.

Resources: Data About the Social World

There are two general sources of data about the social world that are readily available to teachers and that have a variety of applications in different types of classes in most areas of sociology. These sources—federal census data and the local community—are only two among many resources on which teachers can draw. Other resources include:

Films, audiotapes, and videotapes

Simulations and games based on data about the social world

Publications of local, state, and regional governments, as well as business, social movement, political, and voluntary organizations

Radio, television, and print media—national, local, and campus-based

Novels, plays, and poetry

Publications of federal agencies other than the Bureau of the Census

Ideas, reading materials, and experiences of one's students in other courses and in their personal lives

Survey data such as the General Social Surveys of the National Opinion Research Center (see Cutler, 1978)

Census publications and the local community, as well as many of these other resources, can be used as the basis of instruction that actively exploits pertinent data describing students' social world.

Census Data

The Bureau of the Census of the U.S. Department of Commerce issues many books and pamphlets with various instructional uses. Most sociologists are familiar with the decennial census of population and housing, and the other periodic censuses of governments, business, agriculture, manufacturers, and transportation. Listed below are six other statistical publications of the Bureau of the Census that teachers may find especially useful. All are published by the U.S. Government Printing Office (Washington, D. C. 20402) and are found in most academic and public libraries.

Statistical Abstract of the United States.
Issued annually since 1878, the 1978 edition contains more than 1,600 tables and charts on population, housing, income, labor force, social welfare, crime and law enforcement, and dozens of other topics. Introductory and appendix sections provide leads to additional data.

Historical Statistics of the United States: Colonial Times to 1970.
The third and current edition, published in 1975, contains time-series data for 12,500 items of information in most of the major areas covered by the *Statistical Abstract* (above). For example, one table contains sixteen items of information on farms across the period 1850–1970. Another presents school enrollment rates by race and sex for the same period.

Social Indicators, 1976.
Published in December 1977, this 641-page book contains over 375 statistical tables, and for each, a corresponding color chart on current social conditions and trends in the United States. Each major section of the volume contains some international comparisons and data on public perceptions of the social concerns at issue. Major sections treat: family, housing, social security and welfare, health and nutrition, social mobility and participation, and seven other areas. A series of essays interpreting these data is found in *The Annals* (1978); see, also, *Contemporary Sociology* (1978).

Current Population Reports (CPR).
Each month, the Bureau of the Census surveys a probability sample of about 50,000 households throughout the United States. The data obtained are the basis of more than fifty annual *Current Population Reports* dealing with various demographic, social, and economic topics. Most large libraries have an annual, consolidated subscription to the *CPR*; individual reports can be purchased from the Government Printing Office. Two examples suggest the range of the reports: *A Statistical Portrait of Women in the United States* (CPR, P-23, No. 58, April 1976) includes eighty-four tables covering fourteen topics, with most tables having trend data for 1950 through 1974; *Gross Migration by County: 1965–1970* (CPR, P-25, No. 701, May 1977) contains one 135-page table with migration data by sex, race, and age for every county in the United States.

County and City Data Book, 1977.
This volume is a compendium on all counties, cities, urbanized areas, and metropolitan areas in the United States. The contents are also available in a computer punch card or tape format. New editions appear every five years.

Pocket Data Book, USA, 1976.
The fifth edition in its series, this volume contains 655 tables and 92 charts and figures in 444 small-format pages. The content is roughly parallel to the *Statistical Abstract of the United States*. This 1976 edition sells for $4.00 and so can be considered as a supplementary text for student purchase.

These documents can be used by sociology instructors as data bases for: (1) examples or illustrations, (2) handouts in lecture or discussion classes, (3) student papers, and (4) for instructor- or student-generated data sets for analysis by students. The *County and City Data Book* should be especially useful for teachers who design assignments in which they ask their students to explore the communities in which they grew up or with which they are familiar. Additional descriptive information on the sources cited here and some thoughts about their instructional uses can be found in Goldsmid (1979).

The Bureau of the Census issues materials designed to assist teachers and students using census data. *A Student's Workbook on the 1970 Census* acquaints students with the 1970 census of population and housing; about half of this twenty-two-page leaflet discusses census information, uses to which it can be put, and ways of locating needed census data. The rest of the document is six sets of exercises on learning to define data needs, read tables, and use census data. First issued in 1975, the *Workbook* is available from the U.S. Government Printing Office for $.55. The *Workbook* is one of the items in the *Sample Kit from the College Curriculum Support Project* of the Bureau of the Census. On request, the bureau will provide a teacher with this useful kit of fifteen leaflets on census data uses. Requests should be sent to: Chief, Data Access and Use Staff, Data User Services Division, Bureau of the Census, U.S. Department of Commerce, Washington, D. C. 20233. Those writing will be placed on a mailing list to receive samples of new and revised materials developed by the support project. In addition to the *Student Workbook*, the *Sample Kit* includes two case studies involving the student in the use of census data to answer a series of questions about migration patterns and about the location of a playground in a community. Also included are a leaflet on the history of the census and a sample of the 1970 census mailback form.

The Local Community

Some of the census documents described above (as well as data found in local libraries or issued through municipal, county, state, and regional agencies) can be the basis of student assignments focusing on questions about the social structure and process of a community in which students have lived. When students live near their community of origin, such sources can be supplemented by personal interviews and by direct observation. The community in which the college or university is located can also serve as an instructional resource in these and many other ways. Some of the ways in which instructors can draw upon the community include: (1) inviting local officials or organizational representatives to become guest speakers or resource persons for a class; (2) organizing bus tours of a locality, tours designed to show students the physical settings of social relationships dealt with in readings and classes; (3) arranging student internships or seminar-practicum courses; (4) using the community as a source of examples, illustrating cases that may have more meaning to students because they are at hand and shared; (5) using these examples as the foci of written assignments or as raw data used in such assignments; and (6) using these examples to construct a data set for analysis to answer questions about social dynamics.

Communities are useful resources in teaching sociology for a variety of reasons. Typically, data are abundant and easily accessible. The communities themselves are accessible. We all have our experiences (growing up, going to school, forming friendships, attending church, paying taxes, taking jobs) in places, and those places influence the pattern of our experiences. We usually care about our communities—places that we believe constrain us or liberate us, offer or constrict opportunities, places where we feel at home or feel trapped. Communities are also useful resources for sociological instruction because there are so many social myths linked to places: cities are huge and cold and relationships in them impersonal; and largely because cities are cold and impersonal, they are filled with violent crime. In farm areas, people work on farms (in fact, only half of working farm residents work on farms). Communities are also useful data sources because so much important theoretical work in sociology hinges on questions about the meaning of community life—Durkheim's organic and mechanical solidarity is but one example. And finally, the term *community*, as used by sociologists and nonsociologists, is ambiguous. The *community* is variously viewed as a territorial concept, as a field of social interaction, and as a unit of cultural or psychological meaning. For given communities or types of communities at one and many points in time—to what degree do those attributes coincide? Is life different in a community over a twenty-year span of time when the population has remained the same?

Communities are useful resources not only in courses in Urban, Rural, or Community Sociology, but also in courses in Social Change, Social Psychology, and those dealing with most social institutions or processes. Thus the community is often a convenient resource and can be viewed as a point of impact of technologically induced change, as an independent variable affecting religiosity or intergroup contact.

Resources: Locating Audiovisual Materials

In chapter 11, we concluded our discussion of audiovisual aids with a description of articles and books on instructional uses of AVAs in sociology specifically and in college teaching generally. Here we describe sources sociologists can use in locating AV materials: films, videotapes, transparencies, etc. (During 1980, an annotated guide to films useful in sociology instruction (prepared by the ASA Projects on Teaching) will be available through the ASA Teaching Resources Center, Washington, D. C.).

Starting with one's own campus is likely to yield resources that are relatively inexpensive, available, and suited to the students one has. Colleagues who share subject matter concerns are a good first source. (Talking with them about films and other media resources is also a good way of opening a discussion about teaching.) Most campuses have an audiovisual center that can help in the search for AV materials that suit the teacher's instructional needs. Sociologists at smaller schools may want to visit the media center at nearby university campuses, which typically have large selections of motion picture films (and other materials) available for rental.

Beyond the teacher's campus and nearby campuses, there are three major sources of information on AV materials. First, there is the literature on the teaching of sociology (see the resources section concluding this chapter). Second, the instructor's manual for many introductory and social problems textbooks contains lists of films and other AV materials the author considers appropriate for each chapter's content. Third, catalogs of media materials are available in most media centers or can be obtained in a college, university, or public library, or by writing to organizations issuing catalogs. Rental/purchase catalogs are issued annually by commercial media firms, university media centers, and a number of publishing companies. Since rental prices for the same film can vary widely, one should check as many catalogs as are available. Table A. 2 lists a number of major catalogs and indexes.

Table A.2 Major Catalogs and Indexes Listing Audiovisual Materials

Films (16mm)

Educational Film Locator of the Consortium of University Film Centers and the R. R. Bowker Company. 1978 1st ed. New York, NY.: R. R. Bowker Company (1180 Avenue of the Americas, 10036; 2,178 pp.).

For 37,000 films, the *Educational Film Locator* provides running time, topics dealt with, audience level, sound (yes/no), color or black and white, production date, and a one-paragraph description, and indicates which of fifty-two university film centers (in thirty-six states) rents the film. Title and subject listings and cross-listings are provided. Lending policies (fees, restrictions, etc.) for the film centers are stated.

Rental catalogs for selected major university film centers. These catalogs include the same basic information found in the *Educational Film Locator* described above.

California: *Films, 1977–1978: Lifelong Learning.* University of California Extension Media Center, Berkeley, CA. 94720.

Florida: *Film, 1978–1980.* Instructional Support Center, Institutional Systems Development Center, Florida State University, Tallahassee, FL. 32306.

Illinois: *Social Science Films, 1978–1980.* Visual Aids Service, University of Illinois, Urbana, IL. 61801.

Indiana: *Educational Motion Picture Catalog.* Indiana University Audiovisual Center, Bloomington, IN. 47401. (The center is one of the largest rental sources of 16mm film in the United States. Its holdings include many National Educational Television films.)

Minnesota: *Educational Resources Bulletin.* Audiovisual Library Service, University of Minnesota, 3300 University Avenue, S. E., Minneapolis, MN. 55414.

Nebraska: *Catalog.* Instructional Media Center, University of Nebraska at Lincoln, Lincoln, NB. 68508.

New York: *Syracuse University Films.* Film Rental Center, Syracuse Univeristy, 1455 East Colvin Street, Syracuse, NY. 13210.

Utah: *Comprehensive Educational Film Catalog.* Educational Media Center, University of Utah, 207 Milton Bennian Hall, Salt Lake City, UT. 84112.

NICEM Index to 16mm Educational Films. 3 vols. New York: R. R. Bowker Company. (NICEM is the National Center for Educational Media. NICEM Indexes list by title and subject. Maturity level is indicated in the film descriptions provided.)

Catalog. National Film Board of Canada, 1251 Avenue of the Americas, New York, NY. 10020.

Films for Anthropological Teaching. 6th ed. Edited by Karl G. Heider. Washington, D. C.: American Anthropological Association. (Hundreds of annotated film entries are indexed by concepts illustrated—for example, stratification; and by culture area—tribe, ethnic group, etc.)

Video Program Catalogue. Public Television Library, 475 L'Enfant Plaza West, S. W., Washington, D. C. 20024. (This catalog of all PBS productions includes topical listings.)

Britannica Films 1977–1978. Encyclopedia Britannica Educational Corporation, 425 N. Michigan Avenue, Chicago, IL. 60611. (This catalog includes extensive social studies holdings.)

Overhead Transparencies

NICEM Index to Educational Overhead Transparencies. 2 vols. New York: R. R. Bowker Company.

Catalog. Lansford Publishing Company, P.O. Box 8711, 1088 Lincoln Avenue, San Jose, CA. 95155. (The Lansford Publishing Company offers, for sale only, a series of instructional modules comprised of overhead transparencies and written guides; its catalog has a sociology section.)

Audiotapes

NICEM Index to Educational Audio Tapes. New York: R. R. Bowker Company

Pacifica Tape Library Catalog. Pacifica Tape Library, 5316 Venice Boulevard, Los Angeles, CA. 90019. (The general catalog includes a sociology catalog.)

Catalog. Cassettes Unlimited, Roanoke, TX. 76262. (The company offers a sociology catalog.)

Catalog. Association for Educational Communications and Technology, 1201 Sixteenth Street, N. W., Washington, D. C. 20036. (The catalog lists prerecorded, nonmusical tapes.)

Indexes for Other AV Materials

NICEM Indexes. New York: R. R. Bowker Company. (In addition to indexes for 16mm film, overhead transparencies, and audiotapes, NICEM Indexes are available for: 35mm educational filmstrips, educational videotapes, educational records, 8mm motion cartriages, and educational slides.)

Table A.2 (*Continued*)

Multimedia Indexes

A Reference List of Audiovisual Materials Produced by the United States Government, 1978. National Audiovisual Center, National Archives and Records Service, General Services Administration, Washington, D. C. 20409. Publication No. 301-763-1896. (This 396-page index lists more than 6,000 AV materials produced by 175 federal agencies. Materials are available for purchase, rental, and free loan. Media included are: audio cassettes, audiotapes, books, filmstrips, slides, 8mm films. The *Reference List* includes fifteen specific subject headings under "sociology.")

Social Studies School Service, 1978 Catalog. Social Studies School Service, 10000 Culver Boulevard, P. O. Box 802, Culver City, CA. 90230. (This 223-page catalog includes books, filmstrips, duplicating masters, sound filmstrips, simulations and games, records and cassettes, posters, photographs, transparencies, and slides.)

Time-Life Multimedia Educational Resource Catalog. 100 pp. Time-Life Films Multimedia Division, 100 Eisenhower Drive, Paramus, NJ. 07652. Publication No. 201-843-4345. (This 100-page catalog includes 16mm films, filmstrips, and sound filmstrips.)

NICEM Indexes. New York: R. R. Bowker Company. (In addition to media-specific indexes, NICEM multimedia indexes are available in fields such as black history and studies, psychology, and ecology.)

Topical Film Indexes

Rufsvold, Margaret I. *Guides to Educational Media.* 4th ed. Chicago: American Library Association.

1977 (This volume lists scores of bibliographies of films and other media materials in specific subject matter fields—for example, aging, urban studies, family life, black studies, women, political change, and urban problems.)

Resources: The Instructor's, the Department's, the School's

We list below some resource materials useful in teaching sociology, suggesting their availability in a college or university library, computer or media center, in the department's office or library, and on the instructor's own bookshelf. The need for different resources, as well as their appropriate location, will vary by the size of the department, the scope of its offerings, and individual instructor concerns. In assigning resources to categories, we have considered cost and the likely extent of use of a document within the department and institution.

Many of the resources listed here require some investment of money. But others depend only on the willingness of faculty members to share their ideas and reflections on their experience. We have placed an asterisk next to those items that are described in earlier sections of this appendix; prices in parentheses are their approximate costs in mid-1979.

College or University Resources

1. *Change: The Magazine of Learning* (ten issues a year; annual subscription, $18)

2. *The Chronicle of Higher Education* (weekly; annual subscription, $25)

3. Major documents and series from agencies of the U.S. Government (e.g., the decennial *Census of Population and Housing, Current Population Reports* (*), and *Vital Statistics of the United States;* annual reports and statistical yearbooks of departments and regulatory agencies)

4. United Nations documents (e.g., *Demographic Yearbook, Statistical Yearbook,* annual *Report on the World Social Situation, Compendium of Housing Statistics,* and *Yearbook of Labour Statistics*)

5. Human Relations Area Files

6. *Current Contents: Social and Behavioral Sciences* (weekly, annual subscription, $150; lists by journal, subject, and author, the contents of periodicals published during the preceding week; includes journals in education, sociology, and other social sciences)

7. Important books (*) on teaching and curriculum in higher education (e.g., *Change,* 1978; Ericksen, 1974; Cross, 1976; Eble, 1976; McKeachie, 1978; Milton, 1978; Scholl and Inglis, 1977)

8. Films, audiotapes, and videotapes (see chapter 10)

9. Computer languages, packages, and data files useful to sociologists (packages such as SPSS, instructional programs for use on interactive terminals, and computer-readable data sets; examples of data sets are: (1) the punch card or tape files of the Bureau of the Census' *County and City Data Book* (*), (2) the General Social Surveys, National Data Program in the Social Sciences issued by the National Opinion Research Center—see Cutler, 1978, and (3) data sets available through the Inter-University Consortium of Political and Social Science; some articles describing computer-based instructional packages and instructional uses of the computer in sociology are Anderson, 1974; Halley, 1975; and Davis, 1978)

10. *International Encyclopedia of the Social Sciences* (New York: Macmillan, 1968)

11. Major journals in sociology and related social sciences (for extensive listings of such journals, see Rhoades, ca. 1976; Sussman, 1977)

Departmental Resources

1. *Teaching Sociology* (quarterly journal; annual subscription for individuals, $15.; institutions, $26 (*))

2. Major publications of the Bureau of the Census (e.g., *County and City Data Book* (*), *Social Indicators, 1976* (*), *Statistical Abstract of the United States* (*), *Sample Kit for Teachers* (*), *Historical Statistics of the United States* (*))

3. Major publications of U.S. Departments of Health, Education, and Welfare Housing and Urban Development, Labor, Justice, Commerce, and others (e.g., *Monthly Labor Review* and the annually issued *Handbook of Labor Statistics, Crime in the United States—Uniform Crime Reports, Manpower Report of the President,*

Employment and Training Report of the President, Digest of Educational Statistics, and *Social Security Throughout the World*)

4 . Major publications of local, state, and regional governmental agencies for the state in which a school is located (appendix to the *Statistical Abstract of the United States* (*) lists the most recent available statistical abstracts for states; public libraries and local agencies can usually provide lists of data sources and other publications available)

5. Publications series of the Population Reference Bureau (annual subscription, about $25 (*))

6. Major publications available through the ASA Teaching Resource Center (many of these described in the preceding section of this appendix)

7. Other publications of the American Sociological Association (in addition to the scholarly journals published by the ASA, departments might consider: the annually issued *Directory of Members,* $5.00; *Directory of Departments,* $5.00; and the *Guide to Graduate Departments of Sociology,* $4.00; these sources are useful in locating nearby colleagues and in advising students considering graduate school in sociology; other pertinent ASA publications are: *The ASA Teaching Newsletter* (*) and *Careers in Sociology*)

8. Handbooks, guidebooks, and surveys (*) of teaching in higher education (e.g., McKeachie, 1978; Milton, 1978; Grasha, 1977)

9. Catalogs of films, videotapes, and other audiovisual resources held by the campus media center and at other nearby campuses, and larger commercial and academic distributors (see chapter 11 for examples)

10. Books reviewing and analyzing recent research in major subfields of sociology and related disciplines (e.g., *Annual Review of Sociology*—published since 1975—and *Annual Review of Anthropology;* both of these reviews are published by Annual Reviews, Inc., 4139 El Camino Way, Palo Alto, CA. 94306)

11. Copies of journal special issues dealing with topics of recurrent concern to more

than one faculty member (for example, each issue of *The Annals of the American Academy of Political and Social Science* contains articles on some prominent social or political problem; single issues can be purchased separately— 1978 price was $4.50; examples of special issue titles published in the late 1970s are: Urban Black Politics, The New Rural America, The Suburban Seventies, and Social Theory and Social Policy; examples from the late 1960s are: Patterns of Violence, Student Protest, and Evaluating the War on Poverty; the Academy is located at 3938 Chestnut Street, Philadelphia, PA. 19104)

12. Departmental Film Information Exchange (the creation of a file, indexed by course, or sociological concept or public issue, with short reports in a standard format with descriptive and evaluative information on films department members have used; form should include film running time and information on its availability and cost of rental)

13. Other departmental exchanges (files of course syllabi, examinations, test items, transparencies, etc.)

14. Simulations and games, especially those likely to be used in required or frequently offered courses (for resources on simulations and gaming in sociology, see Dukes, 1978)

15. Computer programs used with the Teacher Information Processing System (see chapter 13 for discussion of TIPS)

16. The forms and/or computer-analysis services comprising some of the better student evaluation of teaching programs (e.g., those of the Educational Testing Service, Kansas State University, Purdue University, Cornell University; for descriptions, see chapter 14, Centra, 1979, and Doyle, 1975)

17. A shelf of textbooks for Introductory Sociology and other basic courses might be

created (especially useful in graduate departments that have graduate students teaching; faculty can be asked to contribute texts and other books they would ordinarily discard or not use)

Individual Instructor Resources

1. *Teaching Sociology* (*)

2. *ASA Teaching Newsletter* (*)

3. *Teaching Sociology: A Bibliography* (*)

4. *Statistical Abstract of the United States* (*)

5. Various almanacs and data compendia (e.g., *The World Almanac and Book of Facts, Information Please,* and *CBS News Almanac*)

6. Dictionaries of sociology and social science, specialized fields, English and perhaps other languages (examples of the first category are Theodorson and Theodorson, 1969; Gould and Kolb, 1964)

7. Handbooks in areas of teaching specialization (e.g., *Handbook of Organizations, Handbook of Marriage and the Family,* and *Handbook of Modern Sociology*)

8. Cumulative indexes to journals such as *American Journal of Sociology, American Sociological Review, Social Forces,* and *Social Problems* (when commenting on student papers—or proposals for papers to be prepared—indexes are useful sources of pertinent examples and leads for students; references are also opportunities to make linkages to student interests—for example, "I see you are interested in secondary school teaching; you might want to look at Becker's articles on teachers. . . .")

9. Abstracts in the teacher's specialties (e.g., *Communications Abstracts, Sage Urban Studies Abstracts, Race Relations Abstracts*)

Works Referred To

Adair, John, and Kurt W. Deuschle. "Some
1958   Problems of Physicians on Navajo
        Reservations," *Human Organization*
        16 (Winter): 19–23.

Adams, Raymond S., and Bruce J. Biddle.
1970   *Realities of Teaching: Explorations
        with Videotape.* New York: Holt,
        Rinehart, and Winston.

Adams, Richard N. "On the Effective Use of
1955   Anthropology in Public Health Pro-
        grams." *Human Organization* 13
        (Winter): 5–15.

Albert, C. Rodney, and Rita Hipp.
1976   "Videotape Recording in the Prepa-
        ration of College Sociology
        Teachers." *Teaching Sociology* 3
        (April): 327–38.

Alexander, C. N., Jr., and J. Epstein.
1969   "Problems of Dispositional Infer-
        ence in Person Perception Re-
        search." *Sociometry* 32 (December):
        381–95.

Allport, Gordon W. "The Psychology of Par-
1945   ticipation." *The Psychological Re-
        view* 53 (May): 117–32.

American Sociological Association. "Golden
1979   Fleece Suit Reaches Supreme
        Court." *ASA Footnotes* 7 (May): 1,12.

American Sociological Association. *Guide to
1977a   Graduate Departments of Sociology.*
        Washington, D. C.: ASA.

American Sociological Association. *Guide to
1977b   Graduate Departments of Sociology.*
        Washington, D. C.: ASA.

American Sociological Association Teaching
1977c   Resources Center. *Teaching Re-
        sources Available.* Washington,
        D. C.: ASA. (Publication list.)

American Sociological Association. *Con-
1976a   temporary Sociology.* Washington,
        D. C.: ASA. (Journal).

American Sociological Association. *Directory
1976b   of Members, 1975–1976.* Washing-
        ton, D. C.: ASA.

American Sociological Association. "Un-
1975   dergraduate Sociology Curriculum
        Emphasizes 'Practical Courses.'"
        ASA Footnotes 3 (April): 4.

American Sociologist. "Special Issue: Con-
1980   straints and Opportunities for Soci-
        ology Curricula." *The American Soci-
        ologist* 15 (February): 1–58.

Anderson, Charles H. *Toward a New Sociol-
1971   ogy: A Critical View.* Homewood,
        IL.: Dorsey.

Anderson, Charles H., and John D. Murray,
1971   eds. *The Professors: Work and Life
        Style Among Academicians.* Cam-
        bridge, MA.: Schenkman.

Anderson, Ronald E. "Computer-based Un-
1975   dergraduate Curriculum Materials
        Exchange in the Social Sciences."
        Teaching Sociology 2 (April): 222–23.

Anderson, Ronald E. "Bibliography on Social
1974   Science Computing." *Computing Re-
        views,* Volume 15 (July): 247–61.

Annals. "America in the Seventies: Some So-
1978   cial Indicators." 435 (January): en-
        tire issue.

Anonymous. Personal communication from
1974   two sociology departments in large
        universities.

Antioch College. Experiment in Independent
1958   Study, 1957–1958. Yellow Springs,
        OH.: mimeographed.

Astin, Alexander W., and Calvin B. T. Lee.
1967   "Current Practices in the Evaluation
        and Training of College Teachers."
        In Calvin B. T. Lee (ed.), *Improving
        College Teaching.* Washington, D. C.:
        American Council on Education,
        pp. 296–311.

Attiyeh, R., and K. G. Lumsden. "Some Mod-
1972 ern Myths in Teaching Economics: The U.K. Experience." *American Economic Review* 62:429–33.

Axelrod, Joseph. *The University Teacher as
1973 Artist.* San Francisco: Jossey-Bass.

Baali, Fuad, and Michael C. Moore. "The Ex-
1972 tended Deliberation: Definitions of
Sociology, 1951–1970." *Sociology
and Social Research* 56 (July): 433–39.

Babbie, Earl R. Paper presented at the annual
1977a meeting of the American Sociological Association, Chicago.

Babbie, Earl R. *Society by Agreement: An In-
1977b troduction to Sociology.* Belmont,
CA.: Wadsworth.

Bachrach, Peter, and Morton S. Baratz. *Power
1970 and Poverty: Theory and Practice.*
New York: Oxford University Press.

Baker, Keith. "A New Grantsmanship." *The
1975 American Sociologist* 10 (November):
206–18.

Baker, Paul J. Personal communication, July
1978 18.

Baker, Paul J. "Mass Instruction in Sociology:
1976 On the Domestication of a Pedagogical Monster." *Teaching Sociology* 4
(October): 5–28.

Baker, Paul, J., and Patricia J. Behrens.
1971 "Alternatives to Mass Instruction in Sociology." *The American
Sociologist* 6 (November): 311–17.

Baker, Paul J., and Everett K. Wilson,
1979 eds. *Knowledge Available and
Knowledge Needed to Improve Instruction in Sociology: Proceedings of
a Conference.* Washington, D. C.:
ASA Projects on Teaching, ASA
Teaching Resources Center.

Baldwin, James. "Down at the Cross: Letter
1963 from a Region in My Mind." *The
Fire Next Time.* New York: Dial
Press.

Ballantine, Jeanne H. "Course Improvement
1978 by Systematically Eliciting Student
Reactions." *Teaching Sociology* 5
(January): 167–70.

Ballantine, Jeanne H. "Course Analysis of
1977 Some Introductory Syllabi." In
Charles A. Goldsmid (ed.), *Introduc-
tory Sociology: A Set of Syllabi and
Related Materials.* Washington, D. C.:
ASA Teaching Resources Center
(ASA Section on Undergraduate Ed-
ucation), pp. 5–7.

Barry, Robert M. "Clarifying Objectives."
1978 in Ohmer Milton (ed.), *On College
Teaching.* San Francisco: Jossey-
Bass.

Bart, Pauline, and Linda Frankel. *The Student
1971 Sociologist's Handbook.* Cambridge,
MA.: Schenkman.

Barzun, Jacques. *Teacher in America.* Boston:
1944 Atlantic.

Bassis, Michael S. "The Campus as a Frog
1977 Pond: A Theoretical and Empirical
Reassessment." *American Journal of
Sociology* 82 (May): 1318–26.

Bassis, Michael S., and Joyce P.
1977 Allen. "Teaching Introductory Sociology with TIPS: An Evaluation."
Teaching Sociology 4 (January): 141–
54.

Bassis, Michael S., and Joyce P. Allen. "TIPS:
1976 Individualization and Economy for
Mass Instruction." *Teaching Sociology* 3 (January): 185–90.

Bates, Alan P. "Undergraduate Sociology: A
1965 Problem for the Profession." *Sociological Quarterly* 6 (Winter): 21–36.

Bates, Alan P., and Sue Titus Reid. "The
1971 Sociology Major in Accredited Colleges and Universities." *The American Sociologist* 6 (August): 243–49.

Beard, Ruth. *Teaching and Learning in Higher
1970 Education.* Harmondsworth, England: Penguin.

Beard, Ruth, and Donald A. Bligh. *Research
1971 into Teaching Methods in Higher Education.* 3rd ed. London: Society for
Research into Higher Education,
Ltd.

Becker, Howard S. *Outsiders.* Rev. ed. New
1973 York: The Free Press.

Becker, Howard S., Blanche Geer, and Everett
1968   Hughes. *Making the Grade: The Academic Side of College Life.* New York: Wiley.

Benton, John F., ed. *Town Origins: The Evidence from Medieval England.* Boston: D. C. Heath.
1968

Berger, Peter. *Invitation to Sociology: A Humanistic Perspective.* Garden City, NY.: Doubleday (Anchor).
1963

Bergquist, William H., and Steven R.
1977   Phillips. *A Handbook for Faculty Development, Volume 2.* Washington, D. C.: Council for the Advancement of Small Colleges.

Bergquist, William H., and Steven R.
1975   Phillips. *A Handbook for Faculty Development, Volume 1.* Washington, D. C.: Council for the Advancement of Small Colleges.

Berlyne, D. E. *Conflict, Arousal and Curiosity.* New York: McGraw Hill.
1960

Berryman, Charles. "Secondary Students'
1973   Views of Sociology Courses." *Social Education,* Volume 41 (January): 70–73.

Bess, James L. "Integrating Faculty and Student Life Cycles." *Review of Educational Research* 43 (Fall): 377–403.
1973.

Best, Joel. "The Introductory Sociology Survey." *Teaching Sociology* 4 (April): 271–76.
1977

Bevington, Helen. *The House Was Quiet and the World Was Calm.* New York: Harcourt Brace Jovanovich.
1971

Beyer, Barry K. *Inquiry in the Social Studies Classroom: A Strategy for Teaching.* Columbus, OH.: Merrill.
1971

Bidwell, Charles E. "The Social Psychology of
1973   Teaching." Chapter 13 in Robert M. W. Travers (ed.), *Second Handbook of Research on Teaching.* Chicago: Rand McNally.

Bierstedt, Robert. *The Social Order.* 4th ed.
1974   New York: McGraw-Hill.

Bierstedt, Robert. "Sociology and General
1964   Education." In Charles H. Page (ed.), *Sociology and Contemporary Education.* New York: Random House, pp. 40–55.

Bierstedt, Robert. *The Social Order: An Introduction to Sociology.* 2nd ed. New York: McGraw-Hill.
1963

Bierstedt, Robert. "Nominal and Real
1959   Definitions in Sociological Theory." In Llewellyn Gross (ed.), *Symposium on Sociological Theory.* New York: Harper and Row, pp. 121–44.

Bigge, Morris L. *Learning Theories for Teachers.* New York: Harper and Row.
1964

Billings, Donald B. "PSI Versus the Lecture
1974   Course in the Principles of Economics: A Quasi-Controlled Experiment." *Proceedings of the First National Conference on Personalized Instruction.* Washington, D. C.: Center for Personalized Instruction (Georgetown University).

Birk, Janice M. (Chair), and APA Task Force.
1975   "Guidelines for Nonsexist Use of Language: APA Task Force on Issues of Sexual Bias in Graduate Education." *American Psychologist* 30 (June): 682–84.

Bligh, Donald A. *What's the Use of Lectures?*
1972   Harmondsworth, England: Penguin.

Block, James H., ed. *Mastery Learning: Theory and Practice.* New York: Holt, Rinehart, and Winston, pp. 47–63.
1971

Bloom, Benjamin S. "Learning for Mastery."
1968   *UCLA-CSEIP Evaluation Comment* 1,2. (An adaptation of this essay appears in James H. Block, ed., *Mastery Learning: Theory and Practice.* New York: Holt, Rinehart, and Winston, 1971.)

Bloom, Benjamin S., ed. *Taxonomy of Educational Objectives: Handbook I, Cognitive Domain.* New York: McKay.
1956

Bloom, Benjamin S. "Thought Processes in
1953   Lectures and Discussions." *Journal
of General Education* 7 (April): 160–
69.

Blumstein, Philip W. "Subjective Probability
1973   and Normative Evaluations." *Social
Forces* 52 (September): 98–107.

Bluth, B. J. "Teaching Theory as a Tool of
1975   Analysis." *Teaching Sociology* 2
(April): 147–64.

Bogardus, Emory S. "A Social Distance
1933   Scale." *Sociology and Social Research*
17 (January/February): 265–71.

Bolton, Brian, Dennis Bonge, and John
1979   Marr. "Ratings of Instruction, Examination Performance and Subsequent Enrollment in Psychology
Courses." *Teaching of Psychology* 2
(April): 82–85.

Bono, Stephen, F., Medio, F. J., and Hrapsky,
1977   J. S. "Annotated Review of Articles on Personalized Instruction."
Journal of Personalized Instruction 2
(March): 57–61.

Boocock, Sarane S. "The Social Organization
1978   of the Classroom." In Ralph H.
Turner, James Coleman, and Renee
C. Fox (eds.), *Annual Review of Soci-
ology, Volume 4.* Palo Alto: Annual
Reviews, pp. 1–28.

Boocock, Sarane S. *An Introduction to the Soci-
1972   ology of Learning.* Boston: Hough-
ton-Mifflin.

Booth, James L. *Instructional Technology: Me-
1973   dia, Materials, and Methods Study
Guide.* West Lafayette, IN.: Purdue
University.

Bordin, Edward S. "The Teacher as a Coun-
1969   selor." *Memo to the Faculty* 38 (December). Ann Arbor: Center for Research on Learning and Teaching,
University of Michigan.

Bossert, Steven T. *Tasks and Social Relation-
1979   ships in Classrooms: A Study of Instructional Organization and its Consequences* (ASA Rose Monograph

Series). Cambridge and New York:
Cambridge University Press.

Bowker, Lee, ed. *Data Book on the Institutional
1978   Context of the Teaching of Undergraduate Sociology.* Washington, D. C.:
ASA Projects on Teaching Undergraduate Sociology, ASA Teaching
Resources Center.

Bozeman, B. "Evaluation Research and Col-
1976   lege Teaching." *Teaching Political
Science* 3 (January): 179–95.

Bradshaw, Ted, and Sharon McPherron. *Data
1977   Report on Issues and Resources for the
Undergraduate Sociology Curriculum.*
Washington, D. C.: ASA Projects on
Teaching Undergraduate Sociology,
ASA Teaching Resources Center.

Brasted, Robert C. "The Introductory Course
1975   in Chemistry." Pp. 109–19 in *Excellence in University Teaching: New
Essays.* Columbia, SC.: University
of South Carolina.

Breed, Warren. "Social Control in the News-
1955   room." Social Forces 33 (May): 326–
35.

Bressler, Marvin. "Sociology and Collegiate
1967   General Education." In Paul F. Lazarsfeld, William H. Sewell, and
Harold Wilensky, (eds.), *The Uses of
Sociology.* New York: Basic.

Brilhart, John K. *Effective Group Discussion.*
1974   2nd ed. Dubuque, IA.: Brown.

Bronson, Louise. "Sociology through Slides."
1975   *Community College Social Science
Quarterly* Volume 5 (Summer): 103–
104.

Broom, Leonard, and Philip Selznick.
1977   *Sociology: A Text with Adapted Readings.* 6th ed. New York: Harper and
Row.

Broom, Leonard, and Philip Selznick.
1963   *Sociology: A Text With Adapted Readings.* 3rd ed. New York: Harper and
Row.

Brown, George Isaac. *Human Teaching for Hu-
1971   man Learning: An Introduction to*

Confluent Education. New York: Viking Press.

Brown, James W., R. B. Lewis, and Fred F.
1973   Harcleroad. *A-V Instruction: Technology, Media, and Message.* New York: McGraw-Hill.

Brown, James W., and James W.
1971   Thornton. *College Teaching: A Systematic Approach.* 2nd ed. New York: McGraw-Hill.

Brown, Richard Maxwell. "The American
1969   Vigilante Tradition." Chapter 5 in *Violence in America: Historical and Comparative Perspectives.* New York: Bantam. (Report submitted to the National Commission on the Causes and Prevention of Violence.)

Brown, Ruth Esther. "Introductory Texts: A
1976   Report on the Current Models." *Contemporary Sociology: A Journal of Reviews* 5 (March): 123–30.

Brudner, Harvey J. "Computer-Managed In-
1968   struction." *Science* 162 (November): 970–75.

Bruffee, Kenneth A. "A New Intellectual
1978   Frontier." *The Chronicle of Higher Education* 16 (February 27): 40.

Burchard, Waldo W. "Role Conflicts in Mili-
1954   tary Chaplains." *American Sociological Review* 19 (October): 528–35.

Byrne, Donn. "The Influence of Propinquity
1960   and Opportunities for Interaction on Classroom Relationships." *Human Relations* 13 (February): 63–69.

Cain, Leonard D., Jr. "Life Course and Social
1964   Structure." Pp. 272–309 in Robert E. L. Faris (ed.), *Handbook of Modern Sociology.* Chicago: Rand McNally.

Caine, Robert, David Centa, Cecile Doroff,
1978   Joel H. Horowitz, and Vance Wisenbaker. "Statistics from Whom?" *Teaching Sociology* 6 (October): 37–46.

Cantor, Nathaniel. *The Teaching-Learning*
1953   *Process.* New York: Dryden Press.

Cantor, Nathaniel. *The Dynamics of Learning.*
1950   2nd ed. Buffalo: Foster and Stewart.

Cantor, Nathaniel. "The Teaching and Learn-
1949   ing of Sociology." *American Journal of Sociology* 55 (July): 18–24.

Caplow, Theodore, and Reece J. McGee. *The*
1958   *Academic Market Place.* New York: Basic.

Carlson, C. R. "Feedback for Learning." In
1978   Ohmer Milton (ed.), *On College Teaching.* San Francisco: Jossey-Bass, pp. 125–52.

Carnegie Commission on Higher Education.
1972   *The Fourth Revolution: Instructional Techniques in Higher Education.* New York: McGraw-Hill.

Carr, Stephen. "The City of the Mind." Pp.
1967   197–226 in William R. Ewalt (ed.), *Environment for Man.* Bloomington: Indiana University Press.

Carroll, J. Gregory. "Assessing the Effective-
1977   ness of a Training Program for the University Teaching Assistant." *Teaching of Psychology* 4 (October): 135–38.

Carroll, John B. "A Model of School Learn-
1963   ing." *Teachers College Record* 64: 723–33.

Cash, W. J. *The Mind of the South.* New York:
[1941] Random (Vintage paperback).
1969

Center for Faculty Evaluation and Development
1976   in Higher Education. *Idea: Interpretive Guide: Understanding Student Reactions to Instruction and Courses.* Manhattan, KS.: Center for Faculty Evaluation and Development in Higher Education.

Centers, Richard, and Bertram Raven.
1971   "Conjugal Power Structure: A Re-examination." *American Sociological Review* 36 (April): 264–78.

Centra, John A. *Determining Faculty Effective-*
1979   *ness.* San Francisco: Jossey-Bass.

Centra, John A. "Student Ratings of Instruc-
1977   tion and Their Relationship to Student Learning." *American Educational Research Journal* 14 (Winter): 17–24.

Centra, John A. "Student Ratings of Instruc-
1976   tion and Their Relationship to Stu-
        dent Learning." *Research Bulletin.*
        Princeton, NJ.: Educational Testing
        Service.

Centra, John A. "Colleagues as Raters of
1975   Classroom Instruction." *Journal of
        Higher Education* 46 (May/June): 327–
        37.

Centra, John A. "Self-Ratings of College
1973a   Teachers: A Comparison with Stu-
        dent Ratings." *Journal of Educational
        Measurement* 10: 287–95.

Centra, John A. "The Effectiveness of Student
1973b   Feedback in Modifying College In-
        struction." *Journal of Educational
        Psychology* 65 (December): 395–401.

Centra, John A. "The Relationship between
1973c   Student and Alumni Ratings of
        Teachers." *Research Bulletin* 73–39.
        Princeton, NJ.: Educational Testing
        Service.

Centra, John A. *Strategies for Improving Col-
1972a   lege Teaching.* Washington, D. C.:
        ERIC Clearinghouse on Higher Edu-
        cation, American Association for
        Higher Education.

Centra, John A. Unpublished letter. Pp. 122–
[1972b] 23 in Richard I. Miller, *Developing
1974   Programs for Faculty Evaluation.* San
        Francisco: Jossey-Bass.

Centra, John A., and F. R. Creech. "The Rela-
1976   tionship between Student, Teacher
        and Course Characteristics and Stu-
        dent Ratings of Teacher Effective-
        ness." *Research Bulletin.* Princeton,
        NJ.: Educational Testing Service.

Chandler, Tertius, and Gerald Fox. *3000 Years
1974   of Urban Growth.* New York: Aca-
        demic Press.

Change. "The TIPS Phenomenon." *Change
1977a   Magazine* 9 (Report on Teaching No.
        1, January): 24–25.

Change. (Report on Teaching No. 4, July): en-
1977b   tire issue.

Change. "Custom Tailored TIPS for Stu-
1976   dents." *Change Magazine 8* (March):
        22–23.

Chapin, F. Stuart. "The Use of Graphic
1923   Method in Teaching Sociology." *So-
        cial Forces* 1 (September): 538–43.

Cheatwood, Derral. "The Use of Still Photog-
1978   raphy in Student Projects." *Teaching
        Sociology* 5 (July): 387–408.

Cheatwood, Derral, and T. Lindquist. *The
1976   Human Image: Sociology and Photog-
        raphy.* New Brunswick, NJ.: Trans-
        action.

Chronicle. "20-Year Trends in Higher Educa-
1977   tion" (Fact-File). *The Chronicle of
        Higher Education* 15 (September): 8.

Chu, G. C., and Wilbur Schramm. *Learning
1967   from Television: What the Research
        Says.* Stanford, CA.: Institute for
        Communications Research.

Churchill, R. "Preliminary Report on Reading
1957   Course Study." Yellow Springs,
        OH.: mimeographed.

Clark, Susan G. "An Innovation for Introduc-
1974   tory Sociology." *Teaching Sociology*
        1 (April): 131–42.

Clark, Terry. *Community Structure and Deci-
1968   sion-Making.* San Francisco: Chan-
        dler.

Clifton, A. Kay. "Doin Soc: An Evaluation of
1976   Actively Involving Introductory
        Students in the Work of Sociology."
        Teaching Sociology 3 (January): 138–
        47.

Cline, Hugh F., and Edmund D. Meyers,
1970   Jr. "Problem-Solving Computer
        Systems for Instruction in Sociol-
        ogy." *The American Sociologist* 5
        (November): 365–70.

Coats, William D., and Uldis Smidchens.
1966   "Audience Recall as a Function of
        Speaker Dynamism." *Journal of Ed-
        ucational Psychology* 57: 189–91.

Coch, Lester, and John R. P. French,
1948   Jr. "Overcoming Resistance to
        Change." *Human Relations* 1:512–
        32.

Cohen, Arthur M., Clare Rose, and James W.
1973   Trent. "Teaching Technology and
        Methods." Pp. 1023–28 in Robert

M. W. Travers (ed.), *Second Handbook of Research on Teaching*. Chicago: Rand McNally.

Cohen, Elizabeth G. "Sociology and the
1972   Classroom: Setting the Conditions
          for Teacher-Student Interaction."
          Review of Educational Research 42
          (Fall): 441–52.

Cohen, Morris Raphael. *Reason and Nature:*
[1931]   *The Meaning of Scientific Method.*
1964   New York: Free Press.

Cole, Stephen. *the Sociological Method.* 2nd
1976   ed. Chicago: Rand McNally.

College Marketing Group.   Counts Brochure.
1977   Reading, MA.: College Marketing
          Group.

Collier, John, Jr. *Visual Anthropology: Photog-*
1967   *raphy as a Research Method.* New
          York: Holt, Rinehart, and Winston.

Collins, Randall. "A Conflict Theory of Sexual
1971   Stratification." *Social Problems* 19
          (Summer): 3–12.

Committee on the Undergraduate Program in
1972   Mathematics, Mathematical Associ-
          ation of America. *Suggestions on
          the Teaching of College Mathematics.*
          Hayward, CA.: MAA Special Pro-
          jects Office, Dept. of Mathematics,
          California State University of Hay-
          ward, 94542.

Conklin, George H. "Using the Computer in
1976   Introductory Sociology." *Teaching
          Sociology* 4 (October): 83–97.

Conover, Patrick W. "The Experimental
1974   Teaching of Basic Social Concepts:
          An Improvisational Approach."
          Teaching Sociology 2 (October): 27–
          42.

Contemporary Sociology. "Symposium: Social
1978   Indicators 1976." *Contemporary Soci-
          ology* 7 (November): 712–17.

Cooley, Charles Horton. *Human Nature and
1902   the Social Order.* New York:
          Scribner's.

Coser, Lewis. *The Functions of Social Conflict.*
1956   New York: Free Press.

Costin, Frank. "A Graduate Course in the
1968   Teaching of Psychology: Descrip-
          tion and Evaluation." *Journal of
          Teaching Education* 19 (Winter): 425–
          32.

Costin, Frank, William T. Greenough, and Ro-
1971   bert J. Menges. "Student Ratings
          of College Teaching: Reliability, Va-
          lidity and Usefulness." *Review of
          Educational Research* 41 (December):
          511–35.

Cottrell, Leonard S., Jr. "Individual Adjust-
1942   ment to Age and Sex Roles." *Ameri-
          can Sociological Review* 7 (October):
          617–20.

Cottrell, William F. *Technology, Man, and Pro-
1972   gress.* Columbus, OH.: Merrill.

Cottrell, William F. "Death by Dieselization:
1951   A Case Study in the Reaction to
          Technological Change." *American
          Sociological Review* 16 (June): 358–
          65.

Crittenden, K. S., J. L. Norr, and R. K.
1975   LeBailly. "Size of University
          Classes and Student Evaluations of
          Teaching." *Journal of Higher Educa-
          tion* 46 (July/August): 461–70.

CRM Books. *Society Today.* 2nd ed. Del Mar,
1973   CA.: CRM Books.

Cross, K. Patricia. *Accent on Learning.* San
1976   Francisco: Jossey-Bass.

Cross, K. Patricia. *The Junior College Student:
1968   A Research Description.* Princeton,
          NJ.: Educational Testing Service.

Crow, Mary Lynn. *Teaching on Television.*
1977   Arlington, TX.: Faculty Develop-
          ment Resource Center, University of
          Texas at Arlington.

Crozier, Michel. *The Bureaucratic Phenome-
1964   non.* Chicago: University of Chicago
          Press.

Curry, Thomas J., and Alfred C.
1977   Clarke. *Introducing Visual Sociol-
          ogy.* Dubuque, IA.: Kendall-Hunt.

Cutler, Stephen J. "Instructional Uses of the
1978   General Social Survey." *Contempo-*

rary Sociology 7 (September): 541–45.

Cuzzort, Ray P. *Humanity and Modern Sociological Thought.* New York: Holt, Rinehart, and Winston.
1969

Dahrendorf, Ralf. "On the Origin of Inequality Among Man." In Edward Laumann, Paul Siegel, and Robert M. Hodge (eds.), *The Logic of Social Hierarchies.* Chicago: Markham.
1970

D'Andrade, Roy G. "Sex Differences and Cultural Institutions." Pp. 174–204 in Eleanor E. Maccoby (ed.), *The Development of Sex Differences.* Stanford, CA.: Stanford University Press.
1966

D'Andrea-Burkhart, Vaneeta. "Turning the Tables with Audiovisuals." *Change Magazine* 7 (Report on Teaching No. 4): 70.
1977

Daniels, Glenn. "A User's Look at the Audio-Visual World." Pp. 212–41 in *College Instructor's Vade Mecum.* Preliminary ed. Bowling Green, OH.: Bowling Green State University Professional Development Project, Office of the Graduate School.
1973

Davidson, Raymond L. *Audiovisual Machines.* 2nd ed. Scranton, PA.: International.
1969

Davies, James C. "Toward a Theory of Revolution." *American Sociological Review* 27 (February): 5–19.
1962

Davis, Allison. "The Motivation of the Underprivileged Worker." In William Foote Whyte (ed.), *Industry and Society.* New York: McGraw-Hill, pp. 84–106.
1946

Davis, Ethelyn, Charles A. Goldsmid, and Wilhelmina Perry. *Teaching Sociology. An Annotated Bibliography.* 3rd ed. Washington, D. C.: ASA Teaching Resources Center.
1979

Davis, Ethelyn, Charles A. Goldsmid, and Wilhelmina Perry. *Teaching Sociology: A Bibliography.* 2nd ed. Washington, D. C.: ASA Teaching Resources Center.
1977

Davis, Gerald, and Virginia Ayers. "Photographic Recording of Environmental Behavior." Chapter 6 in William Michaelson (ed.), *Behavioral Research Methods in Environmental Design.* Stroudsburg, PA.: Dowden, Hutchinson, and Ross.
1975

Davis, James A. "Teaching Social Facts with Computers." *Teaching Sociology* 5 (April): 235–58.
1978

Davis, James A. "Using the IMPRESS System to Teach Sociology." Pp. 382–88 in *Proceedings of a Conference on Computers in the Undergraduate Curriculum.* Hanover, NH.: Dartmouth College.
1971

Davis, James A. "The Campus as Frog Pond: An Application of the Theory of Relative Deprivation to Career Decisions of College Men." *American Journal of Sociology* 72 (July): 17–31.
1966

Davis, James R. *Teaching Strategies for the College Classroom.* Boulder, CO.: Westview.
1976

Davis, Kingsley. *The Population of India and Pakistan.* Princeton, NJ.: Princeton University Press.
1951

Davis, Kingsley, and Wilbert E. Moore. "Some Principles of Stratification." *American Sociological Review* 102:242–49.
1945

Davis, Robert H., Allan J. Abedor, and Paul W. F. Witt. *Commitment to Excellence: A Case Study of Educational Innovation.* East Lansing, MI.: Educational Development Program, Michigan State University.
1976

Dean, Dwight G., and Donald M. Valdes. *Experiments in Sociology.* 3rd ed. Englewood Cliffs, NJ.: Prentice-Hall.
1976

Dean, John P. "The Myths of Housing Reform." *American Sociological Review* 14 (April): 281–88.
1949

Debnam, G. "Nondecisions and Power: The
1975   Two Faces of Bachrach and Baratz."
        American Political Science Review 69
        (September): 889–900.

DeFleur, Melvin L., William V. D'Antonio, and
1973   Lois B. DeFleur. *Sociology: Human
        Society*. Glenview, IL.: Scott, Fores-
        man, and Company.

DeLury, George E., ed. *The World Almanac
1973   and Books of Facts: 1973 Edition*. New
        York: Newspaper Enterprise Asso-
        ciation.

Dewey, John. *Human Nature and Conduct: An
[1922] Introduction to Social Psychology*.
1930   New York: Henry Holt (Modern Li-
        brary edition).

Dewey, John. *Democracy and Education*. New
1916   York: Macmillan.

Donahue, Mary, and James L. Spates. *Action
1972   Research Handbook for "Social
        Change in Urban America."* New
        York: Harper and Row.

Douglas, Jack D. *Introduction to Sociology: Sit-
1973   uations and Structures*. New York:
        Free Press.

Doyle, Kenneth O., Jr. *Student Evaluation of
1975   Instruction*. Lexington, MA.: Lex-
        ington.

Doyle, Kenneth O., Jr., and S. E. Whitely.
1974   "Student Ratings as Criteria for Ef-
        fective Teaching." *American Educa-
        tional Research Journal* 11 (Summer):
        259–74.

Dreeben, Robert. "The School as a Work-
1973   place." Chapter 14 in Robert M. W.
        Travers, ed. *Second Handbook of Re-
        search on Teaching*. Chicago: Rand
        McNally.

Dreeben, Robert. *The Nature of Teaching:
1970   Schools and the Work of Teachers*.
        Glenview, IL.: Scott, Foresman, and
        Company.

Dressel, Paul L. *Handbook of Academic Evalua-
1976   tion*. San Francisco: Jossey-Bass.

Dressel, Paul L., and Clarence H.
1961   Nelson. "Testing and Grading
        Policies." In Paul L. Dressel (ed.),
        Evaluation in Higher Education. Bos-
        ton: Houghton Mifflin.

Dressel, Paul L., and Mary M. Thompson.
1973   *Independent Study*. San Francisco:
        Jossey-Bass.

Driscoll, William J. "Independent Study: A
1975   New Emphasis for the 1970s." In
        Thomas H. Buxton and Keith W.
        Prichard (eds.), *Excellence in Univer-
        sity Teaching*. Columbia, SC.: Uni-
        versity of South Carolina Press, pp.
        232–38.

Drucker, A. J. and H. H. Remmers. "Do
1951   Alumni and Students Differ in Their
        Attitudes   Toward   Instructors?"
        Journal of Educational Psychology 42:
        129–43.

Dubin, Robert. *The World of Work*. Engle-
1958   wood Cliffs, NJ.: Prentice-Hall.

Dubin, Robert, and R. Alan Hedley. *The Me-
1969   dium May Be Related to the Message:
        College Instruction by TV*. Eugene,
        OR.: Center for the Advanced Study
        of Educational Administration, Uni-
        versity of Oregon.

Dubin, Robert, and Thomas C. Taveggia. *The
1968   Teaching-Learning Paradox: A Com-
        parative Study of College Teaching
        Methods*. Eugene, OR.: Center for
        the Advanced Study of Educational
        Administration, University of Ore-
        gon.

DuBois, W. E. B. *The Souls of Black Folk*. As
[1897] cited in Peter I. Rose, *They and We:
1974   Racial and Ethnic Relations in the
        United States*. New York: Random
        House, p. 164.

Duchastel, Phillipe C., and Paul F.
1973   Merrill. "The Effects of Behavioral
        Objectives on Learning: A Review
        of Empirical Studies." *Review of Ed-
        ucational Research* 43 (Winter): 53–
        69.

Dukes, Richard L. *Simulation and Gaming and
1978   the Teaching of Sociology*. 2nd ed.
        Washington, D. C.: ASA Teaching
        Resources Center (ASA Projects on
        Teaching)

Dukes, Richard L. "Teaching Introductory
1975   Sociology: The Modular Approach."
        Teaching Sociology 2 (April): 165–
        76.

Dukes, Richard L., and Cathy S. Greenblat.
1979   *Game Generating Games.* Beverly
        Hills, CA.: Sage.

Duncan, Otis Dudley. "Optimum Size of
1957   Cities." Pp. 759–72 in Paul K. Hatt
        and Albert J. Reiss, Jr (eds.), *Cities
        and Society: The Revised Reader in
        Urban Sociology.* New York: Free
        Press.

Dunkin, Michael J., and Bruce J. Biddle. *The
1974   Study of Teaching.* New York: Holt,
        Rinehart, and Winston.

Dunphy, Dexter C. "Planned Environments
1967   for Learning in the Social Sciences:
        Two Innovative Courses at Har-
        vard." *The American Sociologist* 2
        (November): 202–206.

Durkheim, Émile. *Moral Education.* 2nd ed.
[1902– Translated with a new introduction
1903]   by Everett K. Wilson (ed.). New
1973   York: Free Press.

Durkheim, Émile. *The Division of Labor in
[1893] Society.* Translated by George Simp-
1964   son. New York: Free Press.

Durkheim, Émile. *Education and Sociology.*
[1903– Translated with an introduction by
1911]   Sherwood D. Fox. New York: Free
1956   Press.

Durkheim, Émile. *Suicide: A Study in Sociol-
[1897] ogy.* Translated by John A. Spauld-
1951   ing and George Simpson. New
        York: Free Press.

Durkheim, Émile. *Education et sociologie.* Paris:
1922   Librairie Felix Alcan.

Dwyer, Thomas A. "Some Principles for the
1971   Human Use of Computers in Educa-
        tion." *International Journal of Man-
        Machine Studies* 3:219–39.

Earle, Ralph B., Jr., ed. *PSI and Political Sci-
1975   ence: Using the Personalized System of
        Instruction to Teach American Poli-
        tics.* Washington, D. C.: American
        Political Science Association.

Eble, Kenneth E. *The Craft of Teaching.* San
1976   Francisco: Jossey-Bass.

Eble, Kenneth E. *Professors as Teachers.* San
1972   Francisco: Jossey-Bass.

Eble, Kenneth E. *The Recognition and Evalua-
1971a   tion of Teaching.* Washington, D. C.:
        American Association of University
        Professors.

Eble, Kenneth E. *Career Development of the
1971b   Effective College Teacher.* Washing-
        ton, D. C.: American Association of
        University Professors.

Educational Testing Service. *SIR Comparative
1975   Data Guide, 1975–1976.* Princeton,
        NJ.: Educational Testing Service.

Ehman, Lee, Howard Mehlinger, and John
1974   Patrick. *Toward Effective Instruc-
        tion in Secondary Social Studies.* Bos-
        ton: Houghton Mifflin.

Elder, Glen H., Jr. "Age Differentiation and
1975   the Life Course." In Alex Inkeles,
        James Coleman, and Neil Smelser
        (eds.), *Annual Review of Sociology,
        Volume I.* Palo Alto, CA.: Annual
        Reviews, pp. 165–90.

Elgin, Duane, Tom Thomas, Tom Logothetti,
1974   and Sue Cox. *City Size and the
        Quality of Life.* Washington, D. C.:
        U.S. Government Printing Office.
        (Prepared for the NSF RANN Pro-
        gram.)

Elliott, D. H. "Characteristics and Relation-
1950   ships of Various Criteria of College
        and University Teaching." *Purdue
        University Studies in Higher Educa-
        tion* 70: 5–61.

Entwistle, Noel, and Dai Hounsell, eds. *How
1975   Students Learn.* Lancaster: Institute
        for Research and Development in
        Post-Compulsory Education, Uni-
        versity of Lancaster, England.

Ericksen, Maynard L., and R. Brooke Jacobsen.
1973   "On Computer Applications and
        Statistics in Sociology: Toward the
        Passing Away of an Antiquated
        Technology." *Teaching Sociology* 1
        (October): 84–102.

Ericksen, Stanford C.   "The Lecture." *Memo to*
1978   *the Faculty* 60 (April). Ann Arbor:
          Center for Research on Learning
          and Teaching, University of Michi-
          gan.

Ericksen, Stanford C.   *Motivation for Learning:*
1974   *A Guide for the Teacher of the Young*
          Adult. Ann Arbor: University of
          Michigan Press.

Ericksen, Stanford C.   "The Technology Re-
1972   source for Teachers and Students."
          Memo to the Faculty 50 (December).
          Ann Arbor: Center for Research on
          Learning and Teaching, University
          of Michigan.

Ericksen, Stanford C., and James A. Kulik.
1975   "Learning How to Learn Indepen-
          dently." *Memo to the Faculty* 55
          (May). Ann Arbor: Center for Re-
          search on Learning and Teaching,
          University of Michigan.

Ericksen, Stanford C., and James A. Kulik.
1974   "Evaluation of Teaching." *Memo to*
          the Faculty 53 (February). Ann Ar-
          bor: Center for Research on Learn-
          ing and Teaching, University of
          Michigan.

Erickson, Glenn R., and Bette L. Erickson.
1979a   "Improving College Teaching: An
          Evaluation of a Teaching Consulta-
          tion Procedure." *Journal of Higher*
          Education 50:670–73.

Erickson, Glenn R., and Bette L. Erickson.
1979b   "Improving College Teaching: Two
          Evaluation Studies of a Teaching
          Consultation Procedure." Paper
          presented at the annual meeting of
          the American Educational Research
          Association, San Francisco.

Ewens, Bill.   "Developing Programs for Pre-
1976a   paring Sociology Graduate Students
          to Teach." *Teaching Sociology* 3
          (April): 305–26.

Ewens, Bill.   *Preparing for Teaching: Sugges-*
1976b   *tions for Graduate Students of Sociol-*
          ogy. Washington, D. C.: ASA
          Teaching Resources Center.

Ewens, Bill.   *Twenty Suggestions for Improving*
1976c   *the Departmental Procedures for Hir-*
          ing Teachers of Sociology. Washing-
          ton, D. C.: ASA Teaching Resources
          Center (ASA Projects on Teaching).

Ewens, Bill, and Diane Emling.   "Survey Con-
1976   ducted on Teacher Development in
          Sociology." *ASA Footnotes* 4 (Janu-
          ary): 1–4.

Ewens, Bill, and Diane Emling.   *Teacher De-*
1975   *velopment in Sociology: A Survey of*
          Current   Practices   and   Opinions.
          Washington, D. C.: ASA Projects on
          Teaching Undergraduate Sociology,
          ASA Teaching Resources Center.

Falk, R. Frank, and Charles E. Cortese.   "How
1974   to Start a Sociology Computer Labo-
          ratory in a Small College." *Teaching*
          Sociology 1 (April): 242–56.

Feldman, Kenneth A., ed.   *College and Student:*
1972   *Selected Readings in the Social Psy-*
          chology of Higher Education. New
          York: Pergamon.

Feldman, Kenneth A.   "The Superior College
1976   Teacher From the Student's View."
          Research in Higher Education 5:243–
          88.

Fenton, Edwin.   *The New Social Studies.* New
1967   York: Holt, Rinehart, and Winston.

Ferguson, Adam.   *An Essay on the History on*
1819   *Civil Society.* 8th ed. Philadelphia:
          A. Finley.

Fernandez, Ronald.   *The Promise of Sociology.*
1975   New York: Praeger.

Festinger, Leon.   *A Theory of Cognitive Disso-*
1957   *nance.* Stanford, CA.: Stanford Uni-
          versity Press.

Fischer, Claude S.   *The Urban Experience.* New
1976   York: Harcourt Brace Jovanovich.

Fraley, Lawrence E., and Ernest A. Vargas.
1975   "Academic Tradition and Instruc-
          tional   Technology."   *Journal   of*
          Higher Education Volume 46 (Janu-
          ary/February): 1–15.

Francis, Roy G.   "PSI: An Editorial Com-
1974a   ment." *Teaching Sociology* 1 (April):
          160–63.

Francis, Roy G. "The 8mm 'Term Paper:' On
1974b   Helping Sociology Undergraduates
to Make Films." *Teaching Sociology* 2
(October): 57–70.

Frazier, E. Franklin. *The Negro Family in the*
1948   *United States.* New York: Citadel.

French, Robert Mills, ed. *The Community: A*
1969   *Comparative Perspective.* Itasca, IL.:
Peacock.

Frey, Peter W. "Student Ratings of Teaching:
1973   Validity of Several Rating Factors."
Science 182 (October 5): 83–85.

Friedland, William H. "Making Sociology
1969   Relevant: A Teaching-Research Program for Undergraduates." *The*
American Sociologist 4 (May): 104–
10.

Fuller, Francis F., and Brad A. Manning.
1973   "Self-Confrontation Reviewed: A
Conceptualization of Video-Play-
back in Teacher Education." *Review*
of Educational Research 43 (Fall):
469–528.

Gaff, Jerry G. *Toward Faculty Renewal.* San
1975   Francisco: Jossey-Bass.

Gage, N. L. *The Scientific Basis of the Art of*
1978   *Teaching.* New York: Teachers College Press.

Gagné, Robert M. *Essentials of Learning for*
1974   *Instruction.* Hinsdale, IL.: Dryden.

Gagné, Robert M. "Domains of Learning."
1972   *Interchange* 3:1–8.

Gagné, Robert M. *The Conditions of Learning.*
1970   2nd ed. New York: Holt, Rinehart,
and Winston.

Galliher, John F. "The ASA Code of Ethics on
1975   the Protection of Human Beings:
Are Students Human, Too?" *The*
American Sociologist 10 (May): 113–
17.

Gans, Herbert J. "The Positive Functions of
1972   Poverty." *American Journal of Sociol-*
ogy 78 (September): 275–89.

Garfinkel, Harold. *Studies in Ethnomethod-*
1967   *ology.* Englewood Cliffs. NJ.: Prentice-Hall.

Gates, A. I. "Recitation as a Factor in Memo-
1917   rizing." *Archives of Psychology* (September), pp. 1–104.

Gates, Davida P. "Small College Study,
1975   1975." Unpublished data received
through personal communication.

Gates, Davida P. "Sociology in Small Liberal
1969   Arts Colleges." *The American Sociol-*
ogist 4 (November): 324–30.

Geertsen, Reed, ed. *Eighty-one Techniques for*
1979   *Teaching   Sociological   Concepts.*
Washington, D. C.: ASA Teaching
Resources Center (ASA Projects on
Teaching).

Geertsen, Reed. "The Textbook: An ACIDS
1977   Test." *Teaching Sociology* 5 (October): 101–20.

Gelles, Richard J. *"Teaching Sociology* on
1979   Teaching Sociology." Keynote address to meetings of the Section on
Undergraduate Education of the
American Sociological Association,
Boston, August 29. (Copies available from the ASA Teaching Resources Center, 1722 N Street, N.
W., Washington, D. C. 20036.)

Gessner, Peter K. "Evaluation of Instruc-
1973   tion." *Science* 180 (May 11): 566–69.

Gibb, J. R. "The Effects of Group Size and of
1951   Threat Reduction upon Creativity in
a   Problem-Solving   Situation."
American Psychologist 6: 324. (An
abstract.)

Gibbs, Jack P., and Walter T. Martin. "Status
1959   Integration and Suicide in Ceylon."
American Journal of Sociology 64
(May): 585–91.

Gibbs, Jack P., and Walter T. Martin. "A
1958   Theory of Status Integration and Its
Relationship to Suicide." *American*
Sociological Review 23 (April): 140–
47.

Gist, Noel P., and Sylvia Fleis Fava. *Urban*
1974   *Society.* 6th ed. New York: Crowell.

Gleazer, Edmund J., Jr. "Preparation of Jun-
1967   ior College Teachers." *Educational*
Record 48 (Spring): 147–52.

Glenn, Norval D., and Wayne Villemez. "The
1970   Productivity of Sociologists at 45
        American Universities." *The Ameri-
        can Sociologist* 5 (August): 244–52.

Goffman, Erving. *Asylums: Essays on the So-
1961a   cial Situation of Mental Patients and
        Other Inmates.* Garden City, NY.:
        Doubleday Anchor.

Goffman, Erving. *Encounters: Two Studies in
1961b   the Sociology of Interaction.* Indian-
        apolis: Bobbs-Merrill.

Golden, M. Patricia, ed. *The Research Experi-
1976   ence.* Itasca, IL.: Peacock.

Goldsmid, Charles A. "Selected Statistical
1979   Publications of the Census Bureau:
        Description and Review of Instruc-
        tional Uses." *Teaching Sociology* 6
        (April): 269–79.

Goldsmid, Charles A., ed. *Introductory Sociol-
1977a   ogy Courses: A Set of Syllabi and
        Related Materials.* Washington,
        D. C.: ASA Teaching Resources
        Center (ASA Section on Under-
        graduate Education)

Goldsmid, Charles A. "The Teaching of Soci-
1977b   ology, 1975–1976: Annotated Bibli-
        ography and Review." *Teaching So-
        ciology* 4 (April): 341–68.

Goldsmid, Charles A. "Professional Social-
1976a   ization of Teachers of Sociology."
        Teaching Sociology 3 (April): 229–48.

Goldsmid, Charles A. "Resources III: Teach-
1976b   ing Sociology: A Selected Bibliogra-
        phy." *Teaching Sociology* 3 (April):
        357–78.

Goldsmid, Charles A. "Comments and Sug-
1972   gestions Regarding the First Day of
        Classes." With Reactions by Everett
        K. Wilson. Unpublished memoran-
        dum used in Sociology 380, Univer-
        sity of North Carolina at Chapel
        Hill: mimeographed.

Goldsmid, Charles A., and Ethelyn C.
1978   Davis. "The Teaching of Sociology
        1977: Annotated Bibliography and
        Review." *Teaching Sociology* 5
        (April): 325–60.

Goldsmid, Charles A., and Paula L.
1979   Goldsmid. "The Teaching of Soci-
        ology, 1978: Review and Annotated
        Bibliography." *Teaching Sociology* 6
        (April): 291–328.

Goldsmid, Charles A., James E. Gruber, and
1977   Everett K. Wilson. "Perceived At-
        tributes of Superior Teachers."
        *American Educational Research Jour-
        nal* 14 (Fall): 423–40.

Gould, Julius, and William L. Kolb,
1964   eds. *Dictionary of the Social Sci-
        ences.* New York: Free Press.

Grant, Gerald, Peter Elbow, Thomas Ewens,
1979   Zelda Gamson, Wendy Kohli, Wil-
        liam Neumann, Virginia Olesen,
        and David Riesman. *On Compe-
        tence: A Critical Analysis of Com-
        petence-Based Reforms in Higher
        Education.* San Francisco: Jossey-
        Bass.

Grasha, Anthony F. *Assessing and Developing
1977   Faculty Performance: Principles and
        Models.* Cincinnati: Communication
        and Education Associates.

Grasha, Anthony F. "Getting Students In-
1975   volved in the Classroom." In Wil-
        liam Bergquist and Steven Phillips
        (eds.), *A Handbook for Faculty Devel-
        opment, Volume I.* Washington,
        D. C.: Council for the Advancement
        of Small Colleges, pp. 113–21.

Green, Ben A. "Fifteen Reasons Not to Use
1972   the Keller Plan." In J. L. Sayre and
        J. J. Knightly (eds.), *The Personalized
        System of Instruction in Higher Educa-
        tion: Readings on PSI—The Keller
        Plan.* Enid, OK.: Seminary, pp. 46–
        48.

Green, Robert W., ed. *Protestantism and Capi-
1959   talism: The Weber Thesis and Its
        Critics.* Boston: D. C. Heath.

Gustad, John W. "Evaluation of Teaching
1967   Performance: Issues and Possibili-
        ties." In Calvin B. T. Lee (ed.), *Im-
        proving College Teaching.* Washing-
        ton, D. C.: American Council on
        Education, pp. 265–81.

Haas, J. Eugene, and Thomas E. Drabek. *Complex Organizations: A Sociological Perspective*. New York: Macmillan. 1973

Hacker, Helen. "Women as a Minority Group." *Social Forces* 30 (October): 60–69. 1951

Haggard, E. A., and R. J. Rose. "Some Effects of Mental Set and Active Participation in the Conditioning of the Autokinetic Phenomenon." *Journal of Experimental Psychology* 34:45–49. 1944

Haines, Donald B., and Wilbert J. McKeachie. "Cooperative vs. Competitive Discussion Methods in Teaching Introductory Psychology." *Journal of Educational Psychology* 58 (December): 386–90. 1967

Hall, Edward T. *The Hidden Dimension*. New York: Doubleday. 1966

Halley, Fred S. "Programs for Use in Teaching Research Methods for Small Computers." *Teaching Sociology* 2 (April): 218–21. 1975

Hammond, Phillip E., ed. *Sociologists at Work: The Craft of Social Research*. Garden City, NY.: Doubleday Anchor. 1967

Hansen, William L., Allen C. Kelley, and Burton A. Weisbrod. "Economic Efficiency and the Distribution of Benefits from College Instruction." *American Economic Review* 60 (May): 364–69. 1970

Hare, A. Paul. *Handbook of Small Group Research*. 2nd ed. New York: Free Press. 1976

Harper, Dean, and Hanan C. Selvin. "Computer Simulation and the Teaching of Research Methods." *The American Sociologist* 3 (May): 64–70. 1973

Harry, J., and N. S. Goldner. "The Null Relationship between Teaching and Research." *Sociology of Education* 45 (Winter): 47–60. 1972

Hart, Roderick. P. Lecturing as Communication: Problems and Potentialities. West Lafayette, IN.: Purdue University Research Foundation. (A study guide.) 1973a

Hart, Roderick P. Lecturing: Overcoming the Barriers to Communication. West Lafayette, IN.: Purdue University Research Foundation. (A study guide.) 1973b

Hawley, Amos H. "Ecology and Population." *Science* 179 (March 23): 1196–1201. 1973

Hawley, Amos H. *Urban Society: An Ecological Approach*. New York: Ronald Press. 1971

Hawley, Willis D., and Orion White. "Assessing the Quality of Teaching." *News for Teachers of Political Science* 20 (Winter): 8–10. Washington, D. C.: American Political Science Association. 1979

Hedley, Robert A. "Measurement: Social Research Strategies and Their Relevance to Grading." *Teaching Sociology* 6 (October): 21–29. 1978

Heider, Karl G. *Films for Anthropological Teaching*. 6th ed. Washington, D. C.: American Anthropological Association. 1977

Helling, Barbara B. "Looking for Good Teaching: A Guide to Peer Observation." Excerpt from a Danforth Faculty Fellowship Report. Distributed by the ASA Teaching Resources Center, Washington, D. C. 1976

Henry, Mark, and David Ramsett. "The Effects of Computer-Aided Instruction on Learning and Attitudes in Economic Principles Courses." *Journal of Economic Education* 10 (Fall): 26–34. 1978

Herzog, Elizabeth. *About the Poor: Some Facts and Some Fictions* (U.S. Dept. of Health, Education, and Welfare—Children's Bureau Pub. No. 451–1967). Washington, D. C.: U.S. Government Printing Office. 1967

High School Geography Project and Sociologi-
1974   cal Resources for the Social Studies.
        Experiences in Inquiry. Boston: Allyn
        and Bacon.

Hildebrand, Milton. "How to Recommend
1972   Promotion for a Mediocre Teacher
        Without Actually Lying." *Journal of
        Higher Education* 43 (January): 44–
        62.

Hildebrand, Milton, Robert C. Wilson, and
1971   Evelyn R. Dienst. *Evaluating Univer-
        sity Teaching*. Berkeley: Center for
        Research and Development in
        Higher Education, University of
        California.

Hill, Andrew. "Sociology in Two-Year Col-
1979   leges." Unpublished paper pre-
        pared as part of a NSF-sponsored
        study of science education in com-
        munity colleges.

Hill, Richard J.   *A Comparative Study of Lecture
1960   and Discussion*. New York: Fund for
        Adult Education.

Hill, William Fawcett.   *Learning Thru Discus-
1969   sion: Guide for Leaders and Members
        of Discussion Groups*. Beverly Hills,
        CA.: Sage.

Hiller, Harry H. "The Sociological Debate:
1975   Innovating with the Pedagogical
        Role." *Teaching Sociology* 2 (April):
        123–32.

Hind, R. R., Sanford M. Dornbusch, and Wil-
1974   liam R. Scott. "A Theory of Evalu-
        ation Applied to a University Fac-
        ulty." *Sociology of Education* 47:
        114–28.

Hobbes, Thomas.   *Leviathan*. New York: E. P.
[1651]   Dutton.
1914

Hobbs,   Donald   A.,   and   Stuart   J.
1975   Blank. *Sociology and the Human Ex-
        perience*. New York: Wiley.

Hochschild, Arlie, and David Nasatir. Paper
1973   presented at the annual meetings of
        the American Sociological Associa-
        tion.

Hogan, T. P. "Similarity of Student Ratings
1973   Across Instructors, Courses, and
        Time." *Research in Higher Education*
        1:149–54.

Hollingshead, A. B. *Elmtown's Youth*. New
1949   York: Wiley.

Homans, George. *The Human Group*. New
1950   York: Harcourt Brace Jovanovich.

Hoover, Kenneth H.   *College Teaching Today:
1980   A Handbook of Post-Secondary In-
        struction*. Rockleigh, NJ.: Allyn and
        Bacon.

Horan, Patrick M., and Gregory B. Sampson.
1977   "The   Structure   of   University
        Teaching: Some Evidence from So-
        ciology." *The American Sociologist*
        12 (February): 33–41.

Hoult, Thomas F. "Teaching Sociology by Ra-
1958   dio and Television." *Sociology and
        Social Research* 43 (November/De-
        cember): 97–101.

Hovland, Carl I., ed.   *The Order of Presentation
1957   in Persuasion*. New Haven: Yale Uni-
        versity Press.

Howe, M. J. A., and Lorna Colley. "The
1976   Influence of Questions Encountered
        Earlier on Learning from Prose."
        *British Journal of Educational Psychol-
        ogy* 46:149–54.

Hughes, Helen MacGill.   *Inquiries in Sociology*.
1978   2nd ed. New York: Allyn and Bacon.

Hunkins, A. Papers read to the American
1967–   Educational Research Association,
1968   Washington, D. C.

Hurt, H. Thomas, Michael D. Scott, and James
1978   C. McCrosky. *Communication in
        the Classroom*. Reading, MA.: Addi-
        son-Wesley.

Hyman, Herbert H., and John S. Reed. "Black
1969   Matriarchy' Reconsidered: Evidence
        from Secondary Analysis of Sample
        Surveys." *Public Opinion Quarterly*
        33 (Fall): 346–54.

Inkeles, Alex.   *What Is Sociology?* Englewood
1964   Cliffs, NJ.: Prentice-Hall.

Jacobs, Ruth. "Field Work in an Introductory
1975 Family Course." *Improving College
and University Teaching* 23 (Winter):
36–38, 40.

Jamison, Dean, Patrick Suppes, and Stuart
1974 Wells. "The Effectiveness of Alternative Instructional Media: A Survey." *Review of Educational Research*
44 (Winter): 1–67.

Janis, Irving L. "Groupthink." *Psychology To-
1971 day* 5 (November): 43–46, 74–76.

Johnson, Kent R., and Robert S. Ruskin.
1977 *Behavioral Instruction: An Evaluative Review.* Washington, D. C.:
American Psychological Association.

Johnson, Michael P., and Edward J. Walsh.
1978 "Grade Inflation or Better Comprehension: Self-Scheduled Instruction
in Introductory Sociology." *Teaching Sociology* 5 (July): 363–76.

Johnston, James M., and H. S. Pennypacker.
1971 "A Behavioral Approach to College
Teaching." *American Psychologist* 26
(March): 219–44.

Jones, Robert Alun. "The Use of Literature in
1975 Teaching Introductory Sociology."
Teaching Sociology 2 (April): 177–
97.

Karp, David A., and William C. Yoels. "The
1976 College Classroom: Some Observations on the Meanings of Student
Participation." *Sociology and Social
Research* 60 (July): 421–39.

Katona, George. *Organizing and Memorizing.*
1940 New York: Columbia University
Press.

Keller, Fred S. "Good-bye Teacher. . . ."
1968 *Journal of Applied Behavior Analysis* 1
(Spring): 79–89.

Keller, Fred S., and J. G. Sherman. *The Keller
1974 Plan Handbook.* Menlo Park, CA.:
W. A. Benjamin.

Kelley, Allen C. "TIPS and Technical Change
1972 in Classroom Instruction." *American
Economic Review* 62 (May): 422–28.

Kelley, Allen C. "The Economics of Teaching:
1970 The Role of TIPS." Pp. 44–66 in
K. G. Lumsden (ed.), *Recent Re-
search in Economics Education.*
Englewood Cliffs, NJ.: Prentice-
Hall.

Kelley, Allen C. "An Experiment with TIPS:
1968 A Computer-Aided Instructional
System for Undergraduate Education." *American Economic Review* 58
(May): 446–57.

Kemp, Jerrold E. *Planning and Producing Au-
1975 diovisual Materials.* 3rd ed. New
York: Crowell.

Kemp, Jerrold E. *Instructional Design: A Plan
1971 for Unit and Course Development.*
Belmont, CA.: Fearon-Pitman.

Kemper, Theodore. "Why are the Streets So
1979 Dirty?" *Social Forces* 58 (December),
pp. 422–42.

Keniston, Kenneth. *The Uncommitted: Alien-
1965 ated Youth in American Society.* New
York: Harcourt, Brace, and World.

Kennedy, R., and R. J. Kennedy. "Sociology
1942 and American Colleges." *American
Sociological Review* Volume 7 (October): 661–75.

Kibler, Robert J., Donald J. Cegala, David T.
1974 Miles, and Larry L. Baker.
*Objectives for Instruction and Evalua-
tion.* Boston: Allyn and Bacon.

Kirk, M. "The Seminar." Pp. 63–70 in David
1968 Layton (ed.), *University Teaching in
Transition.* Edinburgh: Oliver and
Boyd.

Kirschner, Betty Frankle. "Introducing Stu-
1973 dents to Women's Place in Society:
Women in Introductory Texts."
American Journal of Sociology 78 (January): 1051–54.

Kloss, Robert Marsh, Ron E. Roberts, and Dean
1976 S. Dorn. *Sociology with a Human
Face.* Saint Louis: Mosby.

Knudsen, D. D. and T. R. Vaughan. "Quality
1969 in Graduate Education: A Reevalua-
tion of the Rankings of Sociology

Departments in the Cartter Report." *The American Sociologist* 4 (February): 12–19.

Kohout, Frank J.   "The First Course in Sociology: Models from the Natural Sciences." *Teaching Sociology* 5 (October): 37–48.
1978

Komarovsky, Mirra.   "Teaching College Sociology." *Social Forces* 30 (December): 252–56.
1951

Kozma, Robert B., Lawrence W. Belle, and George W. Williams. *Instructional Techniques in Higher Education.* Englewood Cliffs, NJ.: Educational Technology Pubs.
1978

Kramer, Cheris, Barrie Thorne, and Nancy Henley. "Perspectives on Language and Communication." *Signs: Journal of Women in Culture and Society* 3 (Spring), pp. 638–51.
1978

Krathwohl, David R., Benjamin S. Bloom, and Bertram B. Masia.   *Taxonomy of Educational Objectives—The Classification of Educational Goals, Handbook II: The Affective Domain.* New York: David McKay.
1964

Krauskopf, C. J.   "The Use of Written Responses in the Stimulated Recall Method." Unpublished doctoral dissertation, Ohio State University. *Dissertation Abstracts* 21:1953.
1960

Kulik, James A.   "Student Reactions to Instruction." *Memo to the Faculty* 58 (October). Ann Arbor: Center for Research on Learning and Teaching, University of Michigan.
1976

Kulik, James A., and Chen-Lin C. Kulik. "College Teaching." In P. Peterson and H. J. Walberg (eds.), *Research on Teaching.* Berkeley: McCutchan, pp. 70–93.
1979

Kulik, James A., and Chen-Lin C. Kulik. "Student Ratings of Instruction." *Teaching of Psychology* 1 (December): 51–57.
1974

Kulik, James A., Chen-Lin Kulik, and K. Carmichael "The Keller Plan in
1974

Science Teaching." *Science* 183 (February 1): 379–83.

Kulik, James A., Chen-Lin Kulik, and John E. Milholland. "Evaluation of an Individualized Course in Psychological Statistics." *Proceedings of the First National Conference on Personalized Instruction.* Washington, D. C.: Center for Personalized Instruction.
1974

Kulik, James A., and Wilbert J. McKeachie. "The Evaluation of Teachers in Higher Education." In Fred N. Kerlinger (ed.), *Review of Research in Education,* Volume 3. Itasca, IL.: Peacock.
1975

Kurtz, Richard A., and John R. Maiolo. "Surgery for Sociology: The Need for Introductory Text Opening Chapterectomy." *The American Sociologist* 3 (February): 36–41.
1968

Ladd, Everett C., Jr.   "The Work Experience of American College Professors: Some Data and an Argument." Paper presented at the National Conference on Higher Education, American Association for Higher Education, Chicago (April 17).
1979

Lally, John J., and Bernard Barber.   "'The Compassionate Physician:' Frequency and Social Determinants of Physician-Investigator Concern for Human Subjects." *Social Forces* 53 (December), pp. 289–96.
1974

Landers, Audrey D.   "Evaluating Teachers." In Ohmer Milton (ed.), *On College Teaching.* San Francisco: Jossey-Bass, pp. 355–75.
1978

Larsen, Otto N., and William R. Catton, Jr. *Conceptual Sociology.* 2nd ed. New York: Harper and Row.
1971

Laumann, Edward O., Peter V. Marsden, and Joseph Galaskiewicz. "Community-Elite Influence Structures: Extension of a Network Approach." *American Journal of Sociology* 83 (November): 594–631.
1977

Layton, Donald, ed. *University Teaching in* 1968 *Transition.* Edinburgh: Oliver and Boyd.

Lazarsfeld, Paul F. "The American Soldier: 1949 An Expository Review." *Public Opinion Quarterly* 13 (Fall): 377–404.

Lazarsfeld, Paul F., William H. Sewell, and 1967 Harold L. Wilensky, eds. *The Uses of Sociology.* New York: Basic.

Lazarsfeld, Paul F., Bernard Berelson, and 1948 Hazel Gaudet. *The People's Choice.* New York: Columbia University Press.

Leacock, Stephen. *Sunshine Sketches of a Little* [1912] *Town.* Toronto: McClelland and 1970 Stewart.

Leevy, J. Roy. "Sociology Programs for Tele-1955 vision." *Sociology and Social Research* 39 (March/April): 248–53.

Leevy, J. Roy. "Making Recordings in Social 1944 Institutions for Sociology Classes." *American Sociological Review* 9: 565–66.

Lena, Hugh F., and Bruce London. "An Intro-1979 duction to Sociology Through Fiction Using Kesey's *One Flew Over the Cuckoo's Nest.*" *Teaching Sociology* 6 (January): 123–32.

Lenski, Gerhard. *Human Societies: An Intro-1970 duction to Macrolevel Sociology.* New York: McGraw-Hill.

Lenski, Gerhard. *Power and Privilege: A The-1966 ory of Social Stratification.* New York: McGraw-Hill.

Lenski, Gerhard, and Jean Lenski. *Human So-1974 cieties: An Introduction to Macroso-ciology.* 2nd ed. New York: Mc-Graw-Hill.

Lenski, Gerhard, Jean Lenski, T. P. Schwartz, 1974 and W. Clark Roof. *Instructor's Manual to Accompany Lenski and Lenski's Human Societies.* 2nd ed. New York: McGraw-Hill.

Leslie, Gerald R., Richard F. Larson, and Ben-1976 jamin L. Gorman. *Introductory Sociology; Order and Change in Society.*

2nd ed. New York: Oxford University Press.

Levie, W. Howard, and Kenneth E. Dickie. 1973 "The Analysis and Application of Media." In Robert M. W. Travers (ed.), *Second Handbook of Research on Teaching.* Chicago: Rand McNally, pp. 858–82.

Levine, Arthur. *Handbook on Undergraduate* 1978 *Curriculum.* San Francisco: Jossey-Bass.

Liebert, Roland, J., and Alan E. Bayer. "Goals 1975 in Teaching Undergraduates: Professional Reproduction and Client Centeredness." *The American Sociologist* 10 (November): 195–205.

Liebow, Elliot. *Tally's Corner.* Boston: Little, 1967 Brown, and Company.

Linsky, Arnold S., and Murray A. Straus. 1975 "Student Evaluations, Research Productivity, and Eminence of College Faculty." *Journal of Higher Education* XLVI (January/February): 89–102.

Linsky, Arnold S., and Murray A. Straus. 1973 "Student Evaluations of Teaching: A Comparison of Sociology with Other Disciplines." *Teaching Sociology* 1 (October): 103–18.

Litt, Edgar. "Civic Education, Community 1963 Norms, and Political Indoctrination." *American Sociological Review* 28: 69–75.

Logan, Charles H. "Do Sociologists Teach 1976 Students of Think More Critically?" *Teaching Sociology* 4 (October): 29–48.

Lombardi, John. "Tuition . . . and the Open 1972 Door." *Junior College Journal* 42 (May): 8–11.

Lortie, Dan C. *Schoolteacher: A Sociological* 1975 *Study.* Chicago: University of Chicago Press.

Lortie, Dan C. "Observations on Teaching as 1973 Work." In Robert M. W. Travers (ed.), *Second Handbook of Research on Teaching.* Chicago: Rand McNally, pp. 474–97.

Lowry, Ritchie P., and Robert P. Rankin.
1977   *Sociology: Social Science and Social Concern*. 3rd ed. Lexington, MA.: D. C. Heath.

Ludwig, Mark. "The PSI Social Science Program at Cuyahoga Community College." *Community College Social Science Quarterly* V and VI (Summer/Fall): 25, 26–29.
1975

Lynch, Kevin. *The Image of the City*. Cambridge, MA.: MIT Press.
1960

Lynch, Kevin, and Lloyd Rodwin. "A Theory of Urban Form." In Harold M. Proshansky, William H. Ittelson, and Leanne G. Rivlin (eds.), *Environmental Psychology: Man and His Physical Setting*. New York: Holt, Rinehart, and Winston, pp. 84–100.
1970

MacDaniel, William E. "Individualized Learning: An Application to Teaching Research Methods in Undergraduate Sociology." *Teaching Sociology* 1 (April): 143–59.
1974

McGee, Reece. "Does Teaching Make Any Difference: A Perplexed Essay." *Teaching Sociology* 1 (April): 210–23.
1974

McGee, Reece. *The Academic Janus: The Private College and Its Faculty*. San Francisco: Jossey-Bass.
1971

McGee, Reece, and Associates. *Sociology: An Introduction*. Hinsdale, IL.: Dryden.
1977

McKeachie, Wilbert J. "Student Evaluation of Instruction." *Academe: Bulletin of the AAUP* 65 (October).
1979

McKeachie, Wilbert J. *Teaching Tips: A Guidebook for the Beginning College Teacher*. 7th ed. Lexington, MA.: D. C. Heath.
1978

McKeachie, Wilbert J. "Psychology in America's Bicentennial Year." *American Psychologist* 31 (December): 819–33.
1976

McKeachie, Wilbert J., Yi-Guang Lin, and William Mann. "Student Ratings of Teacher Effectiveness: Validity Studies." *American Educational Research Journal* VIII (May): 435–45.
1971

McKeachie, Wilbert J. *Teaching Tips: A Guidebook for the Beginning College Teacher*. 6th ed. Lexington, MA.: D. C. Heath.
1969

McKee, Paul R., Elmer A. Spreitzer, and Waldemar C. Weber, compilers. *A College Instructor's Vade Mecum*. Preliminary ed. Bowling Green, OH.: Professional Development Project, Office of the Graduate School, Bowling Green State University.
1973

MacKenzie, Norman, Michael Eraut, and Hywel C. Jones. *Teaching and Learning: An Introduction to New Methods and Resources in Higher Education*. Paris: UNESCO International Association of Universities.
1970

MacLean, Norman F. "'This quarter I am Taking McKeon:' A Few Remarks on the Art of Teaching." *University of Chicago Magazine* 66 (January/February): 8–12.
1974

McNall, Scott G. "Peer Teaching: A Description and Evaluation." *Teaching Sociology* (April): 133–46.
1975

McPherron, Sharon. "Introduction." *Teaching Sociology* 5 (October): 7–14. (Special issue on curriculum.)
1977

Maas, James B. "Audio-Visual Materials." *Psychology Teacher's Resource Book: First Course*. Washington, D. C.: American Psychological Association.
1973

Maas, James B., and Thomas R. Owen. *Cornell Inventory for Student Appraisal of Teaching and Courses: Manual of Instructions*. Ithaca, NY.: Cornell University General Stores.
1973

Macrorie, Ken. *Uptaught*. New York: Hayden.
1970

Maier, Norman R. F. *Problem Solving discussion and Conferences: Leadership Methods and Skills*. New York: McGraw-Hill.
1963

Malec, Michael A. *Essential Statistics for Social Research*. New York: Lippincott.
1977

Malec, Michael A. "PSI: A Brief Report and

1975   Reply to Francis." *Teaching Sociology* 2 (April): 212–17.

Mannheim, Karl. *Essays on Sociology of*
1952   *Knowledge.* New York: Oxford University Press.

Mann, Richard D., S. M. Arnold, J. Binder, S.
1970   Cytrynbaum, B. M. Newman, B. Ringwald, J. Ringwald, and R. Rosenwein. *The College Classroom: Conflict, Change and Learning.* New York: Wiley.

Mariampolski, Hyman. "Thoughts about
1978   Reasonable Goals for Introductory Sociology: A Humanistic Perspective." *Teaching Sociology* 5 (January): 141–50.

Marton, F., and R. Säljö. "On Qualitative
1976a   Differences in Learning: I–Outcome and Process." *British Journal of Educational Psychology* 46:4–11.

Marton, F., and R. Säljö. "On Qualitative Dif-
1976b   ferences in Learning: II–Outcome as a Function of the Learner's Conception of the Task." *British Journal of Educational Psychology* 46:115–27.

Marwell, Gerald. "Introducing Introductory
1966   Sociology: The Social Awareness Test." *The American Sociologist* 1 (November): 253–54.

Marwell, Gerald, Weldon Johnson, and Mary
1973   A. Pate. "A Modular Approach to Teaching Introductory Sociology." Paper presented at the 68th annual meetings of the American Sociological Association.

Marx, Gary. *Protest and Prejudice: A Study of*
1969   *Belief in the Black Community.* New York: Harper and Row.

Marx, Karl. The Eighteenth Brumaire of Louis
[1852]   Bonaparte. Reprinted in *Karl Marx*
1958   *and Frederick Engels: Selected Works in Two Volumes*, Volume I. Moscow: Foreign Languages Publishing House, pp. 247–344.

Marx, Karl, and Frederick Engels. "Wage La-
[1849]   bour and Capital." *Selected Works*

1955   I. Moscow: Foreign Languages Publishing House, pp. 79–105.

Matras, Judah. *Social Inequality, Stratification*
1975   *and Mobility.* Englewood Cliffs, NJ.: Prentice-Hall.

Mauksch, Hans O. "Preface." *Teaching Sociol-*
1977   *ogy* 5 (October): 3–6. (Special issue on curriculum.)

Maynard, Richard A. *The Celluloid Curricu-*
1971   *lum: How to Use Movies in the Classroom.* Rochelle Park, NJ.: Hayden.

Mead, George Herbert. *Mind, Self and Society.*
1934   Chicago: University of Chicago Press.

Mead, Margaret, and Paul Byers. *The Small*
1967   *Conference.* The Hague: Mouton.

Means, Richard L. "Textbooks in the Sociol-
1966   ogy of Religion: A Review Article." *Sociological Analysis* 27 (Summer): 101–105.

Mehan, Hugh. *Learning Lessons: Social Orga-*
1979   *nization in the Classroom.* Cambridge, MA.: Harvard University Press.

Merton, Robert K. *Social Theory and Social*
1957   *Structure.* Glencoe, IL.: Free Press.

Merton, Robert K., and Robert Nisbet.
1976   *Contemporary Social Problems.* 4th ed. New York: Harcourt Brace Jovanovich.

Meyer, Marshall W. "Automation and Bu-
1968   reaucratic Structure." *American Journal of Sociology* 74 (November): 256–64.

Michaels, James W. "Classroom Reward
1977   Structures and Academic Performance," *Review of Educational Research* 47 (Winter): 87–98.

Michaels, James W. "A Simple View of the
1976   Grading Issue." *Teaching Sociology* 3 (January): 198–203.

Michelson, William H. *Man and His Urban*
1976   *Environment: A Sociological Approach.* Rev. ed. Reading, MA.: Addison-Wesley.

Middleton, Russell. "Handbook for Teaching
1965   Assistants on Construction and
        Grading of Exams." Mimeo-
        graphed.

Miller, Richard I. *Developing Programs for Fac-*
1974   *ulty Evaluation.* San Francisco: Jos-
        sey-Bass.

Miller, Richard I. *Evaluating Faculty Perfor-*
1972   *mance.* San Francisco: Jossey-Bass.

Mills, C. Wright. *The Sociological Imagination.*
[1959] New York: Grove Press.
1961

Mills, C. Wright. *Images of Man: The Classic*
1960   *Tradition in Sociology.* New York:
        George Braziller.

Mills, C. Wright. "The Professional Ideology
1943   of Social Pathologists." *American
        Journal of Sociology* 49 (September):
        165–80.

Milton, Ohmer, and Associates. *On College*
1978   *Teaching: A Guide to Contemporary
        Practices.* San Francisco: Jossey-
        Bass.

Milton, Ohmer, and John Edgerly. *The Testing*
1977   *and Grading of Students.* New Ro-
        chelle, NY.: Change Magazine.

Mintz, J. J. "The A-T Approach 14 Years
1975   Later: A Review of the Research."
        Journal of College Science Teaching 4
        (March): 247–52.

Mitchell, W. C. "Occupational Role Strains:
1958   The American Elective Public
        Official." *Administrative Science
        Quarterly* 3:210–28.

Monroe, Charles R. *Profile of the Community*
1972   *College.* San Francisco: Jossey-Bass.

Moore, Wilbert E., and Melvin M. Tumin.
1949   "Some Social Functions of Igno-
        rance." *American Sociological Review*
        14 (December): 787–95.

Moos, Rudolf H. *Evaluating Educational Envi-*
1979   *ronments.* San Francisco: Jossey-
        Bass.

Moos, Rudolf H. *The Human Context: Envi-*
1976   *ronmental Determinants of Behavior.*
        New York: Wiley.

Morley, John Viscount. *On Compromise.* Lon-
[1876] don: Macmillan.
1901

Moxley, Robert L. "Teaching Introductory
1974   Sociology: An Exploratory Experi-
        ence Making Use of Senior Under-
        graduate Majors." *Teaching Sociol-
        ogy* 2 (October): 15–26.

Murphy, Raymond. *The American City: An*
1966   *Urban Geography.* New York: Mc-
        Graw-Hill.

Naftulin, D. H., J. E. Ware, and F. A. Donnelly.
1973   "The Doctor Fox Lecture: A Para-
        digm of Educational Seduction."
        Journal of Medical Education 48
        (July): 630–35.

Nasatir, David (with Arlie Hochschild).
1973   "Team Teaching Methodology and
        Content in a Single Course." Un-
        published paper read at ASA meet-
        ings, New York.

National Advisory Commission on Civil
1968   Disorders. *Report.* Washington,
        D. C.: U.S. Government Printing
        Office.

National Audiovisual Association. *Audio-*
Annual *visual Equipment Directory.* Fairfax,
        VA.: NAA.

National Center for Educational Statistics.
1978   *Earned Degrees Conferred, 1975–
        1976: Summary Data.* Washington,
        D. C.: U.S. Government Printing
        Office.

National Institute of Mental Health.
1969   *Sociologists and Anthropologists: Sup-
        ply and Demand in Educational Insti-
        tutions and Other Settings* (Public
        Health Service Publication No.
        1884). Washington, D. C.: U.S.
        Government Printing Office.

National Opinion Research Center. "Jobs and
1947   Occupations: A Popular Evalua-
        tion." *Opinion News* 9 (September):
        3–13.

Neustadt, I. *Teaching Sociology: An Inaugural*
1965   *Lecture.* Leicester, England: Leices-
        ter University Press.

New York Times. "ETS Study of 21,000 College
1973 Students." New York Times (September 10), p. 16.

Newcomb, Charles. "Graphic Representation
1957 of Age and Sex Distribution of Population in the City." In Paul K. Hatt and Albert K. Reiss, Jr. (eds.), *Cities and Society: The Revised Reader in Urban Sociology.* New York: Free Press, pp. 382–92.

Newcomb, Theodore M. *The Acquaintance*
1961 *Process.* New York: Holt, Rinehart, and Winston.

Newcomb, Theodore M., and Everett K.
1966 Wilson, eds. *College Peer Groups: Problems and Prospects for Research.* Chicago: Aldine.

Nisbet, Robert. *Sociology as an Art Form.* New
1976 York: Oxford University Press.

Novak, M. *The Joy of Sports: End Zones, Bases,*
1976 *Baskets, Balls, and the Consecration of the American Spirit.* New York: Basic.

Nuyens, Yvo, and Janin Vansteenkiste,
1978 eds. *Teaching Medical Sociology: Retrospection and Prospection.* Leiden and Boston: Martinus Nijhoff.

Odum, Howard W. *American Sociology: The*
1951 *Story of Sociology in the United States through 1950.* New York: Longmans, Green.

Ogburn, William Fielding, and Otis Dudley
1963 Duncan. "City Size as a Sociological Variable." Pp. 129–47 in Ernest W. Burgess and Donald Bogue (eds.), *Contributions to Urban Sociology.* Chicago: University of Chicago Press.

O'Kane, James M. "Applying Empirical and
1976 Computer Technique in Teaching Undergraduate Sociology." *Improving College and University Teaching* 24 (Winter): 56–58.

Oksanen, Ernest H., and Byron G.
1975 Spencer. "On the Determinants of Student Performance in Introductory Courses in the Social Sciences." *The American Sociologist* 10 (May): 103–109.

Olmstead, Joseph A. *Small-Group Instruction:*
1974 *Theory and Practice.* Alexandria, VA.: Human Resources Research Organization (HumRRO).

Olsen, Marvin E. *The Process of Social Organi-*
1968 *zation.* New York: Holt, Rinehart, and Winston.

Olson, Philip, Jackie Aucoin, and Burke
1976 Fort. *Community and Urban Sociology: A Bibliography and Course Outline.* Prepared under the auspices of the ASA Section on Community. (For further information, contact: Philip Olson, Department of Sociology, University of Missouri-Kansas City, Kansas City, MO. 65110.)

Page, Charles H. "Sociology as an Educa-
1963 tional Enterprise." In Charles H. Page (ed.), *Sociology and Contemporary Education.* New York: Random, pp. 3–39.

Page, Charles H. "Sociology as a Teaching
1959 Enterprise." In Robert K. Merton (ed.), *Sociology Today: Problems and Prospects.* New York: Basic, pp. 579–99.

Panuska, Joseph A. "Open-Endedness as an
1975 Educational Goal." Pp. 94–102 in Thomas H. Buxton and Keith Prichard (eds.), *Excellence in University Teaching: New Essays.* Columbia, SC.: South Carolina Press.

Pape, Max, and D. Paul Miller. "New Ap-
1967 proaches to the Teaching of Sociology: Team Learning and Small Group Dynamics." *The American Sociologist* 2 (May): 93–95.

Parker, Seymour, and Robert Kleiner. "Status
1964 Position, Mobility and Ethnic Identification of the Negro." *Journal of Social Issues* 20 (April): 85–102.

Park, Robert E. "Methods of Teaching: Im-
1941 pressions and a Verdict." *Social Forces* 20 (October): 36–53.

Park, Robert E. "Human Migration and the
1928   Marginal Man." *American Journal of
          Sociology* 33 (May): 881–93.

Park, Robert E. "The Urban Community as a
1925   Spatial Pattern and a Moral Order."
          In E. W. Burgess (ed.), *The Urban
          Community*. Chicago: University of
          Chicago Press, pp. 3–20.

Parsons, Talcott. *The Social System*. New
1951   York: Free Press.

Pavalko, Ronald M., ed. *Sociological Perspec-
1972   tives on Occupations*. Itasca, IL.: Pea-
          cock.

Payne, D. A. *The Assessment of Learning: Cog-
1974   nitive and Affective*. Lexington, MA.:
          D. C. Heath.

Perrucci, Robert, Dean D. Knudsen, and Rus-
1977   sell R. Hamby. *Sociology: Basic
          Structures and Processes*. Dubuque,
          IA.: Brown.

Persell, Carolina Hodges, Floyd Morgan Ham-
1978   mack, and Wagner Thielens, Jr.
          (with   Theodore   Wagenaar).
          *Teaching Sociology of Education: Syl-
          labi and Materials from Undergraduate
          Courses*. (ASA Sociology of Educa-
          tion Section) Washington, D. C.:
          ASA Teaching Resources Center.

Petras, John W., and James R. Hayes. "How
1973   Symbolic Interactionists Can Prac-
          tice What They Preach: Introductory
          Sociology and Knowledge as Emer-
          gence." *Teaching Sociology* 1 (Octo-
          ber): 3–12.

Phenix, Philip H. "Teaching as Celebration."
1975   Pp. 22–29 in Thomas H. Buxton and
          Keith W. Prichard (eds.), *Excellence
          in University Teaching: New Essays*.
          Columbia, SC.: University of South
          Carolina Press.

Piven, Frances Fox, and Richard A. Cloward.
1971   *Regulating the Poor: The Functions of
          Public Welfare*. New York: Pan-
          theon.

Platt, Gerald M., Talcott Parsons, and Rita
1976   Kirshstein. "Faculty   Teaching

Goals, 1968–1973." *Social Problems*
23 (December): 298–307.

Podell, L., M. Vogelfanger, and R. Rogers.
1959   "Sociology in American Colleges—
          Fifteen Years Later." *American Soci-
          ological Review* 24 (February): 87–96.

Pool, Jonathan, ed. *Computer-Assisted Instruc-
1976   tion in Political Science* (Instructional
          Monograph No. 4). Washington,
          D. C.: American Political Science
          Association.

Postlethwait, S. N., J. Novak, and H. T. Mur-
1969   ray, Jr. *The Audio-Tutorial Ap-
          proach to Learning: Independent
          Study and Integrated Experience*. 2nd
          ed. Minneapolis: Burgess.

Pratto, David J., and William E. Knox. "The
1973   Pedagogical Impact of Computer
          Simulation: A Small Group Exam-
          ple." *Social Science Information/In-
          formation sur les Sciences Sociales*
          12:159–72.

Pringle, Bruce M. "Films for Use in Introduc-
1950   tory Sociology." *Sociology and Social
          Research* 43 (November/December):
          97–101.

Proshansky, Harold M., William H. Ittelson,
1970   and Leanne G. Rivlin, eds.
          *Environmental Psychology: Man and
          His Physical Setting*. New York:
          Holt, Rinehart, and Winston.

Psychological Corporation. Some Principles
n.d.   for   Preparing   Multiple-Choice
          Items. (Contact : Psychological Cor-
          poration, 304 East 45th Street, New
          York, NY. 10017.)

Quinney, Valerie. "Using Films in College
1977   Social Science Classes." *Improving
          College and University Teaching* 25
          (Winter): 18–19, 21.

Rayder, N. F. "College Student Ratings of
1968   Instructors." *Journal of Experimental
          Education* 37 (Winter): 76–81.

Redfield,   Robert. "Discussion of C. C.
1947   Taylor's 'Sociology and Common
          Sense.'" *American Sociological Re-
          view* 12 (February): 9–11.

Reid, Sue Titus, and Alan P. Bates.
1971   "Undergraduate Sociology Programs in Accredited Colleges and Universities." *The American Sociologist* 6 (May): 165–75.

Remy, Richard C. "High School Seniors' Attitudes Toward Their Civics and Government Instruction." *Social Education* 36 (October), pp. 590–97.
1972

Report on Higher Education. (Ford Foundation Task Force Report). Washington, D. C.: U.S. Government Printing Office.
1971

Reynolds, Larry T., and Janice M. Reynolds, eds. *The Sociology of Sociology.* New York: David McKay.
1970

Rhoades, Lawrence J., ed. *The Author's Guide to Selected Journals.* Washington, D. C.: ASA.
1976

Rice, Thomas J. "Cognitive Mapping: Small Group Technique in Teaching." *Teaching Sociology* 5 (April): 259–74.
1978

Richard, Michel P., and John Mann. *Exploring Social Space.* New York: Free Press.
1973

Richardson, James T., Ronald S. Frankel, William L. Rankin, and Gregory R. Gaustad. "Computers in the Social and Behavioral Sciences." *The American Sociologist* 6 (May): 143–51.
1971

Riechmann, Sheryl, and Michael A. Malec. "Teacher Development for In-Service Faculty." *Teaching Sociology* 3 (April): 289–304.
1976

Riesman, David, Nathan Glazer, and Reuel Denny. *The Lonely Crowd.* New Haven: Yale University Press.
1953

Rippetoe, Joseph K. "The Undergraduate Education in Sociology: The Case for Experiential Learning." *Teaching Sociology* 4 (April): 239–50.
1977

Robin, Arthur L. "Behavioral Instruction in the College Classroom." *Review of Educational Research* 46 (Summer): 313–54.
1976

Rodin, Miriam. "Can Students Evaluate Good Teaching?" *Change Magazine* Volume 5 (Summer), pp. 66–67.
1973

Rodin, Miriam, and Burton Rodin. "Student Evaluations of Teachers." *Science* 177 (September 29): 1164–66.
1972

Rodman, Hyman. "Desexitizing' the English Language." *The Chronicle of Higher Education* Volume XIV (March 14): 17.
1977

Rodman, Hyman. *Lower-Class Families: The Culture of Poverty in Negro Trinidad.* New York: Oxford University Press.
1971

Rodman, Hyman. "The Lower-Class Value Stretch." *Social Forces* 42 (December): 205–15.
1963

Rogers, Sharon J., William A. Satariano, and Evan D. Rogers. "Self-Scheduled Introductory Sociology: An Evaluation." *Teaching Sociology* 4 (January): 125–40.
1977

Rose, Peter I. *They and We: Racial and Ethnic Relations in the United States.* 2nd ed. New York: Random.
1974

Rosenfeld, Rachel Ann. "Anxiety and Learning." *Teaching Sociology* 5 (January): 151–66.
1978

Rosenthal, Robert, and Lenore F. Jacobson. "Teacher Expectations for the Disadvantaged." *Scientific American* 218 (April): 19–23.
1968

Rothman, Robert A. "Textbooks and the Certification of Knowledge." *The American Sociologist* 6 (May): 125–27.
1971

Ruskin, Robert S. "A Personalized System of Instruction: Basic Components and Current Applications." In Ralph B. Earle, Jr. (ed.), *PSI and Political Science.* Washington, D. C.: American Political Science Association, pp. 1–19.
1975

Ruskin, Robert S. "The Personalized System of Instruction: An Educational Alternative." *ERIC/Higher Education Research Report*, No. 5. Washington, D. C.: American Association for Higher Education.
1974

Ryan, B. A. *PSI—Keller's Personalized System of Instruction: An Appraisal.* Wash-
1974

ington, D. C.: American Psychological Association.

Ryder, Norman. "The Cohort in the Study of
1965   Social Change." *American Sociological Review* 30 (December): 843–61.

St. George, Arthur. "A Computer-Integrated
1978   Course in Research Methods." *Teaching Sociology* 5 (July): 423–44.

Sanders, Norris M. *Classroom Questions: What
1966   Kinds?* New York: Harper and Row.

Sanford, Nevitt, ed. *The American College: A
1962   Psychological and Social Interpretation of the Higher Learning.* New York: Wiley.

Satariano, William A. "Sociologists Affiliated
1976   with Graduate Departments: A Comparison of the Time Devoted to Teaching and Research." *Teaching Sociology* 3 (January): 194–97.

Satariano, William A. "Review of *The Structure of Sociological Theory*, by Jona-
1975   than H. Turner." *Teaching Sociology* 3 (October): 93–95.

Scanzoni, John. *Sexual Bargaining: Power Poli-
1972   tics in the American Marriage.* Englewood Cliffs, NJ.: Prentice-Hall.

Schermerhorn, Richard A. "Techniques and
1958   Instruction in Teaching Sociology on Television." *Sociology and Social Research* 43 (November/December): 108–12.

Schlechty, Phillip C. *Teaching and Social Be-
1976   havior: Toward an Organizational Theory of Instruction.* Boston: Allyn and Bacon.

Schlenker, John. "An Alternative to the Term
1976   Paper in Sociology Classes." *Community College Social Science Quarterly* 6 (Spring): 24–25.

Schmuck, Richard A., and Patricia A.
1975   Schmuck. *Group Processes in the Classroom.* 2nd ed. Dubuque, IA.: Brown.

Schneider, Joseph, and Sally Hacker. "Sex
1973   Role Imagery and the Use of the Generic 'Man' in Introductory Texts: A Case in the Sociology of Sociol-

ogy." *American Sociologist* 8 (February): 12–18.

Scholl, Stephen, and Sandra Inglis,
1977   eds. *Teaching in Higher Education: Readings for Faculty.* Columbus, OH.: Ohio Board of Regents.

Schorr, Alvin. *Slums and Social Insecurity.*
1963   Washington, D. C.: U.S. Department of HEW, U.S. Government Printing Office.

Schulz, David A. "Variations in the Father
1968   Role in Complete Families of the Negro Lower Class." *Social Science Quarterly* 49 (December): 651–59.

Schure, G. H., N. Malamuth, and S. A.
1975   Johnston. "A Computer Simulation of Group Risky Shift for Teaching Undergraduate Research Methods." *Simulation and Games* 6 (June): 202–10.

Schwartz, Barry. "Notes on the Sociology of
1970   Sleep." *The Sociological Quarterly* 11 (Fall): 485–99.

Schwartz, Barry. "The Social Psychology of
1968   Privacy." *American Journal of Sociology* 73 (May): 741–52.

Schwartz, Barry, and Stephen F. Barsky. "The
1977   Home Advantage." *Social Forces* 55 (March): 641–61.

Schwirian, Kent P., ed. *Comparative Urban
1974   Structure: Studies in the Ecology of Cities.* Lexington, MA.: D. C. Heath.

Scott, Robert A. *The Making of Blind Men: A
1969   Study of Adult Socialization.* New York: Russell Sage Foundation.

Segal, Bernard E. "Male Nurses: A Case
1962   Study in Status Contradiction and Prestige Loss.' *Social forces* 41 (October): 31–38.

Seldin, Peter. *How Colleges Evaluate Profes-
1975   sors.* Croton-on-Hudson, NY.: Blythe-Pennington.

Semas, Phillip W. "Students Filing 'Con-
1975   sumer' Suits." *The Chronicle of Higher Education* XI (November), pp. 1, 10.

Shaw, George Bernard. "Maxims for Revolutionists." *Man and Superman*. Baltimore: Penguin.
[1903]
1952

Shaw, George Bernard. *Major Barbara*. Reprinted in *John Bull's Other Island, How He Lied to Her Husband, and Major Barbara*. London: Constable.
1931

Shephard, Jon M. *Basic Sociology: Structures, Interaction and Change*. New York: Harper and Row.
1974

Sherman, J. "PSI: Some Notable Failures." In J. L. Sayre and J. J. Knightly (eds.), *The Personalized System of Instruction in Higher Education: Readings on PSI—The Keller Plan*. Enid, OK.: Seminary Press, pp. 57–61.
1972

Shin, Eui-Hang. "Statistics Requirements for Undergraduate Sociology Majors in Colleges and Universities in the United States." *The American Sociologist* 10 (May): 92–102.
1975

Shostak, Arthur B., ed. *Sociology in Action: Case Studies in Social Problems and Directed Social Change*. Homewood, IL.: Dorsey.
1966

Shulman, Lawrence. "The Dynamics of the First Class." *Learning and Development* 3. (Newsletter of the Centre for Learning and Development, McGill University.)
1971

Sibley, Elbridge. *The Education of Sociologists in the United States*. New York: Russell Sage Foundation.
1963

Siegel, L., L. C. Siegel, P. J. Capretta, R. L. Jones, and H. Berkovitz. "Students' Thoughts During Class: A Criterion for Educational Research." *Journal of Educational Psychology* 54: 45–51.
1963

Silvers, Ronald J. "Letting Go in the Classroom." *Sociological Inquiry* 43 (Spring): 169–78.
1973

Sim, Francis M., Gordon F. DeJohn, Glen Krieder, and David E. Kauffman. "Data Analysis for Sociology Undergraduates: Innovations of Instant Computation." *The American Sociologist* 6 (May): 153–57.
1971

Sime, M., and G. Boyce. "Overt Responses, Knowledge of Results and Learning." *Programmed Learning and Educational Technology* 6: 12–19.
1969

Simmel, Georg. "Exchange." In Donald N. Levine (ed.), *Georg Simmel: On Individuality and Social Forms*. Chicago: University of Chicago Press, pp. 43–69.
[1907]
1971

Simmel, Georg. *The Sociology of Georg Simmel*. Translated with an introduction by Kurt Wolff. Glencoe, IL.: Free Press.
1950

Simons, Helen, and Geoffrey Squires, eds. *Small Group Teaching: Selected Papers*. London: Group for Research and Innovation in Higher Education, Nuffield Foundation.
1976

Simpson, Elizabeth Janes. "The Classification of Educational Objectives in the Psychomotor Domain." *The Psychomotor Domain*, Volume 3. Washington, D. C.: Gryphon House.
1972

Simpson, George Eaton, and J. Milton Yinger. *Racial and Cultural Minorities*. 4th ed. New York: Harper and Row.
1972

Simpson, Richard L. "The Concept of Power: Comment by a Sociologist." *Social Science Quarterly* 48 (December): 287–91.
1967

Skinner, B. F. *The Technology of Teaching*. New York: Appleton-Century-Crofts.
1968

Smith, Adam. "Of Wonder: Of the Effects of Novelty." Pp. 27–35 in Louis Schneider (ed.), *The Scottish Moral Philosophers*. Chicago: University of Chicago.
[1795]
1967

Smith, Don D. "Teaching Introductory Sociology by Film." *Teaching Sociology* 1 (October): 48–61.
1973

Smith, William M. "A Little Technology is Not a Dangerous Thing—for a Large Course." Pp. 10–39 in George L. Wolford and William M. Smith (eds.), *Large Course Instruction*.
1977a

Hanover, NH.: Office of Instructional Services and Educational Research/Department of Psychology, Dartmouth College.

Smith, William M. "The Use of PSI in Large-
1977b Course Instruction." Pp. 40–53 in George L. Wolford and William M. Smith (eds.), *Large Course Instruction*. Hanover, NH.: Office of Instructional Services and Educational Research/Department of Psychology, Dartmouth College.

Sokol, Robert. *Laboratory Manual for Introduc-
1970 tory Sociology: A Data Card Approach*. New York: Harper and Row.

Sokol, Robert. "Research Exercises for Intro-
1968 ductory Sociology: The Data Card Technique." *The American Sociologist* 3 (February): 26–31.

Solomon, Daniel W., Larry Rosenberg, and Wil-
1964 liam E. Bezdeck. "Teacher Behavior and Student Learning." *Journal of Educational Psychology* 55 (February): 23–30.

Solomon, Daniel W., William E. Bezdeck, and
1963 Larry Rosenberg. *Teaching Styles and Learning*. Chicago: Center for the Study of Liberal Education.

Solomon, W. E. "Correlates of Prestige Rank-
1972 ings of Graduate Programs in Sociology." *The American Sociologist* 7 (May): 13–14.

Solomon, W. E., and T. Walters. "The Rela-
1975 tionship Between Productivity and Prestige of Graduate Sociology Departments: Fact or Artifact?" *The American Sociologist* 10 (November): 229–36.

Sommer, Robert. *Personal Space*. Englewood
1969 Cliffs, NJ.: Prentice-Hall.

Sorokin, Pitirim A. *Society, Culture and Per-
1948 sonality*. New York: Harper and Row.

Spanier, G. B., and C. S. Stump. "The Use of
1978 Research in Applied Marriage and Family Textbooks." *Contemporary Sociology* 7 (September): 553–63.

Spector, Malcolm. "The Social Construction
1976 of Social Problems: Six Class Assignments." *Teaching Sociology* 3 (January): 167–84.

Spector, Malcolm, and John I. Kitsuse.
1977 *Constructing Social Problems*. Menlo Park, CA.: Cummings.

Spencer, Herbert. *The Study of Sociology*.
1891 New York: Appleton.

Spencer, R. E., and L. M. Aleamoni. "A Stu-
1970 dent Course Evaluation Questionnaire." *Journal of Educational Measurement* 7 (Fall): 209–10.

Stallings, William M., and S. Singhal. "Some
1970 Observations of the Relationship Between Research Productivity and Students Evaluations of Courses and Teaching." *The American Sociologist* 5 (May): 141–43.

Stasz, Clarice. "Contract Menu Grading."
1976 *Teaching Sociology* 4 (October): 49–66.

Stein, Nancy Wendlandt. "'Just What is Soci-
1977 ology?': The View from the Community College." *Teaching Sociology* 5 (October): 17–36.

Stoll, Clarice S. "Videotape as an Aid in Soci-
1973 ology Instruction." *Teaching Sociology* 1 (October): 38–47.

Stone, Clarence N. *Economic Growth and
1976 Neighborhood Discontent: System Bias in the Urban Renewal Program of Atlanta*. Chapel Hill: University of North Carolina Press.

Stouffer, Samuel A. "An Analysis of Conflict-
1949 ing Social Norms." *American Sociological Review* 14 (December): 707–17.

Stouffer, Samuel A., E. A. Suchman, L. C.
1949 DeVinney, S. A. Star, and R. M. Williams, Jr. *The American Soldier in World War II*, Volume I. Princeton, NJ.: Princeton University Press.

Straus, Murray, and Joel I. Nelson.
1968 *Sociological Analysis: An Empirical*

Approach. New York: Harper and Row.

Strauss, Anselm L. *Images of the American*
1961   *City.* New York: Free Press.

Strauss, Anselm L. *Mirrors and Masks: The*
1959   *Search for Identity.* New York: Free Press.

Streib, Gordon F., and Clement J. Schneider.
1971   *Retirement in American Society: Impact and Process.* Ithaca, NY.: Cornell University Press.

Strodtbeck, Fred L., and L. H. Hook. "The
1961   Social Dimensions of a Twelve-Man Jury Table." *Sociometry* 24 (December): 397–415.

Strodtbeck, Fred L., and Richard D.
1956   Mann. "Sex role Differentiation in Jury Deliberations." *Sociometry* 19 (March): 3–11.

Stuit, D. B., and R. L. Ebel. "Instructor Rating
1952   at a Large State University." *College and University* 27 (January): 247–54.

Sturgis, H. W. "The Relationship of the
1959   Teacher's Knowledge of the Student's Background to the Effectiveness of Teaching. . . ." Unpublished doctoral dissertation, New York University. *Dissertation Abstracts* 19.

Sturgis, Richard B., and Frank Clemente.
1973   "The Productivity of Graduates of 50 Sociology Departments." *The American Sociologist* 9 (November): 169–80.

Sullerot, Evelyn. *Women, Society and Change.*
1971   New York: McGraw-Hill.

Sullivan, A. M., and G. R. Skanes. "Validity
1974   of Student Evaluation of Teaching and the Characteristics of Successful Instructors." *Journal of Educational Psychology* 66 (August): 584–90.

Sussman, Marvin B., ed. *Author's Guide to*
1977   *Journals in Sociology and Related Fields.* New York: Haworth.

Sussman, Marvin B. "The Sociologist as a
1966   Tool of Social Action." Pp. 3–12 in Arthur B. Shostak (ed.), *Sociology in*

Action: Case Studies in Social Problems and Directed Social Change. Homewood, IL.: Dorsey.

Sussman, Marvin B. "Teaching Sociology via
1958   Television: Gains and Losses." *Sociology and Social Research* 43 (November/December): 102–107.

Talese, Gay. *The Kingdom and the Power.* New
1970   York: Bantam.

Taper, Bernard. *Gomillion Versus Lightfoot:*
1962   *Apartheid in Alabama.* New York: McGraw-Hill.

Taveggia, Thomas C. "Goodbye Teacher,
1977   Goodbye Classroom, Hello Learning: A Radical Appraisal of Teaching-Learning Linkages at the College Level." *Journal of Personalized Instruction* 2 (June): 119–22.

Taveggia, Thomas C. "Personalized Instruc-
1976   tion: A Summary of Comparative Research, 1967–1974." *American Journal of Physics* 44 (November): 1028–33.

Taylor, Carl C. "Sociology and Common
1947   Sense." *American Sociological Review* 12 (February): 1–12.

Teaching Sociology. "PSI References." *Teaching*
1974a   *Sociology* 1 (April): 164–66.

Teaching Sociology. "Personalized System of
1974b   Instruction in Sociology." *Teaching Sociology* 1 (April): 131–66.

Thelen, Herbert A. *Dynamics of Groups at*
1954   *Work.* Chicago: University of Chicago Press.

Theodorson, George A., and Achilles G.
1969   Theodorson. *Modern Dictionary of Sociology.* New York: Crowell.

Thompson, George. W. *Discussion Groups in*
1974a   *University Courses: Introduction.* Cincinnati: Faculty Resource Center, University of Cincinnati. (Teaching-learning monograph series.)

Thompson, George W. *Discussion Groups in*
1974b   *University Courses: Ideas and Activities.* Cincinnati: Faculty Resource

Center, University of Cincinnati. (Teaching-learning monograph series.)

Thompson, Ralph. "Learning to Question."
1969   *Journal of Higher Education* 40 (June): 467–72.

Toby, Jackson. "Educational Possibilities of
1972   Consensual Research." *The American Sociologist* 7 (February): 11–13.

Toby, Jackson. "Undermining the Student's
1955   Faith in the Validity of Personal Experience." *American Sociological Review* 20: 717–18.

Toby, Jackson, and Vernon Davies. "On the
1961   Number of Wrong Way Buses." *American Sociological Review* 26: 278–80. (An exchange between Toby and Jackson on Toby, 1955.)

Tocqueville, Alexis de. *The Old Regime and the*
1956   *French Revolution.* Translated by John Bonner. New York: Harper and Row.

Todd, Arthur J. "The Teaching of Sociology."
1920   In Paul Klapper (ed.), *College Teaching.* Yonkers-on-Hudson, NY.: World, pp. 241–55.

Toffler, Alvin. *Future Shock.* New York: Ran-
1970   dom House.

Trent, James W., and Arthur M. Cohen.
1973   "Research on Teaching in Higher Education." In Robert M. W. Travers (ed.), *Second Handbook of Research on Teaching.* Chicago: Rand McNally, pp. 997–1071.

Trumbull, H. Clay. *Teaching and Teachers or*
1887   *the Sunday-School Teacher's Teaching Work and the Other Work of the Sunday School Teacher.* Philadelphia: Wattles.

Tufte, Edward R. *The Qualitative Analysis of*
1970   *Social Problems.* Reading, MA.: Addison-Wesley.

Tumin, Melvin M. "Some Principles of
1953   Stratification: A Critical Analysis." *The American Sociological Review* 17 (August): 387–93.

Turner, Ralph H., and Lewis M.
1972   Killian. *Collective Behavior.* 2nd ed. Englewood Cliffs, NJ.: Prentice-Hall.

Turner, Ralph H., and Lewis M. Killian.
1957   *Collective Behavior.* 1st ed. Englewood Cliffs, NJ.: Prentice-Hall.

"Undergraduate Sociology Curriculum Em-
1975   phasizes 'Practical Courses.'" *ASA Footnotes* 3 (April): 4.

U.S. Bureau of the Census. "School Enroll-
1979   ment—Social and Economic Characteristics of Students, October, 1978. Advance Report." *Current Population Reports,* Series P-20, No. 335 (April).

U.S. Bureau of the Census. *Statistical Abstract*
1978   *of the United States, 1978.* Washington, D. C.: U.S. Government Printing Office.

U.S. Bureau of the Census. *Statistical Abstract*
1976a   *of the United States, 1976.* Washington, D. C.: U.S. G.P.O.

U.S. Bureau of the Census. "A Statistical Por-
1976b   trait of Women in the U.S." (Special Studies). *Current Population Reports,* Series P-23, No. 58 (April). Washington, D. C.: U.S. G.P.O.

U.S. Bureau of the Census. *Historical Statistics*
1975a   *of the United States, Colonial Times to 1970, Part I.* Washington, D. C.: U.S. G.P.O.

U.S. Bureau of the Census. *Statistical Abstract*
1975b   *of the United States, 1975.* Washington, D. C.: U.S. G.P.O.

U.S. Bureau of the Census. "The Population
1974   of the United States: Trends and Prospects, 1950–1990." *Current Population Reports,* Series P-23, No. 49. Washington, D. C.: U.S. G.P.O.

U.S. Bureau of the Census. *County and City*
1973   *Data Book 1972.* Washington, D. C.: U.S. G.P.O.

U.S. Bureau of the Census. *Census of Popula-*
1972   *tion 1970: General Population Characteristics,* Final Report PC(1)-B1

United States Summary. Washington, D. C.: U.S. G.P.O.

U.S. Bureau of the Census. "Religion Reported by the Civilian Population of the United States, March 1957." *Current Population Reports,* Series P-20, No. 79. Washington, D. C.: U.S. G.P.O.
1957

U.S. Department of Commerce. *Social Indicators, 1976.* Washington, D. C.: U.S. G.P.O.
1977

Valdes, Donald M., and Dwight G. Dean, eds. *Sociology in Use: Selected Readings for the Introductory Course.* New York: Macmillan.
1965

Vander Zanden, James W. *Sociology: A Systematic Approach.* 2nd ed. New York: Ronald Press.
1970

Van Valey, Thomas L. "The Computer and Doing Sociology: Tools for the Undergraduate Curriculum." *Teaching Sociology* 4 (April): 277–92.
1977

Van Valey, Thomas L. "Methods or Not: An Examination of Introductory Texts." *Teaching Sociology* 3 (October): 21–32.
1975

Vaughan, Charlotte A., and Richard J. Peterson. "Introductory Sociology: A Behavioral Objectives Approach." *Teaching Sociology* 3 (October): 6–20.
1975

Verner, C., and G. Dickinson. "The Lecture: An Analysis and Reivew of Research." *Adult Education* 17 (Winter): 85–100.
1967

Videosociology. This journal, no longer in existence, published five issues during the dates listed. During the period of publication, the editor was Alexander Blumensteil, then of the Department of Sociology, Boston University (and now a private consultant). Examples of articles and notes include "Introduction to Videotape Recording" and "Videosociology and Small Groups Analysis."
1972–
1974

Vidich, Arthur J., Joseph Bensman, and Maurice R. Stein, eds. *Reflections in Community Studies.* New York: Wiley.
1964

Visual Aids Service. *Social Science Films 1978–1980.* Champaign, IL.: University of Illinois.
1978

Wales, Charles E., and Robert A. Stager. *The Guided Design Approach.* Englewood Cliffs, NJ.: Educational Technology Pubs.
1978

Walker, E. J., and Wilbert J. McKeachie. *Some Thoughts about Teaching and the Beginning Course in Psychology.* Belmont, CA.: Brooks/Cole.
1967

Wallace, Ruth A. "An Alternative to Assembly Line Education: Undergraduate Teaching Assistants." *Teaching Sociology* 2 (October): 3–14.
1974

Waller, Willard. *The Sociology of Teaching.* New York: Wiley.
[1932]
1965

Wallis, George W. "Improving the Teaching of Introductory Sociology and Innovative Classroom Organization." *Teaching Sociology* 1 (October): 25–37.
1973

Ware, J. E., and R. G. Williams. "The Dr. Fox Effect: A Study of Lecture Effectiveness and Ratings of Instruction." *Journal of Medical Education* 50 (February): 149–56.
1975

Warner and Swasey Company. "Let's Declare War on the Cause of Poverty." *Newsweek* (September 5): 1. (An advertisement.)
1966

Warriner, Charles K. "Groups Are Real: A Reaffirmation." *American Sociological Review.* 21 (October): 549–54.
1962

Waskow, Arthur I. *From Race Riot to Sit-In, 1919 and the 1960s: A Study in the Connections between Conflict and Violence.* New York: Doubleday (Anchor).
1967

Watcke, Ronald R. *Students with Reading/Writing Problems: Suggestions for*
1977

Sociology Teachers. Washington, D. C.: ASA Projects on Teaching Undergraduate Sociology, ASA Teaching Resource Center.

Watson, George, and Dickson McGaw.
1975   "Personalizing Instruction in Political Science." Chapter 2 in Ralph B. Earle, Jr. (ed.), *PSI and Political Science.* Washington, D. C.: American Political Science Association.

Watson, Walter, Luis Pardo, and Vladislav
1978   Tomovic. *How to Give an Effective Seminar: A Handbook for Students and Professionals.* Don Mills, Ontario, Canada: General Publishing Co.

Webb, Eugene, Donald T. Campbell, Richard
1966   D. Schwartz, and Lee Sechrist. *Unobtrusive Measures: Nonreactive Reaction in the Social Sciences.* Chicago: Rand McNally.

Weber, Max. *The Protestant Ethic and the Spirit*
[1904– *of Capitalism.* Translated by Talcott
1905]   Parsons. New York: Scribner's.
1958

Weber, Max. *The Methodology of the Social*
[1903– *Sciences.* Translated and edited by
1917]   Edward A. Shils and Henry A.
1949   Finch. New York: Free Press.

Weber, Max. *The Theory of Social and Eco-*
[1921] *nomic Organization.* Translated by
1947   A. J. Henderson and Talcott Parsons. New York: Oxford University Press.

Weber, Max. "Science as a Vocation." In
[1922] Hans H. Gerth and C. Wright Mills
1946   (eds. and trans.), *From Max Weber: Essays in Sociology.* New York: Oxford University Press, pp. 129–58.

Weston, Louise C. *Social Problems Courses: A*
1979   *Set of Syllabi and Related Materials.* Washington, D. C.: ASA Section on Undergraduate Education, ASA Teaching Resource Center.

Whiting, John W. M., Richard Kluckhohn, and
1958   Albert Anthony. "The Function of Male Initiation Rites at Puberty." In Eleanor Maccoby, Theodore M. Newcomb, and Eugene L. Hartley (eds.), *Readings in Social Psychology.* New York: Holt, Rinehart, and Winston, pp. 359–70.

Whyte, William F. "The Social Structure of
1949   the Restaurant." *American Journal of Sociology* 54 (January): 302–10.

Whyte, William F. *Street Corner Society.* Chi-
1943   cago: University of Chicago.

Wieting, Stephen G. "Simulated Research Ex-
1975   periences for Use in Teaching Research Methods." *Teaching Sociology* 3 (October): 33–59.

Williams, R. G., and J. E. Ware. "An Ex-
1977   tended Visit with Dr. Fox: Validity of Student Satisfaction with Instruction Ratings after Repeated Exposures to a Lecturer." *American Educational Research Journal* 14 (Fall): 449–57.

Williams, R. G., and J. E. Ware. "Validity of
1976   Student Ratings of Instruction under Different Incentive Conditions: A Further Study of the Dr. Fox Effect." *Journal of Educational Psychology* 68 (February): 48–56.

Wilson, Everett K. "Sociology: Scholarly Dis-
1977   cipline or Profession." A statement read at ASA Meetings, Chicago (September 8). Washington, D. C.: ASA Teaching Resources Center.

Wilson, Everett K. "The Carolina Course to
1976a   Launch Sociology Instructors: Three Features and Some General Reflections." *Teaching Sociology* 3 (April): 249–64.

Wilson, Everett K. "The Sociologist as Re-
1976b   jected Scrivener or Vital Issues Affecting the Length of Vita." Mimeographed.

Wilson, Everett K. "What Is This Sociology
1975   We Profess?" *Journal of Research and*

Development in Education 9 (October): 3–12.

Wilson, Everett K. *Sociology: Rules, Roles and Relationships.* Rev. ed. Homewood, IL.: Dorsey.
1971a

Wilson, Everett K. *Student's Supplement to Sociology: Rules, Roles, and Relationships.* Rev. ed. Homewood, IL.: Dorsey.
1971c

Wilson, Everett K. "Inductive Methods in Teaching Sociology." In M. M. Krug, John B. Poster, and William B. Grillies, III (eds.), *The New Social Studies: Analysis of Materials and Theory.* Itasca, IL.: Peacock.
1970

Wilson, Everett K. "Disappearing Schools and Scholars." *Antioch Review* 28 (Summer): 133–38.
1968

Wilson, Everett K. "The Entering Student: Attributes and Agents of Change." In Theodore M. Newcomb and Everett K. Wilson (eds.), *College Peer Groups.* Chicago: Aldine, pp. 71–106.
1966

Wilson, Everett K. "Determinants of Participation in Policy Formation in a College Community." *Human Relations* 7 (August): 287–312.
1954

Wilson, Everett K., and Hanan Selvin. *Why Study Sociology: A Note to Undergraduates.* Belmont, CA.: Wadsworth.
1980

Wilson, Robert C., Jerry G. Gaff, Evelyn R. Dienst, Lynn Wood, and James Barry. *College Professors and Their Impact on Students.* New York: Wiley.
1975

Wilson, Robert C, and Lynn Wood. "The Evaluation of University Teaching: Ten Faculty-Initiated Methods for Getting Feedback for Improving Instruction." A memorandum distributed by the ASA Teaching Resources Center, Washington, D. C.
1974

Wilson, Stephen R. "A Course in Small Group Sociology." *The American Sociologist* 8 (May): 71–76.
1973

Wimberly, Robert C., Gary L. Faulkner, and Robert L. Moxley. "Dimensions of Teacher Effectiveness." *Teaching Sociology* 6 (October): 7–20.
1978

Wirth, Louis. "Urbanism as a Way of Life." *American Journal of Sociology* 44 (July): 1–24.
1938

Wittich, William A., and C. F. Shulder. *Instructional Technology: Its Nature and Use.* 5th ed. New York: Harper and Row.
1973

Wolford, George L., and William M. Smith, eds. *Large-Course Instruction.* Hanover, NH.: Office of Instructional Services and Educational Research, Dartmouth College.
1977

Wood, Kenneth, Arnold S. Linsky, and Murray A. Straus. "Class Size and Student Evaluations of Faculty." *Journal of Higher Education* 45 (October): 524–34.
1974

Wright, Grace S. *Subject Offerings and Enrollments in Public Secondary Schools.* Washington, D. C.: U.S. Department of HEW.
1965

Wright, Grace S. *Summary of Offerings and Enrollments in High School Subjects, 1960–1961.* Washington, D. C.: U.S. Department of HEW.
1964

Wright, Sonia. "Work Response to Income Maintenance: Economic, Sociological and Cultural Perspectives." *Social Forces* 53 (June): 553–62.
1975

Wylie, Laurence. *Chanzeau.* Cambridge, MA.: Harvard University Press.
1966

Young, Michael. "Introductory Textbook and Reader Reviews: An Analysis." Unpublished memorandum.
1975

Zeitlin, Maurice. "Political Generations in the Cuban Working Class." *American Journal of Sociology* 71 (March): 493–508.
1966

Zelan, Joseph. "Undergraduate in Sociol-
1974   ogy." *The American Sociologist* 9
          (February): 9–17.

Zeleney, L. D. "Experimental Appraisal of a
1940   Group Learning Plan." *Journal of
          Educational Research* 34 (September):
          37–42.

Zeleney, L. D. "Teaching Sociology by Dis-
1927   cussion Group Method." *Sociology
          and Social Research* 12 (November/
          December): 162–72.

Zillman, D., and Joanne R. Cantor.
1973   "Induction of Curiosity via Rhetori-
          cal Questions and Its Effects on the
          Learning of Factual Materials." *Brit-
          ish Journal of Educational Psychology*
          43 (June): 172–80.

Zopf, Paul E., Jr. *North Carolina: A Demo-
n.d.   graphic Profile.* Chapel Hill: Carolina
          Population Center, University of
          North Carolina.

Acknowledgments

Acknowledgments for illustrative material (figures, tables, and exhibits) appear on the page where
the material appears. Acknowledgments for short
quotations and paraphrases appear below.

Bligh, Donald A. *What's the Use of Lectures?* Harmondsworth, England: Penguin, 1972. Excerpts on
pages 201, 208, 212, 214, 215 (paraphrase of discussion on making a point), 260, 282, 295, and 296 are
reprinted by permission of Donald A. Bligh.

Booth, James L. *Instructional Technology: Media,
Materials, and Methods Study Guide.* West Lafayette,
IN: Purdue University, 1973. Excerpts on pages 256–
257 are reprinted by permission of the Purdue Research Foundation.

Cottrell, William F. "Death by Dieselization: A
Case Study in the Reaction to Technological
Change." *American Sociological Review* 16 (June 1951).
Excerpts on pages 245–246 are reprinted by permis-
sion of the American Sociological Association and
Annice Cottrell.

Ericksen, Stanford C. "The Lecture." *Memo to the
Faculty* 60 (April 1978). Ann Arbor: Center for Re-
search on Learning and Teaching, University of
Michigan. Excerpts on pages 208, 209, and 280 are
reprinted by permission of the Center for Research on
Learning and Teaching.

Gagné, Robert M. *Essentials of Learning for Instruction.* Hinsdale, IL: Dryden, 1974. Copyright © 1974
by The Dryden Press, a division of Holt, Rinehart
and Winston, Inc. Excerpts on pages 298, 299, 301–
302 (paraphrase of five categories of learning outcomes) are reprinted by permission of Holt, Rinehart
and Winston.

Gagné, Robert M. *The Conditions of Learning.* 2nd
ed. New York: Holt, Rinehart and Winston, 1970.
Copyright © 1965, 1970 by Holt, Rinehart and
Winston, Inc. Paraphrase of nine instructional strategies on pages 299–300 and excerpt on page 300 are
reprinted by permission of Holt, Rinehart and
Winston.

Geertsen, Reed. "The Textbook: An ACIDS Test."
Teaching Sociology 5 (October 1977). Excerpts on
pages 194, 197 are reprinted by permission of the
publisher, Sage Publications, Inc. and Reed Geertsen.

Keller, Fred S. "Good-bye Teacher . . ." *Journal of
Applied Behavior Analysis* 1 (Spring 1968). Paraphrase
of five distinctive features of PSI and excerpts on
page 227 are reprinted by permission of the Journal of
Applied Behavior Analysis.

Lenski, Gerhard and Jean Lenski. *Human Societies: An Introduction to Macrosociology.* 2nd ed. New
York: McGraw-Hill, 1974. Excerpts on pages 165 and
240–241 are reprinted by permission of McGraw-Hill
Book Company.

McGee, Reece. "Does Teaching Make Any Difference: A Perplexed Essay." *Teaching Sociology* 1 (April
1974). Excerpts on pages 122, 271, 274, and 275 are
reprinted by permission of the publisher, Sage Publications, Inc.

McKeachie, Wilbert J. *Teaching Tips: A Guidebook
for the Beginning College Teacher.* 7th ed. Lexington,
MA: D. C. Heath, 1978. Excerpts on pages 177, 185,
220, 222, 263, 280, 293, 295, and 296 are reprinted by
permission of D. C. Heath and Company.

McKeachie, Wilbert J. *Teaching Tips: A Guidebook
for the Beginning College Teacher.* 6th ed. Lexington,
MA: D. C. Heath, 1969. Excerpts on page 161 are
reprinted by permission of D. C. Heath and Company.

Sanders, Norris M. *Classroom Questions: What
Kinds?* New York: Harper and Row, 1966. Excerpts on
pages 189 and 191 are reprinted by permission of
Harper and Row Publishers, Inc.

Talese, Gay. *The Kingdom and the Power.* New
York: Bantam, 1970. Excerpts on page 250 are reprinted by permission of Gay Talese.

Vander Zanden, James W. *Sociology: A Systematic
Approach.* 2nd ed. New York: Ronald Press, 1970. Excerpts on pages 189 and 239 are reprinted by permission of John Wiley and Sons, Inc.

Wilson, Everett K. *Sociology: Rules, Roles and
Relationships.* Rev. ed. Homewood, IL: Dorsey,
1971. © 1971 by The Dorsey Press. Excerpts on pages
50 and 113 are reprinted by permission of The
Dorsey Press.

Wilson, Everett K. *Student's Supplement to Sociology: Rules, Roles and Relationships.* Rev. ed.
Homewood, IL: Dorsey, 1971. © 1971 by The Dorsey
Press. Excerpts on pages 264–265 are reprinted by
permission of The Dorsey Press.

NAME INDEX

Abedor, Allan J., 44
Adair, John, 153
Adams, Bert, 246
Adams, Raymond S., 309
Adams, Richard N., 153
Airasian, Peter W., 294
Albert, C. Rodney, 361
Aleamoni, L. M., 355
Allen, Joyce P., 48, 217, 285, 330–32
Allport, Gordon W., 53
Anderson, Charles H., 147, 195, 196, 371
Anderson, Ronald E., 290, 398
Anthony, Albert, 35, 110, 112, 113, 120
Archimedes, 114
Astin, Alexander W., 13, 14, 339, 340, 365
Attiyeh, R., 282
Aucoin, Jackie, 199
Axelrod, Joseph, 218
Ayers, Virginia, 270

Baali, Fuad, 9
Babbie, Earl R., 205, 266
Bachrach, Peter, 270
Baker, Keith, 8, 21
Baker, Paul J., 20, 48, 62, 200, 201, 202, 216, 217, 230, 231, 235, 236, 263, 267
Bakke (case), 244
Baldridge, J. Victor, 195
Baldwin, James, 264, 265
Bales, Robert F., 220
Ballantine, Jeanne H., 62, 171, 186, 198
Bane, C. L., 278
Baratz, Morton S., 270
Barber, Bernard, 41
Barnard, C. I., 184
Barnard, J. D., 278
Barnard, W. H., 278
Barsky, Stephen F., 56
Bart, Pauline, 169, 196
Barzun, Jacques, 202, 203
Bassis, Michael S., 23, 48, 62, 217, 285, 305, 330, 331, 332, 333
Bates, Alan P., 10, 13, 22, 23, 62
Baydo, Gerald, 389
Bayer, Alan E., 62
Beach, L. R., 278
Beard, Ruth, 214, 218, 226, 260, 287
Becker, Howard S., 80, 147, 192, 292, 304, 305
Becker, Leonard, Jr., 196
Behrens, Patricia J., 48
Belle, Lawrence W., 400
Bensman, Joseph, 99, 196
Berelson, Bernard, 87
Berger, Brigitte, 195
Berger, Peter, 77, 100, 195, 196
Bergquist, William, 59, 354, 355, 359, 360, 370, 383
Berlyne, D. E., 295, 296, 298
Berryman, Charles, 142
Best, Joel, 289
Bezdeck, William, E., 24, 281, 295, 304, 308
Biddle, Bruce, J., 305, 307, 308
Bidwell, Charles E., 305
Bierstedt, Robert, 50, 62, 142
Billings, Dwight, 164
Bjorn, Lars, 140
Blau, Peter, 184
Bligh, Donald, 201, 208, 211, 212, 214, 215, 260, 270, 276, 277, 279, 281, 282, 287, 295, 296, 308

Block, James H., 293, 294
Bloom, Benjamin S., 226, 282, 294, 295, 298, 302, 303, 304, 307, 308
Blumstein, Philip W., 80, 154
Bluth, B. J., 225, 259, 267
Blythe, Ronald, 196
Bogardus, Emory S., 40
Bogue, Donald, 423
Bolton, Brian, 349
Bono, Stephen F., 235
Boocock, Sarane S., 24, 58, 304, 305, 323
Booth, James L., 256
Bordin, Edward S., 367
Bossert, Steven T., 400
Bowker, Lee, 340, 341, 365, 392
Bowker, R. R., 396
Boyce, G., 296, 308
Bozeman, Barry, 366
Bradshaw, Ted, 23, 62, 122, 186, 189, 194, 200, 202, 203, 236, 251, 263, 267, 320, 329, 391
Breed, Warren, 250
Bressler, Marvin, 62
Brilhart, John K., 226, 281, 282, 283
Bronson, Louise, 265
Broom, Leonard, 169, 195, 196, 242
Brown, George Isaac, 33, 371
Brown, James W., 203, 215, 218, 263, 269, 270, 287
Brown, Richard Maxwell, 224, 225
Brown, Ruth Esther, 186, 187, 190, 194, 196, 199
Brudner, Harvey J., 332
Bruffee, Kenneth A., 34
Bruner, Jerome, 298
Buckley, Walter, 224
Burchard, Waldo W., 239
Byers, Paul, 270
Byrne, Donn, 76

Cain, Leonard D., Jr., 71, 245
Caine, Robert, 307
Cantor, Joanne R., 296, 298, 308
Cantor, Nathaniel, 305
Caplovitz, David, 169
Caplow, Theodore, 126, 371
Carlson, C. R., 292
Carr, Stephen, 258
Carroll, J. Gregory, 349, 350
Carroll, John B., 294
Casey, J. E., 278
Cash, W. J., 78
Catton, William R., Jr., 191, 195, 259, 265
Centers, Richard, 99
Centra, John A., 348, 349, 350, 352, 355, 368, 369, 399
Chandler, Tertius, 116, 121
Chapin, F. Stuart, 255, 258, 267
Cheatwood, Derral, 255, 265, 267
Chirot, Daniel, 196
Chu, G. C., 286
Churchill, Ruth, 338
Clark, Susan G., 217, 234, 235, 284
Clarke, Alfred C., 255, 259, 265
Clemente, Frank, 345
Clifton, A. Kay, 217
Cline, Hugh F., 289
Cloward, Richard A., 79
Coats, William D., 308
Coch, Lester, 120
Cohen, Arthur M., 269
Cohen, Elizabeth G., 304, 305

Cohen, Morris Raphael, 154
Cole, Stephen, 99, 146, 157, 168, 169, 195, 196
Coleman, James, 195
Colley, Lorna, 295
Collier, John, Jr., 270
Collins, Randall, 114
Conklin, George H., 289
Connecticut, University of, 391
Connor, Eugene (Bull), 243
Conover, Patrick W., 217
Cooley, Charles Horton, 56, 238
Cornell College, 389
Cortese, Charles E., 290
Coser, Lewis, 196, 239
Costin, Frank, 348, 349, 350, 366
Cottrell, Leonard S., Jr., 335
Cottrell, William F., 245, 246, 247, 270
Crittenden, Kathleen S., 350
Cross, K. Patricia, 14, 23, 100, 235, 283, 285, 287, 288, 290, 293, 294, 297, 331, 332, 333, 384, 385, 398
Crow, Mary Lynn, 269
Crozier, Michel, 184, 341
Curry, Thomas J., 255, 259, 265
Cutler, Stephen J., 392, 398
Cuzzort, Ray P., 62

Dahrendorf, Ralf, 206
Daley, Richard J., 244
D'Andrea-Burkhart, Vaneeta, 255, 259, 267
Daniels, Glenn, 270
Davidson, Raymond L., 269
Davis, Allison, 79
Davis, Ethelyn, 19, 23, 48, 122, 329, 366, 388, 390, 400
Davis, Gerald, 270
Davis, James A., 23, 199, 231, 289, 290, 305, 398
Davis, James R., 14, 218
Davis, Kingsley, 11, 157, 206, 207, 220, 223, 224
Davis, Robert H., 44
Dawson, M. D., 278
Dean, Dwight G., 146, 191, 195, 196
Debnam, Geoffray, 270
DeLury, George E., 100
Deuschle, Kurt W., 153
DeVinney, L. C., 428
Dewey, John, 34, 53, 57, 78, 84, 85, 298
Dickie, Kenneth E., 269
Dickinson, G., 215
Dickson, W. J., 184
Donnelly, F. A., 280
Doolittle, Eliza, 313
Dorn, Dean S., 147, 190
Dornbusch, Sanford M., 366, 367
Douglas, Jack D., 145, 154, 169
Doyle, Kenneth O., Jr., 348–55, 366, 368, 369
Drabek, Thomas E., 72, 77
Dreeben, Robert, 125, 305
Dressel, Paul L., 318, 365
Drucker, A. J., 348
Dubin, Robert, 8, 124, 153, 169, 192, 271–77, 280, 281, 286, 338
DuBois, W.E.B., 77
Duchastel, Phillipe C., 297
Dukes, Richard L., 205, 217, 399
Duncan, Otis Dudley, 77, 221
Dunkin, Michael J., 305, 307, 308, 332
Dunphy, Dexter C., 226

Durkheim, Emile, 1, 33, 50, 59, 75, 99, 104, 105, 119, 157, 168, 185, 239, 255, 305, 312, 332, 395

Earle, Ralph B., Jr., 229, 235
Ebel, R. L., 368
Eble, Kenneth E., 22, 169, 192, 202, 215, 216, 218, 226, 241, 269, 365, 367, 368, 384, 385, 386, 398
Edgerly, John, 323, 328
Editors of *Change*, 285, 332, 384, 385
Ehman, Lee, 142
Elder, Glen H., Jr., 245
Elder, Joseph, 45
Elgin, Duane, 68, 69, 77
Elliott, D., 278, 368
Emling, Diane, 7, 8, 15, 339, 341, 365
Engels, Frederick, 158
Ennen, E., 190
Entwistle, Noel
Ericksen, Maynard L., 290
Ericksen, Stanford C., 23, 100, 169, 208, 209, 217, 228, 235, 256, 258, 280, 295, 329, 346, 349, 384, 385, 386, 398
Erickson, Bette L., 44, 349, 350, 354
Erickson, Glenn R., 44, 349, 350, 354
Ewens, Bill, 7, 8, 15, 43, 339, 341, 342, 365

Falk, R. Frank, 290
Faulkner, Garry L., 351, 369
Fava, Sylvia Fleis, 75, 77
Feldman, Kenneth A., 308, 351
Fenton, Edwin, 192
Ferguson, Adam, 85, 110
Festinger, Leon, 87
Fielding, Henry, 243
Filene, Peter, 169, 237
Fort, Burke, 199
Fox, David, 146
Fox, Doctor, 280
Fox, Gerald, 116, 121
Fox, Renee C., 45
Fraley, Lawrence E., 269
Francis, Roy G., 217, 231, 235, 255, 259, 265, 267
Frankel, Linda, 169, 196
Frazier, E. Franklin, 99
French, John R. P., Jr., 120
French, Robert Mills, 246
Frey, Peter W., 23, 349
Fuller, Francis F., 361

Gaff, Jerry G., 59, 383
Gagné, Robert M., 46, 58, 298, 299, 300, 301, 302, 304, 307, 308
Gagnon, John H., 246
Galileo, 154
Galliher, John F., 41
Gans, Herbert J., 79, 196
Garfinkel, Harold, 154
Gates, A. I., 53
Gates, Davida P., 9, 10, 13, 22, 23
Gaudet, Hazel, 87
Geer, Blanche, 80, 192, 292, 304, 305
Geertsen, Reed, 194, 196, 383, 391, 400
Gelles, Richard J., 388, 400
Gerberich, J. R., 278
Gessner, Peter K., 349
Gibb, J. R., 413
Gibbs, Jack P., 97, 154
Gist, Noel P., 75, 77
Glenn, Norval D., 345
Goethe, Johann Wolfgang von, 313
Goffman, Erving, 70, 243

Golden, M. Patricia, 99
Goldman, Peter, 172
Goldner, N. S., 22, 345
Goldsmid, Charles A., 2, 7, 13, 19, 21, 22, 23, 24, 48, 54, 122, 131, 169, 308, 329, 339, 351, 366, 367, 384, 385, 388, 390, 391, 394, 400
Goldsmid, Paula, 23, 122, 170
Gomillion (vs. Lightfoot), 249
Goode, W. J., 363
Gould, Julius, 399
Gouldner, Alvin, 184
Grasha, Anthony F., 365, 370, 398
Green, Ben A., 235
Greenblat, Cathy S., 205
Greenough, William T., 348, 366
Grisham, Vaughn, 138
Gruber, James E., 22, 54, 308, 351
Gulick, Luther H., 184
Gulick, Margaret, 205
Gustad, John W., 340

Haas, J. Eugene, 72, 77
Hacker, Helen, 112
Haggard, E. A., 53
Hall, Donald, 114
Hall, Edward T., 259
Halley, Fred S., 290, 398
Hammack, Floyd Morgan, 199
Hammond, Phillip E., 99
Hansen, William L., 332
Harcleroad, Fred F., 269
Hare, A. Paul, 120, 204, 226, 237, 282, 283
Harper, Dean, 289
Harry, J., 22, 345
Hart, Hornell, 199
Hart, Roderick P., 214, 215
Hatt, Paul K., 207, 236, 265
Hawley, Amos H., 71, 75, 77, 157
Hayes, James R., 57, 217, 305
Hedley, R. Alan, 57, 286, 305, 329
Heider, Karl G., 269, 396
Heise, David, 324
Helms, Jesse, 133
Henry, Mark, 332
Herzog, Elizabeth, 79
Hildebrand, Milton, 335
Hilgard, Ernest R., 192
Hill, Andrew, 400
Hill, Richard J., 278, 281
Hill, William Fawcett, 225, 226
Hiller, Harry H., 80
Hind, R. R., 366, 367
Hipp, Rita, 361
Hobbes, Thomas, 79
Hochschild, Arlie, 32, 138
Hodge, Robert W., 207
Hogan, T. P., 351, 352, 369
Hook, L. H., 75, 248
Hoover, Kenneth M., 400
Hoult, Thomas F., 265, 267
Howe, M. J. A., 295
Hughes, Everett C., 80, 192, 292, 304, 305
Hughes, Helen MacGill, 191
Hull, C. L., 298
Humphrey, Hubert, 264
Hunkins, A., 295
Husband, R. W., 278
Hutchins, Robert, 138
Huxley, Thomas, 203
Hyman, Herbert H., 99

Inglis, Sandra, 329, 360, 365, 384, 385, 387, 398
Inkeles, Alex, 199

Ittelson, William H., 75

Jacobsen, R. Brooke, 290
Jacobson, Lenore F., 313, 332
James, William, 203
Jamison, Dean, 286, 290
Johnson, Kent R., 23, 169, 228, 230, 234, 235, 283, 292, 295
Johnson, Michael P., 217, 235, 284
Johnston, S. A., 289
Jones, Robert Alun, 217

Kafka, Franz, 150
Karp, David A., 24, 57, 305
Katona, George, 293, 295
Keller, Fred S., 31, 41, 200, 226, 227, 228, 231, 235, 319
Kelley, Allen C., 284, 285, 292, 330, 331, 332
Kemp, Jerrold E., 269
Kemper, Theodore, 380
Keniston, Kenneth, 35
Kenkel, William F., 190
Kennedy, John F., 243, 244
Kennedy, R., 10
Kennedy, R. J., 10
Kennedy, Robert F., 244
Kibler, Robert J., 297, 303
Killian, Lewis M., 185
Kindsvatter, (in Scholl & Inglis), 360
King, Larry, 172
King, Martin Luther, 33, 244
Kirschner, Betty Frankle, 9, 194
Kirshstein, Rita, 62
Kloss, Robert Marsh, 147, 190
Kluckhohn, Richard, 35, 110, 112, 113, 120
Knowles, Louis, 172
Knox, William E., 288, 289
Knudsen, Dean D., 190, 195, 345
Kohout, Frank J., 62
Kolb, William L., 399
Komarovsky, Mirra, 149, 168, 307, 342
Kozma, Robert B., 400
Krathwohl, David R., 302
Krauskopf, C. J., 307
Kulik, Chen-Lin C., 276, 277, 281, 291, 292, 293, 349, 351, 352, 366, 369
Kulik, James A., 228, 235, 276, 277, 281, 291–93, 346, 349–54, 366, 369, 373
Kurtz, Richard A., 194, 307

Ladd, Everett C. Jr., 368
Lally, John L., 41
Lancaster, O. E., 278
Landers, Audrey D., 365
Larsen, Otto N., 191, 195, 259, 265
Lasswell, Thomas E., 190
Lazarsfeld, Paul F., 87, 89, 90, 156, 169
LeBailly, R. K., 350
LeBon, Gustave, 185
Lee, Calvin B. T., 13, 14, 339, 340, 365
Leevy, J. Roy, 255, 265, 267
Lena, Hugh F., 270
Lenski, Gerhard, 145, 165, 195, 196, 206, 222, 224, 240, 241, 249, 382
Lenski, Jean, 165, 195, 196, 222, 240, 241, 249
Levie, W. Howard, 269
Lewin, Kurt, 84, 120, 220
Lewis, R. B., 269
Liebert, Roland J., 62
Liebow, Elliott, 79
Lifson, N., 278
Lindquist, T., 265
Lindsay, Paul, 60

Linnaeus, 84
Linsky, Arnold S., 15, 22, 306, 308, 342, 345, 350
Linton, Ralph, 363
Lippitt, Ronald, 120, 184
Lipset, Seymour M., 196, 368
Litt, Edgar, 236
Logan, Charles H., 20, 62, 230
Lombardi, John, 128
London, Bruce, 270
Looman, Wendy J., 270
Lortie, Dan C., 125, 305
Lowry, Ritchie P., 145, 195
Ludwig, Mark, 217, 235, 284
Lumsden, K. G., 282
Lynch, Kevin, 258

MacDaniel, William E., 217, 234, 235, 284
MacLean, Norman F., 344
McCarthy, Senator Joe, 22, 134
McDougall, William, 185
McGaw, Dickson, 229, 237
McGee, Reece, 2, 122, 126, 168, 169, 170, 180, 190, 195, 217, 271, 274, 275, 276, 371
McKeachie, Wilbert J., 37, 100, 160, 161, 169, 177, 181, 185, 192, 201, 217, 220, 222, 226, 235, 237, 263, 269, 270, 276–83, 286, 287, 292–96, 306–08, 323, 325, 328, 333, 349, 351, 354, 357, 366, 384, 385, 386, 387, 398
McNall, Scott G., 195, 196, 217, 293, 383
McPherron, Sharon, 23, 62, 122, 186, 189, 194, 200, 202, 203, 236, 251, 263, 267, 320, 329, 391
Maas, James B., 269, 355, 369
Macrorie, Ken, 236
Maier, Norman R. F., 237
Maiolo, John R., 194, 307
Malamuth, N., 289
Malcolm X, 172
Malec, Michael A., 7, 13, 23, 99, 231, 235, 284
Malthus, Thomas, 36
Mann, Richard D., 24, 77, 181, 308
Mannheim, Karl, 99, 245
Manning, Brad A., 361
Mariampolski, Hyman, 62
Martin, Walter T., 97, 154
Marton, F., 293, 295
Marwell, Gerald, 100, 140, 156, 205, 217
Marx, Gary, 87, 90, 157, 158
Marx, Karl, 59, 77, 158, 184, 206
Masia, Bertram B., 302
Matras, Judah, 77, 206
Mauksch, Hans O., 389
Maynard, Richard A., 269
Mead, George Herbert, 46, 56, 73, 95, 100, 168, 358
Mead, Margaret, 270
Means, Richard L., 198
Mehan, Hugh, 400
Mehlinger, Howard, 142
Menges, Robert J., 348, 366
Merrill, Paul F., 297
Merton, Robert K., 126, 146, 147, 169, 204, 328
Meyer, Marshall W., 320
Meyers, Edmund D., Jr., 289
Michaels, James W., 329, 333
Michelet, Jules, 203
Michelson, William, 75, 258
Millar, David, 290
Middleton, Russell, 323

Miller, D. Paul, 217, 226
Miller, Richard I., 347, 351, 355, 365, 366, 368
Mills, C. Wright, 62, 77, 150, 206, 314
Mills, Theodore, 220
Milton, Ohmer, 226, 235, 323, 325, 328, 329, 384, 385, 387, 398
Mintz, J. J., 255
Mitchell, W. C., 239
Monroe, Charles R., 13, 21
Moore, Michael C., 9
Moore, Wilbert E., 11, 206, 207, 220, 223, 224, 239
Moos, Rudolf H., 75
Morley, John Viscount, 50, 146
Moxley, Robert L., 217, 351, 369, 383
Moynihan, Daniel, 169
Mumford, Lewis, 190, 257
Murphy, Raymond, 254
Murray, John D., 371

Naftulin, D. H., 280
Nasatir, David, 32, 138
Nelson, Clarence H., 318
Nelson, Joel I., 191, 195
Newcomb, Charles, 258
Newcomb, Theodore M., 59, 84, 305
Nisbet, Robert, 62, 169
Nixon, Richard, 244
Norr, James L., 350
North, Cecil C., 207, 236, 265
Novak, M., 60
Nuyens, Yvo, 400

Odum, Howard W., 186
Ogburn, William F., 77, 221, 363
O'Kane, James M., 289
Oksanen, Ernest M., 20
Olmstead, Joseph A., 226, 281
Olsen, Marvin E., 145
Olson, Philip, 199
Owen, Thomas R., 369

Page, Charles H., 62, 307
Pape, Max, 217, 226, 383
Pardo, Luis, 226
Pareto, Vilfredo, 59
Park, Robert E., 77
Parsons, Talcott, 62, 126, 136, 140
Patrick, John, 142
Pavalko, Ronald M., 77
Pavlov, Ivan Petrovich, 82
Payne, D. A., 329
Pearson, Karl, 106
Perry, Wilhelmina, 19, 23, 48, 122, 329, 366, 388, 390, 400
Persell, Carolina Hodges, 199
Peterson, Richard J., 23, 62
Petras, John W., 57, 217, 305
Phenix, Philip H., 188
Phillips, Steven, 59, 354, 355, 359, 360, 370, 383
Pirenne, Henri, 190
Piven, Frances Fox, 79
Plato, 269
Platt, Gerald M., 62
Podell, Lawrence, 10
Pool, Jonathan, 290
Postlethwait, S. N., 170, 255
Pratto, David J., 288, 289
Prewitt, Kenneth, 172
Pringle, Bruce M., 265
Proshansky, Harold M., 75
Proxmire, Senator William, 30, 135, 141
Purdy, Ross, 323

Quinney, Valerie, 265, 287

Ramsett, David, 332
Raven, Bertram, 99
Reed, John Shelton, 99
Reid, Sue Titus, 10, 13, 22, 23
Remmers, H. H., 278, 347, 348
Remy, Richard C., 142
Reynolds, Janice M., 169
Reynolds, Larry T., 169
Rhoades, Lawrence J., 389, 398
Rice, Thomas J., 217, 225, 226, 383
Richardson, James T., 290
Riechmann, Sheryl, 7, 13
Riesman, David, 304, 371, 414
Rivlin, Leanne G., 75
Roberts, Ron E., 147, 190
Robin, Arthur L., 297
Rodin, Burton, 349, 368
Rodin, Miriam, 349, 368
Rodman, Hyman, 79
Rodwin, Lloyd, 258
Roethlisberger, F. J., 184
Rogers, Evan D., 217, 235, 284
Rogers, Roberta, 10
Rogers, Sharon J., 217, 235, 284
Rose, Clare, 269
Rose, Peter I., 77
Rose, R. J., 53
Rosenberg, Larry, 24, 281, 295, 304, 308
Rosenfeld, Rachel Ann, 226, 333
Rosenthal, Robert, 313, 332
Rossi, Peter, 207
Rothman, Robert A., 9
Rufsvold, Margaret I., 397
Ruja, H., 278
Rusker, Dr. Howard, 249
Ruskin, Robert S., 23, 169, 228, 230, 234, 235, 283, 292, 295
Ryan, B. A., 235
Ryder, Norman, 100, 245

St. Augustine, 310
St. George, Arthur, 289, 290
Säljö, R., 293, 295
Sanders, Norris M., 189, 191, 226, 308
Sanford, Nevitt, 308
Satariano, William A., 21, 217, 235, 284
Scanzoni, John, 99, 144, 382
Schermerhorn, Richard A., 265
Schlechty, Phillip C., 58, 125, 305
Schmuck, Patricia A., 24, 77, 165, 169, 226, 237, 283, 304, 305
Schmuck, Richard A., 24, 77, 165, 169, 225, 237, 283, 304, 305
Schneider, Clement J., 90
Scholl, Stephen, 329, 360, 365, 384, 385, 387, 398
Schorr, Alvin, 258
Schramm, Wilbur, 286
Schulz, David A., 99
Schure, G. H., 289
Schwartz, Barry, 56, 239
Schwirian, Kent P., 72, 77
Scott, Robert A., 145, 146
Scott, William R., 366, 367
Seldin, Peter, 339, 365, 366
Selvin, Hanan C., 289, 400
Selznick, Phillip, 169, 195, 196, 242
Semas, Phillip W., 367
Shaw, George Bernard, 143
Sherman, J., 235
Shin, Eui-Hang, 6, 23
Shostak, Arthur B., 146
Shulder, C. F., 269
Shulman, Lawrence, 169

Siegel, L., 282
Siegel, Paul M., 207
Silvers, Ronald J., 80, 226
Sim, Francis M., 289
Sime, M., 296, 308
Simmel, Georg, 37, 39, 57, 77, 78, 85, 114, 140, 270
Simon, Herbert A., 184
Simon, William, 246
Simpson, Elizabeth Janes, 302
Simpson, George Eaton, 77, 99
Simpson, Richard L., 224
Singhal, S., 22
Skanes, G. R., 349
Skinner, B. F., 168, 298
Small, Albion, 186
Smelser, Neil, 195, 361
Smidchens, Uldis, 308
Smith, Adam, 87
Smith, Al, 322
Smith, Don D., 217, 255, 265, 287
Smith, William, 218, 232, 233, 235
Socrates, 269
Sokol, Robert, 80, 191, 195, 288
Solomon, Daniel 24, 278, 281, 295, 304, 308, 349
Solomon, W. E., 21
Sommer, Robert, 77
Spanier, Graham B., 188
Spector, Malcolm, 57, 305
Spence, R. B., 278
Spencer, Byron G., 20
Spencer, Herbert, 102, 185
Spencer, R. E., 355
Stager, Robert A., 400
Stallings, William M., 22
Stasz, Clarice, 329
Stauffer, Robert, 62
Stein, Maurice R., 99
Stinchcombe, Arthur L., 224
Stoll, Clarice S., 255, 259
Stone, Clarence N., 270
Stouffer, Samuel A., 158, 242, 247
Straus, Murray A., 15, 22, 191, 195, 306, 308, 342, 345, 350
Strauss, Anselm, 153, 258
Streib, Gordon F., 90
Strodtbeck, Fred L., 75, 220, 248
Stuit, D. B., 368
Stump, Catherine Surra, 188
Sturgis, Richard B., 345
Sullivan, A. M., 349
Suppes, Patrick, 286
Sussman, Marvin B., 147, 255, 265, 398
Sutherland, Robert, 139

Talese, Gay, 250
Talmon, Yonina, 222

Taper, Bernard, 249
Tarde, Gabriel, 185
Taveggia, Thomas C., 8, 24, 192, 271–77, 280, 281, 292, 338
Taylor, Carl C., 57, 58, 60
Taylor, F. W., 184
Thelen, Herbert, 283
Theodorson, Achilles G., 399
Theodorson, George A., 399
Thielens, Wagner, Jr., 199
Thompson, George W., 218
Thompson, Ralph, 226
Thornberry, Mary C., 44
Thorndike, Robert M., 292
Thornton, James W., 203, 215, 218, 263, 269, 270, 287
Tillich, Paul, 33, 362, 371
Toby, Jackson, 32, 80, 100, 155
Tocqueville, Alexis de, 158
Toffler, Alvin, 114
Tomovic, Vladislav, 226
Trent, James W., 269
Troeltsch, Ernst, 190
Trow, Martin A., 196
Trumbull, H. Clay, 58, 260
Tucker, Sterling, 172
Tufte, Edward R., 169
Tumin, Melvin M., 223, 239
Turner, Ralph H., 185

Valdes, Donald M., 146, 191, 195, 196
Vander Zanden, James W., 172, 189, 239, 242
Van Valey, Thomas L., 6, 9, 20, 186, 187, 194, 199, 290
Vargas, Ernest A., 269
Vaughan, Charlotte A., 23, 62, 389
Vaughan, Ted R., 345
Veblen, Thorstein, 184
Verdet, Paule, 45
Verner, C., 215
Vescoe, Robert, 87
Vidich, Arthur J., 99, 196
Villemez, Wayne, 345
Vincent, John H., 260
Vincent, George, 186
Vogelfanger, Martin, 10
Voland, Ellen, 190

Wales, Charles E., 400
Walker, E. J., 201, 306
Wallace, George, 33
Wallace, Ruth A., 217, 383
Waller, Willard, 24, 305
Wallis, George W., 217
Walsh, Edward J., 217, 235, 284
Walters, T., 21

Ware, J. E., 280, 349
Warner, K. O., 278
Warner, Sam Bass, 221
Warren, Roland L., 221, 278
Warriner, Charles K., 149
Waskow, Arthur I., 243
Watson, George, 229, 237
Watson, Walter, 226
Weaver, B. F., 278
Webb, Eugene, 238
Weber, Max, 59, 88, 184, 190, 238, 255, 336, 380, 381
Weisbrod, Burton A., 332
Wells, Stuart, 286
Wesolowski, W., 224
Weston, Louise C., 199, 391
White, Ralph, 120
Whitely, S. E., 349, 355
Whiting, John W. M., 35, 110, 112, 113, 120
Whyte, William Foote, 75, 184
Wieting, Stephen G., 289, 305
Wilensky, Harold L., 360
Williams, George W., 400
Williams, R. G., 280, 349
Wilson, Everett K., 21, 22, 24, 45, 46, 50, 53, 54, 59, 62, 77, 80, 112, 120, 126, 131, 145, 169, 195, 196, 242, 264, 265, 305, 308, 338, 339, 351, 370, 400
Wilson, Robert C., 22, 215, 305, 307, 367, 370
Wilson, Stephen R., 305
Wimberly, Robert C., 345, 351, 368, 369
Winslow, Robert W., 196
Winslow, Virginia, 196
Wirth, Louis, 183
Witt, Paul W. F., 44
Wittich, William A., 269
Wolensky, Robert, 267
Wolford, George L., 218, 233
Wood, Kenneth, 350
Wood, Lynn, 215, 370
Wright, Burton, 190
Wright, Sonia, 104
Wrong, Dennis, 224
Wylie, Laurence, 32

Yinger, J. Milton, 77, 99
Yoels, William C., 24, 57, 305
Young, Michael, 187, 188

Zeitlin, Maurice, 99, 245
Zelan, Joseph, 62
Zeleny, L. D., 280
Zillman, D., 296, 298, 308
Zimmerman, Carle C., 363
Zopf, Paul E., Jr., 100

SUBJECT INDEX

Achievement, student: evaluation of. *See* Evaluating student achievement; Grading; Tests and testing

ACIDS test (of text selection), 194, 197

Active participation and learning, 34–35, 48, 53–54; classroom ecology and, 363–64; in lectures, 204–08; research on, 279–82, 293, 295; textbooks and, 188–91; *See also* Discussion

Advising, 366–67, 385

Affectivity and learning, 302; critical thinking and, 88; drive to reduce anomolies and, 88

Anxiety, student: learning and, 87; resistance to critical thinking and, 81–82; testing and, 326

Anxiety, teacher: improving instruction and, 379

Assigning teachers to courses, 15–17

Attitude (as a learning outcome), 301–02

Audiovisual aids (AVAs), 251–69; attributes of, 252; chalkboard, 259–62; course planning and, 255–56; graphic examples, 248–49; literature on, 255, 265, 267, 269; overhead projector and transparencies, 252–54, 262–63, 287, 396; photographs, 265; preparation for use of, 256–57; research on, 286–87; selection of, 255, 257–58; sources of materials, 395–97; speaker phones, 382; student production of, 255, 259; teaching sociology and, 258–59, 251–69 *passim*; types of, 252, 254; uses of, 251–52, 255, 258–59

Awards for teaching, 45, 54, 351

Behavioral objectives. *See* Goals

Benign disruption for critical thinking, 84–97; common sense and, 89–90; examples of teaching, 89–97; learning and, 84–87; research on, 297–98; student-teacher relations and, 87–89

Boundaries and social structure, 70–72

Bounding walls (influences on teaching), 125–41; *See also* Teaching sociology, influences on

"Cafeteria" forms for student ratings of teachers, 354–56, 371–73

Case studies, used as examples, 245–47

Census data and teaching, 392–94

Chalkboard (a teaching tool), 208, 259–62

Changes affecting sociology instruction, 2–5; social movements, 2, 134, 138–39

Cheating, problems of, 327–28

Checklists (for): analyzing teaching, 360; evaluating teaching, 347, 370; syllabus, constructing and reviewing, 177–85

Class: communication patterns in, 204–05; mass. *See* Mass classes; size, research on, 282–83; student thoughts during, 282–83

Classroom: ecology of, and participation, 363–64; as instructional setting, 162

Collaborative inquiry: described, 80–81; rarity of, 80; in research and teaching, 34–35; student-teacher relations and, 34–35

Colleague ratings of teaching, 352

Common sense and sociology, 153–59; benign disruption and, 89–90; beyond common sense, tactics of teaching, 155–58; explaining what is contrary to, 158–59; implications of, 153–54

Communication patterns in the classrooms, 204–05

Communication skills and teaching, 280

Community, as a teaching resource, 394–95

Community colleges, 3–5, 13–14, 389

Comparative studies of teaching methods, 271–74, 277–80

Competence, measured apart from conscientiousness, 315

Competence and conscientiousness: evaluating teaching and, 351

Computer assisted instruction (CAI), 287–90, 390

Computer managed instruction (CMI), 287–88

Computers: grading and, 323–24; responding to student work and, 330–32

CONDUIT (a computer information exchange), 290

Constraints on teaching, 15–16, 48, 125–35

Constraints on teaching, options suggested by, 135–40

Corrections, required, 293–94

Course cycle, periodic difficulties, 159–67, 173–74

Course planning: audiovisual aids and, 255–56; student contributions to, 181–83; syllabus and, 177–80 and 171–85 *passim*

Creativity, student, 219–20

Critical thinking, 78–98; affectivity and, 88; anxiety and, 87; benign disruption as a means to achieve, 87–89; confronting problems and, 80; description and explanation as parts of, 78; discrepant data and, 85–87, 92–95, 98; examples of teaching, 89–97; need for teaching skills of, 83–84; research on, 230; resistance to teaching skills of, 81–83; status incongruities and, 95–97; values and, 85

Current situation in teaching sociology, 5–17; publications about, 391–92

Curriculum, sociology, 6, 9, 10, 16, 19, 176–77, 391, 400

Curve, grading on a, 316–19

Data: about social world, and teaching, 392–95; audiovisual aids and, 258–59; census, and teaching, 392–94; discrepant, and teaching critical thinking, 85–87, 92–95, 98; importance of basic social data, 92; use in discussion classes, 224–25; use in examples, 247

Departments of sociology: course syllabi and, 176–77; evaluation of teaching, 336, 339–41, 344; evaluation of what is taught, 344; firing for incompetence in teaching, 17; Chapter 14, *passim*; grading and, 317; hiring new teachers, 341; instructor role constraints and, 129–30; promotion of

faculty, and teaching, 336; statistics requirements and, 307; teaching resources and, 383, 398–99; tenure reviews, and teaching, 340

Disciplines, academic: structure of knowledge in, 306–07

Discussion (a teaching technique), 218–26; defined, 218–19; fixing on problems, procedures, .outcomes, 219; learning skills of, 220–22; preparation for, by teacher and student, 219–20; questions and, 222–24; research on, 277–83; resources about, 225–26; types of, 218; using data in, 224–25

"Dr. Fox" research on teaching, 280

Double standard for research and teaching, Chapter 2, *passim*; adverse effects of, 30–31; evaluation of teaching and, 336; grading and, 325; outcomes of, 29–31; reasons for, 25–29; spurious opposition, 31–34

Dual roles. *See* Double standard for research and teaching

Education: critical thinking and, 83–84; goals of, 52; *See also* Goals

Enrollments, 3–6, 10, 16

Enthusiasm (a teacher attribute), 280; research on, 296

Essay tests, 324–25

Estimating (a form of extending knowledge), 114–19

Ethics and teaching, 41, 51–52, 95, 138–39, 381

Evaluating instructor achievement, 56, 334–78; checklists for, 347, 370; colleague and administrator ratings and, 352; conditions affecting teaching and, 48; current practices of, 338–42; debates on technical issues, 310; departments and, 336, 339–41, 344; increased emphasis on in sociology, 341–42; instructional goals and, 344; need for by teachers, 336–38; publications and, 345; resources about, 365–66, 384, 400; self-ratings of, 352; in sociology, 338–42; sources of evidence, 343; student learning and, 310, 345–47; teacher command of subject matter and, 344–45; types and uses, 342–44; types of evidence, adequacy of, 343; *See also* Awards for teaching; Peer observation and evaluation; Student evaluation of teaching

Evaluating student achievement, 311–33; certifying role of teachers, 312–14; conclusions about, 329–30; debates on technical issues, 310; essay tests, 324–25; guidelines for teacher's testing role, 326–27; language and student inquiry, 150–53; means used for, 319–26; means used in sociology, 319–20; multiple choice tests, 320–24; organization skills, 314–15; purposes of, 311–14; research on, 291–93; resources about, 328–29, 384; student honesty, 327–28; student-teacher relations and, 326–28; syllabus and, 178–79, 181–83; what is measured, 314–15; *See also* Essay tests; Grading; Multiple choice tests; Response; Tests and testing

Evaluation: skills of, needed by students, 335–36; ubiquity and persistence of, 334–35

Examples (as teaching tools), 238–51; case studies as, 245–47; cautionary notes on, 243–46; characteristics of, 240–42; evidence and, 249–51; feedback (response) and, 251; generational experiences and, 134, 139, 243–45; government publications and, 248; graphic, 245, 248–49; mass media as source of, 249; outcomes of using, 240–42; power of, 238–40; of role conflict, 239–40, 42; sources of, 247–49; sports, 55–56; student-teacher interaction and, 251; types, 246–47

Examples of teaching used in *Passing on Sociology*: adolescent initiations (extending knowledge), 110–14; airplane talk (using discrepant data), 95–98; black militancy (common sense), 156–57; black physicians (extending knowledge), 116–19; *c*, the sound of (examples), 241; Caliente (case studies as examples), 245–46; generational experience (selecting examples), 243–45; gerrymandering (graphic examples), 248–49; locational choices (size and social structure), 66–69; marginality (clarifying goal statements, studying social structure), 72–75; market areas (using transparencies), 254; matricentricity (testing explanations), 85–87; moving to new community (common sense), 155; *My Childhood* (use of films), 263–65; newsroom social control (examples and evidence), 249–51; optimum city size (discussion classes), 220–21; population estimates (extending knowledge), 116; population pyramids (using transparencies), 253; "Professor Jones" (clarifying goal statements), 72–75; race and family type (testing explanations), 85–87; role conflict (selecting examples), 239–40, 242; smoking and ads (skills of inquiry), 106–10; social facts (critical thinking), 92–95; socialism and age (competing explanations), 90–92; soldiers' morale (common sense), 156, 158–59; sports (teacher-student communication), 55–56; stratification (lectures and inquiry), 205–08, 220, 222–24; *Suicide* (process of inquiry), 104–05; total institutions (studying social structure), 70–71; total institutions (selecting examples), 240, 243; unionization (extending knowledge), 115–16; vigilante movements (using data), 224–25; what is sociology? (lecture organization), 210–15

Extending knowledge, 110–20; by estimating, 114–19; as intelligence, 110; to new situations, 112–13; steps in, 112–14

Faculty role requirements, influence on teaching, 129–30
Failure, student, 313–14
Feedback. *See* Response
Field experience and student learning, 59
Films, 263–65, 287, 396
Firing faculty for incompetence in teaching, 17; Chapter 14, *passim*

Goals, field-related (sociology), 63–77; boundaries, 70–72; distinctive features of, 64, 76; and learning, research on, 296–97; marginality, 72–75; size, 66–69; social distance, 75–76; social structure, 65–67

Goals of instruction: classifications of, 300–04; evaluation of teaching and, 344; language problems and, 150–53; need to specify precisely, 36–37; operational statement of, 297, 300–04; research on, 297; selection of teaching methods and, 123

Goals of sociology instruction, 10–13; clear and useful statement of, 72; in introductory courses, 61; listing of, 61; literature about, 62; need for clearcut statement of, 46–47, 51, 61; textbooks and, 188–91

Goals transcending sociological content, Chapters 5 and 6, *passim*; critical thinking, 78–98; skill in extending knowledge, 110–20; skill in gaining knowledge, 101–10

Golden Fleece Award, 135, 141

Grading: classroom ecology and, 363–64; craft skills and, 314; curves. *See* Curve, grading on a double standard and, 325; evaluating teaching and, 338, 343; how to, 315–19; inflation, 317–18; measurement problems, 315–19; and Personalised System of Instruction, 226–27, 234; quantity vs. quality, issue of, 315; relative to earlier performance, 316; relative to performance of peers, 316; relative to teacher fixed standard, 316; student-teacher relations and, 326–28; what is measured, 314–15

Graduate students of sociology; preparation for teaching, 16–17, 42–44, 391; as teachers, 8, 16–17

Guided Design (a teaching method), 400

Inquiry (as a teaching approach): textbooks and, 188–91, 198; *See also* Collaborative inquiry
Inquiry, methods of sociological: as a goal in teaching, 101–20
Inquiry, process of sociological, 103–10; aspects of, 103–06; describing and explaining, 106–08; differences observed, initiating inquiry, 103–04; in lectures, 205–08; questions stimulating, 103–04; theory and, 104
Instructional Development and Assessment System (IDEA), 355, 378
IMPRESS, 288–90
Isomorphisms and teaching, 56, 241

Keller Plan. *See* Personalized System of Instruction
Knowledge, gaining and extending as teaching goals, 101–20

Language and teaching sociology: abbreviations, 262; chalkboard and, 260; classification of learnings, and, 303–04; essay tests and, 324; learning objectives and, 303–04; terms with technical and everyday meanings, confusions of, 148–49; terms with unfamiliar values, 150; unfamiliar technical terms, 149; words used to direct student inquiry, 150–53

Learning: classification of outcomes, 300–04; defined, 46–47; essentials of, for instruction, 298–304; as an index of teacher achievement, 345–47; as knowing vs. doing, 47; measurable change and, 46–47; relation to teaching, 46–47; teaching and, research on, Chapter 12 *passim*; theories of, 298–304; variables affecting, 37–38

Lecture, 201–18; active student participation in, 204–08; beginnings of, 209–10; checking effectiveness of, 216; communication patterns in, 204–05; defined, 201; delivering, 216; exposition vs. process of inquiry, 205–08; extent of information in, 208–09; handling content in, 215; instructor domination and, 204–05; organization, making clear, 208; organization, patterns of, 210–14; preparation, 215; principles of effective, 208–10; research on, 276–83; research on, in sociology, 280–81; resources about, 216–18; student interests, linking to, 209–10; use of, 201–16

Mass classes, 48, 200–01, 217, 330–32, 384; *See also* Lecture
Mass media: as source of examples, 249; teaching and, 55
Mastery learning, 293–94
Methods of inquiry. *See* Inquiry, methods of
Methods of teaching, 200–37
Minimum essential learnings in sociology, 10–13; assessing student learning and, 346–47; evaluating teaching and, 344, 346–47
Moral dimensions of teaching, 41, 51–52, 95, 138–39, 381
Multiple choice tests, 320–24; evaluating test items, 323–24; examples of, 320–22; item analysis of, 323–24; for review and teaching, 320

Names, importance of knowing student, 162–63
Nonacademic experiences affecting student learning, 130–34

Objectives. *See* Goals
"Objective tests," 320–24
Obsolescence of teacher's knowledge, 49, 134, 139
Office hours, 184
Overhead projector and transparencies, 252–54, 262–63, 287, 396

Peer observation and evaluation, 358–66
Peer teaching, 293, 295, 383
Personalized System of Instruction: (PSI), 20, 200, 226–35; advice about, 233; assumptions regarding knowledge, 230–31; degree of individualization, 231–32; distinctive features of, 226–27; grading and, 226–27, 234, 316; instructor responsibilities in, 227; research on, 230, 274, 283–84; resources about, 234–35; role of instructor and student in, 232; rote learning and, 230; theoretical base of, 228; trivialization and, 230; types and uses of, 228–30, 232–34; use in sociology, articles about, 235
Personnel actions, teaching skill as a criterion, 17, 43–44, 336, 340

Persuasions about effective sociology instruction, 48–58

Prerequisites (for courses), 10, 12, 180–81

Problem solving. *See* Critical thinking

Problems of sociology instruction, 142–70; analysis over action, 145–47; common sense, limitations of, 153–59; course cycle and, 159–67; diversity of field, 167–68; individualistic views of human behavior, 168; language, difficulties of, 148–53; sociology as a threat to students, 143–44

Professionalism, constraints on teaching and solutions, 136–37

Promotion of faculty, and teaching, 336

Psychological explanations, as a problem of sociology instruction, 168

Questions: before answers, 52–53, 205–08; centrality in research and teaching, 39–40; characteristics of good ones, 40; in discussion classes, 222–24; lectures organized around, 205–08; rhetorical, 296; stimulating inquiry, 103–04; syllabus and, 183–84; textbooks and, 188–91

Quizzing and practice: research on, 290–91, 295–96

Reading, 151

Recruitment and promotion: teaching skills as a criterion, 43–44

Research: adverse effects of poor instruction, 31; role of, contrasted to teaching role, 27

Research and teaching: collaborative inquiry, 34–35; goals of discovery and transmission, 31–33; importance as a criterion, 32–33; needless opposition of, 25, 31–34; processes similar, 33–34

Research on teaching, 271–309; active learning, 293, 295; audiovisual aids, 286–87; benign disruption, 297–98; components of methods, 291–98; computer assisted instruction, 287–90; discussion, 277–83; "Dr. Fox" studies, 280; enthusiasm (a teacher attribute), 296; feedback, prompt, 292–93; lecture, 276–81; mastery learning, 293–94; operational statements of goals, 297; Personalized System of Instruction, 274, 283–84; practice, frequency of, 290–91; questions (as a teaching device), 295–96; quizzing, frequency of, 290–91; required corrections, 293–94; student evaluation of teaching, 348–52; student perceptions of superior instruction, 351–52; student ratings and teacher improvement, 350–51; subject matter, significance of, 296–97; TIPS, 284–85;

Resources for teachers of sociology (on), 18–20, 382–401; audiovisual aids, 255, 265, 267, 269, 395–97; bibliographic, 390–92; books on college teaching described, 383–87, 400–01; census data, 392–94; computer assisted instruction, 289–90; course planning, 177–85; discussion classes, 225–26; evaluating instructor achievement, 265–66, 384; evaluating student achievement, 384; examples, sources of, 247–49; goals of teaching sociol-

ogy, 62; journals, newsletters, organizations described, 388–90; lectures, 216–18; local community as, 394–95; mass classes, 384; more available than we suspect, 57–58; needed by the instructor, 399; needed in the college, 397; needed in the department, 398–99; overview of, 387–88; Personalized System of Instruction, 234–35; scope of the literature, 18–20, 387–88; social world, data about, 392–95; sociology and social action, 145–46; students as resources, 383; syllabi, checklist on construction and review, 177–85; teacher as own resource, 382; TIPS, 332; teaching techniques for mass classes, 217; tests and testing, 328–29

Response (feedback): constructive, 360–61, 365; on essay tests, 325; examples and, 251; frequency of, 290–91; instructional improvement and, 370; in lectures, 210, 216; peer observation and, 364–65; promptness of, 292–93; research on, 290–93

Role constraints on teaching: faculty, 129–30; options suggested by, 137–38; student, 130–34

Roles, differing: gaining and applying knowledge, 146–47

Sampling (in research and teaching), 38–39

Self-fulfilling prophecy, used to enhance learning, 313

Self-paced instruction. *See* Personalized System of Instruction

SETUPS. *See* Supplementary Empirical Teaching Units in Political Science

Simulation games in lectures, 205

Single standard for research and teaching: active inquiry and, 34–35; assessing results in, 41–42; ethics in, 41; identifying pertinent variables, 37–38; sampling, 38–39; specifying problems and goals, 36–37; teacher-student collaboration and, 34–35; for teacher training, 42–44; theory as guide, 37

Size and social structure, 66–69

Size of class, research on, 282–83

Social distance and social structure, 75–76

Social structure, dimensions of, teaching about, 65–76

Society: as affecting sociology instruction, 2–5; *See also* Changes affecting sociology instruction; Teaching sociology, influences on

Sociological concepts, teaching about, Chapter 4; *See also* books on, 390–91

Sociologists: demand for, 2–3; research on teaching and learning by, 304–05; roles of, in gaining and acquiring knowledge, 146–47; as ugly Americans, 127

Sociology: applications of, 50, 145–47; as art, craft and science, 380; common sense and, 153–59; distinctive subject matter of, 64, 76; effective instruction and, 304–05; effective instruction in, 306–07; enrollments. *See* Enrollments; esteem of field on campus, 342; evaluating teaching in, 338–42, Chapter 14 *passim*; field dictates importance of its teaching, 380–81; field of, influ-

ence on its practitioners, 126–27; importance of, 49–51, 381; inquiries in, attributes of, 63–64; perspective of, 238–39; social action and, 145–47; teacher's command of, 49–51; textbooks, 2, 8–9, 185–98; ways of introducing discipline in lectures, 210–14

Sociology courses: collective behavior and social movements, 90–92, 224–25; community conflict, 250–51; family, 85–87; introductory, 143, 391; medical, 400; occupations, 239–40, 242; population, 116, 252, 389–90; race and ethnic relations, 72–75, 85–87; race, poverty and politics, 78–79; research methods, 289; socialization, 110–14; social problems, 391; statistics, 307; stratification, 206–08, 222–24; urban, 66–69, 183–84, 220–21, 245–46, 252, 258, 394–95

Sociology courses, allocating teachers to, 15–17

Status incongruities: teaching critical thinking and, 95–97

Student(s): characteristics of, and teaching, 55–56, 127–34, 137, 319; competition and grading, 316–19; contributions to course planning, 181–83; course syllabus and, 173–75; creativity, 219–20; evaluating. *See* Evaluating student achievement; evaluating teachers. *See* Student evaluation of teaching; failures, 313–14; honesty on tests, 327–28; importance of knowing their names, 162–63; individualistic view of human behavior, 168; inducing change in their intellectual frameworks, 79; issues pertinent to, 209–10; learning as an index of teaching effectiveness, 345–47; learning their names, 169–70; may teach themselves, 274; need for evaluation skills, 335–36; non-academic experiences of, influencing teaching, 130–34; perceptions of superior teachers, 351–52; production of audiovisual aids, 255, 259; rights of, and syllabus, 173; roles of, influence on teaching, 130–34; sociology as a threat to, 143–44; teacher demonstrated concern for, 54; as teachers, 293, 295, 383; thoughts during class, 282–83

Student evaluation of teaching, 347–58, 371–78; "cafeteria" forms for, 354–56, 371–73; colleague and administrator ratings and, 352; constructing ratings forms for, 353–57; course attributes and, 350; information obtainable from, 348; limits of, 280; norms for, 356; rating forms, well designed, 354–56, 371–78; realiability of, 348; research on, 348–52; resources about, 365–66; sample forms, 371–78; selecting questions for, 356–57; selecting rating forms for, 353–57; self-ratings by teachers and, 352; in sociology, 14–15, 306, 339–41, 351; student attributes and, 349; summary, 358; superior teaching as perceived by students, 351–52; teacher attributes and, 349–50; teacher improvement and, 350–51, 357–58; validity of, 348–49

Student-teacher relations: benign disruption and, 87–89; collaborative inquiry, 34–35; communications and, 55–56; generational experiences and, 134, 139, 243–45; grading and, 326–28; problems of teacher manipulation, 95, 156; trust and credibility, 280; use of examples and, 251

Subject matter, significance of: research on, 296–97

Supplementary Empirical Teaching Units in Political Science (SETUPS), 390

Syllabus, 171–85; audiences, 173–77; checklist for constructing and reviewing, 178–80; content and construction, 177–85; content and use, 171–85; course planning and, 177–80; course prerequisites and, 180–81; departments and, 176–77; evaluating teaching and, 343; flexibility regarding, 181–83; for introductory sociology, 391; instructor and, 175–76; as introduction to course, 184–85; load on students and, 183; office hours and, 184; purposes, 173–77; questions and, 183–84; for social problems, 391; students and, 173–75; testing and, 178–79, 181–83

Teacher(s)
advising and, 366–67; as certifying agent, 312–14; competence and conscientiousness, 351; constraints on, 48; course syllabus and, 175–76; dual roles and double standards, Chapter 2 *passim*; effective and responsible, 47–48; extending influence of, 379–81; hiring new, 341; obsolescence of knowledge, 49, 134, 139; office hours, 184; as own resources, 382; professional socialization, Chapter 2 *passim*; promotion and teaching, 336; roles of, 27, 54–55; sharing resources, 382; teaching skills as criterion for recruitment and promotion, 43–44

Teaching: active student participation and learning, 53–54; adverse effects of double standard, 31; awards for, 45, 54, 351; and concern for student growth, 54; defined, 46; effective, and sociology, 304–05; effective, in sociology, 306–07; effective, persuasions about, 48–58; faculty role requirements and, 129–30; as important to student learning, 271–76; improvement of, and student ratings, 350–51, 357–58; isomorphisms and, 56, 241; knowing students and, 55–56; meth-

ods, 200–37; *See also* entries under particular methods; models of, 81; moral dimensions of, 41, 51–52, 95, 138–39, 381; as paradox and perplexity, 271–76; relation to learning, 46–47; role of, contrasted to research, 27; by students, 293, 295; superior, as perceived by students, 351–52; theory as a guide, 37, 304–05; time demands of, 95; training for, 42–44; as transmission, 54; as unimportant to student learning, 271–76

Teaching Analysis by Students (TABS), 354

Teaching and learning: models of, 272, 298–304; research on, Chapter 12 *passim*

Teaching assistants. *See* Graduate students of sociology

Teaching Information Processing System (TIPS), 135, 284–85, 330–32

Teaching methods: commonality among, 191–92; comparative studies of, 191–92, 271–74, 277–80; conclusions about, 290–91; effect of textbooks on, 191–92; operational statements of goals and selection of, 123; preference of teachers for different, 122; problems of changing, 122–23; research on, 276–91; research on components of, 291–98; resources about, 384; selection of, 122; strategy for design and selection of, 123–24; used in sociology, 200–03; *See also* entries under specific methods

Teaching sociology: common sense and, 153–59; concern about, 20–21; current situation, 5–17, Chapter 1 *passim*; effective, persuasions about, 48–58; false beliefs about, 18; high schools, in, 142; hiring new faculty and, 341; ignorance of what is taught, 9–10; institutional contexts of, 391–92; language problems of, 148–53; means of evaluating students, 319–20; methods used in, 200–03; novices, by, 16–17; *See also* Graduate students; preparing for, 42–44, 391; quality of, 14–15; research on, Chapter 12 *passim*; statistical overview, 6–8; subject matter importance, and command of, 49–51, 380–81; tenure reviews and, 340; textbooks and, 185–98; theory as a guide, 37, 304–05; as a threat to students, 143–44; what is taught, 5–13; what should be taught, 10–13; where taught, 13–14; who is taught, 13–14; who teaches, 14–17

Teaching sociology, influences on, 5–17, 125–41; faculty role requirements, 129–30; field of sociology, 126–27; national and international events, 125–26, 135–36; options suggested by constraints, 135–40; student non-academic experiences, 130–34; student populations, 55–56, 127–34, 137, 319; time-linked, 134, 138–40

Television, research on, 286

Tenure reviews in sociology and teaching, 340

TESTAN (computer test item analysis), 323–24

Tests and testing: assessing teacher effectiveness and, 311; as bases of certification, 312–14; as diagnostic tools, 311–12; feedback, research on, 291–93; flexibility and, 181–83; honesty and, 327–28; inevitable for teachers, 311–14; instruments for, 319–26; item analysis, 323–24; measurement problems, 315–19; research on, 291–93, 328–29; student command of facts and skills and, 311–12; student-teacher relations and, 326–28; syllabus and, 178–79, 181–83; teacher role and, 326–28; for teaching and learning, 311–12, 320–21; triadic relations and, 316; uses of, 311–14; *See*

Textbooks (and other written materials), 185–98; availability of, learning about, 186–88; first in sociology, 186; importance of, 191–93; inquiry and, 188–91, 198; learning and teaching and, 8, 188–93, 338; organization of, 197–98; reviews of, 187–88; selecting, 191, 193–98; sources of, 195–96; teacher disagreement with, 161; types of, 195–96; uses of sociology in, 198, 185–98 *passim*

Theory: process of inquiry and, 104; in research and teaching, 37; sociological, and teaching, 37, 304–05

Training for teaching as for research, 42–44

Transparencies and overhead projectors, 252–54, 262–63, 287, 396

Triadic relations and teaching, 35, 316

Validity in research and teaching, 39

Values: critical thinking and, 85; teaching and, 103–04

Variables pertinent to research and teaching, 37–38

Videotaping and observation and evaluation of teaching, 361